D1152775

WITHDRAWN FOR SALE

THE ROUGH GUIDE TO

The Italian Lakes

This fourth edition written and researched by

Lucy Ratcliffe

with additional c

Kiki Deere ar

ROUGH
GUIDES

roughguides.com

Contents

Introduction to
The Italian Lakes

The Italian Lakes are a little slice of paradise. Generations of travellers from the north, descending wearily from the chilly Alpine passes, have come into this Mediterranean vision of figs and palms, bougainvillea and lemon blossom, and been lost for words. Elegant ribbons of blue water stretch out ahead, folded into the sun-baked foothills; after the rigours of the high Alps, the abundance of fine food and wine must have been a revelation. Warming, awe-inspiring and graced with natural beauty, the lakes are still a place to draw breath and wonder.

These days, of course, mass tourism has found the lakes, and the shoreside roads that link every town can be as packed as the ferries that chug to and fro. But the chief reason to visit the area – its spectacular landscapes – remains compelling, and there are plenty of ways to avoid the crowds.

The lakes – deep, slender fjords gouged by glaciers – are sublime. All are oriented north–south, ringed by characterful old villages often wedged onto narrow beaches between rugged cliffs and the water. And those classic lakes images of flower-bedecked balconies, Baroque gardens and splendid waterside villas can be found here in abundance.

Dotted around and between the lakes are some of Italy's finest art cities. Milan is pre-eminent, while Verona, Bergamo, Mantua and others display – in their architecture as well as their art – a civilized, urban vision that stands in marked contrast to the wild, largely rural character of the lakeside hinterlands. Italy only became a unified state in 1861 and, as a result, people often feel more loyalty to their home town than to the nation as a whole – a feeling manifest in the multitude of cuisines, dialects and outlooks that span the region.

Geography, of course, doesn't adhere to political boundaries: the lakes are intimately connected in culture and landscape with the southernmost, Italian-speaking extremities of Switzerland. Lakes Maggiore and Lugano have shorelines in two countries. This book provides full coverage of attractions and travel practicalities on both sides of the border.

ABOVE SWEET FRUIT PICKLES, CREMONA

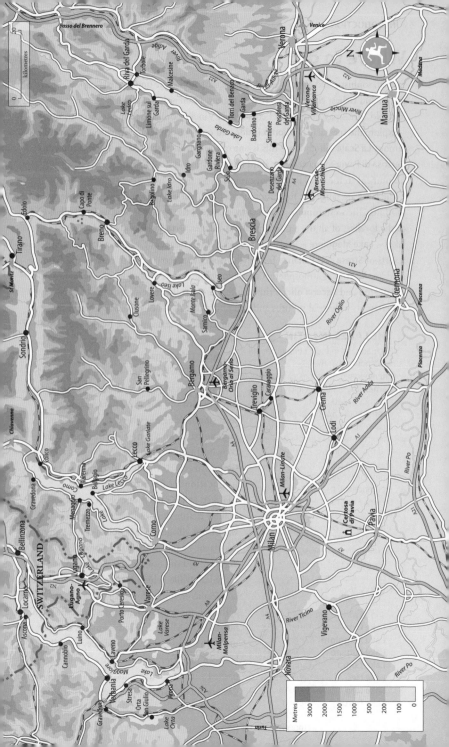

Where to go

Stylish, sophisticated **Milan** needs little introduction – the undisputed "capital" of the north, and richest city of Italy's richest region, Lombardy. Its pilgrimage status is fourfold. Art – pay homage to Leonardo da Vinci's iconic **Last Supper**. Architecture – explore the spectacular **Duomo** inside and out. Music – sample opera at the world-famous **La Scala**. Shopping – this is one of the world's **fashion** capitals. The opulent **Certosa di Pavia** monastery, set amid the rice fields south of Milan, stands as a monument to the city's Renaissance rulers.

The lakes are ranged in formation north of Milan, interleaved between the Prealpine foothills. The westernmost is **Lake Orta**, a pretty little wedge of blue water that holds one of the loveliest of all the region's medieval villages, **Orta San Giulio**. The longest of the lakes – **Lake Maggiore** – lies draped between high ridges of green mountainside. The resorts of **Stresa** and **Pallanza** face idyllic **Isola Bella**, crowned with palaces and Baroque gardens. North lies atmospheric **Cannobio**, while, across the border, the Swiss neighbours of **Locarno** and **Ascona** offer a ritzy allure. **Varese** is the region's most underrated city. Penetrate its industrial suburbs and you find a core of cobbled piazzas and stylish boutiques, made unmissable by the superb gallery of contemporary art at **Villa Panza**.

Nearby **Lake Lugano** lies mostly in Switzerland. Wilder than its neighbours, with long stretches of forested shoreline that plunge directly into the water, it offers a sense of seclusion lacking elsewhere. Cosmopolitan **Lugano** basks on a sunny, south-facing bay, cogwheel trains climb the nearby peak of **Monte Generoso** (1701m), while further north rise the fortifications of **Bellinzona**.

Forked **Lake Como** is one of the best-known holiday destinations in Italy, offering, in waterfront villages such as **Bellagio** and **Varenna**, the classic images of the lakes. **Como** itself is a dignified old silk town with a magnificent cathedral, while behind **Menaggio** and **Tremezzo** coil scenic mountain footpaths.

The hill-town of **Bergamo** rises from the plain northeast of Milan. Its Gothic-medieval upper town, characterized by cobbled alleys winding between high-fronted *palazzi*, is a foodie's delight, packed with fine restaurants, while the **Accademia Carrara** is Lombardy's most prestigious gallery outside Milan.

THE LAKES IN LATIN

On maps and in tourist brochures, you'll notice that the lakes are often referred to by their old **Latin names**. These titles – which are also much used by writers and poets – evoke a sense of pride in local culture and history, forming a linguistic link between the present and the distant past. For this reason, politicians also love them: when the Province of Novara was reorganized in the 1990s, the new province that resulted, covering territory around lakes Maggiore and Orta, was named "Verbano-Cusio-Ossola", deliberately playing on the Latin appellations.

For all practical purposes, though, these names are a curiosity: they are rarely used without their modern equivalents – and never on road signs.

Lake Orta	"Cusio"
Lake Maggiore	"Verbano"
Lake Lugano	"Ceresio"
Lake Como	"Lario"
Lake Iseo	"Sebino"
Lake Idro	"Eridio"
Lake Garda	"Benaco"

CLOCKWISE FROM TOP CAFÉ LIFE, MALCESINE; LAKESIDE SIRMIONE; TORRI DEL BENACO ALIMENTARI

A little east, the squiggle of **Lake Iseo** attracts far fewer visitors and hosts country walks and, on its hilly fringes, prehistoric rock carvings and the prestigious **Franciacorta** vineyards. Nearby stands **Brescia**, a hard-working, business-minded city that boasts fine Roman ruins and, a short way south, the old violin-making town of **Cremona**.

Marking the eastern limit of Lombardy is Italy's largest and most famous lake: **Lake Garda**. The southern shores are flat or gently rolling; highlights here include busy **Sirmione**, on its long peninsula. To the east, a string of old Venetian ports includes gentle **Garda** and little-visited **Torri del Benaco**. Garda's western shore has more classic lake imagery – exotic flower gardens, palm-shaded promenades and fine Art Nouveau villas crowding the waterfront around **Salò** and **Gardone Riviera**.

In the north, Lake Garda's shores are hemmed in by sheer, parallel mountains: the dramatic scenery here takes your breath away. **Gargnano** village – beloved of D.H. Lawrence – is a highlight on the trip north past **Limone** to the splendid, once-Austrian resort of **Riva del Garda** at the head of the lake. As well as a sense of history, Riva, and its neighbour, **Torbole**, have watersports aplenty, and there are good walks on the crest of **Monte Baldo** nearby, above **Malcesine**.

Then there's **Verona**, a laidback, romantically minded city a stone's throw from Lake Garda with, at its core, the glorious Roman **Arena**, scene of a famous summer opera festival. Roaming Verona's alleys, dipping into the local taverns and restaurants, is a rare pleasure.

Just to the south, the dignified old town of **Mantua** (Mantova in Italian) makes a compelling side-trip, with spectacular Renaissance frescoes and lotus-fringed lakes.

When to go

The best months to visit are **June** and, especially, **September**. At these times, visitor numbers are below their peak, but the weather is lovely: sunshine pouring from blue skies, temperatures that are toasty but not scorching, and magically clear, cool evenings.

The hottest months, **July** and **August**, are when the lakes are at their most crowded: weekends in particular can see roads jam-packed with traffic. The cities, especially Milan, can be sweltering, with temperatures topping 35°C for days on end. Spectacular – but short-lived – thunderstorms are common in late August.

Italians take the first two or three weeks of August as their annual holiday; this means the urban centres – Milan, Verona, Bergamo – can feel somewhat artificial, as the only people around are foreign tourists. Many restaurants, bars and shops close altogether. In this, the Swiss are more flexible: head across to Lugano or Locarno in August and you'll find that life continues more or less as normal.

The season on the lakes runs from **Easter** to **October**. Outside these months you'll find that tourism shuts down: many hotels and restaurants close for the winter, ferry services are reduced or halted and attractions open for shorter hours, if at all. Skies are often grey, with chill winds sweeping down from the peaks. Nonetheless, the lakes retain their romance – morning mist hangs on the waters, snow carpets the lakeside ridges. With prices low and few tourists around, **winter** can be a great time to visit.

Author picks

Despite more than ten years living, working and travelling in this beautiful region, our Italian Lakes authors still can't agree on which lake is best. Nevertheless, after much discussion, they've managed to pinpoint some favourite places:

Charming waterside villages There are dozens, but for sheer lakes romance these four are hard to beat: Gargnano on Lake Garda (p.298), Cannobio on Lake Maggiore (p.136), Orta San Giulio on Lake Orta (p.104) and – the all-round champion – Varenna on Lake Como (p.220).

Contemporary art Milan's Triennale (p.66) is a showcase for contemporary art and design, while if abstract painting floats your boat, head for the stunning Villa Panza gallery in Varese (p.157).

Renaissance splendour After Leonardo's *Last Supper* (p.79), next stop is Bergamo's Accademia Carrara (p.238) – but make time for Masolino's frescoes at Castiglione Olona (p.161) and Brescia's Santa Giulia museum (p.262), then head for the beauty of Cremona (p.267), Verona (p.315) and Mantua (p.339).

Sunny waterfront piazzas There are so many to savour – Cernobbio's (p.199) is a beauty, and Salò's (p.291) goes on forever, but Piazza Motta in Ascona (p.140) never fails to wow.

Best mountain drive For the sheer pleasure of switchbacks, forest climbs and stupendous summit views, plot a route up Monte Sighignola (p.175) – or for rugged Alpine scenery, tackle the Four Lakes Drive (p.296).

Walking country For the diversity of trails – from simple lakeside strolls to testing Alpine treks – the slopes behind Tremezzo (p.203), Menaggio (p.207) and Malcesine (p.309) take top slot.

Only accessible by boat There's no other way to reach the Swiss Customs Museum (p.174), the lavish gardens of Isola del Garda (p.281) and Isola Bella (p.126) or the graceful Baroque church of San Giulio (p.107).

> Our author recommendations don't end here. We've flagged up our favourite places – a perfectly sited hotel, an atmospheric café, a special restaurant – throughout the guide, highlighted with the ★ symbol.

TOP ISOLA BELLA **BOTTOM** LAKE GARDA

15

things not to miss

It's not possible to see everything that the Italian Lakes have to offer in one trip – and we don't suggest you try. What follows, in no particular order, is a selective taste of the region's highlights: beautiful villages, epic attractions and scenic journeys. All highlights have a page reference to take you straight into the guide, where you can find out more. Coloured numbers refer to chapters in the Guide section.

1 SIRMIONE, LAKE GARDA
Page 282
One of Lake Garda's most bewitchingly beautiful waterfront villages, sheltering behind crenellated walls, offers views, history and an air of calm relaxation.

2 WATERFRONT CAFÉS
Page 32
Wherever you go, the temptation is to nab a sunny lakeside table in a waterfront café and take in the views.

3 SHOPPING IN MILAN
Page 92
From slick designer boutiques to bargain-basement factory outlets, Milan is one of the world's best shopping destinations.

4 STRESA, LAKE MAGGIORE
Page 117
On Italy's longest lake, slender Maggiore, the beautiful resort of Stresa gazes out at island gardens floating offshore.

11 LAKE COMO
Page 186

Take a ferry across this idyllic lake, between the waterside villages of Bellagio, Menaggio and Varenna.

12 LAGO MAGGIORE EXPRESS
Page 119

A varied and beautiful circular journey by boat and train from Lake Maggiore up into the high Alps, crossing into Switzerland by scenic narrow-gauge train.

13 THE LAST SUPPER
Page 79

Book well in advance to see Leonardo da Vinci's masterpiece, tucked away on a refectory wall in Milan.

14 MANTUA
Page 340

One of Renaissance Italy's most prominent city-states, sleepy, elegant Mantua is a patchwork of cobbled lanes and piazzas with the vast Palazzo Ducale at its centre.

15 FOUR LAKES DRIVE
Page 296

A scenic full-day drive on a looping route through Alpine landscapes above Lake Garda, venturing out to Lake Idro and beyond.

Itineraries

The Italian Lakes aren't only about touring: many people choose one or other of the lakes and then base themselves there to explore locally. But if you fancy mixing things up – and if you have your own transport: train and bus links from lake to lake aren't great – there's nothing to stop you taking in the whole region at a single bite.

A WEEKEND IN MILAN

DAY ONE

The Duomo Kick off in the heart of the city at the iconic cathedral. Be sure to make time to clamber among the rooftop spires. **See p.56**

Quadrilatero d'Oro Feast your eyes or empty your wallet among cobbled lanes housing the world's top fashion showrooms. **See p.71**

Pinacoteca di Brera The fine collection at Milan's top art gallery will have you bewitched: these are some of Italy's greatest works of art. **See p.67**

Dinner Sample Milanese specialities such as *ossobuco alla Milanese* and *risotto alla Milanese* in traditional trattorie and *osterie*. **See p.86**

DAY TWO

The Last Supper Having reserved your slot months before, admire Leonardo's masterpiece at Santa Maria delle Grazie. **See p.79**

Sant'Ambrogio The lovely Romanesque church dedicated to the city's patron saint is an intimate haven. **See p.80**

Corso di Porta Ticinese Explore the charming churches of San Lorenzo and Sant'Eustorgio on this ancient thoroughfare. **See p.73**

Dinner Browse the waterfront bars and restaurants in the Navigli, Milan's last remaining canal neighbourhood. **See p.86**

THE GREAT OUTDOORS

❶ **Lake Orta** Rent a rowing boat for a lazy afternoon on the water. **See p.104**

❷ **Mottarone** Cable-car access to mountain-bike trails and footpaths galore. **See p.125**

❸ **Monte Generoso** Vintage rack-railway clanking high above Lake Lugano. **See p.176**

❹ **Cadenabbia** The Greenway del Lago path offers easy lakeside strolls. **See p.204**

❺ **Menaggio** Well-resourced trailhead for Lake Como's finest mountain walks. **See p.207**

❻ **Iseo** Stroll along the ancient Via Valeriana above Lake Iseo. **See p.253**

❼ **Tremosine** Venture on horseback into Alpine meadows high above Lake Garda. **See p.300**

❽ **Monte Baldo** An epic cable-car ride for walks and bike trails. **See p.310**

FOODIE HIGHLIGHTS

You'd be unlikely to plot a Lakes itinerary around specific restaurants – part of the joy is discovering some unsung family-run trattoria in the hills, after all – but here are a few favourites, mixed in with choice delis and foodie treats.

❶ **Pasticceria Grandazzi, Domodossola** Exquisite handmade chocolate creations

ABOVE COLONNE DI SAN LORENZO, MILAN; ISOLA BELLA, LAKE MAGGIORE

emerge from a tiny workshop in this northern town. **See p.147**

❷ Villa Crespi, Orta San Giulio Top-class fine dining at an opulent oriental-style folly above Lake Orta. **See p.110**

❸ La Sorgente, Vico Morcote Laidback village restaurant above Lake Lugano with a sense of style. **See p.177**

❹ Peck, Milan Swoon at the mouth-watering culinary delicacies in this multi storey deli and café. **See p.94**

❺ La Dogana del Buongusto, Milan Feast on exceptional home-made specialities at this bustling restaurant and wine bar. **See p.87**

❻ Silvio, Bellagio Cheerful welcome guaranteed at this modern fish restaurant on Lake Como. **See p.216**

❼ Vineria Cozzi, Bergamo Historic wine bar and restaurant serving excellent regional dishes in a series of inviting dining rooms. **See p.241**

❽ Due Colombe, Franciacorta Michelin-starred restaurant offering delectable gourmet cuisine in an ancient farmhouse. **See p.255**

❾ Cascina Capuzza, Selva Capuzza Delicious local ingredients (including their own wines and olive oil) served amid vineyards near Lake Garda. **See p.290**

❿ Enoteca Cangrande, Verona Wonderful array of wines and Veronese nibbles at this welcoming, always-packed wine bar off the main Piazza Brà. **See p.336**

GARDENS OF THE LAKES

Visit these celebrated gardens to fill a two-week botanical jaunt around the lakes.

❶ Isola Bella Famously beautiful island garden in Italian Baroque style, tiered high above Lake Maggiore. **See p.126**

❷ Isola Madre Outstanding English garden on Lake Maggiore, packed with exotics. **See p.128**

❸ Villa Táranto Superbly varied English gardens, with dahlias and miles of trails to explore. **See p.131**

❹ Isole di Brissago Pristine botanical gardens in Swiss waters. Roam the footpaths, then grab a siesta under the palms. **See p.139**

❺ Villa del Balbianello Lovely waterside lawns on Lake Como – the epitome of lakes romance. **See p.202**

❻ Villa Carlotta Acres of beautifully presented rhododendrons, camellias and azaleas cover slopes overlooking Lake Como. **See p.206**

❼ Villa Melzi Landscaped English gardens beside Bellagio, with promenades of plane trees and even a sequoia. **See p.213**

❽ Villa Monastero Atmospheric garden of succulents and exotics, steeply tiered on Lake Como's eastern shore. **See p.222**

❾ Parco Giardino Sigurtà Expansive lawns and tranquil woods spread above the River Mincio, by Lake Garda. **See p.288**

❿ Giardino Giusti Romantic Renaissance gardens in the heart of Verona. **See p.331**

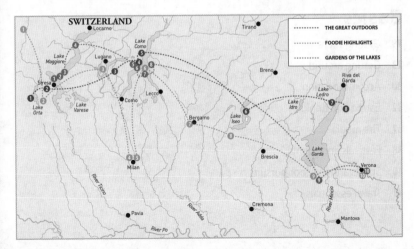

Basics

Getting there

The Italian Lakes region is well connected with airports all around the world. Intercontinental flights head for Milan's Malpensa, which also serves many European routings, as does Milan's other airport, Linate. The smaller airports at Bergamo, Brescia, Verona, and Lugano in Switzerland, are also within striking distance of Milan and the lakes. Travelling by train, car or even bus from the UK is a viable, greener, more leisurely option, though still not competitive in terms of price.

Flight availability and prices depend on when you travel. It's cheaper to fly midweek; flights at the beginning and end of the week are in demand from businesspeople and holiday-makers alike. Easter, public holidays and the beginning and end of August see airports at their busiest. Flights to the region are also booked up well in advance around Milan's fashion and design shows in January, April and September, while in August most people choose to avoid the humid heat of the city, so flights can be easier to come by. The best advice is to reserve your flight as far ahead as possible: good-value last-minute tickets are rare.

The **internet** is the best place to start looking for flights, but don't ignore **specialist agents** either (see p.22): many offer youth fares and a range of other travel-related services such as insurance, car rental and tours. Italy is also a common stop on European and worldwide **tours**, and you should have no problem including the region in a tailor-made itinerary if off-the-peg tickets are not suitable.

Flights from the UK and Ireland

The fastest and most economical way of reaching the Italian Lakes is by air. It takes just under two hours to fly from southern England to the heart of the region, and good bus, train and road routes ensure swift onward transport. If you're planning to tour the area, consider flying into one airport and out of another.

The **no-frills airlines**, such as easyJet and Ryanair, fly regularly from London and many regional airports to Orio al Serio, Venice Treviso and Turin. Of the major **full-service carriers**, British Airways offers the most choice, while Alitalia flies to Milan from the UK. SWISS has daily flights to Lugano-Agno (via Zürich).

From the Irish Republic, Aer Lingus and Alitalia have services to Milan and Ryanair flies from Shannon to Bergamo-Orio al Serio.

Tickets and prices

If you book far enough in advance on the **no-frills airlines**, or bag one of their frequent special offers, you can get tickets for less than £50 return from the UK (including taxes, with hand-luggage only) for an off-peak flight. The cheapest **full-service** tickets normally cost around £120–160 (including taxes) to Milan or Verona for a return fare in low season; be prepared to pay £250–350 in high season, when the cheaper seats get booked up months in advance.

It is possible to find deals for around €100 for direct return flights **from Ireland** if you book early, but prices are usually significantly higher (€300–500). It might make more sense to pick up an inexpensive flight to England or the Continent and get a connecting flight from there.

Flights from the US and Canada

Alitalia offers the widest choice of direct flights between North America and Italy, and Delta, US Airways, Continental and American Airways also offer direct options. In addition, many European carriers fly to Milan (via their capitals or via Rome) from major US and Canadian cities.

Fares don't vary much so you can usually base your choice on flight timings, routes, gateway cities, ticket restrictions and even the airline's

---

A BETTER KIND OF TRAVEL

At Rough Guides we are passionately committed to travel. We feel that travelling is the best way to understand the world we live in and the people we share it with – plus tourism has brought a great deal of benefit to developing economies around the world over the last few decades. But the growth in tourism has also damaged some places irreparably, and climate change is exacerbated by most forms of transport, especially flying. All Rough Guides' trips are carbon-offset, and every year we donate money to a variety of charities devoted to combating the effects of climate change.

reputation for comfort and service. Flight time is around nine hours from New York, Boston and the eastern Canadian cities, twelve hours from Chicago and fifteen hours from Los Angeles. The cheapest return fares to Milan, travelling midweek in low season, start at around $800 from New York or Boston, rising to about $1000 during the summer. Add another $150–300 for flights from LA, Miami and Chicago. Numerous airlines, including Air Canada and United, have flights from Toronto via Rome to Milan for a low-season fare of around Can$1200 midweek, increasing to around $2500 in high season without taxes.

Flights from Australia, New Zealand and South Africa

There are no direct flights to Italy from Australia or New Zealand, but there are some good deals to be had which include **stopovers** in East

AIRPORTS AND ROUTES

It's worth spending a moment establishing which is the most **convenient** of the region's numerous airports for your holiday, so that you can cut down travelling time when you arrive. Milan has two airports, both of which receive regular flights from the UK and Ireland. **Malpensa** (MXP), 45km northwest of the city – also the region's intercontinental airport – is just 15km from the southern tip of Lake Maggiore and convenient for lakes Orta and Como, too (see p.81). **Linate** (LIN), 7km east of the city, is your best bet if you're starting or ending your trip in Milan itself (see p.81). **Orio al Serio** (BGY), just outside Bergamo, is also billed as Milan, although it's about an hour's travel from the city centre. It is, however, conveniently located halfway between lakes Como and Garda, near the smaller Lake Iseo (see p.239). The smaller **Brescia-Montichiari** (VBS) airport, confusingly otherwise known as "Verona (Brescia)" airport and "Gabriele d'Annunzio" airport, is 20km southeast of Brescia, just 12km from Lake Garda, though it's actually quite a long way out of Verona – 52km southwest (see p.264). Much closer to Verona itself is **Verona-Villafranca** (VRN), also called "Valerio Catullo" (see p.331). Venice and Turin are outside the scope of this book, but their airports (Turin and both Venice Marco Polo and Venice Treviso) are under an hour away from the western and eastern lakes respectively (see p.331). In Switzerland, the small **Lugano-Agno** (LUG) airport is ten minutes from the town centre and convenient for lakes Maggiore and Como, as well as Lake Lugano itself (see p.170).

DISTANCES

The table below shows the distance from the different airports to a main town on each of the lakes. Distances have been worked out along major roads and the estimated times based on travelling by car at a steady 100km per hour. Tolls vary depending on the route but are always inexpensive. At the time of writing, for example, the 58km from Linate to Como cost €5.80, while the 130km journey from Malpensa to Sirmione on Lake Garda was €10.40.

Arrival airport/ final destination	Stresa (Lake Maggiore)	Lugano (Lake Lugano)	Milan city centre	Como (Lake Como)	Bergamo city centre	Sirmione (Lake Garda)	Verona city centre
Milan-Malpensa (MXP)	45km (30min)	65km (45min)	48km (35min)	43km (30min)	72km (55min)	150km (1hr 40min)	178km (2hr)
Milan-Linate (LIN)	100km (1hr 10min)	87km (1hr)	7km (20min)	65km (45min)	45km (30min)	124km (1hr 25min)	152km (1hr 45min)
Lugano-Agno (LUG)	90km (1hr 45min)	4km (10min)	86km (1hr)	25km (15min)	95km (1hr 15min)	185km (2hr)	215km (2hr 25min)
Bergamo-Orio al Serio (BGY)	124km (1hr 25min)	112km (1hr 15min)	40km (30min)	88km (1hr)	5km (15min)	81km (55min)	108km (1hr 15min)
Brescia-Montichiari (VBS)	186km (2hr)	172km (1hr 55min)	105km (1hr 15min)	150km (1hr 40min)	66km (45min)	22km (15min)	50km (35min)
Verona-Villafranca (VRN)	242km (2hr 35min)	230km (2hr 45min)	155km (1hr 15min)	206km (2hr 25min)	122km (1hr 40min)	42km (30min)	13km (10min)

Asia or European airline hubs. Return **fares** to Milan from the main cities in **Australia** cost Aus\$1800–2100 in low season, and Aus\$2000–2500 in high season.

Fares to Milan from **New Zealand** cost from NZ\$2100 in low season to NZ\$3500 in high season. It's also worth considering flying to one of the European hubs such as London or Berlin and looking for a low-cost flight from there.

Various carriers run from **South Africa** to Italy, usually with a stop in their European or Middle Eastern hub, although Etihad has several weekly direct flights from Johannesburg and Cape Town to Milan. The best-value carriers are Etihad, Lufthansa and KLM, although BA, Turkish Airlines and South African Airways can be competitive if bought far enough in advance. Return flights start at around ZAR5800.

Trains from the UK

Travelling **by train** to Italy won't save you money, but it can be an enjoyable and leisurely way of getting to the country. The choice of routes and fares is complex, but most trains pass through Paris and head south through Switzerland towards Milan. A **return fare** to Milan, using Eurostar and the high-speed Artesia TGV through France, starts at £120 and takes around eleven hours. Booking ninety days or more in advance will give you more choice of services and you should bag any special offers that are going. Using slower trains won't cut the cost very significantly and neither will the cross-Channel ferry route. Bear in mind that if you travel via Paris on Eurostar you have to change stations from the Gare du Nord to the Gare de Lyon. Most trains cross the Alps during the night, though with a very early start you can get from London to Milan in a day and catch some Alpine scenery. Alternatively, head for Zürich, stay overnight and take a Eurocity train to Milan in the morning. Details on the options for international rail routes are reliably explained on the wonderful website Ⓦseat61.com.

Buses from the UK and Ireland

The days when **bus travel** was the cheapest way of getting to Italy have long gone and it's difficult to see why anyone would choose to get there this way. National Express Eurolines have direct services **from London** to Milan and Turin, with less frequent services to Brescia and Verona, all for around £120 return (mid-season). They have occasional bargain offers for tickets booked a week or more in advance and there are small discounts for passengers under 26 or over 60. The Milan and Turin service departs four times a week and takes 24–26 hours; the journeys to Brescia and Verona take a similar length of time but departures are a little less frequent. Eurolines also has a regular service **from Dublin**, Cork, Limerick and Belfast to London, from where you can get a connection to Italy.

Driving from the UK and Ireland

There's no one fixed route to Italy if you're travelling with your own vehicle. The best cross-Channel route will depend on your starting point, but any travel agent can provide up-to-date ferry schedules and make advance bookings – essential for high season. There are several excellent online **route-planning services** which calculate not only the best route but also toll booth and petrol prices, as well as listing service stations; the AA and RAC sites are good, but the quickest and easiest to use is the Michelin service (Ⓦviamichelin.co.uk).

As regards **routes from northern France**, the Alpine route via Germany and Switzerland entering Italy at Chiasso by Lake Como is the shortest as the crow flies. Alternatively, you could push down further into France and then cross the Alps at the Mont Blanc tunnel to Courmayeur and the A5, or at Fréjus from where the A32 heads to Turin and from there the A4 continues into Lombardy.

There are **direct motorail train services** to Alessandria in Piemonte (one hour's drive southwest of Milan) from 'S Hertogenbosch (convenient for the Hook of Holland ferry port; Ⓦautoslaaptrein.nl) in the Netherlands. Seven German railway stations (Ⓦdbautozug.de), including Dusseldorf, Hildesheim, Lorrach and Berlin, are boarding points for motorail train services to Alessandria, Bolzano and Verona. Car-carrying trains head under the Alps from Kandersteg (near Bern) to Iselle (near Domodossola), through the Lötschberg Tunnel and the Simplon Tunnel (Ⓦbls.ch).

Remember that **motorways** in France, Switzerland and Germany – not to mention Italy – are **toll roads**, so you'll need to factor these in when calculating costs; €50 should cover a trip from the UK to Lake Como, for example. In France and Italy you get a ticket when you join the motorway and pay when you exit, while in Switzerland you need a *vignette* which you display in your windscreen, granting the right to drive anywhere on the Swiss motorway network for up to a year; this costs Fr.40, available from customs officials as you enter the country.

The Channel Tunnel

Eurotunnel runs shuttle trains for vehicles between Folkestone and Coquelles, near Calais, via the **Channel Tunnel**. You can just turn up and go, though booking is advisable. Boarding is quick and easy – there are up to four departures per hour (one per hour midnight to 6am) – and the journey takes a smooth, hassle-free 35–45 minutes. **Fares** vary a lot; travelling between 10pm and 6am can cut costs, while travelling at weekends, or in July and August, adds a premium. A two-week return in the peak summer period can be £110–180 per car, though last-minute fares are likely to be much higher.

AIRLINES

Aer Lingus ⓦ aerlingus.com.
Air Canada ⓦ aircanada.ca.
Air France ⓦ airfrance.com.
Air One ⓦ flyairone.com.
Alitalia ⓦ alitalia.com.
American Airlines ⓦ aa.com.
British Airways ⓦ britishairways.com.
Delta Air Lines ⓦ delta.com.
easyJet ⓦ easyjet.com.
Etihad ⓦ etihad.com.
KLM ⓦ klm.com.
Lufthansa ⓦ lufthansa.com.
Qantas ⓦ qantas.com.au.
Ryanair ⓦ ryanair.com.
South African Airways ⓦ flysaa.com.
SWISS ⓦ swiss.com.
Turkish Airlines ⓦ turkishairlines.com.
United Airlines ⓦ united.com.

TRAVEL AGENTS

CIT Australia ☎ 1300 361 500, ⓦ cittravel.com.au. Italian specialists, with packages to Milan, as well as the lakes.
Flight Centres Australia ☎ 13 31 33, New Zealand ☎ 09 358 4310, ⓦ flightcentre.com.au. Discount international airfares and holiday packages.
Joe Walsh Tours Eire ☎ 01 241 0800, ⓦ joewalshtours.ie. General budget fares agent.
North South Travel UK ☎ 01245 608 291, ⓦ northsouthtravel .co.uk. Friendly, competitive travel agency whose profits are used to promote sustainable tourism.
Premier Travel Eire ☎ 028 7126 3333, ⓦ premiertravel.uk.com. Discount flight specialists with hotel, insurance and car-rental deals.
STA Travel UK ☎ 0871 2300 040, US ☎ 1 800 781 4040, Australia ☎ 134 782, New Zealand ☎ 0800 474 400, South Africa ☎ 0861 781 781, ⓦ statravel.co.uk. Worldwide specialists in independent travel; also student IDs, travel insurance, car rental, rail passes, and more. Good discounts for students and under-26s.
Travel Cuts Canada US & Canada ☎ 1 866 246 9762, ⓦ travelcuts.com. Canadian student-travel organization.

TOUR OPERATORS

Adventure Travel Company New Zealand ☎ 09 355 9135, ⓦ adventuretravel.co.nz. Hotels and car rental, plus walking and cycling tours in the Italian Lakes.
Adventures Abroad US ☎ 1 800 665 3998, ⓦ adventures -abroad.com. Small-group cultural and walking tours.
Arblaster & Clarke UK ☎ 01730 263 111, ⓦ winetours.co.uk. Upmarket outfit which organizes opera, gourmet and wine-tasting breaks.
Backroads US ☎ 1 800 462 2848 or ☎ 510 527 1555, ⓦ backroads.com. Activity holidays including lakeside walking holidays.
Butterfield & Robinson US ☎ 1 800 678 11477, ⓦ butter field.com. Escorted cycling and walking tours in Italy, featuring Lakes trip.

PACKAGES AND ORGANIZED TOURS

Package tours may not sound like your kind of travel, but don't dismiss the idea out of hand. In addition to the fully escorted variety, many agents (see above) can put together very flexible deals, sometimes amounting to no more than a flight plus car and accommodation. If you're planning a trip geared around special interests, such packages can sometimes work out cheaper – and are certainly less hassle – than the same arrangements made on arrival.

An increasing number of operators organize **specialist holidays** such as walking tours, art and architecture trips, and Italian food and wine jaunts, as well as short breaks to coincide with opera festivals and even football matches. Prices vary widely, so check what you are getting for your money (many don't include the cost of the airfare).

There's also a plethora of operators selling **short-break deals**, especially to Milan and Verona: for these, reckon on spending upwards of £250 per person for three nights in Milan in a three-star hotel during low season and upwards of £300 between April and October, though special offers can sometimes cut prices drastically, especially for late bookings.

If you want to rent a car in Italy (see p.26), check with tour operators, airlines and flight agents before you leave, as some **fly-drive** deals work out very cheaply.

Central Holidays US ☎ 1 800 539 7098, ⓦ centralholidays.com. Wide range of independent and escorted tours plus city breaks.

Citalia UK ☎ 0871 200 2004, ⓦ citalia.co.uk. Hotel packages around the main lakes plus tailor-made itineraries, city breaks in Milan and Verona, and car rental.

Classic Journeys US ☎ 1 800 200 3887, ⓦ classicjourneys.com. Gentle hikes around lakes Maggiore, Lugano and Como.

Country Walkers US ☎ 1 800 464 9255, ⓦ countrywalkers.com. Small-group walking tours around the lakes with local guides.

Crystal Holidays UK ☎ 0871 231 5661, ⓦ crystalholidays.co.uk. Hotel packages on the lakes, and in Milan and Verona.

Europe Through the Back Door US ☎ 425 771 8303, ⓦ ricksteves.com. Rick Steves offers an informative website to help with planning independent trips and also offers a range of tours.

Italian Connection UK ☎ 01424 728 900, ⓦ italian-connection .co.uk. Tailor-made holidays throughout the region, including accommodation and car rental.

Italian Connection US ☎ 1 800 462 7911, ⓦ italian-connection .com. Hiking and gourmet holidays that take in the western lakes.

Martin Randall Travel UK ☎ 020 8742 3355, ⓦ martinrandall .com. Small-group cultural holidays led by experts on art, archeology or music. At the time of writing, they were offering tours of lakeside gardens and Verona and Milan opera.

Saga Holidays UK ☎ 0800 096 0074, ⓦ travel.saga.co.uk. Tours of the lakes aimed at people who are 50 and over.

Sunvil Discovery UK ☎ 020 8758 4722, ⓦ sunvil.co.uk/discovery. Tailor-made specialists offering a high-quality range of accommodation around the region, including hotels on Lake Maggiore, Lake Como, Lake Garda and in central Verona.

Walkabout Gourmet Adventures Australia ☎ 02 9871 5526, ⓦ walkaboutgourmet.com. Classy food, wine and walking tours.

RAIL CONTACTS

Eurostar ☎ 0843 218 6186, ⓦ eurostar.com.
International Rail ☎ 0870 231 0791, ⓦ internationalrail.com. Friendly company offering a wide variety of rail options including Eurostar, international sleepers and ferry crossings.
The Man in Seat Sixty-One ⓦ seat61.com. Up-to-date, user-friendly advice on how to use rail systems around the world.
Voyages SNCF ☎ 08448 485 848, ⓦ uk.voyages-sncf.com. Informative agent selling tickets for rail journeys to Italy, with discounted fares for under-26s. Also agents for InterRail and Eurostar.

BUS CONTACTS

Eurolines ☎ 08717 818181, ⓦ eurolines.co.uk.

FERRY CONTACTS

SeaView ⓦ seaview.co.uk. Up-to-date list of ferry companies and their routes.

CHANNEL TUNNEL

Eurotunnel UK ☎ 0844 335 3535, International ☎ +333 2100 2061, ⓦ eurotunnel.com.

Getting around

Whether you choose to spend your lakes holiday taking ferries from one village to another or wish to venture further afield, you'll have plenty of modes of transport to choose from. Public transport is comprehensive, with ferries, buses and trains covering the region, and prices are low, although getting from one lake to another can be fiddly. Naturally, you'll have more flexibility with your own transport, allowing you to travel at your own pace and to out-of-the-way places, though this can be outweighed by the stress of driving. Roads are good throughout the region, although they get very crowded on summer weekends and public holidays.

All the lakes are crisscrossed by good-value regular **ferry services** throughout the year, with car-ferries traversing the middle of the three big lakes. **Trains** link the larger towns away from the lakes. Milan is the main hub, while **buses** connect smaller centres and trace the lakeside roads to serve the waterfront villages. This is also **motorbike and bicycle** territory, so if you're happier on two wheels you won't be alone.

We've detailed train, bus and ferry frequencies in the "Arrival and departure" sections throughout the Guide: note that these refer to regular working-day schedules (Monday to Saturday); services can be reduced or even nonexistent on **Sundays**. Bus and train timetables are also affected by school holidays, and some services don't run during **August**.

In Italy

Public transport in Italy is good value for money and efficient. Most Italians still choose to drive, however, and you may want to follow suit if you wish to explore beyond the lakes themselves.

By car

Italy is a car-loving nation: its population spends an awful lot of money on new vehicles and takes every possible opportunity to use them. The result is busy roads full of new – or newish – cars travelling at high speeds. The **road network**, though, is generally good, with a comprehensive motorway (autostrada) system running the length and breadth of the region. The best plan is to avoid driving on public holidays or Friday and Sunday nights in summer when nature-starved townsfolk head for the lakes and mountains – and back again. Town centres should be avoided as much as possible, too, as congestion, a proliferation of one-way systems, limited-access areas ("ZTL") and confusing signage can make them a headache. The centres of many of the lake villages are closed to traffic, although access is usually allowed if you have a hotel reservation. Driving in Milan and on its notorious *Tangenziale* (ring road) is best avoided especially during the morning and evening rush hours (Mon–Sat 7–9am & 5–8pm).

To combat the pollution problems of some of Italy's big towns, **No-Car Days** are becoming increasingly common. On these designated days, between the allotted hours, only authorized cars are allowed to circulate. On Sundays this will usually mean just public transport and taxis. In some towns – most notably Bergamo's Città Alta – the *centro storico* is closed to unauthorized vehicles every Sunday as well as Friday and Saturday mornings in summer: you'll need to use the well-organized public transport instead.

Rules of the road

Italian driving laws are straightforward. Drive on the right; observe the speed limits – 50kph in built-up areas, 110kph on dual carriageways and 130kph on motorways (for camper vans, these limits are 50kph, 80kph and 100kph respectively); and don't drink and drive. Police checkpoints are relatively common in holiday areas and speed cameras are popping up everywhere. Similarly, cameras record any unauthorized vehicles entering the "Zona Traffico Limitato" (ZTL) areas of old towns and fines are high. Drivers also need to have their dipped headlights on when using any road outside a built-up area and carry a warning triangle and a fluorescent jacket, in case of breakdown.

As regards **documentation**, if you're bringing your own car, as well as current insurance, you need a valid driving licence and an international driving permit if you're a non-EU licence holder. If you hold a UK pre-1991 driving licence you'll need an inter-national driving permit or to update your licence to a photocard version. It's compulsory to carry your car documents (not photocopies) and passport while you're driving, and you can be fined on the spot if you cannot present them when stopped by the police – not an uncommon occurrence. For more information, consult ⓦtheaa.com.

Signage

Confusingly for UK visitors, motorway **signage** is on a green background and main-road information on

---

CROSSING THE ROAD

Don't assume that as a **pedestrian** you're safe in Italy; even on crossings with traffic lights you can be subject to some close calls. Drivers will not automatically stop at pedestrian crossings. Look both ways before crossing, even when there's a green light for you, as it will probably also be giving the go-ahead to a line of traffic.

---

blue. In most cases you'd do best to have a map or use a satellite navigation system rather than just follow signs, as they can be, at best, erratic and, at worst, indecipherable. Abbreviations are common, so if you get a few of the main ones under your belt, navigating will be a whole lot easier: MI is Milan, BG Bergamo, BS Brescia, VR Verona, TO Turin and CH Switzerland. Motorways are often more prominently named by their start and finish points on some signs than by their A-number – for example, the signs to "GENOVA-GRAVELLONA T." are in fact indicating the A26 which leads to Lake Maggiore. To be properly prepared, check the end point of the motorway in the direction you're going before you head off.

Another common sight that can leave visitors perplexed is **flashing traffic lights** at crossroads. This happens in locations where the lights are needed for traffic control during the day, but where there is not enough night-time traffic to warrant continued control. The lights basically serve to alert you to a junction; they do not give anyone the right of way, you just have to look and go when it's clear.

You will no doubt encounter a route or two undergoing **roadworks**. Slow down and follow the temporary yellow road lines. Whenever possible try and work out any temporary signs too – motorway exits, for example, are frequently closed (*chiuso*) if they are affected by works, but this will be well signed for up to 100km beforehand.

Fuel

Most **petrol stations** give you the choice of self-service (*fai da te*), or, for a few cents more, someone will fill the tank. Petrol stations often have the same working hours as shops, which means they'll be closed for a couple of hours at midday, will shut up shop at around 7pm and are likely to be closed on Sundays. Outside these times many have a self-service facility payable into a machine between the pumps by bank note or, more rarely, credit card; these are often not well advertised so you might need to go onto the forecourt to check. It's worth bearing in mind that petrol is considerably **cheaper in Switzerland**. Unsurprisingly, there are hardly any petrol stations within about 20km of the border on the Italian side, so do as the locals do, and pop over the border (you might need your passport). Alternatively, if you're visiting Swiss lakes and mountains be sure to fill your tank while you're there.

Lakeside driving

Most of the **roads around the lakes** are narrow and you'll often find yourself fast up against the mountainside with the lake on the other side just a few metres away. Some of the roads give stunning views across the water; others, hemmed in by campsites, Baroque palaces or lemon groves, keep you tantalizingly just out of sight of the lake. The roads at the southern end of the lakes, nearer the major urban centres, can get very busy in summer; you could find yourself in gridlock for several miles on a sunny Sunday afternoon.

The roads along some parts of the lakes are cut into the mountains with single-bore tunnels or *gallerie*, with one lane in each direction and no central divider. Beware of driving with sunglasses on, as you can be plunged from sunshine into scary blackness with little warning.

Motorway driving

All **motorways** (autostrade) are toll-roads. Take a ticket as you come on and pay on exit; the amount due is flashed up on a screen in front of you. Paying by cash is the most straightforward option – booths are marked "cash/*contanti*" and colour-coded white. To pay by credit card, follow the "Viacard" sign (blue). Avoid the Telepass lane (yellow), which is for drivers holding post-paid electronic cards. Be alert as you get into lane as traffic zigzags in and out at high speed to get pole position at the shortest-looking queue. Since other roads can be frustratingly slow and heaving with freight traffic, the very reasonable tolls are well worth it over long distances, but be prepared for queues at exits at peak times.

You're most likely to use the A4 Turin–Venice motorway, which travels south of the lakes and skirts Milan to the north. Running north, the A8 and A9 head out from Milan to Varese and Lake Como respectively, while the A21 and A22 feed traffic south to Cremona and Mantua. Milan's ring road – the *Tangenziale* – is divided into the A50 Tangenziale Ovest (west, which also covers the southern part) and the A51 Tangenziale Est (the eastern part); the A4 comprises the northern stretch.

Italian motorway driving is aggressive, with excessive speeds and tailgating all too common. The inside lane is often taken by large freight vehicles (part of Italy's severe pollution problem comes from the fact that so much commercial traffic uses the road rather than the rail system), while the outside lane frequently resembles a Formula One testing track. Your best bet is to drive within the speed limit, observe all the rules and be alert to juggernauts or Audis swinging out in front of you without any warning.

Parking

Parking can be a problem. On the lakes, most towns and villages have pay-and-display areas just outside the centre, but these can get very full during high season. Parking at night is easier than during the day, but check the signs to make sure you're not parked in a street that turns into a market in the morning or on the one day of the week when it's cleaned in the small hours; otherwise you're likely to be towed.

Parking attendants are especially active in tourist areas and if you get fed up with driving around and settle for a space in a *zona di rimozione* (tow-away zone), don't expect your car to be there when you get back. In **Milan**, don't be surprised to see parking just about anywhere, notably on pavements, seemingly working tram lines and bus stops, but you'd be unwise to follow suit.

Towns generally operate a colour-coded parking scheme: **blue-zone** parking spaces (delineated by a blue line) usually have a maximum stay of one or

---

MOTORWAYS (AUTOSTRADE) IN THE LAKES REGION

A4 "Torino–Venezia/Trieste" Turin–Milan–Bergamo–Brescia–Verona–Venice.

A8 "Milano–Varese" Milan–Varese.

A9 "Lainate–Chiasso" Milan–Como–Switzerland (Lugano).

A21 "Torino–Brescia" Cremona–Brescia.

A22 "Modena–Brennero" Mantua–Verona–Lake Garda's east shore.

A26 "Genova–Gravellona Toce" West side of Lake Maggiore–Domodossola (signposted for the "Passo del Sempione").

two hours; they cost €1–1.50 per hour (pay at meters, attendants wearing authorizing badges or buy scratch-cards from local tobacconists), but are sometimes free at lunchtimes, after 8pm and on Sundays. Much coveted **white-zone** spaces (white lines) are free, while **yellow-zone** areas (yellow lines) are reserved for residents.

Breakdown and safety

If your vehicle **breaks down**, dial ☎ 116 and tell the operator where you are, the type of car you're in, and your registration number: the nearest office of the Automobile Club d'Italia (ACI) will send someone out to fix your car – although it's not a free service and can work out very expensive if you need a tow. For this reason, if you're bringing your own vehicle you might consider arranging cover with a motoring organization in your home country. Any ACI office in Italy can tell you where to get **spare parts** for your particular car.

Never leave anything visible in the car when you're not using it. Thefts are particularly common at motorway service areas and in tourist centres.

Car rental

Renting a car in Italy is pricey, especially in high season, at around £265/US$430 per week for a small hatchback, with unlimited mileage if booked in advance. The major chains have offices in all the larger towns and the airports, as well as Milan's Stazione Centrale; addresses are detailed in the "Arrival and departure" sections throughout the Guide. Generally the best deals are to be had by arranging things in advance, through one of the agents listed below or with specialist tour operators when you book your flight or holiday. You need to be over 21 to rent a car in Italy and will need a credit card with enough available funds (around €1000) to act as a deposit when picking up your vehicle; otherwise you will have to take out comprehensive insurance.

If you're planning to head into **Switzerland** on your trip – to go round the top of Lake Maggiore, say, or spend a day or two around Lugano or Bellinzona – always check the rules with your rental company in advance. Switzerland is not in the EU, although it's surrounded by EU countries. Border controls, especially at heavily used crossing points, can lead to long lines of traffic, even though regulations are a formality and searches are very infrequent. However, you'd do well to be certain before you depart that you're not going to break customs regulations or passport/visa requirements on your way back in.

Camper van rental

Camper van or mobile-home holidays are becoming increasingly popular in Italy and the rental market is opening up to meet the demand. To add to the obvious convenience of this type of holiday, facilities in campsites are usually dependable (see p.31), and more and more resorts have created free camper van parking areas (*sosta camper*). The following are just a selection of the companies offering new (or newish) vehicles for rent. Prices are usually around €1200 for a two-berth vehicle for a week in high season, with unlimited mileage.

CAMPERVAN RENTAL AGENCIES

Blu rent ☎ 39 0171 601 702, ⓦ blurent.com.
Comocaravan ☎ 39 031 521 215, ⓦ comocaravan.it. Website in Italian only.
Maggiore ☎ 39 0323 556 137, ⓦ magicamper.com. Website in Italian only.

MOTORING ORGANIZATIONS

Australia AAA ☎ 02 6247 7311, ⓦ aaa.asn.au.
Canada CAA ☎ 613 820-1890, ⓦ caa.ca.
Ireland AA ☎ 01 617 9999, ⓦ aaireland.ie.
Italy TCI ☎ 0840 888 802, ⓦ www.touringclub.it.
New Zealand AA ☎ 0800 500 444, ⓦ aa.co.nz.
UK AA ☎ 0161 333 0004, ⓦ theaa.co.uk; RAC ☎ 0800 550 055, ⓦ rac.co.uk.
US AAA ☎ 1 800 222 4357, ⓦ aaa.com.

By rail

The **railway network** around Lombardy is good, especially if you want to travel between the provincial towns. It is not so comprehensive, however, when it comes to the lakes, where railway lines often serve one shoreline only and you'll have to switch to ferries or buses. Milan is naturally the hub of the system and you may find it quicker to head into the city and then out again rather than fiddle around with connections at smaller stations. Services are usually on time, efficient and good value for money.

The majority of trains are run by the state-run Ferrovie dello Stato (FS) under the brand name **Trenitalia**, but there are also a few other companies operating services in the region, for example the **Ferrovia Vigezzina** (ⓦ vigezzina.com), which operates the Domodossola to Locarno route, and the **Ferrovie Nord** (ⓦ trenord.it), which runs many services around Varese, Lake Maggiore and Como, and from Brescia past Lake Iseo, as well as operating the Malpensa Express from Malpensa airport into Milan.

Standards of trains and carriages vary. At the top of the range are the **Pendolino** (CiS), a trans-Alpine service between Italy and Switzerland with very smart trains; the **Eurostar Italia** (ES), which runs between major cities, is slightly faster and more efficient than the **Intercity** (IC); the **Eurocity** trains connect Milan with centres such as Paris, Vienna, Hamburg and Barcelona. Reservations are usually required for all of these services and a supplement in the region of thirty percent of the ordinary fare is payable. Make sure you get the correct ticket for the service before boarding, otherwise you'll have to cough up a large surcharge to the conductor.

Diretto (D) and **Interregionale (IR)** trains are the common-or-garden long-distance trains, calling only at larger stations. Although reservations are not required for these trains, it's worth booking seats, especially in summer, when they can get very crowded. **Reservations** can be made at any major train station or travel agent in Italy or via Italian State Railways agents in the UK (see p.23). Lastly, there are the **Regionale (R)** services, which stop just about everywhere.

For **information** on the above trains call ☎89 20 21 or visit the Trenitalia website at ⓦ trenitalia.com. The website ⓦ seat61.com has excellent tips on how to use the Trenitalia website.

Timetables and fares

Timings and route information for the Trenitalia network are posted up at train stations, and we give a rough idea of frequencies and journey times in the "Arrival and departure" sections throughout the guide. If you're travelling extensively it would be worth investing in a copy of the twice-yearly *Orario delle ferrovie* (€3.50), the timetable for the main rail routes, on sale at most newspaper stands.

Fares are inexpensive, calculated by the kilometre and easy to work out for each journey. The timetables give the prices per kilometre, but as a rough guide, a second-class one-way fare from Milan to Verona currently costs about €25 by Intercity and Eurostar, €14 on Interregionale. Return tickets are valid within two months of the outward journey, but as two one-way tickets cost the same it's hardly worth bothering. **Children** aged 4–12 qualify for a fifty percent discount on all journeys, and children under 4 (not occupying a seat) travel free.

All stations have yellow **validating machines** in which passengers must stamp their ticket before embarking on their journey. Look out for them as you come onto the platform: if you fail to validate your ticket you'll be given an on-the-spot fine.

Rail passes

Because fares are so reasonable in Italy, a **rail pass** is only really worth considering if you plan to visit Italy as part of a wider tour of Europe. The Europe-wide **InterRail** pass (ⓦ interrail.eu) is available to European citizens travelling around a combination of countries in Europe, including Italy. And for non-EU citizens, **Eurail** passes (ⓦ eurail.com) give unlimited travel in Europe, including the Trenitalia network. With any of these passes you will be liable for supplements of €10 per journey on the faster trains, which will still need to be reserved in advance.

By bus

The train lines are complemented by regular **bus services** (*autobus* or *pullman*), which run up and down the lake shores and link towns and villages across the region. Remember, however, that in

---

READING TIMETABLES

On timetables – and parking signs too – *Lavorativo* or **feriale** is the word for the Monday to Saturday service, represented by two crossed hammers; **festivo** means that a train runs only on Sundays and holidays, symbolized by a Christian cross. Also pay attention to the **timetable notes**, specifying the dates between which some services run (*Si effettua dal … al …*), or whether a service is seasonal (*periodico*, denoted by a vertical squiggle).

Some other common terms on timetables are below.

escluso sabato not including Saturdays
si effettua fino all' … running until…
si effettua dal … starting from…
giornalmente daily
prenotazione obbligatoria compulsory reservation
estivo summer
invernale winter
Fer5 Monday to Friday
Fer6 Monday to Saturday

out-of-the-way villages, schedules can be sketchy and are drastically reduced – sometimes nonexistent – at weekends, especially on Sundays. On lakes Maggiore and Garda the situation is complicated by the fact that the shorelines lie in different regions and so tourist offices will not necessarily have information on the bus routes on the other side.

Timetables are usually displayed by the stop, or details can be picked up from tourist offices. There is no national bus company; dozens of private companies cover the lakes area. Buy **tickets** immediately before you travel from the bus station ticket office, or on the bus itself. If you want to get off, ask "*posso scendere?*"; "the next stop" is "*la prossima fermata*". The details of the whereabouts of **bus terminals** (*autostazione*) – often within walking distance of the train station – are detailed in the Guide. In smaller towns and villages, most buses pull in at the central piazza or on the main road just outside the centre.

City buses are always cheap, usually costing a flat fare of little more than €1. **Tickets** are available from a variety of sources, commonly newsagents and tobacconists (*tabacchi*), but also from anywhere displaying a sticker saying "tickets" or "*biglietti*", including many campsite shops and hotel front desks. Once on board, you must register your ticket in the machine at the back of the bus. The whole system is based on trust, though in most cities checks for fare-dodging are regularly made, and hefty spot-fines are levied against offenders.

By ferry

The four biggest lakes are all well served by **ferries,** which zigzag from shore to shore, docking at jetties that are usually conveniently positioned on the main lakeside piazzas or in the centre of the larger towns' promenades. Some of the regular boats are slow; if you're in a hurry, pay extra for a **hydrofoil**.

Car ferries also operate on Lake Maggiore (Intra–Laveno), Lake Como (Cadenabbia–Menaggio–Bellagio–Varenna) and Lake Garda (Maderno–Torri del Benaco and Limone–Malcesine). These can be a good way to minimize driving along slow, traffic-congested lakeside roads.

Timetables and fares are available at all tourist offices and the ticket booths on the jetties themselves. Prices vary from lake to lake, but fares are relatively inexpensive: Como to Bellagio, for example, is €10.40 one-way. There are some **discounts** for EU citizens over 65 and for children; details of passes are given in the relevant chapters.

For schedules and prices, check ⓦnavigazionelaghi .it, which covers the services on lakes Maggiore, Como and Garda; ⓦlakelugano.ch for Lake Lugano; and ⓦnavigazionelagoiseo.it for Lake Iseo.

By bicycle and motorbike

Cycling is a very popular sport and mode of transport in northern Italy. If you're intending to do a fair amount of touring by bike you could think about bringing your own machine from home – most flights take bikes (double-check with your carrier before you purchase a ticket). Alternatively, you could **rent** on the ground; bikes are often available for around €3 per hour in towns and lake resorts. Milan has a good-value **bike-sharing** system (see p.83). The flat topography of the Bassa Padana around Mantua is perfect cycling territory, and the paths along the rice fields make ideal cycle tracks (see p.349). Many local tourist authorities have leaflets detailing recommended routes.

The serious cyclist might consider staying at one of a chain of hotels that cater specifically for cycling enthusiasts. Each hotel has a secure room for your bike, a maintenance workshop, overnight laundry facilities, suggested itineraries and group-tour possibilities, a doctor at hand and even a special cyclists' diet. There is a handful of affiliated hotels in the lakes region; call ☎39 0541 307 531, or see ⓦitalybikehotels.it for further information and a list of hotels.

An alternative is to tour by **motorbike** (*moto*), and there are several professional outfits in Milan where you can rent by the day or the week (see p.83). Crash helmets are compulsory; police rigorously enforce this rule. In Milan, you could copy the locals and scoot around on a **moped**, or *motorino* (see p.83).

PUBLIC TRANSPORT IN LOMBARDY

The website ⓦ**www.en.regione.lombardia.it.** (click on "Move in Lombardy") is a very useful site combining **timetables** for different forms of public transport in Lombardy. Type in your start point and destination and the site will come up with different options, including bus, train, cable car and ferry connections. The downside is that it sticks strictly to the administrative region of Lombardy and so the eastern shore of Lake Garda and the western shore of Lake Maggiore and Lake Orta are not included.

In Switzerland

The efficiency of the massively comprehensive Swiss public transport system remains one of the wonders of the modern world. You can get anywhere you want quickly, easily and relatively cheaply, and it's clean, safe and pleasant. Services always depart on the dot, and train timetables are well integrated with those of the ferries and postbuses, which operate on routes not covered by rail, including the more remote villages and valleys. Cyclists are well served by the Swiss instinct for encouraging green thinking in all things.

By train

Swiss Federal Railways, or **FFS** (*Ferrovie federali svizzere*), maintains a modern, integrated, ecologically sound transport system, and travelling by train in Switzerland is invariably comfortable and hassle-free. There's a confusing array of different **Swiss travel passes** and you'll need to do your sums carefully to see if they're worth your while. Full details are at ⓦsbb.ch, where there is also a complete timetable with English-language information on connection timings, platform numbers and even the kind of refreshments available on board. Most main stations keep a public copy to consult.

Just about the only people you'll see lugging suitcases or rucksacks through train compartments in Switzerland are foreigners. Many Swiss register their heavy bags at the **station baggage counter** before boarding (Fr.22/€18 per item). This is a great service to take advantage of if you want to move on during the day but don't fancy carting your gear from locker to locker.

By bus and boat

Backing up the train network is a yet more comprehensive system of **buses**, which get to every single village and hamlet in the country. In addition, all Swiss travel passes are valid for travel on buses as well as trains. Bus stations are nearly always located in the forecourt of train stations. Even more handily, the bus and train **timetables** are coordinated, ensuring watertight connections from one to the other.

Boats on Lake Maggiore run smoothly from Italian waters to Swiss, as do those on Lake Lugano – which lies mostly in Switzerland.

Driving in Switzerland

Switzerland's road network is comprehensive and well planned. However, Swiss transport policy means that **cars** are slowly being given the squeeze, with tough city parking regulations and strict law enforcement.

The minimum driving age is 18, international licences are recognized for one year's driving in Switzerland and, as across Europe, **third-party insurance** is compulsory. It's obligatory to carry both a red warning triangle and the registration documents of the vehicle. If you intend driving on Swiss **motorways**, you have to stick a **vignette** inside your windscreen. These cost Fr.40/€33 for any vehicle up to 3.5 tonnes, are bought most easily from the customs officials when you first cross the border (also at post offices and petrol stations), and remain valid until January 31 of the following year. Trailers or caravans must have their own, additional *vignette*. Getting caught without one lays you open to a significant fine. However, it's quite easy to avoid motorways altogether and stick to ordinary main roads, which are free and – outside urban centres at least – reasonably fast.

Switzerland drives on the **right**, **seatbelts** are compulsory for all, and penalties for **drink-driving** are tough (one glass of beer has you on the limit). **Speed limits** are 120kph on motorways, 80kph on main roads and 50kph in urban areas. Like Italy, Swiss motorways are **signed in green**, while main roads are signed in blue; it's common to see a green sign and a blue sign to the same place pointing in opposite directions. At junctions, yellow diamonds painted on the road show who has **priority**; if in doubt, always let trams and buses go first, and give way to traffic coming from your right. On gradients, vehicles heading **uphill** have priority over those coming down; some narrow mountain tracks have controlled times for ascent and descent.

Parking

Parking in Switzerland is hellish, and can be very limited and prohibitively expensive. In cities, full car parks will quite often harbour queues of cars, their engines off, drivers waiting – sometimes for over an hour – for the next person to finish their shopping and so liberate a space.

On-street parking and open **car parks** are colour-coded. Spaces delineated with white lines – the **White Zone** – are the most common, time-limited places controlled either by individual meters or, more usually, a prominently marked central pay-point or *parchimetro collettivo*, taking coins only. Outside the hours posted on the pay-point, and where there isn't a machine at all (in a small village, say), White Zone spaces are free, unless there's a sign reserving them. You can park in **Blue Zone** spaces if you have a special parking disc (available for free from tourist offices, police stations and banks, and generally supplied in the glove box of rental cars). Spin the wheel round to show your time of arrival and leave it on your dashboard: this gives you ninety minutes' free parking if you arrive between 8am and 11.30am or between 1.30pm and 6pm. Between 11.30am and 1.30pm doesn't count so you're safe until 2.30pm; if you arrive after 6pm, you're OK until 9am next day. Rarer **Red Zone** spaces are free for up to fifteen hours, as long as you display the disc. Spaces marked in **yellow** indicate private parking for, say, staff of a nearby company or perhaps guests of a local hotel; the only way to know is to ask. Illegal parking of any kind is much less tolerated in Switzerland than Italy, and fines for minor transgressions are common.

Car rental

Car rental in Switzerland can be nastily expensive. You can cut costs by renting in advance from the big international agencies. They all cover Switzerland, with offices in all major towns, most minor ones, and at all airports. **One-way rentals** are simple to arrange, although they may attract a handling fee. Remember to check that there are no restrictions to taking the car across international borders if you're intending to head for Italy; remember, too, to have your passport, and visa if necessary, at the ready for the border crossings.

Cycling and mountain-biking in Switzerland

If you're arriving in Switzerland with **your own bike**, there are various methods of transporting it on public transport; check the national railway website (⦿ sbb .ch) for more information. Alternatively, there is a well-organized nationwide **bike rental** system. New seven-gear country bike or quality 21-gear mountain bikes are available from Rent-A-Bike (⦿ rentabike.ch) located at most Swiss train stations (look for *bici da noleggiare*). If there's no dedicated bike office, you can normally rent from left-luggage counters. **Prices** are Fr.27/€22 for a half-day (the cut-off time is 1.30pm) or Fr.35/€29 for a full day. The popular option of one-way rental attracts a Fr.8/€6.50 surcharge on a one-day rental (free thereafter); you must let staff know where and when you intend to drop the bike off when you rent. Kids' bikes and seats for children which you can attach to an adult's bike are also available. Station bike rental is massively popular, especially in summer, and if you're planning to rent you should always **reserve** as far as possible in advance (normally, a day or two is OK). Look for the bike-train leaflet at stations, which has a list of stations, phone numbers and the number of rental bikes at each one.

Accommodation

Whether you prefer to stay in a nineteenth-century villa, a modern hotel designed by one of Europe's top architects, a sixteenth-century farmhouse, or under canvas, you'll be spoilt for choice.

While never especially cheap, tourist accommodation in Italy is strictly regulated; hotels and campsites are star rated and required to post their prices up clearly. Booking ahead is more than advisable, especially during July and August. Although some tourist offices will help you find a room if you turn up on spec, others will just hand you a photocopy of all the options and expect you to sort yourself out. Advance reservations can be made through **online agents** like ⦿ venere .it or with travel agents, but we've given contact details throughout the Guide if you want to reserve directly. Make sure you get **confirmation** of the booking by fax or email – in the cities it's not uncommon to arrive and find all knowledge of your booking is denied. Although a level of English is commonly spoken, we have included some phrases to help overcome language barriers (see p.364). Note that some hotels may ask you to email or fax credit card details to secure a booking.

The following sites are useful for alternative/ informal accommodation: **Airbnb** (⦿ airbnb.com), **CouchSurfing** (⦿ couchsurfing.org) and **Vacation Rentals by Owner** (⦿ vrbo.com).

Hotels

Hotels in Italy come tagged with a confusing variety of names, and, although the differences are minimal these days, you will still find various terms used for what are basically private hotel facilities. A **locanda** was historically the most basic option, although these days the word is often used by boutique hotels and the like to conjure up images of simple, traditional hospitality. **Pensione, albergo** or **hotel** are all commonly used and more or less interchangeable. **Prices** vary greatly between the tourist hot spots and more rural areas, but a no-frills double hotel room starts at around €80 in most areas, while somewhere more comfortable and atmospheric will set you back around €120 and upwards. The official star system is based on facilities (TV in rooms, swimming pool, and so on) rather than character or comfort. The prices in this guide are for the **cheapest double room in high season**.

In season, on the lakes it's not unusual to have to stay for a minimum of three nights, and many proprietors will add the price of **breakfast** to your bill whether you want it or not; try to ask for accommodation only – you can always eat more cheaply – and often better – in a bar. Be warned, too, that some places will also insist on **half** or **full board** during the summer although, on the whole, besides the top-end hotels, the quality can be disappointing and not worth the saving. Note that people travelling alone may sometimes be clobbered for the price of a double room even when they only need a single, though it can also work the other way round – if all their **single rooms** are taken, a hotelier may well put you in a double room but only charge the single rate.

Hostels, convents and monasteries

There are several **hostels** in the lakes area. For two people travelling together they don't always represent a massive saving on the cheapest double hotel room, however, but if you're on your own – or with a family – hostels can work out a lot cheaper. Many have inexpensive restaurants and self-catering kitchens that enable you to cut costs even further and, in general, they are more sociable.

Virtually all of the Italian hostels in this area are members of the official **Hostelling International** (HI; Ⓦ hihostels.com) and charge around €20 per night for a dormitory bed. Strictly speaking you need to be a member of that organization in order to use them – you can join through your home country's hostelling organization. You need to reserve well ahead in summer, most efficiently by using HI's Booking Network which, for a small fee, enables you to book (including online) from your home country up to six months in advance.

An online agency, Monastery Stays (Ⓦ monasterystays.com), offers a centralized booking service for numerous **convents** and **monasteries** around the region. There are no restrictions on age, sex or faith, all rooms have private bathrooms and few places have early curfews.

Agriturismo and bed and breakfast

The **agriturismo** scheme has grown considerably in recent years and enables farmers to rent out converted barns and farm buildings to tourists – and, increasingly, city-bound Italians – through a centralized booking agency. The lakes region has a good selection of options; the agricultural area to the south, particularly around Mantua and Cremona, is perhaps the best hunting ground, as more and more *cascine* and rice-growing estates diversify. Some establishments offer self-contained apartments, others have rooms with or without en-suite bathrooms; **rates** start at around €80 per night for self-contained places with two beds. There's often a wide range of **activities** on offer, such as horseriding, fishing and cycling, plus escorted walks and excursions. For a full list of properties, consult Ⓦ agriturismo.com or Ⓦ agriturismo.it.

Bed and breakfast schemes are a relatively new arrival; the best ones are a good way to get a flavour of Italian home life, though they're not necessarily cheaper than an inexpensive hotel, and they rarely accept credit cards. Most establishments in this region charge €50–100 for a double room.

For a comprehensive list of B&Bs, check Ⓦ bbitalia.it or Ⓦ bbplanet.com.

Camping

Camping is popular in Italy and there are hundreds of sites around the lakes and in the surrounding mountains catering for Italians and holidaying Europeans alike. Camper vans have become popular in recent years and most campsites offer space for these as well as tents (see p.26); some of the larger sites also offer space for accommodation in chalets or caravans. Campsites are generally open from April to September. The majority are well equipped and often have swimming pools, games areas and usually a bar and small supermarket. Sites are graded with a star rating system, which, as with hotels, refers to facilities available rather than standard of upkeep. In high season on the lakes you can expect to pay a daily **rate** of €7–12 per person plus €5–15 per tent or caravan and €5 per vehicle.

We have listed some campsites in the guide; otherwise local tourist offices have details of nearby sites, and the exhaustive Italian camping website Ⓦ camping.it has information by region and booking facilities.

Villas and apartments

If you fancy lazing away your holiday on a lakeside in your own space, you should consider renting a **villa** for a week or two. Often enjoying marvellous lakefront locations, they can prove a cost-effective way of putting up a family or a group of friends. Rented **apartments** are becoming an increasingly popular way of experiencing Italy's towns and cities, too. Available for anything from a couple of nights to a month or so, they are usually equipped for self-catering and there's nothing like shopping for

ACCOMMODATION IN SWITZERLAND

Accommodation in Switzerland is of a universally high standard: hotels are famous for having some of the best service in the world, rented accommodation and campsites are usually spotless and, although perhaps a little pricey by European standards, establishments are invariably conscientiously run and hospitable. Tourist offices always have lists of hotels, hostels, campsites and apartments in their area, and outside office hours they normally have a display board on the street with details of the local hotels, often with a courtesy phone.

Most **hotels** in the country (and some hostels) are regulated by the Swiss Hotel Association which awards stars (between zero and five) according to strict guidelines on everything from room size to the presence or absence of bubble bath. ⓦswisshotels.com has the full listing and – more significantly – plenty of last-minute offers for cut-price multi-night deals. As well as the **youth hostels** that are part of the Hostelling International network (ⓦyouthhostel.ch), Switzerland has a rival group of independent hostels that work together as the Swiss Backpacker umbrella organization (ⓦbackpacker.ch). Often less institutional than the competition, these lively places don't require membership and are usually located in prime positions. When it comes to **camping** (ⓦswisscamps.ch), prices are reasonable at Fr.6–8 per person, plus Fr.8–12 for a tent; booking ahead is recommended at all times of the year.

supplies in a local market to make you feel part of Italian daily life, even on a short break.

In addition to the specialist accommodation companies below, you could try the tour operators, who rent villas either on their own or in conjunction with a flight or fly-drive package (see p.22).

VILLA AND APARTMENT COMPANIES

Cottages to Castles UK ☎ 01622 775 217, ⓦ cottagestocastles .com. Property rental company with a few apartments in the lakes area.
Interhome UK ☎ 01483 863500, ⓦ interhome.co.uk. Swiss company renting apartments and villas in the region at competitive prices.
Italian Breaks UK ☎ 020 8666 0407, ⓦ italianbreaks.com. Lovely selection of lakeside villas, many with pools and great views.
Italian Life UK ☎ 0800 085 7732, ⓦ italianlife.co.uk. Database of properties featuring apartments mainly around Lake Garda.

Eating and drinking

The importance Italians attach to food and drink makes any holiday in the country a treat. Although you should be sure to try local specialities, the sheer variety of Italian cooking should mean there's something for most tastes – and, although Ticino's Swiss-Italian cooking has its differences, many styles and ingredients are common to both sides of the border. The region is also a treasure-trove for wine lovers, with Franciacorta, Valpolicella and the lesser-known Valtellina vineyards all within easy reach of the lakes.

Restaurants

Full meals are generally served in either a trattoria or a *ristorante*. Traditionally, a **trattoria** is a cheaper and more basic purveyor of homestyle cooking (*cucina casalinga*), while a **ristorante** is more upmarket, though the two names are often interchangeable. Other types of eating places include **osterie**, basically an old-fashioned restaurant or inn-like place specializing in home cooking, though some upmarket places with pretensions to established antiquity borrow the name. In mid-range establishments, pasta dishes go for €5–10, while the main fish or meat courses will normally cost between €10 and €15.

Italy is a latecomer to the boom in non-indigenous eating, partly owing to its lack of any substantial colonial legacy but also because of the innate chauvinism of Italian eating habits. The exceptions are the Chinese restaurants that crop up in every town, the ubiquitous burger bars, and the growing numbers of Japanese and North African restaurants in larger towns. Milan is the largest, most cosmopolitan city in the region and is very proud of its "fusion" cooking, ostensibly pan-Pacific flavours, usually served in restaurants with minimalist Asian decor.

Understanding the menu

Perhaps the most striking thing about eating in Italy is how deeply embedded in the culture it really is. Food is celebrated with gusto: **traditional meals** tend to consist of many courses and can seem to last forever, starting with an antipasto, followed by a risotto or a pasta dish, leading on to a fish or meat course, cheese, and finished with fresh fruit and coffee. Even everyday meals are a scaled-down version of the full-blown affair.

Traditionally, **lunch** (*pranzo*) and dinner (*cena*) start with **antipasto** (literally "before the meal"), a course consisting of various cold cuts of meat, seafood and cold vegetable dishes, generally costing €5–10. Some places offer self-service antipasto buffets. The next course, the **primo**, consists of a soup, risotto or pasta dish, and is followed by the **secondo** – the meat or fish course, usually served alone, except for perhaps a wedge of lemon or tomato. Note that by law, any ingredients that have been frozen need to be marked (usually with an asterisk) on the menu; you might decide that it's better to try the local fish rather than one flown in from the South Atlantic, for example. Vegetables or salads – **contorni** – are ordered and served separately, and there often won't be much choice: potatoes will usually come as fries (*patate fritte*), but you can also find boiled (*lesse*) or roast (*arrostite*) potatoes, while salads are either green (*verde*) or mixed (*mista*) and vegetables (*verdure*) usually come very well boiled. Afterwards, you nearly always get a choice of fresh local fruit (*frutta*) and a selection of **desserts** (*dolci*) – sometimes just ice cream or *macedonia* (fresh fruit salad), but often home-made items, like apple or pear cake (*torta di mela/pera*) or *tiramisù*. **Cheeses** (*formaggi*) are always worth a shot if you have any room left; ask to try a selection of local varieties.

You will need quite an appetite to tackle all these courses and if your stomach – or wallet – isn't up to it, it's perfectly acceptable to have less. If you're not sure of the size of the portions, start with a pasta or rice dish and ask to order the *secondo* when you've finished the first. And, although it's not a very Italian thing to do, don't feel shy about just having an

antipasto and a *primo*; they're probably the best way of trying local specialities anyway. If there's no menu, the verbal list of what's available can be bewildering; if you don't understand, just ask for what you want – if it's something simple they can usually rustle it up. Everywhere will have pasta with tomato sauce (*pomodoro*) or meat sauce (*al ragù*).

At the end of the meal ask for the **bill** (*il conto*); bear in mind that almost everywhere you'll pay a cover charge (*coperto*) of €1–5 a head. In many trattorias the bill amounts to little more than an illegible scrap of paper; if you want to check it, ask for a **receipt** (*ricevuta*). In more expensive places, service (*servizio*) will often be added on top of the cover charge, generally about ten percent. If service isn't included it's common just to leave a few coins as a **tip**, unless you're particularly pleased with the service, in which case, leave up to ten percent.

In the "Language" section you'll find a detailed **menu reader** of Italian terms (see p.367).

Breakfast

Most Italians start their day in a bar, their **breakfast** (*colazione*) consisting of a coffee and a brioche or *cornetto* – a croissant often filled with jam, custard or chocolate, which you usually help yourself to from the counter and eat standing at the bar. It will cost between €1.30 and €1.60. Breakfast in a hotel can be a limp affair of watery coffee, bread and processed meats, often not worth the price.

Ice cream

Italian **ice cream** (*gelato*), with its dense texture and high proportion of butter fat, is justifiably famous: a cone (*un cono*) is an indispensable accessory to the evening *passeggiata*. Most bars have a selection, but for real choice go to a **gelateria**, where the range is a tribute to the Italian imagination and flair for display. There's no problem locating the finest *gelateria* in town – it's the one that draws the crowds – and we've noted the really special places throughout the guide. If in doubt, go for the places that make their own ice cream, denoted by the sign "Produzione Propria". There's usually a veritable cornucopia of flavours ranging from the classics – like lemon (*limone*) and pistachio (*pistacchio*) – through staples including *stracciatella* (vanilla with chocolate chips), straw-berry (*fragola*) and *fiordilatte* (similar to vanilla), to house specialities that might include cinnamon (*cannella*), chocolate with chilli pepper (*cioccolato con peperoncino*) or even pumpkin (*zucca*).

NO SMOKING

It is illegal in Italy (and the Swiss canton of Ticino) to smoke in **restaurants and bars**. Any establishment that wants to allow smoking has to follow very stringent rules for isolating a separate room – including doors and special air-conditioning. Needless to say, this is beyond the pocket of most places and so the majority remain no-smoking throughout. Conversely, the pavement outside has become a popular gathering-point for smokers.

LAKE CUISINE

Forget pizzas and tomato-based sauces: lake cuisine specializes in risotto, polenta, fresh-caught fish and wild mushrooms in butter. The historical emphasis here has been on hearty fare to fuel a day's hard work, making the most of local ingredients, be they fish from the lakes, corn from the fields, or frogs from the marshes.

RICE AND PASTA

The shortgrain rice used for **risotto** is grown in the paddy fields of the Bassa Padana south and east of Milan. Different areas add their own ingredients: yellow *risotto alla Milanese* is infused with saffron; small prawns (*gamberetti*) and trout (*trota*) are common on the lakes, while frogs' legs, pumpkin (*zucca*) and wild mushrooms (*funghi*) are all favourites.

Pasta usually comes as *tortelloni* (pasta pockets, similar to ravioli) stuffed with lake fish, sausage meat or vegetables and drizzled with *burro sfuso* (butter melted with sage). Verona is celebrated for its gnocchi, and you'll find *bigoli* (thick wheat spaghetti) on many menus.

POLENTA

Lombardy's most famous ingredient is **polenta** (similar to US-style grits) – cornmeal that is slow-cooked over a low heat to a thick, creamy mash, dolloped into a bowl and topped with cheese or served as an accompaniment to meat or fish. It is also often allowed to cool, then sliced into fingers to be grilled until crispy and golden and drizzled with oil.

FISH

The tastiest lake **fish** include tench (*tinca*) and perch (*persico*) – the former a speciality of Lake Iseo when stuffed and baked, the latter fried in breadcrumbs. Lake Como's shad (*missoltini*) is dried in the sun then preserved in oil and vinegar. Menus from Como to Verona include pike (*luccio*) – at its best when cooked in local olive oil, with capers and shallots – and lavaret (*lavarello*), deliciously prepared with sage, then grilled with butter. Whitefish (*coregone*) is a meaty affair, while eel (*anguilla*), chub (*cavedano*) and bleak (*alborella*) are less ubiquitous.

MEATS

Across the region, **veal** and **pork** are the main meats, although beef, rabbit and donkey are not uncommon. Ordering a plate of *affettati misti* is a great way of trying several local speciality cold cuts in one dish. Varieties of **salami** include wild boar (*cinghiale*) in Piemonte and goose (*oca*) around Pavia.

CHEESES

Lombardy is also one of the largest **cheese-making** regions in the country. As well as creamy Mascarpone and blue-veined Gorgonzola, the numerous other local cheeses include the tangy, soft Taleggio, crumbly, aged Grana Padana – the local version of Parmesan – and the fragrant yellow Brescian cheese, Bagoss.

DESSERTS

The dairy products of the region are put to heavenly use in the Veneto's *tiramisù* (pick-me-up), while Piemonte's *zabaione* is a delicious sugary concoction with eggs and marsala wine. Panettone, the soft eggy cake with sultanas eaten at Christmas, originated in Milan, although Verona has its own version known as Pandoro.

Pizza and snacks

Pizza is now a worldwide phenomenon, but Italy remains the best place to eat it. When good, the creations served up here are wholly different from the soggy concoctions that have taken over the international fast-food market, though it has to be said that some of the joints in the lakeside villages feel they can fob off undiscerning tourists with deeply inferior versions. For a quality pizza, opt for somewhere with a wood-fired oven (*forno a legna*) rather than an electric one, so that the pizzas arrive blasted and bubbling on the surface and with a distinctive charcoal taste. This adherence to tradition means that it's unusual to find a good pizzeria open at lunchtime; it takes hours for a wood-fired oven to heat up to the necessary temperature. In Italy, pizza usually comes thin and flat, not deep-pan, and the choice of toppings is fairly limited, with none of the dubious pineapple and sweetcorn variations.

Pizzerias range from a stand-up counter selling slices to a fully fledged sit-down restaurant, and on the whole they don't sell much else besides pizza, soft drinks and beer. A basic cheese and tomato *margherita* costs around €6, a fancier variety €6–10, and it's quite acceptable to cut it into slices and eat it with your fingers. Consult our food glossary (see p.367) for the different kinds of pizza.

For a lunchtime snack **sandwiches** (panini) can be pretty substantial, a bread roll packed with any number of fillings. A sandwich bar (*paninoteca*) in larger towns and cities, and in smaller places a grocer's shop (*alimentari*) will normally make you up whatever you want. Bars may also offer *tramezzini*, ready-made sliced white bread with mixed fillings. Toasted sandwiches (*toast*) are common, too: in a *paninoteca* you can get whatever you want toasted; in ordinary bars it's more likely to be a variation on cheese or ham with tomato.

Other sources of quick snacks are **markets**, where fresh, flavoursome produce is sold, often including cheese, cold meats, spit-roast chicken and *arancini* (deep-fried balls of rice with meat – *rosso* – or butter and cheese – *bianco* – filling). **Bread shops** (*panetterie*) often serve slices of pizza or *focaccia* (bread with oil and salt topped with rosemary, olives or tomato). **Supermarkets**, also, are an obvious stop for a picnic lunch: the major chains Esselunga, Carrefour and Auchan are on the outskirts of larger towns, while GS, Unes! and Sma are often in the centre.

In recent years the very civilized habit of having a few nibbles with your late-afternoon **aperitivo** (aperitif) has taken on a whole new meaning. In the 1990s some bars began to supplement the usual olives and things on cocktail sticks with cold pasta salads and quiches to attract more customers. Before long the trend had spread and bars now groan with cold buffets at what has become known as "**happy hour**" – although it typically lasts from 6pm until 9pm. As with most things in these parts, the fad started in Milan but the waves have spread outwards, and bars throughout the region these days offer a fine variety of finger food to accompany your *prosecco*. If you've had a large lunch, a discreet plateful or two may be all you feel like for an evening meal – and it's available for just the price of a drink.

Drinking

A mezzo caraffa (half-litre carafe) may be a standard accompaniment to any meal but there's not a great emphasis on dedicated **drinking** in Italy. You'll rarely see drunks in public, young people don't

devote their nights to getting wasted, and women especially are frowned upon if they're seen to be overindulging. Nonetheless, there's a wide choice of alcoholic drinks available, soft drinks come in multifarious hues; and there's also mineral water and crushed-ice drinks – you'll certainly never be stuck if you want to slake your thirst.

Where to drink

Traditional **bars** are less social centres than functional, brightly lit places, with a bar, a Gaggia coffee machine and a picture of the local football team on the wall. This is the place to come for a coffee in the morning, and a quick beer or a cup of tea in the afternoon – people don't generally idle away evenings in bars; indeed it's often difficult to find this kind of bar open much after 8pm. It's cheapest to drink standing at the counter, in which case you usually pay first at the cash desk (*cassa*), present your receipt (*scontrino*) to the barperson and give your order. There's always a list of prices (*listino prezzi*) behind the bar. If there's waiter service, just sit where you like, though bear in mind that to do this will cost up to twice as much as positioning yourself at the bar, especially if you sit outside (*fuori*) – the difference is shown on the price list as *tavolo* (table).

The larger resorts and towns offer a much greater variety of places to sit and drink in the evening, sometimes with live music or DJs. The more energetic or late-opening of these have taken to calling themselves **pubs**, a spillover from the outrageous success of Irish pubs, at least one of which you'll find, packed to the rafters, in almost every small town. Beer, particularly in its draught form, *alla spina*, has become fashionable in recent years. Real enthusiasts of the grape should head for an

VEGETARIANS AND VEGANS

Although your diet will probably be based around pasta, Italy isn't a bad country to travel in if you're a **vegetarian**. As well as the ubiquitous tomato sauce, there are numerous other pasta sauces without meat, some superb vegetable antipasti, and if you eat fish and seafood you should have no problem at all. Salads, too, are fresh and good. The only real difficulty is one of comprehension: outside the cities and resorts Italians still don't really understand someone not eating meat, and stating the obvious doesn't always get the point across. Saying you're a vegetarian (*Sono vegetariano/a*) and asking if a dish has meat in it (*c'è carne dentro?*) might still turn up a poultry or prosciutto dish. Asking for it *"senza carne e pesce"* should make things sufficiently clear. **Vegans** will have a much harder time, though pizzas without cheese (*marinara* – nothing to do with fish – is a common option) are a good standby, vegetable soup (*minestrone*) is usually just that, and the fruit is excellent.

enoteca, though many of these are as much restaurants as bars, as well as being a good place to buy a few bottles of the local brew.

Coffee, tea and soft drinks

One of the most distinctive smells in an Italian street is that of fresh **coffee**. The basic choice is either small and black (*espresso*, or just *caffè*), which costs around €1 a cup, or white and frothy (cappuccino, for about €1.30), but there are scores of variations; note that Italians only drink cappuccino in the morning. If you want your espresso a little longer and weaker, ask for a *caffè lungo* or, for an espresso with hot water added to make it more like a filter coffee, an *Americano*; with a drop of milk is *caffè macchiato*; very milky is *latte macchiato or caffè latte* (ordering just a *"latte"* Starbucks-style will get you a glass of milk). Coffee with a shot of alcohol – and you can ask for just about anything – is *caffè corretto*. Many places also sell decaffeinated coffee (*decaffeinato*); while in summer you might want to have your coffee on Ice (*caffè freddo*). Whichever variation you order, it'll be cheaper – and more authentically Italian – if you drink it standing at the bar (*al banco*).

If you don't like coffee, there's always **tea**. In summer you can drink this cold too (*tè freddo*) – excellent for taking the heat off. Hot tea (*tè*) comes with lemon (*con limone*) unless you ask for milk (*con latte*). Milk itself is drunk hot as often as cold, or you can get it as a milkshake – *frappé* or *frullato*. A small selection of herbal teas (*infusioni*) are generally available: camomile (*camomilla*) and peppermint (*infuso di menta*) are the most common.

There are various **soft drinks** (*analcolici*) to choose from. Slightly fizzy, bitter drinks like San Bittèr or Crodino are common, especially at *aperitivo* time. A **spremuta** is a fresh fruit juice, squeezed at the bar, usually orange, lemon or grapefruit. There are also crushed-ice *granite*, offered in several flavours and available with or without ice cream on

top. Otherwise you'll find the usual range of fizzy drinks and concentrated juices. Coke is as prevalent as it is everywhere, though the diet or light versions less so; the home-grown Italian version, Chinotto, is less sweet. **Tap water** (*acqua del rubinetto*) is quite drinkable, and you won't pay for a glass in a bar, though Italians prefer **mineral water** (*acqua minerale*) and drink more of it than any other country in Europe. It can be drunk either still (*senza gas* or *naturale*) or sparkling (*con gas* or *frizzante*).

Beer and spirits

Beer (*birra*) is always a lager-type brew which usually comes in one-third or two-third litre bottles, or on tap (*alla spina*), measure for measure more expensive than the bottled variety. A small beer is a *piccola* (20cl or 25cl), a larger one (usually 40cl) a *media*. The cheapest and most common brands are the Italian Moretti, Peroni and Dreher, all of which are very drinkable; if this is what you want, either state the brand name or ask for *birra nazionale* or *birra chiara* – otherwise you could end up with a more expensive imported beer. You may also come across darker beers (*birra nera* or *birra rossa*), which have a sweeter, maltier taste and in appearance resemble stout or bitter.

All the usual **spirits** are on sale, known mostly by their generic names. The home-grown Italian firewater is **grappa**, originally from Bassano di Grappa in the Veneto but now available just about everywhere. It's made from the leftovers from the winemaking process (skins, stalks and the like) and is just the thing on a cool evening.

You'll also find **fortified wines** like Martini, Cinzano and Campari. Ask for a Campari-soda and you'll get a ready-mixed version from a little bottle; Campari Bitter is a shot of Campari with soda. You might also try Cynar – an artichoke-based sherry often drunk as an aperitif with water. There's also a daunting selection of **liqueurs**. An *amaro* is a

ITALIAN WINE LABELS

The labelling of **Italian wine** is confusing. The **Denominazione d'Origine Controllata (DOC)** system was introduced in the 1960s followed by the **Denominazione d'Origine Controllata e Garantita (DOCG)** in the 1980s as a way of guaranteeing quality but it quickly became a mixed blessing. Though it's undoubtedly true that the DOC and DOCG system helped lift standards of Italian wines, the laws have come under fire from both growers and critics for their rigidity, constraints and anomalies. They leave no room for the experimentation and modern methods that northern Italy, for one, specializes in. Increasingly, producers eager to experiment began to disregard the regulations and make new wines that were sometimes among Italy's best, though they were officially labelled only table wine (*vino da tavola*). The **Indicazione Geografica Tipica (IGT)** was introduced in 1992 to enable producers to use geographical names and grape varieties on labels to help describe their wines – something that has benefited the less traditional producers in particular.

general term for an after-dinner liqueur or *digestivo*. Two of the more bitter are Ramazzotti and Montenegro, while Amaretto is much sweeter with a strong taste of almond and Sambuca a sticky-sweet aniseed concoction, traditionally served with a coffee bean in it and set on fire (though, increasingly, this is something put on to impress tourists). A shot of clear grappa is a common accompaniment to a coffee and can range from a warming palate cleanser to throat-burning firewater, while another sweet alternative, originally from Sorrento, is *limoncello* or *limoncino*, a lemon-based liqueur. Strega is another drink you'll see behind every bar: yellow, herb-and-saffron-based stuff in tall, elongated bottles: about as sweet as it looks but not unpleasant.

Wine

The hillsides around the lakes are spread with vineyards producing the kind of decent, ordinary stuff you'll find as house **wine** in the region's restaurants. These include the Merlot reds from the Sottoceneri, around Lugano, and Valcalepio and Scanzo from the Bergamasc valleys, which are often served by the *caraffa* – available in quarter (*quarto*), half (*mezzo*) and litre (*un litro*) measures.

There are also some internationally celebrated wine-producing areas around the lakes and it's worth trying a bottle of these very affordable local gems. The world-class sparkling wine produced in the hills of the **Franciacorta** between Bergamo and Brescia has made its name in recent years using the *metodo classico* of the French Champagne region. Although the elegant, bubbly Cuvée (Cà del Bosco and Bellavista are two of the best) is the most renowned product of this area, velvety reds and well-perfumed whites are also worth trying (usually labelled Terre di Franciacorta). For a very different type of sparkling wine, try the slightly fizzy red

Bonarda from the little-known **Oltropò Pavese** region, across the Po River south of Pavia.

In the east of the lakes region, around the southern and eastern shores of **Lake Garda**, light reds and aromatic whites admirably accompany local lake fish and risottos; Bardolino and Bianco di Custoza are names to look out for, along with the DOC labels of Garda Classico, Lugana and San Martino della Battaglia. Recioto di Soave and Soave Superiore from around Verona are some of the oldest types of wine hereabouts, with evidence of their cultivation dating back to the fifth century. The wine's deep yellow colour and honey bouquet make the perfect partner for a slice of local *pandoro*. The **Valpolicella** district, north of Verona, produces some of northern Italy's best-known red wines.

On the south-facing mountain slopes in the north of Lombardy, the **Valtellina Superiore** (divided into the different geographic zones of Sassella, Inferno, Grumello and Valgella) cultivates the Nebbiola grape (known here as Chiavennasca), creating strong red wines with a characteristic perfume that perfectly complement the mountain meats and salamis of the area.

The media

The decentralized press of Italy and Switzerland serves to emphasize the strength of regionalism in the countries. Local TV is popular, too, in the light of little competition from the national channels.

Newspapers and online media

The **Italian press** is largely regionally based, with just a few newspapers available across the country.

The centre-left *La Repubblica* (Ⓦrepubblica.it) and authoritative *Corriere della Sera* (Ⓦcorriere.it) are the two most widely read, published nationwide with local supplements, but originating in Milan. *La Stampa* (Ⓦlastampa.it), the daily of Turin, is a rather stuffy, establishment broadsheet. Most people's choice of reading matter, however, bears witness to how intensely regionalist Italy remains; the majority buy their local rag – like *L'Eco di Bergamo* or *Il Corriere di Como*, for example – rather than bother with anything more universal in outlook. Many of the imprints you see on newsstands are the official mouthpieces for political parties: *L'Unità* was the party organ of the former Communist Party, while *La Padania* is the press of the right-wing, regionalist Lega Nord party. The traditionally radical *Il Manifesto* has always been regarded as one of the most serious and influential sources of Italian journalism, while the independent *Il Fatto Quotidiano* was set up in 2009 specifically to address the issues of editorial freedom and legitimacy and was sold out before 8am on the first morning. Perhaps the most avidly read newspapers of all, however, are the specialist sports papers, most notably the *Corriere dello Sport* (Ⓦcorrieredellosport.it) and the pink *Gazzetta dello Sport* (Ⓦgazzetta.it) – both essential reading if you want an insight into the Italian football scene.

Switzerland has lots of **newspapers** – more than 200 nationwide – but again almost without exception they're parochial local news-sheets, reporting cantonal and municipal affairs in some detail, but relegating the rest of Switzerland, let alone the world, to a few inside columns. Zürich's *Neue Zürcher Zeitung*, or *NZZ* (Ⓦnzz.ch), is the best known. Conservative and highbrow in the extreme, it nonetheless has gained its reputation by reporting Swiss and world events with scrupulously high journalistic standards. The local Italian-language *Corriere del Ticino* (Ⓦcdt.ch) and German-language *Tessiner Zeitung* (Ⓦtessinerzeitung.ch) are provincial small-fry in comparison.

English-language newspapers can be found for around three times their home cover price in all the larger towns and most of the more established resorts.

TV and radio

Italian TV is appalling, with ghastly quiz shows, mindless variety programmes and cathartic chat-shows squeezed in between countless artless advertisements. Of the three national channels, RAI 1, 2 and 3, RAI 3 has some worthwhile

programmes and plays eclectic and interesting music, although the intelligent, satirical shows are often indecipherable to foreigners who have anything less than an encyclopedic knowledge of Italian politics from the last fifty years. **Swiss television** is similarly undemanding, with a diet of game shows, made-for-TV movies (dubbed) and lots of local news and local-interest programming, including from Radiotelevisione Svizzera Italiana (RSI). **Satellite television** is widely distributed across the region, and hotels with three stars and above usually offer a mix of BBC World News, CNN, and French-, German- and Spanish-language news channels, as well as MTV and Eurosport.

Radio is highly deregulated in Italy, with the FM waves crowded to the extent that you continually pick up new stations whether you want to or not – with the Catholic Radio Maria popping up with an uncanny frequency. On the whole the RAI stations are again the more professional – though even with them daytime listening is virtually undiluted Euro-pop. For intelligent discussion programmes try Radio Popolare (FM 107.6). Each language area of **Switzerland** has three regional **radio stations**, one channel devoted to each of news, classical music and popular music (see Ⓦsrgssr.ch), as well as a fistful of community stations.

Most **global** stations broadcast online: see **BBC** (Ⓦbbc.co.uk/worldserviceradio), **Radio Canada** (Ⓦrcinet.ca) and **Voice of America** (Ⓦvoa.gov).

Festivals and events

Although religion is rarely at the forefront of celebrations in the north of Italy, the origins of many festivities lie in the Church calendar. Epiphany, Carnival, Easter and Christmas, as well as local patron saints' days, are all a good excuse to break the daily routine. The lakes region is also well blessed with music festivals and events, including several good jazz festivals, lakeside classical music concerts, and the world-famous opera seasons in both Verona and Milan. Last, but by no means least in terms of the economy of the region, are Milan's big fashion and design fairs, which draw fashionistas and design gurus from around the world.

Notable festivals in honour of local saints include **Santa Lucia** (December 13), which is particularly celebrated around Bergamo and Brescia and sees the setting-up of handicraft stalls and local produce markets. A street fair is also central to celebrations of the patron saint of Milan, **Sant'Ambrogio** on December 7, when the *Oh Bej, Oh Bej!* stalls of handicrafts, antiques and Christmas gifts fill the streets around the saint's eponymous church. Recently there's been a revival of interest in **Carnival** (*Carnevale*), the last fling before Lent. One of the best places to witness Carnival celebrations is the village of Bagolino above Lake Idro: locals dress up in traditional costume and there is much music-making and dancing.

Food-inspired *feste* are lower-key, but no less enjoyable, affairs, usually celebrating the local speciality of the region to the accompaniment of dancing, music from a local band and noisy fireworks at the end of the evening. There are literally hundreds of food festivals, sometimes advertised as *sagre* – most are modest affairs, primarily aimed at locals and little publicized, but look in the local papers or ask at the tourist office during summer and autumn and you're bound to find something going on.

One other type of festival to keep an eye out for are the summer **political** shindigs, like the **Festa de l'Unità**, usually taking place in the evenings and advertised by posters all over the region. Begun initially to recruit members to the different political parties, they have become something akin to a village fête but with a healthy Italian twist. The food tents are a great way to try tasty local dishes washed down with a cup of wine. There's usually bingo going on in one corner, the sort of dancing that will make teenagers cringe and the odd coconut shy or two. In larger towns these have become more sophisticated affairs with big-name national bands playing.

Efficient as ever, Switzerland Tourism maintains an encyclopedic events calendar at Ⓦ myswitzerland .com, detailing hundreds of pageants big and small, while the Italian Tourist Board have a slightly temperamental search engine organized by region on their site Ⓦ enit.it.

Calendar of festivals and events

There are literally hundreds of local festivals around the lakes and sometimes the best ones are those that you come across unexpectedly. Below are some of the highlights, but note that **dates change** from year to year, so it's best to contact the local tourist office for specific details.

JANUARY

6 Milan. Epifania, a costumed parade of the Three Kings from the Duomo to Sant'Eustorgio, the resting place of the bones of the Magi. Across the region, La Befana, the good witch, who brings toys and sweets to children who've been good and coal to those who haven't, is celebrated.

17 Mantua. San Antonio is celebrated with a human chess game, stalls and street celebrations.

FEBRUARY

Second/third week Milan. Carnevale Ambrosiano: the city's patron saint is celebrated with children's fancy-dress processions and religious services, and the traditional biscuits, *chiacchiere*, are available in the city's *pasticcerie*.

Second/third week Carnevale sees Carnival festivities across the region, especially lively at Lecco and Bagolino, which celebrate with processions, floats and traditional dancing.

End of Feb/March Verona. Baccanale del Gnoco (Gnocchi Festival). Parades and floats around the San Zeno neighbourhood led by the newly voted King Gnoco.

15 Brescia SS Faustino and Giovita. Fireworks, food stalls and music to celebrate the city's patron saint's day.

Last week Milan. Spring Fashion Week, presenting the summer's must-have clothes.

MARCH

8 Festa della Donna – International Women's Day – on which women are given bunches of mimosa.

Third week Milan. At the Salone Internazionale del Mobile the world's designers come to check out the latest in furnishing and design throughout the city.

Last Thurs Verona. At Vinitalia, wine enthusiasts from around the world converge to try each other's wares.

APRIL

20 Como. Light and illumination displays honour Volta's presentation to the Royal Society in London in 1800 of a device to produce energy.

Third Sun Milan. During the Mercato dei Fiori, Milan's canal district is strewn with blooms.

Fourth week Pavia. La Grande Feria di Pavia Sapori sees typical Pavian food, wine and handicrafts on display throughout town.

MAY

Second week Brescia. In the Mille Miglia, vintage cars set off on their 1600-kilometre race around the country.

Last Sun All Italy. On International Wine Day, wine estates open their cellars to the public.

JUNE

First Sun Milan. Festa sui Navigli boat race, food and craft stalls in Milan's canal district.

Second/third week Valeggio sul Mincio, Verona. This attractive small village, with its numerous restaurants, draws lovers of pumpkin ravioli, and the weekend of the Tortelloni Festival sees the speciality at its best.

Second half Bellinzona. Piazza Blues, a free open-air jazz festival.

Third Sun Menaggio, Lake Como. Annual fish fry-up.

Third Sun Milan. Sagra di San Cristoforo, a candlelit boat parade with fireworks, dancing and music along the canals.

Fourth Fri Verona. The opera season starts in the Roman arena (see Ⓦ arena.it).

JULY

All month Clusone. The twenty-year-old festival Clusone Jazz attracts some big names to this quiet little town near Lake Iseo.

First half of July Lugano. A free jazz festival, Estival Jazz, is held alfresco in the main squares in Lugano.

15 Cremona. Inter-district rivalry fuels the Palio dell'oca goose race, plus there are processions with floats, and lots of local produce on offer.

AUGUST

15 Laveno, Lake Maggiore. Illuminated Boat Race held in Laveno; the lights and fireworks are clearly visible from the other side of the lake around Stresa.

SEPTEMBER

First week Monza, Milan. Italian Formula One Grand Prix.

12 Verona. Street entertainment and general partying to celebrate the birthday of the town's most famous lover, Juliet.

21 Varenna, Lake Como. Polenta and fish festival.

Last week Lake Como. Ancient rivalries are played out in the gondola race between Lecco, Varenna and Bellagio.

Last Sun Desenzano del Garda, Lake Garda. Autumn festival that sees the village alive with street entertainment and local food and wine.

Last week Milan. The fashionistas hit town again for Autumn Fashion Week, and the traffic comes to a standstill.

OCTOBER

Fourth weekend Cremona. During the Torrone Festival, nougat is celebrated in the town that claims to have invented it.

DECEMBER

All month Riva del Garda, Lake Garda. Each of the town's piazzas is decorated on the theme of a fairytale (Ⓦ nottedifiaba.it).

All month Arco, Lake Garda. Celebrations of the Austrian connection with the village focus on a Christmas market.

First week Milan. Opera season starts with an all-star opening night at La Scala.

Second week Verona. Christmas market in Piazza Bra.

7 Milan. Oh Bej, Oh Bej! The city's patron saint, Sant'Ambrogio, is celebrated with a huge street market around his church and a day off work and school for all.

13 Bergamo, Brescia and Cremona. At Santa Lucia, children are given presents and sweets, and there are candlelit processions.

Sports and outdoor pursuits

The Italian Lakes region and the Ticino district of Switzerland provide opportunities for activities ranging from swimming, sailing, golf and windsurfing to exploring the surrounding mountains on foot, bike, or even hang-glider. Spectator sports are popular in Italy, especially the hallowed calcio (football), and there is undying national passion for frenetic motor and cycle races.

Spectator sports

Calcio, or football, is the national sport, followed fanatically by millions of Italians, and if you're at all interested in the game, it would be a shame to leave the country without attending a *partita* (football match). The **season** starts around the middle of August, and finishes in June. **Il campionato** is split into four principal divisions with the twenty teams in the Serie A being the most prestigious. Matches are normally played on Sunday afternoons, although Saturday, Sunday-evening and Monday games are becoming more common, too. The top-flight sides in this part of the country are Milan's two teams, Milan and Inter, both of which have consolidated their positions near the top of Serie A in recent years and who usually spend the season vying for top place with Turin's Juventus. At the other end of the table, Bergamo's main team Atalanta, Brescia and Verona can usually be found hovering between relegation or promotion between Serie A and B. See Ⓦ legaseriea.it for results, a calendar of events and English links to the official team websites.

Inevitably, **tickets** for Serie A matches are not cheap, starting at about €15 for "Curva" seats where the *tifosi* or serious fans go, rising to €40–50 for "Tribuna" seats along the side of the pitch, and anything up to €100 for the more comfortable "Poltroncina" cushioned seats in the centre of the Tribuna. Once at the football match, get into the atmosphere by knocking back *borghetti* – little vials of cold coffee with a drop of spirit added.

The chosen sport after football in northern Italy is **cycling**. Popular as a participatory and spectator sport alike, at weekends especially, you'll often see a club group out, dressed in bright team kit, whirring along on their slender machines taking the hairpin bends of the pre-Alps at death-defying speeds.

The annual **Giro d'Italia**, in the second half of May, is a prestigious event that attracts scores of international participants each year, closing down roads and finishing in Milan. It has a long history and the region is very proud that several local boys, brought up on the punishing pre-Alp roads, have been winners of the pink jersey.

In a country that has produced Ferrari, Maserati, Alfa Romeo and Fiat, it should come as no surprise that **motor racing** gives Italians such a buzz. The **Formula One** track at Monza, near Milan, holds the Italian Grand Prix in September every year, and numerous companies organize packages that include flights, entrance tickets and accommodation.

Basketball is a surprisingly popular sport in Italy. It was introduced from the United States after World War II and most cities now have a team. Italy is now ranked among the foremost basketball teams in the world.

Participatory sports

Lake Garda is the best option for **watersports**: Torbole is famous for windsurfing but is also well organized for kayaking, dinghy sailing and water-skiing on the lake, and canyoning excursions in the mountains behind. Gargnano, also on Lake Garda, holds the annual Centomiglia **sailing** race at the beginning of September, and sailing is similarly popular on the other lakes, with many outlets – such as at Sarnico on Lake Iseo, Dongo on Lake Como and Cannero on Lake Maggiore – offering boats, boards and gear for rental, with and without tuition. All around the lakes, public lidos (most free of charge) provide perfect **swimming** conditions: it's a good idea to bring rubber-soled shoes though for the stony beaches.

The hills and mountains above all the lakes make perfect **walking** and **mountain-biking** country: tour operators offer many independent or escorted tours throughout the region, but it's just as easy to strike out alone. Tourist offices keep details of walks in the vicinity, while those in popular walking areas – such as Menaggio on Lake Como or Cannobio on Lake Maggiore – stock hiking maps and detailed route descriptions, and can advise on particular trails to follow. Ask at the tourist offices in Ascona and Locarno for their resources for walkers, including details of circular trails between stations on the Centovalli railway nearby. Several high peaks in the area are easily reached by public transport, including Monte Baldo above Malcesine (Lake Garda), Monte Generoso above Lugano (Lake Lugano) and the Mottarone above Stresa (Lake Maggiore); when skies are clear, taking the train or cable car up in order to follow trails around their summits can offer breathtaking panoramic views. The Mottarone in particular has some excellent mountain-bike routes.

By contrast, the flatter lands to the south of the region, around Mantua, Cremona and Pavia, are perfect for leisurely **cycle rides** or strolls. Tourist offices in all three cities keep details: one especially good route is the full-day bike ride between Peschiera del Garda and Mantua, following the River Mincio all the way.

Horseriding (*maneggio*) is becoming increasingly popular in rural areas and most tourist offices have lists of local stables. Many *agriturismi* also have riding facilities, and sometimes offer daily or weekly treks and night rides. Note that Italians rarely wear or provide riding hats.

In the winter months, it's possible to spend a day **skiing** or **snowboarding**. Resorts in this area (universally small, with limited facilities) are found chiefly above Bergamo – and thus are often crammed with weekending Milanese – as well as the much more remote high valleys above Locarno; small pistes are also created on slopes such as Monte Tamaro above Lugano, Monte Baldo above Malcesine and in the side-valleys of the Val Camonica and Val Sabbia above Brescia. Though great for a few hours of fun, these resorts can't match the snow cover, facilities and ambience of the major winter-sports centres of Piemonte, Trentino and Switzerland. There is information in English on Italian resorts and conditions at Ⓦ skiinfo.it. For details of skiing in Ticino, check Ⓦ ticino.ch.

Golf is popular around the lakes, although not such a common sport in Italy in general. There are some beautifully located courses; lists with links are available at Ⓦ golflombardia.it, Ⓦ visitgarda.com and Ⓦ distrettolaghi.it.

Travel essentials

Costs

The north of Italy has always been fairly expensive, with **prices** in line with northern Europe rather than the Mediterranean south. In recent years, inflation caused by the introduction of the euro and a wavering economy have conspired to increase prices still further. Public transport and entrance to sights is usually relatively inexpensive, but restaurant and hotel prices are similar to the UK or parts of the US. As an indication you should be able to survive on a **budget** of about €65–75 per day if you stay in a hostel, have lunchtime snacks and a cheap evening meal. If you stay in a mid-range hotel and eat out twice a day, you'll spend closer to €140–150 per day without transport or entrance fees.

Prices in the **Swiss Ticino** are similar to those in northern Italy, and the banking infrastructure works along the same lines, so the advice below for carrying and exchanging money is also relevant once you cross the border; remember that Switzerland is not in the Eurozone, although it will accept euros as payment.

Full-time students are entitled to special **discounts** on museum and gallery entrance in Italy as long as they have recognized ID cards. University photo ID might open some doors, but they are not as readily accepted as the **International Student ID Card** (ISIC, ⓦ isiccard.com), which also entitles the bearer to some discounts on accommodation, entertainment and even language courses. At some tourist sights, **children** under 12 are allowed in free. At the other end of the scale, European citizens who are **over 60** – or sometimes 65 – are often allowed into sights at a reduced rate. It's always worth carrying proof of your age and asking "*C'è sconto per gli anziani?*" ("Is there a discount for senior citizens?"). Bear in mind also that state museums across Italy are free on the first Sunday of the month.

Crime and personal safety

Both Italy and Switzerland are safe countries and you should feel comfortable walking around town centres and resorts, even in the evening. That said, in the bigger towns, like Milan and Verona, tourists can be targeted by **pickpockets**: crowded streets or markets, big train stations and busy tourist areas are the places to be on your guard: don't flash anything of value, keep a firm hand on your camera, and carry shoulder bags, as Italian women do, slung across your body.

Keep an eye out for two or three people begging together, often with an infant or small child in tow; they will usually have a piece of cardboard explaining their predicament which will be adroitly used to cover one of them whipping away your valuables. On the whole, it's common sense to avoid badly lit areas completely at night. Confronted with a robber, your best bet is to submit meekly. If driving, never leave anything valuable in your vehicle, and try to park on well-lit, well-used streets or in garages with security men. Motorway

service stations have a particularly high rate of petty crime, so make sure you always leave your vehicle locked with all valuables out of sight.

If the worst happens, you'll need to report to the **police**. In Italy, these come in many forms: the **Vigili Urbani**, with their white pith helmets and natty gloves, are mainly concerned with directing traffic and issuing parking fines, whereas the **Polizia Stradale** patrol the motorways. You may, however, have dealings with the **Carabinieri**, in their military-style uniforms and white shoulder-belts, who deal with general crime, public order and drug control. These are the ones Italians are most rude about, but a lot of jokes concerning their supposed stupidity stem from the usual north–south prejudice. The Carabinieri tend to come from southern Italy – joining the police is one way to escape the poverty trap – and they are posted away from home so as to be well out of the sphere of influence of their families. The **Polizia Statale**, the other general crime-fighting force, enjoy a fierce rivalry with the Carabinieri and are the ones you'll perhaps have most chance of coming into contact with, since **thefts** should be reported to them. You'll find the address of the **questura** or police station in the local telephone directory (in smaller places it may be just a local *commissariato*); alternatively ask your hotel or the tourist office for details. The *questura* is where you go to get a *denuncia*, the official report of anything that's been lost or stolen that you will need for any insurance claim; take a book and be prepared for a long wait.

By contrast with Italy, **Switzerland** has only one small force of plain-clothes federal police (*polizia*), as most police duties are managed by the cantonal authorities. Ticino's **Polizia Cantonale** has its own website, ⓦ www4.ti.ch/di/pol/polizia-cantonale, with contact details for every local police station.

Electricity

The supply is 220V, though anything requiring 240V will work. Most plugs have two round pins, though you'll find the older three-pin plug in some places: a multi-plug adapter is very useful.

Entry requirements

British, Irish and other **EU citizens** can enter Italy on production of a valid passport, although if you're planning to live and work in the country a *permesso di soggiorno* (resident's permit) is needed. Citizens of the **United States, Canada, Australia and New Zealand** need only a valid passport, too, but are

EMERGENCIES

For help in an **emergency**, call one of the following national emergency telephone numbers:

ITALY

- ☎ 112 **Police** (Carabinieri)
- ☎ 113 **Local police** (Polizia Statale)
- ☎ 115 **Fire brigade** (Vigili del Fuoco)
- ☎ 116 **Roadside assistance** (Soccorso Stradale)
- ☎ 118 **Ambulance** (Ambulanza)

SWITZERLAND

- ☎ 117 **Police**
- ☎ 118 **Fire, ambulance and accidents**
- ☎ 140 **Roadside assistance**

limited to stays of three months. Likewise, EU nationals and citizens of the US, Canada, Australia and New Zealand need only a valid passport to visit **Switzerland**, where stays are limited for all to a maximum of three months. **South Africans** need to obtain visas in advance; other nationals should consult the relevant embassy about visa requirements.

In Italy, you're legally required to register with the police within three days of entering the country, though if you're staying at a hotel this will be done for you and, even if it isn't, most police officers would be amazed at any attempt to register yourself down at the local station while on holiday. However, if you're going to be staying around for a while, you'd be advised to comply.

ITALIAN EMBASSIES AND CONSULATES ABROAD

Australia ⓦ www.ambcanberra.esteri.it.
Canada ⓦ www.ambottawa.esteri.it.
Ireland ⓦ www.ambdublino.esteri.it.
New Zealand ⓦ www.ambwellington.esteri.it.
South Africa ⓦ www.ambpretoria.esteri.it.
UK ⓦ www.amblondra.esteri.it.
US ⓦ www.ambwashingtondc.esteri.it.

SWISS EMBASSIES ABROAD

See ⓦ eda.admin.ch.

Health

As a member of the European Union, Italy has free reciprocal **health agreements** with other member states. EU citizens are entitled to free treatment within Italy's public health-care system on production of a **European Health Insurance Card** (EHIC), which British citizens can obtain by calling ☎ 0191 218 1999, or applying online at ⓦ nhs.uk. Allow up to 21 days for delivery. The EHIC is free of charge and valid for at least three years, and it basically entitles you to the same treatment as an Italian. The Australian Medicare system also has a reciprocal health-care arrangement with Italy. American and South African visitors should take out health insurance.

Vaccinations are not required, and neither Italy – nor neighbouring Switzerland – present any more health worries than anywhere else in Europe. In Italy, although the **water** is safe to drink, most Italians drink bottled water, in some areas because there is a very high limescale content in the supply but, more often than not, simply out of habit. Public water fountains (usually button- or tap-operated) in squares and city streets are common, though look out for *acqua non potabile* signs, indicating that the water is unsafe to drink.

It's wise to take high-factor **suncream** to protect against sunburn – the gentle breezes on the lakes and in the mountains can make the strength of the sun deceptive. **Mosquitoes** can be a problem between June and October, especially in Milan and the southern parts of the lakes, so you might want to pack insect repellent, sprays and/or plug-ins.

In Italy

For most holiday ailments, your first port of call should be a **pharmacy** (*farmacia*). Italian pharmacists are well qualified to give you advice on minor ailments and can dispense many medicines that need prescriptions in other countries. There's generally at least one pharmacy open all night in the bigger towns. A rota system operates and you should find the address of the one currently open on any *farmacia* door or listed in the local paper.

If your condition is more serious or you're involved in an accident, head for the *pronto soccorso* (**accident and emergency department**) of the nearest hospital or, in extreme cases, phone ☎ 118 and ask for *ospedale* or *ambulanza*. Casualty departments are organized according to the triage system, which means that you will be seen whatever your condition, but more serious cases will be treated first. You may be charged for the service if the hospital staff feel that your condition was not really urgent, but this is still the quickest and most effective way of getting the best treatment: the fee will usually be around €30. Whenever possible, make sure you take your passport with you and your European Health

Insurance Card, if you're eligible, to enable you to get prescriptions for medicines at the local rate (about ten percent of the full price). If at all possible, try to avoid going to the **dentist** (*dentista*) while you're in Italy or Switzerland. These aren't covered by the health service, and for the smallest problem you'll pay through the teeth. If it's an emergency that really can't wait until you get home, visit the *pronto soccorso* in the big towns or take local advice in the smaller ones.

In Switzerland

Although Switzerland isn't a member of the EU, citizens of European member states are entitled to **emergency health care** in the country under the same terms as Swiss residents. This effectively means that, on production of an EHIC (see p.43), the care will be subsidized but you will have to contribute to the costs: for example, there is a small charge for bed and board if you have to stay in hospital, although medical treatment is free. If you need an ambulance, you will be required to pay fifty percent of the cost (as local residents do) and there is usually a small standard charge for any prescribed drugs.

Insurance

Even though EU health care privileges apply in Italy, you'd do well to take out an **insurance policy** before travelling to cover against theft, loss, illness or injury. A typical policy usually provides cover for the loss of baggage, tickets and – up to a certain limit – cash or cheques, as well as cancellation or curtailment of your journey. Most policies exclude so-called dangerous sports unless an extra premium is paid; around the lakes this can mean windsurfing, canyoning and trekking. Many policies can be chopped and changed to exclude coverage you don't need – for example, sickness and accident benefits can often be excluded or included at will. If you do

take medical coverage, ascertain whether benefits will be paid as treatment proceeds or only after your return home, and whether there is a 24-hour medical emergency number. When securing baggage cover, make sure that the per-article limit – typically under £500 – will cover your most valuable possession. If you need to make a claim, keep receipts for medicines and medical treatment, and in the event you have anything stolen, you must obtain an official statement from the police (*polizia* or *carabinieri*).

Mail

Post office (Ⓦ poste.it) **opening hours** in Italy are usually Monday to Saturday 8.30am to 1pm, and it pays to get there early, as large queues invariably form around mid-morning. Unless you need registered post (*raccomandata*) or have parcels to send though, you won't need to waste your holiday time in post office queues. **Stamps** (*francobolli*) are sold in *tabacchi*, too, as well as in some gift shops in tourist resorts; they will often also weigh your letter. If your letter is urgent make sure you mark it "*posta prioritaria*"; this service is included in the basic price of €0.65 to anywhere in Europe. Sending a standard-sized envelope or a postcard costs €0.85 to the US, Australia and New Zealand.

Post offices (❶0800 888 777, Ⓦ post.ch) in **Switzerland** are generally open Monday to Friday 7.30am to noon and 1.30 to 6.30pm, and Saturday 8 to 11am, although watch out for slight regional variations and restricted hours in smaller branches. Sending a postcard or a 20g letter costs Fr.1.40 to Europe, Fr.1.90 worldwide.

Maps

The **town plans** throughout this guide should be fine for most purposes, and practically all tourist offices give out maps of their local area for free. The clearest and best-value **road maps** for Italy are produced by Touring Club Italiano (TCI). The fold-up 1:200,000 scale map of Lombardy is excellent and includes the neighbouring areas of Piemonte, Veneto and Switzerland covered in this guide. If you prefer an atlas format, go for their *Atlante Stradale d'Italia* (*Nord*) on the same scale; this covers everywhere in the country north of Florence and features profiles of the motorways, including the facilities at individual service stations. For **hiking** you'll need at least a scale of 1:50,000. Studio FMB and the TCI cover the major mountain areas of northern Italy to this scale. Both the Istituto Geografico Centrale and Kompass series cover the area with more detailed 1:25,000 maps.

For Switzerland, the most respected commercial series is that published by the Federal Office of Topography (Ⓦswisstopo.ch). They do a full range starting at 1:1 million, detailed 1:100,000 regional maps and 1:50,000 and 1:25,000 hikers' maps, as well as specialist maps on different scales highlighting cycling and inline-skating routes, ski runs, historic sites, vineyards and cultural attractions.

Money

Italy's **currency** is the euro (€), which is split into 100 cents (c). The currency in Switzerland is the Swiss franc (*franco svizzero*), commonly abbreviated to "Fr." – but you may also see "fr", "sFr", "Sfr", "SF", "FS", or the official bank abbreviation "CHF". Each franc is divided into 100 *centesimi* (c). This being border territory, however, you can pay for just about everything in the Ticino in euros (cash or card). All hotels in Switzerland advertise rates in francs and euros (check closely which column you're referring to), as do the boat companies and even restaurants and shops. Note that the euro equivalent price is always worked out when you buy according to the daily CHF–EUR exchange rate, so it can vary slightly from the advertised figure.

Banking hours are normally Monday to Friday mornings from 8.30am until 1.30pm, and for an hour in the afternoon (usually between 2.30 and 4pm). There are local variations on this and banks are usually open only in the morning on the day before a public holiday.

Debit and credit cards

Although it's a good idea to have some **cash** when you first arrive, one of the easiest ways of accessing funds while you're abroad is with your **debit card** direct from an ATM cash machine (*bancomat*). While the flat transaction fee is usually quite small,

most cards can only issue a maximum of €250 per day; check with your bank before you leave home to make sure your card is set up to work abroad, as some banks have an increased security system that means your card will not work abroad unless you have informed them that you are travelling. Debit cards from the UK can be used to purchase goods in shops.

Credit cards can also be used in ATMs with a PIN number that's designed to be used overseas but remember that cash advances on credit cards are treated as loans with interest accruing daily from the date of withdrawal, and there may be a transaction fee on top of this. Note that payment by card (*carta*) is not as prevalent as in the UK and US; many budget hotels aren't set up to take cards, and even some upmarket restaurants insist on cash, although you shouldn't have too many problems in the main tourist centres. MasterCard, Visa and American Express are the most widely accepted cards in Italy and Switzerland.

Travellers' cheques and Cash Passports

A safe alternative to cash and cards, American Express (Ⓦamericanexpress.com), Thomas Cook (Ⓦthomascook.com) and Visa (Ⓦvisa.co.uk) **travellers' cheques** can be cashed in most Italian banks. However, they are becoming less common and many travellers find that **Cash Passports** – a prepaid currency card that is loaded up before travelling and can be used in some shops and most ATMs in Italy – are a secure, convenient alternative. Thomas Cook (Ⓦcashpassport.com), Travelex (Ⓦtravelex.co.uk) and various banks offer the service.

Opening hours

In Italy, most **shops and businesses** open Monday to Saturday from around 9am until 1pm, and from about 3/4pm until 6/7pm, though some places still close on Saturday afternoons and Monday mornings. Exceptions are banks (see left) and post offices (see opposite). Traditionally, everything except bars and restaurants closes on Sunday, though *pasticcerie* are open in the mornings; while in Milan and tourist areas, Sunday shopping is becoming more common and around Christmas

---

CLOSED ON MONDAYS

Most museums and sights are **closed on Mondays**; see the relevant sections in the guide for specific opening hours.

time, in particular, there are extended openings. Opening hours for state-run **museums** are generally Tuesday to Saturday 9am until 7pm, and Sunday 9am until 1pm. Most other museums roughly follow this pattern too, although they are more likely to close for a couple of hours in the afternoon, and have shorter opening times in winter. The majority of churches open in the early morning, around 7 or 8am for Mass, and close around noon, opening up again at 4pm and closing at 7 or 8pm.

Shop opening hours in Switzerland are customarily Monday to Saturday 9am to 5.30/6pm, with some now opening on Sundays. A few places take Monday morning off. **Cafés** that serve full meals (which is most of them) will only do so at the customary mealtimes: roughly noon to 2pm and 6 to 10pm. Outside of those hours, you'll generally be able to find only snacks. Closing times of all establishments are regulated by each individual municipality: Lugano, for example, stipulates midnight, though places can stay open an hour later than normal on Friday and Saturday nights.

Phones

Mobile/cell phones in Italy and Switzerland work on the GSM European standard, usually compatible with phones from the UK, the rest of Europe, Australia and New Zealand, but not the US and Canada, which use a different system. You'll hardly ever see an Italian without their *telefonino*, but if you want to join them, make sure you have a booster package or have made the necessary "roaming" arrangements with your provider. International SIM cards also work well and are a good-value option, but you will not be able to activate an Italian SIM without an Italian tax code (*codice fiscale*).

Public telephones, run by Telecom Italia, come in various forms, usually with clear instructions in English. Coin-operated machines are increasingly hard to find so you will probably have to buy a **telephone card** (*carta* or *scheda telefonica*), available from *tabacchi* and newsstands. Numbers beginning ☎800 are free, ☎170 will get you through to an English-speaking operator, ☎176 to international directory enquiries. **Phone tariffs** are among the most expensive in Europe, especially if you're calling long-distance or internationally. You can cut costs hugely by buying a **phone card**, on sale for upwards of €5 from newspaper stands; you don't insert it into the phone but dial a central freephone number and then a pin code given on the reverse of the card.

> ### DRESS CODE
> The rules for **visiting churches** are strictly enforced everywhere: **dress modestly**, which means no shorts (not even Bermuda-length ones) for men or women, and covered shoulders for women, and try to avoid wandering around during a service.

Public holidays

It is worth trying to avoid travelling on the eve of a **national holiday**, as roads and public transport are usually packed. On the country's official national holidays, everything closes down – including many museums – although bars and restaurants are likely to stay open in resorts. If a holiday falls on a Tuesday or Thursday, it is common for people to take the Monday or Friday as a *ponte* – or bridge – and so enjoy a long weekend. In August, particularly during the weeks either side of **Ferragosto** (August 15), most townsfolk flee to the coast, lakes or mountains, leaving many towns half-deserted, with shops, bars and restaurants closed and a reduced public transport service. Meanwhile, the lakeside villages fill up with the townies, and the routes around the lakes reach near-saturation point.

CALENDAR OF PUBLIC HOLIDAYS

The following dates are holidays in both Italy and Switzerland, unless otherwise stated.

January 1 Primo dell'anno; New Year's Day.
January 6 Epifania; Epiphany.
Pasquetta Easter Monday.
April 25 Giorno della Liberazione; Liberation Day, in Italy only.
May 1 Festa dei Lavoratori; Labour Day.
June 2 Festa della Repubblica; Republic Day, in Italy only.
August 1 Festa nazionale; Swiss National Day, in Switzerland only.
August 15 Ferragosto; Assumption of the Blessed Virgin Mary.
November 1 Ognissanti; All Souls Day.
December 8 Immacolata; Immaculate Conception of the Blessed Virgin Mary.
December 25 Natale; Christmas.
December 26 Santo Stefano; St Stephen's Day.

Time

Italy and Switzerland are always one hour ahead of Britain, seven hours ahead of US Eastern Standard Time and ten hours ahead of Pacific Standard Time.

Tipping

Service is generally included on restaurant bills in Italy, but if not, a couple of euros will suffice. You only need to tip taxi drivers, concierge and so on, if they have been particularly helpful. In **Switzerland**, all bar, restaurant and hotel bills are calculated with fifteen percent service included: tipping is officially abolished. Nonetheless, unless service was truly diabolical, everyone rounds things up at least to the nearest franc; in restaurants, it's common to add a few francs.

Toilets

Public facilities have improved around tourist sites in recent years, although the main options remain train and bus stations, or nipping into a bar or café for the loo followed by a quick drink. In stations and motorway services, there might be an attendant who should keep the facilities stocked with paper (*carta*) and will expect a tip of a few cents. Most places are relatively clean, though hole-in-the-floor versions are still common for public toilets and it's advisable not to be without your own tissue. By law, basins in public places in Italy have to be designed so that you don't need to touch the taps: in modern bathrooms this requires waving your hands under the tap to start the flow; in older ones, there is usually a foot pedal.

Tourist information

There is no shortage of information on the lakes region. The national tourist offices (Ⓦenit.it) are an obvious starting point. Their websites hold a wealth of information, and once you're on the ground, you'll find plenty of brochures, maps and leaflets at tourist offices throughout the district. There are also hundreds of other **websites**, covering every aspect of Italian and Swiss life (see p.49).

In Italy

Most towns and villages have a **tourist office** and there are branches at the major airports and stations. They vary in degrees of usefulness (and helpfulness), but usually provide at least a town plan and local listings guide. In smaller villages, there is sometimes a "Pro Loco" office (representing a consortium of local businesses) that has much the same kind of information, but the staff are unlikely to speak English.

Opening hours vary: offices in larger cities and resorts are likely to be open Monday to Saturday 9am to 1pm and 4 to 7pm – and sometimes on Sunday mornings – while smaller offices may open weekdays only. In peak season, however, many offices will stay open over lunch. Pro Loco times are notoriously erratic – some open for only a couple of hours a day, even in summer. Some of the lake resorts have information boards outside the offices, which can be helpful if you need numbers or directions when everything is closed.

In Switzerland

The efficient **Switzerland Tourism** (Ⓦmy switzerland.com) is only too happy to supply you with exhaustive information on all things Swiss; its partner **Ticino Tourism** (Ⓦticino.ch) covers Italian-speaking Switzerland. All towns, and a sizeable number of villages, have a tourist office (*ente turistico*), where staff speak at least some English and are scrupulously helpful.

INTERNATIONAL CALLS

CALLING ITALY AND SWITZERLAND FROM HOME

Dial your international access code (00 from the UK, Ireland & New Zealand, 011 from the US & Canada, 0011 from Australia), followed by **39** for Italy, then the area code and number **including the initial zero**. For Switzerland you need the international access code followed by **41** for Switzerland, followed by the local number **excluding the initial zero**.

CALLING HOME FROM ITALY

Note that the initial zero is omitted from the area code when dialling the UK, Ireland, Australia and New Zealand.

Australia international access code + 61
New Zealand international access code + 64
UK international access code + 44
US and Canada international access code + 1
Ireland international access code + 353
South Africa international access code + 27

From April to October tourist offices are usually **open** Monday to Saturday from 9am to 6pm, and Sunday from 9am to 3pm, although some may close a little earlier. Out of season they are likely to shut up shop between noon and 2pm and all day on Sundays.

Travellers with disabilities

Italy isn't generally geared towards disabled travellers, though people are usually helpful and progress is gradually being made in accessible accommodation, transport and public buildings. In Switzerland, on the other hand, you'll find most tourist facilities have been designed with everybody, not just the able-bodied, in mind, and there's a wealth of information to help you plan your trip.

In Italy

Public transport access can be challenging in Italy, although low-level buses are gradually being introduced in towns and some trains have disabled facilities. Happily, however, the ferries on the lakes are wheelchair accessible. Recent legislation means that adapted **accommodation** shouldn't be too much of a problem and spacious, specially designed toilets are becoming increasingly common in **bars, restaurants and hotels**. The cobbled streets in old town and village centres can present their own problems as can access to **sights**, including galleries and museums. Even in the bigger cities – like Milan and Verona – high kerbs, ad hoc parking and constant building works can make life difficult for those in wheelchairs and the partially sighted. On the plus side, some of the lake resorts, particularly on **Lake Maggiore**, have been a favourite with senior citizens for decades and so some hotels and restaurants have slightly better facilities for those with reduced mobility.

In Switzerland

Switzerland Tourism publishes a very useful hotel guide specifically for visitors with disabilities (W myswitzerland.com/en-gb/transporttravel /physically_challenged.html), listing and assessing **hotels** around the country according to their access for people with limited mobility or in wheelchairs. If you contact the Call Center Handicap team of Swiss Federal Railways at least two hours before you want to travel, giving them your full name, phone number, date of travel, desired departure and arrival times, and the nature of your disability, they can arrange for people to help you on and off the **train** and access the "Mobilifts" at most stations; this is a free service. All fast trains (single- and double-decker), and most regional trains have spaces within second-class carriages to park wheelchairs, identified by a wheelchair pictogram. **Boats** are generally easy to board and often have facilities such as disabled toilets; and private narrow-gauge train companies including FART (the Centovalli line from Locarno) are converting carriages for passengers with disabilities. The Call Center Handicap office has full details.

CONTACTS FOR TRAVELLERS WITH DISABILITIES

Access-Able W access-able.com. Online resource for US travellers with disabilities.

Accessible Italy Italy T 378 0549 941111, W accessibleitaly.com. Italian operation offering an English-speaking accessible accommodation advice, organized tours and tailor-made trips.

Accessible Journeys 35 W Sellers Ave, Ridley Park, PA 19078, US T 1 800 846 4537, W disabilitytravel.com. Travel tips and programmes for groups or individual travellers from the US, including an Italian Lakes tour.

Call Center Handicap Mobil Services Handicap, Bahnhofplatz 1, CH-3900 Brig, Switzerland T 0800 007 102 or T +41 51 225 7150, W sbb.ch. Full details of accessibility on all forms of public transport; they can also make arrangements for travel anywhere in Switzerland.

Disabled Persons Assembly 4/173–175 Victoria St, Wellington, NZ T 04 801 9100, W dpa.org.nz. NZ resource centre with lists of travel agencies and tour operators for people with disabilities.

Holiday Care 2nd floor, Imperial Building, Victoria Rd, Horley, Surrey RH6 7PZ, UK T 01293 774 535, Minicom T 01293 776 943, W holidaycare.org.uk. Provides free lists of accessible accommodation outside the UK.

Irish Wheelchair Association Blackheath Drive, Clontarf, Dublin 3, Eire T 01 833 8241, W iwa.ie. Useful information for wheelchair users about travelling abroad.

Society for the Advancement of Travelers with Handicaps (SATH) 347 5th Ave, New York, NY 10016, US T 212 447 7284, W sath.org. Information on the accessibility of specific airlines and advice on travelling with certain conditions.

Travelling with children

Children are adored in Italy and will be made a fuss of in the street, and welcomed and catered for in bars and restaurants. Hotels normally charge around thirty percent extra to put a bed or cot in your room, though kids pay less on trains and can generally expect discounts for museum entry: prices vary, but 11–18-year-olds are usually admitted at half price on production of some form of ID (although sometimes this applies only to EU citizens). Under-11s – or sometimes only under-6s – have free entry.

Supplies for **babies** and small children are pricey: nappies and milk formula can cost up to three times as much as in other parts of Europe. Discreet

---

TOP 5 FAMILY-FRIENDLY DESTINATIONS

Northern Lake Garda Beaches, bikes, boat trips and adventure sports. See p.290

Varenna, Lake Como Tiny alleyways and a ruined hilltop castle complete with its own ghost. See p.220

Città Alta, Bergamo Ancient piazzas, cobbled lanes and a funicular to zip you up and down. See p.228

Gardaland Shaded, well-organized theme park. See p.285

Aquadventure Park An exhilarating climbing wall, as well as rope-walks, mountain-bike trails and waterslides. See p.125

---

breastfeeding is widely accepted – even smiled upon – but nappy changing facilities are few and far between. Branches of the children's clothes and accessories chain Prenatal have changing facilities and a feeding area, but otherwise you may find you have to be creative. It is rare to find any facilities in stations, department stores or public toilets, although that said, people will usually go out of their way to help you.

For **older children**, most towns and villages have central playgrounds, while the theme parks of Gardaland (see p.285) will no doubt entertain. Once you're on the lakes, there is plenty to keep children of all ages occupied, from pedaloes to windsurfing and from paddling to dinghy-sailing.

The only **hazards** when travelling with children to the lakes are the heat and sun. Very-high-factor sun creams are quite difficult to find, although pharmacies usually sell sun block. Bonnets or straw hats are plentiful in local markets. Take advantage of the periods of less intense sun – mornings and evenings – for travelling, and use the quiet of siesta-time to recover flagging energy. The rhythms of the southern climate soon modify established patterns, and you'll find it more natural carrying on later into the night, past normal bedtimes.

INTERNET RESOURCES

Ⓦ **holidayswithkids.com.au** The website of the popular *Holidays With Kids* magazine. Advice for frazzled parents on kid-friendly destinations and accommodation, as well as tours.

Ⓦ **italyfamilyhotels.it** An organization of hotels across Italy geared up with facilities, from cots and bottle warmers in rooms to babysitter, play areas and special menus. New hotels are constantly joining; at the time of writing there were two close to Lake Garda.

Ⓦ **travelforkids.com** US site offering advice on planning holidays with children.

Websites

REGIONAL TOURIST SITES

Bergamo Ⓦ www.provincia.bergamo.it/turismo.

Brescia Ⓦ bresciaturism.it.

Cremona Ⓦ www.provincia.cremona.it.

Lake Como Ⓦ www.lakecomo.it.

Lake Garda Ⓦ visitgarda.com.

Lake Iseo Ⓦ agenzialagoiseofranciacorta.it.

Lake Lugano Ⓦ lugano-tourism.ch.

Lake Maggiore (east shore) and Varese Ⓦ vareselandoftourism.it.

Lake Maggiore (north shore) Ⓦ ascona-locarno.com.

Lake Orta & Lake Maggiore (west) Ⓦ distrettolaghi.it.

Mantua Ⓦ turismo.mantova.it.

Milan Ⓦ www.tourism.milan.it.

Verona Ⓦ tourism.verona.it.

GENERAL ITALY SITES

Ⓦ **corriere.it** Online version of the Milan daily with some interesting general articles translated into English and a regularly updated weather forecast.

Ⓦ **italianlakes.com** An attractive site run by an expat American couple that's full of helpful tips and resources.

Ⓦ **italymagazine.com** Aimed at expats, with articles on life in Italy plus some good links and a forum for posting queries.

Ⓦ **parks.it** Good, detailed English-language info on national and regional parks, plus some wildlife information.

GENERAL SWITZERLAND SITES

Ⓦ **museums.ch** Catalogue and description of all museums nationwide.

Ⓦ **www.swissembassy.org.uk** Engaging information in English about the country and its politics put together by the Swiss Embassy in London.

Ⓦ **swissinfo.ch** Useful news site reporting on all things Swiss.

Ⓦ **ticino.ch** Vast array of useful stuff on Ticino canton.

Milan

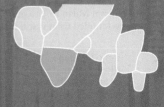

ROOF OF MILAN'S DUOMO

Milan

1

Milan stands at the foot of the Alps, amid Lombardy's rich agricultural plains, guarding the route south from central Europe to Rome. Since its Celtic beginnings, the Lombard capital has been a hub of trade and business, as well as an important manufacturing and political centre. The home of the country's Stock Exchange and banks, and the centre of Italian broadcasting, publishing and marketing, twenty-first-century Milan has in many ways more of a claim to be Italy's capital city than Rome. Yet it is smaller and more compact than a capital city, which makes a day or two exploring its ancient monuments and contemporary fashion and design scenes a must on any visit to the region.

Milan's rich history has also bequeathed it a wealth of art and monuments, not least its spectacular **Duomo**, some splendid **ancient churches**, the medieval **Castello Sforzesco** and the world-famous **La Scala** opera house. Chief among its artistic treasures and justifying a visit alone is Leonardo da Vinci's masterpiece of Renaissance art, **The Last Supper**. More superlative artworks by the likes of Mantegna, Veronese and Tintoretto can be seen at the city's premier art gallery, the **Pinacoteca di Brera**. Milan's other major draw is **shopping**. The second half of the twentieth century saw the city become a catwalk for the world's top **fashion** designers and also home to the most important **design** and manufacturing companies in the world. Milan's high proportion of beautiful people – from fashionistas and their wealthy clients to would-be models and *veline* (scantily dressed TV presenters) – means that this is a place where appearance counts and there's no better place to do a spot of people-watching than in the city's bars, especially at **aperitivo** time, an extended happy hour that's become something of an institution.

If you begin to tire of the city or want to slow down a gear or two, head for nearby **Pavia**, a comfortable provincial town on the River Ticino that once held the hunting lodge and summer residence of the Sforza family. Close by, and an easy day-trip away, is the stunning **Certosa**, the Carthusian monastery that Gian Galeazzo Visconti founded as his mausoleum.

Brief history

Milan first stepped into the historical limelight in the fourth century when Emperor Constantine issued the **Edict of Milan** here, granting Christians throughout the Roman Empire the freedom to worship for the first time. The city, under its charismatic bishop, Ambrogio (Ambrose), swiftly became a major centre of Christianity – many of today's churches stand on the sites, or even retain parts, of fourth-century predecessors.

Medieval Milan

Medieval Milan rose to prominence under the ruthless regime of the Visconti dynasty, who founded what is still the city's most recognized building, the florid late-Gothic

THE LAST SUPPER

Highlights

❶ Roof of Milan's Duomo Wander amid the tracery of the world's largest Gothic cathedral and enjoy views of the city and the mountains beyond. **See p.60**

❷ Pinacoteca di Brera This venerable art gallery, opened in 1809, holds a peerless collection of northern Italian masterpieces. **See p.67**

❸ The Last Supper Leonardo da Vinci's mural for the refectory wall of Santa Maria delle Grazie is one of the greatest masterpieces of the Renaissance. **See p.79**

❹ Sant'Ambrogio This beautiful church dedicated to the city's patron saint provided

the prototype for many of the region's Romanesque basilicas. **See p.80**

❺ Aperitivo Unwind with Milan's signature drink – Campari – and a plate of nibbles during the city's extended happy hour. **See p.88**

❻ Shopping in Milan Whether looking for top-label chic or bargain designer threads, you'll be spoilt for choice in Italy's fashion capital. **See p.92**

❼ Certosa di Pavia Rising out of the rice fields near Pavia, this Carthusian monastery is a wonderful fusion of Gothic and Renaissance architecture. **See p.99**

HIGHLIGHTS ARE MARKED ON THE MAP ON P.54

1

Duomo, and built the first, heavily fortified nucleus of the **Castello** – which, under their successors, the Sforza, was extended to house what became one of the most luxurious courts of the Renaissance. This was a period of much building and rebuilding, notably under the last Sforza, Lodovico, who employed the architect **Bramante** to improve the city's churches. He also commissioned **Leonardo da Vinci** to paint *The Last Supper* and design war-machines to aid him in his struggles with foreign powers and other Italian states.

Foreign rule

Leonardo's inventions didn't prevent Milan falling to the French in 1499, marking the beginning of almost four centuries of foreign rule. Two hundred years of Spanish dominance – beginning in the mid-sixteenth century – were mainly characterized by high taxes, plague and the construction of a new defensive wall around the city. Later, the Austrian Habsburgs took control; their major legacies were the **Teatro della Scala** and the **Brera** art gallery, which, during Milan's short spell under Napoleon, was filled with paintings looted from churches and private collections and opened to the public.

MILAN & AROUND

HIGHLIGHTS

1 Roof of Milan's Duomo
2 Pinacoteca di Brera
3 The Last Supper
4 Sant'Ambrogio
5 Aperitivo
6 Shopping in Milan
7 Certosa di Pavia

- - - Ecopass Border

0   4
kilometres

UGLY DUCKLING

Milan's reputation for being ugly and **industrial** is mainly unfounded. True, the postwar suburbs are not attractive places, but the centre is a collage of architectural styles displaying the city's history in a comfortably wanderable **maze of pedestrianized streets**, although Allied bombing raids in the summer of 1943 more or less put paid to what the nineteenth century and Fascist town planners had left of the medieval centre. **Bomb damage** still riddles the city, as many sites were issued with preservation orders limiting what could be built, while the 1950s and 1960s saw the construction of rather too many unimaginative office blocks. Beside them, however, lie **Roman remains**, **medieval piazzas** and **Neoclassical palaces**, not to mention the city's **ancient canals**.

Fascism

Mussolini made his mark on the city, too. Arrive by train and you emerge into the massive white megalith of the **Stazione Centrale** built on the dictator's orders; while the town council offices are housed in the pompous **Arengario** from which he would address crowds gathered in Piazza Duomo. And it was on the innocuous roundabout of Piazzale Loreto that the dead dictator was strung up for display to the baying mob as proof of his demise in April 1945.

Postwar

The city's postwar development was characterized by the boom periods of the 1950s and 1980s. The industry that launched the so-called "miracle of Milan" in the 1950s led to the construction of the hundreds of small factories and the infamous dreary **suburbs** that still encircle the city today. Most of the factories stopped production during the last few decades, and the city's wealth now comes from banking and its position at the top of the world's **fashion** and **design** industries.

Political axis

Politically, too, Milan has been at the centre of Italy's postwar history. A bomb in Piazza Fontana in 1969 that killed sixteen people signalled the beginning of the dark and bloody period in the country's history known as the **Anni di piombi**, when murky secret-service goings-on led to over one hundred deaths from bomb attacks. In the 1980s, the corruption and political scandals of the Craxi period once again focused attention on Milan, the centre of the country's institutional corruption, gaining it the nickname **Tangentopoli** or "Bribesville". The subsequent dismantling of the existing political system paved the way for the birth and rapid success of Forza Italia, the political party founded by the self-promoting media magnate **Silvio Berlusconi**, which has ruled the country for longer than any other postwar government. Berlusconi is Milan born and bred and has his financial and power base in the media and publishing companies of the city – not to mention being owner of the football team, AC Milan. And as history repeats itself, in the last year or so Milan appears once again at the centre of a new wave of scandal and corruption sweeping the country.

Orientation

We have divided the centre up into areas radiating out from the obvious focal point of **Piazza Duomo**, which as well as hosting the city's iconic Duomo leads on to the elegant Galleria Vittorio Emanuele and the Piazza della Scala, home to the world-famous opera house. Heading northwest along the shopping street of Via Dante takes you to the imperious **Castello Sforzesco** and the extensive **Parco Sempione** beyond. North, the well-heeled neighbourhoods of **Moscova** and **Brera** are the stomping ground of Milan's most style-conscious citizens. Here you'll find the fine art collection of the Pinacoteca di Brera near the so-called Quadrilatero d'Oro (Golden Quadrangle), a concentration

1

HIDDEN MILAN

Much of the best that Milan has to offer is hidden away from view behind imposing facades and heavy doors. If you get a chance, sneak a look behind a door that's been left ajar and you might catch a glimpse of a wonderful garden or a courtyard full of flowers. The city also harbours some peaceful corners, listed below, where you can relax with a book or a sandwich and recharge your batteries before continuing your sightseeing.

Roof of the Duomo p.60
Giardino Botanico p.70
Giardini della Villa Reale p.72
Ospedale Maggiore p.73

Rotonda della Besana p.73
Bramante courtyard, Santa Maria delle Grazie p.78

---

of top designer fashion boutiques. Slightly further north is Milan's most pleasant park, the Giardini Pubblici. **Southeast of the Duomo** is one of Milan's studenty areas, home to the city's medieval hospital, the Ospedale Maggiore, and the burial ground of the Rotonda del Besana. Southwest, the shopping streets of Via Torino take you to the **Ticinese** district, a focal point at *aperitivo* time, and home to a couple of the city's most beautiful ancient churches. Continuing south on to the **Navigli** leads to the bar and restaurant area around the city's remaining canals. West of the cathedral stands the church of Santa Maria delle Grazie and the adjacent refectory building, holding Leonardo da Vinci's *The Last Supper*. There's more Leonardo at the Museo Nazionale della Scienza e della Tecnologia, while the basilica of Milan's Christian father Sant'Ambrogio is a couple of blocks away.

Piazza del Duomo

The hub of the city is **Piazza del Duomo**, a large, mostly pedestrianized square that's rarely quiet at any time of day, lorded over by the exaggerated spires of the **Duomo**, Milan's cathedral. Milanese hurry out of the metro station deftly avoiding the buskers and ice-cream vendors; harassed tour guides gather together their flocks; loafers meet for a chat; and elegant women stiletto-click across the square.

The piazza was given its present form in 1860 when medieval buildings were demolished to allow grander, unobstructed views of the cathedral. Mussolini added the bombastic Palazzo dell'Arengario building to the cathedral's left which now houses the city's collection of twentieth-century art in the **Museo del Novecento**.

The Duomo

Piazza del Duomo • Daily 7am–6.30pm; May–Sept Fri & Sat until 9.30pm • ⓦ duomomilano.it • **Battistero San Giovanni alle Fonti** Tues–Sun 10am–6pm • €6; ticket grants entry to Museum • **Scurolo di San Carlo** Daily 7am–6.30pm • Free **The roof** Daily 9am–6.30pm; last ticket 6pm • €7 to walk, €12 for the lift • **Museum** Tues–Sun 10am–6pm • €6; ticket grants entry to Battistero • Combined ticket for entry to Roof, Museum and Battistero €15/€11 if ascending roof on foot • Tickets can be purchased online at ⓦ ticketone.it • ⓜ Duomo

The **Duomo** is the world's largest Gothic cathedral and the third-largest Roman Catholic church in the world – after St Peter's in Rome and Seville's cathedral. It was begun in 1386 under the Viscontis, but not completed until nearly five centuries later, when the finishing touches to the facade were finally added in 1813. Many of the masters of their day worked on its construction: Milanese architects and craftsmen such as the Solari clan, Giovanni Antonio Amadeo and Pellegrino Tibaldi, as well as outsiders like Filarete and Martino Bassi. Understandably, it is characterized by a hotchpotch of styles that range from Gothic to Classical. From the **outside** at least, it's an incredible building, notable as much for its strange confection of Baroque and

Gothic decoration, including 3500-odd statues, as its sheer size. The marble, chosen by the Viscontis in preference to the usual material of brick, was brought on specially built canals from the quarries of Candoglia, near Lake Maggiore, and continues to be used in renovation today. A seven-year-long facelift was completed in 2008, having repaired the damage done by centuries of smoke and pollution and leaving the cathedral resplendent once more.

The interior
The **interior** of the Duomo is striking for its size and atmosphere. The five aisles are separated by 52 towering piers (one for each week of the year), while a green, almost subterranean half-light filters through the stained-glass windows, lending the marble columns a bone-like hue that led the French writer Suarés to compare the interior to "the hollow of a colossal beast".

By the entrance, the narrow brass strip embedded in the pavement with the signs of the zodiac alongside is Europe's largest sundial, laid out in 1786. A beam of light still falls on it through a hole in the ceiling, though changes in the Earth's rotation mean that it's no longer accurate.

The Battistero San Giovanni alle Fonti
To the right of the entrance you'll find the archeological remains of the fourth-century **Battistero San Giovanni alle Fonti**, where the city's patron saint Sant'Ambrogio baptized St Augustine in 387 AD. Augustine had arrived in Milan three years earlier with his illegitimate son, and after sampling various religions, including paganism, was eventually converted to Christianity by Ambrose, then the city's bishop. The remains of the baptistry were discovered during excavations for a bomb shelter in the 1940s, and more was unearthed later during work for the metro system in the 1950s, also revealing the foundations for the fourth-century basilica of Santa Tecla and some first-century Roman baths.

At the far end of the church, suspended high above the chancel, a little red light marks the most important of the Duomo's holy relics – a nail from Christ's cross, which was crafted into the bit for the bridle of Emperor Constantine's horse. The cross is lowered once a year, on September 14, the Feast of the Cross, by a device invented by Leonardo da Vinci.

The Scurolo di San Carlo
Close by, beneath the presbytery, is the **Scurolo di San Carlo**, an octagonal crypt housing the remains of San Carlo Borromeo, the zealous sixteenth-century cardinal who was canonized for his unflinching work among the poor of the city, especially during the Plague of 1630, and whose reforms antagonized the higher echelons of the corrupt Church. He lies here in a glass coffin, clothed, bejewelled, masked and gloved, wearing a gold crown attributed to Cellini.

The Treasury
Adjacent to Borromeo's resting-place, the **treasury** features extravagant silverwork, Byzantine ivory carvings and heavily embroidered vestments. Nearby is the Duomo's most surprising exhibit: British artist Mark Wallinger's haunting video installation **Via Dolorosa**, commissioned by the diocese of Milan in a bold attempt to resurrect the role of the Church as a patron of the arts. A large screen shows the last eighteen minutes of Zeffirelli's *Jesus of Nazareth*, with ninety percent of the image blacked out, leaving just a narrow frame visible round the sides.

St Bartholomew
To the right of the chancel, by the door to the Palazzo Reale, the sixteenth-century **statue of St Bartholomew**, with his flayed skin thrown like a toga over his shoulder, is

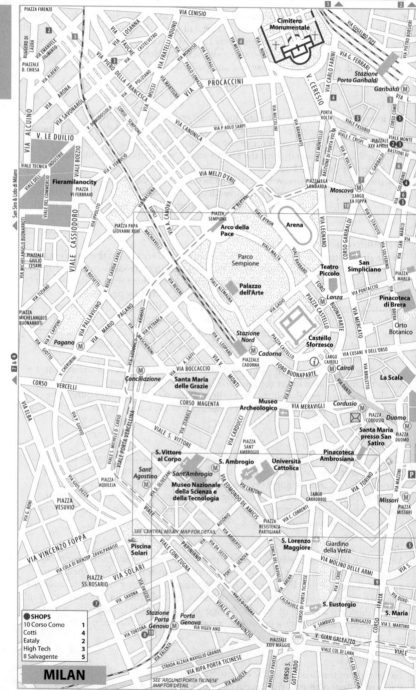

●SHOPS

10 Corso Como	1
Cotti	4
Eataly	2
High Tech	3
Il Salvagente	5

MILAN

1

RESTAURANTS AND CAFÉS

Al Fresco	7
Al Mercato	5
Bello e Buono	9
Da Marcone	11
Da Noi In	8
Don Juan	10
Gelateria Marghera	4
Joe Cipolla	3
Osteria dell'Acquabella	12
Ratanà	2
Sartori	1
Zio Pesce	6

GAY BARS AND CLUBS

Blanco	12
Lelephant	14
Mono	11
Plastic	18
Tropical Island	13

--- Ecopass Border

BARS AND CLUBS

Blue Note	2
Brasserie Bruxelles	8
Byblos	4
Club Haus '80's	1
Dry	6
Hollywood	5
Magazzini Generali	17
Moscatelli	10
Nottingham Forest	15
Pandenus	9
Pravda	16
Radetzky Café	7
Roialto	3

ACCOMMODATION

Antica Locanda Solferino	6
B&B Porta Garibaldi	5
BioCity Hotel	1
Città di Milano	7
Enterprise Hotel	2
Espressohotel	8
Gogol'Ostello	3
Hotel Magna Pars Suites	9
La Favia Four Rooms	4
Petit Palais	10

1

one of the church's more gruesome statues, with veins, muscles and bones sculpted with anatomical accuracy, the draped skin retaining the form of knee, foot, toes and toenails.

The roof

Outside again, from the northwest end of the cathedral you can get to the **Duomo roof**, one of the highlights of the city. Here you can stroll around the rooftop forest of tracery, pinnacles and statues while enjoying fine views of the city and, on clear days, even the Alps. The lacy marble of the central spire is crowned by a gilded statue of the Madonna, or **Madonnina**. The 4.16-metre-high statue has become a symbol of the city – a kind of guardian – inspiring numerous popular songs and ballads. When the Pirelli Tower, near the station, usurped the cathedral's position as the tallest building in town in the late 1950s, the city's clergy insisted on a replica of the Madonnina being placed on top in order to ensure the well-being of Milan.

Museo del Duomo

Located in a separate building by the Palazzo Reale, the **Museo del Duomo** houses a large collection of historical treasures including sculptures, stained glass windows, paintings, tapestries and embroideries from the fifteenth to the twentieth centuries. The Tesoro del Duomo showcases a collection of antique objects, including ivory diptychs dating back to the period from the fifth to the ninth century.

Museo del Novecento

Palazzo dell'Arengario, Via Guglielo Marconi 1 • Mon 2.30–7.30pm, Tues, Wed, Fri & Sun 9.30am–7.30pm, Thurs & Sat 9.30am–10.30pm • €5 • ☏ 02 8844 4061, ⓦ museodelnovecento.org • Ⓜ Duomo

Housing about 350 works of art, the **Museo del Novecento** brings together the city's collection of twentieth-century art. The museum houses masterpieces by Giorgio Morandi, Lucio Fontana and Giorgio di Chirico. Works are displayed in chronological order, beginning with avant-garde movements of the early twentieth century before moving on to Futurism, while also covering important movements of twentieth-century Italian art including Milan's Arte Povera, represented by works by Piero Manzoni and Jannis Kounellis, among others. Linked by a glass bridge, the gallery spaces spill into the adjacent Palazzo Reale and there are great views of Piazza Duomo from the top floor which houses Lucio Fontana's Neon Structure.

Around Piazza del Duomo

Roads fan out from the Piazza del Duomo like bicycle spokes, with the **Galleria Vittorio Emanuele II** linking the piazza to the famous opera house, **La Scala**. A number of other worthwhile sights just a few steps from the Duomo include Bramante's first work in Milan, the ingeniously designed **Santa Maria presso San Satiro**; Da Vinci's Codex and some important paintings at the **Pinacoteca Ambrosiana**; and the unassuming **Piazza Mercanti**, the centre of the medieval city.

Galleria Vittorio Emanuele II

Almost as famous a Milanese sight as the Duomo is the opulent **Galleria Vittorio Emanuele II**, to the north of the cathedral. This nineteenth-century equivalent of a shopping mall was such a success that the model was copied in Rome, Turin and Naples. Intended as a covered walkway between the Piazza del Duomo and Piazza della Scala, the cruciform glass-domed arcade was designed in 1865 by Giuseppe Mengoni, who died when he fell from the roof a few days before the inaugural ceremony, also leaving his remodelling of the Piazza del Duomo incomplete. The circular mosaic beneath the glass cupola is composed of the symbols that made up the cities of the newly unified Italy: Romulus and Remus for Rome, a fleur-de-lys for Florence, the white shield with a red cross for Milan and a bull for Turin – it's considered good luck to spin round three times on the bull's testicles, hence the indentation in the floor.

Nicknamed the "salotto" – or drawing room – of Milan, the Galleria was once the focal point for parading Milanese on their *passeggiata*. These days, visitors rather than locals are more likely to swallow the extortionate prices at the gallery's cafés, which include the historic *Zucca*, with its glorious 1920s tiled interior at one end, and the newer, stylish *Gucci Café* – the label's first foray into catering – at the other. Shops, too, are aimed at visitors to the city, with top designer labels jostling next to pricey souvenir outlets. Somehow, however, the Galleria still manages to retain its original dignity, helped along by quietly elegant boutiques selling handmade leather gloves or carefully turned hats, and the handsome ninety-year-old Prada store in the centre.

Teatro alla Scala

The world-famous **Teatro alla Scala** opera house, popularly known as La Scala, was commissioned by Empress Maria Theresa of Austria from the architect Giuseppe Piermarini and built on the site of the burnt-down church of Santa Maria della Scala. The main branch of Galleria Vittorio Emanuele leads through to Piazza della Scala fronted by the rather plain Neoclassical facade of the theatre. It opened in 1778 and is still to a great extent, the social and cultural centre of Milan's elite. Every year on the opening night – 7 December, the festival of Milan's patron saint, Sant'Ambrogio – when fur coats and dinner jackets are out in force, there are demonstrations from political and social groups, ranging from animal rights' campaigners to local factory workers complaining about redundancies. Tickets (see p.91) are pricey and can be hard to come by, but there are several avenues to try.

La Scala museum

Largo Ghiringhelli 1, Piazza Scala • Daily 9am–12.30pm & 1.30–5.30pm • €6 • ⓦ teatroallascala.org • ⓜ Duomo

Tucked in next door to La Scala is the theatre's small museum, featuring costumes, sets, composers' death masks, plaster casts of conductors' hands and a rugged statue of Puccini in a capacious overcoat. A visit to the auditorium is included in the ticket, providing there is no rehearsal taking place; times when the auditorium is empty are listed daily outside the entrance to the museum. Down in the south of the city, near Porta Genova, the costume and scenery workshop offers guided visits (see p.62).

LA SCALA'S ROLL CALL

Many of the leading names in Italian opera had their major works premiered here, including Bellini, Donizetti and Rossini, but it is **Giuseppe Verdi** who is most closely associated with the opera house and whose fame was consolidated in 1842 with the first performance of *Nabucco* and its perfectly timed patriotic sentiments.

As the heyday of Italian *opera seria* petered out with Puccini's *Turandot*, the early years of the twentieth century saw foreign composers welcomed to La Scala for the first time. The post-World War II period in particular saw a breathtaking roll call of top composers and performers: Schoenberg, Lucio Berio, Rudolf Nureyev and Maria Callas all had close relationships with the theatre. Perhaps the most influential conductor of all time, **Toscanini**, devoted more than fifty years to the theatre and led the orchestra when the opera house reopened in 1946 after being bombed out. These days La Scala is about to embark on a new season of transformation. In 2015 Riccardo Chailly replaced Daniel Barenboim as musical director, and has pledged to put the Italian repertoire centre-stage once again under the baton of today's great conductors.

1

Ansaldo workshops

Via Bergognone 34 • Tues & Thurs guided tours 3pm • €5; booking essential • ☎ 02 4335 3521 • Ⓜ Pta Genova

The former Ansaldo steel plant now houses La Scala's scenery and costume department, which can be visited by reserving in advance. The guided tours take visitors to a huge facility with three pavilions, where handmade works are carried out for productions. This is where artists design costumes, wigs, set designs, costume design and carpentry works – to name a few. The workshops are home to 60,000 stage costumes, and more than 150 workers including set designers, dressmakers and blacksmiths are based here.

Gallerie d'Italia

Via Manzoni 10 • Tues–Sun 9.30am–7.30pm, Thurs until 10.30pm • €8 • Ⓦ gallerieditalia.com • Ⓜ Montenapoleone

Housed in a splendid eighteenth-century Neoclassical *palazzo* that has maintained its original decoration unchanged, the wonderful **Gallerie d'Italia** is worth visiting for the building alone. Formally a bank – note the cashier desks within – the gallery now houses an exceptional collection of Italian art that once belonged to great collections such as those of the Emperor of Austria and the Kings of Italy. The two hundred works on display span just over a century of Italian art from 1798 to 1911, from Antonio Canova's bas-reliefs to masterpieces by Futurist Umberto Boccioni. The emphasis is on nineteenth-century Lombard paintings that aimed to confirm Milan's importance as the country's centre for artistic production at the time.

Santa Maria presso San Satiro

Via Torino 17/19 • Daily 8–11am & 3.30–6.30pm; Oct–March until 6pm • Ⓜ Duomo

South of Piazza del Duomo, tucked away off the busy shopping street of Via Torino, is the charming church of **Santa Maria presso San Satiro**, a study in ingenuity by Milan's foremost Renaissance architect, Bramante, in 1478. It was built up against (*presso*) the ninth-century chapel of San Satiro to celebrate a miracle when the Virgin painted on the outside wall of the chapel was knifed and supposedly started bleeding. The site was originally to have been larger, but there were problems acquiring the land of present-day Via Falcone behind. Undeterred, Bramante continued with a Greek-cross plan and solved the space problem by falsifying the perspective with the wonderful trompe l'oeil apse on the back wall. The fresco in the lunette above the altar records the story of the vandalizing of the Madonna. The octagonal chapel of San Satiro stands to the left of the altar and includes traces of Byzantine frescoes in the niches round the sides. Bramante's plans for the facade were never realized and the current one dates from the nineteenth century.

Biblioteca Pinacoteca Ambrosiana

Piazza Pio XI 2 • Tues–Sun 10am–6pm • €15 • ☎ 02 806 921, Ⓦ ambrosiana.it • Ⓜ Duomo or Cordusio

The **Biblioteca Pinacoteca Ambrosiana** was founded by another member of the Borromeo family, Cardinal Federico Borromeo, in the early seventeenth century. In the face of Protestant reforms, the Cardinal was concerned to defend Catholic traditions not only through doctrine and liturgy, but also by educating the faithful about their Catholic origins. To this end he set about collecting paintings and ancient manuscripts, assembling one of the largest libraries in Europe. You can visit the original reading room and other rooms but the main draw, however, is the largest bound collection of Leonardo da Vinci's drawings and writings, known as the **Codice Atlantico Leonardo**.

The extensive **art collection** may include many mediocre works of the Lombard school but there are some real gems, such as a rare painting by Leonardo da Vinci,

1

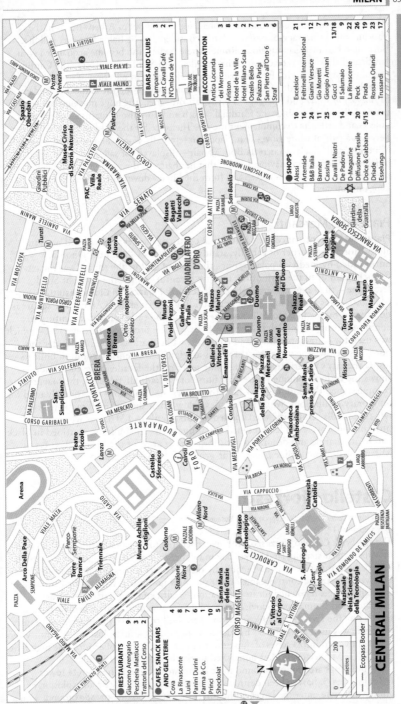

CENTRAL MILAN

N

0   200
metres

—— Ecopass Border

RESTAURANTS
Giacomo Arengario 9
Pescheria Mattiucci 3
Trattoria del Corso 2

CAFES, SNACK BARS AND GELATERIE
Cova 4
La Rinascente 8
Luini 7
Panini Durini 6
Parma & Co. 1
Princi 10
Shockolat 5

BARS AND CLUBS
Camparino 3
Just Cavalli Café 2
N'Ombra de Vin 1

ACCOMMODATION
Antica Locanda
dei Mercanti 3
Ariston 8
Hotel de la Ville 4
Hotel Milano Scala 2
Ostello Bello 7
Palazzo Parigi 1
San Pietro all'Orto 6 5
Straf 6

SHOPS
Alessi 10
Artemide 16
B&B Italia 24
Banner 11
Cassina 25
Cavalli i Nastri 8
De Padova 14
Diffusione Tessile 20
Dolce & Gabbana 5/15
Driade 6
Esselunga 2

Excelsior 21
Feltrinelli International 1
Gianni Versace 12
Gio Moretti 7
Giorgio Armani 3
Gucci 13/18
Il Salumaio 9
La Rinascente 22
Peck 26
Prada 19
Rossana Orlandi 23
Trussardi 17

Portrait of a Musician, a cartoon by Raphael for the School of Athens fresco in the Vatican, and a Caravaggio, *Basket of Fruit*, considered to be Italy's first-ever still life. Borromeo had met Caravaggio in Rome, where he had also become acquainted with Jan Brueghel, who was teaching at the Accademia di San Luca in 1593. The Cardinal was obviously taken with Flemish painting, building up a collection of works by Brueghel the Elder and Paul Brill, the highlights of which are the fantastical landscapes of *Allegory of Water* and *Allegory of Fire* by Jan Brueghel. The huge **museum** has been continually added to since the Cardinal's death and now also contains a collection of objects and artefacts to complement the art. The prize for the quirkiest exhibit is shared between a pair of white gloves that Napoleon reputedly wore when he met his Waterloo, and a lock of Lucrezia Borgia's hair – displayed for safe-keeping in a glass phial ever since Byron (having decided that her hair was the most beautiful he had ever seen) extracted a strand as a keepsake from the library downstairs, where it used to be kept unprotected.

Piazza dei Mercanti

Piazza dei Mercanti, once the commercial centre of medieval Milan and now an almost forgotten corner of the city, stands northwest of Piazza del Duomo. Surrounded by medieval palaces, once the seats of guilds, the square was the city's financial hub until the turn of the twentieth century, when the Borsa or Stock Exchange – then housed in the sixteenth-century **Palazzo dei Giureconsulti** on Via Mercanti – was moved north to a new building in Piazza degli Affari. The square is dominated by the **Palazzo della Ragione**, built in the early thirteenth century to a common European model: on the first floor was the **Broletto** – or town hall – which was used for council meetings and tribunals, while markets were held under the porticoes below. The uppermost storey is an eighteenth-century addition built to house the city's notary archive. The stone relief on the facade above the arcade shows the forlorn-looking figure on a horse of Oldrado di Tressano, the mayor who commissioned the building in 1228. These days the Broletto is occasionally used for temporary exhibitions, while the arcades below often shelter small markets or fair-trade stalls. Opposite, the **Loggia degli Orsi**, built in 1316, was where council proclamations were made and sentences announced. The building is striped in black and white marble and decorated with the coats of arms of the various districts of Milan – just about visible beneath the grime left by Milanese smog.

Castello Sforzesco

Piazza Castello • Daily 7am–7pm, closes 6pm in winter • **Museums** Tues–Sun 9am–5.30pm • Combined ticket €3, free after 2pm on Fri • Ⓜ milanocastello.it • Ⓜ Cairoli

The red-brick **Castello Sforzesco**, with its crenellated towers and fortified walls, is one of Milan's most striking landmarks. Begun by the Viscontis in 1368, it was destroyed by rebellious mobs in 1447 and rebuilt by the Viscontis' successors, the Sforzas. Under Lodovico Sforza the court became one of the most powerful, luxurious and cultured of the Renaissance, renowned for its ostentatious wealth and court artists, such as Leonardo and Bramante. Lodovico's days of glory came to an end when Milan was invaded by the French in 1499, and from then until the end of the nineteenth century the castle was used as a barracks by successive occupying armies. Just over a century ago it was converted into a series of museums to house municipal collections, the highlight of which is Michelangelo's last unfinished work, the *Rondanini Pietà*.

The buildings are grouped around three courtyards: through the **Filarete Tower** (rebuilt in 1905, having been destroyed in the sixteenth century by an explosion of gunpowder) you enter the larger of the three, the dusty-looking **parade ground**, with a good bookshop to your left. It is not until you're through the gateway opposite that you begin to get the sense of a Renaissance castle: this is the **Corte Ducale**, which formed the centre of the residential quarters and is now the home of the castle's museums. The **Rocchetta**, to your left, was the most secure part of the fortress and is used for temporary exhibitions. The gateway ahead leads to the Parco Sempione, once the castle's garden and hunting grounds and now the city's largest park.

Museo d'Arte Antica

The itinerary of the castle museums begins through the **Museo d'Arte Antica** (Museum of Ancient Art), just next to the ticket office in the Corte Ducale. A succession of rooms showcase an extensive collection of artefacts, including mosaics, bas-reliefs and column fragments, saved from the city's churches and archeological excavations.

More interesting than these, though, are the castle rooms themselves, especially the **Sala delle Asse**, designed by Leonardo da Vinci; his black-and-white preparatory sketches were discovered in the 1950s during the elegant reorganization of the museums by the architecture studio BBPR (see p.72) and can be seen on the walls.

After some rather dull armoury you reach the museum's star exhibit: Michelangelo's **Rondanini Pietà**, which the artist worked on for the last nine years of his life. It's an unfinished but oddly powerful work; much of the marble is unpolished and a third arm, indicating a change of position for Christ's body, hangs limply from a block of stone to his right.

Museum of Decorative Arts

Upstairs, the **Museo delle Arti Decorative** (Museum of Decorative Arts) holds exhibits of furniture and decorative arts through the ages, including fascinating early works by the great Milanese designer, Gio Ponti, which show his evolution from the elegant lines of the Domus Nova dining suite in the 1920s to the modern design classic of the Superleggera chair.

Castle Art Gallery

Beginning in the **Torre Falconiere** (the falconry tower) next door, is the castle's art collection containing numerous paintings by Lombard artists, such as Foppa and Bramantino, as well as Venetian works, including some Canalettos. The best are all grouped together in Room XIII and include Antonello da Messina's *Saint Benedict*, originally part of a five-piece polyptych, of which the central painting, a *Madonna and Child*, and the left-hand panel, *Saint John the Baptist*, are in the Uffizi Gallery in Florence. The Duke of Milan, Galeazza Maria Sforza, had tried to engage Antonello as his court portrait painter, but he preferred to stay and complete his masterpiece in the church of San Cassiano in Venice. In his *Saint Benedict* the artist shows his talent as a portraitist, bestowing this formal, stylized figure with a truly human face. Nearby are Giovanni Bellini's touching *Madonna and Child* and Mantegna's decorative *Madonna in Glory and Saints*, both minor works by the artists on subjects they returned to on several occasions.

The Egyptian and prehistoric collections

Across the courtyard, in the castle cellars are two small, rather eclectic collections. The **Egyptian collection** has impressive displays of mummies, sarcophagi and papyrus fragments from *The Book of the Dead*, while the deftly lit **prehistoric collection** consists of an assortment of finds from the Iron Age burial grounds of the Golasecca civilization, south of Lake Maggiore.

1

Parco Sempione

Park Dawn to dusk • **Acquario Civico** Tues–Sun 9am–1pm & 2–5.30pm • Free • Ⓦ acquariocivicomilano.eu • Ⓜ Lanza

The **Parco Sempione**, the city centre's largest area of greenery, was laid out in the castle's old hunting grounds and orchards. It can make a refreshing break from the city's traffic-choked roads, with a playground for younger kids, grass to sprawl or kick a football on and a café or two. The park does have its sleazy side so you might feel more comfortable visiting when the locals do – at the weekend or early summer evenings.

The northern end of the park is topped by what was intended by Napoleon and his urban planners to be a triumphal arch to mark the road from Milan to Paris. It was finally finished by the Austrians thirty years later in 1838, and renamed the **Arco della Pace**, the Arch of Peace, once the chariot had been turned round to face Milan rather than Paris. A little round to the east is another monument to Napoleon's imperial aspirations in the **Arena Civica**, a Colosseum-inspired area where mock chariot races and naval battles were held. These days it's used for sports events and the odd summer pop concert. Next door, the recently refurbished **Aquario Civico** is a pretty Liberty building with a small collection of tanks that will keep children entertained for a spell.

Triennale

Viale Alemagna 6 • Tues–Sun 10.30am–8.30pm, Thurs until 11pm • €8 • Ⓦ triennale.it • Ⓜ Cadorna or Cairoli

The Palazzo dell'Arte or **Triennale**, on the western reaches of the park, make a refreshing diversion from the greenery. Designed by Giovanni Muzio in 1931, the building played a pivotal role in the development of Milan's importance in the world of design, providing a permanent home to the tri-annual design exhibition held here since the 1930s. The majestic lines of the building and its light airy interior are reason enough for a visit, but the *palazzo* also holds the **Triennale Design Museum** and other good-quality temporary exhibitions of design, architecture and contemporary art. There's a great café-bar, *DesignCafé*, which overflows downstairs into the park in the summer.

Studio Museo Achille Castiglioni

Piazza Castello 27 • Tues, Wed, Fri & Sat guided tours 10am, 11am & noon, Thurs 6.30pm, 7.30pm & 8.30pm • €10 • ☏ 02 805 3606, Ⓦ fondazioneachillecastiglioni.it • Ⓜ Cadorna or Cairoli

The **Studio Museo Achille Castiglioni** is stuffed with found objects, plans and sketches as well as prototypes of the works of one of Milan's best-known industrial designers. The guided tours (1hr) are sometimes given by Castiglioni's wife or daughter.

Torre Branca

Viale Camoes 2 • Mid-May to mid-Sept Tues, Thurs & Fri 3–7pm & 8.30pm–midnight, Wed 10.30am–12.30pm, 3–7pm & 8.30pm–midnight, Sat 10.30am–2pm, 2.30–7.30pm & 8.30pm–midnight; mid-Sept to mid-May Wed 10.30am–12.30pm & 4–6.30pm, Sat 10.30am–1pm, 3–6.30pm & 8.30pm–midnight, Sun 10.30am–2pm & 2.30–7pm • €5, free Wed for over-65s • ☏ 02 331 4120 • Ⓜ Cadorna or Cairoli

The **Torre Branca** was designed by Gio Ponti on the occasion of the fifth Triennale in 1933. A lift takes you up the outside to the top of the tower, 100m high and from where, on a clear day, there are vertiginous views across Milan to the Alps to the north and the Apennines to the south. The base of the tower is the venue for one of Milan's signature bars, *Just Cavalli Café* (see p.91), which struts into full gear on summer evenings.

Brera

1

To the north of the centre, the medieval streets of **Brera** are full of boutiques, bars and restaurants, popular with an image-conscious, stylish crowd.

Via Brera runs through the centre of the city's over-hyped arty quarter. This is home to Milan's most famous art gallery, the **Pinacoteca di Brera**, part of a cultural complex founded in the eighteenth century, under the patronage of Empress Maria Theresa of Austria, and including a Fine Arts Academy, an observatory and a botanical garden. There was a time when this area was a hotbed of artistic talent: in the 1960s, *Bar Jamaica*, on Via Brera, was the haunt of Piero Manzoni and other members of the Milan branch of the Arte Povera movement, but these days you're more likely to meet the expat Americans or wealthy Milanese teenagers who frequent the bars and pavement cafés in this part of town. The students from the Accademia di Belle Arti help to provide a touch of colour to the neighbourhood in the daytime, but Bohemianism is not a style that the Milanese take to with ease. In the evening the pedestrian streets are lined with fortune-tellers, portrait painters and more fake Gucci and D&G goods than you could shake a handbag at.

Pinacoteca di Brera

Via Brera 28 • Tues–Sun 8.30am–7.15pm • €6 • ☎ 02 722 631, ⓦ brera.beniculturali.it • Ⓜ Montenapoleone or Lanza

The Brera district gives its name to Milan's prestigious art gallery, the **Pinacoteca di Brera**, the most important collection of North Italian art anywhere. Originally consisting of plaster casts and drawings put together as a study aid for students from the Fine Arts academy, the collection was added to by works looted from the churches and aristocratic collections of French-occupied Italy when Napoleon decided to make it a public museum. Opened in 1809, the collection has gradually grown over the years, to the extent that plans are now being discussed to extend the gallery to the nearby Palazzo Citterio.

It's a fine gallery – well organized, in chronological order, with good explanatory notes – but it's also large, and your visit will probably be more enjoyable if you're selective. There's a good audioguide available (€5), although it does rather gallop through the highlights.

Room VI

Exiting the three rooms of early medieval works brings you face to face with the stunningly powerful *The Dead Christ*, a painting by Andrea Mantegna, the court artist in fifteenth-century Mantua responsible for the Camera degli Sposi (see p.346). It's an ingenious composition – Christ, lying on a wooden slab being prepared for burial, viewed from the wrinkled and pierced soles of his feet upwards. We are drawn into the scene not just by the foreshortening technique but by Christ's serene expression and the realism in the colouring and details of his wounds. One of Mantegna's sons had died around the time he was working on this painting and it seems that the desolation in the women's faces and the powerful sense of bereavement emanating from the work were autobiographical. In the same room, the *Pietà* by Mantegna's brother-in-law, Giovanni Gentile, is another beautifully balanced work of grief and pain that has been deemed "one of the most moving paintings in the history of art".

Room VIII

Next door in Room VIII, the impressive *St Mark Preaching in St Euphemia Square* introduces an exotic note, the square bustling with turbaned men, veiled women, camels and even a giraffe. Gentile Bellini, who had lived and worked in Constantinople for several years, died before the painting was complete, so it was finished off by his brother Giovanni for the Scuola Grande di San Marco in Venice.

1

Room IX

In room IX visitors will find Paolo Veronese's depiction of *Supper in the House of Simon*; it got him into trouble with the Inquisition, who considered the introduction of frolicking animals and unruly kids unsuitable subject matter for a religious painting. Tintoretto's *Pietà* was more starkly in tune with requirements of the time, a scene of intense concentration and grief over Christ's body, painted in the 1560s. Nearby in the same room is another Tintoretto, painted around the same time and one of the highlights of Venetian Renaissance painting: *The Finding of the Body of Saint Mark in Alexandria* shows the moment when the frantic search for the saint's body is interrupted by the appearance of Saint Mark himself, on the left of the picture, to identify his own corpse. The dramatic use of perspective – with the tombs disappearing into the background – coupled with the mystical use of light and shadow create a truly operatic ensemble.

Room XXIV

Works by Lombard masters showing the transition from medieval to Renaissance art take you through to a number of rooms featuring artists from Le Marche and Emilia Romagna. You might want to skip through these, saving yourself for Room XXIV, the pride of the Brera collection, containing three paintings ranked among the highest expression of Renaissance culture in art. Piero della Francesca's haunting *Madonna and Child with Angels, SS and Federigo da Montefeltro* is the most arresting, with its stylized composition and geometric harmony. Kneeling on the right is the commissioner of the painting, the powerful Duke of Urbino in a full suit of armour reflecting the light from an open window just out of the picture. The painting is full of symbolism, such as the ostrich egg suspended above the Virgin, an image of fertility and also the Montefeltro family emblem. On the wall opposite, *Christ at the Column* is the only known painting by the architect Bramante, painted for the Chiaravalle monastery to the south of the city. The resemblance between the architectural detail of the painting and the very similar motifs used by the architect in Santa Maria presso San Satiro (see p.62) is striking. Take a look, too, at Raphael's altarpiece, the *Marriage of the Virgin*, whose lucid, languid Renaissance mood stands in sharp contrast to the grim realism of Caravaggio's deeply human *Supper at Emmaus* (Room XXIX), set in a dark tavern.

The rest of the gallery

Less well known but equally naturalistic are the paintings of Lombardy's brilliant eighteenth-century realist, Ceruti – known as *Il Pitocchetto* (The Little Beggar) for his unfashionable sympathy with the poor, who stare out with reproachful dignity from his canvases (Room XXXVI). As his main champion, Roberto Longhi, said, his figures are "dangerously larger than life", not easily transformed into "gay drawing room ornaments", a description that could easily apply to the Canalettos and Crespis on the surrounding walls. Francesco Hayez's Romantic-era *The Kiss* (Room XXXVII) is one of the most reproduced of the gallery's paintings, but the artist's fine portrait of the writer Alessandro Manzoni, in the same room, is far less saccharine. The collection ends with the unfinished *Fuimaria* (Room XXXVII) by Giuseppe Pelizza da Volpedo, a composition showing the emerging people-power of the time and the artist's socialist ideals – themes that he developed for *The Fourth Estate* in the Museo del Novecento (see p.60), adopted as an emblem of the power of the populace.

There is also a small collection of modern work from the Jesi donation on display in Room X, which is particularly strong on the Futurists but includes paintings by Morandi, Modigliani, De Chirico and Carrà, as well as abstract sculpture by Marino Marini and Medardo Rosso.

CLOCKWISE FROM TOP THE NAVIGLI AT NIGHT (P.76); *THE KISS*, FRANCESCO HAYEZ (P.68); CERTOSA DI PAVIA (P.99) >

1

Orto Botanico di Brera

Via Brera 28 (entrance on Via Privata Fratelli Gabba) • Mon–Fri 9am–noon & 2–4pm, Sat 10am–4pm • Free • Ⓜ Montenapoleone

Hidden behind the Pinacoteca, the delightful **Giardino Botanico** provides a wonderful bolthole if you want a break from pounding the cobbled pavements. No more than about an acre in size, the gardens were founded in 1774 by the Empress Maria Theresa of Austria to teach botany to the students of the nearby science colleges and are still used today by the college students. One part of the gardens is given over to flower beds and floral experiments, while the other consists of an attractive patch of grass shaded by trees, including a giant *Ginkgo biloba*, apparently the largest in the world and dating back to the opening of the gardens.

Moscova

Stylish bars and traditional trattorias continue north of Brera through the neighbourhood of **Moscova**, renowned as the haunt of journalists – the offices of the *Corriere della Sera* are located here. A good area for shopping and window browsing, the local delicatessens and small boutiques of Corso Garibaldi, Via Solferino and Via San Marco lead up to the bastion of Piazza XXV Aprile which marks the northern extent of the Spanish walls and the beginning of **Corso Como**, a trendy street full of bars, clubs and stylish shops that, in turn, gives onto the train and bus station of Porto Garibaldi.

Via Manzoni

Elegant **Via Manzoni** sets the tone for the neighbourhoods northeast of the Piazza Duomo. Patrician *palazzi* line the Roman thoroughfare north from La Scala to Porta Nuova, one of the medieval entrances to the city. Named after the nineteenth-century author who lived and died in a house just off the street, Via Manzoni also houses the **Museo Poldi Pezzoli**, an eclectic legacy of the nineteenth-century mania for collecting.

Museo Poldi Pezzoli

Via Manzoni 12 • Mon & Wed–Sun 10am–6pm • €9 • Ⓦ museopoldipezzoli.it • Ⓜ Montenapoleone

Many of the aristocratic houses of Via Manzoni have become banks, museums and hotels; one of them, the opulent *Grand Hotel et de Milan*, was where the composer Giuseppe Verdi lived for the last twenty years of his life and died. Another of the *palazzi* worth seeking out is at no. 12, where the **Museo Poldi Pezzoli** houses an extensive collection of artefacts assembled in the nineteenth century by the collector Gian Giacomo Poldi Pezzoli. Much of the house was destroyed by Allied bombs and only Gian Giacomo's study was left unscathed; the reconstruction is somewhat soulless in places, but the early twentieth-century photographs of the original in each room help evoke the atmosphere of the past. There's a lot to take in, with room upon room of timepieces, archeological remains, Venetian glassware and jewellery, but dipping in where you fancy, you can become entranced by individual pieces – exquisite Lombard embroidery, for example, or a seventeenth-century carved ivory chest. The Salone Dorato upstairs contains a number of striking paintings, including a portrait of a portly *San Nicola da Tolentino* by Piero della Francesca, part of an altarpiece on which he worked intermittently for fifteen years. St Nicholas looks across at two works by Botticelli, one a gentle *Madonna del Libro*, the other a mesmerizing *Deposition*, painted towards the end of his life in response to the monk Savonarola's crusade against his earlier, more humanistic canvases. Also in the room is the museum's best-known painting, *Portrait of a Young Woman* by Pollaiuolo, whose anatomical studies are evidenced in the subtle suggestion of bone structure beneath the skin of this ideal Renaissance woman.

The Quadrilatero d'Oro

Bordered by Via Manzoni to the west and Via Montenapoleone, Via Sant'Andrea and Via della Spiga on the other sides, the so-called **Quadrilatero d'Oro** (Golden Quadrangle) is home to the shops of all the big international and Italian fashion names (see p.92), along with design studios and contemporary art galleries. This is Milan in its element and the area is well worth a wander if only to see the city's better-heeled residents in their favourite habitat.

For a break from the latest trends, head for the **Museo Bagatti Valsecchi** for a glimpse of Renaissance living through nineteenth-century eyes.

Museo Bagatti Valsecchi

Via Santo Spirito 10 • Tues–Sun 1–5.45pm • €9 • ⓦ museobagattivalsecchi.org • ⓜ Montenapoleone or San Babilia

In a house linking Via Santo Spirito with Via Gesù 5, just off Via Montenapoleone, is the **Museo Bagatti Valsecchi**, an absorbing private museum affording an intriguing insight into the tastes of the Bagatti Valsecchi brothers, Giuseppe and Fausto. Taking the nineteenth-century fashion for collecting to an extreme, they built a Renaissance-style home, inspired by the Palazzo Ducale in Mantua, in which to house their Renaissance collections. Nineteenth-century reproductions were artfully executed to integrate harmoniously with the original Renaissance tapestries, furniture and other works of art that decorated the premises.

The brothers lived in separate apartments sharing the drawing room, dining room and a gallery of weapons and armour. All the rooms are richly decorated with carved fireplaces, painted ceilings and heavy wall-hangings and paintings. The fireplace in the drawing room perfectly illustrates the brothers' eclectic approach to decoration: the main surround is sixteenth-century Venetian, the frescoes in the middle are from Cremona, while the whole ensemble is topped off with the Bagatti Valsecchi coat-of-arms. Modern conveniences were incorporated into the house but not allowed to ruin the harmony, so the shower in the bathroom is disguised in a niche, and the piano, which had not yet been invented in the sixteenth century, is discreetly incorporated within a cabinet. Among the miscellany of paintings, ceramics, armoury, ironwork and musical instruments are touching domestic details like the nursery furniture for Giuseppe's children.

Giardini Pubblici and art galleries

Park Daily 7am until dusk • **Galleria d'Arte Moderna** Tues–Sun 9am–1pm & 2–5.30pm • €5 • ⓦ gam-milano.com • **Padiglione d'Arte Contemporanea** Tues–Sun 9.30am–7.30pm, Thurs closes 10.30pm • €8 • ⓦ pacmilano.it • ⓜ Palestro, Turati or Pta Venezia

The **Giardini Pubblici**, designed by Piermarini shortly after he completed La Scala, stretch from Piazza Cavour over to Porta Venezia. Re-landscaped in the nineteenth century to give it a more rustic look, the park, with its shady avenues and small lake, is ideal for a break from the busy streets. There are playgrounds plus other child-friendly weekend activities, such as creative workshops, interactive games and sporting activities (check the Italian-only website ⓦ gam-milano.com for a calendar of events).

Across the road from the park, housed in Napoleon's former town residence, the Villa Belgiojoso Bonaparte or **Villa Reale**, is the **Galleria d'Arte Moderna** at Via Palestro 16, housing a collection of Italian and European artworks from the eighteenth- to the twentieth-centuries.

In the grounds, the **Padiglione d'Arte Contemporanea** or PAC, is a venue for good, temporary exhibitions of contemporary art. The elegant, luminous spaces of the pavilion were designed by the architect Ignazio Gardella and opened in 1979 only to be destroyed in July 1993 by a Mafia bomb that killed five people; the bomb was actually intended for journalists at the Palazzo dei Giornali in nearby Piazza Cavour. The pavilion was reconstructed, again by Gardella, and reopened in 1996.

Behind the art galleries, the **Giardini della Villa Reale** offer an urban oasis reserved for those with children under 13. With a small area of swings, lawns, shady trees and a little pond with ducks and giant carp, it makes a perfect bolthole, especially if you have under-5s in tow.

Southeast from Piazza Duomo

The area southeast from Piazza Duomo is characterized by a jumble of architectural styles typical of Milan's city centre. Medieval streets give way to 1930s and post-World War II constructions, the most striking example of which is the 1950s **Torre Velasca**, which guards the start of the Roman road from Milan to Rome. The streets are populated by a comfortable mix of students from the Arts faculties of Milan's university, lawyers from the **Palazzo di Giustizia** and medical professionals from the city's university hospital. The area's biggest draw is the medieval hospital, the **Ospedale Maggiore**, which was rebuilt after being destroyed by World War II bombs, as was San Nazaro Maggiore, one of Milan's original Christian basilicas. Nearby, the cemetery chapel of the **Rotonda della Besana** has taken to its secular role with dignity, providing an attractive backdrop for interesting temporary exhibitions.

Torre Velasca

Directly south of the Duomo, just off Corso Porta Romana, Piazza Velasca holds one of the city's most iconic twentieth-century buildings, the **Torre Velasca**. At 105m high, the Brutalist structure towers above the city, inspiring loathing and admiration in equal measure. It was built between 1956 and 1958 by the studio BBPR – the "R" of which was Ernesto Rogers, a close relative of the British architect Richard Rogers, who used to work in the studio in university holidays. The top-heavy structure was an ingenious way of wangling more real estate out of a narrow plot and strict planning rules, but it was also an elegant reference to the medieval towers that characterize the cityscape of so many Italian towns. Just as these domestic fortresses housed businesses, warehouses and shops on the lower floors and homes on the upper floors, so Torre Velasca is a mixed-use block, with offices in the narrower part of the tower and residential accommodation in the overhanging section above.

Basilica di San Nazaro Maggiore

Piazza San Nazaro in Brolo • Mon–Fri 8am–noon & 3.30–7pm, Sat 8.30am–12.30pm & 3.30–7pm, Sun 9am–12.30pm & 4–7pm • Free

Rebuilt several times after being destroyed by fires and World War II bombs, **Basilica San Nazaro Maggiore** is one of the four churches founded in the fourth century by Sant'Ambrogio outside the city walls. Its most notable feature is the octagonal chapel designed by Bramantino for the treacherous *condottiere* Giangiacomo Trivulzio, who led the French attack on Milan to spite his rival

Lodovico Sforza and was rewarded by being made the city's French governor. Not one to be relegated to the sidelines, Giangiacomo had his *cappella* built as a vestibule rather than as the more usual side-chapel, so that everyone had to pass through it on their way into the church. His tomb is contained in a niche of the chapel, along with other family members, and the epitaph, written by Giangiacomo himself, reads: "He who never rested now rests: silence."

Ospedale Maggiore (Ca' Grande)

The **Ospedale Maggiore**, built by Francesco Sforza in the mid-fifteenth century, stands just behind the basilica of San Nazaro Maggiore. Used as a hospital until 1939, today the building houses the offices of the university hospital and several faculties. The Ospedale Maggiore united all Milan's smaller hospitals and charitable institutions on one site, hence the name Ca' Grande, or "Big House". Opened at the same time as the Lazaretto, the plague hospital established outside the walls near the current Porta Venezia, the huge Ospedale was an attempt to control the outbreaks of the deadly disease and improve the city's health services. In a thoroughly modern design by the Florentine architect Filarete, a series of courtyards – eight in all – provided separate wings for men and women.

Over the years, local architects adapted and altered Filarete's original design, creating a mix of styles. The right side of the wide facade shows the original fifteenth-century brickwork with Lombard terracotta decorations, while to the left, the style is Neoclassical. Inside, in the main courtyard, Filarete's Renaissance arcade survives, with the additions of a Baroque loggia and stone busts. All but razed to the ground by Allied bombs in World War II, the courtyards to the right were reconstructed using original plans and masonry, and now make a pleasant spot to rest.

Rotonda della Besana

The Giardino della Guastalla, laid out in 1555, leads through to Milan's main synagogue, and lies behind the Ospedale Maggiore. Four blocks east, past the monolithic Palazzo di Giustizia law courts and the city's main hospital, stands the peaceful **Rotonda della Besana**, the Ospedale Maggiore's cemetery, opened in 1695 and designed by Francesco Raffagno. At the centre, the Greek-cross chapel of San Michele ai Nuovi Sepolcri, built in 1713, was turned into the hospital laundry in the early nineteenth century. Now deconsecrated, the tranquil space is used for temporary exhibitions, while the surrounding grass and cool arcaded porticoes make a perfect spot for a picnic.

Corso Porta Ticinese

Past the chain stores of Via Torino, leading southwest away from the Duomo to the canals, the city takes on a different, slightly more alternative air. The main thoroughfare, **Corso Porta Ticinese**, is a fashionable and popular area lined with small boutiques and bars. The area really comes into its own at *aperitivo* time, especially during summer when people spill onto the pedestrian streets from the numerous bars and cafés. The neighbourhood also boasts two of Milan's most important churches – and most rewarding sights – **San Lorenzo Maggiore** and **Sant'Eustorgio**.

The Ticinese district has always played an important role in the history of the city. It was here, just outside the walls, that in Roman times a giant amphitheatre was built, as well as some of the first paleo-Christian places of worship. In the Middle Ages this was one of the main gateways into the city from the important town of Pavia and the monastic complexes scattered across the Po plain to the south. Later, when the canals

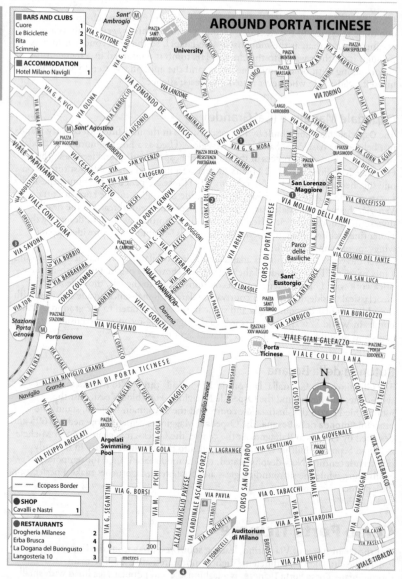

AROUND PORTA TICINESE

were at the height of their trading success, goods were brought through the Porta Ticinese to the city centre.

San Lorenzo Maggiore

Corso di Porto Ticinese 35 • **Church** Mon–Sat 7.30am–6.45pm, Sun 9am–7pm • Free • **Cappella di San Aquilino** Daily 9am–6.30pm • €2 • W sanlorenzomaggiore.com • Tram 3

Towards the northern end of Corso Ticinese stands **San Lorenzo Maggiore**, considered by Leonardo da Vinci to be the most beautiful church in Milan. One of the four churches founded by Sant'Ambrogio in the city in the fourth century, it was the largest centrally planned church in the western Roman Empire, built with masonry salvaged from various Roman buildings, most notably the amphitheatre. The sixteen Corinthian columns outside – the **Colonne di San Lorenzo** – were probably scavenged from a bath or temple complex and placed here as a portico to the church in the fourth century. The current building is a sixteenth-century renovation of an eleventh-century church, which in turn replaced the original after several fires. Inside, the octagonal plan – a sixteenth-century remodelling of the original square – gives the church an intimate feel, while the light streaming down from the four large windows in the dome makes a refreshing change from the penumbra of the city's sombre medieval places of worship. Note the two inverted columns flanking the main altar; although it's not entirely clear why the columns are upside down, it is believed placing them in such a way was representative of the power Christianity had over paganism and earthly authorities.

To the right of the altar, the **Cappella di San Aquilino** was probably built as an imperial mausoleum in the fourth century. The lunettes in the Roman octagonal room hold beautiful fourth-century mosaics, which would originally have covered all the walls, while beneath the relics of San Aquilino, steps lead down to what is left of the original foundations, a jigsaw of fragments of Roman architecture.

Piazza della Vetra

Shady **Piazza della Vetra,** which lies behind San Lorenzo, was a site for public executions until the mid-nineteenth century and the park here makes a good spot for a breather. It also allows fabulous views of the back of San Lorenzo, showing the mishmash of building styles that make up the basilica.

Sant'Eustorgio

Piazza Sant'Eustorgio 1 • Portinari chapel Tues–Sun 10am–6pm • €6, combined ticket with Cappella di San Aquilino, Cappella Portinari & Museo Diocesano €12 • ⓦ santeustorgio.it • Trams 3 & 9

Heading south through the Parco della Vetra, or straight down Corso Ticinese, you come to **Sant'Eustorgio**, a fourth-century church, built to house the bones of the Magi which are said to have been brought here by Sant'Ambrogio. It was rebuilt in the eleventh century, and in the twelfth century was virtually destroyed by Barbarossa, who seized the Magi's bones and deposited them in Cologne cathedral. Some were returned in 1903 and are kept in a Roman sarcophagus in the right transept. Every year at Epiphany (6 Jan), the bones are taken to the Duomo and paraded back to the church by men in slightly pantomime-like satin costumes of the Three Kings.

The simple Romanesque nave and the medieval and Renaissance private chapels jostling for position on the right of the church are only half the story. The primary reason for visiting Sant'Eustorgio is to see the **Portinari chapel**, accessed round to the left of the main entrance. En route, you can dip down under the nave to see remnants from the Roman burial ground that the church was built on, including several surprisingly well-preserved funeral monuments, tombs and the odd bone or two. The dignified sacristy offers an impressive collection of reliquaries from different periods: note San Carlo Borromeo's shirt rolled up in one and the many B-movie-like paintings of St Peter the Martyr's untimely end.

The Portinari chapel

The beautiful **Portinari chapel** consciously recalls Brunelleschi's San Lorenzo in Florence, with two domed rooms, the smaller one housing the altar. It has been credited with being Milan's first real Renaissance building because of its simple

1

geometric design. The mixture of Lombard terracotta sculpture and Florentine monochromatic simplicity makes for an enchanting fusion of styles. It was commissioned from the Florentine architect Michelozzi in the 1460s by one Pigello Portinari, an agent of the Medici bank, to house the remains of St Peter the Martyr. Peter, one of Catholicism's less attractive saints, was excommunicated for allegedly entertaining women in his cell, then cleared of the charge and given a job as an Inquisitor. His death was particularly nasty – he was axed in the head by a member of the Cathar sect that he was persecuting near Lake Como – but the martyrdom led to almost immediate canonization and the dubious honour of being deemed Patron Saint of Inquisitors. St Peter the Martyr's wildly elaborate tomb is crowded with reliefs showing scenes of his various miracles and supported by statues of the eight *Virtues*. The wonderful frescoes on the walls and ceiling are attributed to Foppa; the gold-cloaked figure half hiding from the scene in the right-hand lunette of the right wall is said to be a self-portrait. The rainbow-coloured scales on the dome above the gaily dancing angels lead up to the Portinari coat-of-arms in the lantern directly above the spot where the banker is buried.

The Navigli

The southern end of Corso di Porta Ticinese is guarded by the nineteenth-century **Arco di Porta Ticinese**, an Ionic-style gateway, on the site of a medieval entrance to the city, built to celebrate Napoleon's victory at Marengo. It marks the beginning of the canal – or **Navigli** – neighbourhood, once a bustling industrial area and these days a focus for the nightlife of the city. Alongside, the forlorn-looking **Darsena**, or Basin, was the busiest part of the city's canal system (see opposite), the main dock area for goods entering and leaving the city. This unloved body of stagnant water has been promised a new lease of life by an international architectural competition, which will remodel the basin and link it with newly created parks and bridges. This will hopefully spur the way for investment in the rest of the canal area, which although full of lively restaurants, bars and clubs in the evenings, promises much more than it currently offers to daytime visitors.

Naviglio Grande and Naviglio Pavese

South from the Darsena, the **Naviglio Grande** and the **Naviglio Pavese**, respectively the first and last of the city's canals to be completed, lead into the plains of Lombardy. Although the bohemian atmosphere of the area is somewhat over-hyped, it certainly shows a different side to Milan; this was Milan with its sleeves rolled up, the working city at its grittiest. Some of the warehouses and traditional

---

MARKETS, FESTIVALS AND EVENTS ON THE NAVIGLI

Throughout the year the Navigli hosts markets, festivals and events that keep the waterways busy. The useful website Ⓦ naviglilive.it lists further information on events along the canal.

Arte sul Naviglio Grande (mid-May 9am–6.30pm). An open-air event where over 200 painters and artists exhibit their artwork; local galleries, workshops and restaurants remain open for the weekend.

Cimento Invernale (Jan). Every January a handful of courageous souls brave the Navigli's ice-cold waters in a 150m race.

Fiera dell'Antiquariato (last Sun of the month excluding July 9am–6pm). Stretching over 2km, this popular antiques market offers a mixture of bric-a-brac and genuine antiques, including furniture, books, prints, watches and porcelain.

Fiori sul Naviglio (April). Along the shores of the Naviglio Grande, this flower festival is a true feast of colours, with a wonderful floral display adorning the towpaths and a selection of artisans' crafts on show.

tenement blocks, or *case ringhere*, have been refurbished and become prime real estate, although you'll still find plenty of unreconstructed corners too. Some craftsmen and artists have moved in and although the overpriced craft and antique

MILAN'S CANALS

Canals play an important part in the history of Milan and hold a special place in the hearts of the Milanese. Comparisons with Amsterdam and Venice seem improbable these days, but less than fifty years ago the city was still a viable port and only one hundred years ago, several of the main arteries – including **Via Senato** and **Via San Marco** – were busy waterways. Rivers and canals still run under much of Milan and there are ghostly reminders in the names of streets and alleyways, such as the Conca del Naviglio (canal basin) in the south, the Tombone di San Marco (St Mark's lock) in Brera and Via Laghetto (the pool or wharf where the Duomo building materials arrived by canal), near the Ospedale Maggiore. There is much talk of uncovering the city's old canals as a nostalgic nod to the time when Milan was a great military and manufacturing power, although in reality it is little more than political posturing.

HISTORY

The first section of the **canal system** was started in the **eleventh century** and was gradually developed and added to over the centuries to enable Milan to become one of the most important ports in the country, despite its inland position. The process of covering over the canals began in the 1930s to make way for the city's trams and trolley buses. By the mid-1970s, only the **Naviglio Grande** and the **Naviglio Pavese**, to the south of the city, were left in the centre; the last working boat plied the waters in 1977.

Milan is surrounded by rivers and it was only logical for the city's powers to want to harness these natural resources for both **trade** and **military purposes**. In the twelfth century, the first canals connected irrigation channels and the various defensive moats of the city. Later, in 1386, the Naviglio Grande was opened, linking the city to the River Ticino and thus Lake Maggiore and Switzerland. It was Gian Galeazzo Visconti, however, who was really responsible for the development of the system. Looking for a way to transport the building materials for the Duomo, especially marble from Lake Maggiore, he invited proposals for solving the different logistical problems involved: Leonardo da Vinci is said to have had a hand in the invention of a system of locks. During the building of the cathedral, boats carrying construction materials – marked with "**AUF**" for "*ad usum fabricae*" – had precedence over all other water traffic.

Different rivers and canals were added to the system over the centuries, with the Spanish developing the Darsena to the south in 1603 and Napoleon's regime finally managing to make the Naviglio Pavese navigable all the way to Pavia and down to the Po river, and so to the sea. During the industrial revolution at the end of the nineteenth century, raw materials such as coal, iron and silk were brought into the city, and handmade finished products transported out with an ease that ensured Milan's commercial and economic domination of the region. In the 1950s, desperately needed materials were floated in for reconstructing the badly bombed city and it wasn't until the 1970s that the remaining canals finally fell into disuse.

The canals were not just reserved for business. Ruling families used the extensive network of waterways to visit one another and journey between their summer and winter residences. Prospero and Miranda escaped along the Navigli in **The Tempest**, and they were still being used by visitors on the Grand Tour in the eighteenth century; **Goethe**, for example, describes the discomfort and hazards of journeying by canal.

EXPLORING THE CANALS

The best way to explore the canals these days is to don a pair of walking shoes or rent a **bike** (see p.83), pack some mosquito repellent, and head off down the towpaths into the paddy fields of Lombardy. Alternatively, you could take a relaxing **boat trip**; these run between April and mid-September when the canals are not being dredged or cleaned. For more information ask at the tourist office or check ⓦnaviglilombardi.it and ⓦamicideinavigli.it.

1

shops won't hold your attention for long, a wander round the streets popping into open courtyards will give you a feel of the neighbourhood. One of the few specific sights is the prettified **Vicolo dei Lavandai**, or Washerwomen's Alleyway, near the beginning of the Naviglio Grande, where washerwomen scrubbed smalls in the murky canal waters.

Porta Genova

Five minutes' walk west from the Naviglio Grande is **Porta Genova**, the station for Milan's southern outskirts. It is also the name given to one of Milan's up-and-coming areas, another ex-industrial district that is slowly being regenerated. Across the tracks from the train station, disused warehouses and factories are being reclaimed by photographers, fashion houses and designers. Giorgio Armani has an exhibition space and workshops here, as does Prada.

Santa Maria delle Grazie to Sant'Ambrogio

To the south of the Castello Sforzesco, beyond the busy streets of the financial district, skirted by Corso Magenta, are some of Milan's richest cultural pickings. Nineteenth-century *palazzi* and smart residential blocks have replaced the religious communities that once populated the area and it's their treasures that really bring visitors into this part of town. The church of **Santa Maria delle Grazie** is famous for the mural of *The Last Supper* by Leonardo da Vinci painted on the refectory wall of the adjacent Dominican monastery.

There are more works by da Vinci at the **Museo Nazionale della Scienza e della Tecnologia** where displays bring to life the engineering projects of the fifteenth-century genius. More ancient exhibits are on display at the **Museo Archeologico** and in the courtyard of the beautiful church to Milan's patron saint, **Sant'Ambrogio**.

Santa Maria delle Grazie

Piazza Santa Maria delle Grazie 2 · Ⓜ Cadorna or Conciliazione

The beautiful terracotta-and-brick church of **Santa Maria delle Grazie** was first built in Gothic style by the fifteenth-century architect Guiniforte Solari. It was part of the Dominican monastery that headed the Inquisition for over one hundred years in the late-fifteenth and sixteenth centuries. Ludovico Sforza set about making changes to the complex, conceiving the church as a grand dynastic mausoleum. Included in these improvements was a painting for the wall of the monks' refectory, which has become one of the world's most famous works of art, Leonardo da Vinci's *The Last Supper*.

A dissatisfied Lodovico Sforza, who wanted a funerary chapel for his wife, Beatrice d'Este, had the church partially rebuilt by Bramante, who tore down Solari's chancel and replaced it with a massive dome supported by an airy Renaissance cube. Lodovico

---

EVIL PERSONIFIED

Leonardo spent two years on the mural of *The Last Supper*, wandering the streets of Milan searching for and sketching models. When the monks complained that the **face of Judas** was still unfinished, Leonardo replied that he had been searching for over a year among the city's criminals for a sufficiently evil face, and that if he didn't find one he would use the face of the prior. Whether or not Judas's face is modelled on the prior's is unrecorded, but Leonardo's Judas does seem, as Vasari wrote, "the very embodiment of treachery and inhumanity".

also intended to replace the nave and facade, but was unable to do so before Milan fell to the French, leaving an odd combination of styles – Solari's Gothic vaults, decorated in powdery blues, reds and ochre, illuminated by the light that floods through the windows of Bramante's dome. A side door leads into Bramante's cool and tranquil cloisters, from which there's a good view of the sixteen-sided drum the architect placed around his dome.

The Last Supper

Henry James likened Leonardo's *The Last Supper* – signposted "Cenacolo Vinciano" – to an "illustrious invalid" that people visited with "leave-taking sighs and almost death-bed or tip-toe precautions"; certainly it's hard, when you visit the fragile painting, not to feel that it's the last time you'll see it. A twenty-year restoration process recently re-established the original colours using contemporary descriptions and copies, but that the work survived at all is something of a miracle. Leonardo's decision to use oil paint rather than the more usual faster-drying – and longer-lasting – fresco technique with watercolours led to the painting disintegrating within five years of its completion. A couple of centuries later, Napoleonic troops billeted here used the wall for target practice. And, in 1943, an Allied bomb destroyed the building, amazingly leaving only *The Last Supper*'s wall standing.

The painting

The Last Supper was a conventional theme for refectory walls, but Leonardo's decision to capture the moment when Christ announces that one of his disciples will betray him imbues the work with an unprecedented sense of drama. The composition is divided into four groups with Christ as the calm central focus. The serenity of the landscape behind echoes his peace of mind while it also provides his figure with the luminosity that allowed Leonardo to dispense with the traditional halo with which Christ was usually portrayed. The decision to set the table at the front of the composition draws us into the scene, and the trestle table, simple tablecloth tied to the table at the corners and crockery are said to have been the same as those used by the monks, thus emphasizing that this was just an extension of the refectory itself. The use of perspective adds a depth and realism to the painting unseen in previous versions of the theme, while the architectural angles draw our eyes up to the coats-of-arms of the Sforza family – and patrons – above.

Goethe commented on how very Italian the painting was in that so much is said through the expressions of the characters' hands; the group of Matthew, Thaddaeus and Simon on the far right of the mural could be discussing a football match or the latest government scandal in any bar in Italy today. The only disciple not gesticulating or protesting in some way is the recoiling Judas, who has one hand clenched, while a bread roll has just dropped dramatically out of the other. Christ is calmly reaching out to share his bread with him while his other hand falls open in a gesture of sacrifice.

If you feel you need any confirmation of the emotional tenor or accomplishment of the painting, take a look at the contemporary *Crucifixion* by Montorfano on the wall at the other end of the refectory: not a bad fresco in itself, but destined always to pale into mediocrity beside da Vinci's masterpiece.

INFORMATION AND TOURS   **THE LAST SUPPER**

Visiting one of the world's great paintings and most resonant images doesn't come easy: visits must be booked at least two weeks in advance, more like a month or three in summer and for weekends. If it's fully booked when you ring, try asking about cancellations on the day: people don't always turn up for the early-morning slots so it might be worth chancing your luck and enquiring at the desk. At your allotted hour, once you've passed through a series of air-filtering systems along the rebuilt sides of what was the monastery's largest courtyard, your fifteen-minute slot face-to-face with the masterpiece begins.

Viewing times Tues–Sun 8.15am–7pm (last entry 6.45pm). **Reservations** Mon–Sat 8.30am–6.30pm on ☎ 02 9280 0360 or Ⓦ cenacolovinciano.net.

Admission €6.50, plus €1.50 obligatory booking fee. **Tours** Alternatively, try the city tours (see p.83), where entrance to view the painting can be included.

Museo Archeologico

Corso Magenta 15 • Tues–Sun 9am–5.30pm • €5, free Tues 2–5pm & daily after 4.30pm • ☎ 02 8844 5208 • Ⓜ Cadorna

Remains of Roman buildings can be found across the city centre but the **Museo Archeologico** presents more domestic examples of the heritage. The museum, housed in the ex-Monastero Maggiore (don't miss the beautiful Church of San Maurizio next door, also accessible from the museum) is worth a quick visit if you wish to delve deeper into the city's Roman heritage. The displays of glass phials, kitchen utensils and jewellery from Roman Milan are compelling. The itinerary continues in the inner cloister, home to the remains of a Roman dwelling dating back to the first- to third-century AD, and beautiful frescoes from the thirteenth to fourteenth centuries. From here a walkway leads to a building on Via Nirone, which houses findings from the Early Middle Ages, Etruscan and Greek eras.

Museo Nazionale della Scienza e della Tecnologia

Via S. Vittore 21 • Mid-June to mid-Sept Tues–Fri 9.30am–5pm, Sat & Sun 9.30am–6.30pm; mid-Sept to mid-June Tues–Fri 10am–6pm, Sat & Sun 10am–7pm; • €10, submarine entrance extra €8 • Ⓦ museoscienza.org • Ⓜ Sant'Ambrogio

A couple of blocks south of Santa Maria delle Grazie, the **Museo Nazionale della Scienza e della Tecnologia** is housed in the sixteenth-century Olivetan monastery of San Vittore. This is a wet-weather museum with a huge miscellany of exhibits of varying quality; school-age children, in particular, are likely to enjoy exploring the labyrinth of displays spanning molecular science to early Vespas, taking in astronomy, telecommunications, the history of the car, musical instruments and much more on the way. The collection even includes several hangars housing steam engines, a submarine, aeroplanes, and a full-sized galleon from 1850.

The **Leonardo da Vinci** gallery on the first floor contains sketches and models of many of his inventions, as well as reconstructions of some of his wackier contraptions, including the famous flying machine and an automatic weaving machine. It is a dry, no-nonsense display dating from the 1950s, but it offers an insight into the prodigious mind of this most Renaissance of men.

Weekends see the museum buzzing with children involved in the numerous free organized activities that are on offer – from ceramics courses to making plastic. Most are run in Italian but it's worth enquiring – a day or two in advance – if you're interested.

Basilica di Sant'Ambrogio

Piazza Sant'Ambrogio 15 • Mon–Sat 10am–noon & 2.30–6pm, Sun 3–5pm • Free • Ⓦ basilicasantambrogio.it • Ⓜ Sant'Ambrogio

The **Basilica di Sant'Ambrogio** was founded in the fourth century by Milan's patron saint. The present twelfth-century church, the blueprint for many of Lombardy's

---

SANT'AMBROGIO (SAINT AMBROSE)

Sant'Ambrogio or Saint Ambrose, as he's known in English, is even today an important name in the city: the Milanese refer to themselves as Ambrosiani, have named a chain of banks after him, and celebrate his feast day, **December 7**, with the opening of the Scala season and a big street market around the church. Ambrose's remains still lie in the church's crypt, but there's nothing left of the original church in which his most famous convert, St Augustine, first heard him preach.

Romanesque basilicas, is, however, one of the city's loveliest, reached through a colonnaded quadrangle with column capitals carved with rearing horses, contorted dragons and an assortment of bizarre predators. Inside, to the left of the nave, a freestanding Byzantine pillar is topped with a "magic" bronze serpent, flicked into a loop and symbolizing Aaron's rod – an ancient tradition held that on the Day of Judgement it would crawl back to the Valley of Jesophat. Look, too, at the pulpit, a superb piece of Romanesque carving decorated with reliefs of wild animals and the occasional human, most of whom are intent upon devouring one another. There are older relics further down the nave, notably the ciborium, reliefed with the figures of saints Gervasius and Protasius – martyred Roman soldiers whose clothed bodies flank that of St Ambrose in the crypt. A nineteenth-century autopsy revealed that they had been killed by having their throats cut. Similar investigations into St Ambrose's remains restored the reputation of the anonymous fifth-century artist responsible for the mosaic portrait of the saint in the Cappella di San Vittorio in Ciel d'Oro (to the right of the sacristy). Until then it was assumed that Ambrose owed his crooked face to a slip of the artist's hand, but the examination of his skull revealed an abnormally deep-set tooth, suggesting that his face would indeed have been slightly deformed.

ARRIVAL AND DEPARTURE MILAN

BY PLANE

Milan has two main airports – Malpensa and Linate – with regular connections to domestic as well as major European and international destinations. Airport enquiries (☎02 232 323) is the same for both Linate and Malpensa airports. Bergamo-Orio al Serio (see p.239) is also touted as Milan and is a comfortable 50mins away.

Malpensa (ⓦsea-aeroportimilano.it) 50km northwest of the city near Lake Maggiore, Malpensa is connected by direct buses, operated by Autostradale (ⓦautostradale.com) and Air Pullman (ⓦmalpensashuttle.com), with the Stazione Centrale, Milan's main train station (every 15min 3.45am–12.30am; 1hr; €10), and by a fast train, the Malpensa Express, with Milano Cadorna-Stazione Nord (every 30min 4.28am–11.28pm; 50min; ⓦmalpensaexpress.it; €11) and Milano Centrale (every 30min 9.25am–3.25pm and then hourly until 11.25pm; 43min; €10), also stopping off at Milano Porta Garibaldi. A taxi from Malpensa to the centre (around 40min) costs around €90 when the traffic is not too heavy. You can book a taxi at ⓦtaximilano.it.

Linate (ⓦsea-aeroportimilano.it) Milan's other airport, Linate, is just 7km east of the city centre: airport buses connect it with the Piazza Luigi di Savoia, on the east side of Stazione Centrale (every 30min 5.30am–11pm; 30min; €5). Ordinary ATM urban transport buses (73) also run every ten minutes from 5.35am until 12.35am (30min; €1.50) between Linate and Corso Europa (ⓦSan Babila). Tickets should be bought before you get on the bus from the airport newsagent. A taxi to the centre will cost around €25. There are also daily bus services between Linate and Malpensa (5 daily; 75mins).

Destinations Amsterdam (5 daily; 1hr 45min); Catania (6 daily; 1hr 50min); Dublin (daily; 2hr 25min); London (7 daily; 1hr 55min); Paris (6 daily; 1hr 25min); Rome (7 daily; 1hr 10min).

BY TRAIN

Most international and domestic trains pull in at the monumental Stazione Centrale, northeast of the city centre on Piazza Duca d'Aosta, at the hub of the metro network on lines M2 and M3. Other services, especially those from stations in the Milan region – Bergamo, Pavia, Como and the other western lakes – terminate at smaller stations around the city: Garibaldi, Lambrate, Porta Genova and Milano Nord, all on M2 (the metro stop for Milano Nord is "Cadorna"), although these often also stop at Stazione Centrale. There are separate train enquiries details for Ferrovie dello Stato (☎892 021, ⓦtrenitalia.com) and for TreNord (☎02 7249 4949, ⓦtrenord.it).

MILANO LAMBRATE

Destinations Bergamo (hourly; 45min); Brescia (hourly; 1hr 20min); Certosa di Pavia (9 daily; 20min); Cremona (3 daily; 1hr 25min); Desenzano (2 daily; 1hr); Pavia (every 25min; 25min); Peschiera (2 daily; 1hr 10min); Verona (hourly; 1hr 35min).

MILANO NORD CADORNA

Destinations Como (every 30min; 1hr 5min); Varese (every 30min; 1hr).

MILANO PORTA GARIBALDI

Destinations Arona (8 daily; 1hr); Bergamo (every 40min; 55min); Chiasso (hourly; 1hr 15min); Como (7 daily; 30min); Cremona (3 daily; 1hr 30min); Domodossola (9 daily; 2hr); Lecco (hourly; 1hr); Luino (4 daily; 1hr 40min);

1

Stresa (9 daily; 1hr 30min); Varese (hourly; 1hr); Verbania-Pallanza (9 daily; 1hr 35min).

MILANO STAZIONE CENTRALE

Destinations Arona (5 daily; 1hr); Bergamo (hourly; 50min); Brescia (every 45min; 1hr 15min); Certosa di Pavia (every 2hr; 30min); Chiasso (hourly; 50min); Como (hourly; 40min); Cremona (7 daily; 1hr 40min); Desenzano (every 30min; 1hr 10min); Domodossola (hourly; 1hr 30min); Lecco (every 2hr; 50min); Pavia (every 30min; 25min); Peschiera (hourly; 1hr 17min); Stresa (9 daily; 1hr 10min); Varenna (every 2hr; 1hr 10min); Verbania-Pallanza (9 daily; 1hr 20min); Verona (hourly; 1hr 35min).

BY BUS

International and long-distance buses, and many regional buses, arrive at and depart from Lampugnano bus station on Via Giulio Latta (ⓂLampugnano).

Private buses also run regularly, linking Malpensa to several of the regional towns around the lakes. Tickets are available from the Airport 2000 desk in the airport or on

the buses themselves: Arona, Stresa and Verbania (5 daily; must be reserved by midday the day before travelling, 48hr in advance for weekends and public holidays; ☎0323 552 172, ⓦsafduemila.com; €15). Gallarate train station, linked to Malpensa airport 5km away by regular local bus services, is on the main train line from Milan to Lake Maggiore (including Arona, Stresa and Intra), as well as the Varese branch line.

BY CAR

If you're arriving by car, try to time your arrival to avoid the morning and evening rush hours (approximately 7.30–10am & 4.30–7pm) when Milan's ring road, the infamous Tangenziale, is often gridlocked. Signage is copious, if not always very clear, and the ring road links onto the autostradas for Bergamo, Brescia, Verona and Lake Garda (A4), Varese and Lake Maggiore (A8), Lake Como (A9) and the "Autostrada del Sole" (A1) for Cremona and Mantua. We also provide information about the Ecopass zone, car rental and advice on parking in Milan (see p.23).

GETTING AROUND

Milan's street-plan resembles a spider's web, with roads radiating out from the central Piazza Duomo. The bulk of the city is encircled by two concentric ring roads following the medieval and Spanish walls of the city, while the suburbs and industrial estates spill out towards a third ring, the Tangenziale, which links the main motorways. The city centre is just about compact enough to explore on foot and you'll probably only want to use the easy-to-master **public transport** system when you're flagging or going out of the way. The network of trams, buses and metro is cheap and, on the whole, efficient, although wildcat strikes are frequent on the metro.

BY PUBLIC TRANSPORT

The orange ATM map (*Pianta dei Trasporti Pubblici*) shows the routes and numbers of all buses and trams, as well as the metro system. The fast, if gloomy, metro is good for crossing the city quickly, while the well-organized bus and tram routes are more pleasant for short hops. Most bus and

tram stops display the route and direction of travel, and the front of each metro train shows the station at the end of the line. For all public transport enquiries (☎02 4860 7607, ⓦatm-mi.it) the information offices at the Duomo or Stazione Centrale metro stations are helpful, and have English-speaking staff.

MILAN METRO

Metro The metro is made up of five lines, the red MM1, green MM2, yellow MM3, lilac MM5 and blue *passante ferroviario*; the main intersections are Stazione Centrale, Duomo, Cadorna (Milano Nord) and Loreto (see map, p.82). Buses, trams and the metro run from around 6am to midnight, after which nightbuses take over, following the metro routes until 1am, with some also operating throughout the night.

Tickets Valid for 90 minutes, tickets cost €1.50 and can be used for one metro trip and as many bus and tram rides as you want. Stations have automatic ticket machines, and tickets are also on sale at tobacconists, bars and at the metro station newsagents; most outlets close at 8pm, so it's best to buy a few tickets in advance if you intend to use public transport after this time, or get a carnet of ten for €13.80. You can also buy a one-day (€4.50) or two-day pass (€8.25). Remember to validate your ticket in the orange machines when you enter the metro and board buses and trams, as inspections are common.

BY TAXI

Taxis don't cruise the streets, so don't bother trying to flag one down. Your best bet is to phone one of the following numbers (operators speak English): ☎ 02 6767, ☎ 02 4040 or ☎ 02 8585, say where you are and the operator will check how long before a cab can get to you (usually under 5min) and then give you a code to quote to the driver. Alternatively, there are a number of taxi ranks around town – including in Piazza Duomo, Largo Cairoli, Piazza San Babila and Stazione Centrale. All cabs are metered and prices are reasonable, although in the daytime Milan's traffic-logged streets can quickly start to push fares up.

BY CAR

Driving your own car in the city is best avoided: the streets are congested and parking is nigh on impossible in the evenings and on Saturdays. If you do bring a car, you need to know that the Area C – an initiative to cut pollution and congestion in the city centre – is in force (Mon–Fri 7am–7.30pm, Thurs until 6pm; €5) in the area from Cerchia de Bastione to Cerchia dei Bastioni. The pass must be bought on the day of entry or up to midnight of the day afterwards. Payments can be made at authorized

newsagents and tobacconists, or, in English, over the phone (☎ 02 4868 4001) or online (❽ comune.milano.it/areac).

Parking For parking you're probably best off heading for one of the numerous central car parks, costing around €2.50 per hour, less if you stay longer than four hours. Central options include Autosilo Diaz, Piazza Diaz 6, just south of Piazza Duomo; Garage Traversi, on Via Bagutta, close to Piazza San Babila; Parking Majno, on Viale Majno near Porta Venezia. Prices vary from zone to zone but are displayed on the sign. Blue lines along the street denote "pay and display" parking. Parking in prohibited zones is not worth it; you'll be fined if caught and have your car impounded by the police.

Car rental All the international companies have car rental offices at the airports and in the city centre including Avis (☎ 02 8940 9016), Europcar (☎ 02 8646 3454), Hertz (☎ 02 6698 5151) and Maggiore (☎ 02 669 0934).

BY BIKE

Milan has a convenient bike-sharing system in the city centre, Bike MI (see below). Cycling is a very pleasant way of exploring Milan: the terrain is flat, there is little of the aggression that you see on the streets of London or New York, and it is easy to head off down a quiet side road and get away from it all; do be careful with the tram lines though. Several hotels also offer bicycles or you can rent by the day or week; you'll need a passport or ID card and often a credit card, as well. If you fancy something a little more powerful, you could rent a scooter, but you have to be 18 or over and will need to rent a helmet too.

BIKE RENTAL OUTLETS

AWS Via Ponte Seveso 33 ☎ 02 6707 2145, ❽ awsbici.com. City and mountain bikes (€12/day).
Bike Mi ☎ 02 4860 7607, ❽ bikemi.com. Register for a temporary subscription by phone, online or at ATM points like Duomo, Stazione Centrale and Cadorna. Payment can only be by credit card. Rental is for a maximum of two hours at a time and it's €2.50/24hr and €6/week.
Motorcycle tours and rentals Via del Ricordo 31 ☎ 02 2720 1556, ❽ mototouring.com. Scooters and motorbikes. From €50/day.

INFORMATION

Online guides *Milano Mese* (❽ visitamilano.it.) is a monthly booklet published by the tourist office that gives a good rundown of temporary exhibitions and events, while *Where Milan* (❽ wheremilan.com) features lifestyle and city events.
Tourist office Piazza Castello 1 (Mon–Fri 9am–6pm, Sat

9am–1.30pm & 2–6pm, Sun 9am–1.30pm 2–5pm; ☎ 02 7740 4343, ❽ visitamilanoit). Offers literature on the city and around, as well as information on guided tours.
Tourist booths Stazione Centrale (Mon–Fri 9am–5pm, Sat & Sun 9am–12.30pm; ☎ 02 7740 4318).

TOURS

The central tourist office has information and sells tickets for various English-speaking tours. You can also take a tour of the San Siro stadium (see p.95).

1

Canal boat cruises Naviglio Lombardi (☎ 02 9227 3118, ⓦ naviglilombardi.it/navigare/in-barca) organises five cruise itineraries along the Navigli (€12/person) mainly from April–Oct.

City Sightseeing Milano ⓦ milano.city-sightseeing .it. A hop-on hop-off bus tour with two different routes around central Milan in an open-top bus. Daily every

30–45min 9.30am–7.20pm; €25/24hr, multi-language headphone commentaries included.

Gran Tour di Milano ⓦ zaniviaggi.it. The Gran Tour di Milano is a coach and walking tour (Tues–Sun 9.30am; 3hr 30min; €65) that includes entrance to the castle, La Scala museum and *The Last Supper*. Advance booking highly recommended.

ACCOMMODATION

Much of Milan's **accommodation** is geared towards business-travellers and, as a result, prices are high, rooms can be characterless and many hotels are booked up all year round. You'd be wise to **reserve ahead**, especially during the spring (mid-Feb) and autumn (from late-Sept) fashion weeks and during the Salone del Mobile in April. Hotel **prices** can more than double during these periods. In August, on the other hand, visitors are so scarce that some hotels shut up shop for the month and those that don't might be prepared to negotiate over prices.

HOTELS

The hotels below have been divided into three areas – the Station area, covering places within a twenty-minute walk of the Stazione Centrale, and districts north and south of Piazza Duomo. The area around Stazione Centrale, and across to Porta Venezia, is home to a good proportion of the city's cheaper hotels, and although many cater to the area's considerable red-light trade, you should be fine at any of the chosen places below. As you go towards the centre, prices rise, but deals can be had in some of the side streets off the city's main thoroughfares.

STAZIONE CENTRALE AND AROUND

★ **BioCity Hotel** Via Edolo 18 ☎ 02 6670 3595, ⓦ biocityhotel.it; Ⓜ Sondrio or Ⓜ Central F.S; map pp.58–59. An excellent budget choice with immaculate, tastefully furnished rooms 750m north of Stazione Centrale. The hotel prides itself in being eco-friendly – complimentary beauty products are biological and biodegradable, bathrooms feature recycled toilet paper while breakfast includes homemade cakes, organic jams and eggs. **€89**

NORTH OF PIAZZA DUOMO

Antica Locanda dei Mercanti Via San Tomaso 6 ☎ 02 805 4080, ⓦ locanda.it; Ⓜ Cairoli; map p.63. Tucked away by the Sforzesco Castle in a smart eighteenth-century building is this elegant *locanda*. Bright, airy rooms have hardwood floors, light coloured furnishings and modern amenities – some also have lovely private terraces where guests can enjoy breakfast **€225**

Antica Locanda Solferino Via Castelfidardo 2 ☎ 02 657 0129, ⓦ anticalocandasolferino.it; Ⓜ Moscova; map pp.58–59. An intimate, atmosphereic nineteenth-century *palazzo* in the side streets of Brera popular with actors, singers and other celebs for several generations. Ask for a room away from the street. **€260**

Enterprise Hotel Corso Sempione 91 ☎ 02 318 181, ⓦ enterprisehotel.com; tram 1; map pp.58–59.

A comfortable business hotels north of Parco Sempione offering functional a/c soundproof rooms with modern amenities and tea and coffee making facilities. The large buffet breakfast is excellent. **€232**

Espressohotel Via Francesco Baracca 19 ☎ 02 4537 7800, ⓦ espressohotel.it; bus 73; map pp.58–59. Just 600m from Linate airport, this is one of the country's first "social" hotels – the idea is to encourage guests to socialise and share their experiences in the city through complimentary iPads. **€100**

Hotel de la Ville Via Ulrico Hoepli ☎ 02 879 131, ⓦ delavillemilano.com; Ⓜ Duomo or Ⓜ San Babila; map p.63. Just a few steps from La Scala, this large hotel offers a selection of classic and contemporary rooms, some in better shape than others, along with a compact gym, steam room, sauna and small swimming pool with sun deck. **€260**

Hotel Milano Scala Via dell'Orso 7 ☎ 02 870 961, ⓦ hotelmilanoscala.it; Ⓜ Cairoli or Ⓜ Montenapoleone; map p.63. A stone's throw away from La Scala, this four-star hotel has attractive rooms decorated with large images of opera, dance and backstage scenes from the Historical Archives of La Scala. The suites are each named after a different opera, and most feature whirlpool tubs and scented candles. Breakfast is accompanied by harp music – a soothing way to start the day. **€250**

Palazzo Parigi Corso di Porta Nuova 1 ☎ 02 625 625, ⓦ palazzoparigi.com; Ⓜ Montenapoleone or Ⓜ Turati; map p.63. This newly opened five-star hotel in the heart of Milan features sumptuous marble interiors, with rich wood furniture and luxurious fabrics. Well-appointed rooms with modern amenities, all have private open-air terraces with garden or city views, while convivial *Caffè Parigi*, with seating in a leafy garden, is the perfect spot for coffee or an afternoon tea. **€560**

Straf Via San Raffaele 3 ☎ 02 805 081, ⓦ straf.it; Ⓜ Duomo; map p.63. A stylish minimalist hotel with bare cement walls, oxidized copper and black slate fittings. The

A MILANESE PICNIC

There are **street markets** throughout the city every day except Sunday. The perfect places to assemble a picnic, they sell all the cheese, salami and fruit you might need; a complete list is given daily in the *Corriere della Sera* under "Mercati". Alternatively, the *mercato comunale* in Piazza Wagner has similar fresh produce to the street markets, but under one, large and colourful roof. There is also an Esselunga supermarket at Viale Piave 38, near Porta Venezia, while the excellent food emporium Eataly on Piazza XXV Aprile houses restaurants and cafés, and sells local produce, from freshly baked bread to speciality cold-cuts.

bathrooms are fitted with designer sinks and stylish mirrors while the hotel bar, also open to non-guests, features recycled furniture and hosts renowned DJ sets and live music events. **€341**

SOUTH OF PIAZZA DUOMO

Ariston Largo Carobbio 2 ☎02 7200 0556, ⓦ aristonhotel.com; ⓜ Duomo, then tram 2, 3 or 14; map p.63. A moderate three-star hotel within walking distance of the Duomo and the Navigli. Rooms are a little cramped, but all are en suite and there's a decent breakfast included. Book a room on the eighth floor for good city views. **€150**

Hotel Magna Pars Suites Via Forcella 6 ☎02 833 8371, ⓦ magnapars-suitesmilano.it; ⓜ Pta Genova; map pp.58–59. In the Navigli area just a few steps from bustling Via Tortona, stylish rooms in a former perfume factory that has been converted into a swish architectural complex. The chic suites open onto a leafy interior courtyard and facilities include a fitness centre, steam room and roof deck. **€580**

Hotel Milano Navigli Piazza Sant'Eustorgio 2 ☎02 3655 375, ⓦ hotelmilanonavigli.com; ⓜ Pta Genova; map p.74. In an enviable location 300m from the bustling Navigli, this three-star business hotel offers spick-and-span rooms decorated in earthy colours. The top floor rooms have lovely views over the piazza and beyond. **€180**

Petit Palais Via Molino delle Armi 1 ☎02 584 891, ⓦ petitpalais.it; ⓜ Missori; map pp.58–59. A small luxury hotel in a seventeenth-century mansion just a few hundred yards from the Navigli. Rooms are decorated with period furniture, Murano chandeliers and oriental rugs; all have modern amenities including tea and coffee making facilities, a/c and satellite TV. **€300**

B&BS AND APARTMENTS

As many of the mid-range hotels are rather dingy you may want to look into B&B alternatives. Check out the website ⓦ bed-and-breakfast.it for more options.

B&B Porta Garibaldi Viale Pasubio 8 ☎02 2906 1419 or ☎335 804 4030, ⓦ portagaribaldi.it; ⓜ Pta Garibaldi; map pp.58–59. This colourful B&B close to Porta Garibaldi station features a comfortable mini-apartment with kitchenette. The friendly owner lives next

door and is always happy to help with suggestions. Complimentary bicycles, too. **€100**

Five Stars ☎338 1820 717, ⓦ ifivestars.it Five tastefully furnished apartments sleeping from four to eight people. All the apartments feature modern amenities and the friendly landlady will make you feel at home– guests will find complimentary food upon arrival as well as tea, coffee and toiletries. **€70**

★**LaFavia Four Rooms** Via Carlo Farini 4 ☎0347 784 2212, ⓦ lafavia4rooms.com; ⓜ Pta Garibaldi; map pp.58–59. A charming B&B in a nineteenth-century building with warm and welcoming rooms decorated in different styles, featuring retro armchairs and lamps, hand-woven carpets and designer wallpaper. Breakfast is served on the leafy roof terrace garden. **€110**

San Pietro all'Orto 6 Via San Pietro all'Orto 6 ☎02 781 147, ⓦ allegroitalia.it; ⓜ San Babila; map p.63. In an enviable location just a few steps from the Duomo, this secure hotel offers luxurious modern apartments fitted out in Armani Home furnishings; all have flatscreen TVs and fully equipped kitchenettes. **€700**

HOSTELS AND CAMPSITES

Città di Milano Via G. Airaghi 61 ☎02 4820 7017, ⓦ campingmilano.it; ⓜ M1 to De Angeli, then bus 72; map pp.58–59. Next to an aquapark and the nearest campsite to the centre, but still a metro trip and a bus ride away. Open all year. Camping for two **€6.50**, doubles **€70**, bungalows **€90**

Gogol'Ostello Via Chieti 1 ☎02 3675 5522, ⓦ gogolostello.it; tram 1; map pp.58–59. This pleasant hostel and literary café to the north of Parco Sempione hosts cultural events including book presentations and theatre performances. Communal areas are warm and colourful with books scattered here and there, while the dorms are neat and tidy. Bike rental, too (€10/day). Dorms **€28**, doubles **€40**

★**Ostello Bello** Via Medici 4 ☎02 3658 2720, ⓦ ostellobello.com; ⓜ Missori; map p.63. An award-winning hostel with mismatched coloured furniture, terraces with hammocks and a communal area dotted with curios including guitars and a pair of old wooden skis. Welcoming dorms have reading lamps and lockers, and there's a cosy kitchen for guests' use. Dorms **€30**, doubles **€98**

1

EATING AND DRINKING

Milan may seem to live at a faster pace than much of Italy but it takes its food just as seriously. There are **restaurants** and **cafés** to suit every pocket and more choices of cuisine than you'll find almost anywhere else in the country. Whether you're looking for a neighbourhood trattoria, want to watch models pick at their salads or fancy well-priced international cuisine, Milan has it all. If you don't fancy a sit-down meal, make the most of the Milanese custom of **aperitivo** (see box, p.88) to curb your hunger.

LUNCH AND SNACK BARS

Weekday lunchtime is an ideal time to sample good-value cuisine: unprepossessing-looking bars throughout the city centre serve tasty pasta dishes or set menus at modest prices to local office workers.

Al Mercato Via Sant'Eufemia 16 ☎ 02 8723 7167, ☼ al -mercato.it; Ⓜ Crocetta or Ⓜ Missori; map pp.58–59. Milan's best burger joint features a glass-panelled kitchen where customers can watch the chefs at work. The casual burger bar serves towering burgers and street food, while the tiny restaurant menu offers a range of dishes including lamb, duck, tuna and fish curries. Mains €16. Daily 12.30– 3pm & 7.30–11pm; closed Sun eve.

★ **Bello e Buono** Viale Sabotino 14 ☎ 02 9455 3407, ☼ belloebuonogastronomia.it; Ⓜ Porta Romana; map pp.58–59. This itty-bitty laidback place attracting students from nearby Bocconi University offers exceptional home cooking at incredible prices. Expect traditional Mediterranean recipes that have been passed down from generation to generation – the *melanzane parmigiana* (€7.50) are to die for. The pasta and bread are homemade, too and lunch is a bargain €6. Mon–Sat 10.30am–1am.

La Rinascente Food Hall, Top floor, Piazza Duomo ☎ 02 866 371, ☼ rinascente.it; Ⓜ Duomo; map p.63. Enjoy one of the best views in town with a plate of nibbles or a full-blown meal to match, although the service is not always of the same quality. The space is divided between the city's best breadmakers, mozzarella specialists, sushi chefs, experts in Milanese cooking and chocolatiers to provide a gourmet pick-and-mix to please any tastes. Choose a table on the terrace outside and you can almost reach over and feed the gargoyles on the Duomo roof. Daily 10am–midnight.

Luini Via S. Radegonda 16 ☼ luini.it; Ⓜ Duomo; map p.63. A city institution that has been going strong since 1949. The real draw here are the freshly made *panzerotti* (deep-fried or oven baked mini-*calzone* that come in eleven different types of fillings), traditionally served steaming hot and enjoyed in the nearby square of Piazza San Fedele. Mon 10am–3pm, Tues–Sat 10am–8pm.

Panini Durini Corso Magenta 31 ☎ 02 8909 4056, ☼ paninidurini.it; Ⓜ Cadorna or Ⓜ Sant'Ambrogio; map p.63. A light and airy café serving over forty types of sandwiches (€5) with all manner of fillings including roast beef, turkey, mortadella, speck, salami, salmon and parma ham. There are also tasty vegetarian options, salads (€6) and light lunches (€10). Mon–Sat 7.30am–10pm & 7.30am–8.30pm.

Parma & Co. Via Delio Tessa 2 ☎ 02 8909 6720, ☼ parmaeco.it; Ⓜ Lanza; map p.63. A welcoming deli that specialises in cold cuts from Parma (meat platters €10), traditionally served with *torta fritta* (fried dough parcels). Mains (€12) include cold roast beef (€10) and freshly made pasta (€10) – all from Parma. Mon–Sat 10am–3pm & 5–11pm, Sun noon–4pm.

Princi Via Speronari 6 ☎ 02 874 797, ☼ princi.co.uk; Ⓜ Duomo; map p.63. This smart café tucked off a side street by the Duomo displays neat rows of sweet and savoury delights, including mouth-watering cakes (€3.50) and pizza slices (€3.50). Mon–Fri 7am–8pm, Sat 8am–8pm, Sun 9am–7.30pm.

CAFÉS & GELATERIE

Milan has traditional cafés and *salons de thé* galore; bourgeois, staid and very comfortable, they serve morning coffee, lunchtime snacks and afternoon tea. We've listed a selection of the best below, as well as some of the city's most famous ice-cream parlours, or *gelaterie*. Milan also has many cafés and bars that are more popular for *aperitivi* and evening drinks (see p.89).

Cova Via Montenapoleone 8 ☎ 02 7600 0578, ☼ pasticceriacova.it; Ⓜ Montenapoleone; map p.63. A historic tearoom dating back to 1817 with *fin-de-siècle* decor. Famed for its irresistible chocolate delicacies, it doesn't come cheap – a coffee at the bar will set you back €1.10, which increases to a whopping €5 at the table. Mon–Sat 7.45am–8.30pm.

Gelateria Marghera Via Marghera 33 ☎ 02 468 641; Ⓜ Wagner or Ⓜ De Angeli; map pp.58–59. One of Milan's best *gelaterie* displaying large tubs of tasty ice cream (€2.60); flavours include seasonal fruits as well as the classics. Be prepared to queue. Sun–Thurs 10am–10.30pm, Fri & Sat until 1am.

Sartori Piazza Luigi di Savoia ☼ gelateriasartori.it; Ⓜ Stazione Centrale; map pp.58–59. This legendary kiosk by the airport buses just outside Stazione Centrale, has been going strong since 1937. With over thirty flavours – including pistachio, *zabaglione* and *torroncino* – there's plenty of choice. There are five flavours of refreshing slush puppies, such as lemon and nut (€2), too. March to mid-Oct daily 11am–1am.

★ **Shockolat** Via Boccaccio 9 ☎ 02 4810 0597, ☼ shockolat.it; Ⓜ Cadorna; map p.63. A sleek, stylish café and *gelaterie* offering twenty-six delicious flavours, including seven chocolate options (€2.50) such as orange chocolate, rum chocolate and ginger chocolate. Their ice cream is blended with unusual ingredients such as chilli, aniseed and vinegar. The café also offers delectable cakes that can be enjoyed at the tables on the ground floor or on the mezzanine. Mon–Fri 7.30am–1am, Sat 8am–1am & Sun 10am–1am.

RESTAURANTS

Predictably, the centre of Milan has numerous pricey, expense-account establishments, but usually, just round the corner, there is somewhere more atmospheric or better value. To the south of the centre, the streets around the Ticinese and Navigli are full of bustling restaurants and bars attracting a young crowd. The districts of Brera and Moscova are also popular in the evening, as is the up and coming district of Isola north of Porta Garibaldi.

Al Fresco Via Savona 50 ☎ 02 4953 3630, ⓦ alfrescomilano.it; ⓜ Porta Genova; map pp.58–59. Located in a former warehouse in the Tortona district, this breezy restaurant offers seating in a verdant interior courtyard filled with cherry trees, wisteria and honeysuckle. Part bistro, part greenhouse, the creatively presented dishes are wholesome and the menu includes a selection of homemade pastries and desserts. Antipasti €5, primi €10, secondi €15. Tues–Sun 12.30–4pm & 7.30pm–1am.

Da Marcone Via Lodovico Muratori 50 ☎ 02 5501 6966, ⓦ damarcone.it; ⓜ Lodi; map pp.58–59. A good value neighbourhood restaurant to the south of the city centre lined with black and white 1960s photos. The refreshingly short menu changes daily and features two meat and two fish dishes, as well as a vegetarian option. Primi €8, secondi €14. Mon–Sat noon–2.30pm & 7.30–11pm.

Da Noi In Via Forcella 6 ☎ 02 8338 3799, ⓦ magnapars -suitesmilano.it/en/da-noi-in; ⓜ Porta Genova; map pp.58–59. This elegant restaurant in the *Magna Pars Suites Hotel* is run by a renowned Piedmontese chef. The Italian dishes are prepared using high-quality seasonal ingredients. Sit in the smart, understated interior or within the building's leafy courtyard; on cold winter evenings two fireplaces complement the intimate setting. Antipasti €17, primi €17, secondi €24. Mon–Sat 12.30–2.30pm & 7.30–10.30pm.

Don Juan Via Altaguardia 2 ☎ 02 5843 0805, ⓦ ristorantedonjuan.com; ⓜ Porta Romana; map pp.58–59. Traditional Argentine steakhouse serving excellent beef sirloin steak (€25) and tender skirt steak (€24) grilled before customers' very eyes. The wine list features fifty Argentine wines, while the dessert menu includes a mouth-watering custard flan (€7). Mon–Sat 7pm–midnight.

★**Drogheria Milanese** Via Conca del Naviglio 7 ☎ 02 5811 4843, ⓦ drogheriamilanese.it; ⓜ Sant'Ambrogio or ⓜ Sant'Agostino; map p.74. This fashionable bistro-style restaurant has a welcoming interior with low hanging light bulbs and a long communal table. The menu features Mediterranean and international dishes, including pasta, burgers and fish (mains €12.50); most dishes can be ordered in half-portions – great for sampling different options. Daily noon–3.30pm & 6pm–midnight.

Erba Brusca Alzaia Naviglio Pavese 286 ☎ 02 8738 0711, ⓦ erbabrusca.it; 15min from ⓜ Abbiategrasso; map p.74. Near the banks of the Naviglio Pavese, this welcoming restaurant with alfresco seating shaded by a pergola serves international dishes with a twist. Organic meat is sourced from local farmers and the dishes are seasoned with herbs from the lovely garden at the back. Primi €12, secondi €16. Wed–Sun noon–3pm & 8–11pm, Sun lunch until 4pm.

Giacomo Arengario Via Guglielo Marconi 1 ☎ 02 7209 3814, ⓦ giacomoarengario.com; ⓜ Duomo; map p.63. On the top floor of the Museo del Novecento, this smart restaurant boasts incredible views of the Duomo. At such a prime location the dishes (mains €30) don't come cheap, although the view is worth the splurge. Daily noon–midnight.

Joe Cipolla Via San Marco 29 ☎ 02 4548 8837, ⓦ joecipolla.it; ⓜ Moscova map pp.58–59. Named after Joe Cipolla, a 1920s gangster and Al Capone's cook, this cosy restaurant jam-packed with black and white 1920s photos and old American ads specialises in meat dishes. Meat is cooked in a wood-fired oven, the portions are huge and the dishes are very reasonably priced. The rib eye steak (€18.80) is a real winner. There's a sister restaurant at Via Vigevano 33 (ⓜ Porta Genova). Mon–Sat 7pm–midnight.

★**La Dogana del Buongusto** Via Molino delle Armi 48 ☎ 02 8324 2444, ⓦ ladoganadelbuongusto.it; ⓜ Sant'Ambrogio or ⓜ Crocetta; map p.74. Warm and welcoming family-run restaurant serving exceptional cuisine in a rustic interior with cavernous exposed brick walls, wooden ceilings and old world knick-knacks. The hearty cold cut platters (€10) include wild boar and deer ham, while the menu encompasses excellent Milanese dishes. The 30cm meat brochette (€15) is a must try. Mon–Fri 12.30–2.30pm & 7.30pm–12.30am, Sat 7.30pm–1.30am.

★**Langosteria 10** Via Savona 10 ☎ 02 5811 1649, ⓦ langosteria10.it; ⓜ Porta Genova or ⓜ Sant'Agostino; map p.74. This atmospheric restaurant with an understated interior serves some of Milan's best fish and seafood dishes. The oyster bar is the perfect spot for a pre- or postprandial drink, while seating is in a series of individually furnished rooms

1

featuring maritime ornaments, including an upturned boat. The Catalan-style king crabs are superb, as are the scampi with foie gras. Mains €30. Mon–Sat 7pm–midnight, oyster bar until 1am.

★**Osteria dell'Acquabella** Via San Rocco 11 ☎02 5830 9653, ⓦacquabella.it; ⓜPorta Romana; map pp.58–59. A bustling neighbourhood *osteria* that serves excellent Milanese dishes including risotto (€7), *cotoletta* (€14) and *ossobuco* (€20). The wine list includes over 180 wines, and service is friendly and efficient. If you're after a taste of the "real" Milan, then this is it. Tues–Fri noon–3pm & 8–10.30pm, Sat & Mon 8–10.30pm.

Pescheria Mattiucci Via Vincenzo Monti 56 ☎02 4800 9316, ⓦpescheriamattiucci.com; ⓜConciliazione or ⓜPagano; map p.63. A charming little fishmonger's and restaurant, set on two floors decorated with quaint curios. The cuisine is mainly Mediterranean, with an emphasis on Neapolitan dishes. The varied menu includes stuffed calamari with fried courgettes (€12), while the raw fish starter (€24) is large enough to share. Mon 11am–3pm, Tues–Thurs & Sat 11am–3pm & 6–11pm, Fri 9am–3pm & 6–11pm.

Ratanà Via de Castillia 28 ☎02 8712 8855, ⓦratana.it; ⓜGioia; map pp.58–59. This fashionable restaurant in up-and-coming Isola offers regional dishes with a contemporary twist – home-made pasta, risotto, freshwater fish and meat dishes that customers can enjoy in the bistro-style interior, at the bar or in the welcoming garden. Primi €15, secondi €25. Wed–Sun 12.30–2.30pm & 6.30–11.30pm.

Trattoria del Corso Corso Garibaldi 12 ☎02 7200 4525, ⓦdaerre.com; ⓜLanza; map p.63. A popular trattoria with tables spilling out onto the pavement serving beef bourguignon (€20), cheese fondue (€22), *raclette* (€25) and *pierrade* (€25), along with regional specialities such as *ossobuco alla Milanese* (€20). Spaghetti carbonara (€10) is served in a parmesan wafer with a fresh egg on top. Tues–Sun noon–4pm & 5–11.30pm.

Zio Pesce Via Andrea Maffei 12 ☎02 4979 4967, ⓦziopesce.it; ⓜCrocetta or ⓜPorta Romana; map pp.58–59. A cosy fish restaurant with colourful paraphernalia, such as lanterns, oars and fishing nets, decorating the walls. Fish and seafood are bought fresh from the market each morning, which means the menu changes daily. Try the tasty *frittura di pesce* (€17.50) as a starter. Primi €10, secondi €17. Mon–Sat 7pm–midnight.

NIGHTLIFE

Milan is renowned as having some of the best **nightlife** in Italy. Although hardly cutting-edge, it's a diverse scene that offers something for just about everyone. There are plenty of places catering for those who want to see and be seen but there are also laidback joints where the music and company are just as important. Milan's nightlife traditionally centres on two main areas: the designer-label streets around **Corso Como** and south around Via Brera and the canal-side **Navigli** and the adjacent Ticinese quarter, south of the city, where a more mixed clientele enjoys the lively bars, restaurants and nightclubs, some hosting regular live bands. But there are numerous other pockets like around **Porta Venezia**, Corso Sempione and Porta Romana, as well as **Isola**, north of Porta Garibaldi, where trendy bars and restaurants have started to spring up. Milan's relatively small size and car and scooter culture mean that people are happy to drive to places **out of the centre**, so some of the more popular bars and clubs that we recommend below may require a bus, bike or a quick taxi ride.

APERITIVO TIME

An Italian custom that has been honed to a fine art in Milan is the **aperitivo**, or pre-dinner drink. Between 6pm and 9pm the city unwinds over a drink and a bite to eat: counters often groan under the weight of hot and cold food, all of which is included in the price of your drink (somewhere between €3 and €10, depending on the establishment). Here are some of the city's best spots for an *aperitivo*.

Moscatelli Corso Garibaldi 93 ☎02 655 4602; map pp.58–59. A popular wine bar offering a rich *apertivo* buffet including focaccia breads, cold cuts and pasta. Mon–Sat 7.30am–midnight.

Pandenus Via Tadino 15 ☎02 2952 8016, ⓦpandenus.it; ⓜPorta Venezia; map pp.58–59. A happening little bar just off Corso Buenos Aires that buzzes at *aperitivo* time, when customers enjoying a drink or two spill onto the pavement. Daily 7am–10.30pm.

Roialto Via Piero della Francesca 55 ☎02 3493 6616, ⓦroialtogroup.it; map pp.58–59. One of the city's best spots for *aperitivo*, this upmarket bar with a summer terrace offers a great variety of fresh food cooked on the spot. Tues–Sun 6pm–2am.

CLOCKWISE FROM TOP GALLERIA VITTORIO EMANUELLE II (P.60); ANTIQUE MARKET, NAVIGLIO GRANDE (P.76); RISOTTO ALLA MILANESE (P.34); PRADA (P.93) >

1

BARS

Many bars metamorphose as the day – and night – progresses, serving coffee and food in the day and becoming clubs in all but name and entry charge later in the evening. Most of the following bars open at around 11am and don't close their doors until 2am at the earliest. They are at their busiest from *aperitivo*-time onwards. For a truly Milanese experience, don't forget to check out the bars in the city's top fashion showrooms (see p.92).

Brasserie Bruxelles Viale Abruzzi 33 ☎02 2941 9148, ⓦ brasseriebruxelles.eu; ⓜ Lima; map pp.58–59. This welcoming pub decked out in chocolate-coloured furniture offers over one hundred bottles of Belgian beer and seven on tap, including a selection of Trappist beers and farmhouse ales. Football matches are regularly screened here too. Daily 6pm–2am.

Camparino Piazza Duomo 21 ☎02 8646 4435, ⓦ camparino.it; ⓜ Duomo; map p.63. Founded by the Campari family, this historic bar right on Piazza Duomo serves potent Campari drinks (€5). The interior retains a historic feel, with lovely Art Nouveau mosaics and an inlaid counter featuring beautiful pieces of Murano glass. The restaurant above was once frequented by artists and painters including Verdi, Puccini and Toscanini. Tues–Sun 7.30am–8pm.

Cuore Via G Mora 3 ☎02 5811 8311, ⓦ cuoremilano.it; ⓜ Sant'Ambrogio; map p.74. Hidden away down a side street opposite San Lorenzo Maggiore, this cool, friendly bar is well worth including in your night out. Good jazz and rock & roll tunes as well as occasional live bands and DJs set the mixed crowd at their ease. Daily 6.30pm–2am.

Dry Via Solferino 33 ☎02 6379 3414, ⓦ drymilano.it; ⓜ Moscova; map pp.58–59. This trendy bar in the heart of the fashionable Brera district serves imaginative cocktails (€8) and tasty pizzas (€9) to nibble on. Tues–Sun 7pm–1am.

Le Biciclette Conca del Naviglio 10 ⓦ lebiciclette .eu; ⓜ S. Ambrogio; map p.74. Located in a former cycle repair centre, this fashionable bar with cushioned seating and hanging bikes has long been one of the city's most sought-after bars for an *aperitivo* (€7). Its most popular days have now passed, though it still attracts quite a crowd. The Sunday brunch features eggs and hamburgers but doesn't come cheap at €22 per head. Mon & Sun 6pm–midnight, Tues–Sat 6pm–2am.

N'Ombra de Vin Via San Marco 2 ☎02 6599 650, ⓦ nombradevin.it; ⓜ Lanza; map p.63. This popular wine bar-cum-bistro with tables spilling onto the street attracts well-heeled *milanesi* who flock here at *aperitivo* time. The cool, cavernous cellar is lined with thousands of wine bottles (there are over 3000 labels) from Italy and further afield. Daily 10am–2am.

Nottingham Forest Viale Piave 1 ☎02 798 311, ⓦ nottingham-forest.com; ⓜ Porta Venezia; map pp.58–59. Arguably one of Milan's best cocktail bars shaking up all manner of creatively presented drinks (€12), each served in different funky glasses and containers (there's even a cocktail served in a first aid kit) in an intimate environment. Tues–Sat 6.30pm–2am, Sun 6pm–1am.

Pravda Via Carlo Vittadini 6 ⓜ Porta Romana; map pp.58–59. Offering over 150 types of vodka from across the world, this is a definite favourite among Milanese students who flock here for potent cocktails made with fresh fruit and juices (€7), and typically enjoyed on the little pavement outside. Daily 6.30pm–1am.

★**Rita** Via Angelo Fumagalli 1 ☎02 837 2865; ⓜ Pta Genova; map p.74. This discreet little bar just off Porta Ticinese shakes up creative cocktails using the freshest ingredients around. *Aperitivo* (6.30–10pm) includes delicious finger food as well as tapas-sized portions of Mediterranean dishes that change daily. Highly recommended. Daily 6.30pm–2am.

Radetzky Café Corso Garibaldi 105 ☎02 657 2645, ⓦ radetzky.it; ⓜ Moscova; map pp.58–59. This place has become a bit of an institution where stylish Milanese come to see and be seen; it won't break your wallet though (a beer will set you back €5). Tables spill out onto the pavement in the summer months, with the bar particularly buzzing at happy hour from 7pm. Daily 8am–1.30am.

LIVE MUSIC VENUES AND CLUBS

The city's clubs are at their hippest midweek, particularly Mondays and Thursdays – at weekends out-of-towners flood in and any self-respecting Milanese trendy either stays at home or hits a bar. Many places have obscure door policies, often dependent on the whim of the bouncer; assuming you get in, you can expect to pay €15–30 entry, which usually includes your first drink. Most clubs don't open until around 11pm, but are likely to carry on through until 4am. As for live music, Milan scores high on jazz and the pop scene is relatively good by Italian standards: there are regular gigs by local bands and the city is a stop on the circuit for big-name bands too.

Blue Note Via Borsieri 37 ⓦ bluenotemilano .com; ⓜ Isola. Top-name jazz club located in the alternative neighbourhood of Isola, just north of Stazione Garibaldi. Quality bookings and a relaxed atmosphere make this place a top venue. There's a small restaurant, as well as the bar. Tues–Sun 6pm–midnight.

Byblos Via Messina 38 ⓦ byblosmilano.com; ⓜ Pta Garibaldi; map pp.58–59. Fashionable club with a large open-air terrace and a dancefloor packed with trendy Milanese. Thurs–Sun 11pm–4.30am.

Club Haus '80's Via Valtellina 21 ⓦ clubhaus80s.com; ⓜ Maciachini or ⓜ Zara; map pp.58–59. A fun club with themed 1980s nights. The music varies from disco and electronica to new wave, pop and house. There's a nightly dress code so expect to see partygoers with funky hats and glow in the dark accessories. Fri & Sat 11.30pm–5am.

Hollywood Corso Como 15 ⓦ discotecahollywood .com; ⓜ Pta Garibaldi; map pp.58–59. This Milan institution has been going strong for two decades – it remains the place to go if you want to be surrounded by beautiful people. Tues–Sat 11pm–4am, Sun 9.30pm–4am.

Just Cavalli Café Via Luigi Camoens, c/o Torre Branca ⓦ milano.cavalliclub.com; ⓜ Cadorna; map p.63. On summer nights *Just Cavalli Café* becomes an upmarket open-air club in the heart of the city where well-heeled Milanese meet to see and be seen in the fashion capital. Check online for music listings and be prepared for the pricey cocktail list (May–Sept €10; Oct–April €15). Daily noon–2am.

Magazzini Generali Via Pietrasanta 14 ⓣ 02 5521 1313, ⓦ magazzinigenerali.it; tram 24; map pp.58–59. Ex-warehouse that has become a Milan institution with a mixture of popular club nights and live music. Wed, Fri & Sat 11pm–5am.

Scimmie Via Ascanio Sforza 49 ⓦ scimmie.it; ⓜ Pta Genova FS; map p.74. This Ticinese club is one of Milan's most popular venues, with a different band every night and jazz-fusion predominating. Small and intimate, with a restaurant – and a barge on the canal in summer. Mon–Tues & Thurs–Sat 8pm–2am.

GAY AND LESBIAN MILAN

Milan is one of Italy's most gay-friendly cities with little of the religious- and socially-fuelled homophobia of the south. Many of the city's bars and clubs welcome a mixed crowd, but they often hold specific **gay nights**, too. Naturally, see-and-be-seen venues are Milan's forte, though there is also a choice of more relaxed and more hardcore establishments as well. The **lesbian scene** is less developed, with just a few dedicated venues. Whatever your taste, Milan's high proportion of would-be models and style-setters certainly means the city has more than its fair share of eye candy.

BARS, CLUBS AND SAUNAS

Many of the city's more hardcore gay venues are located on or near Via Sammartini, not far from the Stazione Centrale. There are numerous other establishments around town, though it's not uncommon to have to travel a little out of the centre. One essential item when visiting Milan's exclusively gay venues is the Arci Club Card, which most establishments require as a condition of entry. It can be bought (€15 annual membership) on the door at any place that requires it or online through Arcigay (ⓦ arcigaymilano.org).

Blanco Piazza Lavater 18 ⓣ 02 2940 5284, ⓦ blancomilano.com; ⓜ Porta Venezia or ⓜ Lima; map pp.58–59. Stylish, gay-friendly café and bar with white decor, which attracts an artsy crowd including designers, creative types and fashionistas from the nearby D&G headquarters. Mojitos (€8) are the bar's signature drink, accompanied by a good selection of snacks. Thursdays see a gay crowd at *aperitivo* time (6.30–9.30pm). Mon 7am–midnight, Tues–Fri 7am–8pm, Sat 7am–2am, Sun 6pm–1am.

Elephant Via Melzo 22 ⓣ 02 2951 8768; ⓜ Porta Venezia; map pp.58–59. One of the city's most popular gay bars hosting drag shows and DJs after 10pm. Tues–Sat 6.30pm–3am, Sun 6.30pm–2am.

Mono Via Lecco 6 ⓣ 02 2940 9330; ⓜ Porta Venezia; map pp.58–59. A gay vintage cocktail bar with 1960s decor and a happy hour from 6.30–9.30pm. The musical flavour is indie, rock and electro with DJ sets on Thursday, Friday and Saturday. Tues & Sun 6.30pm–1am, Wed & Thurs 6.30pm–1.30am, Fri & Sat 6.30pm–2am.

Plastic Via Gargano 15 ⓣ 02 8719 6630, ⓦ anglerecords.com; ⓜ Brenta; map pp.58–59. This gay friendly club has been going strong since the 1980s; it attracts a mixed crowd who come here to mingle and dance until the early hours. Fri 11pm–5am, Sat midnight–5am, Sun 11pm–3am.

Tropical Island Bastioni di Porta Venezia ⓣ 02 2951 1599; ⓜ Porta Venezia; map pp.58–59. A popular *chiringuito* (pop-up bar) on the edge of the park of Palestro that gets busy at *aperitivo* time because of its good cocktails (€7). The bar attracts a gay crowd on Wednesday and Fridays. Daily 6pm–2am.

OPERA, MUSIC, THEATRE AND CINEMA

For many, Milan is synonymous with opera, and a night at La Scala is unlikely to disappoint, but there is also a good programme of classical music organized throughout the year. Milan's reputation for ground-breaking theatre in the 1980s and 1990s has waned in recent years, but there are still several quality venues. You can also choose from a range of cinemas.

LA SCALA

Many of Milan's tourists are in the city for just one reason – La Scala, at Via dei Filodrammatici 2 (info ⓣ 02 7200 3744), one of the world's most prestigious opera houses. The opera season runs from 7 December through to July, and there are usually also classical concerts and ballet performances between September and November. The average price of a ticket is about €70 and seats often sell out months in advance.

1

Advance tickets Tickets can be bought in advance on the phone or online (📞 02 860 775, 🌐 teatroallascala.org). The website has a useful seating plan with a twenty percent advance booking fee; book two months before the performance, or in person at the Central Box Office, Galleria del Sagrato, underground in the corridors of the Duomo metro station, opposite the ATM office (Sept–July daily noon–6pm), a month before. Ticket collection for reservations is possible from two hours before the start of the performance at the opera house.

Same day sales Some tickets for each performance are set aside for sale on the day; 140 tickets are available for operas and ballets, and 80 for concerts, with a maximum purchase of two tickets per person. The system changes frequently, but at the time of writing a list of names is compiled at the box office at 1pm, with tickets to be collected at 5.30pm: check the website or ask at the box office for the latest information.

CLASSICAL MUSIC

Milan offers several good programmes of classical music throughout the year.

Auditorium di Milano Largo G Mahler 1 🌐 laverdi.org; Ⓜ Prta Genova. In the Navigli district, these comfortable modern surroundings are home to the Verdi orchestra and some wonderful concerts, including jazz.

Conservatorio Giuseppe Verdi Via Conservatorio 12 🌐 consmilano.it; Ⓜ San Babila. This prestigious music school organizes regular concerts in the deconsecrated Santa Maria della Passione next door.

THEATRE

The heyday of Milan's theatre was in the 1980s, when Giorgio Strehler put the city on the map for contemporary performances of the classics at the Piccolo theatre.

Piccolo Teatro Strehler Largo Greppi 1 📞 02 4241 1889, 🌐 piccoloteatro.org; Ⓜ Lanza. Also known as the Nuovo Piccolo, this is a classical theatre with a traditional repertoire (usually performed in Italian) and still one of the best in Italy. Closed Aug.

CINEMA

Around the Duomo there are umpteen cinema complexes screening all the latest blockbusters, more often than not dubbed into Italian. There are, however, a few places that show films in their original language (with Italian subtitles). In the summer months, outdoor films are shown at several venues around the city; see the newspapers for listings.

Fondazione Cineteca Italiana Viale Vittorio Veneto 2 🌐 cinetecamilano.it; Ⓜ Pta. Venezia. Part of the arts centre Spazio Oberdan, with a good programme of international art-house movies.

Sound and Motion Pictures 🌐 spaziocinema.info /sound-motion. Current original-language films shown every month; usually Mondays at the Anteo (Via Milazzo 9; Ⓜ Garibaldi), Tuesdays at Arcobaleno Film Centre (Viale Tunisia 11; Ⓜ Porta Venezia) and Thursdays at Mexico (Via Savona 57; Ⓜ Porta Genova), but the venue does change.

SHOPPING

Milan is synonymous with **shopping**: whether you're here to indulge in the ultimate consumer experience or want to bag a designer bargain, there are few places on earth with more to offer. The city's reputation as a **fashion** Mecca means you can find boutiques from all the world's top clothes and accessories designers within a hop, skip and a high-heeled teeter from each other. If your pockets are not quite deep enough, you could always rummage through last season's leftovers at the many factory stores around town, or check out the city's wide range of medium- and budget-range clothes shops. Milan also excels in furniture and **design**, with showrooms from the world's top companies, plus a handful of shops offering a selection of brands and labels under one roof.

Opening hours Most shops open Tuesday to Saturday 10am to 12.30pm and 3.30pm to 7pm, plus Monday afternoons, although some larger places stay open at lunchtime and on Sunday afternoons. Opening hours for in-house cafés vary, but in general they follow the store hours, and prices are in line with the rest of the city's watering holes.

Sales There are official dates for sales, set by the town council a week or two in advance, so all shops make their reductions at the same time. The summer sale usually lasts from early July through August, while the winter one starts around the second week of January and lasts for a month; as always bargains are best on the first day – when there are big crowds and queues – or at the tail end, when shops are desperate to get rid of stock.

FASHION

Twice a year Milan is brought to a standstill by the world's fashionistas who flock to show and be shown the latest collections in the spring and autumn fashion shows. Milan has been associated with top-end fashion since the 1970s, when local designers broke with the staid atmosphere of Italy's traditional fashion home at the Palazzo Pitti in Florence. It was during the 1980s, however, that the worldwide thirst for designer labels consolidated the international reputations of home-grown talent such as Armani, Gucci, Prada, Versace and Dolce & Gabbana.

Where to go The top-name fashion stores are mainly concentrated in three areas. The "Quadrilatero d'Oro" – Via Montenapoleone, Via della Spiga and around – is the place for Versace, Prada et al. Corso di Porta Ticinese houses the funkier, more youth-oriented shops, with a handful of interesting, independent stores, as well as international names like Diesel, Carhartt and Stussy. If your budget is smaller, head to Corso Vittorio Emanuele, Via Torino or Corso Buenos Aires for large branches of Italian mid-range chainstores, including Max Mara, Benetton and Stefanel, plus international high-street giants Gap, H&M and Zara.

MULTI-LABEL BOUTIQUES

If you're a little daunted by the full collections or simply don't have the time or energy to visit all the showrooms, help is at hand. Right in the heart of the city and the Quadrilatero there are a couple of shops offering a selection of the best of the season from various top designers.

Banner Via Sant'Andrea 8 ⓦ bannerboutique.it; ⓜ Montenapoleone; map p.63. Boutique offering garments by international avant-garde labels, including Alexander Wang, Moncler and Stella McCartney in a store designed by the ubiquitous Milanese architect Gae Aulenti.

Excelsior Galleria del Corso 4 ⓣ excelsiormilano.com; ⓜ San Babila; map p.63. A smart department store with food, fashion and design to suit all tastes.

Gio Moretti Via della Spiga 4 ⓦ giomoretti.com; ⓜ montenapoleone/San Babila; map p.63. Sleek shop selling mainstream designer clothing by Jil Sander, John Paul Gaultier and DKNY among others.

La Rinascente Piazza Duomo 14 ⓦ rinascente.it; ⓜ Duomo; map p.63. This swish department store offers a host of international designers displayed in a shopper-friendly layout.

DESIGNER STORES

Cavalli i Nastri Via Brera 2 and Via Gian Giacomo Mora 3 & 12 ⓦ cavallienastri.com; ⓜ Montenapoleone; map p.63. The ultimate in vintage chic offering exquisite pieces to compliment any wardrobe or home from their Brera and Ticenese showrooms.

Dolce & Gabbana Menswear, Corso Venezia 15 ⓦ dolcegabbana.com; Womenswear and shoes, Via della Spiga 26; ⓜ San Babila; map p.63. Go through to the courtyard on the ground floor of the eighteenth-century palace at Corso Venezia 15 to find a space dedicated to enhancing your shopping experience. There's an old-fashioned barber's, a small grooming centre and the *Bar Martini*, popular with beautiful people of all nationalities.

Gianni Versace Via Montenapoleone 11 ⓦ versace .com; ⓜ Montenapoleone or San Babila; map p.63. Unusually for Versace, this store, spread over five storeys, is nothing if not understated. The clean lines provide a perfect backdrop for the luxurious ostentation of the clothes, shoes and accessories in glinting gold and swirling colours.

Giorgio Armani Via Manzoni 31 ⓦ armani.com; ⓜ Montenapoleone; map p.63. This temple to all things

Giorgio is more a mini-shopping centre than a shop. There are boutiques for all his ranges – womens- and menswear, furnishings and homeware – accompanied by *Armani Café*, a relaxed pavement café, and *Nobu*, a pricey, hi-tech Japanese restaurant that's been one of *the* places in town to be seen for years. With a book corner selling design and coffee-table books, a florists' and a chocolate counter offering monogrammed sugary confections, you really won't need to spend your money anywhere else in town.

Gucci Via Montenapoleone 5–7 & Galleria Vittorio Emanuele II ⓦ gucci.com; ⓜ Montenapoleone or San Babila; map p.63. Every desirable fashion item imaginable is available in the warren of sleek show rooms in Montenapoleone, while the newer store in the Galleria Vittorio Emanuele II has the *Gucci Café*, where you can get a freshly squeezed fruit juice or a coffee accompanied by an exquisite chocolate – sporting the famous GG symbol, of course – in an atmosphere of elegant minimalism.

Prada Galleria Vittorio Emanuele II ⓦ prada.com; ⓜ Duomo; map p.63. The original Prada store, dating from 1913, stands on a side corner in the centre of the Galleria Vittorio Emanuele II. Much of the elegant interior is original, including the monochrome marble floor and the polished wood display cabinets, but the best bit is the central staircase swirling down past the leather goods to the men's and women's collections in the basement. Accessories, including shoes: Via della Spiga 18. Menswear: Via Montenapoleone 6. Womenswear: Via Montenapoleone 8.

Trussardi Piazza Scala 5 ⓦ trussardi.com; ⓜ Duomo; map p.63. A spacious boutique spread across three floors. The uber-chic *Trussardi Alla Scala Café* occupies the ground floor, with a huge video-wall to keep you entertained while you sip your coffee. On the floor above the soft leather bags and crisp home lines is the formal but well-priced restaurant, and one floor higher still is a gallery space that's worth checking out for contemporary art and fashion exhibitions.

FACTORY STORES

There's a selection of outlets or factory stores in and around Milan for designer labels at affordable prices. A couple of these are centrally located.

D-Magazine Via Manzoni 44 ⓦ dmagazine.it; ⓜ montenapoleone; map p.63. Rails of different designer labels in the heart of the golden quadrangle.

Diffusione Tessile Galleria San Carlo 6 ⓦ diffusione tessile.it; ⓜ San Babila; map p.63. Good discounts on the range of Max Mara brands operating under the name of DTIntrend.

Il Salvagente Via F Bronzetti 16, 15min east of San Babila by bus ⓦ salvagentemilano.it; bus 54 or 61; map pp.58–59. The grande dame of Milan's outlet stores where, with a little rummaging, you can bag a designer label for around a third of its original price.

1

DESIGN AND FURNITURE

To pick up Gio Ponti, Castiglione, or Alessi designer furniture, make for the broad streets off San Babila: Corso Europa, Via Durini, Corso Venezia and Corso Monforte are home to the furniture and lighting showrooms that made Milan the design capital of the world in the 1950s.

CONCEPT STORES

For a relaxed, but very Milanese, shopping experience, try a concept store that sells a bit of everything designer.

10 Corso Como Corso Como 10 ⓦ 10corsocomo.com; Ⓜ Moscova or Garibaldi FS; map pp.58–59. A Milan institution selling a small range of carefully selected design and fashion items, as well as books and music, with a café and art gallery, too. Outlet store round the corner at Via Tazzoli 3.

High Tech Piazza XXV Aprile 12 ⓦ cargomilano.it; Ⓜ Moscova or Garibaldi FS; map pp.58–59. A warren of designer, imitation and global knick-knacks and furniture; perfect for present buying.

La Rinascente Piazza Duomo 14 ⓦ rinascente.it; Ⓜ Duomo; map p.63. The basement of this department store offers an accessible array of the best design pieces from around the world with an emphasis on Italian creations.

Rossana Orlandi Via Matteo Bandello 14-16 ⓦ rossanaorlandi.com; Ⓜ S.Ambrogio; map p.63. A converted tie factory housing a seductive mix of new designer and vintage furniture and accessories, as well as a contemporary art gallery.

BRAND STORES

Alessi Via Manzoni 14 ⓦ alessi.com; Ⓜ Montenapoleone; map p.63. A whole store full of Alessi's colourful and entertaining homewares.

Artemide Corso Monforte 19 ⓦ artemide.com; Ⓜ San Babila; map p.63. This company, largely responsible for Italy's international reputation for lighting design, has a showroom exhibiting all their lines, from the classics such as De Lucchi's Tolomeo and Richard Sapper's Tizio, to the season's latest.

B&B Italia Via Durini 14 ⓦ bebitalia.it; Ⓜ San Babila; map p.63. International name that specializes in stylish contemporary furniture by big names in Italian modern design.

Cassina Via Durini 16 ⓦ cassina.it; Ⓜ San Babila; map p.63. The showroom of this legendary Milanese company, which worked with all the greats in Italian design in the 1950s, is always worth a visit for both new designs and

their range of twentieth-century design classics including Eames, De Stijl and Rennie Mackintosh chairs.

De Padova Corso Venezia 14 ⓦ depadova.it; Ⓜ San Babila; map p.63. Two floors of elegant own-brand furniture and homeware creatively displayed in a stylish showroom. Their collections are designed by big names including Vico Magestretti and Patricia Urquiola.

Driade Via Manzoni 30 ⓦ driade.com; Ⓜ Monte napoleone; map p.63. A wonderful multi-brand store with their own designs, as well as work by designers like Ron Arad and Philippe Starck. The collection includes furniture, tableware, kitchen and bathroom accessories, but the real treat here is the showroom housed in an elegant nineteenth-century *palazzo*.

FOOD AND DRINK

Cotti Via Solferino 42 ⓦ enotecacotti.it; Ⓜ Moscova; map pp.58–59. A treasure-trove of wines and liqueurs from across the country is accompanied by an array of gourmet treats – both sweet and savoury.

Il Salumaio Via Santo Spirito 10 & Via Gesù 5 ⓦ ilsalumaiodimontenapoleone.it; Ⓜ Montenapoleone; map p.63. The selection of savoury delicacies and handmade pasta are to die for in this upmarket delicatessen, with a smart restaurant and tables outside in the courtyard.

Peck Via Spadari 9 ⓦ peck.it; Ⓜ Duomo; map p.63. Three floors of top-priced Italian delicacies, from olive oil and home-made chocolate to mouth-watering prosciutto, cheeses, and an impressive wine cellar. There's also a café on the first floor and a swish cocktail bar and restaurant round the corner at Via Cantù 3.

MARKETS

Fiera di Sinigaglia Via Valenza ⓦ fieradisinigaglia.it; Ⓜ P.Genova; map p.74. This hugely popular flea market by the Naviglio Grande is also Milan's oldest, attracting custom since the 1800s. Here you will find anything and everything from coins to designer-knitwear seconds. Sat 8am–6pm.

Mercatino d'Antiquariato di Brera Via Fiori Chiari; Ⓜ Lanza; map p.63. This upbeat market in the picturesque district of Brera displays bric-a-brac and antiques, including porcelain, blown glass, paintings and jewellery. Every third Sun of the month 9am–6pm, except Aug.

Mercato Comunale Piazza Wagner; Ⓜ Wagner; map p.63. The city's main fresh-food market has had a makeover and is now, once again, the place to head for a glorious array of picnic supplies or take-home food gifts. Closed Sun & Mon pm.

SPORT

Really there's just one spectator sport that you'd come to Milan for and that's **football**. Home to two of the country's top teams, San Siro stadium is a big draw for anyone even vaguely interested in the beautiful game. If you want to work off some of those pasta calories while you're in town, your best bets are **jogging**, cycling or swimming. Although the city centre's green spaces are not vast, the Parco Sempione or a couple of laps of the Giardini Pubblici should suffice for an early-morning run. **Cycling** is a very popular way of getting around the city (see p.83). There are a couple of conveniently located indoor **swimming pools**, and in summer the open-air pools offer a way of keeping cool and doing some exercise at the same time.

FOOTBALL

Milan has two rival football teams – Inter Milan and AC Milan – which share the G. Meazza or San Siro stadium, playing on alternate Sundays. In 1899 AC (*Associazione Calcio* or "Football Association") Milan was founded by players from the Milan Cricket and Football Club. Eight years later, a splinter group broke away to form Inter in reaction to a ruling banning foreigners playing in the championships. Inter – or the Internationals – were traditionally supported by the middle classes, while AC Milan, with its socialist red stripe, claimed the loyalty of the city's working class. This distinction was blown apart in the mid-1980s when the ardent capitalist Silvio Berlusconi bought the ailing AC and revived its fortunes, leaving many an AC fan with a moral quandary. Recent years have seen the two clubs vying for top positions in *Serie A* and their twice-yearly derbies are a highlight of the city's calendar and well worth experiencing live.

Tours There are hourly guided tours around the G. Meazza stadium at Via Piccolomini 5 (museum daily 9.30am–6pm; €7; tours €17 including museum entry; ☎ 02 404 2432, ⓦ sansirotour.com; Ⓜ Lotto, then a longish walk). Match tickets can be bought here.

Tickets Other ticket outlets are New Milan Point, in Piazza San Fedele 2 (☎ 02 4548 6224) for AC Milan games (ⓦ acmilan.it); and for Inter games (ⓦ inter.it) at Ricordi

Media Stores in the Feltrinelli bookstore at Via Ugo Foscolo 3 by the Gallerie Vittorio Emanuele II (Mon–Thurs 9.30am–9.30pm, Fri & Sat 9.30am–10pm, Sun 10am–8pm; ☎ 02 7200 7031).

SWIMMING

In the wintertime there are three main options for a swim: the Olympic-sized Piscina Cozzi (☎ 02 659 9703; Ⓜ Repubblica/Pta Venezia), at Viale Tunisia 35, near to the Stazione Centrale; Piscina Solari (☎ 02 469 5278; Ⓜ S Agostino), at Via Montevideo 20, to the south of the city; and the Lido di Milano (☎ 02 392 791 or ☎ 02 66 100; Ⓜ Lotto), which has both indoor and open-air pools, out to the west at Piazzale Lotto 15.

Open-air pools From June to mid-September, however, swimming becomes less exercise and more a way of cooling down. The 1930s-built neighbourhood open-air pools with their sunbathing areas, playgrounds and late-night bars, can get very crowded, especially during weekends and late afternoon, but are a great place to wash away the muggy heat of the Milanese summer. Among the nicest are Argelati, at Via Segantini 6, by the Navigli (☎ 02 5810 0012; Ⓜ Pta Genova) and Romano in Città Studi, at Via Ampère 20 (☎ 02 7060 0224; Ⓜ Piola). Prices are €5 during the week and €5.50 at weekends; for more information see ⓦ milanosport.it.

DIRECTORY

Consulates Australia, Via Borgogna 2 ☎ 02 7767 4200, ⓦ italy.embassy.gov.au; Canada, Piazza Cavour 3 ☎ 02 6269 4238, ⓦ voyage.gc.ca; Ireland, Piazza San Pietro in Gessate 2 ☎ 02 5518 7569, ⓦ ambasciata-irlanda .it; New Zealand, Via Terraggio, 17, ☎ 02 7217 0001, ⓦ nzembassy.com/italy; South Africa, Vicolo San Giovanni sul Muro 4 ☎ 02 885 8581, ⓦ sudafrica.it; UK, Via San Paolo 7 ☎ 02 723 001, ⓦ ukinitaly.fco.gov.uk/en; US, Via Principe Amedeo 2/10 ☎ 02 290 351, ⓦ milan .usconsulate.gov.

Doctors English-speaking doctors are available at the private International Health Center (Galleria Strasburgo 3; ☎ 02 7634 0720, ⓦ ihc.it; Ⓜ San Babila) and the Centro Medico Visconti di Modrone (Via Visconti di Modrone 7; ☎ 02 783 241, ⓦ cmvm.com).

Exchange Banks usually offer the best rates, but out of normal banking hours you can change money and travellers' cheques at the Stazione Centrale office (daily 7.45am–10.15pm). The airports all have exchange facilities.

Hospital There is a 24hr casualty service at the Ospedale

Maggiore Policlinico, Via Francesco Sforza 33 (☎ 02 55 03), a short walk from Piazza Duomo. Emergency ☎ 118.

Internet There are internet cafés dotted throughout town, especially around Duomo, generally charging around €2/hr.

Left luggage Stazione Centrale (daily 6am–11pm; €6/5hr, then small increments per hour). Stazione Nord (Cadorna) has no left luggage service.

Pharmacy The Stazione Centrale (☎ 02 669 0735), which has English-speaking assistants, and Carlo Erba, on Piazza Duomo (☎ 02 8646 4832); both have 24hr services. Rotas are published in *Corriere della Sera*, and are usually posted on *farmacia* doors.

Police ☎ 113. Head office at Via Fatebenefratelli 11 (☎ 02 62 261), near the Pinacoteca di Brera.

Post office Via Cordusio 4, off Piazza Cordusio – not the building marked "Poste", but around the corner (Mon–Fri 8am–7pm, Sat 8.30am–noon). Unless you have a parcel to send, it's much easier and quicker to buy stamps from the many *tabacchini* around the city.

Pavia

Fifty-five kilometres south of Milan and the furthest west of the string of historic towns that spread across the Lombardy plain, **Pavia** is close enough to Milan to be seen on a day-trip, but still retains a clear identity of its own. A comfortable provincial town with an illustrious history, it boasts one of the masterpieces of Italian architecture in the nearby Carthusian monastery, the **Certosa di Pavia**.

Pavia was founded on an easily defendable stretch of land alongside the confluence of the Po and Ticino rivers and was always an important staging post en route to the Alps and beyond. Medieval Pavia was known as the city of a hundred towers, and although only a handful remain – one of the best collapsed in 1989 – the medieval aspect is still strong, with numerous Romanesque and Gothic churches tucked away in a web of narrow streets and cobbled squares. The town is not, however, stranded in the past – its ancient university continues to thrive, ensuring an animated street life and reasonably lively night-time scene.

Brief history

Pavia reached its zenith in the Dark Ages when it was capital of the Kingdom of the Lombards. After their downfall it remained a centre of power, and the succession of emperors – including Charlemagne in 774 and Frederick Barbarossa in 1155 – who ruled northern Italy continued to come to the town to receive the Lombards' traditional iron crown. This all came to an end in the fourteenth century when Pavia was handed over to the Visconti and became a satellite of Milan. The Visconti, and later the Sforza, did, however, found the university and provide the town with its prime attraction – the nearby Certosa di Pavia. In 1525, the Battle of Pavia, just north of the city, put an end to French domination of the territory (once the Sforza dynasty had died out, the French had taken over) and resulted in the following two hundred years of Spanish rule over Milan and Pavia.

Just wandering around town is the nicest way to spend time here: pick any side street and you're almost bound to stumble on something of interest – a lofty medieval tower, a pretty Romanesque or Gothic church, or just a silent, sleepy piazza. Getting lost is difficult as the town is still based around its Roman axes of the *decumanus* running east–west: Corso Cavour, which becomes Corso Mazzini; and the *cardo* running north–south: Strada Nuova. The River Ticino borders the south of the city centre.

Piazza della Vittoria and the Duomo

The large cobbled rectangle of **Piazza della Vittoria**, lined with bars, *gelaterie* and restaurants, stands in the centre of the old town. At the square's southern end, the Broletto, medieval Pavia's town hall, abuts the rear of the rambling and unwieldy **Duomo**. An early Renaissance sprawl of protruding curves and jutting angles designed by Rocchi and Amadeo, possibly with contributions from Bramante and da Vinci, the cathedral is best known for its huge nineteenth-century cupola, which dominates the skyline of the city. The facade was only added in 1933. Beside the west front of the Duomo, facing Piazza del Duomo, are the remnants of the eleventh-century Torre Civica, a campanile that collapsed without warning in March 1989, killing four people.

San Teodoro

Piazza San Teodoro • Daily 8.30am–noon & 3am–6.30pm, Sun opens at 9am • Free

Southwest of the piazza, the narrow, cobbled streets lead to the neighbourhood church of **San Teodoro**. The twelfth-century basilica was clumsily restored at the

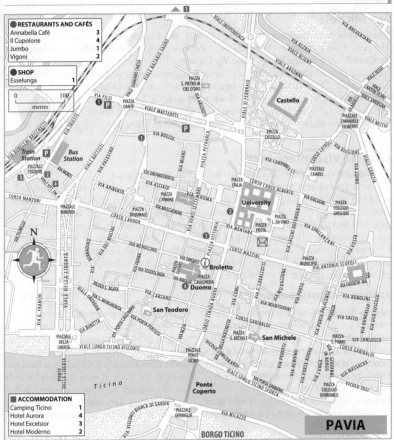

RESTAURANTS AND CAFÉS
Annabella Café   3
Il Cupolone   4
Jumbo   1
Vigoni   2

SHOP
Esselunga   1

ACCOMMODATION
Camping Ticino   1
Hotel Aurora   4
Hotel Excelsior   3
Hotel Moderno   2

end of the nineteenth century, though it's not without charm. The main reason for visiting is to see the fresco on the left-hand side of the nave near the entrance: the *View of Pavia* by Bernardino Lanazani illustrates the city in 1522 with its hundreds of civic towers built by Pavia's noble families in order to show their superiority over their rivals. In the nineteenth century there were still eighty left, but now only three remain.

Ponte Coperto and Borgo Ticino

The **Ponte Coperto**, the covered bridge, crosses the Ticino just to the south of the basilica. The current bridge was rebuilt slightly downriver in the 1940s after the medieval one was bombed; you can still see remnants of the old one jutting out into the water.

The bridge leads over to the **Borgo Ticino**, the riverside neighbourhood traditionally inhabited by fishermen and *raniere* (frog catchers); these days there are several restaurants popular with locals. Note the marks on the walls showing the flood levels over the last century. An attractive open park runs along the shore of both banks west of the bridge, a popular sunbathing and picnic spot in summer.

1

San Michele

Piazza San Michele • Mon 8.30am–noon & 2.30–7pm, Tues–Sat 8.30am–7pm, Sun 9am–8pm • ⓦ sanmichelepavia.it

The best of the town's churches is the beautiful Romanesque **San Michele**, a five-minute walk northeast from the bridge along Via Capsoni. This is where the kings of Northern Italy were crowned and Federico I, or Barbarossa, came to receive the title here in 1155. The friezes and capitals on its broad sandstone facade are carved into a menagerie of snake-tailed fish, griffins, dragons and other beasts, some locked in a struggle with humans, representing the fight between good and evil. Sadly, the sandstone is being worn away despite restoration work in the 1960s and some of the figures are being lost for good.

Castello Visconteo

Viale XI Febbraio 35 • Tues–Sun 10am–1pm & 2–6pm • €6 • ☎ 03 823 3853 • ⓦ museicivici.pavia.it

The austere-looking **Castello Visconteo**, initiated by Galeazzo II Visconti in 1360 and added to by the Sforza, originally housed luxurious apartments, the majority of which were in the wing of the quadrangle destroyed by the French in 1527. The castle was used as a barracks until 1921, and although it's been restored, the rooms that remain are unmemorable. The well-organized **Museo Civico** inside includes an art gallery with a handful of Venetian paintings, an archeology collection with Roman jewellery, pottery and glassware, and a museum of sculpture displaying architectural fragments, mosaics and sculptures rescued from the town's demolished churches.

ARRIVAL AND INFORMATION

PAVIA

By train There are regional trains that connect Milan to Pavia, although the S13 train line operated by Trenord is the most efficient way of travelling here. It connects a number of stations, including Milan Porta Garibaldi, Milan Repubblica and Milan Porta Venezia to Pavia (every 30min; 45min). The same train also connects the Certosa di Pavia to Pavia (every 30min; 8min).

By bus Bus services from Milan Famagosta metro station drop you at the bus station round the corner from the train station in Pavia, on the western edge of the town centre. Destinations Certosa (every 30min; 10min); Milan Famagosta (every 30min; 37min); Linate airport (8 daily; 1hr).

Tourist office In the Palazzo del Broletto, at Piazza della Vittoria in the centre of town (March–Oct Mon–Fri 9am–1pm & 2–5pm, Sat & Sun 10am–1pm & 2–6pm; Nov–Feb Mon–Fri 9am–1pm & 2–5pm, Sat & Sun 9am–1pm ☎ 0382 079 943, ⓦ paviaturismo.it).

ACCOMMODATION

Pavia's hotels are a rather bland mix of business hotels and standard three-stars that tend to take the overspill from Milan's commercial fairs, so finding somewhere appealing to stay can be more difficult than you might imagine. Most of the options listed here are near the station.

Camping Ticino Via Mascherpa 10/16 ☎ 0382 527 094, ⓦ campingticino.it. This campsite is 3km northwest of town – take bus 4 from the train station. The site is set in lovely countryside and has a pool and wooden chalets sleeping two for rent (€45). April–Sept. Camping **€4**

Hotel Aurora Viale Vittorio Emanuele II 25 ☎ 0382 23 664, ⓦ hotel-aurora.eu. Probably the best hotel of the bunch. Clean and comfortable rooms have chocolate-coloured decor and modern amenities. Breakfast is an extra €6. **€105**

Hotel Excelsior Piazzale Stazione 25 ☎ 0382 28 596, ⓦ excelsiorpavia.com. This moderate three-star hotel with fairly dark interiors offers spacious a/c rooms just across the road from the train station. **€100**

Hotel Moderno Viale Vittorio Emanuele 41 ☎ 0382 303 401, ⓦ hotelmoderno.it. This four-star hotel with friendly staff offers comfortable rooms, a small health centre with a steam room and jacuzzi, and complimentary bicycles. **€180**

EATING AND DRINKING

Round the corner from the bus station on Viale Cesare Battisti 41, a branch of the supermarket Esselunga is a handy place to put together the ingredients for a riverside picnic.

Annabella Café Corso Strada Nuova 86 ☎ 03 8253 9592, ⓦ annabellacafe.com. Pavia's historical *Al Demetrio* *Café*, established in 1758, has had a complete revamp and is now a popular café that morphs into a cocktail bar in the evenings. It has a decent lunch menu, too, with mains at €10. Happy hour 6.30–10pm. Daily 7.30pm–2am.

Il Cupolone Via Cardinal Riboldi 2 ☎ 03 8230 3519, ⓦ hostariailcupolone.it. Pavia's oldest restaurant serves up seasonal regional food in a traditional atmosphere, close to the cathedral. Leave room for the home-made desserts. Wed–Mon noon–3pm & 7–10.30pm; Mon dinner only.

Jumbo Via Lanfranco 14/12 ☎ 03 822 8617. An informal restaurant and café attracting students with tasty sandwiches and burgers that come in all sizes, including double, triple, quadruple and "massive jumbo". Burgers from €5. Daily 11am–3pm & 7pm–midnight.

Vigoni Corso Strada Nuova 110 ☎ 0382 22 103, ⓦ tortavigoni.it. This historic *pasticceria* is where Italy's much loved *torta paradiso* (a delicate sponge cake made with lemon zest and butter, then sprinkled with icing sugar) was allegedly invented in 1878. Mon–Sat 8am–7.30pm, Sun 8am–1pm & 3–7.30pm.

Certosa di Pavia

10km north of Pavia • Tues–Sun: Nov–Feb 9–11.30am & 2.30–4.30pm; Oct & March 9–11.30am & 2.30–5pm; April & Sept 9–11.30am & 2.30–5.30pm; May–Aug 9–11.30am & 2.30–6pm • Free

The **Certosa di Pavia** (Charterhouse of Pavia) is one of the most extravagant monasteries in Europe, commissioned by the Duke of Milan, Gian Galeazzo Visconti, in 1396 as the family mausoleum. Visconti intended the church here to resemble Milan's late-Gothic cathedral and the same architects and craftsmen worked on the building throughout its construction. It took a century to build, and by the time it was finished, tastes had changed – and the Visconti had been replaced by the Sforza. As a work of art, the monastery is one of the most important testimonies to the transformation from late-Gothic to Renaissance and Mannerist styles, but it also affords a fascinating insight into the lives and beliefs of the Carthusian monks. After the suppression of Catholicism in the latter half of the eighteenth century came the confiscation of ecclesiastical lands by the new secular state of Italy in 1881. It was not until 1968 that a handful of Cistercian monks moved back into the complex and gradually restored it.

You can see the church unaccompanied, but to visit the rest of the monastery, you need to join a **guided tour** of just under an hour (free but contributions welcomed), led by one of the monks released from the strict vow of silence. Tours run regularly – basically when enough people have gathered. They're in Italian, but well worth doing – even if you don't understand a word – as it allows you to visit the best parts of the monastery complex.

The church

The monastery lies at the end of a tree-lined avenue, part of a former Visconti hunting range that stretched all the way from Pavia's *castello*. Encircled by a high wall, the complex is entered through a central gateway bearing a motif that recurs throughout the monastery – "GRA-CAR" or "Gratiarum Carthusiae", a reference to the fact that the Carthusian monastery is dedicated to Santa Maria delle Grazie, who appears in numerous works of art in the church. Beyond the gateway is a gracious courtyard, with the seventeenth-century Ducal Palace on the right-hand side and outbuildings along the left. Rising up before you is the fantastical **facade** of the church, festooned with inlaid marble, twisted columns, statues and friezes. Despite more than a century's work by leading architects, the facade remains unfinished: the tympanum was never added, giving the church its stocky, truncated look.

The Milanese architect Guiniforte Solari was the first to work on the facade, starting in 1472 with the medallions of emperors and figures from antiquity around the base. The following layers of reliefs and statues of prophets and saints were created by the Mantegazza brothers, while the richest decorations – in particular the Bible scenes round the two windows – are attributed to Amadeo, who included a self-portrait in the bottom left-hand corner holding a pair of architect's compasses. Lombardo is responsible for the decoration in the upper, slightly simpler, layers.

1

The interior

Inside, the Gothic design of the **church** was a deliberate reference to Milan's Duomo, but it has a lighter, more joyous feel, with its painted ceiling, and light streaming in through the one hundred windows high up in the walls. Halfway down the right-hand aisle, a trompe l'oeil of a Carthusian monk peeping through a window seems to watch visitors as they move around the church. The elaborate seventeenth-century gates to the transept and highly decorated altar, at the far end, are opened when a tour is about to start.

The sculptural highlights of the church lie in the two wings of the transept. In the centre of the north transept lies the stone **funerary monument** of the greatest of the dukes of Milan, Ludovico il Moro, and his wife Beatrice d'Este, neither of whom are actually buried here. Ludovico commissioned the piece for the church of Santa Maria delle Grazie in Milan, where Beatrice is still buried, but it was moved here in 1564, forty years after his death; Ludovico himself is buried in France, where he died as a prisoner. The exquisite detail of the statue, by another of the ubiquitous Solari clan – Gian Cristoforo – is an important document of sixteenth-century fashions with its tasselled latticework dress and glam-rock platform shoes. Many of the church's artworks are by Bergognone, including the fresco behind the funerary monument of the *Crowning of the Virgin* flanked by Francesco Sforza and his son, Ludovico il Moro. The south transept contains the magnificent **mausoleum** of the founder of the monastery, Gian Galeazzo Visconti, by Cristoforo Romano, including a carving of Gian Galeazzo presenting a model of the Certosa to the Virgin. Both he and his wife, Isabella di Valois, are buried here.

The monastery

Opposite the mausoleum is the door to the delightful **small cloister**, a reminder that the monastery was built for the contemplative Carthusian order rather than simply as a vehicle for wealthy families to buy their salvation. With fine terracotta decoration and a charming geometric garden, this was where monks shared the communal part of their lives, meeting here to pace the courtyard during their weekly ration of talking time. The reliefs around the pleasing terracotta and marble washing area on the far side are early works by Amadeo, showing Christ washing the feet of a leper, and were used by the monks to perform ablutions before entering the nearby **refectory**. Here the monks would eat together on Sundays and holy days and remain in silence while being read Bible passages from the pulpit, accessed via a staircase hidden in the wooden panelling in the middle of the room. The dining room is divided by a blind wall, which allowed the monastery to feed visiting pilgrims and lay agricultural workers without compromising the rules of their closed order. The room was used as the main church of the complex for the first hundred years of existence while the church was completed, and a crude *Madonna and Child* fresco remains on the far wall.

Leading off the side of the small cloister, the breathtaking **great cloister** was the centre of the monks' lives. Lining three sides of the huge green courtyard are the monks' individual houses, each consisting of two rooms, a chapel, a garden and a loggia, with a bedroom above. The hatches to the side of the entrances were for food to be passed through to the monks without any communication.

The final call is the Certosa **shop**, stocked with honey, chocolate, souvenirs and the famous Chartreuse liqueur.

ARRIVAL AND DEPARTURE	CERTOSA DI PAVIA

By train Arriving by train, turn left out of the station and walk around the Certosa walls until you reach the entrance – about a 15min walk. There are regional trains that connect Milan to the Certosa di Pavia although the S13 train line operated by Trenord is the most efficient way of travelling here. It connects a number of stations, including Milan Porta Garibaldi, Milan Repubblica and Milan Porta Venezia to the Certosa di Pavia (every 30min; 37min). The same train also connects the Certosa di Pavia to Pavia (every 30min; 8min).

By bus Buses drop you a 15min walk from the Certosa.

Destinations Pavia (every 30min; 10min); Milan Famagosta (every 30min; 27min).

EATING AND DRINKING

Locanda Vecchia Pavia al Molino Via al Monumento 5 ☎0382 925 894, ⓦvecchiapaviaalmulino.it. Located in the old monastery mill, this pleasant formal restaurant set in beautiful grounds serves traditional Italian cuisine. The menu includes dishes invented by monks – such as *risotto alla certosina* (risotto with frogs, freshwater shrimps, peas and sturgeon; €18). Tues–Sun 12.15–2.15pm & 8–10.30pm; April–Oct closed Tues lunch; Nov–March closed Sun dinner.

Lake Orta

CROSSING LAKE ORTA BY MOTORBOAT

Lake Orta

The westernmost of the major Italian lakes, lying wholly within Piemonte, Lake Orta (Lago d'Orta) appears an afterthought, a little croissant-shaped tarn that is closer to the Matterhorn than Milan. Perhaps that's why it is relatively quiet, seeing a fraction of the numbers who pile into Stresa nearby. To find it, you have to make a special journey; Orta is not somewhere you stumble across. Base yourself here for a refreshingly low-key take on an Italian Lakes holiday – and for the chance to appreciate the romance of Orta San Giulio village after dark.

Dubbed *Lacus Cusius* by the Romans, after the local Usii tribe – and still referred to as **Cusio** – Orta is unique among the subalpine lakes for having no outflow in the south. Only the small Nigoglia stream leaves the lake, and it flows northwards through the town of Omegna, giving the stubborn Omegnesi their motto: "The Nigoglia flows uphill, and we'll do whatever we please!"

Yet Omegna and most of the other lakeside towns are not especially attractive. Aside from the beauty of the lake itself, with its deep blue waters and green fringe of mountains, the main reason to come this way is for **Orta San Giulio**, the single most captivating medieval village on this – or, perhaps, any – Italian lake. Part of the allure is the **Isola San Giulio** just offshore, once a nest of dragons, now adorned with a monastery and eleventh-century church. The romance of the place is unforgettable, with narrow, cobbled lanes running through the town, and the towers and facades of the island suspended in the foreground of a lake-and-mountain view that constantly changes in the clear, shifting sunlight.

Orta San Giulio

ORTA SAN GIULIO is the cat's whiskers. It has everything, this medieval village, well kept but largely unrenovated. Narrow, cobbled streets snake between tall, pastel-washed *palazzi* with elaborate wrought-iron balconies. Life centres on the waterfront **Piazza Motta**, which looks directly across at Orta's prime attraction – the **Isola San Giulio**. This wooded islet, 400m offshore, shelters a closed community of nuns, their convent built around a beautiful medieval church. The harmonious ensemble of town, piazza and island is pure theatre, especially at night, when floodlights on the island pick out an arch here, a loggia there, rising to a pinnacle of graceful architecture. Charm isn't the half of it: Orta is bewitching.

The town is, inevitably, popular, although – summer Sundays apart, when approach roads can see heavy traffic – it's rarely crowded. Orta accommodates its visitors with grace and good humour, and retains a small town's easy approach to life, best sampled midweek or out of season. Note, though, that many businesses close in January.

Piazza Motta

The pace of life in Orta is slow, with everything revolving around the main square, **Piazza Motta**, dubbed the *salotto*, or drawing-room – a broad, deep piazza ringed

Boats on Lake Orta p.107   **A lakeside walk around Orta San Giulio** p.109

ORTA SAN GIULIO

Highlights

❶ Orta San Giulio Just about the most romantic Italian Lakes village you could ever hope to find. **See p.104**

❷ Piazza Motta Orta San Giulio's picture-perfect lakefront square is ringed by frescoed facades and framed with chestnut trees. **See p.104**

❸ Sacro Monte di San Francesco Head up to the forested slopes above Orta San Giulio for pleasant walks and airy views. **See p.106**

❹ Isola San Giulio Tiny lake island sporting an ancient church and atmospheric footpath. **See p.106**

❺ Taking to the water However you manage it, a voyage on tiny Lake Orta is a splendid way to appreciate the natural beauty of the surroundings. **See p.107**

❻ Pella Pleasant little lakeside village opposite Orta San Giulio which repays gentle exploration. **See p.111**

❼ Alessi shop, Crusinallo Outlet store for the legendary Alessi brand of cookware, hidden away at the head of Lake Orta. **See p.111**

HIGHLIGHTS ARE MARKED ON THE MAP ON P.106

around on three sides by elegant facades and open on the fourth, with the lake and island visible behind a screen of horse-chestnut trees. Orta's Wednesday **market** has been held here since 1228. *Gelaterie*, terrace cafés and restaurants share space under the arcades with art galleries, designer boutiques and fancy delis. On the north side is the **Palazzo della Comunità**, or **Palazzotto**, Orta's titchy town hall, built in 1582 and supported on a portico, with faded frescoes of crests and sundials.

Via Olina

From Piazza Motta, the main street – cobbled, and barely two or three metres wide – heads northwards as **Via Olina**, lined with tall sixteenth- and seventeenth-century buildings. Cafés, restaurants and shops pack the street at ground level; above are many graceful wrought-iron balconies. Orta's oldest street is the quieter **Via Bersani**, running parallel to Via Olina slightly higher up; it is accessed from Piazza Motta by the **Salita della Motta**, a broad, stepped lane that climbs steeply east towards the fifteenth-century church of **Santa Maria Assunta**, renovated in Baroque style and dramatically floodlit at night.

Sacro Monte di San Francesco

Above Orta San Giulio, reached on foot from the town's church of Santa Maria Assunta or from its own signposted parking area above the Via Panoramica, is the **Sacro Monte di San Francesco**, a tight little skein of 21 chapels that winds around the hilltop, built from 1590 to 1785. Each chapel holds a tableau of painted terracotta statues acting out a scene from the life of St Francis of Assisi. Artistry takes second place to didactic clarity. The chapels make up a devotional route still followed by pilgrims, though just as many visitors come simply to picnic, admire the views of the lake and inhale the pine-scented air.

LAKE ORTA

Isola San Giulio

The **Isola San Giulio**, a tiny, car-free island just offshore, is dominated by a stern, white convent and the more graceful tower of a medieval basilica. According to legend, the island was the realm of dragons and serpents until 390 AD, when Julius, a Christian from Greece, arrived. He asked to be rowed to the island, but no boatman brave enough came forward. Julius crossed alone, using his staff as a rudder and his cloak as a sail, banished the monsters, founded a sanctuary and thus earned himself a sainthood. He died in 392, and was laid to rest in the church he'd built. In its place now stands a tenth- and

HIGHLIGHTS

1. Orta San Giulio
2. Piazza Motta
3. Sacro Monte di San Francesco
4. Isola San Giulio
5. Taking to the water
6. Pella
7. Alessi shop, Crusinallo

BOATS ON LAKE ORTA

Passenger **boats** crisscross Lake Orta, though the main focus of interest is the five-minute voyage between Orta San Giulio and the Isola San Giulio. At Orta San Giulio's landing-stage on Piazza Motta, there's no differentiation between the "official" boats of Navigazione Lago d'Orta (☎ 345 517 0005, ⓦ navigazionelagodorta.it), which run frequently at weekends but sporadically on weekdays (€3.15 return), and the **motorboats** operated by a consortium of local owners, which scoot across more or less on demand (about €4.50 return; ☎ 333 605 0288, ⓦ motoscafisti.com). You can also charter your own motorboat (around €55/30min) or **rent a rowingboat** (roughly €14/hr for two people).

Elsewhere, the "official" boats run continuously on a circuit around the central part of the lake, crossing from Orta to the island, then to Pella and one or two of its neighbours, before returning to Orta; this could comprise a nice little half-hour **sightseeing tour** (€4.90; ticket valid all day). A longer cruise (2hr 30min) heads north once a day to **Omegna** (€7.35 return), giving an hour or so there before returning to Orta. Extra services run on Thursdays, Omegna's market day. A one-day pass for the whole lake costs €8.90.

"Official" boats run daily in **summer** (late March to mid-Oct) and in **winter** on Sundays only (Sat & Sun in late Oct) or not at all (Dec–Feb). The motorboat captains waiting by the quay at Orta will put together any kind of lake tour on request.

eleventh-century successor, with a fine Romanesque bell tower that is easily visible from the mainland.

All boats dock at the island's southern point, beside the **Basilica di San Giulio**. From the church, the only **street** – a picturesque cobbled lane – leads around the island; it's a twenty-minute walk, past the various buildings which make up the Benedictine convent, home to more than sixty nuns. In an attempt to preserve the tranquillity of the island, the sisters have put up double-sided signs in four languages at regular intervals along the walking route; if you walk clockwise, the path is the **Street of Meditation**; anticlockwise, it is the **Street of Silence**. Needless to say, the rather Buddhic contemplations on each sign are ignored by virtually everyone. Partway round is a pleasant little café-restaurant.

Note that you'll be refused admission to the church if you're wearing shorts or a short skirt. The municipality (on request from the scandalized nuns) has banned swimming at the island's landing-stage.

Basilica di San Giulio

Isola San Giulio • April–Sept Mon noon–6pm, Tues–Sun 9.30am–6pm; Oct–March Mon 2–5pm, Tues–Sun 9.30am–noon & 2–5pm • Free

For a small church, the basilica has an impressively lofty interior. Much of the decoration, including the vaulting, dates from a Baroque eighteenth-century refit, but frescoes from as early as the fourteenth century survive all round the walls, many of them naïve in design but remarkably well preserved. The fine **pulpit**, made in the early twelfth century from dark stone quarried nearby at Oira, is covered in symbols of the four evangelists and images of good winning over evil; note the crocodile locked in battle with the phoenix. The saint's remains can be viewed in the crypt.

ARRIVAL AND DEPARTURE   **ORTA SAN GIULIO**

By train Orta-Miasino train station is served by 6–8 trains a day on the obscure branch line between Novara (40min) and Domodossola (1hr 5min). If you're coming from Milano Centrale, change at Novara. Timetables for this part of Piemonte are downloadable at ⓦ trenitalia.com. The station is in the hills around 3km east of Orta San Giulio. Turn left out of the station onto the main road and walk

downhill for about twenty minutes to reach the town.

By bus Three buses a day arrive from Stresa (1hr) and Baveno (50min), terminating at Piazzale Prarondo. Timetables for the areas of Piemonte covered in this chapter are at ⓦ vcoinbus.it.

By car Orta's town centre is closed to traffic. From the roundabout on the main lakeside road, beside the

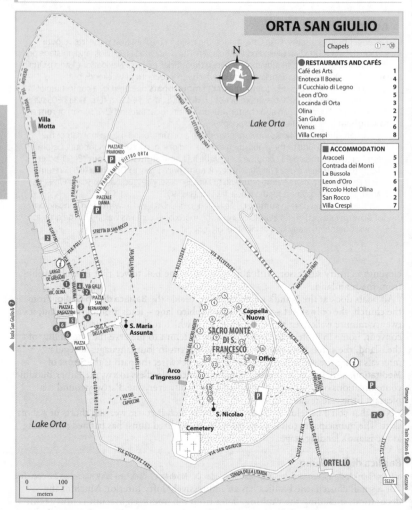

ORTA SAN GIULIO

Chapels	① — ~②⓪

● **RESTAURANTS AND CAFÉS**	
Café des Arts	1
Enoteca Il Boeuc	4
Il Cucchiaio di Legno	9
Leon d'Oro	5
Locanda di Orta	3
Olina	2
San Giulio	7
Venus	6
Villa Crespi	8

■ **ACCOMMODATION**	
Aracoeli	5
Contrada dei Monti	3
La Bussola	1
Leon d'Oro	6
Piccolo Hotel Olina	4
San Rocco	2
Villa Crespi	7

Oriental-style *Villa Crespi* hotel, the Via Panoramica runs past the tourist office and a left turn for the Sacro Monte; 700m further are big parking areas and subterranean garages around Piazzale Prarondo and Piazzale Diania, on the hillside above Orta. This is as far as you're allowed to drive – from here pick any footpath heading downhill to find yourself after a few minutes in the old quarter. The parking on titchy Piazza San Bernardino, 600m past the big car parks, is residents-only.

GETTING AROUND

By car Cameras record the number plate of every vehicle driving in the historic centre. You're allowed to drive in if you're unloading at a hotel, but should always advise reception staff in advance. Bear in mind the streets are extremely narrow; anything much bigger than a Fiat Punto won't get through. Most hotels will arrange pick-ups and drop-offs on request.

By boat Ferries and motorboats travel frequently between Orta San Giulio and Isola San Giulio (see box, p.107).

By trenino Orta's motorized tourist train – dubbed the *trenino* (May–Sept daily 9am–7pm; March, April & Oct daily 9am–5.30pm; Nov–Feb Sat & Sun 9.30am–5.30pm; ⓦ treninodiorta.it) – makes a more or less continuous circuit from the tourist office on Via

A LAKESIDE WALK AROUND ORTA SAN GIULIO

One of Orta San Giulio's most pleasant **walks** begins from the tourist office hut on Via Panoramica. Walk down the road for 100m or so, then cut right off the road into the woods. This leads you down to the shore, for the waterside stroll around Orta's peninsula on the scenic **Lungolago 11 Settembre 2001** footpath, past a handful of little houses and some prime spots for quiet sunbathing and swimming. It eventually delivers you (about 30min in total) past the privately owned Villa Motta to the *Hotel San Rocco*, at the northern edge of Orta town centre. You can continue through the town and beyond to complete a circumambulation of the whole peninsula (1hr).

2

Panoramica down to Piazza Motta and back, to the parking garages around Piazzale Prarondo and back, and occasionally up to the Sacro Monte. The fare is €2.50 one-way, €4 return (less for children). It's cheesy, but in practical terms can be invaluable for conquering Orta's steep slopes – though if you want to transport heavy bags it will be at the discretion of the *trenino* driver; officially, that's what Orta's taxis (☎346 211 1587) are for. On some runs, the *trenino* also heads out to the train station.

INFORMATION

Orta San Giulio tourist office Bizarrely located in a hut on the Via Panoramica, way up above the town centre, 100m from *Villa Crespi* (variable hours: usually Tues–Thurs 11am–noon & 2.30–5pm, Fri–Sun 10.30am–noon & 2.30–5pm; ☎0322 905 163, ⓦdistrettolaghi.it).

Municipal tourist office There's a small information office in the town hall (*municipio*), hidden in the old lanes north of Piazza Motta, at Via Bossi 11 (Mon–Thurs 11am–1pm & 2–4pm, Sat & Sun 10am–1pm & 2–4pm; ☎0322 90 155, ⓦwww.comune.ortasangiulio.no.it). **Useful website** ⓦorta.net.

ACCOMMODATION

Orta's **accommodation** is generally good, but limited: you should always **book in advance**, at any budget. Many places offer free parking on request. At the time of writing the grand old *Albergo Orta*, plum on the main square, was closed and boarded-up after more than 140 years in business, its future uncertain.

HOTELS

★**Aracoeli** Piazza Motta 34 ☎0322 905 173, ⓦortainfo.com. Eye-popping little design hotel (pronounced *ara-chaylee*) tucked into one corner of the main square; check-in is down the street at the "Hello Orta" office, 40 Via Olina. There are only seven rooms, on four floors (with a lift), each stylishly presented with plain white walls, designer furniture, a/c and huge walk-in showers. Go for the lusciously large "Room of One's Own", up under the eaves, with two double futons on the floor, billowing white drapes and stunning lake views over the rooftops. Breakfast is gourmet. **€135**

Contrada dei Monti Via dei Monti 10 ☎0322 905 114, ⓦlacontradadeimonti.it. Comfortable, well-kept little hotel in an eighteenth-century house on one of the steep lanes leading off the main drag – and consequently better value than its neighbours. Rooms are fresh and stylish, with soft fabrics and warm colours, many of them overlooking a little internal courtyard where breakfast is served in summer. Closed Jan. **€110**

La Bussola Via Panoramica 24 ☎0322 911 913, ⓦhotelbussolaorta.it. Conveniently located (for drivers) near the large car parks above the town centre, this family-run three-star with private parking benefits from spacious, clutter-free rooms, a sense of style and epic hillside views out over the lake and island. Splash out on the attic suite (around €270–330). **€135**

Leon d'Oro Piazza Motta 42 ☎0322 911 991, ⓦalbergoleondoro.it. Long-standing old *albergo* directly on the waterfront behind the main square, with renovated three-star rooms offering some great lake views. Owned by the same family as the *Contrada dei Monti*. **€110**

Piccolo Hotel Olina Via Olina 40 ☎0322 905 656, ⓦortainfo.com. Little hotel alongside the *Olina* restaurant in the historic centre, with twelve contemporary designed rooms of varying sizes – very clean and attractive. Also has an annexe nearby on Via Poli. Closed Nov to mid-Dec. **€95**

★**San Rocco** Via Gippini 11 ☎0322 911 977, ⓦhotelsanrocco.it. A seventeenth-century former convent on the lakefront. Its secluded location offers fine views westwards to the island – and the lakeside swimming pool is to die for. Most rooms sport minimalist interiors in chocolate and cream, with Italian design touches in lighting, bathrooms and furniture. The real glory lies in the adjacent *Villa Gippini* rooms, with marble floors and frescoed ceilings set off by stylish textiles and contemporary art. The presidential suite – in rosewood, with a frescoed bathroom opening to the lake – wows. **€230**

2

Villa Crespi Via Fava 18 ☎ 0322 911 902, ⓦ villacrespi .it. This extraordinary building, located away from the lake in its own grounds, resembles a Moorish palace. It dates from 1879, when Cristoforo Crespi, a cotton-trader who made his fortune in Baghdad, returned to Orta and built a palace to remind him of the East. Reception features Arab arches, stucco and carved wood, the rooms retain their inlaid parquet flooring, and decor is exceptional, with antique furniture, frescoed ceilings and luxurious bathrooms. With only eight rooms and six suites, an air of exclusivity prevails. Closed Jan to mid-Feb. **€370**

CAMPING

Camping Orta Via Domodossola 28 ☎ 0322 90 267, ⓦ campingorta.it. Good-quality site about 1km north of Orta, sandwiched between the main road and the lake, with nice facilities and a private beach. Also has bungalows and caravans for weekly rent. Open year-round. Pitch **€27**; caravan/week **€700**; bungalow/week **€900**

APARTMENTS AND ROOMS

Hello Orta Via Olina 40 ☎ 0322 905 656, ⓦ ortainfo .com. Orta San Giulio has many en-suite rooms and self-catering apartments for rent, most notably from the little "Hello Orta" office in town. *Casa Vacanze Olina* includes houses and flats sleeping from two to five people (generally €300–400 for three nights in high season), while *La Casa sul Lago* is a large villa divided up into several apartments (seven-night minimum stay in high season). Both must be booked through the office.

Orta Lake Flats Via Giovanetti 34 ☎ 338 366 7403, ⓦ ortalakeflats.com. Another good option for self-catering rooms, holiday houses and apartments in Orta (generally €300–400 for three nights in high season).

EATING AND DRINKING

Café des Arts Via Olina 13 ☎ 366 931 6952. A romantic little café-bar – dark wood, ladder-back chairs and candles – that offers a small, moderately priced menu of Piemontese specialities with jazzy musical accompaniment. Closed Mon.

Enoteca Il Boeuc Via Bersani 28 ☎ 339 584 0039. Cosy little wine bar on a back street which serves tasty Piedmontese nosh to accompany well-chosen wine. Closed Tues.

★**Il Cucchiaio di Legno** Via Prisciola 10 ☎ 0322 905 280, ⓦ ilcucchiaiodilegno.com. Appealing little agriturismo located in the hilly Legro district, roughly 400m beyond (south of) the train station, which serves up hearty cooking with a rustic air – lake fish, of course, but also plenty of seasonal dishes relying on local farm-fresh ingredients. Relax on the vine-shaded terrace. Menu around €25. Closed Mon–Wed.

★**Leon d'Oro** Piazza Motta 42 ☎ 0322 911 991, ⓦ albergoleondoro.it. Landmark restaurant in a corner of the main square, featuring a long line of candlelit tables directly on the water, looking out to the floodlit island. The food is local, served with grace and informality. Mains €10–20. Open daily.

Locanda di Orta Via Olina 18 ☎ 0322 905 188, ⓦ locandaorta.com. Upmarket little restaurant shoehorned into an old courtyard building in the centre, serving artistically presented Mediterranean-influenced cuisine off a small but expensive menu (reckon on €50 a head). The food is similarly good but less pricey at the informal rooftop bistro – with lakes-and-mountains views thrown in. Open daily.

Olina Via Olina 40 ☎ 0322 905 656, ⓦ ortainfo.com. A fine restaurant, serving excellent local specialities beautifully cooked and presented, along with thoughtful extras like aperitifs on the house, plus good vegetarian options. Daily special €12; two-course menu €23. Closed Wed.

San Giulio Isola San Giulio ☎ 0322 90 234, ⓦ ristorantesangiulio.it. A peaceful little hideaway on the island, with a waterside terrace and motorboat shuttles in the evenings. Come for the atmosphere more than the regional Piedmontese food, which is perfectly fine but nothing exceptional. Closed Tues.

Venus Piazza Motta 59 ☎ 0322 90 256. Another prominent terrace restaurant on the main square which sprawls over the cobbles in front of the landing-stage. Its ice cream is excellent, and its inexpensive menus of local specialities (from €25) are well presented. Mains €7–19. Closed Mon.

Villa Crespi Via Fava 18 ☎ 0322 911 902, ⓦ villacrespi .it. Orta's finest hotel hosts a glittering, Michelin-starred restaurant. You can choose à la carte, opt for modest set *menùs* or, for a meal to remember, go for the chef's ten-stage *menù degustazione*, which starts around €150, with pairings for each course from the cellar's five hundred wines adding around €80 on top. Closed Tues, Wed lunch.

Around Lake Orta

Beyond Orta San Giulio, the remainder of the lake is disappointingly humdrum, largely given over to suburban towns and light industry. Explore by boat, then strike out on footpaths and mule tracks up the wooded slopes overlooking the water.

Ordinary-looking **PETTENASCO**, just north of Orta, hosts a clutch of New-Age retreats. It is also the start of the road up to the Mottarone summit (see p.125), which coils up through the village of **Armeno**.

Vacciago

A few kilometres south of Orta, in the township of **VACCIAGO** below Ameno, the **Collezione Calderara** (mid-May to mid-Oct Tues–Fri 3–7pm, Sat & Sun 10am–noon & 3–7pm; free; ⓦfondazionecalderara.it) displays European and non-European contemporary art in the seventeenth-century villa of the painter Antonio Calderara (1903–78). Drop in to see Calderara's beautiful landscapes of Lake Orta.

Pella

Sleepy **PELLA**, directly opposite Orta San Giulio, is handy for a light lunch on a cross-lake trip: wander back from the lakefront to discover its frescoed church, decorated with strange truncated pilasters in the apse. There's a scattering of modest little beaches nearby, backed by steep wooded slopes. Drop into one of the local pizzerias, or plump for the handmade ice cream at *Gelateria Antica Torre* (ⓦgelateriaanticatorre.com), housed in a prominent medieval tower on the lakefront.

San Maurizio d'Opaglio

Among the roster of Italian design companies headquartered on or near Lake Orta is Giacomini, specialists in bathroom fittings. They are based at **SAN MAURIZIO D'OPAGLIO** on the western shore, where they celebrate their heritage at the town's quirky **Museo del Rubinetto** (Tap Museum; Fri–Sun 3–6pm; free; ⓦmuseodel rubinetto.it).

Nearby on this wooded slope is the Baroque **Madonna del Sasso** church, perched atop a rocky crag and clearly visible from Orta San Giulio.

Omegna

At the northern tip of Lake Orta stands the busy little town of **OMEGNA**, with a photogenic old quarter good for window-shopping. Omegna is home to chic cookware firms Bialetti (designers of the iconic Moka Express stovetop espresso-maker), Lagostina and Alessi: alongside the Alessi factory, signposted just north of the centre in **Crusinallo**, is the **Alessi Shop** (Mon–Sat 9.30am–6pm; June–Sept also Sun 2.30–6.30pm; ⓦalessi.com), an outlet store offering the full designer range, heavily discounted.

Traffic streams through Omegna to join the autostrada 7km north at **Gravellona Toce**. North of Gravellona, the highway – signed for the **Passo del Sempione** (Simplon Pass) – reaches into the Alpine territory of the **Val d'Ossola**, a web of mountain valleys surrounded by walls of sheer peaks marking the Swiss border. On a lakes-based stay, the only reason to venture this far north is for the town of **Domodossola**, 33km north of Gravellona Toce (see p.147).

Lake Maggiore

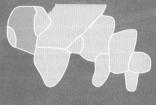

LOCARNO

Lake Maggiore

For generations of overland travellers, Lake Maggiore (Lago Maggiore) has been a first taste of Italy. Roads and rail lines from Switzerland run down beside its shores – and for travellers weary of the cool grandeur of the Alps, the first glimpse of limpid blue waters, green hills and exotic vegetation are evidence of arrival in the warm south. Unmistakeably Mediterranean in atmosphere, with palms and oleanders lining the lakeside promenades and a peaceful, serene air, Maggiore may not be somewhere for thrill-seekers, but it is seductively relaxing. Orange blossom, vines, clear air and the verbena that flourishes on Maggiore's shores – giving rise to the lake's alternative name Verbano – continue to draw visitors, and you'll need to book in advance in peak season.

Maggiore's main sights cluster around the **Golfo Borromeo** in mid-lake; here lie the grand old resorts of **Stresa** and **Pallanza**, with the Baroque gardens of the **Isole Borromee** floating enticingly just offshore. The southern part of the lake, beyond the cliffside hermitage of **Santa Caterina**, is guarded by the **Rocca Borromeo**, while to the north, the lake narrows between high peaks, sheltering romantic hideaways like **Cannero**, **Cannobio** and – across the Swiss border – **Ascona**. The northern end of the lake is dominated by the cultivated Swiss town of **Locarno**, while to the east the unsung city of **Varese**, caught between lakes Maggiore, Lugano and Como, is a refreshing place to draw breath away from the crowds.

Note that in winter (Nov–Easter) many hotels across the region close down and attractions may be shut.

INFORMATION

This chapter covers territory in both Switzerland and Italy. The northernmost part of Lake Maggiore is in the Swiss canton of **Ticino** (Ⓦ ascona-locarno.com). On the Italian side, the east bank is in Lombardy's province of **Varese** (Ⓦ vareselandoftourism.com). The west bank (all of which lies in Piemonte) is divided between the provinces of Novara and Verbano-Cusio-Ossola – the **Distretto Turistico dei Laghi** (Ⓦ distrettolaghi.it) manages tourism for the whole western shore, as well as for Lake Orta and the valleys around Domodossola. All phone numbers prefixed ☎ 091 are Swiss; all other numbers (beginning ☎ 03 in this chapter) are Italian. International dialling is straightforward (see p.47).

GETTING AROUND

Timetables for **trains, buses and boats** along the western shore of Lake Maggiore are at Ⓦ vcoinbus.it. For the whole lake (and wider region of Lombardy), go to Ⓦ www.muoversi.regione.lombardia.it. There's full details of boat services at Ⓦ navigazionelaghi.it. Swiss public transport timetables are online at Ⓦ sbb.ch/en. Check timetables carefully for notes and arcane symbols (see p.27). You'll need your passport to travel between Italy and Switzerland. By **car**, border posts are staffed but delays are rare.

ISOLA MADRE

Highlights

❶ Lago Maggiore Express A memorable three-stage journey by train and boat through splendid scenery of lakes and mountains, crossing between Italy and Switzerland. **See p.119**

❷ Isola Madre Charming formal gardens near Stresa, part of the Borromeo islands group. **See p.128**

❸ Pallanza Genial, slow-paced lake resort which beats Stresa for peace and quiet. **See p.129**

❹ Cannobio Characterful old town in the north that just wins out over its neighbour Cannero for lake-appeal. **See p.136**

❺ Ascona Another beautiful corner in the north of Lake Maggiore, this time facing south from Switzerland. **See p.140**

❻ Locarno-Cardada Sensational Alpine views reached with a futuristic cable car and chairlift above the Swiss resort of Locarno. **See p.144**

❼ Villa Panza Contemporary art in a fine Baroque villa – well worth the trip to elegant, showy Varese. **See p.157**

❽ Castiglione Olona Exceptional Tuscan Renaissance frescoes in this small country town outside Varese. **See p.160**

HIGHLIGHTS ARE MARKED ON THE MAP ON P.116

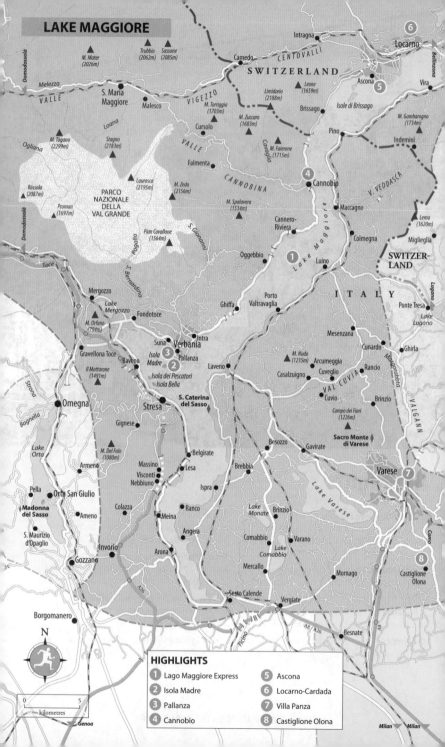

Stresa

Most of Maggiore's visitors head for the western shore, where a bulging bay disturbs the lake's smooth parallel lines. Long dubbed the **Golfo Borromeo**, for the regional pre-eminence of the Borromeo – a family of bankers, raised to nobility in the 1450s and still prominent locally – the bay holds some of the region's best-loved attractions, notably **STRESA**, the legendary *grande dame* of Italian lake resorts.

During the nineteenth-century boom in tourism, Stresa remained largely unvisited: boats called in at the Borromeo islands, but bypassed the shoreline. Then, in 1906, the Simplon Tunnel between Switzerland and Italy opened, the final link in a chain of railways that connected Lake Geneva to Milan, and thus northern Europe to the Mediterranean. International trains, including the *Orient Express*, were routed through Stresa, which quickly became a favoured holiday retreat for Europe's nobility and royalty, hosting high society all through the heady 1920s and 1930s.

Today, Stresa is a busy little place, but its greatest days have passed. Apart from a rump of grand hotels, the sophistication has mostly waned in favour of some nice window-shopping in the narrow lanes and lakeside lawns, kept trim and neat.

3

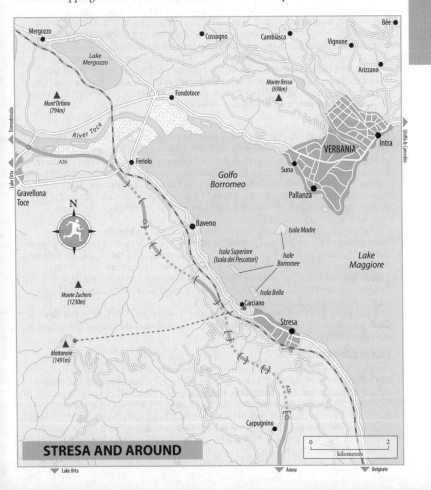

STRESA AND AROUND

BOATS ON LAKE MAGGIORE

Lake Maggiore has an extensive ferry network; it's easy (indeed, preferable) to get to most places by boat. Service is provided by **NLM**, Navigazione Lago Maggiore (☎800 551 801, ⓦnavigazionelaghi.it), who have more than thirty landing-stages, all of which sell tickets (the smaller booths tend to open only ten or fifteen minutes before a boat is due in). Boats run year-round, although outside the summer season (April–Sept) services are greatly reduced or, on many routes, halted.

ROUTES

Because the lake is so long, the timetable is divided up into four broad sectors: the lower lake, between **Arona** and **Angera**; the central area between **Stresa** and **Intra**, including **Pallanza** and the islands; the northern section around **Cannobio**, **Cannero** and **Luino**; and the Swiss basin (*Bacino Svizzero*) around **Ascona** and **Locarno**.

Within each sector there is reasonably frequent service (roughly every 30–60mins). Boats run between sectors, less frequently; quiet corners such as **Ghiffa** or **Ranco** may get just two a day.

Most boats are ordinary passenger vessels. "AL" on the timetable denotes an **aliscafo** (hydrofoil) – a faster ride (also marked "SR", *servizio rapido*) that must be **reserved in advance** and commands a small supplement. Services start around 7am, and finish by 8pm, although the lake's only **traghetto** (car-ferry), which also takes foot passengers, shuttles continuously between Intra and Laveno from 5am to midnight. Supplementing the main timetable, extra boats shuttle frequently between **Carciano** (near Stresa) and Isola Bella.

You can easily put together a sightseeing itinerary using the widely available timetable leaflets. Check carefully the various symbols and colour-coded notes to identify each route's days of operation; several routes change on **Wednesdays** (to take account of the market at Luino) and some boats run only on *festivi* (Sun and holidays). Services marked with a knife and fork have a **restaurant** on board, serving a set meal (€15).

FARES AND PASSES

Fares are charged on a complicated sliding scale. Each route is assigned a number, according to the distance involved; you then cross-check on the relevant chart for how much that route-number (or *tratta*) costs. Children aged 4–12 and people over 65 qualify for a discount. Make sure you're checking the chart for individual travellers, marked *individuali* or *singoli* – not the one headlined *comitive e scuole* (groups and school parties). As an example, Stresa to Pallanza is *tratta* 5, which costs €5 direct, or €8.90 if you stop off on the way. Isola Bella to Isola Madre is *tratta* 4 (€4.30/€8.20), while Stresa to Cannero is *tratta* 8 (€8.40/€14.10). You pay a small surcharge to use the hydrofoil.

For all these, a return ticket costs twice the price of a one-way. A **biglietto di libera circolazione** (ticket for unlimited journeys) is also priced per tratta; a day-pass covering Stresa and the three islands, for example, is €16.90. Taking an ordinary-sized **car** on the ferry between Intra and Laveno costs €7.80 including the driver, plus €3.40 per passenger.

International tickets cost more: for example, from Stresa to Ascona costs €18.70, from Pallanza to Locarno €20.20, from Cannobio to the Isole di Brissago €10.10, with return tickets capped at around €30. Don't forget your **passport**.

Boats operating on the **Swiss** side of the lake have separate fares (see p.141). A **Holiday Card** gives unlimited journeys on the whole lake, including Switzerland, for €65 (three days) or €83 (seven days).

PRIVATE OPERATORS

Completely separate from the "official" boats, **motorboat** owners at towns all round the lake – many of whom get together in local consortia – offer transport on request. It can sometimes be difficult to tell who's who, as these skippers often tout for business from prominent booths directly beside official landing-stages. The difference is in the signboards: *Servizio pubblico di linea* refers to the official boats, while *Servizio pubblico non di linea* means the motorboats. Rates are very negotiable, and depend on demand – but if you want to drop everything and be taken on a solo voyage to a destination of your choice, reckon on around €100 per hour.

Piazza Cadorna and the lakefront

Stresa's mellow, chiefly pedestrianized town centre, set back from the *imbarcadero*, comprises half a dozen streets clustered around the little **Piazza Cadorna**, a triangular space filled with café tables dedicated to the mass consumption of outsized ice-cream sundaes.

Otherwise, take a stroll along the elegant promenade – marred slightly by traffic passing alongside – which stretches for over 500m along the lakefront, flanked, for the most part, by gardens. Just beyond the grounds of the palatial *Grand Hotel des Îles Borromées*, the main road dips inland, leaving the lakefront path to continue around the little headland at **Carciano**, served by boats and the cable car up to the Mottarone summit (see p.125). Views of Isola Bella just offshore are magical (see p.126), and it's a short boat journey to reach the cliffside church of **Santa Caterina del Sasso** (see p.151).

Sala Canonica

Piazza Matteotti 6 • April–Sept Fri–Sun 10am–1pm, also July & Aug Mon–Sat 3–5pm • Free • ☎ 0323 939 252

Within Stresa's pint-sized town hall, a room has been given over to display sculptures by **Pietro Canonica** (1869–1959). A regular visitor to the town, Canonica was known for securing commissions from European nobility and aristocracy, and statues by him

3

LAGO MAGGIORE EXPRESS

For its simplicity, diversity and superb scenery, the **Lago Maggiore Express** ticket (🌐 lagomaggioreexpress.eu) is one of the best round-trip excursions on the lakes. It comprises three sectors, all of them great journeys in their own right: a long **boat trip** on Maggiore, the stunning **Centovalli railway** between Locarno and Domodossola (see p.147), and a **fast train** on the historic Simplon main line between Domodossola and Stresa. The schedules are flexible; you can start and end wherever you like. The whole thing could take as little as six hours – or you could dawdle over it for a couple of days. Note that this is not a tour; you are on your own, using **public transport**. Carry your **passport** (the route crosses into Switzerland) and also check the timetables carefully for the validity of each part of the trip. You must reserve ahead for any **hydrofoil** journeys (and pay a small supplement).

ITINERARIES

A dizzying seventeen **itineraries** have been devised, starting from different towns, running in opposite directions and covering various days of validity – but all that matters is your starting-point. From this key bit of information, the website makes it easy to research your options. Alternatively you could leave it until you arrive; local tourist offices have full details of the various routings applicable from their town. We've given **example routings** throughout this chapter within the town listings of Stresa, Pallanza and other popular starting-points.

WHEN TO GO

The journey is possible only over the **summer** (July–Sept daily), plus a few weeks either side in mid-June and early October (Thurs–Sun only). Note that even when daily service is indicated, beware **Wednesdays**, when timetables change to take account of the big weekly market in Luino (see p.149), rendering some routings impossible. There are also different itineraries in play depending on which way round you choose to cover the circuit (clockwise or anti-clockwise). Double-check that you're consulting the right itinerary for the day of your intended trip.

FARES

The complete round-trip in **one day**, in either direction and from any starting-point, costs €32 (from Switzerland, about Fr.48). The **two-day** pass, which allows you to break your journey overnight anywhere on the route and also includes free boat travel on the whole of Lake Maggiore, is €42 (Fr.58). On certain boats – marked on the timetables – **lunch** is served for a set price (€15).

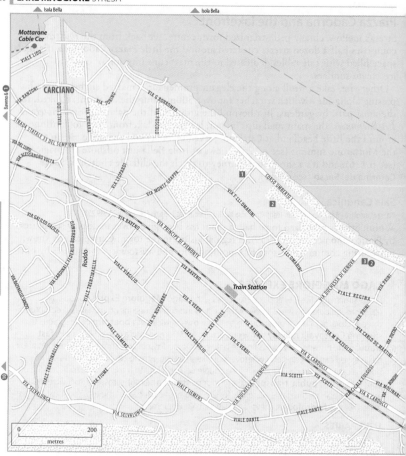

remain on public display around Italy and further afield, in Turkey, Egypt and South America. His works combine realism with a symbolist style – a rather striking, emotional counterpoint to the blandness of the resort Stresa has become.

ARRIVAL AND DEPARTURE

STRESA

By plane Milan-Malpensa Airport is around 45km south. SAF's Alibus runs six times daily (April–Sept only) from Malpensa (Terminals 1 and 2), along the western shore of Lake Maggiore, including stops at Stresa and Baveno (€12; booking essential 48hr ahead by phone or online; ☎0323 552 172, Ⓦsafduemila.com). Buses also run all year round from Malpensa (Terminals 1 and 2) to Gravellona Toce (€12; Ⓦcomazzialibus.com), 9km north of Stresa.

By train Stresa is an hour from Milano Centrale on the high-speed trains that continue to Baveno and Domodossola; slower trains also run from Milano Centrale and Milano Porta Garibaldi. Stresa's train station is behind the town centre on Via Principe di Piemonte; taxis wait

outside, or you could walk right to the crossroads, then left on Via Duchessa di Genova for 200m down to the lakefront. Timetables are at Ⓦvcoinbus.it.

Destinations Domodossola (approx hourly; 20min); Milano Centrale (approx hourly; 55min).

By bus Buses stop on the main lakefront road. Tim etables are at Ⓦvcoinbus.it.

Destinations Orta San Giulio (3 daily; 1hr); Pallanza & Intra (about every 30min; 25min).

By car The lakefront SS33 road is a slow, scenic drive through every village – or you could opt for the A26 autostrada, which has exits at Carpugnino, south of Stresa in the hills, and at Baveno, about 8km further north.

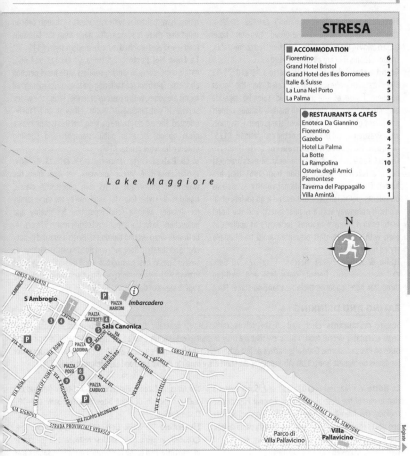

STRESA

■ ACCOMMODATION	
Fiorentino	6
Grand Hotel Bristol	1
Grand Hotel des Iles Borromees	2
Italie & Suisse	4
La Luna Nel Porto	5
La Palma	3

● RESTAURANTS & CAFÉS	
Enoteca Da Giannino	6
Fiorentino	8
Gazebo	4
Hotel La Palma	2
La Botte	5
La Rampolina	10
Osteria degli Amici	9
Piemontese	7
Taverna del Pappagallo	3
Villa Amintà	1

By boat Stresa is the linchpin of the dense network of boat routes around the islands, as well as a stop for boats heading north from Arona and south from Locarno. Timetables are at ⓦ vcoinbus.it. The *imbarcadero* is very central, on Piazza Marconi, directly across the road from Stresa's town centre. There's a large parking area alongside. Additional boats to Isola Bella depart from Carciano, 750m north. Private operators include ⓦ isoleborromee.com and ⓦ isolelagomaggiore.com (both based at Carciano) and ⓦ summerboats.it (based at Baveno).

Destinations Arona (approx hourly; 1hr); Intra (every 30min; 55min); Isola Bella (every 30min; 10min); Isola dei Pescatori (every 30min; 15min); Isola Madre (every 30min; 30min); Pallanza (every 30min; 35min); Santa Caterina (hourly; 15min); Villa Taranto (every 30min; 45min).

INFORMATION

Online ⓦ stresatravelnotes.blogspot.it.
Tourist office Piazza Marconi 16, beside the *imbarcadero* (daily 10am–12.30pm & 3–6.30pm; mid-Oct to mid-March closed Sat afternoon & Sun; ☏ 0323 31 308, ⓦ stresaturismo.it & ⓦ distrettolaghi.it).

ACCOMMODATION

A decent alternative to staying in Stresa itself is to abandon the mainland and opt instead for one of the hotels on the Borromeo islands, specifically the charming Isola dei Pescatori (see p.128). All of them offer a motorboat shuttle service for guests on request to and from waterfront towns around the bay.

Fiorentino Via A.M. Bolongaro 9 ☎0323 30 254, ⓦhotelfiorentino.com. House-proud two-star hotel tucked away in the town centre, with fourteen comfortable, spacious rooms that are all en suite. €90

Grand Hotel Bristol Corso Umberto I 73 ☎0323 32 601, ⓦzaccherahotels.com. Located on the quiet northern fringe of the town amid splendid lakeside grounds. Interiors are plush, with marble, antique carpets and Tiffany glass – but this is a four-star property, so prices are less astronomical than some of the competition. €125

★ **Grand Hotel des Iles Borromées** Corso Umberto I 67 ☎0323 938 938, ⓦborromees.it. Stresa's grandest hotel, a lakefront palace dating from 1861 that has hosted European and international royalty as well as presidents, politicians, celebrities and high society of all kinds. Hemingway was a regular guest, and the hotel features in *A Farewell to Arms*. Today, it's as opulent as ever, with every comfort presented amid traditionally styled luxury. €250

Italie & Suisse Piazza Marconi 1 ☎0323 30 540, ⓦitaliesuisse.com. Decent, convenient and well-run three-star hotel opposite the Stresa landing-stage. Most

rooms have balconies with lake views – though bear in mind that there is some traffic noise from the lakefront road – and are furnished in fresh, modern style. €115

La Luna Nel Porto Corso Italia 60 ☎0323 934 466, ⓦlalunanelporto.it. Bright, spotless little hotel perched above the lakefront road offering great value for money: all rooms are suites, with a balcony or terrace facing the water. Service is outstanding – warm, efficient and family-oriented. There is no private parking, but this is otherwise a great option, close to public transport and strolling distance from the centre. €160

★ **La Palma** Corso Umberto I 33 ☎0323 32 401, ⓦhlapalma.it. A Stresa landmark, set back from the waterfront promenade in its own gardens. A classic, traditionally styled four-star hotel, run by the same family for decades, with a solid reputation for quality and innovation. Go for the upper-level corner rooms 514 or 614, both with wrap-around balconies. There's a spa and beauty centre on the sixth floor, airy and flooded with sunshine, as well as Stresa's best rooftop bar – and this is the only hotel in town with a swimming pool directly on the lake, offering superb views of the islands. €150

EATING AND DRINKING

Stresa's **restaurants** cater well to the town's conservative, generally undemanding clientele – most places serve acceptably decent food, with a few that are truly memorable. Make time for an ice cream or aperitif at one of the cafés on Piazza Cadorna. Good alternatives lie just offshore, on the Isola dei Pescatori, with free motorboat shuttle service for diners on request (see p.128). Also consider the short drive north to *Piccolo Lago* on Lake Mergozzo (see p.129).

La Botte Via Mazzini 6 ☎0323 30 462. Snug trattoria that is one of the best places to try regional Piemontese cooking; the friendly host serves up local game, polenta and goat's cheeses as well as a variety of tasty pasta dishes. There's no terrace, but the ambience is warm and welcoming. Mains €8–15. Closed Thurs.

★ **Enoteca Da Giannino** Piazza Cadorna 9 ☎0323 30 781, ⓦenotecadagiannino.it. Sociable little corner on the main square, with a lounge-bar atmosphere – stylish, contemporary interior, comfy chairs, a long list of wines by

the glass, a dozen varieties of gin-and-tonic (around €8) and a selection of light bites to accompany (€4–10). Open daily.

Fiorentino Via A.M. Bolongaro 9 ☎0323 30 254, ⓦhotelfiorentino.com. Modest restaurant in the centre of town attached to the family-run hotel of the same name – keenly priced soup, spaghetti and decent *secondi*. *Menù* €16. Open daily.

Gazebo Hotel Moderno, Via Cavour 31 ☎0323 933 773, ⓦhms.it. Of the cluster of open-air terrace restaurants on

---

LAGO MAGGIORE EXPRESS FROM STRESA

The **Lago Maggiore Express** excursion ticket (see p.119) is a great way to explore the region. From **Stresa** (on **Itinerary 7**), the clockwise routing begins with a morning train (8.30, 9.30 or 10.30am). You get a break for coffee in Domodossola before the scenic narrow-gauge train ride to Locarno, arriving in time for lunch (or opt for a later service). A boat departs Locarno at 4.15pm for the three-hour cruise back to Stresa.

The anticlockwise alternative involves departing Stresa by boat at 11.15am (eating lunch on board), taking a couple of hours in Locarno and a quick change at Domodossola, arriving back at Stresa around 7.30 or 8.30pm for dinner.

These details were accurate at the time of writing – check for up-to-date schedules before you set out (and note that timetables are slightly different on Wednesdays, when Itinerary 15 applies instead). It's easy to put together a trip starting from other points on the lake, too.

> ### STRESA'S MUSICAL EVENTS
>
> The **Stresa Festival** (ⓦ stresafestival.eu) features prestigious classical music concerts from May to September at venues in the town, on all three islands (including piano recitals in the spectacular setting of the Isola Bella *palazzo*), at various medieval churches including Santa Caterina del Sasso, and elsewhere. Look out, also, for regular **jazz** gigs every two or three weeks from April to October, and July's classical **Baveno Festival Umberto Giordano** (ⓦ festivalgiordano.it).

this pedestrianized street, *Gazebo* is nicer than most. The food is broadly similar to that of its near neighbours – soups, pasta and lake fish – but the service is genial and the atmosphere pleasant. *Menù* around €25. Open evenings only 7–9.30pm.

★ **Hotel La Palma** Corso Umberto I 33 ☎ 0323 32 401, ⓦ hlapalma.it. This upmarket tourist hotel scores with its stunning seventh-floor rooftop lounge bar and restaurant, which also sports an open-air jacuzzi. It's a lovely place for a quiet sunny lunch of salad, pasta or grilled sea bass, under shade, with spectacular views (mains €12–15) – but it comes into its own at the cocktail hour around sunset: nowhere in town can match it for views and chilled-out atmosphere. Open daily.

La Rampolina Via per Somero 13, Campino ☎ 0323 923 415, ⓦ larampolina.com. If you fancy a break from predictable lakeside dining, head up into the hills behind Stresa for this lovely local tavern-cum-pizzeria-cum-wine bar, with stunning views over lakes and mountains. The owners are super-friendly and the cooking will warm your cockles – hearty local Piemontese fare (mains €8–17) and crispy wood-fired pizzas (€6–10). Closed Mon.

Osteria degli Amici Via A.M. Bolongaro 31 ☎ 0323 30 453. Across the main square, on tiny Piazza Possi, this cosy nook is a simple place with an attractive vine-covered terrace, serving tasty *risotti* and fish (mains €12–17), plus excellent pizza (€6–10). Service can be a tad slow. Closed Wed.

Piemontese Via Mazzini 25 ☎ 0323 30 235, ⓦ ristorantepiemontese.com. Some of the best cooking Stresa has to offer – light, artfully presented traditional Piedmont dishes, including lake fish and mountain cheeses, served in an elegant dark-wood dining room or pleasant garden. Two-course menu €23, or à la carte mains €12–20. Closed Mon & Dec–Feb.

Taverna del Pappagallo Via Principessa Margherita 46 ☎ 0323 30 411, ⓦ tavernapappagallo.com. Busy, intimate pizzeria with an open wood fire and excellent, low-priced pizzas (€6–11) alongside simple, traditional Piedmontese cooking (mains €10–17). Closed Wed.

Villa Amintà Via Sempione Nord 123 ☎ 0323 933 818, ⓦ villa-aminta.it. Showy five-star deluxe spa hotel on the lakefront road 1km north of Stresa. Come here less for the rooms than for the terrace restaurant *Le Isole*, which offers the finest view of Lake Maggiore's islands. Book well in advance for a table at the balustrade; the panorama, gazing over the floodlit *palazzo* of Isola Bella to the right, Isola dei Pescatori to the left, Isola Madre set back between them, and the lights of Pallanza glittering opposite, is pure lakes romance. The menu of lake staples – with notably good fish – is around €50. Open daily.

Parco della Villa Pallavicino

Park March–Oct daily 9am–7pm, last entry 5pm • €9.50 • ⓦ parcozoopallavicino.it **Trenino del Parco** April–Sept daily 9.30am–4.30pm • €4 return

Around 500m south of Stresa's town centre is the lakeside **Parco della Villa Pallavicino**, a patch of green around a fine nineteenth-century house, featuring a botanic garden and animals such as deer, zebra and wallabies wandering around, safari-park-style. There's also a playground, a restaurant and several picnic areas. In peak season, the *Trenino del Parco* – a little motorized tourist train – does the run to the park from Stresa's *imbarcadero*.

Belgirate

A few boats a day serve Belgirate on a zigzag route between Stresa and Arona

About 5km south of Stresa, the charming old village of **BELGIRATE** marks a "pretty turn" (*bella girata*), where the road rounds a little headland. From Stresa's waterfront, you could walk the attractive hillside **trail L2** (2hr); this takes in a semi-ruined Roman road to Passera, a stretch of woodland, several country churches and a mule track that heads down to Belgirate's twelfth-century church. The tourist-office leaflet *Trekking alle pendici del Mottarone* has a map and English outline.

Mottarone

Ⓦ stresa-mottarone.it

Towering behind Stresa, separating Lake Maggiore from Lake Orta, is the **Mottarone** mountain, rising to 1491m. It's hardly the most sensational of peaks, but nonetheless undeserving of the derision heaped upon it by John Ruskin – he referred to it as "the stupidest of mountains" and thought the views dull. Either Ruskin's mood or the weather must have been bad, for in truth the views are impressive, stretching from Monte Rosa on the Swiss border across to the Adamello, taking in most of Lake Maggiore on the way. Its wooded western slopes are a favourite destination for family outings. The tourist office has leaflets detailing walks in the area.

A **cable car** serves the mountain from **CARCIANO**, on the lakefront about 750m north of Stresa; it's an epic twenty-minute ride, swinging high above the forested slopes, which delivers you to a point just below the summit, offering stupendous east-facing views across Maggiore. A chairlift (free with cable-car ticket) – or a ten-minute walk – covers the last bit to the very top, where 360-degree panoramas open up.

Beside the midway cable-car stop is the **Alpinia Botanic Garden** (April–Oct daily 9.30am–6pm; €3), with fountain, lake and lookout point, and beside the top station is the **Alpyland** family fun park (Mon–Fri 10am–5pm, Sat & Sun 10am–6pm; €5), with a toboggan run and cafés.

ARRIVAL AND GETTING AROUND   **MOTTARONE**

By cable car From the Carciano ferry stop, 750m north of Stresa by the lido (ample parking alongside). Runs every 20min: April–Oct daily 9.30am–5.30pm (€19 return); Dec–March daily 8am–5pm (€13.50 return plus optional ski passes available).

By car If you're driving up from Stresa, be aware that access above Alpino (part of Gignese village) is by a private road that was laid by the Borromeo family in the fifteenth century; they charge a toll of €6 per car to reach the summit. The road up from the Orta side is free.

By bike You can rent mountain bikes at the cable-car base station (€25/day including cable-car ticket; Ⓦ bicico.it).

On foot The easy walk up the mountain, signposted as path 1, takes four hours.

Baveno

BAVENO, 4km north of Stresa, is a soporific little town, catching some of its bigger neighbour's overspill but not offering a great deal itself. It made – and, to a certain extent, still makes – a living from its **quarries**, which show themselves in stark white gashes in the slopes behind the town. Aside from quartz, the most famous stone to be quarried here is **pink Baveno granite**, used in the building of St Paul's in Rome and the Galleria Vittorio Emanuele in Milan – one of sixty-odd varieties found nearby (including a particular local mineral, bavenite).

Baveno's Art Nouveau landing-stage is one of the nicest on the lake. Directly opposite, across the main road, is the central Piazza Dante Alighieri, surrounded by a tight-packed web of picturesque residential alleys. Baveno holds some fine nineteenth-century villas – in 1879 Queen Victoria stayed in what is now called the Villa Branca – and Baveno's church, **Santi Gervasio e Protasio**, retains its eleventh-century square facade, with Roman inscriptions adorning many of the reused stones and a fifth-century baptistry alongside.

Sporty families will love the **Aquadventure Park**, just north of Baveno at Strada Cavalli 18 (June–Aug daily 10am–1pm & 4–8pm; April, May, Sept & Oct Sat & Sun 10am–5pm; activities €7–12; Ⓦ aquadventurepark.com), with a climbing wall, rope walks, a mountain-bike trail, swimming pools and waterslides.

ARRIVAL AND INFORMATION	BAVENO
By train Baveno is three minutes from Stresa. Timetables are at ⓦvcoinbus.it.	**Tourist office** Piazza della Chiesa 8, opposite the *imbarcadero* (April–Sept Mon–Sat 9am–12.30pm
By bus Several buses shuttle between Baveno and Stresa daily (10min).	& 3–6pm, Sun 9am–noon; restricted hours in winter; ☎0323 924 632, ⓦbavenoturismo.it & ⓦdistrettolaghi
By boat Several boats serving Stresa each day stop at Baveno.	.it).

Isole Borromee (Borromeo islands)

However fanciful the Isola Bella may be, it still is beautiful. Anything springing out of that blue water, with that scenery around it, must be.

Charles Dickens, Pictures from Italy (1846)

Lake Maggiore's leading attractions are three lush **islands** rising from the waters of the bay between Stresa and Pallanza. All three are often dubbed the **ISOLE BORROMEE**, although, strictly speaking, only two are Borromeo property.

Each island is markedly different. The most celebrated is **Isola Bella**, just offshore at Stresa and taken up by a Baroque *palazzo* and formal terraced gardens that are the epitome of Italian lake beauty. Behind, in open water nearer to Pallanza, is the larger **Isola Madre**, occupied by a modest villa, with gardens that are wilder than its twin. These two were acquired by the Borromeo family in the sixteenth century. A stone's throw northwest of Isola Bella is the slender **Isola Superiore**, also known as **Isola dei Pescatori** – once the residence of fisherfolk and still a pleasant little nook, with its narrow lanes and old houses.

Romantics will be knocked for six. The atmospheric journey by boat from Stresa, as the Baroque terraces of Isola Bella rise from the water, is fantasy brought to life. Views of the *palazzo* from different angles, as your boat circles to approach the porticoes and shuttered windows of Isola dei Pescatori, are delightful. The drawback, inevitably, is the **crowds**. All summer long, the islands are crawling with people; boats are packed to the gunwales and the quays are shoulder-to-shoulder. Both Isola Bella (outside the *palazzo* walls) and Isola dei Pescatori feature souvenir shops and touristy cafés, alongside the odd worthwhile restaurant and hideaway. Nowhere can you escape company entirely, although you'll have the best chance on Isola Madre, the quietest of the three.

ARRIVAL AND DEPARTURE	ISOLE BORROMEE
By boat Public ferries (ⓦnavigazionelaghi.it; see p.118) shuttle frequently in both directions between all three islands, connecting to Stresa, Carciano, Baveno and Pallanza	on the mainland. In addition, private boat operators at every landing-stage offer excursions to any or all of the islands, for negotiable rates depending on demand.

Isola Bella

Mid-March to mid-Oct daily 9am–5.30pm • €13, free to members of the British Royal Horticultural Society; joint ticket with Isola Madre €18.50; joint ticket with Isola Madre & Rocca Borromeo in Angera (see p.152) €22 • Audioguide €5 • Book online or by phone at least a day ahead for personal guided tour of the palace in English (€45; takes 45min) • ☎0323 30 556, ⓦisoleborromee.it

The poet Robert Southey reckoned **Isola Bella** "one of the most costly efforts of bad taste in all Italy". Bad taste or good, it is undoubtedly an extravagant display of wealth and power. In the mid-sixteenth century the Borromeo family, who had already acquired Isola Madre, turned their attention to what was a rocky islet of fishermen's houses, known at the time as Isola Inferiore. They bought up land piecemeal, slowly moving residents off the island and renaming it in 1630 "Isola Isabella", after the wife of Carlo III Borromeo – a mouthful that was soon shortened to Isola Bella.

Under Carlo's guidance, the architect Giovanni Angelo Crivelli designed terraces for the gardens and laid foundations for a grand house at the northern end of the island. In 1659, Carlo's son, Vitaliano VI Borromeo, hired a new architect, Francesco Castelli, and the *palazzo* as it stands today began to take shape, with its grand salons, chapels and sumptuous galleries. Andrea Biffi took over in 1671, and it was under his stewardship that the palace and its monumental gardens became imbued with the High Baroque taste. Vitaliano died in 1690 with most of the work completed, although the vast, unfinished Salone dominating the northern wing of the palace, based on the plans of the San Lorenzo basilica in Milan, was redesigned in 1781 and only completed under Vitaliano X Borromeo as late as 1958.

Visiting needs a tolerant frame of mind. Even if grand houses and formal gardens are right up your alley, your patience may still be tested by the size and bustle of the crowds. The best advice is to organize your transport so you're already on the island when the *palazzo* opens in the morning; that way, you can have perhaps half an hour before the first of the tour groups arrives.

The palazzo

A tour begins at the piazza in front of the stepped harbour, enclosed by three wings of the *palazzo*. To the right is the Borromeos' **private chapel**, built in the 1840s and housing the twin-arched tomb of Vitaliano and Giovanni Borromeo carved from Carrara marble. Opposite, past the ticket office, is the **main staircase**, completed in 1680 with a barrel vault and, on the walls, large stucco crests. At the top, the **Sala delle Medaglie** (room 3) is named after ten gilded wooden tondi on the walls. This was used as a banqueting chamber; a Murano crystal chandelier (1769) hangs above. On one side is the **Sala del Trono** (Throne Room); on the other is the **Salone** (room 5), the largest room in the palace, three storeys high, with pillars supporting the dome vault. The colour scheme is stunning – areas of white stucco interspersed with fields of turquoise – with windows that look out over the water.

Beyond the Sala della Musica is the **Sala di Napoleone** (room 7), where the great man slept with his wife Josephine during a stay in 1797. A sequence of smaller rooms extends round to room 12, the **Stanza dello Zuccarelli**, named after the artist who has several landscapes displayed here, alongside three sixteenth-century English tapestries.

After room 14, the grand **Sala da Ballo** (Ballroom), stairs descend to six **grottoes** (rooms 15–20), facing north down at the water level, each of which has walls, ceiling and floor covered by decorative patterns and mosaics in coloured stones. They were intended to be retreats from the summer heat, and the effect is rather like exploring your way through dark, naturalistic caves – a mirror-image of the formal, furnished rooms above. After the Sixth Grotto, stairs head up again to the final sequence of rooms, ending with the long **Galleria degli Arazzi** (Tapestry Gallery, room 24), lined with exquisite Flemish tapestries.

The gardens

You exit the palace in front of the **Atrio di Diana** (Diana's Atrium), a polygonal structure arranged around a statue of the goddess, with twin staircases leading up to a balustraded terrace. Beyond is the large, open **Piano della Canfora** (Camphor Terrace), which takes its name from a camphor tree planted by Vitaliano IX Borromeo in 1819.

Exits to the right deliver you to the remnants of the old village that once occupied the island, but ahead lie the famous Italianate Baroque **gardens**, dotted with fountains and statues, and filled with orange and lemon trees, camellias, magnolias, box trees, laurels, cypresses and much more. The centrepiece, dead ahead, is the **Teatro Massimo**, a three-storey confection of shell-, mirror- and marble-encrusted grottoes, topped with a suitably melodramatic unicorn, mini-obelisks, and various Greek gods and cherubs in attendance. A flight of steps leads up to the topmost **terrace**, where you can stand at the balustrade, 37m above the lake waters, and enjoy uninterrupted views on all sides.

Below, the easternmost end of the island is taken up with the suitably named **Giardino d'Amore**, a parterre of four symmetrical beds framed by cone-shaped coniferous yews, with the octagonal Torre della Noria on the south side and Torre dei Venti on the north.

Isola dei Pescatori (Isola Superiore)

Hemingway's favourite island of the three, **Isola dei Pescatori** (or Isola Superiore), lies within spitting distance of Isola Bella and the shore. Despite the invasions of sightseers, there are no sights as such, although the island has kept its cluster of old houses (about fifty people live here year-round) and retains a certain charm. Ramble your way along the tight little alleyways behind the harbourfront; along with the obligatory trinket stands and cafés, there are a few ordinary bars and shops, and it's not hard to find a good spot for a scenic, waterside picnic.

3

ACCOMMODATION AND EATING   ISOLA DEI PESCATORI (ISOLA SUPERIORE)

No public ferries visit Isola dei Pescatori after about 7.20pm, but any of these restaurants will shuttle you for free to and from the shore by private motorboat when you book a table for dinner.

Belvedere Via di Mezzo ☎0323 32 292, ⓦbelvedere -isolapescatori.it. Busy mid-range hotel at the western end of the island with decent restaurant attached, offering views out over open water from beneath the vine-shaded pergola and a menu of local cuisine from lake fish to organic risotto. Booking essential. Restaurant open daily April–Oct. €100

★**Casabella** Via del Marinaio 1 ☎0323 33 471, ⓦisola-pescatori.it. Outstanding family-run restaurant for great food in a rumbustious, authentically local atmosphere. Plump for lake fish or artfully presented Piedmont beef and rabbit dishes (mains €20–25). Booking essential. *Casabella* also boasts one cosy double room upstairs for guests – spacious, clean, with a

comfortably chunky wooden bed and double windows overlooking the water. After dark, and in the early morning, is what sells it, when the crowds are absent. Restaurant open daily. €120

★**Verbano** Via Ugo Ara 2 ☎0323 30 408, ⓦhotelv erbano.it. Romantic little three-star hotel occupying the eastern end of the island. The twelve rooms are handsomely furnished, with lake views. In the early morning and evening, once the day-trippers have gone, the island reverts to calm and tranquillity: this is a perfect bolthole in any season. There's also a charming, moderately priced restaurant with shaded terraces at the water's edge, serving refined local cuisine – fish and seafood, pastas and meat mains. Booking essential. Restaurant open daily. €170

Isola Madre

Mid-March to mid-Oct daily 9am–5.30pm • €11, free to members of the British Royal Horticultural Society; joint ticket with Isola Bella €18.50; joint ticket with Isola Bella & Rocca Borromeo in Angera (see p.152) €22 • ☎0323 30 556, ⓦisoleborromee.it

Out in the bay is **Isola Madre**, larger but less visited than Isola Bella, with a small, tasteful *palazzo* and extensive gardens. The island was inhabited as early as 846 AD, when it was known for its olive trees and was dubbed the Isola San Vittore. By 998 it had become Isola Maggiore. It passed to the Borromeo family in the sixteenth century, and works proceeded slowly to build the villa and the azalea-rich, English-style gardens around it. By 1704 the island was being called Isola Madre, most likely after Margherita Trivulzio, mother of Renato I Borromeo.

The villa and gardens

The original landing-stage is on the north side of the island, from where a long, stepped avenue leads up to the house, but today, ferries dock on the south side. Steps rise to a terrace level; to the left is a short walk around to a café-restaurant (where private boats dock), while the entrance to the villa grounds is to the right. The free handout map describes a long circuit of the gardens, beginning at the ticket gate with the south-facing **Viale Africa**, lined with tropical exotics including lemons, magnolias and carob trees. Head up the steps to your left to reach the house, or continue ahead along the **Piano delle Camelie** through the garden; don't miss the **Piazzale dei Pappagalli**, home to a colony of parrots and peacocks and a magnificent, thirty-metre-high fragrant magnolia. In front of the house is the **Loggia del Cashmir**, where rises the largest Kashmir cypress tree in Europe, over two hundred years old.

The Borromeo family have furnished the **villa** with various historical bits and bobs taken from their other houses – a doll collection here, a four-poster bed there; this is much more appealing than Isola Bella, with none of the pomposity. Room 6 holds scenery and puppets from the eighteenth-century **Teatro delle Marionette**, while room 15 is the beautiful **Salotto Veneziano** (Venetian Drawing-Room), with elaborate Rococo wall decoration imitating a floral canopy.

Outside, turn right for the charming **Piazzale della Cappella**, centred on a pond with pink, red, white and yellow water-lilies and a hibiscus. Coffee, mimosa and banana plants add to the allure, with the little **Mortuary Chapel** on one side, dating from 1858. Steps lead down to the landing-stage past the **Viale delle Palme**, a line of giant palms interspersed with *Ginkgo biloba*.

3

Lake Mergozzo

Around the bay from Stresa and Baveno, Lake Maggiore ends at an expanse of reeds and marshes at the mouth of the River Toce. The main road bends right to hug the shore towards Verbania, while the autostrada and rail line dodge either side of the bulbous **Mont'Orfano** (794m) – named for its orphan status, remote from nearby peaks – on their way north to Domodossola. Omegna, at the head of Lake Orta (see p.111), lies 7km south of **Gravellona Toce**, the main town hereabouts.

Behind the marshes, and loomed over by Mont'Orfano, is the titchy **Lake Mergozzo** (**Lago di Mergozzo**), which formed part of Maggiore until silt from the Toce built up in the ninth century. It is now a freestanding tarn cut off from its giant neighbour, cool, clean and very deep. A road runs along its eastern shore, while the steep, wooded western slopes hold the scenic Sentiero Azzurro footpath linking the hamlet of Montorfano in fifteen minutes with **MERGOZZO** at the head of the lake, a picturesque old village with some interesting lanes to poke around in. Mergozzo would be a perfect location for a romantic little bistro at the water's edge; hopes rise when you spot terrace tables, but crash when you realize they belong only to the tacky *Birreria Freelance* pub. Mergozzo's hotels are similarly disappointing.

EATING   **LAKE MERGOZZO**

★**Piccolo Lago** Via Filippo Turati 87, on the lakeshore road between Fondotoce and Mergozzo ☎0323 586 792, ⊛piccololago.it. In the same family for more than forty years, this sleek fine-dining restaurant is now run by chef Marco Sacco and his sommelier brother Carlo. The modern, airy interior sports picture windows over the water, and service is smooth and discreet. Marco's cuisine combines rustic Piemonte mountain cooking with more sophisticated lake cuisine – for example, Mergozzo trout, lightly smoked in-house, or a flan of the local Bettelmatt cheese with a pear mustard. Pasta (such as chestnut-flour tagliatelle) is all home-made. Mains €22–38. *Menùs* €90 (five courses) or €130 (eight courses), with wine pairings (€50–70 extra). Closed Mon & Tues–Fri lunch.

Pallanza (Verbania)

The largest town on this part of the lake, **Verbania** is a modern conceit, formed in 1939 in a fit of Fascist zeal by "uniting" the old lakeside neighbours of Pallanza and Intra with nearby Suna, Fondotoce and a few inland villages and giving the project a grandiose title intended to evoke the Roman name for Lake Maggiore, *Lacus Verbanus*. The outcome is that Verbania is a will-o'-the-wisp; despite its appearance on maps and

VERBANIA

PALLANZA

ACCOMMODATION

Grand Hotel Majestic	5
Novara	3
Ostello Villa Congreve	4
Pallanza	2
Pesce d'Oro	1

RESTAURANTS & CAFÉS

Antica Osteria Monte Rosso	2
Bolongaro	5
Estremadura	3
Hostaria Dam a Traa	1
Il Burchiello	6
Il Portale	4
Milano	7

bus timetables, no actual town exists with that name. Pallanza, Intra and the others maintain their own clear identities and territories.

With a picturesque old quarter set back from its *imbarcadero*, **INTRA** is a bustling commercial town and transport hub, looking east across the lake. By contrast, its neighbour **PALLANZA** is a lovely, placid little resort, facing south over the bay and revelling in some beautiful views, exceptional sunsets and a balmy winter climate. The main road cuts inland, bypassing the centre of Pallanza, which has, as a result, one of the quietest and most attractive waterfronts on the whole of Maggiore. There's very little to do other than relax in the sunshine, sample the local restaurants, take the odd boat-trip and stroll in the lavish gardens of **Villa Taranto** nearby – a perfect Italian Lakes holiday.

Piazza Garibaldi

Pallanza's pedestrianized waterfront is centred on the dapper **Piazza Garibaldi**; boats dock here, most hotels are within a short stroll, and the tourist office is nearby. The broad piazza is flanked by terrace cafés and restaurants. It's a sociable spot; families and old-timers chat their afternoons away under the trees, while the kids play in the fountains. As dusk falls, join in the *passeggiata* to and fro along the lakeside Viale delle Magnolie in front of the piazza.

Museo del Paesaggio

Via Ruga 44 • Closed for restoration at the time of writing, with exhibits moved to Villa Giulia beside the tourist office; formerly April–Oct Tues–Sun 10am–noon & 3.30–6.30pm • €5 • ⓦ museodelpaesaggio.it

Pallanza's attractions are few; nose your way around the alleys, and up Via Ruga to the **Museo del Paesaggio**, which holds late nineteenth- and early twentieth-century landscape paintings of the area, as well as sculpture and some archeological finds.

Madonna di Campagna

Via alla Chiesa • Daily 9am–noon & 4–6pm • Free

Via Ruga – and the pedestrian zone – end at **Piazza Gramsci**, site of the post office and bus stops. Beyond here, well north of the centre on Viale Azari, is the Renaissance **Madonna di Campagna**, with an unusual octagonal arcaded lantern and Romanesque bell tower and, inside, sixteenth-century frescoes attributed to the school of Gerolamo Lanino.

Villa Taranto

Via Vittorio Veneto 111 • Mid-March to Oct daily 8.30am–6.30pm (Oct closes 4pm) • €10 • ⓦ villataranto.it

Pallanza's major attraction is the garden of **Villa Taranto**. The house, built in 1875, was bought in 1931 by Captain Neil McEacharn, scion of a wealthy Scottish industrial family, who spotted an advert for it in *The Times*. Over decades, McEacharn landscaped and cultivated the grounds of the villa, planting seeds gathered from around the world and establishing an extraordinarily rich and varied botanical garden. He died at Villa Taranto in 1964 and is buried in a mausoleum in the grounds.

The villa has its own landing-stage, a stop for virtually all Stresa–Intra **boats**, though it can also be reached from Pallanza **on foot** or **by bike** on Via Vittorio Veneto (the walk takes about 30min). Via Veneto is a narrow, lakefront road which leads from the old harbour around the headland; it is one-way for cars towards Pallanza – but most traffic is diverted elsewhere and virtually no vehicles use it. On the way, you'll pass the tiny **Isolino di San Giovanni**, an offshore islet owned by the Borromeo; its villa, once a favoured haunt of Toscanini, has no public access.

Exploring the gardens

You arrive at Villa Taranto's *imbarcadero*, with a free parking area alongside. The **ticket office** stands at the entrance gate beside a pleasant terrace **café-restaurant**. There are 7km of paths winding around these beautiful grounds, with the free map leading you past the delightful **Fontana dei Putti** (cherub fountain) to the dahlia garden and the greenhouses holding giant Amazonian lilies. Further round is the **Valletta**, a little valley created in 1935, with a charming arched bridge, and a set of **terraced gardens** with a field of **lotus** flowers. Give yourself at least an hour, if not a half-day, to take it all in. The villa itself – now off-limits at one end of the gardens – is the seat of the Provincia di Verbano-Cusio-Ossola.

Villa Giulia and Villa San Remigio

Apart from Villa Taranto, Pallanza has two more fine **gardens**. Beside the main tourist office is **Villa Giulia**, built in 1847 and renovated in Art Nouveau fashion in 1904; its grounds, landscaped in English style, are open to the public during daylight hours. The villa itself now hosts concerts and cultural events.

Signposted on the slopes above Pallanza is **Villa San Remigio**, with rhododendron-rich gardens designed in 1916. Visits, which include the fine Romanesque hilltop **oratory** – with its eleventh-century frescoes – are possible only by booking with the tourist office.

ARRIVAL AND DEPARTURE

PALLANZA (VERBANIA)

By plane Milan-Malpensa Airport is around 55km south. SAF's Alibus runs six times daily (April–Sept only) from Malpensa (Terminals 1 and 2) to Suna, Pallanza and Intra (€15; booking essential 48hr ahead by phone or online; ☏ 0323 552 172, ⊕ safduemila.com). Buses also run all year round from Malpensa (Terminals 1 and 2) to Gravellona Toce (€12; ⊕ comazzialibus.com), 10km west of Pallanza.

By train "Verbania-Pallanza FS" train station – on the Stresa–Domodossola main line, with fast service from Milan (Centrale and Porta Garibaldi) – lies 8km west of town, on the main road between Fondotoce and Gravellona, served by taxis or bus 2 every thirty minutes. Timetables are at ⊕ vcoinbus.it.

Destinations Domodossola (approx hourly; 20min); Milan (approx hourly; 1hr 15min).

By bus Buses serve Cannero and Cannobio, with some continuing across the Swiss border to Brissago, while others connect Pallanza with Stresa and Omegna on Lake Orta. Timetables are at ⊕ vcoinbus.it.

Destinations Cannero (hourly; 25min); Cannobio (hourly; 35min); Omegna (about every 30min; 35min); Stresa (about every 30min; 25min).

By car From the A26 autostrada, the Verbania exit is actually located near Gravellona Toce, 10km west of Pallanza itself. Approaching from Varese, take the SS394 to Laveno (22km; see p.150), from where the lake's only car ferry (which also takes foot passengers) shuttles continuously to and from Intra.

By boat Verbania has three different landing-stages, none of which has Verbania in its name: Pallanza is the most useful; there's another at Villa Taranto; and Intra is a major stop for boats heading up and down the shoreline as well as on a separate route across the lake to Laveno (not to be confused with Baveno). All three stops have frequent boats (see p.118) from Stresa and the islands. Timetables are at ⊕ vcoinbus.it. Private motorboat operators based at Pallanza include ⊕ lagomaggioreboat.it.

GETTING AROUND AND INFORMATION

Bike and scooter rental Rent a bike (€10/4hr, €15/day) or 50cc scooter (€40/4hr, €45/day) from Vagamondo, Corso Europa 41 in Pallanza (☏ 0323 504 419, ⊕ vagamondo.com) – or for slightly more options at similar prices (as well as a pick-up point on the Pallanza waterfront), consult the mobile operation Living Lake (☏ 329 569 2378, ⊕ livinglake.it).

Tourist office Corso Zanitello 8, beside the old harbour

(April–Sept Mon–Fri 9am–1pm & 3–5.30pm, Sat 9.30am–12.30pm & 3–5.30pm, Sun 9.30am–12.30pm; shorter hours in winter; ☏ 0323 503 249, ⊕ verbania-turismo.it & ⊕ distrettolaghi.it). There is also a smaller Pro Loco office at the Pallanza *imbarcadero*, Via delle Magnolie 1 (temporarily closed at the time of writing; formerly daily 9.30am–12.30pm & 3–6pm; ☏ 0323 557 676).

ACCOMMODATION

Camping Conca d'Oro Via Quarantadue Martiri 26 ☏ 0323 28 116, ⊕ concadoro.it. Best of five campsites clustered near each other between Fondotoce and Feriolo, a few kilometres west of Pallanza, with beach

access and decent facilities. Closed Oct–March. Pitch €44

★ **Grand Hotel Majestic** Via V. Veneto 32 ☏ 0323 504 305, ⊕ grandhotelmajestic.it. A grand hotel that lives up to the name, this traditional establishment has a magnificent waterfront location, impressive history (dating from 1870), *belle époque* architecture, beautiful grounds, state-of-the-art facilities and staff who are formal but accommodating. Rooms are furnished in classic style, many with balconies, and most with lake views. Most significantly, almost no traffic passes within earshot; the road outside is a one-way lane used chiefly by walkers and cyclists. This raises it well above similarly styled hotels on this and other lakes. Come to hear the lake waters lapping and the parquet floors creaking. €210

Novara Piazza Garibaldi 30 ☎0323 503 527, ⓦ hotelnovara.com. Well-kept little hotel in the centre of Pallanza, on the main square just a few steps from the lake. Rooms are compact but clean and attractive, and the welcome is warm. €80

Ostello Villa Congreve (HI hostel) Via delle Rose 7 ☎0323 501 648, ⓦ ostelloverbania.com. Lake Maggiore's only hostel, a short, signposted walk uphill from the tourist office. It's a friendly place set in an old hillside villa, with small dorms (including breakfast) and private doubles (with shared/en-suite bath); the staff also organize activities in the area. Dorms €21; doubles €46

Pallanza Viale Magnolie 8 ☎0323 503 202, ⓦ pallanzahotels.com. An excellent four-star hotel, on the Pallanza waterfront just across from the *imbarcadero*. The building dates from the early 1900s, but has been entirely renovated inside – rooms are characterful and spacious. Make sure you have a lake view, preferably on a balconied upper floor; windows face southwest towards Isola Madre and Baveno, and the late afternoons are sensational, as the sun, framed in the Toce valley, sinks behind the peaks of Monte Rosa. Service is cheerful and efficient, and there is parking available (though the spaces on the street are free). €140

Pesce d'Oro Via Troubetzkoy 136 ☎0323 504 445, ⓦ hotelpescedoro.it. About ten minutes' walk west of Pallanza in the little township of Suna, this is a decent three-star family hotel in a former monastery dating from the sixteenth century. Rooms are good, if a little generic, but their personal touch marks this place out as special – the Piazza family have been owners and managers for 30 years, and have created a warm, friendly environment for their guests. €105

EATING AND DRINKING

The best of Pallanza's **restaurants** lie just off the main square, with several notably good options available. The ones in plain view are perfectly good – but, as everywhere, those slightly hidden away tend to be even better. If you're after a meal to remember, also consider the short drive west to Piccolo Lago on Lake Mergozzo (see p.129).

Antica Osteria Monte Rosso Via Troubetzkoy 128 ☎0323 506 056. Highly acclaimed local restaurant in Suna, 1km west of Pallanza, with a terrace overlooking the lake. It's a traditional interior – tiled floor, old wooden chairs – but the cooking is upmarket, with an innovative approach to local styles. Expect around €50 a head, less than that at lunchtime. Open daily.

Bolongaro Piazza Garibaldi 9 ☎0323 503 254. Popular, highly accomplished pizza restaurant on the main square, with moderate prices and a welter of options. Pizzas €6–8, mains €8–17. Open daily.

★ **Estremadura** Via Troubetzkoy 142 ☎0323 504 282.

Cheerful little café-bar on the lakefront in Suna, 1km west of Pallanza, that is renowned for the owner Cinzia Ferro, who in 2014 won an Italian bar competition. Her national fame focused particularly on her cocktail skills – choose from 400 expertly prepared varieties, alongside beers, spirits, a long wine list and accompanying snacks and light bites. Daily 6pm–2am.

Hostaria Dam a Traa Via Troubetzkoy 106 ☎0323 557 152, ⓦ damatraa.com. Popular local wine-bar-cum-restaurant on the busy waterfront in Suna, 1km west of Pallanza, with a chic interior and sunny terrace tables. Closed Mon & Sat lunch.

LAGO MAGGIORE EXPRESS FROM PALLANZA

The **Lago Maggiore Express** excursion ticket is a great way to explore the region (see p.119). From **Pallanza** (on **Itinerary 9**), the clockwise routing starts at 8.20am with a short boat ride to Baveno, where you pick up the train to Domodossola. After a break for coffee, you join the scenic Centovalli railway – either straight to Locarno, arriving for lunch, or with a midway break at the mountain village of Santa Maria Maggiore, where you can grab a bite. Either way, your boat departs Locarno at 4.15pm, arriving back at Pallanza at 6.50pm.

The alternative routing anticlockwise involves an 11.35am lunch-boat departure to Locarno, where you have a short mid-afternoon break, continuing by train and boat to arrive back in Pallanza at 7.40pm.

These details were accurate at the time of writing – check for up-to-date schedules before you set out (and note that timetables are slightly different on Wednesdays, when Itinerary 15 applies instead). It's easy to put together a trip starting from other points on the lake, too.

Il Burchiello Corso Zanitello 3 ☎0323 504 503. A fresh, friendly little restaurant with a contemporary feel that specializes in fish and seafood – try the fettucine with octopus, or just go for the catch of the day. Their menus start from around €17, and they host live music on Fridays. Closed Wed.

Il Portale Vicolo Sassello 3 ☎0323 505 486, ⓦristoranteilportale.it. Discreet little place shoehorned into an alley off the main square, serving expertly prepared nouvelle-style cuisine. Expect welcome little touches such as no cover charge. Mains €16–25. Closed Tues.

Milano Corso Zanitello 2 ☎0323 556 816, ⓦristorante milanolagomaggiore.it. An expensive restaurant in a quiet, romantic setting, with terrace tables overlooking the old harbour. Their small *menù* of fish and pasta staples is done exceptionally well, but expect a bill of €75 per head and upwards. Closed Mon eve & Tues.

North to Locarno

North of Verbania, Lake Maggiore becomes wilder, narrower, more mountainous – and much less visited. Nonetheless, it pulls off a couple of gems just before the Swiss frontier: **Cannero** and especially **Cannobio** are as charming as anywhere on the lake.

Further north across the **Swiss border** (which is abruptly signposted hereabouts as *"confine"* or just "CH", the international abbreviation for Switzerland), the botanical island gardens on the **Isole di Brissago** are a mini-version of those on the more famous Isole Borromee at Stresa. They are overlooked by the picturesque, south-facing resort of **Ascona**, while at the top of the lake stands **Locarno**, a cultured town of elegant architecture, good food and great shopping.

Ghiffa

Occupying a small headland 5km north of Intra, **GHIFFA** has some of the lake's longest sightlines, south beyond Stresa, north as far as Maccagno. The former Panizzara hat factory, 500m north of the landing-stage – now largely converted into apartments – contains the diverting **Museo dell'Arte del Cappello** (Hat Museum; April–Oct Sat & Sun 3.30–6.30pm, July & Aug also Tues & Thurs same times; €1.50; ⓦmuseodellartedelcappello.it). Roads coil up to Ronco, access point for the **Sacro Monte di Ghiffa** (ⓦsacrimonti.net), a trio of seventeenth-century chapels within a nature reserve (ⓦparks.it).

ARRIVAL AND GETTING AROUND
GHIFFA

By bus Buses run approximately hourly from Pallanza (15min).

By boat Two boats daily (summer only) arrive from Stresa (1hr) and Verbania (30min), and two from Cannero (40min).

Bike and boat rental Intra's Living Lake (☎329 569 2378, ⓦlivinglake.it) rent bikes (€16/day), 125cc Vespas (€65/day) and small motorboats (€110/half day) at Hotel Ghiffa.

ACCOMMODATION

★**Hotel Ghiffa** Corso Belvedere 88 ☎0323 59 285, ⓦhotelghiffa.com. An old-fashioned charmer, standing on the lake side of the main road. Its public areas retain their nineteenth-century character – parquet floors, high ceilings, picture windows, gently ticking clocks – as do many of the rooms; the best are the spacious corner rooms on the second floor. Some on the first floor have their own terraces with panoramic lake views, while up on the fourth floor, under the eaves, smaller modernized rooms have compact, private sun-decks facing the lake. Private parking. **€185**

Cannero

Roughly 9km north of Ghiffa, **CANNERO RIVIERA** – it plays on its suffix – is a beautiful little corner, bypassed both by the main road (which keeps to a higher contour, well above shore level) and by most of Maggiore's crowds. It's a leisure resort, for sure, with a large campsite drawing in holidaying families, but also has more than a touch of class about it. The town occupies a little bulge of land, split by the Rio Cannero, which flows off Monte Spalavera (1534m) behind the town. This whole stretch of shore

– mostly south-facing and shielded by the mountains – is lush with subtropical flora; lemon, orange and olive trees all flourish, as do palms, magnolias, azaleas, mimosa, bougainvillea and camellias. Cannero's pretty waterfront promenade is idyllic almost to the point of sedation; come here for a meal, and find yourself lulled into lingering.

Museo Etnografico

Via Dante • July & Aug Tues 9.30am–12.30pm, Fri & Sat 8–10.30pm, Sun 5–7pm; April–Oct days & hours vary • €1

Just down from the tourist office in the Villa Laura, the **Museo Etnografico** is a modest folk museum of local history, with displays on domestic life, the brush industry that once supported the area and traditional crafts.

Castelli di Cannero (Castelli di Malpàga)

Just offshore are two islets, on which rise the photogenic **Castelli di Malpàga**, destroyed by the Visconti in 1414 and partially rebuilt by the Borromeo in 1521. At the time of writing they were undergoing restoration; ask around at the landing-stage to see if access is possible, and for a motorboat to take you out, or rent your own at the *Lido* campsite (about €20/hr).

3

ARRIVAL AND DEPARTURE | CANNERO

By bus Buses run approximately hourly from Verbania (both Pallanza and Intra) to Cannero (25min) and Cannobio (35min). Some continue north across the border to Brissago, from where Swiss buses head on to Ascona and Locarno. Timetables are at ⓦ vcoinbus.it.

By boat Cannero has regular ferry links south to Intra (40min) and onwards to the islands and Stresa, and north to Luino (15min) and Cannobio (45min). Timetables are at ⓦ vcoinbus.it.

INFORMATION AND ACTIVITIES

Pro Loco tourist office Via Orsi 1 (March–Oct Mon–Sat 9am–noon & 4–7pm, Sun 9.30am–noon; ☏ 0323 788 943, ⓦ cannero.it).
By boat One local motorboat operator based in

Cannero, offering trips on request, is Taxi Banano (☏ 339 834 3322, ⓦ taxibanano.it). Rent a self-drive motorboat (€35/hr) or a kayak (€8/day) on Cannero's west-facing beach (☏ 333 190 9035).

ACCOMMODATION AND EATING

Arancio Amaro Via Dante 39 ☏ 0323 788 398, ⓦ arancioamaro.it. This refurbished, family-run place with eight rooms on the Cannero waterfront is now reborn as a swanky little boutique hotel. Expect sleek lines, contemporary decor and fabrics, and a rather appealing, witty air of updated elegance. There's private parking too. The terrace restaurant has refined tasting menus focused around fish and seafood, from around €45 including wine – or opt for expertly prepared and

presented pastas (around €15) and mains (€19–24). €190
Camping Lido Viale del Lido 5 ☏ 0323 787 148, ⓦ campinglidocannero.com. Campsite on the beach on the south side of the headland, recently renovated, with a playground and family activities. Pitch €26
★ **Hotel Cannero** Lungolago 2 ☏ 0323 788 046, ⓦ hotel cannero.com. A refined, posh lake hotel of the old school with private parking and a pool, located directly opposite the ferry landing-stage. It occupies a former monastery and the

---

LAGO MAGGIORE EXPRESS FROM CANNERO OR CANNOBIO

The **Lago Maggiore Express** excursion ticket is a great way to explore the region (see p.119). From **Cannero** or **Cannobio** on **Itinerary 3**, you start with a boat to Locarno (departs Cannero around 7.30am, Cannobio around 8.30am). There's a brief stop in Locarno before the Centovalli ride to Domodossola. Linger in Domodossola for lunch, then board a fast train to Stresa – or get an earlier train and grab a bite in Stresa instead. Then either get an mid-afternoon boat back to Cannero (5.10pm) and Cannobio (5.55pm), or delay to visit Isola Bella and/or Isola Madre – only possible if you've pre-booked for the late-afternoon hydrofoil.

These details were accurate at the time of writing – check for up-to-date schedules before you set out (and note that Itinerary 3 doesn't operate on Wednesdays). It's easy to put together a trip starting from other points on the lake, too.

linked Casa del Barone alongside, dating from 1700. Its public areas and rooms, many with balcony, are quiet and tasteful, rates are a bargain and service is outstanding – genial, intelligent and understated. The waterfront terrace restaurant

is an atmospheric place for excellent, reasonably priced food – pasta, lake fish, and so on – alongside romantic views across the lake. The *Europa* restaurant next door is in a similar vein. Closed Nov–Feb. **€130**

Cannobio

North of Cannero, the narrow lakeshore road skirts Monte Carza (1116m) for 7km to **CANNOBIO**, one of Lake Maggiore's most appealing places to stay. A centre of lake commerce for over a thousand years, Cannobio has a beautiful, and very long, promenade of elegant, pastel-washed facades, most now occupied by terrace cafés. On Sunday mornings, the local **market** takes over the broad, granite-paved waterfront piazza, selling anything from fresh produce to leather goods. Behind, stepped and cobbled alleyways climb steeply into a tightly tangled old village of fifteenth- and sixteenth-century architecture, characterized by arcades, frescoes and charming little piazzas. It's a perfect place to spend a relaxed few days. Part of the pleasure is noshing your way through the town's cafés and restaurants.

Cannobio's campsites and an unusually good Lido **beach** (awarded an EU Blue Flag for cleanliness) – as well as the fact that it is the first town inside Italy on the drive south from Switzerland – attract many holidaying families from the north, especially German and Swiss-German; you'll find that English is the third or fourth language here. The town's only sight as such is the **Santuario della Pietà**, a Bramante-inspired church beside the landing-stage with a curious openwork cupola, built to house a painting of the *Pietà* which suddenly began to bleed in 1522.

Val Cannobina

Extending behind Cannobio, the wooded **Val Cannobina** offers beautiful views, little-visited stone-built hamlets and a clutch of good countryside restaurants. Buses climb high into the valley on one route to **Falmenta**, marooned in the jagged shadow of Monte Vadà (1836m), and on another to **Cursolo**, from where a scenic seven-kilometre walk heads past Finero to **Malesco** in the Val Vigezzo, a stop on the Domodossola–Locarno train line. Near Finero, **Provola** lies within the **Parco Nazionale Val Grande** (ⓦparcovalgrande.it), Italy's largest protected wilderness area; lonesome trails head from here through beech woods in the upper Cannobina valley to a mountain hut at Alpe Uovo, just below the Bocchetta di Terza pass (1836m). The tourist office has details of many more walks, including along the Linea Cadorna, a well-preserved World War I defence line that snaked across the peaks from the Val d'Ossola down to Cannobio.

Orrido di Sant'Anna

Around 2.5km into the valley from central Cannóbio, near Traffiume, a turn-off signs the **Orrido di Sant'Anna**, a spectacular rocky gorge surrounded by wooded slopes that is a popular picnic spot. Beside the Roman bridge and the chapel is a small river beach and a wonderfully sited restaurant, the *Sant'Anna* (see p.139). An attractive cycle route runs along the riverside from the centre of Cannobio, also easily covered on foot.

ARRIVAL AND DEPARTURE
CANNOBIO

By bus Buses run approximately hourly from Verbania (Pallanza and Intra) to Cannobio (35min). Some continue north across the border to Brissago, from where Swiss buses head on to Ascona and Locarno. Timetables

are at ⓦvcoinbus.it.
By boat Cannobio has regular ferry links up and down the lake, as well as good service across to Luino (see p.149) on the eastern shore. Timetables are at ⓦvcoinbus.it.

GETTING AROUND AND INFORMATION

By bus Cannobio's evening-only CityBus has departures every 30min (June–Aug Tues–Sun 6.30pm–1am) on a

circuit from the Infopoint kiosk by the lido, along the waterfront, then all the way out of town to the Orrido di

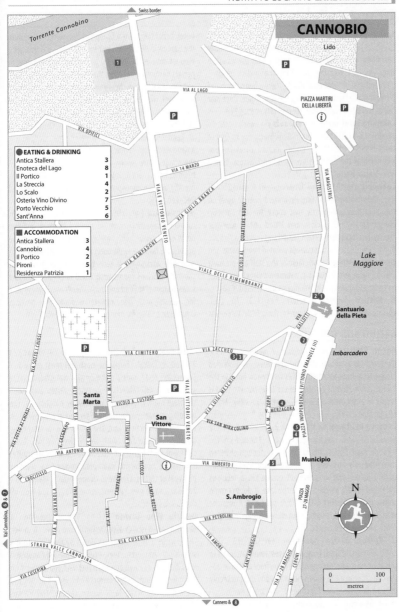

CANNOBIO

EATING & DRINKING

Antica Stallera	3
Enoteca del Lago	8
Il Portico	1
La Streccia	4
Lo Scalo	2
Osteria Vino Divino	7
Porto Vecchio	5
Sant'Anna	6

ACCOMMODATION

Antica Stallera	3
Cannobio	4
Il Portico	2
Pironi	5
Residenza Patrizia	1

Sant'Anna and back; a ticket is €1.50.

By bike and boat Intra's Living Lake (☏ 329 569 2378, ⓦ livinglake.it) rent bikes (€16/day) and 125cc Vespas (€65/day) at the Infopoint kiosk by the lido.

Tourist information A Pro Loco office is behind the San Vittore church off the main road, at Via A. Giovanola 25 (Mon–Sat 9am–noon & 4–7pm, Sun 9am–noon; ☏ 0323 71 212, ⓦ procannobio.it). There's also an official "Infopoint" kiosk by the lido car park, on Piazza Martiri della Libertà (April–Oct daily 10am–10pm; ☏ 0323 060 088, ⓦ distrettolaghi.it). More information at ⓦ www .lagomaggioreferien.com.

3

ACCOMMODATION

Antica Stallera Via P. Zaccheo 7 ☎0323 71 595, ⓦanticastallera.com. A friendly hotel occupying a former post-house and stables, built in 1650 within the village, a short way back from the waterfront. The modern rooms – quiet and en suite – are comfortable, there is free parking and the vine-shaded restaurant terrace is lovely. A great three-star choice, run by the same family for over fifty years. €118

Camping Internazionale Paradis Via Casali Darbedo 12 ☎0323 71 227, ⓦcampinglagomaggiore.it. One of several family-friendly campsites located cheek-by-jowl just north of the town centre, with beach access. Closed Nov–March. Pitch €34

Cannobio Piazza Vittorio Emanuele III 6 ☎0323 739 639, ⓦhotelcannobio.com. Prominent historic hotel on the quiet lakefront piazza, just above the old harbour. Everything is airy, spacious and kitted out to four-star quality, but lacks that certain something – and you'll have to hold your nose for the cut-out painted headboards and gaudy colour scheme. Nonetheless, the staff are pleasant and attentive, every room has a romantic view (some have balconies, too) and the location can't be bettered. €180

Il Portico Piazza Santuario ☎0323 70 598, ⓦhotelilportico.com. Another cracking little three-star hotel, benefiting from a tiptop location directly alongside the Santuario della Pietà; opt for room 207 and you get a view of cobbles, slate roofs, the church and the lake in perfect harmony. The rooms themselves are nothing fancy, but the location, the cheery welcome and the great hotel restaurant, tucked into a vaulted passageway off the lakefront promenade, conspire to seduce. €119

★**Pironi** Via Marconi 35 ☎0323 70 624, ⓦpironihotel .it. Cannobio's loveliest hotel – a real charmer, wedged into a narrow fifteenth-century ex-convent on a cobbled lane in the village centre. Rooms are light, bright and attractive – room 12 has its own private frescoed balcony – the staff are friendly, and the atmosphere is fresh and appealing. Closed Dec–Feb. €150

★**Residenza Patrizia** Via Veneto ☎0323 739 713, ⓦresidenzapatrizia.com. A swanky modern building north of the centre, with holiday apartments and – on the uppermost floors – eight hotel rooms. Everything is done with flair and style; hi-tech bathrooms with multi-jet showers, spacious rooms with wood floors and designer sofas, balconies to front and back. There's a swimming pool for guests and free private underground parking. Outstanding value for money. Closed Jan & Feb. €160

EATING AND DRINKING

Antica Stallera Via P. Zaccheo 7 ☎0323 71 595, ⓦanticastallera.com. Pleasant, enclosed, vine-shaded terrace restaurant attached to this family-run hotel in the village centre. There's no view of the lake, but the food is local and a full meal is unlikely to break the bank. Mains €9–18. Open daily.

Enoteca del Lago Via Nazionale 2, Carmine Inferiore ☎0323 70 595, ⓦenotecalago.com. Located on the lakeside road 3km south of Cannobio, though shielded from road noise, this is a gourmet restaurant serving top-quality Italian and international cuisine on a fabulous balconied terrace perched above the lake. It doesn't come cheap, though; expect €70 or more per head. Across the road is the pleasant *enoteca*, with wine-tastings and sales. Closed Tues & Wed lunch.

Il Portico Piazza Santuario ☎0323 70 598, ⓦhotelilportico.com. Cosy terrace restaurant attached to this hotel on a quiet section of the waterfront piazza beside the church, with a €13 daily lunch *menù* and decent, keenly priced à-la-carte options (mains €9–20). Open daily.

★**La Streccia** Via Merzagora 5 ☎0323 70 575, ⓦristorantelastreccia.it. Good, typical Piemonte food served in a rustic, low-ceilinged *osteria* in the heart of Cannobio, up one of the steep cobbled alleys leading back from the lakefront (*streccia* is a local word for alley). Local produce – cheese, meats, mushrooms – features strongly, as do regional wines. Mains €15–18; two-course *menù* €20. Closed Thurs.

★**Lo Scalo** Piazza Vittorio Emanuele III 32 ☎0323 71 480, ⓦloscalo.com. The best and most refined of Cannobio's restaurants, plum on the waterfront piazza – white linen tablecloths, crystal flutes and posh clientele mark it out from its cheaper neighbours. The building is lovely, a fourteenth-century *palazzo* with an atmospheric portico, and the cuisine is outstanding, classic Piemonte fare with innovative touches; black tagliolini with lobster, or skewer of quail with truffles and purple potato, for example, followed by suckling pig, veal or turbot. The *menù* changes daily. Mains €13–26; four-course *menù degustazione* €48. Closed Mon all day & Tues lunch.

Osteria Vino Divino Strada Valle Cannobina 1 ☎0323 71 919, ⓦosteriavinodivino.com. A quiet, shady little spot in the forest down by the river, with a surprisingly hip, urban feel – turn off the Val Cannobina road 2km out of town at a right fork and you're met with designer furniture, arty interiors and trendy haircuts. The specialities are wine, local Alpine cheese, and various kinds of salamis and cured meats, all sampled to the accompaniment of the rushing river. Mains €11–23; four-course *menù* €43. Open evenings only, plus Sun lunch. Closed Wed & Jan–Feb.

Porto Vecchio Hotel Cannobio, Piazza Vittorio Emanuele III 6 ☎0323 739 998. Although physically part of the hotel, the restaurant is under separate management – which is perhaps why it suffers from occasionally sloppy, over-informal service standards. It is, nonetheless, worth eating here (or just stopping in for an aperitif) simply for the heavenly lakeside terrace, one of the most captivating on all of Maggiore – shaded, quiet, with expansive views. The food is fine, fairly standard, moderately priced north Italian cuisine. Book a table by the balustrade for a romantic *tête-à-tête*. Open daily.

Sant'Anna Via Sant'Anna 30, overlooking the gorge ☎ 0323 70 682. A perfect little country restaurant, perched spectacularly on a crag above the Orrido di Sant'Anna. Choices like pâté, porcini mushrooms and lamb in a red wine and chestnut sauce make a delicious change from lake fish – and you could easily eat for €25–30 here. Booking essential. Served by the evening CityBus (see p.136) to and from Cannobio town centre. Closed Mon (except July & Aug).

Brissago

North of Cannobio, the lakeside road continues on a tight and narrow course around the cliffs that tumble down from Monte Giove (1298m) and the Monte Limidario massif (2187m). After 5km or so of slightly hair-raising driving, you **cross into Switzerland** – whereupon the road widens and improves. The first Swiss town, **BRISSAGO**, 2km further, is a rather soulless little place, determinedly neat and tidy and packed with holiday flats. It's best known for its large **cigar factory**, producer of fine Brissago smokes for over a century. If you're heading on to Ascona or Locarno, you can pick up maps and information at Brissago's **tourist office** on the main street.

The road continues through Porto Ronco, from where boats cross to the **Isole di Brissago** (see below), and on for 6km to **Ascona** and then **Locarno**. This whole area lies in Switzerland's Italian-speaking canton of Ticino, which has its own, unique history (see p.164).

ARRIVAL AND INFORMATION BRISSAGO

By bus A few Italian buses each day from Pallanza, Cannero and Cannobio continue over the border to terminate at Brissago. Timetables at ⓦ vcoinbus.it. Swiss buses start from Brissago on an hourly run to Ascona (15min) and Locarno (30min). Timetables at ⓦ sbb.ch/en.

By boat Brissago is linked into boat routings around the lake, with fairly frequent boats shuttling to the Isole di Brissago. Timetables at ⓦ navigazionelaghi.it.

Tourist office Via Leoncavallo 25 (March–Oct Mon–Fri 9am–6pm; June & Sept also Sat 9am–noon; July & Aug also Sat 9am–noon & 2–6pm; ☎ 0848 091 091, ⓦ ascona -locarno.com).

Isole di Brissago

April–Oct daily 9am–6pm • Fr.8 in addition to boat ticket • ☎ 091 791 4361, ⓦ isolebrissago.ch

The **ISOLE DI BRISSAGO** are twin islands 4km south of Ascona. These tiny dots of green in the shimmering lake overflow with luxuriant subtropical flora basking in the hot sun. The small island, Sant'Apollinare, has no public access, but the main island, San Pancrazio – about ten minutes' stroll end to end – is given over to a fine botanical garden, housing some 1700 species from around the world (note that the signs identifying each plant species lack an English translation). At one end stands an attractive 1929 villa, now a hotel and restaurant; a long lunch here, followed by a siesta under the palms, makes for an unexpectedly Mediterranean-like afternoon.

ARRIVAL AND DEPARTURE ISOLE DI BRISSAGO

By boat Boats run approximately hourly from Locarno (40min) and Ascona (10min), and more regular shuttles run from Porto Ronco (5min), the nearest point on the mainland. Timetables are at ⓦ isolebrissago.ch.

ACCOMMODATION AND EATING

Isole di Brissago ☎ 091 791 4362, ⓦ isolebrissago.ch. Villa Emden, the only house on the island, has a rather nice restaurant, very posh-looking, with white tablecloths and silver service, but unusually affordable, with mains – salads, pasta dishes and the like – either side of Fr.15. It's now also possible to stay overnight on the island; ten renovated upper-floor hotel rooms in the villa are simply furnished and – as you'd expect – blissfully peaceful. Not cheap, mind. **Fr.330**

Ascona

On the south-facing side of the Maggia delta, 14km north of Cannobio and 3km southwest of Locarno, **ASCONA** has been a magnet for idealistic, sun-starved northerners for more than a century. Since the 1890s, this fishing hamlet has grown into a cultured, artistically inclined small town, an enticing Swiss blend of character, natural beauty and good shopping. Swiss-German holidaymakers, in particular, love it.

But the influx of German-speakers, as summer tourists and second-home-owners, has been so great in recent years that Ascona can feel like it has lost its way. Since most of the visitors have, at best, rudimentary Italian, staff in hotels and restaurants are now accustomed to speak to guests in German first. Even the poshest menus are bilingual. Shops frequently advertise special offers in German before Italian. With general Ticinese disquiet at German-speaking dominance of Swiss affairs, Asconesi are becoming uneasy; voices are being raised for the cantonal government to step in and force Ascona's businesses to use Italian.

Piazza Motta

Ascona's *tour de force* is **Piazza Motta**, the cobbled lakefront promenade, south-facing and fully 500m long; its airy views past the Brissago islands down the lake, flanked by wooded peaks, are sensational. There are few better places anywhere – on any of the lakes – to watch the day drift by; the morning mists on the water, the clarity of light at midday, the sunsets and peaceful twilight are simply mesmerizing.

Museo Comunale d'Arte Moderna

Via Borgo 34 • March–Dec Tues–Sat 10am–noon & 3–6pm, Sun 10.30am–12.30pm • Fr.10 • ⓦ museoascona.ch

Ascona's attractive cobbled lanes leading back from the lakefront are full of artisans' galleries, upmarket jewellers and designer craft shops. The **Museo Comunale d'Arte Moderna**, in a sixteenth-century *palazzo*, has a high-quality collection focused on Marianne von Werefkin, one of the artists attracted to Ascona in its heyday and joint founder of Munich's expressionist *Blaue Reiter* movement; look out for her terrifying, Munch-like *Il Cenciaiolo* (The Rag-Man, 1920).

Monte Verità

Via Collina • Casa Selma daily 8am–8pm • Free • Rest of museum closed for renovation at time of writing • ⓦ monteverita.org

Word of Ascona began to spread a century or more ago, when a slow but steady influx began of philosophers, theosophists and spiritualists, most of whom believed that a return to nature was the best remedy for the moral disintegration of Western society. At the turn of the twentieth century, the artists Henri Oedenkoven and Ida Hofmann established an esoteric, vegetarian artists' colony on the hill of **Monte Verità** beside Ascona. An array of European fringe intellectuals followed; in 1913, Rudolf von Laban set up his nudist School of Natural and Expressive Dance within the Monte Verità community, attracting Isadora Duncan among others. During and after World War I, artists and pacifists flocked to Ascona.

The Bauhaus-style complex atop the wooded hill has now been revamped as a hotel and conference centre, but a few original buildings are preserved as a **museum** of the movement, including the wooden **Casa Anatta**, with two floors given over to papers and photos commemorating the artists' exploits. A short signposted walk into the woods brings you first to the tiny **Casa Selma**, used as the community's retreat, and then to the **Elisarion**, housing a circular painting by Elisar von Kupffer depicting the spiritual liberations of communal life.

Casa del Tè

Monte Verità • April–Oct Wed–Sun 1.30–6pm; Nov–March Sat & Sun 1.30–5pm • Free • Tea Ceremony: April–Oct first & third Tues of month 5pm; Nov–March first & third Sat of month 10.30am • Fr.38; booking essential • ☎ 079 551 1636, ⓦ casa-del-te.ch

Beside the hotel and conference centre is the small **Casa del Tè** (Tea House), essentially a shop selling exotic varieties of East Asian tea, which you can sample in the hotel café. Twice a month they stage an authentic **Japanese Tea Ceremony**, conforming to the unchanging strictures of sixteenth-century tea master Sen Rikyu.

ARRIVAL AND INFORMATION
ASCONA

By bus From Brissago (where Italian buses terminate), Swiss bus 316 runs hourly to Ascona (20min) and Locarno (30min). Bus 1 shuttles between Ascona and Locarno (every 15min; 15min). A day pass is Fr.6.90. See Ⓦcentovalli.ch for details.

By boat As well as frequent shuttles to the Isole di Brissago (15min), Ascona has roughly hourly boats to and from Locarno (20min), as well as fairly

regular services to/from Cannobio (50min), Luino (1hr) and points further south in Italy. Details at Ⓦnavigazionelaghi.it.

Tourist office Viale Papio 5, at the top of the old quarter (April–Oct Mon–Fri 9am–6pm, Sat 10am–6pm, Sun 10am–2pm; Nov–March Mon–Fri 9.30am–noon & 1.30–5pm, Sat 10am–2pm; ☎0848 091 091, Ⓦascona-locarno.com).

ACCOMMODATION

Ascona has literally dozens of **hotels**, with nine on the waterfront piazza alone, as well as a sprinkling of top-end luxury resort-style hotels. But although the upmarket hotels are as good as any in Switzerland (or Italy), mid-range options can be fairly ho-hum – and bargains are hard to find.

Art Hotel Riposo Scalinata della Ruga 4 ☎091 791 3164, Ⓦhotelriposo.ch. Swanky new design hotel, perched just above the old quarter, a stroll from the waterfront. The style is an appealing mix of classic – deep sofas, frescoed ceilings – and contemporary – vivid colours, hi-tech bathrooms. Rooftop views to the lake are pure romance. **Fr.230**

Castello Seeschloss Piazza Motta ☎091 791 0161, Ⓦcastello-seeschloss.ch. Four-star option at one end of the lakefront piazza, with tastefully appointed classic interiors. Also a member of the highly regarded Romantik Hotels group. **Fr.250**

Eden Roc Via Albarelle 16 ☎091 785 7171, Ⓦedenroc.ch. If money is no object, this – one of Switzerland's top

luxury hotels – makes for a memorable hideaway, with a variety of traditional and contemporary styled rooms and a host of amenities. **Fr.490**

Osteria Ticino Via Muraccio 20 ☎091 791 3581, Ⓦosteria-ticino.ch. One option that lets you duck under Ascona's high prices. This modest little place, a short walk outside the old quarter, has 15 double rooms in a plain but comfortable modern style, and the family who run it are ready to help. **Fr.190**

Tamaro Piazza Motta 35 ☎091 785 4848, Ⓦhoteltamaroascona.com. A decent, welcoming, family-run three-star hotel, with 44 rooms and an unbeatable location plum on the lakefront piazza. **Fr.240**

EATING AND DRINKING

Eating is a case of following your nose; Ascona's old quarter is given over to high-quality consumption of one kind or another, and the long waterfront piazza is lined with terrace café-restaurants. Otherwise, Locarno is within easy reach – or, if you have a car, consider the *Fattoria l'Amorosa* country restaurant (see p.183), roughly 20mins' drive from Ascona near Gudo.

BOATS ON THE SWISS SIDE OF LAKE MAGGIORE

Boats run by NLM (April–Oct only; Ⓦnavigazionelaghi.it) crisscross the Swiss shores of the lake, as well as continuing down the lake into Italy (see p.118).

A **point-to-point** one-way ticket from Locarno to Ascona is Fr.10.10, or Locarno to Isole di Brissago Fr.16.80 – though for all but the shortest hops, a **one-day pass** is the most economical choice; unlimited journeys within Zone A (Locarno to Ascona) or within Zone B (Ascona to Brissago) costs Fr.20.70, or throughout the whole Swiss basin Fr.36.60 (three days Fr.73.20). Families and those over 65 qualify for discounts. **International** fares are pricier; examples include Locarno to Stresa Fr.52.40 return, or Ascona to Pallanza Fr.39 return. Using the hydrofoil – for which you must **reserve in advance** – adds a small supplement.

A **Holiday Card** gives unlimited journeys on the whole lake, including Italy, for Fr.93 (three days) or Fr.140 (seven days). The **Ticino Discovery Card** (April–Oct only; Fr.87; Ⓦcartaturisticaticino.ch) covers free journeys on the Swiss part of the lake for three days in a week, as well as discounts for cable cars, museums and other attractions.

Al Torchio Contrada Maggiore ☎091 791 7126. Rustic little restaurant hidden away in the lanes, with a pleasant shaded courtyard. Notably strong on local specialities, with lamb and game lightened by fish and seafood pasta dishes. *Menù* around Fr.35. Closed Tues in winter.

Antico Ristorante Borromeo Via Collegio 16 ☎091 791 9281. A popular spot, offering a small, carefully chosen *menù*, an attractive vaulted interior, a private garden and – best of all – excellent, cheerful service. Expect a welter of Swiss and Italian dishes, from risotto and *osso buco* to lake fish and Alpine cheeses. Mains Fr.18–39. Closed Mon (except June–Aug open Mon eve).

Caffè Borghetto Via Carrà dei Nasi 18 ☎091 791 0968. Easy-going Old Town lounge bar and café-patisserie, out of the hubbub – come for the handmade Mastrolucibello ice cream. Open from breakfast until midnight (Sept–May closes 7.30pm). Closed Sun afternoon & Mon.

Della Carrà Via Carrà dei Nasi 10 ☎091 791 4452, ⓦ ristorantedellacarra.ch. Posh restaurant in a higher price bracket than others listed in this section, with an atmospheric courtyard and a reputation for Mediterranean cooking of high quality, including fish and seafood starters and its own charcuterie. Mains Fr.22–49. Closed Sun & Mon.

Elvezia Piazza Motta 15 ☎091 791 1514, ⓦhotel -elvezia.ch. An Ascona institution, in the same family for more than a century, offering a perfect spot on the waterfront piazza for inexpensive wood-fired pizza (Fr.17–22) and fish dishes, with a spacious terrace and keen prices (mains Fr.18–41). Open daily.

3

Locarno

The charming Swiss town of **LOCARNO** enjoys a grand location, on the broad sweeping curve of a bay at the top of Lake Maggiore. The arcades and piazzas of the town centre overlook subtropical gardens of palms, camellias, bougainvillea, cypress, oleanders and magnolias, which flourish on the lakeside promenades and cover the wooded slopes which crowd in above the town centre.

Locarno found its feet in the nineteenth century as the most elegant of Swiss resorts. In 1925 its backdrop of *belle époque* hotels and piazza cafés served as the setting for the **Treaty of Locarno**, signed by the European powers in a failed effort to secure peace following World War I. These days, Locarno focuses its considerable resources on tourism; the cobbled alleys of the Old Town, lined with Renaissance facades, can get overrun with the rich and wannabe-famous on summer weekends, yet still – in the midst of the hubbub – the place manages to retain its poise.

The UNESCO World Heritage Site of **Bellinzona** (see p.180) is easily reached by road or a short train journey 15km east of Locarno. From Bellinzona, high-speed trains and a motorway offer rapid connections south to **Lake Lugano** (see p.164) and **Lake Como** (see p.186).

Piazza Grande

The focus of town is **Piazza Grande**, an attractive arcaded square just off the lakefront that is lined with pavement cafés and serves as meeting point, social club and public catwalk. Warm summer nights deliver some great people-watching, as exquisitely groomed locals parade to and fro, with all the cafés abuzz and fragrant breezes bringing in the scent of flowers from the lakeside gardens, which extend south for 1km or so to the fragrant **Parco delle Camelie**, planted with 900 varieties of camellia.

Old Town

From the west end of Piazza Grande, lanes run up to Via Cittadella in the **Old Town** and the Baroque **Chiesa Nuova**, adorned with a huge statue of St Christopher outside. The quiet arcaded courtyard, reached through a side door, is a charming spot to draw breath away from the bustle. From here it's pleasant to lose yourself in the bustle; don't miss Suini, an unprettified locals' deli at Via San Francesco 3 (closed Sun afternoon & Mon), which is packed with Alpine cheeses, cured meats, olive oils, fresh pasta and countless other culinary souvenirs.

Opposite the deli, the atmospheric Via di Sant'Antonio brings you to the rather sombre church of **Sant'Antonio**, dating from the seventeenth century but rebuilt following a fatal roof collapse in 1863. Beside the church, the eighteenth-century

Casa Rusca (Tues–Sun 10am–noon & 2–5pm; Fr.8; ⓦlocarno.ch) houses a worthwhile art museum focusing on the twentieth-century Swiss artist Jean Arp.

Alleys lead south to the tall **San Francesco**, consecrated as part of a monastery in the fourteenth century. Sixteenth-century renovation added frescoes, most of which are now fading badly. Further down sits the stout thirteenth-century **Castello Visconteo**, now home to the **Museo Archeologico** (April–Oct Tues–Sun 10am–noon & 2–5pm; Fr.8; ⓦlocarno.ch), worth visiting if only for its collection of beautiful Roman glassware and ceramics.

Muralto

Lanes lead back from the lakefront landing-stage into the contiguous urban district of **Muralto**, home to the Madonna del Sasso funicular station and – one minute further – Locarno's **train station**. On the far side of the station, 100m east, rises the austere twelfth-century Romanesque basilica of **San Vittore**, built over a church first mentioned in the tenth century and now surrounded by housing developments. Medieval fresco-fragments inside and the Renaissance relief of St Victor on the bell tower are a diverting contrast to the trackside views. From here, a pleasant walk along the *lungolago* (lakefront promenade) leads back into town.

Madonna del Sasso

Church Daily 6.30am–7pm • Free • ⓦmadonnadelsasso.org • **Funicular** Daily 8am–8pm (later in summer); every 15 min • Fr.7.20 return

Most striking of all Locarno's sights is the pilgrimage church of **Madonna del Sasso**, an impressive ochre vision floating above the town centre in the district of **Orselina**. It stands on a wooded crag – *sasso* means rock – and was consecrated in 1487 on the spot where, seven years earlier, the Virgin had appeared to a Franciscan brother. The twenty-minute walk up through the wooded ravine of the Torrente Ramogno and past a handful of decaying shrines is atmospheric enough in itself; or you could take the **funicular** from just west of the train station. The low, Baroque interior of the church features a number of paintings, two of which stand out: Bramantino's emotionally charged *Fuga in Egitto* (Flight to Egypt, 1522) and local artist Antonio Ciseri's *Trasporto di Cristo al Sepolcro* (1870). Don't miss the epic views from the cloister, beside the church door.

Cardada and Cimetta

Cable car Daily 8.15am–6.15pm; every 30min (autumn/winter hours slightly curtailed) • **Cimetta chairlift** Daily 9.30am–5pm (Dec–March closed Mon–Thurs) • To Cimetta Fr.36 return, to Cardada Fr.28 return • ⓦ cardada.ch

In high summer, when sweltering Locarno (210m) gets too much, it's easy to escape into the cool, wooded hills above. Opposite the top station of the Madonna del Sasso funicular in **Orselina** (395m) is the base station of a futuristic cable car that rises on an ear-poppingly steep course to the plateau of **Cardada** (1350m), set amid fragrant pine woods. A short stroll left from the top station brings you to the "Observation Platform", a gracefully designed catwalk suspended off a huge A-frame; a stupendous view takes in Ascona, the lake and the mountains. There are a couple of simple restaurants up here and some easy strolls in the pine forest – many of them wheelchair accessible.

Turn right from the top station, and wander for ten minutes or so through the woods to a spectacular chairlift that whisks you even higher, up to the flower-strewn meadows of **Cimetta** (1672m), where there's a restaurant/guesthouse with a terrace view that you won't forget in a hurry. This is a popular hang-gliders' take-off point, too.

If you're approaching from Locarno, ask at the base-station of the Madonna del Sasso funicular for a ticket to the top; this discounts the fare and includes half-price car parking in Locarno as well.

Valle Maggia

ⓦ vallemaggia.ch

The valleys around Locarno offer exceptional mountain scenery, not least in the wild **VALLE MAGGIA**, which comprises a complex valley system stretching north into the high Alps. Roads divide 30km north of Locarno at **Bignasco** (438m). One route heads northwest into the Val Bavona, hemmed in by sheer scarps and waterfalls, leading to a cable car rising to the glacial eyrie of **Robiei** (1905m). There's a terrace restaurant beside the top station (ⓦ robiei.ch).

From Bignasco, another road struggles northeast into the Val Lavizzara to **Mogno** (1180m), where you'll spot the tilted circular roof of the church of San Giovanni Battista, designed by Ticinese architect Mario Botta and completed in 1996. It's a dazzling achievement – this small building, set on a marble plaza, boasts a supremely

---

FESTIVALS IN LOCARNO AND ASCONA

Events and festivities in Locarno and Ascona run all summer long (see ⓦ ascona-locarno.com). The season kicks off in June with Ascona's **Street Artists Festival**, followed in late June by the popular **JazzAscona** festival (ⓦ jazzascona.ch). In July, Locarno hosts **Moon and Stars** (ⓦ moonandstars.ch), a run of open-air rock and pop gigs by major stars.

In among several more festivals of music and performance, the **Locarno International Film Festival** (ⓦ pardo.ch), in early August, is rated among the top five film festivals in the world. Catch major offerings on the huge open-air screen in Piazza Grande, playing to 7500 people nightly (Fr.24), or at one of the 12 daily screenings in the city's cinemas (Fr.15).

Over late August and September, Ascona presents its **Settimane Musicali** ("Music Weeks"), a series of prestigious classical concerts staged around the region.

LAGO MAGGIORE EXPRESS FROM LOCARNO

The **Lago Maggiore Express** excursion ticket is a great way to explore the region (see p.119). Both directions from **Locarno** are well timed, with enticing stopovers. **Itinerary 14** starts with a morning train through the Centovalli to Domodossola, where a choice of connections bring you on to Stresa for lunch. You could then include a boat trip to Isola Bella before heading directly back to Locarno, arriving around 7pm. In reverse, **Itinerary 4** has a cruise to Stresa by mid-morning boat or hydrofoil. This allows a decent break for lunch before an afternoon train to Domodossola, and a short break there before joining the Centovalli line back to Locarno, arriving at 6.20 or 7.20pm.

These details were accurate at the time of writing – check for up-to-date schedules before you set out. Variations are also possible from **Ascona**.

elegant interior, bare and silent, encircled in striped marble, with the altar bathed in sunlight. It is worth the journey.

3

Verzasca Dam

ⓦ tenero-tourism.ch

About 3km east of Locarno above the town of Tenero, a road coils up into the Val Verzasca to meet the gigantic **Verzasca Dam**, scene of the world's highest commercial bungy jump (ⓦ trekking.ch). You can park beside it and walk out onto the dam; on one side is a dizzying 220-metre drop down to bare rock, on the other a tranquil, blue lake is framed by classic Alpine scenery. Expect sweaty palms.

ARRIVAL AND DEPARTURE
LOCARNO

By train Locarno's train station is 100m north of the ferry landing-stage and 150m northeast of Piazza Grande. Mainline trains to and from Bellinzona (20min) – where you can change for Lugano, Como and Milan – depart frequently from ground level. From separate platforms below ground, the local transport company Ferrovie Autolinee Regionali Ticinesi – unfortunately abbreviated to FART – operates trains on the narrow-gauge Centovalli line towards Domodossola (see p.147). Schedules are searchable at ⓦ sbb.ch/en.

By bus From Brissago (where Italian buses terminate) Swiss bus 316 runs hourly to Locarno (30min). Bus 1 shuttles between Ascona and Locarno (every 15min; 15min). A day pass is Fr.6.90. See ⓦ centovalli .ch for details.

By boat Locarno has roughly hourly boats to and from Ascona (20min), as well as fairly regular services to/ from Cannobio (1hr 10min), Luino (1hr 20min) and points further south in Italy (see p.118). Details at ⓦ navigazionelaghi.it.

INFORMATION AND TOURS

Tourist office In the Casino complex on the edge of Piazza Grande, at Largo Zorzi 1 (April–Oct Mon–Fri 9am–6pm, Sat 10am–6pm, Sun 10am–1.30pm & 2.30–5pm; Nov–March Mon–Fri 9.30am–noon & 1.30–5pm, Sat 10am–noon & 1.30–5pm; ☏ 0848 091 091, ⓦ ascona-locarno.com).

Segway tours One neat way to explore is on a two-hour guided tour by Segway (Fr.90/person). Book ahead – preferably the day before, but last-minute is sometimes possible – through *Albergo Losone* (☏ 091 785 7000, ⓦ albergolosone.ch); the hotel, midway between Ascona and Locarno at Via dei Pioppi 14, is also the meeting point. Tours go with a minimum of two people. You'll need your driving licence.

ACCOMMODATION

Locarno's **accommodation** is strongest in the mid-range bracket, with a good choice of hotels in and near the city, and facilities of a pretty high standard. However, if you're after a spot of luxury, your best bet is to dodge Locarno and instead head over to Ascona (see p.140) or Lugano (see p.166).

Albergo Castello Schlosshotel Via San Francesco 7a ☏ 091 751 2361, ⓦ hotelcastello.ch. Thirty-two large old-fashioned rooms in a well-kept Old Town pile, run by the same family for knocking on a century. It stands in a quiet corner, amid gardens off mostly pedestrianized lanes beside the Visconti fortress; upper rooms have balconies with lake views. Closed Nov–March. **Fr.185**

★ **Ca' Serafina** Lodano ☎091 756 5060, ⓦcaserafina
.com. For a break from the lakes, book well ahead for this
outstanding five-room *pensione* in the rural hamlet of
Lodano, 15km north of Locarno. Rooms are rustic, spacious
and all en suite, and the charming owner, Alexa Thio,
speaks English. Dine at *Locanda Poncini*, a lovely little
restaurant down the road in Maggia village. **Fr.200**

Camping Delta Via Respini 7 ☎091 751 6081,
ⓦcampingdelta.com. Quality campsite, a 15min walk
south from the town centre along the lakeshore
promenade. Closed Nov–Feb. Pitch **Fr.67**

Città Vecchia Via Torretta 13 ☎091 751 4554,
ⓦcittavecchia.ch. Centrally placed B&B pension-style
hotel, with dorms (Fr.40pp) and simple, shared bathrooms.
Closed Nov–Feb. **Fr.100**

Du Lac Via Ramogna 3 ☎091 751 2921, ⓦdu-lac
-locarno.ch. Location, location, location. This three-star
"*garni*" hotel (meaning one which has no restaurant and
only serves breakfast for guests) is unbeatably central,
steps from the landing-stage, at the edge of Piazza Grande

and within a minute's stroll of the train station. The rooms
are pleasant and well soundproofed, but don't expect much
in the way of personal service. **Fr.210**

Nessi Via Varenna 79 ☎091 751 7741, ⓦgarninessi.ch.
Welcoming little family-run three-star a short way west of
the centre, with pool and private underground parking.
Rooms are fresh and decent, with better, bigger ones on
higher floors. Closed Jan. **Fr.195**

Palagiovani Ostello/Jugendherberge (HI hostel)
Via Varenna 18 ☎091 756 1500, ⓦyouthhostel.ch
/locarno. Modern hostel with dorms and bike rental, but
it's in an awkward western location – take bus 1 or 7 from
the station to Cinque Vie. Closed Dec–Feb. Dorms **Fr.43**;
doubles **Fr.90**

Vecchia Locarno Via Motta 10 ☎091 751 6502,
ⓦvecchia-locarno.ch. Well-run Old Town gem that has
benefited from a renovation, with twenty simple
shared-bath and en-suite rooms – singles, doubles and
a triple – above the cheerful *Govinda* courtyard
restaurant. **Fr.110**

EATING AND DRINKING

Piazza Grande is full of cafés and pizzerias buzzing from morning until after midnight, and there are plenty of atmospheric
places in the Old Town alleys. Fresh fish plucked from the lake is Locarno's speciality – look out for trout (*trota*), perch
(*persico*), pike (*luccio*) and whitefish (*coregone*). Out of town, aim for the *Fattoria l'Amorosa* agriturismo near Gudo, roughly
fifteen minutes' drive northeast of Locarno (see p.183).

Cantina/Osteria Canetti Piazza Grande 1 ☎091
751 0797. Plain local cooking (around Fr.18) in a much-
loved popular diner, with the added bonus of live
accordion on Fri and Sat nights – but in 2014 a
Fr.17m complete rebuild of the property was announced,
which may mean substantial changes when you visit.
Closed Sun.

★ **Casa del Popolo** Piazzetta Corporazioni ☎091
751 1208. Unpretentious, always-busy Old Town terrace
restaurant and pizzeria, with a long menu of simple,
hearty Swiss-Italian food – pizzas (Fr.19–26) and home-
made pasta, plus fish and meaty mains (Fr.26–38).
Open daily.

Cittadella Via Cittadella 18 ☎091 751 5885,
ⓦcittadella.ch. The popular trattoria at ground level is
excellent, serving pizzas, pasta and simple fish dishes
(Fr.15–38), while upstairs the formal restaurant
concentrates on fish and seafood – and does it well (four-
course *menù* Fr.75). Open daily.

Funicolare Via Santuario 4, Orselina ☎091 743 1833.
Quiet, simple place beside the funicular top station that
benefits from a spectacular secluded terrace garden
overlooking Madonna del Sasso at which to savour their
inexpensive fish specialities. Closed Thurs in winter &
Nov–Jan.

★ **Govinda** Via Motta 10 ☎091 752 3852, ⓦgovinda
-locarno.ch. Pleasant little café-restaurant in the Old Town

serving organic Indian cuisine – all vegetarian – from a
daily-changing buffet selection (each dish Fr.6–8). *Menùs*
start from around Fr.25. Mon–Thurs 9am–6.30pm, Fri &
Sat 9am–10.30pm.

Lungolago Via Bramantino 1 ☎091 751 5246,
ⓦlungolago.ch. Classy, dimly-lit bar, pizzeria and
paninoteca where flamboyantly sociable locals go to flee
the invasion of white-knee'd northerners. Mains Fr.21–40.
Open daily.

Manora Via della Stazione 1, Muralto ☎091 743 7676,
ⓦmanor.ch. Good self-service salads and plain cooking in
this busy buffet fast-food-style restaurant across from the
train station. Open daily until 9pm.

Osteria del Centenario Viale Verbano 17, Muralto
☎091 743 8222. One of Locarno's best restaurants,
serving internationally acclaimed nouvelle cuisine
in an appealing blend of French and Italian styles. A
lakeside terrace and three-figure bills come as standard.
Closed Sun.

Pozzo Piazza Sant'Antonio ☎091 751 5088,
ⓦbarpozzo.com. Friendly local café-bar on a quiet Old
Town square. Open daily.

Svizzero Largo Zorzi 18 ☎091 751 2874. Best of the
many pizzerias and diners on Piazza Grande, with
affordable fresh-made pasta, wood-fired pizza and plenty
of Italian staples. Bustling from breakfast till the small
hours. Open daily.

The Centovalli railway

Ⓦ centovalli.ch & Ⓦ vigezzina.com

Locarno is the eastern terminus of the scenic **Centovalli railway** to Domodossola, known in its Italian section through the Val Vigezzo as the **Ferrovia Vigezzina**. Little trains run by the Swiss FART company and its Italian SSIF counterpart depart from beneath Locarno station into the spectacular valley – so named for its "hundred" side valleys – most of the time winding slowly on precarious bridges and viaducts above ravine-like depths. Sit on the left for the best views. The area is renowned for its natural beauty, and, with a walking map from Locarno tourist office, you could get out at any of the villages en route, pick up a trail and head off into the hills. There's no lack of cafés and simple accommodation. One neat way to see the route is with the **Lago Maggiore Express** pass (see p.119).

Tiny **VERSCIO**, 4km northwest of Locarno, is a lovely stone-built village which houses the **Teatro Dimitri** (Ⓦ teatrodimitri.ch), an international mime school founded by the Ascona-born clown Dimitri, protégé of Marcel Marceau. The small theatre stages performances all summer long. Some 3km down the line is **INTRAGNA**, whose graceful seventy-metre bridge was the scene of Switzerland's first-ever bungy jump, and remains a choice spot for leaping.

After the border at **Cámedo** (passport needed), trains roll on through rustic villages of the Italian **Val Vigezzo** to the highest point of the line at **SANTA MARIA MAGGIORE** (836m) before easing down into Domodossola.

Domodossola

The busy, characterful Italian town of **DOMODOSSOLA** stands at the fulcrum of three major rail routes: Swiss main line trains run west to Bern and Geneva; Italian ones speed south to Stresa and Milan; and little mountain trains depart from underground platforms on the scenic route east to Locarno through the Val Vigezzo and **Centovalli** (see above).

If you have time to kill between connections, walk directly away from the station westwards on Corso Ferraris and Corso Fratelli di Dio for 200m into the old part of town, set around a series of attractively crumbling arcaded piazzas. **Piazza Mercato** is the finest – conveniently laid with café tables – and also stages the town's Saturday market. From here, pedestrianized Via Briona, lined with many pleasant cafés and restaurants, leads to Piazza Cavour, from where Via Marconi returns to the station.

ARRIVAL AND INFORMATION   DOMODOSSOLA

By train Aside from the narrow-gauge trains on the Centovalli/Vigezzina line from Locarno (1hr 40min), Domodossola also has mainline services from Stresa (35min) and Milan (1hr 30min). Timetables are at

Ⓦ vcoinbus.it.
Tourist office Piazza Stazione (Mon–Fri 8.30am–12.30pm & 2–6pm, Sat 8.30am–12.30pm; ☏ 0324 248 265, Ⓦ prodomodossola.it).

EATING AND DRINKING

Il Giardino Via Gramsci 21 ☏ 0324 243 587. Pleasant little restaurant serving mid-priced fish and risotto on its vine-shaded terrace. Open daily.

La Meridiana Via Rosmini 11 ☏ 0324 240 858, Ⓦ ristorantelameridiana.it. Moderately priced Spanish specialities, as well as fish and pasta dishes. Closed Mon.

★ Pasticceria Grandazzi Via Castellazzo 23 ☏ 0324 243 040, Ⓦ pasticceriagrandazzi.com. For particularly luscious edible souvenirs, head 250m north of Piazza

Cavour on Via Binda, then turn right onto Via Castellazzo to find this superb chocolatier; munch on their chocolate paintbrushes or take away a chocolate toolbox, complete with delicious spanners and "rusty" nails, dusted with cocoa. Tues–Sat 9am–12.30pm & 3–7pm, Sun 9am–12.30pm.

Piazzetta Piazza Matteotti 5 ☏ 0324 481 006, Ⓦ giardinasrl.it. A cheery, inexpensive joint for good-value pizza, located directly in front of the station. Closed Tues in winter.

Eastern Lake Maggiore

The **eastern shore** of Lake Maggiore has some appealingly quiet hideaways and great opportunities for mountain hikes and drives. Not far south of the Swiss border, **Luino** is heavily promoted for its huge weekly market and as an access point for mountain drives and walks. **Laveno**, opposite Verbania, has a touch of character, but the highlight of the area is the hermitage of **Santa Caterina del Sasso**, wedged into the rocky cliffs opposite Stresa.

Maccagno and the Gambarogno

MACCAGNO, just inside Italy on Maggiore's northeastern shore, is a dour working village, split in two by the River Giona. The **Swiss border** at Zenna lies 9km north; just before you get there, in **Pino**, La Darsena (May–Sept; ⓦladarsenawindsurf.com) takes advantage of the breezy conditions to offer windsurfing and kiteboarding courses, as well as rental (€18/hour).

Over the border in Switzerland, the 13km stretch opposite Ascona and Locarno is known as the **Gambarogno**, a line of shoreside villages backed by rugged mountains. **VIRA** is the main settlement, from where a road climbs above San Nazzaro to the splendid hillside **Parco Botanico del Gambarogno** (daily during daylight hours; Fr.5; ⓦparcobotanico.ch), one of Europe's finest collections of magnolias and camellias, alongside azaleas, rhododendrons, peonies and more – best viewed in springtime.

Maccagno and the **Val Veddasca**, which climbs behind the town, are linked to the Gambarogno by testing mountain roads and stiff hiking trails. An improbably steep track leads straight out from Maccagno into the hills, from where there are paths up to the dam on little **Lake Delio**. Trails also lead inland from Maccagno to **Curiglia**, beyond which, from Ponte di Piero, a precipitous mule track climbs to picturesque **Monteviasco**, 500m above. There's no road to Monteviasco, and until the recent arrival of a cable car, the mule track was its only link with the world.

ARRIVAL AND DEPARTURE — MACCAGNO AND THE GAMBAROGNO

By train Magadino, Vira and Maccagno are stops on the Luino–Bellinzona rail line (about every 2hr; 10–30min from Luino). Timetables at ⓦtilo.ch.

By bus Roughly hourly buses connect Luino and Maccagno; timetables at ⓦwww.muoversi.regione .lombardia.it. Vira has buses to Magadino (from where boats serve Locarno) and up to Indemini – timetables at ⓦsbb.ch/en.

By boat Vira, Maccagno and other villages are linked into ferry routes around the lake. Timetables at ⓦnavigazionelaghi.it.

INFORMATION

Maccagno tourist office Via Garibaldi 1 (Tues–Sat 9am–12.30pm & 4–7pm; July & Aug also Sun 9.30am–12.30pm; closed Jan & Feb; ☏0332 562 009, ⓦprolocomaccagno.it).

Vira tourist office Via Cantonale (July & Aug Mon–Fri 8am–6pm, Sat 9am–noon; rest of year Mon–Fri 8am–noon & 2–6pm, Sat 9am–noon; Nov–May closed Sat; ☏091 795 1866, ⓦgambarognoturismo.ch).

Indémini

For drivers, a road also climbs from Maccagno through the woods to Lake Delio; the views are breathtaking, looking back at Cannobio, 1000m below on the lake. Beyond the pass at **La Forcora**, this route links up with another that crosses the border at the isolated Swiss hamlet of **INDÉMINI** (930m), 18km from Maccagno. This stone-built village clinging to the valley sides has recently attracted artists and sculptors; workshops are often open. The simple *Ristorante Indeminese* is a great lunch stop. Beyond, it's a drive of 17km over the bleak Alpe di Neggia pass (1395m) – with a mountain inn boasting spectacular views – down to Vira on the lakeshore.

ARRIVAL AND DEPARTURE

INDÉMINI

By bus An Italian bus links Maccagno with the mountain border village of Biegno (3–5 daily; 50min); walking the 500m of no-man's-land brings you into Indémini, from where a Swiss bus runs down to the ferry at Magadino, beside Vira (2 daily; 1hr).

ACCOMMODATION AND EATING

Ristorante Indeminese ☎091 795 1222, ⓦ ristorante-indeminese.ch. This charming little tavern restaurant, in the tiniest of mountain villages, offers heartwarming Swiss-Italian Alpine cooking, from game and polenta to home-made pasta. There are sublime views of mountains and valleys from the balcony, and there's even a little self-catering apartment where you can hole up for the night. **Fr.70**

Luino

Roughly 14km south of the Swiss border, the commercial town of **LUINO** is besieged every **Wednesday** by people pouring in for what is, purportedly, the largest weekly **market** in Europe, a frantically busy emporium seemingly dominated by handbags, clothes, shoes and novelty toys. More interesting stalls – tucked away down side streets – sell homeware or silks and laces, and your nose will lead you to the food section, piled high with cheeses from all over Italy and Switzerland, endless varieties of salami and prosciutto, Sicilian olives and fresh-baked breads. Roads are jam-packed from breakfast-time onwards and parking restrictions are strictly enforced; if you haven't got a space by 8am, don't bother looking. Extra boats and buses serve Luino all day long. The town has a decent choice of hotels – including one of the best on this side of the lake.

ARRIVAL AND INFORMATION

LUINO

By train Shoreline trains connect Luino to the Swiss city of Bellinzona in the north, also running south to Laveno and Malpensa Airport (change at Gallarate for Milan Porta Garibaldi). Timetables are at ⓦ tilo.ch.
Destinations Bellinzona (approx every 2hr; 45min); Laveno (approx every 2hr; 30min); Malpensa (approx every 2hr; 1hr 25min).
By bus Buses connect Luino with towns up and down the shoreline; see ⓦ www.muoversi.regione.lombardia.it.
By boat There are boats (see p.118) from Luino to Cannobio and other points on the Italian shore as well as Ascona and Locarno in Switzerland.
Luino tourist office Viale della Vittoria (Mon–Sat 9am–noon & 2.30–6pm, Sun 9am–noon; Nov–March Mon–Sat 9am–noon & 2–5.30pm; ☎0332 530 019, ⓦ vareselandoftourism.com).

ACCOMMODATION

★**Camin Hotel Colmegna** Via Palazzi 1, 3km north of Luino in the hamlet of Colmegna ☎0332 510 855, ⓦ caminhotel.com. Though this eighteenth-century building is on the busy shoreside road, soundproofing ensures noise is negligible. The easy-going family owners keep their bright lakeview rooms spotless. Immediately beyond the hotel, the shoreside road enters a tunnel beneath the hill; the hotel's extensive gardens, which flank the hill, are quiet and peaceful. Wander past the private beach to a secluded path facing west across the lake. The terrace restaurant is a delight, with a good, moderately priced menu of local specialities, plus barbecues and buffets on summer evenings; book ahead. **€180**

VARESE HOTELS WELCOME CARD

The Varese Hotels Association "Federalberghi Varese" offers the free **Welcome Card** to guests staying at any of its hotels, which comprise dozens of options in all price categories along the eastern shore of Lake Maggiore, as well as in rural villages, Varese itself and even towns on Lake Lugano. The card gives all kinds of perks, from reduced admission to museums and historic houses, and discounted fares on boats, cable cars and mountain railways, to money off the bill at a clutch of shops and restaurants – and even reduced tariffs for golf courses and rental cars. More details at ⓦ varesehotels.it.

Laveno

LAVENO is a modest little industrial town and transport hub 25km south of Luino, linked with its contiguous neighbour to the south, Mombello.

If you're day-tripping by boat, turn left after you disembark to find the tourist office on little **Piazza Italia**; they can give you a map and a leaflet for a self-guided walking tour through the streets of the old quarter around Piazza Fontana, with its eighteenth-century villas and churches, and along the scenic waterfront. From Via Tinelli, an ancient **cable car** (Mon–Fri 11am–6.30pm, Sat 11am–10.30pm, Sun 10am–10.30pm; €10; ⓦfuniviedellagomaggiore.it) rises to Poggio Sant'Elsa near the summit of Sasso del Ferro. South along the lakefront road, in the district of Cerro, the **Museo Internazionale Design Ceramico** (Lungolago Perabò 5; Tues 10am–12.30pm, Wed–Sun 10am–12.30pm & 2.30–5.30pm; €5; ⓦmidec.org) focuses on Laveno's ceramics history, displaying a strong collection of Art Nouveau and modernist pieces in a fine sixteenth-century courtyarded villa.

ARRIVAL AND INFORMATION

LAVENO

By train Laveno has two stations. Laveno-Mombello Nord is a terminus for trains from Varese and Milan Cadorna/Nord. The other station, Laveno-Mombello, lies 1km south of the centre, served by trains on the Bellinzona-Luino-Malpensa Airport line; change at Gallarate for Milano Porta Garibaldi. Timetables are at ⓦwww.muoversi.regione.lombardia.it.

By boat Car ferries – which also take foot passengers

– shuttle continuously between Laveno and Verbania-Intra (see p.132) on the western shore of the lake. They dock directly in front of Laveno-Mombello Nord train station.

Laveno tourist office Piazza Italia 2 (Mon, Tues, Thurs & Fri 9am–noon & 2.30–5.30pm, Sat & Sun 9am–7pm; shorter hours in winter; ☎0332 668 785, ⓦvareselandoftourism.com).

Val Cúvia

From Laveno major roads head south to Varese and Malpensa airport. A good reason to drive this way is to branch off into the pretty **Val Cúvia** that runs parallel to the shore between Monte Nudo (1236m) and the protected area of Campo dei Fiori (1226m), which extends as far as the outskirts of Varese.

Villa della Porta Bozzolo

Casalzuigno • Wed–Sun 10am–6pm; Oct & Nov closes 5pm; closed Dec–Feb • €6; free to UK National Trust cardholders • ⓦfondoambiente.it

Partway along the valley-floor road, flanked by forests of chestnut near **CASALZUIGNO**, stands the **Villa della Porta Bozzolo**, a magnificent eighteenth-century Lombard country villa 10km from Laveno (and 16km from Luino). It's a pleasure to wander in the cool rooms of the house and through to the older seventeenth-century wing. Salons to the left of the entrance hold a billiard table and a piano, but the most impressive room is the **library**, with a huge desk on a dais. Upstairs are stone-flagged bedrooms with their original furnishings. The terraced Italian **gardens** are splendid, featuring an avenue of oaks, a frescoed temple, and more.

Arcumeggia

Just east of the turn-off to the villa, a minor road climbs for 3km to **ARCUMEGGIA** – a steep, narrow lane which switchbacks dangerously; you'll barely be able to get out of first gear. In the 1950s, the locals invited leading Italian artists of the day to fresco the village's stone cottages; the combination of the mountain setting and the art is an alluring one. Beyond Arcumeggia, mountain roads continue over the ridge and down to Porto Valtravaglia on the lake.

ARRIVAL AND DEPARTURE

VAL CÚVIA

By bus A bus from Luino runs through Val Cúvia towards Cittiglio station, one stop southeast of Laveno, stopping at Villa

della Porta Bozzolo on the way (approx every 2hr; 30min). Timetables at ⓦwww.muoversi.regione.lombardia.it.

Santa Caterina del Sasso

Leggiuno • April to mid-Sept daily 9am–noon & 2–6pm; March & Oct closes 5pm; Nov–Feb Sat & Sun 9am–noon & 2–5pm • Free • ⓦ santacaterinadelsasso.com

Tucked into the cliffs on the eastern, Lombard shore of the lake, the hermitage of **SANTA CATERINA DEL SASSO** has regular boats to and from Stresa. This beautiful little monastic complex – visible only from the water – is well worth a visit for its frescoes and its sense of tranquillity, but make sure you come at opening time; for most of the day, crowds swamp the place.

The site dates back to 1170, when Alberto Besozzi, from nearby Arolo, was shipwrecked in a storm, invoked the help of St Catherine of Alexandria and survived. He subsequently withdrew to a cave here, in the cliff of Sasso Bàllaro, to devote his life to prayer. Local townspeople began construction of a votive chapel shortly afterwards, and the complex grew. By 1620 fourteen monks lived here, but a suppression decree in 1770 forced the last six out. The sanctuary crumbled until it was declared a national monument in 1914 and restored. Today, it is home to a small community of Benedictine monks and oblates.

Exploring Santa Caterina

The complex is tiny; you could walk from one end to the other in three minutes. The steps from above and below meet at the lovely **entrance gallery** (1624), with arches looking out over the lake, which leads to the **South Convent**. Inside, opposite the gift shop, is the Gothic **Chapterhouse**, decorated with frescoes including a pristine image from 1439 of St Eligius healing a horse. A door gives onto a small courtyard; ahead, beneath the four Gothic arches of the **Small Convent** (1315) is the **church**, with its stubby Romanesque bell tower and graceful Renaissance porch. Dating from 1587, this is a movingly quiet and holy space. A fresco of *God the Father*, dated 1610, adorns the Baroque vault above the high altar; around the church are other, older examples. A rear chapel, dedicated to the Blessed Alberto, is known as the **Chapel of the Rocks**; five massive boulders fell through the roof around 1700 and became lodged, as if miraculously, above this chapel, supported by the vaulting. They stayed that way for two centuries, finally crashing to the floor in 1910 (and were removed in 1983).

ARRIVAL AND DEPARTURE	**SANTA CATERINA DEL SASSO**
By car From the well-signed car park at Quicchio (or Quiquio), located along a turn-off from the main SP69 road between Cellina and Reno, you could take the panoramic flight of 268 steps down the cliffside to the hermitage – or	opt for the lift (which costs 50c). **By boat** Boats shuttle regularly to and from Stresa. There are 80 steps up from the landing-stage to the church.

Southern Lake Maggiore

South of Stresa and Santa Caterina, the southern reaches of Lake Maggiore peter out bathetically into reedy inlets; horizons are low and undistinguished, and there are few attractions compared to the natural beauty further north. On the western shore, the few little communities beyond Stresa are pretty enough, but blighted somewhat by the traffic on the lakeside road; the major town of this part of the lake, **Arona**, remains eminently missable. The eastern shore is notable chiefly for the stout **Rocca Borromeo** castle, which dominates **Angera**.

Arona

South of Stresa, the road hugs the lakeshore for 16km to **ARONA**, the major town at the south end of the lake. It's a busy, humdrum place which makes few concessions to tourism.

From the *imbarcadero*, head right onto the old quarter's central shopping street, **Via Cavour**, past upmarket handbag and fashion boutiques. Via Cavour ends at the broad **Piazza del Popolo**, Arona's prettiest square, adorned with the Gothic arches of the fifteenth-century **Casa del Podestà** – but tainted by having traffic channelled along one side. The views from here across the water to the Rocca Borromeo castle above Angera are sensational.

Sancarlone (Colosso di San Carlo Borromeo)
April–Sept daily 9am–12.30pm & 2–6.15pm; March & Oct–Dec Sat & Sun 9am–12.30pm & 2–4.30pm • €4

On the slopes high above Arona rises a 35-metre-high, hollow, bronze **statue of San Carlo Borromeo**, a sixteenth-century archbishop of Milan. Borromeo was canonized in 1610 and the statue completed 88 years later. You can climb steps inside to look out of his eyes and – bizarrely – his ears and nose too, as he blesses the town.

ARRIVAL AND INFORMATION
ARONA

By plane Milan-Malpensa Airport is around 35km south. SAF's Alibus runs from Malpensa Terminals 1 and 2 to Arona (6 daily April–Sept only; 40min; €7; booking essential 48hr ahead by phone or online; ☏0323 552 172, ⓦsafduemila.com).

By train Arona is on the main train line from Milan to Stresa. Timetables are at ⓦvcoinbus.it. The train station is at the other end of Corso della Repubblica from the *imbarcadero*, past 300m of car parks.

Destinations Milan (approx hourly; 55min); Stresa

(every 30min; 15min).

By boat Arona and Angera are linked by regular boats (see p.118) and there are also a few services a day north to Stresa and up as far as Locarno. The main waterfront road Corso della Repubblica passes in front of Arona's *imbarcadero*.

Tourist office Opposite the train station, Largo Vidale 1 (Tues–Sun 9.30am–12.30pm, Thurs–Sat also 3–6pm; ☏0322 243 601, ⓦcomune.arona.no.it & ⓦdistrettolaghi.it).

ACCOMMODATION AND EATING

Barchetta Via Repubblica 34 ☏0322 243 356. Busy modern café in a good location for a coffee and a bun opposite the landing-stage. Open daily.

Florida Piazza del Popolo 32 ☏0322 46 212, ⓦhotelflorida-arona.it. Let the genial manager of this pleasant small hotel show you to the airy old rooms, some of which have balconies on Arona's most attractive square. **€70**

Osteria degli Acrobati Piazza San Graziano 30 ☏0322

240 395. A popular rustic-style restaurant in the old quarter which doubles as a friendly, congenial spot for light bites. Open daily.

Taverna del Pittore Piazza del Popolo 39 ☏0322 243 366, ⓦristorantetavernadelpittore.it. Arona's top restaurant – a rather stiffly formal place to savour top-quality lake cuisine, artfully presented, for €50 and up. Book ahead for a terrace table with a view over the lake to Angera's castle. Closed Mon.

Angera

Directly opposite Arona, tucked into a creek on the Lombard shore, is the smaller, more enticing town of **ANGERA**. Now quiet, this was once an important port on the lake, dominated by a rocky spur above the harbour which was fortified by the Romans and subsequently developed into a key military base. Come for the castle, though after a visit you could fill an hour or two rambling through the unadorned lanes of the old quarter.

Rocca d'Angera (Rocca Borromeo)
Mid-March to mid-Oct daily 9am–5.30pm • €8.50; joint ticket with Isola Bella & Isola Madre (see p.126) €22 • ☏0331 931 300, ⓦisoleborromee.it

Signposted on the hilltop above Angera looms the **Rocca Borromeo**, a rare example of a medieval fortress totally preserved in its original form. Built in the eleventh century and expanded by the Visconti in the fourteenth, the castle was bought in 1449, along with Angera town, by Vitaliano I Borromeo for the vast sum of 12,800 lire; it became a

FROM TOP FRESCOES, SANTA CATERINA DEL SASSO (P.151); VILLA PANZA (P.157) >

key point of defence for the Lombards against the Swiss. Extensively refurbished in the seventeenth century, it remains a fine old building, its towers and swallow-tail battlements crowning the wooded hill.

From the car park just below the walls, you walk up to enter the castle; ahead is the café, while under the arch (which forms part of the fifteenth-century **Borromeo Wing**), is the giftshop and steep, cobbled internal courtyard. You climb the slope in front of the **Della Scala Wing**, faced in bleak Angera stone; in the left corner is the mighty **Torre Principale**, dating from the twelfth century. As you come round to the left, you face the **Visconti Wing**, with arched windows and a small double staircase. Left of here, pass through an elegant seventeenth-century triple-arched portico in the Borromeo Wing and turn to the right to climb the staircase into the fortress.

Sala di Giustizia

At the top of the stairs, ahead lie half a dozen grand rooms filled with Borromeo family portraits, but if you double back on yourself you'll find the stunning **Sala della Giustizia** (Law Court), a large room with two fluted cross-vaults. Its six bays, each with mullioned windows, are covered by a thirteenth-century fresco cycle showing the Visconti success at the Battle of Desio in 1277, with the military exploits related, in the upper registers, to the signs of the zodiac. Wooden stairs at the far end climb to the top of the Torre Principale, for spectacular lake views.

The museum and gardens

Ground-floor rooms in the various wings of the castle are given over to the diverting **Museo della Bambola e del Giocattolo** (Museum of Dolls and Toys), one of the most complete collections in Europe, while the esplanade showcases a carefully planted **medieval garden**.

ARRIVAL AND INFORMATION — ANGERA

By car The road journey from Arona is 16km around the end of the lake, past malls, multiplex cinemas and camping superstores, crossing a bridge over the Ticino at Sesto Calende (see p.155).

By boat Arona and Angera are linked by regular boats (see p.118) and Angera also has a few services daily north to Stresa and up as far as Locarno. Boats dock in Angera at Piazzale della Vittoria, alongside the long Piazza Garibaldi.

Tourist office Set back from the lakefront square, Via Marconi 2 (May–Sept Mon & Wed 2.30–5pm, Thurs–Sun 9.30am–5pm; ⊤0331 931 915, Ⓦcomune.angera.va.it & Ⓦvareselandoftourism.com).

Ranco

On the quiet lakeside road a kilometre or two north of Angera is **RANCO**, just about the sleepiest of all the lake's sleepy little corners. Virtually no traffic passes – Ranco lies 2.5km down a turning off the main lakeside highway – and there are just two or three boats a day, in the morning to Stresa and in the evening to Arona. There is literally nothing to do, other than bask in the sun and stroll through the well-tended waterside gardens.

Otherwise, there is little reason to turn off the main road north out of Angera, which passes a series of placid communities including **Ispra**, headquarters for research institutes attached to the European Commission. Just past **Cellina** is a turn-off west to a clifftop car park, from where steps and a lift lead down to the hermitage of **Santa Caterina del Sasso** (see p.151). Laveno (see p.150) lies 22km north of Angera.

ACCOMMODATION AND EATING — RANCO

Il Sole Piazza Venezia 5 ⊤0331 976 507, Ⓦilsolediranco.it. Stuffy old hotel in this backwater village which capitalizes fully on Ranco's soporific air with a range of traditionally styled suites, though tired in parts and a little fussy for some tastes. The grounds are beautiful, and the restaurant is still worth trying out, though not as good as it once was (three-course *menù* €50; mains €20–35). Restaurant closed Mon & Tues. **€190**

Sesto Calende

Roughly 9km south of Arona and Angera, at the point where the River Ticino drains Lake Maggiore southwards, **SESTO CALENDE** feels like a return from tourist isolation to the hectic normality of provincial town life. There's no real reason to head this way – lake ferries don't come down this far anyhow – but if you're driving and prefer to avoid the autostrada, you could stop in for an hour or two. Road and rail traffic is siphoned onto a single bridge over the river, which marks the Lombardy/Piedmont border; the **old quarter** clusters along the northern (Lombard) bank, in a handful of squares and lanes leading back from the narrow riverside Viale Italia. North of the centre, hunt out the tenth-century church of **San Donato**, with sixteenth-century artworks and frescoes.

ARRIVAL AND INFORMATION   SESTO CALENDE

By train Sesto Calende is on the main train line between Milan and Stresa, and also has regional links with Laveno and Luino. Timetables are at ⓦwww.muoversi.regione.lombardia.it.

Tourist office Viale Italia 6 (March–Oct daily 9am–1pm, Fri–Sun also 2–7pm; ☏0331 919 874, ⓦprosestocalende.it & ⓦvareselandoftourism.com).

EATING AND DRINKING

Al Portichetto Piazza Garibaldi 15 ☏0331 923 671, ⓦristorantealportichetto.it. Popular, high-quality restaurant on the old quarter's main square, serving fresh lake fish and seasonal dishes for moderate prices. Often busy, though service standards remain high; this is a great choice. Open daily.

Varese

VARESE gets short shrift from visitors, despite its location plum in the centre of the Lakes region – roughly equidistant from Como, Lugano and Lake Maggiore, and easily reached from all three. The reasons for heading inland to this commercial hub aren't immediately obvious, yet Varese, the so-called "**Città Giardino**" (Garden City), can offer gardens, a notable **Sacro Monte** of hillside chapels, superb contemporary art at **Villa Panza**, and the unexpected wonder of Florentine Renaissance frescoes in rural **Castiglione Olona**.

When the railway arrived from Milan – the State line in 1865, and the Nord line in 1886 – Varese became a favoured spot for wealthy Milanese to build their holiday homes. The fashion coincided with the flowering of Art Nouveau (known in Italy as "**Liberty**"), and to this day Varese's outskirts are filled with superb examples of Liberty architecture, in villas and grand hotels.

And the links with Milan went deeper; for Italians, Varese has long been indelibly associated with high fashion, principally shoes. Although the famous Trolli shoe family sold up to Benetton in 1995, and most of the city's shoe manufacturers have now departed, Varese retains its air of cool, fashion-conscious sophistication.

Piazza Monte Grappa

Varese's compact and elegant historic centre comprises a tight cluster of pedestrianized streets spreading north from the main **Piazza Monte Grappa**, a spread of angular Fascist architecture dating from 1927. The stone-paved **Corso Matteotti** leads out of the square, with chic boutiques and cafés crowding beneath its arcades; well worth a stroll.

San Vittore
Piazza Canonica • ⓦbasvit.it

To one side of Corso Matteotti rises **San Vittore**, built in the late sixteenth century and adorned with a Neoclassical facade; its domed **campanile** is a seventeenth-century addition, and still bears the scars of the 1859 battle for the town, when Garibaldi faced

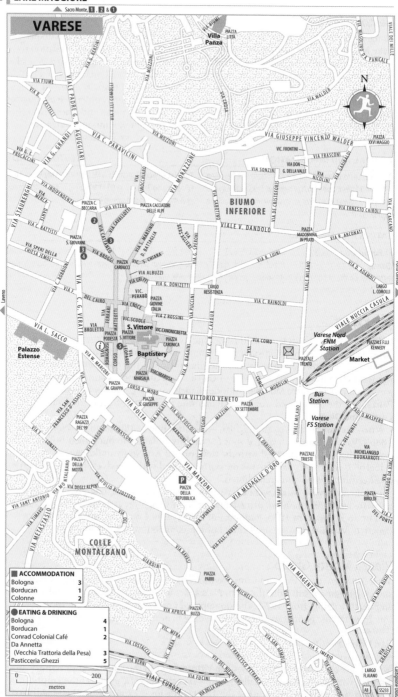

▲ Sacro Monte, **1**, **2** & **1**

VARESE

ACCOMMODATION

Bologna	3
Borducan	1
Colonne	2

EATING & DRINKING

Bologna	4
Borducan	1
Conrad Colonial Café	2
Da Annetta (Vecchia Trattoria della Pesa)	3
Pasticceria Ghezzi	5

down the Austrian army. Inside the church, the first chapel on the left holds a painting of a topless *Mary Magdalene* by Il Morazzone, painted in 1627 but long hidden from view on the grounds of decency. On the south side of the church, the twelfth-century **baptistry** (unlocked on request) – unusually quadrangular, not octagonal, and with a matroneum above the presbytery – holds a seventh-century font, recessed into the floor beneath a monolithic (and unfinished) tenth-century replacement. The remarkably fresh interior frescoes, dating from around 1325, include, on the south wall, all twelve apostles rendered in artistic style with personalized faces, and a *Crucifixion* on the east wall showing bird-like angels swooping down to an expressively suffering Christ.

Palazzo Estense

Via Sacco 5 • Palazzo closed to visitors; gardens open daily during daylight hours • Free

A five-minute walk from Piazza Monte Grappa, along Via Marcobi and Via Sacco, stands **Palazzo Estense**, built in the 1760s by Francesco III d'Este, duke of Modena, and now Varese's town hall. Its extensive **gardens** are modelled on Vienna's Schönbrunn, with fountains and formal terraces. Adjacent is the wilder, lusher English-style garden of the **Villa Mirabello**, replete with grottoes, arbours and babbling streams.

3

Villa Panza

Piazza Litta 1 • Tues–Sun 10am–6pm; closed Jan • €9; free to UK National Trust cardholders • ⓦ fondoambiente.it • Signposted from the centre, with free parking; city bus A from the train station and Piazza Monte Grappa (every 30min)

A little north of Varese city centre, set amid Liberty villas in the hillside suburb of Biumo Superiore, is one of the region's most original art galleries. The sober, elegant, eighteenth-century Villa Menafoglio-Litta-Panza – or **Villa Panza** for short – donated to the nation in 1996 by its last owner, Count Giuseppe Panza, stands among beautiful gardens, with views of the Alps. Adorning its interior is the Count's world-class **contemporary art** collection. Give yourself a couple of hours to take it in – and pick up a free **audioguide**; the English commentary is outstanding, explaining works that might otherwise appear meaningless.

The main house

Almost all the paintings in the **main house** are monochrome canvases by postwar American artists, big blocks of purple or silver or green, hanging – at first glance, incongruously – in rooms with ornate stucco ceilings and refined Baroque furnishings.

The **ground floor** includes a billiard room (room 4), hung with deep monochromes by Californian Phil Sims, and a sumptuous Empire Dining Hall (room 8), designed in 1829, with frescoes, a stucco ceiling, Classical columns and, now, two stunning acrylics – one black, one silver – by David Simpson.

On the **upper floor**, the left-hand wing has been cleared of furniture: one highlight is the Yellow Room (room 18), housing three large-scale works in black, white and yellow by Ford Beckman. The opposite wing retains furnishings from its time as the Panza family home. The most memorable space here is the dining room (room 27), with eight ethereal paintings by David Simpson, a fine sixteenth-century Tuscan table in walnut, and several African and pre-Columbian figurines set on the fifteenth-century Umbrian sideboard. This room, and the drawing room alongside, showcase the Count's remarkable taste for leavening an aristocratic lifestyle with what was, when he started buying it in the 1950s, deeply unfashionable art.

The rustici

The villa's **rustici** (outbuildings) house works that are site-specific – that is, the artists were invited to Villa Panza and created pieces designed to be seen in their specific location. Many are now owned by the Guggenheim Foundation.

Connecting to the villa's upper-floor galleries are rooms showcasing works by **Dan Flavin** (1933–96), the first artist to work exclusively with artificial light, in the form of fluorescent tubes. Off the first corridor (room 32) are rooms suffused with light from pink, red or blue tubes, in different configurations. Beyond is Flavin's *Varese Corridor* (room 36), a striking installation (press the button by the door to turn it on and off), with more rooms to either side. Don't miss works here by the conceptual artist Robert Irwin, notably the ghostly, intriguing *Varese Scrim* (room 43), as well as the extraordinary *Sky Space* by James Turrell (room 47). Room 48 holds a sound sculpture by Michael Brewster.

Stairs lead down to temporary exhibits. Make time for room 56 here, featuring a light installation by German artist Maria Nordman; you wait for a few minutes in a dim chamber before proceeding into the main room – apparently pitch-dark. Allowing your senses to adjust over, perhaps, ten minutes is a fittingly memorable conclusion to the villa's surprises.

ARRIVAL AND INFORMATION   VARESE

By plane Varese is only 25km north of Milan-Malpensa Airport. At the time of writing, rail access involved changing midway at Gallarate or Saronno, but by the time you read this a new line may be open, with trains running direct between Varese and Malpensa Airport.

By train Varese's two train stations stand east of the centre. The Stazione FS, on Piazzale Trieste, handles services from Milan Porta Garibaldi (hourly; 1hr), and is due to have direct trains from Lugano on a new line via Mendrisio by the time you read this. Nearby, accessed from Viale Casula, is the Stazione FNM (listed on timetables as "Varese Nord"), midway on the line between Milan Cadorna Nord and Laveno-Mombello Nord (see p.150).

Timetables are at ⓦ www.muoversi.regione.lombardia.it.
By bus Varese's bus station, situated alongside the Stazione FS, has services around the region, but for most journeys, trains are quicker and/or easier. Timetables are at ⓦ www.muoversi.regione.lombardia.it.
By car Varese is at the head of the A8 autostrada, an easy 45km north of Milan (and 25km north of Milan-Malpensa airport). It is also 25km west of Como, 22km east of Laveno and 33km south of Lugano.
Varese tourist office Via Romagnosi 9 (April–Sept Mon–Sat 9.30am–1pm & 2–6.30pm (Tues 3–5pm), Sun 9.30am–1pm; Oct–March Mon–Sat 9.30am–5.30pm; ☎ 0332 281 913, ⓦ varesecittagiardino.it).

ACCOMMODATION

There's not much reason to stay in the city centre; you'd do better to aim instead for one of the historic hotels on the Sacro Monte hillside. The Varese Hotels Welcome Card, offered by all local hotels, is worth picking up, as it gives a range of perks and discounts on attractions all round the lake (see p.149).

Bologna Via Broggi 7 ☎ 0332 234 362, ⓦ albergobologna.it. Decent little family-run hotel and restaurant on the edge of the pedestrianized centre, set into what was a convent dating from 1550. Frills are few but the rooms are adequate and there is private parking. **€95**

★**Borducan** Via Beata Caterina Moriggi 43 ☎ 0332 220 567, ⓦ hotelborducan.com. Quiet four-star Liberty-style villa hotel on the Sacro Monte hillside, now completely renovated, with ten individually styled rooms, often split-level (connected by spiral stairs), some with

balconies – but only modestly sized. This is an old building of great character; think creaking staircases, polished woods and welcoming service. We cover the hotel's history in our review of its famous bar (see below). **€120**

Colonne Via Fincará 37 ☎ 0332 220 404, ⓦ colonnehotelva.it. Another four-star hotel, located alongside the Sacro Monte funicular top station, a short walk from the *Borducan* – and freshly updated in 2014. Rooms here are airy and very pleasant, especially those with balconies for the view over Varese, but they don't quite share the *Borducan's* touch of historic class. **€140**

EATING AND DRINKING

Bologna Via Broggi 7 ☎ 0332 234 362, ⓦ albergobologna.it. A cheerful, family-run restaurant in the city centre with excellent food at moderate prices. *Menùs* from €25 to €35. Closed Sat & every third Sun of month.

★**Borducan** Via Beata Caterina Moriggi 43 ☎ 0332 220 567, ⓦ hotelborducan.com. The original owner of this villa near the Sacro Monte, Davide Bregonzio, accompanied Garibaldi to Sicily in 1860, sailing on, after the battles, to North Africa. He brought luscious Algerian

oranges back to Varese, and after trying out different recipes, in 1872 hit on a mellow liqueur that blended orange oil with the aromatic herbs found on Varese's hillsides. Bregonzio called his creation *"Elixir Al Borducan"* after the Arabic word for orange, and opened a bar to sell it. That bar is the *Borducan* restaurant and hotel, owned today by Bregonzio's great-great-grandniece, and it remains the one place where you can sample the liqueur – which is still made only in Varese, though now from organic Sicilian oranges. It's perfect for a sunset tipple before dinner on the terrace. Open daily.

Conrad Colonial Café Via Cattaneo 1 ☎ 0332 235 742. Popular, mid-range café-bar done up in vaguely colonial style – bamboo screens and the like – that attracts a lively, sociable crowd, who often bar-hop between similar places nearby, around Piazza Carducci. Open daily 5.30pm to 2am.

Da Annetta (Vecchia Trattoria della Pesa) Via Cattaneo 14 ☎ 0332 287 070, ⓦ daannetta.it. Classy, contemporary urban restaurant, featuring exposed brick, a slate floor, armchairs and sofas in the bar. The owners have created a warm, almost farmhouse style in the middle of the city – expect refined cuisine, using local, market-fresh ingredients, but at mid-level prices. Next door, at no.12, the upmarket *Sweetly* café – part of the same business – tempts with gourmet chocolates, wine, light bites and coffee. Open daily.

Pasticceria Ghezzi Corso Matteotti 36 ☎ 0332 235 179. A mirrored, chandeliered café-patisserie on Varese's main street, dating from 1924. It's renowned for its brioches and – especially – its *Dolce Varese*, a tasty concoction of chopped almonds and dried fruit. Closed Sun & Mon.

Sacro Monte di Varese

ⓦ sacromonte.it

On the northern outskirts rises the **Sacro Monte di Varese**, one of several "holy mountains" – comprising a series of hillside shrines dedicated to Mary – that were established across Lombardy and Piedmont during the Counter-Reformation. This hill, thickly wooded and topped by a convent, has been a centre of Christianity since the Dark Ages. In 1604, fourteen chapels were built in a coiling line up the hillside, each filled with frescoes and statuary on the Mystery of the Rosary, beginning with the Annunciation and ending with the Assumption. The route, known as the **Via Sacra** – a broad, leafy path, still with its original cobbles and boasting fine views – is these days used as much by Sunday walkers as by devotees praying at each chapel. The path rises steeply, gaining 260m over a distance of 2.2km.

The start lies 5km north of Varese, accessed via Viale Aguggiari and marked by the **Primo Arco** (First Arch) and **Prima Cappella** (First Chapel). All the chapels are locked; to see inside press the light switch and peer through the window. At the top, the path ends at a bombastic nineteenth-century **Statue of Moses**, above which rise the blank walls of a convent that has housed a closed community of nuns since 1492.

The convent church, **Santuario di Santa Maria del Monte** (daily 8am–noon & 2–6pm) – rebuilt in 1474 over the remnants of a fourth-century original – is accessed from a small piazza bearing a statue of Pope Paul VI. Its Baroque interior holds a revered medieval Black Madonna in wood, while the adjacent **Cappella delle Beate** houses the shrine of Caterina and Giuliana, two local girls who founded the convent. A concealed upper corridor allows the nuns to pray unseen.

Santa Maria del Monte

On the other side of the church is **SANTA MARIA DEL MONTE** village, looking out over the valley – a hundred or so people live here. Just below the church, **Museo Baroffio** (April–Oct Thurs, Sat & Sun 9.30am–12.30pm & 3–6.30pm; May–Sept also Tues & Wed 3–6.30pm; €4; ⓦ museobaroffio.it) holds some minor artworks, while **Museo Pogliaghi** (April–Oct Sat & Sun 9am–6pm; €4; ⓦ casamuseopogliaghi.it) commemorates the life and work of painter and sculptor Lodovico Pogliaghi (1857–1950) and also displays his collection of Classical and Renaissance art. A joint ticket for both museums is €5. A short walk down through the alleys brings you to a knot of hotel/restaurants beside the beautiful Liberty-style **funicular** station.

ARRIVAL AND DEPARTURE	**SACRO MONTE DI VARESE**

By bus Bus C (every 20min; €1.30) runs from Varese city centre to the Prima Cappella. From there it continues either up the hill into Santa Maria del Monte village (Mon–Fri) or to the base station of the funicular in Vellone (Sat & Sun).

By funicular Aug daily 10am–7.30pm; March–July, Sept & Oct Sat 1–7pm, Sun 10am–7pm; Nov–Feb Sun 10am–6pm; closed late Dec; €1 one-way; ⓦ avtvarese.it.

3

HIKING THE VIA VERDE VARESINA ("3V")

The mountainous area of the Provincia di Varese, lying between lakes Lugano and Maggiore, is the setting for the **Via Verde Varesina**, or "3V", one of the region's best long-distance footpaths. It was conceived to link the European E1 trail, which runs from Norway to Sicily (passing through Porto Ceresio on Lake Lugano), with the Grande Traversata Alpina, which ends on the western shore of Lake Maggiore. The 3V comprises **ten stages** – 134.5km in total – following a looping route from Porto Ceresio to the Sacro Monte di Varese, then on to Laveno, Arcumeggia and Luino, up to Monte Lema and down to Maccagno. All ten stages (complete with English route descriptions), plus five variations, are shown in detail on an excellent 1:35,000 **map** produced by DeAgostini for the Provincia di Varese, available from tourist offices. The ten traditional stages are all graded T (for "Tourist" – that is, easy); some of the variations are slightly harder. More information is at ⓦ provincia.va.it/3v.

Campo dei Fiori

ⓦ parcocampodeifiori.it

Narrow roads continue past Santa Maria del Monte into the broadleaf forests of the **Parco Regionale del Campo dei Fiori**, a swathe of green mountainside centred on the peak of Campo dei Fiori (1226m), atop which stand an observatory and meteorology station. This is beautiful country for leg-stretching walks and picnics-with-a-view. Partway up, you may notice a turn in the road by a red-and-white barrier alongside a gatekeeper's stone lodge. This marks a private road leading a short way into the forests to the **Albergo Campo dei Fiori**, a grand hillside hotel built in 1912 by the architect Giuseppe Sommaruga and visible from all over Varese. A caretaker family live in one wing, but otherwise this fine building, complete with all its original Art Nouveau fittings, has been left to crumble since it closed in 1968. Beautiful railings by Sommaruga are covered in rust and grime. The top station of the hotel's funicular nearby and panoramic restaurant above – both disused – are graceful Liberty buildings in utter disrepair amid the encroaching forest.

The reason for this tragic neglect centres on the thicket of aerials and satellite dishes atop the abandoned hotel. The Castiglioni family which owns the site (along with the prestigious motorcycle firm Cagiva) gain more by renting roof-space to TV and communications companies than they would by refurbishing the hotel and opening it to the public. So they let the place rot, with scandalous impunity.

The Varesotto

Varese's hinterland, the **Varesotto**, is chiefly worth driving through to get somewhere more interesting, but it holds a handful of attractions.

West of Varese, down on the plain lies the small **Lago di Varese** – prettier from a distance than close to – on the northern fringes of the the **Parco Naturale Lombardo della Valle del Ticino**, which extends to Sesto Calende (see p.155) and which, bizarrely, also includes Milan-Malpensa international airport.

North of Varese, the SS233 road to the Swiss border at Ponte Tresa heads through the deep **Val Ganna**, passing, after 14km, the little **Lago di Ghirla**, which offers plenty of walking opportunities. Ponte Tresa lies 7km north on Lake Lugano (see p.178).

Northeast of Varese, the SS344 leads into the Val Ceresio and on to Porto Ceresio, on another arm of Lake Lugano (see p.177). On the way, just outside Bisuschio, drop into the Renaissance **Villa Cicogna Mozzoni** (guided tours April–Oct Sun 9.30am–noon & 2.30–7pm; ⓦ villacicognamozzoni.it), with a splendid formal garden.

Castiglione Olona

ⓦ prolococastiglioneolona.it • Bus B45 from Varese bus station (Mon–Sat 4 daily; 1 on Sun; 20min)

Deep in the Olona valley 8km south of Varese, **CASTIGLIONE OLONA** was rebuilt in

Tuscan style in the fifteenth century and hosts superb **frescoes** by a master of the Florentine Renaissance, **Masolino**. They are worth going well out of your way to see – but road signage is poor. From Varese, head south on the SS233 (towards Saronno) for 8km to the modern part of Castiglione Olona. After passing a church on the right, at the next set of traffic lights turn right onto Via IV Novembre and follow the hill down into the atmospheric old quarter.

Castiglione Olona owes its prominence to local boy **Cardinal Branda Castiglioni** (1350–1443). Branda taught law at Pavia University, was appointed Bishop of Piacenza, travelled to Hungary as legate of Pope John XXIII, and was a major player at the ecumenical councils of Pisa (1409), Constance (1414–18) and Basel (after 1431). From the 1420s onwards, he rebuilt his home town according to Renaissance principles and commissioned art to decorate its churches and mansions.

On the main Piazza Garibaldi stands the **Palazzo Branda Castiglioni** (Tues–Sat 9am–noon & 3–6pm, Sun 10.30am–12.30pm & 3–6pm; Oct–March closed Sun morning; €3), a fourteenth-century house where the cardinal was born and died. Upstairs is the bedroom, with allegorical frescoes dating from 1423, and study, frescoed by Masolino with a Hungarian landscape. Across the square, the **Chiesa di Villa** was built in the 1430s in the style of the great Florentine architect Brunelleschi – a cube topped by a cylinder that conceals the dome. Two enormous statues of St Christopher and St Anthony flank the main door.

The Collegiata: Masolino's frescoes

Via Branda 1 • April–Sept Tues–Sun 10am–1pm & 3–6pm; Oct–March Tues–Sat 9.30am–12.30pm & 2.30–5.30pm • €6 • Ⓦ museocollegiata.it

Via Branda heads up the hill as a cobbled lane, rising steeply to the **Collegiata**, built by the cardinal in 1422 on the ruins of the old castle. The portal, added later, was originally too tall; you can see where the rose window had to be raised to make space. The presbytery has frescoes by Masolino on the life of Mary, while over the altar hangs an unusual eight-armed Flemish candelabrum from the 1420s, depicting St George killing the dragon.

What lifts a visit out of the ordinary are the frescoes in the adjacent **Baptistry**. Formerly the Castiglioni family chapel, this small building holds what is considered Masolino's masterpiece – a fresco cycle painted in 1435 on the life of John the Baptist. The colours are rich and bright, the texture and detailing wonderfully clear.

The cycle begins to one side of the **west wall**, with two faded scenes of the visitation. The **north wall**, alongside, shows what is probably the birth and naming of John (Zacharias is shown writing the word Johannes). Scenes in the presbytery show John in the desert, talking to Jesus. The top of the **east wall** has a beautiful depiction of Jesus' baptism in the River Jordan. Still on the east wall, to the right of the window is shown John condemning Herod – who summons his guards – and the impatient Herodias. Further round, John languishes in prison. The highlight is the glorious **south wall**. Beneath a Renaissance scene of columns and porticoes, Salome dances. Next, the head of John is brought in to a stone-faced Herodias, seated amongst her frantic daughters. Above, John's companions are shown burying him in a cave.

Other frescoed vignettes include, on the soffit of the arch, St Jerome translating the Bible, while the west wall has an unusual view of fifteenth-century Rome, centred on the Pantheon.

Across the cloister from the Baptistry, a little **café** serves as a perfect spot to draw breath.

Lake Lugano

TWILIGHT REFLECTIONS ON LAKE LUGANO

Lake Lugano

Divided from its larger twin Lake Como by the international border, Lake Lugano (Lago di Lugano, also often referred to by its old Latin name, Ceresio) is, if anything, even prettier. With mountains that are often steeper than those of Como, the lake is noticeably less developed; aside from the stylish city of Lugano – which is less than half the size of Como – there are no big towns at all on its shores, which are, in any case, frequently too steep for even the Swiss to be able to build roads. The main part of the lake is in Switzerland, though it twists out into Italy on both sides. Boats, buses and trains pass from one to the other with minimal fuss.

Lugano is the biggest city in the Swiss canton (region) of **Ticino** (ⓦticino.ch), whose stunning natural beauty – lush wooded hills rising from azure water, palms swaying against deep-blue skies, red roofs framed by purple bougainvillea – often seems to blind outsiders with romance.

Aside from **Lugano** itself – and the beauty of the lake – attractions are low-key and largely rural. Jutting out into the lake a stone's throw from the city is the sun-drenched **Ceresio peninsula**, dotted with idyllic country villages and crisscrossed by some lovely walks. The rack-railway up to **Monte Generoso** (1701m) offers some jaw-dropping panoramic views as well as a host of walking routes into the nearby valleys, including the idyllic **Valle di Muggio**. And north of Lugano, beyond the Monte Ceneri range (1961m), lies the Ticinese capital **Bellinzona**, a charmingly unfussy city dominated by three well-preserved medieval castles.

INFORMATION

This chapter covers territory in both Switzerland and Italy. All **phone numbers** prefixed ☎091 are **Swiss**; all other numbers (beginning ☎03 in this chapter) are **Italian**. International dialling is straightforward (see p.47).

GETTING AROUND

Timetables for **trains, buses, boats and cable cars** throughout Switzerland (and beyond) are at ⓦsbb.ch/en, with a useful rundown of cross-border train services between Lugano and Milan at ⓦtilo.ch and links for mountain railways at ⓦutpt.ch. There are full details of boat services at ⓦlakelugano.ch. Check timetables carefully for notes and arcane symbols (see p.27). You'll need your passport to travel between Italy and Switzerland. By **car**, border posts are staffed but delays are rare.

Brief history

Although linguistically and temperamentally Italian, Ticino has been **Swiss** since the early 1500s, when Uri, Schwyz and Unterwalden – three cantons of Central Switzerland – moved to secure the southern approaches of the Gotthard Pass against the dukes of Milan. For three centuries the Ticinesi remained under the thumb of the tyrannical northerners, until **Napoleon** arrived in 1798 to reorganize the area under his new Cisalpine Republic. But faced with a mere exchange of overlords, the Ticinesi held out for independence, and under the banner *Liberi e Svizzeri!* ("Free and Swiss!"), the **Republic of Ticino** joined Switzerland as a new canton in 1803.

MEADOW, MONTE GENEROSO

Highlights

❶ Lugano Elegant Swiss lakefront city, with bags of style, sass and charm. **See p.166**

❷ Santa Maria degli Angioli Plain little church in Lugano which holds one of the finest Renaissance artworks anywhere in the region – a spectacular fresco by Bernardino Luini. **See p.168**

❸ Gandria Lovely lakeside village a short distance from Lugano – but a world away in spirit. Hole up and enjoy the tranquillity. **See p.173**

❹ Monte Sighignola The "Balcony of Italy" offers breathtaking views west over Lake Lugano and the Alps, but is only reachable on a tortuous road climbing its eastern flank. **See p.175**

❺ Monte Generoso High rocky peak served by rack-railway, with panoramic views from the summit. **See p.176**

❻ Alprose chocolate factory Unromantic industrial complex in Caslano which nonetheless offers the unbeatable combination of watching the factory production, buying at a discount – and eating as much chocolate as you like. **See p.178**

❼ Bellinzona Three medieval castles form a defensive chain above this attractive, little-visited city in the Alpine foothills. **See p.180**

HIGHLIGHTS ARE MARKED ON THE MAP ON P.167

BOATS ON LAKE LUGANO

Idyllic **Lake Lugano** merits taking to the water simply for the pleasure of it. SNL (T 091 971 5223, W lakelugano.ch) name their main landing-stage, opposite the tourist office, **Lugano-Centrale** (or just "Lugano"); a few services depart from **Lugano-Giardino** 100m to the east. Within the city, boats also call in at **Paradiso** to the south and Cassarate further east.

ROUTES

Between April and October, boats run roughly hourly to **Gandria**, while others depart less frequently south to **Campione d'Italia** and **Morcote**, stopping at points on the way. A few continue to **Porto Ceresio** and on around the peninsula to **Ponte Tresa**. One boat a day heads east to **Porlezza**.

Cruises operate around various bays – or the whole lake – throughout the day, some with commentary in English, others offering on-board meals, drinks and/or music. In **winter**, a skeleton service operates to Morcote, with a few boats each week to Campione and Gandria.

FARES AND PASSES

From Lugano, short trips to Gandria or Campione cost Fr.13–18, longer voyages to Porlezza or Ponte Tresa Fr.24–29. In general a lake pass is a good bet; unlimited journeys for one/three/seven days cost Fr.49/59/76. The **Ticino Discovery Card** (April–Oct only; Fr.87; W cartaturisticaticino.ch) covers free journeys on the lake for three days in a week, as well as discounts for cable cars, museums and other attractions.

Since then, the Ticinesi remain resolutely Swiss, and have little truck with foreigners calling them Italian, although it's almost impossible for an outsider to tell the locals apart from the almost 60,000 Italian *frontalieri* who cross into Ticino daily to work for salaries well below the Swiss average. A cruel irony of life here is that Ticino suffers Switzerland's highest **unemployment** rates even while its service industries thrive, staffed by Italians and paid for by thousands of German and Swiss-German tourists and second-home owners. As an ethnic and linguistic minority of eight percent in their own country, and nothing more than a quaint irrelevance to the urban hotshots of Milan next door, the Ticinesi constantly have to struggle to get their voices heard.

Lugano

With its compact cluster of attractive piazzas and tree-lined promenades, **LUGANO** is the most alluring of Switzerland's lake resorts. It's a sassy place, full of style – much less famous than its near-neighbour Como, but smaller, cleaner and even a little bit sexier. While Como looks north, Lugano basks on a south-facing bay of the cerulean blue **Lake Lugano**, framed on all sides by wooded, sugarloaf hills rising sheer from the water. There is none of Como's waterfront clutter. Both **Monte Brè** to the northeast and **Monte San Salvatore** to the south are served by funiculars, and both give spectacular views over to the snow-capped Alps. Even Milanese urban style-junkies, who give very little quarter to their own provincial towns, are prepared to bring friends over to Lugano for some shopping, a lakeside drink and a good meal.

Lugano stands alongside Zürich and Geneva as a Swiss banking centre, and the city centre reflects this. These old alleys and winding lanes are full of commerce, whether in the form of enticing delicatessens and boutiques or graceful, villa-style hotels and apartment buildings. Explore churches and art galleries, or indulge in a stroll under the lakeside palms. The twilight views over the lake from the summit of Monte Brè, with a warm southerly breeze blowing and the toot and rumble of cars rising from a bed of twinkling lights, could melt the hardest of hearts.

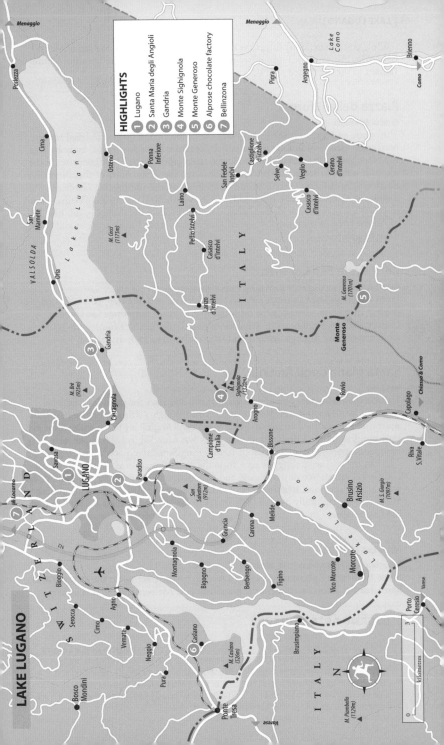

LAKE LUGANO

HIGHLIGHTS

1. Lugano
2. Santa Maria degli Angioli
3. Gandria
4. Monte Sighignola
5. Monte Generoso
6. Alprose chocolate factory
7. Bellinzona

While you're here, don't forget the epic rack-railway journey to the top of **Monte Generoso**, just south of Lugano (see p.176) – and the cable car up beautiful **Monte Tamaro** to the north (see p.179).

Piazza della Riforma

Ⓦ piazzariformalugano.ch

The centre of Lugano is the broad **Piazza della Riforma**, a huge café-lined square perfect for people-watching over a coffee. The lake lies a few metres away behind the Neoclassical **Palazzo Civico**, while the steep lanes of the Old Town rise on the opposite side of the square. Wandering through the dense maze of shopping alleys northwest of Riforma, you're bound to stumble on the photogenic Gabbani delicatessen, a fixture here since 1937, with two shops flanking Via Pessina – both interiors are crammed with fine *salsicce* made especially for the shop, cabinets full of Alpine cheeses from the farmers of Alto Ticino, fresh bread, pastries and foodie delights galore.

Cattedrale San Lorenzo

Via San Lorenzo • Irregular hours at time of writing, due to renovation work • Ⓦ lugano.ch

From bustling Piazza Cioccaro just past the Gabbani deli, the stepped Via Cattedrale doglegs steeply up, alongside the funicular line, to reach **Cattedrale San Lorenzo**, characterized by an impressive Renaissance portal, fragments of fourteenth- to sixteenth-century interior frescoes, and spectacular views from its terrace.

Santa Maria degli Angioli

Piazza Luini

The narrow **Via Nassa** – one of Switzerland's top addresses for chic, designer-label fashion – heads southwest from Piazza Riforma through a string of picturesque little squares to the medieval church of **Santa Maria degli Angioli** on Piazza Luini. This plain little building beside a disused funicular track was founded in 1490 as part of a Franciscan monastery (suppressed in 1848 during Switzerland's civil war).

Inside, the wall separating the nave from the chancel is covered by a monumental Leonardo-esque fresco of the Passion and Crucifixion painted in 1529 by **Bernadino Luini**, one of the finest Renaissance artworks in the region. It includes a magnificent St Sebastian, graphically pierced by arrows. On the left-hand wall is Luini's fresco of the Last Supper.

Museo d'Arte

Riva Caccia 5 • Tues–Sun 10am–6pm • Fr.12 • Ⓦ mdam.ch

Some 100m south of Santa Maria degli Angioli on the lakefront is the **Museo d'Arte**, housed at the time of writing in the grandiose Villa Malpensata, but due to have

---

LUGANO ARTE E CULTURA

Following extensive building works due for completion in 2015, the church of Santa Maria degli Angioli stands alongside the huge new lakefront arts centre **Lugano Arte e Cultura**, known as **LAC** (Ⓦ luganolac.ch). As well as a theatre, concert hall and panoramic rooftop restaurant, the new complex houses the **Museo d'Arte**, showcasing its collections and continuing its cycle of stellar touring exhibitions. The **Museo delle Culture** (Museum of Cultures, displaying non-European art and artefacts) will move into the art museum's former home at Villa Malpensata. Check online for the latest news.

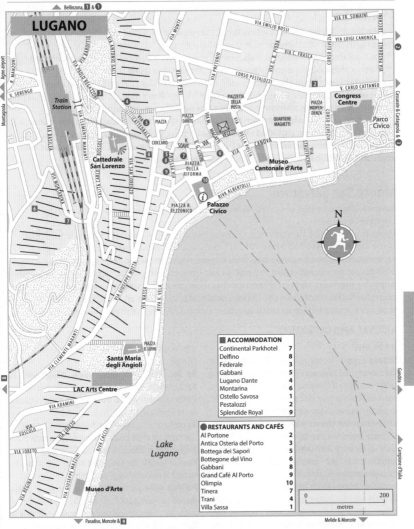

LUGANO

Bellinzona,

Agno airport

Montagnola

Train Station

Cattedrale San Lorenzo

Santa Maria degli Angioli

LAC Arts Centre

Museo d'Arte

Lake Lugano

Cattedrale San Lorenzo

Piazza Dante

Piazza della Riforma

Museo Cantonale d'Arte

Palazzo Civico

Paradiso, Morcote &

Melide & Morcote

N

■ ACCOMMODATION	
Continental Parkhotel	7
Delfino	8
Federale	5
Gabbani	5
Lugano Dante	4
Montarina	6
Ostello Savosa	1
Pestalozzi	2
Splendide Royal	9

● RESTAURANTS AND CAFÉS	
Al Portone	2
Antica Osteria del Porto	3
Bottega dei Sapori	5
Bottegone del Vino	6
Gabbani	8
Grand Café Al Porto	9
Olimpia	10
Tinera	7
Trani	4
Villa Sassa	1

0   200
metres

moved to the new LAC cultural centre nearby by the time you read this (see box opposite). It stages several major temporary exhibitions a year, often headline shows of work by major twentieth-century artists.

Museo Cantonale d'Arte

Via Canova 10 • Tues 2–5pm, Wed–Sun 10am–5pm • Fr.8–12 • Ⓦ museo-cantonale-arte.ch

Five minutes' walk east from Piazza Riforma brings you to the **Museo Cantonale d'Arte**, a fine old villa housing a permanent collection including paintings by Klee, Renoir, Turner, Degas and Pissaro alongside work by Swiss and Italian artists of the nineteenth and twentieth centuries. It also stages regular temporary shows, ranging from sculpture to photography; check the website for what's on.

Monte Brè

Funicular: June–Oct daily 9am–7pm (July & Aug until 11pm Fri & Sat), rest of year daily 9.15am–5pm; closed Jan & Feb · Fr.25 return, ask about discounted combi tickets including boat journey; free with Ticino Discovery Card · ⓦ montebre.ch

From Cassarate, ten minutes' walk east of the centre, a funicular rises to **Monte Brè** (925m), a sheer 660m directly above the city (also accessible by car), offering spectacular views from the summit café over the lake, the curve of Lugano's bay overlooked by San Salvatore, and the snowy Monte Rosa massif. Bracing hikes lead off all over the mountain and there are plenty of options for mountain-biking.

Brè village, dotted with outdoor art installations, is a short walk from the summit. The tourist office runs a **guided walk** (June–Oct Fri 1–6pm; Fr.10; ⓦ luganotourism.ch) in English through the village every Friday afternoon in summer, including boat ride and cable car. Booking essential, up to one hour beforehand.

Monte San Salvatore

Funicular: mid-March to Oct daily 9am–6pm (mid-June to mid-Sept until 11pm) · Fr.28 return, free with Ticino Discovery Card · ⓦ montesansalvatore.ch

From the district of Paradiso, ten minutes' walk south of central Lugano, a funicular climbs to **Monte San Salvatore** (912m), the sugarloaf mountain which rises in plain view directly above Lugano's bay. This rugged rock pinnacle offers especially good 360-degree panoramas from the roof of the little church on the summit, a short climb from the funicular station, which also has a decent café-restaurant. This is the starting point for **walks** south into the **Ceresio peninsula**; it's about an hour and twenty minutes through Carona village to reach Morcote (see p.177) on the tip of the peninsula.

ARRIVAL AND DEPARTURE
LUGANO

BY PLANE

Lugano airport 4km west in Agno. Shuttle buses wait for flight arrivals; the driver will drop you at your hotel or any point in the centre (Fr.10 including luggage). On departure, you must book a pick-up the day before (☏ 079 221 4243, ⓦ shuttle-bus.com). A taxi is around Fr.35.

Milan-Malpensa airport 40km southwest in Italy. The Malpensa Express bus runs from both terminals to Lugano (daily approx every 2hrs; 1hr 10min; Fr.25). Reservation is advisable, but not essential (☏ 091 858 2326, ⓦ malpensaexpress.ch). By the time you read this, a new train line linking Malpensa Airport with Lugano may be open.

By train Lugano is on the trans-Alpine high-speed rail line between Zürich and Milan; trains arrive frequently from Como San Giovanni (40min), Milano Centrale (55min) and Bellinzona (25min). Newly built track, which may be open by the time you read this, links to Varese. Lugano station is perched high above the city centre and lake. A funicular linking the station to pedestrianized Piazza Cioccaro in the centre was under long-term renovation at the time of writing, replaced by the frequent FuniBus (daily 5.20am–11.55pm; Fr.1.10; ⓦ tplsa.ch). If you prefer to walk (10min), cross the road outside the station and follow steps down to Via Cattedrale, which coils down to Piazza Cioccaro.

By bus Local buses access inland villages such as Montagnola (every 30min; 20min) or Vico Morcote (hourly; 40min; change at Olivella). Buses also run about six times a day to Gandria (20min).

By car Lugano has two exits off Switzerland's N2 autostrada (the extension of the Italian A9), roughly 23km north of the Italian border at Chiasso and less than 30km north of Como. There's a fiendish one-way system in operation in the city centre, and parking is in very short supply.

Parking Make sure your hotel has spaces, or resign yourself to shelling out Fr.25–30 a day at one of the car parks. For a one-day visit, use the Fornaci P+R (Park & Ride), located alongside Lugano-Sud autostrada exit: the car park entry ticket is valid for 24 hours on all Lugano public transport, including the P+R buses 1 or F into the centre (Mon–Sat 6.30am–11pm; every 15–30min). To exit the car park costs Fr.6.90.

By boat Ferries cover a network of routes (see p.166). Motorboat operators, for private jaunts around the lake (reckon on about Fr.100/hr), include Motoscafi Riuniti on the Lugano waterfront (☏ 091 922 9340; ⓦ motoscafiriuniti.ch).

INFORMATION AND ACTIVITIES

Tourist information The tourist office is located opposite the main landing-stage, in the Palazzo Civico on Riva Albertolli (April–Oct Mon–Fri 9am–7pm, Sat 9am–6pm, Sun 10am–5pm; Nov–March Mon–Fri 9am–noon & 1.30–5.30pm, Sat 10am–12.30pm & 1.30–5pm; ☏ 058 866 6600, ⓦ luganotourism.ch). There's also a

LUGANO'S FESTIVALS

The **Lugano Festival** (Ⓦluganofestival.ch), running from April into June, features classical soloists and orchestras. July sees the star-studded free concerts of **Estival Jazz** (Ⓦestivaljazz .ch). The **Ceresio Estate** classical music season runs throughout July and August, flanking two big **firework** displays over the lake: Campione throws down the gauntlet in late July and Lugano responds on August 1 (Swiss National Day). The **Blues to Bop Festival** in late August (Ⓦbluestobop.ch) showcases international blues, jazz, rock and gospel artists.

branch office inside the train station (Mon–Sat 9am–6pm).

Rent a bike At the train station (daily 8.45am–5.45pm; ☎051 221 5642, Ⓦrentabike.ch; Fr.35/day).

Guided walks There are free guided walks in English around the city (May–Oct Mon, Wed & Thurs 10am; 2hr) and through parks and gardens (May–Oct Tues 10am; 2hr; not mid-July to mid-Aug), starting from the tourist office.

ACCOMMODATION

There are plenty of accommodation options in the city centre; it can be hard to find a bargain, but – in characteristic Swiss fashion – quality at all price levels is very high. For some lakefront peace and quiet, consider staying just outside the city in Gandria (see p.173).

Continental Parkhotel Via Basilea 28 ☎091 966 1112, Ⓦcontinentalparkhotel.com. A vintage nineteenth-century facade, alongside the railway tracks but set back within its own grounds, conceals a completely renovated interior. Rooms – mostly three-star, with a few deluxe options – are blandly contemporary, but everything is well designed and Swissly efficient. Train buffs could request a corner room overlooking the level crossing and railway station, which is two minutes' walk away. Free parking. **Fr.210**

Delfino Via Casserinetta 6 ☎091 985 9999, Ⓦdelfinolugano.ch. Pleasant, welcoming small family-run hotel, with secure private parking and a pool. Something of an institution, and with a good reputation to uphold; rooms are functional rather than characterful, and the food is of a high standard. **Fr.180**

Federale Via Regazzoni 8 ☎091 910 0808, Ⓦhotel-federale.ch. Classic old townhouse hotel set in a quiet, leafy district immediately below the station, well away from traffic and with lake views from upper floors; rooms are full of character and good value. Private parking. **Fr.200**

★ **Gabbani** Piazza Cioccaro 1 ☎091 921 3470, Ⓦhotel-gabbani.ch. This stylish art hotel occupies the upper floors of a former convent in the old town lanes, above one of the outlets of Gabbani, Lugano's most famous deli. Each of the fourteen rooms features contemporary styling in wood and marble, with names – Orange, Walnut, Honey, Chocolate – reflecting individual design touches. And wow, is the food good. **Fr.220**

Lugano Dante Piazza Cioccaro 5 ☎091 910 5700, Ⓦhotel-luganodante.com. Quality business hotel bang in the heart of the pedestrianized city centre, with good service, comfortable rooms and no trouble from street noise. There's a free shuttle to and from Lugano airport, and private parking. **Fr.305**

Montarina Via Montarina 1 ☎091 966 7272, Ⓦmontarina.ch. Efficient low-budget place in a nice garden just behind the train station, with helpful management and clean rooms – those in the annexe are en suite, those in the main building share bathrooms. Rates include breakfast. Dorms **Fr.40**; doubles **Fr.125**

Ostello Savosa (HI hostel) Via Cantonale 13, Savosa ☎091 966 2728, Ⓦyouthhostel.ch. One of Switzerland's best hostels, set in its own parkland complete with a swimming pool. It has 132 beds spread across various rooms, including 17 doubles, plus family rooms and apartments. To get there, walk left out of the station for 300m to the Genzana bus stop, then take bus 5 (direction Vezia) to Crocifisso. Closed mid-Dec to mid-Jan. Dorms **Fr.42**; doubles **Fr.96**

Pestalozzi Piazza Indipendenza 9 ☎091 921 4646, Ⓦpestalozzi-lugano.ch. Very nice family-run two-star, smart, swanky and renovated – and it's right in the centre, 150m from the lakeshore. Some rooms have balconies and lake views. Those with an en-suite bathroom are more expensive. **Fr.120**

Splendide Royal Riva Caccia 7 ☎091 985 7711, Ⓦsplendide.ch. Lugano's premier city-centre luxury hotel, with traditionally styled public spaces and guest rooms that live up to the hotel's name. Accept nothing less than one of the vast rooms on the top floor, offering some of the best views in the city. Private parking. **Fr.405**

CAMPSITE

Camping La Piodella Via alla Foce 14, Muzzano ☎091 994 7788, Ⓦcampingtcs.ch. Of the five campsites clustered together on the lake at Agno (see p.178), a little way west of Lugano, this is perhaps the best, open year-round and with a pool, watersports and plenty of activities. Pitch **Fr.35**

4

EATING AND DRINKING

The many cafés and restaurants around Piazza Riforma offer good, inexpensive food at lunch and dinner; for classier options, head deeper into the city – or, if you're after a bite on the go, choose from the fresh-made panini, pizzas and other pastry bites on offer throughout the middle of the day from the Gabbani deli's street-side counters on Via Pessina. Restaurants in Gandria, Campione and other spots around the lake are within easy reach.

CAFÉS

Bottega dei Sapori Via Cattedrale 6 ☎091 921 4733, ⓦbottegadeisapori.ch. Bright and breezy little café-bar on a busy little street – great for coffee on the go, gourmet filled panini (around Fr.10–12) or a light lunch. Mon & Tues 7.30am–7.30pm, Wed–Fri 7.30am–9pm, Sat 9am–7.30pm.

Grand Café Al Porto Via Pessina 3 ☎091 910 5130, ⓦgrand-cafe-lugano.ch. Venerable grand café in the lanes behind Piazza Riforma, built on the site of a medieval convent and boasting Florentine-style frescoes in the old refectory (now used for private parties). The patio, under its cupola, is the perfect place for genteel morning coffee or afternoon tea – pricey, at somewhere north of Fr.25. Mon–Sat 8am–6.30pm.

RESTAURANTS

Al Portone Viale Cassarate 3 ☎078 722 9324, ⓦristorante-alportone.ch. Fine-dining restaurant that manages to sustain a pleasantly relaxed ambience alongside its inventive, artfully showcased new Italian cuisine and detail-perfect contemporary design ethic. This kind of quality commands top prices: the seven-course *menù degustazione* is Fr.120; à la carte mains are Fr.25–55. Tues–Fri noon–2.30pm & 6.30–10pm, Sat 6.30–10pm.

Antica Osteria del Porto Via Foce 9 ☎091 971 4200, ⓦosteriadelporto.ch. Busy, amiable little riverside terrace restaurant by the marina, a short walk east of the city centre, serving Ticino-inspired cuisine to a relaxed array of Luganesi families. *Menùs* around Fr.40. Sept–May closed Tues.

4

CROSSING THE SWISS-ITALIAN BORDER

On the map, the border between **Lugano** and **Como** appears an afterthought – yet, in truth, this has been an international frontier for five hundred years. It represents a profound cleft of culture and history; Lugano has been Swiss since the dukes of Milan lost Ticino to the invading northerners in 1512. Even today, with Switzerland staying out of the European Union, the frontier remains significant.

Crossing and recrossing the border can give fascinating insight into what it is, exactly, that makes Lake Como so unequivocally Italian and Lake Lugano so **unequivocally Swiss**. The city of Lugano is wealthier, certainly, and lacks the remnants of Fascist and post-Fascist urban design on show in Como. The **food** on Lake Como is classic Lombard fare – *missoltini* (dried fish), polenta, *pizzoccheri* (buckwheat tagliatelle) – whereas Lugano's cooking displays northern influence in its rich dressings, cured meats and Alpine cheeses. In **art and architecture**, the impact of the Italian Renaissance did seep northwards across the border, but from then to the late eighteenth century, while Europe's nobility were busy putting up opulent villas on Como's shores, Lugano was a backwater, under continuous occupation by a trans-Alpine German-speaking army. Lugano's history is revolutionary, whereas Como's is authoritarian.

Today, one way to tell which side of the border you're on is by the extent and type of new building, and by the upkeep of older buildings; Italy crumbles under the weight of history and poor urban planning, while Ticino has gained a reputation for **world-class** contemporary architecture.

And armies of northerners continue to arrive. Lugano can seem tranquil in comparison with the battalions of tour-buses and camper vans that parade up and down Como's shores all summer long.

DAY-TRIPS BETWEEN LUGANO AND COMO

With a bit of timetable planning, it's easy to pop to and fro between Lake Lugano and Lake Como in a day. Frequent trains go from Lugano south to Como (40min). From there you can link to Menaggio, halfway up the lake, by bus C10 (hourly; 1hr 10min) – or, much nicer, by boat (frequent; 2hr). From Menaggio, bus C12 (about every 2hrs) climbs westwards past Porlezza and back to Lugano (55min). If you work things so you leave Menaggio about 2.30pm, you could get off the bus midway at Porlezza in good time to catch the afternoon boat back to Lugano. The last bus from Menaggio is at 5.30pm. Doing the route in reverse lets you stay late in Como for dinner; trains run to Lugano until midnight. Don't forget your passport.

Bottegone del Vino Via Magatti 3 ☎091 922 7689. Popular old-style wine bar beside the post office, with waiters in aprons and a huge range of wines on offer by the glass or bottle. A chalkboard features the special of the day. Always busy, always crowded. Closed Sun.

★**Gabbani** Piazza Cioccaro 1 ☎091 911 3083, ⓦgabbani.com. Lugano's most celebrated deli has now expanded across the lane from its original outlet at Via Pessina 12; the new building, tucked beneath a portico alongside Piazza Cioccaro, houses a specialist cheesemonger's, bakery and wine shop as well as an informal café-bar at ground level and a chic, rustic-styled restaurant upstairs serving unfussy Mediterranean cuisine of the highest quality. *Menùs* around Fr.32. Closed Sun.

Olimpia Piazza Riforma 1 ☎091 922 7488, ⓦristorante olimpia.ch. A Lugano landmark, occupying one wing of the Palazzo Civico on Piazza Riforma – and the best of the main square's many cafés for its good, inexpensive food. Italian staples, steaks and a few more interesting dishes rarely go for more than Fr.30. Daily 11am–midnight.

Tinera Via dei Gorini 2 ☎091 923 5219. Popular, rustic *grotto*-style restaurant off Piazza Riforma, specializing in keenly priced Ticinese and Lombard dishes such as polenta and *pollo alla cacciatora* (spicy chicken stew), along with an array of excellent local Merlots served, unusually, in bowls. *Menùs* around Fr.23. Closed Sun & Mon.

Trani Via Cattedrale 12 ☎091 922 0505, ⓦtrani.ch. Friendly little local *osteria*, tucked away in a quiet corner off the cathedral lane, with a pleasant, sky-lit interior and tables laid out on the steps. Stop in for excellent pasta – including gnocchi (Fr.22) and saffron lasagne (Fr.21) – as well as good perch, bass and vegetarian options (around Fr.35). Mon–Sat 10am–1am.

Villa Sassa Via Tesserete 10 ☎091 911 4111, ⓦvillasassa .ch. Outstanding haute-cuisine restaurant attached to this luxury hotel in the hills just north of the city centre. The restaurant terrace offers a spectacular view over the city and the lake. The romance is kept up by the service – white-tuxedoed waiters gliding by – and the food, formal European/international cuisine with a North Italian twist; superb lake fish, delicately flavoured filled pastas and the like. Expect at least Fr.75 a head. Daily 7–10.30pm.

Around Lake Lugano

The possibilities for getting out into the countryside around Lugano are plentiful; the tourist office has sheets detailing fifty-odd cycling routes and walking trails out of the city, for all abilities. The best area to head for is the hilly countryside of the **Ceresio peninsula**, extending southwards behind the San Salvatore mountain opposite Lugano, and well served by boats and buses.

East of Lugano across the Italian border is a cluster of attractive villages on the way to **Porlezza**, beyond which lies Menaggio on Lake Como. West of Lugano in the **Malcantone** district, before the border at Ponte Tresa, there's the memorable attraction of a Swiss chocolate factory at little **Caslano**, while to the south, the **Mendrisiotto** offers walks and country villages nudged up against the Italian border.

Gandria

ⓦviva-gandria.ch

From Castagnola, just east of Lugano city centre, a pleasant stroll heads east around the base of Monte Brè, joining the Sentiero di Gandria footpath through the **Parco degli Olivi**, a Mediterranean-style lakefront park shaded by olive trees, cypress, laurels and oleander.

After less than an hour's walk from Lugano – or a few minutes by car – you come to picturesque **GANDRIA**, a village of 200 people which rises straight from the water 4km east of the city (and is served by regular boats). Wandering down through the alleys – far too narrow for traffic; cars must park on the slopes above the village – past palm trees growing out of the rocky walls and the atmospheric little church of **San Vigilio**, you come to the landing-stage, around which is crowded a handful of charming terrace **restaurants**; there are few quieter, more alluring corners at which to hole up. Views down this little-explored eastern arm of Lake Lugano frame the pinnacle of Monte dei Pizzoni – and, beside it, Monte Bronzone – sweeping down into the water, with precipitous wooded slopes opposite that are almost completely devoid of habitation. High on the hillside opposite you can see Lanzo d'Intelvi's *Albergo Belvedere* (see p.175). The silence is wonderful.

Swiss Customs Museum

Cantine di Gandria · April–Oct daily 1.30–5.30pm · Free · Ⓦ customsmuseum.admin.ch

Opposite Gandria, with its own landing-stage served by boats from Gandria as well as Lugano (there are no roads here), is the **Museo delle Dogane Svizzere** (Swiss Customs Museum). Its collection of smuggler-related bits and bobs, including a mini-submarine that was once used to bring illicit salami into Switzerland, makes for a diverting hour or two.

ARRIVAL AND INFORMATION

GANDRIA

By bus Bus 490 shuttles 6–8 times a day from Lugano (20min).

By boat Gandria has roughly hourly ferries from Lugano (25min) in summer, with a less frequent service in winter.

Gandria info point In the village (Easter–Oct daily 11am–8pm; ☏ 079 331 3065, Ⓦ luganotourism.ch).

ACCOMMODATION AND EATING

Grotto dei Pescatori Caprino ☏ 091 923 9867. Alluring little *grotto* (rustic tavern), located near the hamlet of Caprino, across the lake from Gandria – and inaccessible by road. The only way to get here is by boat; a handful head over from Lugano, and smaller craft shuttle across from Gandria. The means of arrival and the isolation are the main attractions, but the atmosphere – and the food – match up; tables are laid out under the shade of the trees, directly on the waterfront. Plump for the succulent perch in butter and sage, or a heartier dish such as beef with polenta (meals around Fr.30). A taxi boat from Lugano is about Fr.40. Closed Oct–April.

Hotel Moosmann Gandria ☏ 091 971 7261, Ⓦ hotel-moosmann-gandria.ch. Very quiet, small family-run hotel at the edge of the village, with a selection of spotless but unrenovated rooms with lovely lake views. No road access. Closed Nov–March. **Fr.160**

Locanda Gandriese Gandria ☏ 091 971 4181, Ⓦ locanda.com. Browse your way through the handful of broadly similar lakefront restaurants beside Gandria's landing-stage – but also factor in this posh, upmarket restaurant a stroll away in the village lanes. The menu covers a range of Swiss-Italian favourites, risotto and veal escalope filled out with nine choices of accompaniments for polenta, both vegetarian and meaty. Mains Fr.18–40. They also have four simple rooms. Closed Nov–Feb. **Fr.120**

East to Lake Como

From Gandria, the main road continues east for 1.3km to the international border. After 500m of no-man's-land, you emerge into the **VALSOLDA**, a stretch of Italian lakeside villages headed by **Oria** and **Albogasio**, both of them cheerful little places – thoroughly Italian, and quite unlike Gandria just the other side of the frontier. **San Mamete** is especially picturesque, with its twelfth-century bell tower.

Porlezza

Quarter of an hour east of Gandria by road, and 8km from the border, is **PORLEZZA**, the main town on this Italian branch of Lake Lugano. It's a fairly uninspiring place, but the views west over the water, framed by forested mountains, are sensational. Take a five-minute stroll through the old quarter, and a three-minute stroll along the lakefront, then settle down with an ice cream. **Menaggio**, on the shores of Lake Como (see p.207), lies only 11km east.

ARRIVAL AND INFORMATION

PORLEZZA

By bus Reasonably regular buses serve Porlezza on the route between Lugano (30min) and Menaggio (25min).

By boat One boat a day serves Porlezza from Lugano, returning shortly afterwards.

Tourist office By the landing-stage (Mon–Sat 9am–noon; ☏ 334 144 3183, Ⓦ comune.porlezza.co.it).

Osteno

Ⓦ osteno.it

Continue around the end of the lake from Porlezza, and after 6km or so – still inside Italy, and on a narrow, scenic road hugging the water – you come to **OSTENO**, an unprettified, end-of-the-road village gazing across at the shark's-tooth peaks above the

Valsolda. The church holds a marble sculpture of the Virgin and Child by the fifteenth-century artist Andrea Bregno – but the main reason to head this way is for the quiet. One boat a day stops here on the way from Lugano to Porlezza on request, returning again an hour or so later, and a couple of waterfront bars offer refreshment.

Above Osteno, a narrow road scrambles its way up the mountainside towards Laino, where it meets the main road through the Val d'Intelvi. At the junction, turn left through San Fedele Intelvi to drop down through 8km of hairpins to Argegno on Lake Como (see p.200) – or turn right to climb towards Lanzo d'Intelvi and, eventually, the Sighignola summit.

Monte Sighignola
No public transport

Dubbed the "Balcony of Italy", **Monte Sighignola** (1320m) offers truly epic views over Lugano and the Swiss Alps. It stands plum on the Swiss-Italian border, at the head of the Val d'Intelvi (which leads down to Lake Como) and a full thousand metres directly above the lakeside village of Campione d'Italia far below. A road goes to the top; whether you approach from Lake Como or Lake Lugano, it's a wonderful drive, mostly climbing through dense, cool forest.

The two routes meet just above **San Fedele Intelvi** – a fairly charmless town in stunning surroundings – above which, beyond Pellio, breathtaking views open up to Porlezza as the road twists and turns. **Lanzo d'Intelvi**, 6km past San Fedele, has a little cluster of Alpine-style village hotels as well as a turning to the *Albergo Belvedere* (walbergobelvedere.it) perched on the forested hillside gazing down at Gandria. Climb another 6km, on a twisting forest lane above Lanzo, to eventually reach the summit car park at Sighignola, where there's a snack bar and stupendous vistas over the bay of Lugano, reaching as far as Luino, Varese and, if conditions are good, even Mont Blanc. Plans to build a cable car up here from Campione ran out of steam years ago, but the concrete pylons survive, mouldering on the hillside. Linger for sunset, if you can. In winter, there's some modest skiing.

Campione d'Italia

Visible across the lake from Lugano below the towering heights of Monte Sighignola, the enclave of **CAMPIONE D'ITALIA** opted out of Ticino's independence campaign in 1798 and so remained Italian when all around it became Swiss. The village – for that's all it is, even though it's very swish – is a bit mixed up. It is Italian, administered as part of the Provincia di Como, but uses Swiss francs rather than euros (and it's a good place for a meal, since restaurant prices are much lower than in Lugano). The police are Italian, but their cars have Swiss plates. Switzerland runs the phones but Italy handles the post. And there is no passport control.

Casino
Piazzale Milano • Mon–Thurs noon–4am, Fri & Sat noon–5am, Sun 11am–4am • w casinocampione.it

Just north of Bissone, the lakeshore road enters Italy at a distinctive modern gateway arch marking Campione's border; you must follow Corso Italia on a strict one-way system around the town centre before turning back along the lakeshore. As you do so, you pass beneath Campione's landmark building: its giant **casino**, designed by Ticinese architect Mario Botta. Unlimited stakes apply here, and – despite liberalization of Swiss gaming law – this is still where Lugano's many high rollers come to dally after dark.

Piazza Roma

Boats from Lugano (and around the lake) dock at Campione's main **Piazza Roma**, a step from the Casino and flanked by busy terrace cafés; this is an atmospheric spot. Medieval Campione was renowned for its stonemasons, the Maestri Campionesi, whose skills were sought for buildings all over northern Italy; the only example that has survived unscathed in Campione is the little church of **San Pietro** (entirely glassed-in for protection), just off Piazza Roma. From here, Via Marco da Campione runs south along the lake, back to the arch.

Santa Maria dei Ghirli

April–Oct daily 9am–6pm; Nov–March Sat & Sun 9am–4.30pm

About 700m south of Piazza Roma, and 100m before the arch, is the rather lovely church of **Santa Maria dei Ghirli**. *Ghirli* ("swallows") refers to Campione's well-travelled masons, who returned home only rarely. The church – which shows its best side to the lake – is filled with thirteenth-century **frescoes**; especially striking are the scenes on the south wall, showing Salome and Herodias in medieval courtly dress.

ARRIVAL AND INFORMATION	CAMPIONE D'ITALIA

By bus Bus 439 serves Campione hourly from Lugano (15min).

By boat Roughly six boats daily arrive from Lugano (20min).

Tourist office Corso Italia 2 (Mon, Tues, Thurs & Fri 8.30am–1pm & 2–6pm, Wed 8.30am–1pm; ☎ 091 649 5051, ⓦ campioneitalia.com).

EATING AND DRINKING

Da Candida Via Marco 4 ☎ 091 649 7541, ⓦ dacandida .net. Campione's poshest restaurant, an institution here since 1886. The chef prepares his own foie gras, and imports his own oysters and other seafood from Brittany; expect classic upmarket Italian cooking and a bill well into three figures. Tues 7–11pm, Wed–Sun noon–2pm & 7–11pm. Closed most of Aug.

Monello Piazza Roma 2 ☎ 091 649 4997. Fast-paced, popular waterfront pizza/pasta restaurant beside the landing-stage, with good pizzas from around Fr.14. Tues–Sun noon–3pm & 6.30pm–midnight.

Taverna Piazza Roma 1 ☎ 091 649 4797, ⓦ ristorantetaverna.com. Another good choice from the selection of busy, cheerful and unmistakeably Italian cafés on the main square – a century-old establishment with a solid reputation for quality, notably in their salt-baked fresh lake fish. Mon noon–2.30pm & 7–11.30pm, Wed 7–11.30pm, Thurs–Sun noon–2.30pm & 7–11.30pm.

Monte Generoso

Rack railway and summit facilities closed at time of writing • ⓦ montegeneroso.ch

From alongside **Capolago** train station (274m) at the southern end of Lake Lugano, a rack railway climbs on a slow, scenic route up to **MONTE GENEROSO** (1704m). Once the restoration works have been completed (reportedly 2016), this trip is worth taking for the views alone; from the summit – a short walk above the Vetta (top) station – you can see out across a sizeable part of northern Italy, in an amazing panorama. Milan and Turin are both visible; Bellagio on Lake Como is in plain sight, as is Arona on Lake Maggiore and the distinctive pyramidal Matterhorn; and you can even see as far as the mountain pass in the Apennines above Genoa. The restaurant by the top station is the starting-point for an array of **walks**, including down to Mendrisio one way (2hr 40min) or Muggio another (2hr 15min). We cover both in the "Mendrisiotto" section (see p.179).

Hermann Hesse Museum

Montagnola • March–Oct daily 10.30am–5.30pm; Nov–Feb Sat & Sun 10.30am–5.30pm • Fr.8.50 • ⓦ hessemontagnola.ch • Bus 436 from Via Sorengo behind Lugano station

Behind Monte San Salvatore on the Collina d'Oro – named 'Hill of Gold' for its sun-drenched tranquillity – sits **MONTAGNOLA** village. The writer Hermann Hesse lived in Montagnola from 1919 until his death in 1962, and wrote most of his classic works here, including *Steppenwolf* and *The Glass Bead Game*. His villa Casa Camuzzi now houses the **Museo Hermann Hesse**, an interesting little spot, though the displays – Hesse's umbrella, Hesse's table – are modest. What makes a visit worthwhile is an excellent 45-minute video in English on the writer's life in Montagnola, which the staff can set up for you. They also have details of a self-guided walk through the village and surrounding woods. The *Boccadoro* literary café next door (run by the museum) offers refreshment.

Swissminiatur

Mid-March to Oct daily 9am–6pm • Fr.19 • ⓦ swissminiatur.ch • Train from Lugano (every 30min; 6min) or bus 439 (hourly; 8min)

Halfway down Lake Lugano, at the point where the train tracks, main road and autostrada all cross the water on a low bridge, the village of **MELIDE** is home to the kitschy **Swissminiatur**. This small park features 1:25 scale models of just about every attraction in Switzerland, from Geneva's cathedral to Alpine peaks, with moving model boats, trains and cable cars livening up the static displays. A wander past all 113 exhibits could fill a slow hour or two.

Morcote and Vico Morcote

At the Ceresio peninsula's southern tip, 4km south of Melide, lies the captivating village of **MORCOTE**, once a fishing community and now eking out a living as a lakeside attraction, served by regular boats from Lugano. Its antiques shops and photogenic arcaded houses – many from the sixteenth and seventeenth centuries – are strung along the shoreline road. Just around the headland are gates into the **Parco Scherrer** (mid-March to mid-Oct daily 10am–5pm; July & Aug until 6pm; Fr.7), a romantic hillside garden of lush flora and exotic follies. Stepped lanes lead up the hill behind to **Santa Maria del Sasso** (Mon–Fri 8am–6pm, Sat & Sun 9am–6pm; Nov–March closed Mon–Fri mornings), an atmospheric church with sixteenth-century frescoes and great views.

Morcote's waterfront is shoulder-to-shoulder cafés – pleasant enough, but fairly generic (and often crowded). Aim instead for the tinier village of **VICO MORCOTE**, on the hillside above and 1km north; unlike in Morcote, here you can stand alone in the cobbled street to absorb the atmosphere – and there's a sprinkling of decent restaurants to tempt you to linger.

ARRIVAL AND INFORMATION — MORCOTE AND VICO MORCOTE

By bus Vico Morcote has a few buses shuttling up from Morcote, Olivella or Melide on the lakeshore.

By boat Four boats a day serve Morcote from Lugano (50min).

Tourist office Riva dal Garavèll 16 (April–Oct Mon–Fri 8.30am–12.30pm & 1.30–5.30pm, Sat & Sun 10am–noon & 1.30–5pm; ☎ 058 866 4960, ⓦ morcoteturismo.ch).

EATING AND DRINKING

Osteria Al Böcc La Piazza, Vico Morcote ☎ 091 980 2627, ⓦ bocc.ch. Splendid family-run wine bar-restaurant in an attractive corner of this old village, specializing in polenta served seven different ways. Plenty for vegetarians too. Expect a bill around Fr.25 per head. Mon & Thurs–Sun 10.30am–2.30pm & 5.30pm–midnight.

Ristorante La Sorgente Portic da Süra 18, Vico Morcote ☎ 091 996 2301, ⓦ lasorgente.ch. Stone tables set out on a lovely little terrace and a cool, white-walled interior set the scene for this bastion of Slow Food in a delightful semi-rural location above the lake. Lunch on salad and prosciutto (around Fr.30) or sample their handmade pasta alongside dishes such as grilled octopus (*menùs* Fr.60–85). The best bet, if you can afford it, is to splash out on their *Menù del territorio* (around Fr.70), a four-course blowout of local ingredients and styles. July & Aug closed Mon, Tues lunch & Sat lunch. Rest of year closed Mon & Tues.

Porto Ceresio and around

From Capolago, a minor road cuts west through the medieval village of **Riva San Vitale** and skirts the perimeter of **Monte San Giorgio**, a wooded mountain that is a UNESCO

World Natural Heritage Site for its unspoilt environment and fossils. From **Brusino Arsizio**, an attractive village 5km from Riva, with a handful of lazy terrace cafés, a **cable car** rises to Serpiano on a shoulder of the mountain for lonesome forest rambling. Before you reach Brusino, the road rounds the headland of **Pojana**, occupied by the shady terrace of the simple *Terminus* café-restaurant, offering stunning views north past Lugano to the high Alps.

The Italian border lies 2km beyond Brusino; 1500m further brings you to the genial lakefront town of **PORTO CERESIO**, gazing back at Morcote. In a moment of inspiration, the town built itself a boardwalk on stilts over the water to facilitate the lovely late-afternoon *passeggiata*, which extends either side of the main lakefront **Piazza Bossi** and takes in several enticing little pockets of west-facing sandy beach. There's not much else to do; boats stop in here two or three times a day from Lugano, but the town is more oriented towards its Italian neighbours – Varese (see p.155) lies just 10km south.

ARRIVAL AND INFORMATION   PORTO CERESIO

By bus Swiss buses run hourly north to Capolago (15min), Italian ones run hourly south to Varese (40min).
By boat Boats run two or three times a day from Lugano (1hr).

Tourist office Piazzale Luraschi (June–Sept Mon, Tues & Thurs 10am–12.30pm & 2.30–6.30pm, Fri & Sat 2.30–6.30pm, Sun 10am–12.30pm & 3–6.30pm; ☏ 0332 939 303, ⓦ comune.portoceresio.va.it).

The Malcantone

Narrow-gauge trains start from open platforms opposite Lugano's main rail station on a scenic route west through the **Malcantone** district, bound for Ponte Tresa. After leaving Lugano, they circle the pint-sized airport at **AGNO**, above which stands Monte Lema, endpoint of a long, beautiful hiking trail from Monte Tamaro (see p.179).

Caslano chocolate factory
Via Rompada 36 • Mon–Fri 9am–5.30pm, Sat & Sun 9am–4.30pm • Fr.3 • ⓦ alprose.ch

After Agno, trains head on to the undistinguished town of **CASLANO**, unlikely home of the **Alprose chocolate factory**; from Caslano station, follow the tracks in the direction of Ponte Tresa for about 200m and cut left into the industrial estate. As you enter the factory you're greeted, Willy Wonka-style, by an attendant who will swoop a breadstick through a fountain bubbling with fragrant molten chocolate, and hand it to you. The museum comprises some old coin-op machines and knick-knacks, but the main attraction is the chance to watch the mixing machines and production-line conveyor belts in action (Mon–Fri only) from a partly enclosed catwalk above the factory floor. The on-site shop stocks the full Alprose range at a discount – and has unlimited free chocolate for sampling. Eat as much as you want.

Ponte Tresa
Caslano is loomed over by the bulbous **Monte Caslano**, which almost chokes this corner of the lake; there is just a narrow, reedy strait between the mountain and the opposite, Italian, shore allowing boats to access **PONTE TRESA**, the rail terminus 3km south of Caslano. This is a schizophrenic little place, divided by the **international border**. The Swiss half of town is placid and neat, but crossing the bridge over the River Tresa for which the town was named throws you into its Italian twin – a mini-maelstrom of cars negotiating a complex one-way system around busy shops, even busier for the huge Saturday morning market.

From Ponte Tresa the main road heads south 25km to **Varese** (see p.155), while minor roads run parallel on both the Swiss and Italian riverbanks for 10km west to **Luino** on Lake Maggiore (see p.149). South around the lakeshore lies **Porto Ceresio** (see p.177).

ARRIVAL AND INFORMATION
THE MALCANTONE

By train Frequent (every 15min) narrow-gauge trains from Lugano serve Caslano (20min) and Ponte Tresa (25min). Details at ⓦflpsa.ch.

By boat Two boats daily serve Caslano from Lugano (1hr 25min).

Tourist office Piazza Lago, Caslano (Mon–Fri 8am–noon & 1.30–5.30pm; ☎091 606 2986, ⓦmalcantone.ch).

The Mendrisiotto

South of Lake Lugano, main roads and trains shoot through the hot, dry region known as the **Mendrisiotto**, after **MENDRISIO**, largest town in the area and a major wine-growing centre. There's not a great deal to stop for in the town, although its centre is picturesque. The main draw is the giant **Foxtown outlet mall** (daily 11am–7pm; ⓦfoxtown.com), prominently signposted alongside the autostrada, where you can pick up designer-label fashions – Prada, Gucci, Versace, Dolce & Gabbana, and more – at up to seventy percent off.

Near Mendrisio, the village of Morbio Inferiore marks a branch road that climbs into the last valley in Switzerland, the tranquil **Valle di Muggio** (ⓦvalledimuggio.ch). Thickly wooded, with seemingly inaccessible hamlets clinging to the steep side opposite the road, this is a lovely, rarely visited backwater. A steep trail leads up to Monte Generoso, while **MUGGIO** (666m), 7km into the valley, has a few taverns where you can grab a bite.

Some 6km beyond Mendrisio, and 23km south of Lugano, the Italian frontier is marked by **CHIASSO**, an unprepossessing border town with a large train station on the edge of a desultory town centre. Swarms of motorized and foot traffic pass through during the morning and evening rush hours. Como's suburbs begin immediately on the other side, trickling on for 5km to the city centre and lakefront (see p.189).

ARRIVAL AND INFORMATION
THE MENDRISIOTTO

By train Mendrisio is on the Lugano-Chiasso main line, served by frequent trains (every 30min; 20min).

By bus A few buses a day serve Muggio from Chiasso, and both Monte and Muggio from Mendrisio

(change at Castel San Pietro).

Mendrisio info point Inside the Foxtown mall (daily 11am–7pm; ☎091 641 3050, ⓦmendrisiottoturismo.ch).

ACCOMMODATION AND EATING
VALLE DI MUGGIO

Ostello di Scudellate Scudellate ☎091 684 1388, ⓦostellodiscudellate.com. A basic mountain hostel in a high-altitude village on a shoulder of Monte Generoso, with 26 beds packed into three rooms and good access to Alpine trails. Dorms <u>Fr.22</u>

Osteria La Montanara Monte ☎091 684 1479. A welcoming little inn in a country hamlet across the valley from Muggio, serving rustic country fare such as venison and other game, home-cured meats, freshly-baked bread and local wines. Also has three simple guest rooms. <u>Fr.80</u>

Monte Tamaro

Gondola April–Oct daily 8.30am–5pm • Fr.23, half-price with Ticino Discovery Card • ⓦmontetamaro.ch • Trains run every 30min to Rivera from Como (50min) and Lugano (15min) on the route to Bellinzona (15min)

North of Lugano, where the autostrada and railway plunge into tunnels beneath Monte Ceneri, gondolas rise from the town of **Rivera** (469m) up to **Alpe Foppa** (1530m), located on a shoulder of **Monte Tamaro** (1961m). By the top gondola station, alongside a little restaurant, is the church of **Santa Maria degli Angeli**, designed by the Ticinese architect Mario Botta in 1990. It's an effortlessly graceful building of porphyry stone, with symmetrical stairs, arches, a long walkway and extensive views from the belvedere.

The church is worth the journey by itself, but you'll also find loads of family-friendly activities, including an adventure park and pool, and also plenty of **walks** up here – not least from Alpe Foppa to the Tamaro summit (1hr 40min) or down to Rivera (2hr 15min). The most spectacular heads on an isolated route (4hr 30min) along a ridge west to **Monte Lema** (1624m; ⓦmontelema.ch), from where a cable car runs down to Miglieglia, which is in turn linked by bus to Lugano. Ask at the base station about a combination ticket covering the route.

Bellinzona

Few people bother with **BELLINZONA** – but that's their loss, since this graceful old town is the perfect place to draw breath away from the lakeside bustle. A fortress since Roman times, Bellinzona occupies a prime valley-floor position, holding the keys to the great Alpine passes of the Novena, Gottardo, Lucomagno and San Bernardino. In 1242 it was bought by the Visconti family, dukes of Milan, who built a new **castle** atop the hill plum in the middle of the valley, while their allies, the Rusconi family of Como, built another castle slightly up the hillside. In the 1420s the newly independent Swiss confederates north of the Gotthard Pass, who had successfully thrown off Habsburg rule, began a violent campaign against the Milanese forces, which spurred the Sforza dynasty – then in the ascendant in Milan – to reinforce the two castles and build a third, even higher up the hillside. A massive chain of fortifications cut right across the Ticino valley… to no avail, since the Swiss won Bellinzona by treaty in 1503. Three centuries of domination and oppression followed, with Swiss overlords posted to Bellinzona to keep control of the peasantry, until Ticino won its independence in 1803.

Bellinzona lacks a lake, but it also lacks the pace, the crowds and the touristic sheen of its bigger neighbours. Its medieval architecture and picturesque churches are crowned by a trio of castles – **Castelgrande**, **Montebello** and **Sasso Corbaro** – together listed as UNESCO World Heritage. If you can, combine a trip with a visit to Bellinzona's **Saturday market** (7.30am–1pm) – one of the best in Ticino, which sees the Old Town packed with stalls selling breads, local cheeses, wine, fruit, veg, handicrafts and more.

Around Piazza Collegiata

The Old Town centres on the Renaissance buildings of **Piazza Collegiata**, dominated by the Collegiata church, built by the same architect who worked on Como's cathedral and decorated with Baroque frescoes and stucco. Narrow lanes branch out all around; arcaded **Piazza Nosetto** is just south, with the Cà Rossa house on the way featuring a striking red terracotta facade – a style fashionable in early nineteenth-century Milan. From Piazza Nosetto, a gateway leads into the courtyard of the **Palazzo Civico**, a splendid Renaissance building rebuilt in the 1920s along with its loggias, which coil attractively around both upper floors.

Castelgrande

Castle courtyard Mon 10am–6pm, Tues–Sun 9am–10pm • Free • **Museum** Daily 10am–6pm; Nov–March 11am–4pm • Fr.5; joint ticket for all castle museums plus Villa Cedri Fr.15

High on Bellinzona's central rock rise the massive towers and walls of **Castelgrande**, the most impressive of the town's three medieval castles. The whole complex has been sympathetically restored by architect Aurelio Galfetti, who added a public **lift**, dramatically recessed deep into the bedrock of the hill behind the central Piazza del Sole, which emerges at a purpose-built modern fortification on an upper terrace of the castle. The castle grounds are serene, overlooked by the slender thirteenth-century

White Tower, with two upper windows on all four faces, and the fourteenth-century **Black Tower**, with three windows on its longer side. Despite their names, both, like the castle itself, are grey granite, and between them run lines of distinctive Lombard-style **swallow-tail battlements**.

Off Castelgrande's central lawns is an entrance to the **Museo Storico**, offering a tour through Bellinzona's past, including an excellent audiovisual show (in English).

Montebello

Castle courtyard April–Oct daily 10am–6pm • Free • **Museum** April–Oct daily 10am–6pm • Fr.5; joint ticket for all castle museums plus Villa Cedri Fr.15

Behind the Collegiata church, a path rises to the picturesque **Castello di Montebello**, some 90m higher in elevation than Castelgrande. From a vantage point on the ramparts, it's easy to trace the line of defensive fortifications which link the two castles across the width of the Ticino valley. The castle itself is impressive, with a fifteenth-century courtyard and residential palace surrounding an older central portion dating from the thirteenth century, the latter now housing a **museum** of Gothic and Renaissance architecture.

Sasso Corbaro

Castle courtyard April–Oct daily 10am–6pm • Free • **Museum** April–Oct daily 10am–6pm • Fr.5; joint ticket for all castle museums plus Villa Cedri Fr.15 • Bus 4 runs between the town centre and Artore, near the castle

A stiff 45-minute climb brings you to **Castello di Sasso Corbaro**, 230m above Bellinzona, designed and built in six months in 1479 by a military engineer brought in from Florence. It shelters a vine-shaded courtyard *osteria* and has a spectacular rampart panorama; its **museum** includes a gallery showing changing exhibits by contemporary Ticinese artists.

Villa dei Cedri and around

Piazza San Biagio 9 • Tues–Fri 2–6pm, Sat & Sun 11am–6pm • Fr.8; joint ticket for all castle museums plus Villa Cedri Fr.15 • ⓦ villacedri.ch

Peaceful **Piazza Indipendenza** is 100m south of the tourist office and sports a 1903 obelisk commemorating the first century of Ticinese independence. On the east side of the square is the small church of **San Rocco**, built in 1330 and renovated in 1478. Following Via Lugano south for 600m brings you to Piazza San Biagio, and the gates of the **Villa dei Cedri** art gallery. Explore the beautiful grounds then head in to the museum, which focuses on early modern Swiss and Lombard art. The frescoed church of **San Biagio** beside the villa dates from the twelfth century, while beside a convent 100m west across the tracks is **Santa Maria delle Grazie**, with an enormous, late fifteenth-century interior fresco of the Crucifixion.

ARRIVAL AND INFORMATION

BELLINZONA

By train Bellinzona is on the main north–south trans-Alpine rail route, served by fast trains from Lugano (every 15min; 25min), Como (hourly; 1hr) and Milan (approx hourly; 1hr 35min), as well as the branch lines from Locarno (3–4 hourly; 20min) and Luino (approx hourly; 50min) on Lake Maggiore. The station lies a short walk northeast of the old quarter.

By car Bellinzona is about 22km north of Lugano – use the N2 autostrada (Bellinzona-Sud exit) or opt for the slower but more scenic road over Monte Ceneri. It also lies about 15km east of Locarno (see p.142) via often-packed main roads; instead try the quieter Via Cantonale which runs between Tenero and Sementina.

Tourist office In the Palazzo Civico on Piazza Nosetto (April–Oct Mon–Fri 9am–6.30pm, Sat 9am–2pm, Sun 10am–2pm; Nov–March Mon–Fri 9am–noon & 1.30–6.30pm, Sat 9am–noon; ☎091 825 2131, ⓦ bellinzonaturismo.ch).

WALKS AROUND BELLINZONA

There are plenty of picturesque **walks** near Bellinzona. One of the best begins in nearby **Roveredo** (served by postbuses from Bellinzona), from where an old cart track on the "quiet" side of the river heads through tiny San Giulio and into the woods opposite San Vittore, before crossing the river at a little bridge in Lumino and heading on through the forest to Arbedo on the outskirts of Bellinzona. You'll come across plenty of peaceful cafés on the way. Side roads off the main Via San Gottardo lead through Arbedo and under the tracks to the picturesque church of San Paolo, also known as the "Chiesa Rossa", an ancient red-washed building standing lost and forgotten beside industrial warehouses on Via del Carmagnola backing onto the tracks (total 2hr walking). Buses can run you the final 1.5km south into Bellinzona's centre.

ACCOMMODATION AND EATING

Castelgrande Castelgrande ☎091 814 8781, ⓦristorantecastelgrande.ch. Formal restaurant showcasing a slightly uncomfortable mix of contemporary styling and traditional cuisine. The setting, within the castle but with superb city views, and the quality of the cooking and presentation may seduce. Five-course *menù* Fr.120 including wine pairings. Sept–June Tues–Sun 7–10pm.

★**Fattoria l'Amorosa** Via Moyar, Sementina-Gudo ☎091 840 29 50, ⓦamorosa.ch. Wonderful agriturismo ten minutes' drive south of Bellinzona, amid hillside vineyards on a minor road between Sementina and Gudo. To stay, choose between eight tasteful rooms with rustic Tuscan-style decor, or the separate cottage Isabella, where kids can sleep on a platform under the eaves and the basement bathroom features a super-size granite bath. Balconies and picture windows take advantage of the views. The restaurant is a great rural discovery, with *menùs* of refined local cuisine from Fr.50 to Fr.75 – plus top-rated wines (and balsamic vinegars) produced on-site. Nov– March restaurant closed Sun eve & all day Mon. <u>Fr.230</u>

Grotto Castelgrande Castelgrande ☎091 814 8781, ⓦristorantecastelgrande.ch. Rustic tavern-style food (under the same management as the castle restaurant) served on a shady open terrace overlooking the castle vineyards. The menu is all Ticinese classics, with main dishes around Fr.18 and two- or three-course *menùs* Fr.25– 32. Tues–Sat 11am–11pm, Sun 11.30am–2pm.

Hotel Internazionale Viale Stazione 35 ☎091 825 4333, ⓦhotel-internazionale.ch. Updated business-style hotel in a convenient central location directly opposite the train station, with good service and a decent range of airy and comfortable, if slightly bland, rooms. <u>Fr.200</u>

Osteria Sasso Corbaro Salita ai Castelli ☎091 825 5532, ⓦosteriasassocorbaro.com. Atmospheric spot within Bellinzona's topmost castle, serving up authentic Ticinese food at stone tables in the shady castle courtyard, or in a great hall within – expect risotto with woodland mushrooms, veal in cream sauce or shoulder of lamb. At lunch, two courses are Fr.40; in the evening, mains are Fr.18–45 or three courses for Fr.70. Tues–Sat noon–2pm & 7–9pm, Sun noon–2pm. Closed Nov–March.

4

Lake Como

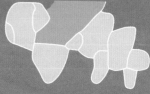

VILLA CARLOTTA

5

Lake Como

Of all the Italian lakes, slender, forked Lake Como (Lago di Como) comes most heavily praised; it is "a treasure which the earth keeps to itself", wrote Wordsworth. This has been the retreat of choice for hard-pressed urbanites for a couple of thousand years at least; Virgil knew of the lake, then called *Lacus Larius* (and still referred to today as Lario), while the Roman general Pliny had two villas here, one near Lenno, the other at Bellagio, and wrote in glowing terms of the natural beauty all around. The combination of forested mountains and blue water remains bewitching.

Lake Como (ⓦwww.lakecomo.com) came into its own in the Romantic era, when artists, writers, composers and boatfuls of creative wannabes sought inspiration from the magnificence of the surroundings and the simplicity of the working life led by local fisherfolk and craftspeople. In parts, that atmosphere survives; the lake that inspired the poets can still be found – a cobbled piazza here, a romantic view there – but the demands of tourism mean that you should perhaps tone down your expectations. Many parts of the lake are given over to low- and mid-budget holiday-making, with campsites and generic, if serviceable, two- and three-star hotels setting the tone in several places. Nonetheless, making your way in a stately fashion by steamer can still feel wonderfully romantic – and halfway up the lake, old-fashioned luxury hotels from the grand old days of tourism preserve an aristocratic air of nostalgia.

The area's principal towns – **Como** and **Lecco** – mark the southernmost points of both forks of the lake. Near Como gather a few fairly low-key lakeside villages – **Cernobbio** is nicest – on the approach to the central part of the lake, where the main resorts cluster. Here, around the most popular and beautiful of Lake Como's shores, those classic images of blue water, forested mountains, terrace cafés and stately steamers abound. The best-known names are **Bellagio** and **Menaggio** – both will delight unrepentant romantics – and yet the lake can still surprise; to seduce a cynic, whisk them off to lesser-known **Varenna**, perhaps Lake Como's most captivating hideaway.

GETTING AROUND

Timetables for **trains, buses and boats** are at ⓦ www.muoversi.regione.lombardia.it.

By train There are three approaches to Lake Como by rail. Two lines serve Como – a fast main line from Milano Centrale which stops at Como (approx hourly; 40min) on the way to Lugano in Switzerland, and a slower regional route from Milano Cadorna (approx hourly; 1hr) which terminates at Como. Trains also run roughly hourly from Milano Centrale all along Lake Como's eastern shore, serving Lecco (20min), Varenna (1hr) and other villages.

By car The SS340 along Lake Como's western shore is mostly a slow, scenic drive through every lakeside

VARENNA

Highlights

❶ Duomo, Como Italy's most elegant fusion of the Gothic and the Renaissance, in this mighty cathedral towering above Como's old quarter. **See p.191**

❷ Villa Carlotta Supremely photogenic lakeside villa, featuring romantic statuary and lush gardens. **See p.206**

❸ Menaggio Charming, popular lakeside resort that holds itself with considerable grace and manages to combine *dolce far niente* with tough hiking trails through the mountains. **See p.207**

❹ Bellagio Legendary lake beauty, a swoon-worthy old village crammed onto its own peninsula, offering romance and elegance in equal measure. **See p.211**

❺ End of the War Museum The best of Lake Como's small local museums, telling the amazing story of wartime resistance to Fascism, in the very place where the partisans were active. **See p.218**

❻ Piona At the lake's farthest corner, this tiny suntrap cove offers another view of Lake Como; unpretentious, downbeat, easy-going – and refreshingly ordinary. **See p.219**

❼ Varenna Bewitchingly seductive lake village on the lesser-visited eastern shore, draped with idyllic gardens and overlooked by a mighty castle on the slopes above. **See p.220**

HIGHLIGHTS ARE MARKED ON THE MAP ON P.188

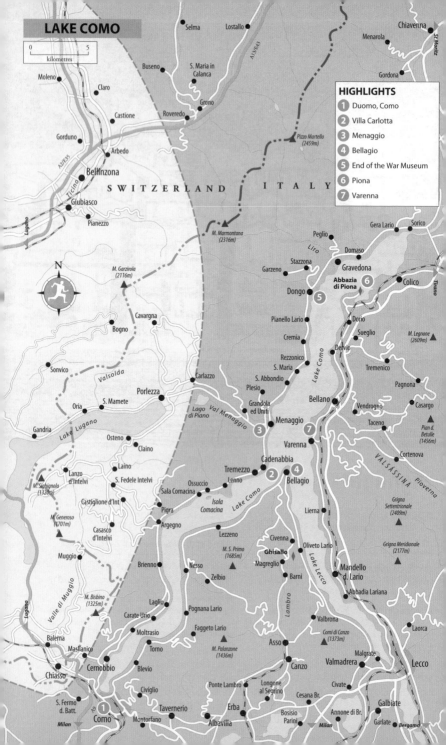

5

BOATS ON LAKE COMO

Seeing **Lake Como** from the water is not to be missed – indeed, with summer traffic on the narrow lakefront roads, getting around by boat makes a good deal of sense. Boats are run by the Gestione Navigazione Laghi (☏ 800 551 801, ⓦ navigazionelaghi.it), who have booths for information and tickets at most landing-stages around the lake. Boats run year-round, with the greatest frequency in high season (June–Sept); at other times, services are reduced or, on some routes, halted.

ROUTES

It's easy to put together any kind of itinerary, using the widely available timetable leaflets. However, check carefully the various symbols and colour-coded notes to identify each route's days of operation, and be sure to differentiate between timings for the **battello** (ship), which stops everywhere; the **aliscafo/servizio rapido** (hydrofoil/fast service), which stops at major points only; and the **autotraghetto** (car ferry, also for foot passengers), which shuttles across the central part of the lake. Daily services run between about 7.30am and 8.30pm, though the car ferries start earlier and finish later.

CRUISES

The only genuine **cruises** are dinner-dance excursions from Como on summer Saturdays (9pm–1.30am; €49.50 including dinner). Nonetheless, timetables highlight several *Giri Turistici* (tourist trips) which use regular scheduled services as sightseeing cruises; the one-hour journey from Como to Torno or Urio and back, for instance (€7.60; disembarkation prohibited). On some routes (marked on the timetable with a knife and fork), you can eat on board – a fixed menu for €16.

FARES AND PASSES

Tickets are charged on a complicated sliding scale, set out in a chart at the ticket booths (and online). Each route is assigned a number, according to the distance involved; you then cross-check on the list for how much that route-number (or *tratta*) costs. As an example, a one-way ticket from Como to Bellagio is given as *tratta* 6, which costs €10.40 (or €14.80 on the hydrofoil), whereas Tremezzo to Varenna is *tratta* 3, equal to €4.60 (or €7.10 on the hydrofoil). The most expensive one-way ticket, *tratta* 8 (Como to Colico, for instance), is €12.60/€17.50. The charge for taking an ordinary-sized **car** on the car-ferry between Cadenabbia, Bellagio, Menaggio and/or Varenna is €8.60 one-way, including the driver.

A **return ticket** costs double. EU citizens over 65 get a twenty-percent **discount** (Mon–Fri only). Ask at ticket offices about a **special offer** discounting admission to one of the lake's grand houses if you arrive by boat. You pay a **surcharge** of €1 if you buy your ticket on board, and bags or suitcases over 60cm long may also attract a supplement.

A **pass for unlimited journeys** (*biglietto di libera circolazione*; not valid on hydrofoils) is also priced according to *tratte*. A one-day pass covering six *tratte* (ie anywhere between Como and Bellagio) costs €23.30, or a pass for the whole lake costs €28. The six-day equivalents are €70/€84.

---

village, though some places (Cernobbio, Menaggio, Pianello) are bypassed by tunnels. On the eastern shore, the SS36 superstrada ("highway") zips from Lecco to Colico mostly in tunnels, with a few exits along the way; the SP72 lakeside road is a slower, quieter drive. To reach Bellagio, the lakeside SS583 from Como and Lecco is narrow and tortuous; it's easier to cross to Bellagio by ferry instead.

By boat Much the nicest way to get around (see above); full details of services at ⓦ navigazionelaghi.it.

Como

As the nearest resort to Milan and a popular stop-off on the autostrada to and from Switzerland, **COMO** is both much visited and, on the outskirts at least, fairly industrialized. The main industry is a rarefied one – Como supplies luxury silk to fashion houses in Milan, Paris and New York – but that doesn't make the suburban factories any more endearing.

5

Once you penetrate through to the lakeshore, however, things look up. The atmospheric **Città Murata** – Como's formerly walled old quarter, a dense grid of narrow, pedestrianized lanes – offers great window-shopping and relaxed, sociable dining. The **Duomo** is a strikingly beautiful and artistically significant building, blending elements of Gothic and Renaissance. A **funicular** climbs the wooded slopes nearby to offer wonderful views and there's a smattering of historical interest elsewhere around town. In the main, though, Como gets on with life quite regardless of the lake on its doorstep and retains considerable poise. Stay for a couple of days to soak up the atmosphere.

Piazza Cavour

The most obvious place to start is **Piazza Cavour**, a rather forbidding square on the lakefront dominated by unsightly modern hotels and banks – though the *Hotel Metropole Suisse* sports a fine nineteenth-century facade whose lowest two storeys were reworked by Como-born architect Giuseppe Terragni in 1927. Terrace cafés abound. From Piazza Cavour, the rectangular **Città Murata**, or walled town, spreads southeast, in parts bounded by its old walls but frequently with no formal delineation. Northeast of Piazza Cavour, the lakefront road curves around to the **funicular** station below Brunate (see p.195), while northwest of Piazza Cavour is a pleasant lakefront park – good for strolling, and also with historical attractions including the Volta museum (see p.194).

Piazza Duomo

A short walk away from the lake on bustling Via Plinio brings you to Como's architectural set piece, **Piazza Duomo**. The city's commercial life continues here quite

5

COMO'S NEW WATERFRONT

At the time of writing, work was continuing on **renovations** of Como's cramped waterfront. The lakeside promenade has been widened, and there are to be flood barriers sunk into the pavement that can be raised when water levels rise significantly (two-metre floods, high enough to swamp Piazza Cavour, are not unknown). More trees will be planted, and there is talk of perhaps diverting traffic away from the lakeside road. Work has gone more slowly than expected, but may be finished by the time you read this.

regardless of history or tourism; rather prosaically, men's outfitters and a department store share this modestly sized square with the magnificent west front of the **Duomo**, remarkable for its melding of the Gothic and Renaissance styles. Also facing the piazza, adjacent to the Duomo and connected to it, are the Gothic-Renaissance **Broletto** – the former law courts, prettily striped in pink, white and grey, with a fifteenth-century balcony designed for municipal orators – and the tall, imposing **campanile**, with an angled roof protecting its clock-face.

The Duomo

Piazza Duomo • Mon–Sat 10.30am–5pm, Sun 1–4.30pm • Free • ⓦ cattedraledicomo.it

Como's cathedral replaced the ninth-century church of Santa Maria Maggiore, remnants of which survive in the south wall. Work began in the 1390s, while **Gothic** held sway – first with the interior and then, from 1457, the west facade. By 1487, when the side walls were being built and the facade completed (both under the supervision of sculptor Tommaso Rodari), **Renaissance** ideas had taken hold, as shown in the choice of statuary adorning the facade. The main apse and vestries were begun in the 1510s, at the height of the Renaissance. The south and north apses date from later within the Renaissance – the middle decades of the seventeenth century – while the cathedral was only completed in 1744 with the addition of a **late-Baroque** cupola. Yet, remarkably, the vision for the building remained harmonious throughout; the overriding impression is of cross-stylistic elegance.

Duomo exterior

The Duomo's soaring **west facade** facing the piazza shows a Gothic spirit, in its fairy-tale pinnacles, rose window and buffoonish gargoyles, but it was completed in Renaissance style with rounded rather than pointed arches to the portals. Four vertical lines of saints climb each pilaster on the facade. At top centre is a figure of the resurrected Christ, while occupying small roundels on either side of the main door, below an elegant row of pointed niches, are depictions of Adam (on one side) and Eve (on the other).

The most surprising figures flank the main door: on the left is the Roman author Pliny the Elder, on the right his adoptive son Pliny the Younger – both of them pagans. Associating non-Christians with a house of God would have been unthinkable in 1396, when work on the facade began; yet by the 1480s, when Giovanni Rodari carved these statues – and by 1498, when his sons Tommaso and Jacopo designed their settings on this wall – Christian Renaissance humanists were drawing huge influence from such classical luminaries as the Plinys. The fact that both were also born in Como seems to have secured their inclusion here as honorary saints. The presence of Pliny Junior remains particularly questionable; his connection with Christianity extended little beyond torturing two deaconesses to better understand what he termed "this depraved superstition".

Round the corner, the Duomo's north door, designed by the Rodaris in 1507, is known as the "**Door of the Frog**", for the frog which is carved – coincidentally, alongside the words *Sanctus Paulus* – into the left-hand side of the portal. Centuries of curious fingers have rubbed the little beast smooth.

5

Duomo interior: west end

Just inside the Duomo are two **holy-water fonts**, placed either side of the main door, supported by splendid Romanesque lions. Alongside is the freestanding Renaissance **Baptistry**, built in 1590 as a small circular temple.

The exterior's Gothic-Renaissance fusion continues here. Gothic columns divide the nave and aisles, but the first two intercolumnar spaces have been hung with rich Renaissance **tapestries**, made in the sixteenth and seventeenth centuries, chiefly in Ferrara and Florence. Facing each other across the nave are Guasparri di Bartolomeo Papini's *Sacrifice of Isaac* and *Cain and Abel* (both 1598), while alongside the former is the *Presentation of the Virgin in the Temple*, possibly produced in Brussels in 1569 from figures by Dürer, and featuring striking use of perspective.

Of the cathedral's **paintings**, the south (right) wall features – behind the third column – the gilded St Abbondio altarpiece flanked by a languid *Flight to Egypt* (1526) by Gaudenzio Ferrari, filled with detail and composed on a diagonal axis to emphasize movement, and an absorbing *Adoration of the Magi* (1526) by Bernardino Luini, which includes such exotica as an elephant and a giraffe. Directly opposite, across the church, hangs Luini's *Adoration of the Shepherds* (1526), while a little further along the south wall is his melancholy, heavy-lidded *Madonna* for the St Jerome altarpiece (1521), both works showing the artist's debt to Leonardo.

Duomo interior: east end

Where two large **organs** face each other across the nave, the Gothic construction ends; the east end of the cathedral was completed under the influence of the Renaissance,

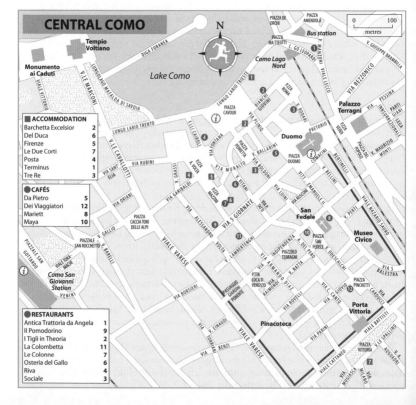

5

with a distinctive lightness and symmetry of design. The **north apse** holds the colourful Altar of the Crucifixion, while the **south apse** has the Baroque Altar of Our Lady of the Assumption, completed in 1686 with twisting columns in black Varenna marble. The Renaissance **main apse** features the Altar of the Maestri Campionesi, consecrated in 1317 as the main altar of the old Santa Maria Maggiore church, and itself demonstrating another transition in style – from the Romanesque, as seen in the figures of the saints, to the Gothic, exemplified by the flower-ornamented arches which frame them. Overhead soars the spectacular Baroque **cupola**, designed in the 1730s by the master architect Filippo Juvarra, its apparently small lantern illuminating virtually the whole building.

The Città Murata

Within the narrow streets of the **Città Murata** – Como's once-walled old quarter – the few museums and historical attractions are trumped by the atmosphere of simply strolling the lanes.

San Fedele

Piazza San Fedele • Daily 8am–noon & 3.30–7pm • Free • ⓦ parrocchiasanfedelecomo.it

Several medieval frontages survive on the irregularly shaped **Piazza San Fedele**, formerly the city's corn market – reached from the Duomo via bustling Via Vittorio Emanuele II. Squashed into a corner of the square, its facade and campanile partly obscured by an arcaded building stuck in front, is the church of **San Fedele**, once Como's cathedral. Its origins are uncertain: it was probably begun in the tenth century and completed in the twelfth, though was subsequently altered. The atmospherically dim interior features a pentagonal apse and some rather beautiful seventeenth-century frescoes.

Museo Civico

Piazza Medaglie d'Oro 1 • Tues–Sat 9.30am–12.30pm & 2–5pm, Sun 10am–1pm • €4 • ⓦ museicivici.comune.como.it

Framing one corner of Piazza Medaglie d'Oro, the elegant Palazzo Giovio and Palazzo Olginati together form the **Museo Civico**. From the ticket desk, doors open to a peaceful internal courtyard, lined with Roman columns and capitals. Inside, turning left at the top of the stairs brings you past displays of Roman glass, the mummy of Isiuret, a ninth-century BC priestess (with both feet sticking out of her sarcophagus), and Greek vases. Back at the stairs, head the other way for rooms devoted to prehistoric finds. Corridors at two points cross to the adjacent *palazzo*, which displays items related to Garibaldi and the Risorgimento.

Pinacoteca Civica

Via Diaz 84 • Tues–Sat 9.30am–12.30pm & 2–5pm, Sun 10am–1pm • €4 • ⓦ museicivici.comune.como.it

The pedestrianized shopping street Via Cantù offers a view towards the towering **Porta Vittoria** gate at the eastern edge of the old town, with four storeys of open arches (its internal wooden structure is long gone). Via Giovio continues to the next corner (Via Diaz), where you'll see the **Pinacoteca** at no. 84, a small collection of medieval paintings housed in the dour seventeenth-century Palazzo Volpi. A pleasant stroll back along Via Diaz returns you to the waterfront squares.

Beyond the Città Murata

Just beyond the Città Murata lie several architectural highlights – or you could ramble a path around on the lakefront promenade around the curve of Como's bay, from Villa Olmo in the west to Villa Geno in the east.

5

Casa del Fascio (Palazzo Terragni)

Piazza del Popolo • Interior accessible only on guided tours: May–Oct Sat 4pm & 4.30pm; €5

Just behind the Duomo, across the railway tracks, stands the definitive expression of Rationalism by Como-born architect Giuseppe Terragni. Built as the **Casa del Fascio** – a headquarters for the local Fascist party – in the 1930s, it has since been renamed the **Palazzo Terragni** and now houses the Guardia di Finanza. From a distance, the angular building is almost transparent; you can see right through its loggia to the wooded hills behind. This kind of light, deftly functional architecture broke new ground, yet it stands – by happy coincidence – directly opposite another, equally good example of geometry applied to produce architectural harmony: the apse of the Duomo, 418 years its senior.

Tempio Voltiano

Viale Marconi • Tues–Sun 10am–noon & 3–6pm (Oct–March shorter afternoon hours 2–4pm) • €4 • ⓦ museicivici.comune .como.it

From Piazza Cavour, Como's waterfront promenade curls west into a little park hosting a sequence of moving Holocaust memorials leading you onwards to a curious temple-like building, the **Tempio Voltiano**. This holds a museum dedicated to Alessandro Volta, a pioneer in electricity who gave his name to the volt – some of the instruments he used to conduct his experiments are displayed inside.

Monumento ai Caduti

Viale Puecher • Interior accessible only May–Oct Sun 3–6pm; €3

Como's **Monumento ai Caduti**, an angular memorial to the dead of World War I, stands alongside the Tempio Voltiano. It was designed by Futurist architect Antonio Sant'Elia, another Como native, but built – after Sant'Elia was killed in action at the age of 28 in 1916 – by Terragni. Soaring rigidly above the lakeside park, it stands in stark contrast to its surroundings.

Villa Olmo

Via per Cernobbio • **Gardens** Mon–Sat 8am–11pm (Oct–April 9am–7pm) • Free • ⓦ culturacomo.it **Lido** June–Sept daily 9am–7pm • €7 • ⓦ lidovillaolmo.it

Como's pretty lakeside walk extends west around the bay from the city centre to **Villa Olmo**, a Neoclassical pile which hosts conferences and top-flight art exhibitions. Whatever is on, its **gardens** are worth a wander, with lovely waterside promenades and views, as well as a **lido** alongside.

COMO SILK

Como is one of the world's great **silk** cities. By the 1500s – a millennium after the secret of sericulture had leaked into Europe from China – silkworm farming was a major industry in and around Como; the city boasted an ideal temperate climate, plenty of fresh water and – crucially – abundant supplies of mulberry leaves (a silkworm's staple diet) from farms in the nearby Po Valley. Como only stopped producing raw silk in the middle of the last century, but it retained its expertise in high-quality finishing of silk items. Today, some eight hundred firms in and around the city – now supplied with Chinese raw silk – are involved in the design, manufacture, printing and dyeing of silk pieces for all the world's big-name fashion houses. Track the history of the industry at Como's excellent **Museo Didattico della Seta** (Educational Silk Museum), by the university on Via Castelnuovo (Tues–Fri 9am–noon & 3–6pm; €10; ⓦ museosetacomo.com) – complete with original looms and printing blocks – and then drop by one of the city's many fashion boutiques for designer silk ties and scarves; A. Picci, a short walk from the Duomo at Via Vittorio Emanuele II 54, is a fine choice. The tourist office can direct you to others, including discount factory outlets.

5

Brunate

Funicular Piazza Alcide de Gasperi • Daily 6am–10.30pm, every 15–30min; June–Aug until midnight • €5.30 return • ⓦ funicolarecomo.it

Northeast from Piazza Cavour along the lakefront, past the bus and train stations fronting Piazza Matteotti, you'll spot signs for the base-station of Como's **funicular**. The little carriages take seven minutes to creep up the hillside alongside the splendid gardens of nineteenth-century villas to **BRUNATE**, a small hilltop resort that has a few bars and restaurants and great views of the lake. Brunate is also a good starting-point for **walks**; the tourist office has free leaflets detailing routes, including Trail 1 – *La Dorsale del Triangolo Lariano*, a two-day trek of 30km through the mountains on mule tracks and easy paths to Bellagio (also downloadable at ⓦ menaggio.com). Shorter loops are possible: for example, a **three-hour walk** follows Trail 1 from Brunate (715m) past San Maurizio (906m) and the forests at Baita Carla (997m) to pick up Trail 15 which cuts left down to Torno on the lake, where a boat or the C30 bus returns you to Como.

Villa Geno

Viale Geno 12 • Grounds: daily 10am–9pm (winter until 6pm) • Free

From the base-station of the Brunate funicular, it's about ten pleasant minutes' stroll further round the quiet lakefront promenade to the compact late-eighteenth-century **Villa Geno**, occupying a jutting headland with good views back to Como. The villa's grounds include a little area to take a dip in the lake.

Sant'Abbondio

Via Regina • Daily 8am–6pm (winter closes 4.30pm) • Free • ⓦ santabbondio.eu • Bus 9

It's a short walk from Piazza Vittoria, on the eastern side of Porta Vittoria, to reach the strikingly attractive Romanesque church of **Sant'Abbondio**, an eleventh-century building erected on the site of a church recorded as early as the fifth century. The exterior has two elegant square campaniles, while the plain, solemn interior of this relatively small church has five soaring aisles divided by columns. The focus of attention is the ornate presbytery, dominated by a cycle of vivid fourteenth-century frescoes on the life of Christ.

ARRIVAL AND DEPARTURE

COMO

BY PLANE

From Milan-Malpensa Airport Take a "Malpensa Express" stopping train (check it's not an non-stop service) towards Milan but change midway at Saronno (15min), where you can catch another train to Como Lago (40min). By car from Malpensa it's a quick and easy drive to Como via the A8 and A9 autostradas.

BY TRAIN

Timetables are at ⓦ www.muoversi.regione.lombardia.it.
Como San Giovanni station ("Como S.G.") Served by fast trains on the main line between Milano Centrale (approx hourly; 40min) and Lugano (approx hourly; 40min), and slower trains on the S10 line from Lugano and the S11 line between Milano Porta Garibaldi and Chiasso. One or two trains a day arrive from Lecco (1hr 10min). The station overlooks Piazzale San Gottardo, about ten minutes' walk west of the city centre; from the station, head down a grandiose flight of 54 steps through a patch of parkland (poorly lit after dark) to a large sculpture of a splayed hand, from where you cross the two main roads and then continue ahead on Via Garibaldi into the old town. Buses

are frequent, and taxis are always available.

Como Lago station (also called Como Lago Nord, or Como Nord Lago) The terminus for stopping trains on a frequent branch line from Milano Cadorna station (approx hourly; 1hr). It is conveniently located on the lakefront Piazza Matteotti just across from the bus station, a short walk from the old town. The penultimate stop is Como Borghi, located on Piazzale Gerbetto, five minutes' walk southeast of Piazza Vittoria.

BY BUS

Como's bus station is central, beside the lakefront on Piazza Matteotti. Timetables are at ⓦ www.muoversi.regione.lombardia.it. The main local company is ASF Autolinee (ⓦ asfautolinee.it) – their routes into Como include the C10, running the length of the western lakeshore from Colico (2hr 15min), Menaggio (1hr 10min), Cadenabbia (1hr 5min), Tremezzo (1hr), Lenno (55min) and points in between; the C30 from Bellagio (1hr 10min); the C40/D41 from Lecco (1hr 10min); and the C46/D46 from Bergamo (2hr). FNM Autoservizi (ⓦ fnmautoservizi.it) runs the C77 from Varese (1hr 10min).

5

GIROLARIO: FROM COMO TO BELLAGIO

The **GiroLario** day pass (June–Sept only; €15) covers a discounted boat journey from Como to Bellagio, another boat from Bellagio to Lecco, and a less romantic hour's bus ride from Lecco back to Como. It is outlined in detail at ⓦ navigazionelaghi.it. Because the buses run late (last bus Lecco–Como 8.30pm in Aug, or 10.15pm in June, July & Sept), you can dawdle – or, alternatively, not start out from Como until mid-afternoon and still be back for dinner. However, you're not allowed to break the journey (other than at Bellagio and Lecco) and you can't backtrack. The route is also possible from and to Lecco.

BY CAR

Driving from Milan on the A9 autostrada, exit at Como Sud to get tangled in suburban traffic, or at Como Monte Olimpino for a gentler approach to the city from the northwest. Approaching from Lugano/Chiasso on the Swiss N2 autostrada, take the Como Nord exit, a narrow sliproad branching unexpectedly from the left-hand lane immediately after the border. Considering the large numbers of *frontalieri* – people who live in Como but drive to work in Switzerland – you'd do well to avoid trying to cross the border southwards during the weekday rush (roughly 4–6pm).

Parking If you're planning a day-trip to Como but can't face the search for parking, consider driving instead to the Tavernola landing-stage, about 1km north of the city centre; parking here is free, and regular boats shuttle to and from Como all day long (8min).

BY BOAT

Boats dock at one or other of the jetties facing Piazza Cavour, with service from points all round the lake (see p.189), including close-at-hand villages such as Cernobbio (15min) and mid-lake destinations including Bellagio (2hr 10min), Menaggio (2hr 25min) and Varenna (2hr 40min). Timetables are at ⓦ navigazionelaghi.it.

INFORMATION

Tourist office Piazza Cavour 17 (Mon–Sat 9am–1pm & 2–5pm; ☎ 031 269 712, ⓦ lakecomo.com). There are city info points on Via Comacini, beside the Duomo (Mon–Fri 10am–1pm & 2.30–5.30pm, Sat & Sun 10am–1pm & 2–6pm; ☎ 031 264 215, ⓦ comotourism.it) and on platform 1 in the main San Giovanni train station (daily 9am–5pm; ☎ 031 449 9539).

Useful websites ⓦ turismo.como.it, ⓦ camminacitta.it.

TOURS AND ACTIVITIES

Guided walks The municipality runs free themed guided walks in English on various days in summer (April–Oct; ⓦ comotourism.it), including a sightseeing walking tour at night, tours of medieval Como and an itinerary focused on the life of Alessandro Volta. Check dates and times online or at the city info point beside the Duomo. There are also guided walks through Como's neighbourhoods of Rationalist architecture, starting from the city info point beside the Duomo (May–Oct Sat 5pm; €8; 1hr 30min).

Private boat trips Motorboat operators, for private jaunts, include Tasell on the Piazza Cavour waterfront (☎ 031 304 084, ⓦ tasell.com).

Sightseeing flights Seaplanes buzz regularly above Como, taking off and landing from the Aero Club hangar on the lakefront (☎ 031 574 495, ⓦ aeroclubcomo.com), the largest seaplane facility in Europe, in operation since 1913. Book ahead for a sightseeing flight (roughly €250/hr).

ACCOMMODATION

HOTELS

Barchetta Excelsior Piazza Cavour 1 ☎ 031 3221, ⓦ hotelbarchetta.it; map p.192. Venerable old four-star hotel in a perfect city-centre location overlooking the main lakefront square. Many rooms, done up in classic, traditional style, have balconies. €̄170

★**Del Duca** Piazza Mazzini 12 ☎ 031 264 859, ⓦ albergodelduca.it; map p.192. Great little three-star hotel full of cheery, down-to-earth local atmosphere, on a picturesque old-town square a short walk from the lake and the Duomo. The seven rooms are made special by windows onto the piazza, windowboxes and, in some rooms, two-person showers. Some less desirable rooms overlook only the titchy internal courtyard. Private parking. €̄110

Firenze Piazza Volta 16 ☎ 031 300 333, ⓦ albergofirenze.it; map p.192. Pleasant mid-range option on the spacious Piazza Volta, just back from the lakefront, with comfortable, smartly modernized rooms set mainly around a quiet internal courtyard. Some have balconies over the square. Private parking. €̄125

Le Due Corti Piazza Vittoria 12 ☎ 031 328 111, ⓦ hotelduecorti.com; map p.192. Despite (or perhaps because of) its location well away from the lake – which is ten minutes' walk across town – this is a great place to stay; romantic without being stuffy. Built as a monastery in the

5

seventeenth century, and serving for a time as a post-house, its rustic-style rooms arranged around an internal courtyard feature exposed stonework, full-spec bathrooms and old prints on the walls. Private parking. €140

★**Posta** Via Garibaldi 2 ☎031 276 9011, ⓦpostadesignhotel.com; map p.192. A dour 1930s facade by Como-born Rationalist architect Giuseppe Terragni preludes a spanking new interior, completely reworked in 2014. Fourteen rooms all feature top-class contemporary design, from original art to super-stylish marble bathrooms – this is a very classy bolthole, bang in the middle of the city beside Piazza Volta. €170

Quarcino Salita Quarcino 4 ☎031 303 934, ⓦhotelquarcino.it; map p.190. A family-run hotel near the funicular on the northeast side of the old town, with quiet rooms, some with their own balconies overlooking the hillside. The family rooms and suites are particularly good value (€115–135) and there is parking available. €90

Terminus Lungo Lario Trieste 14 ☎031 329 111, ⓦalbergoterminus.it; map p.192. A classy, upmarket city-centre hotel, on the lake and just a short stroll from the Duomo. The whole building is done out in Liberty style – the Italian version of Art Nouveau – with rich grained woods and brightly patterned fabrics. Plump for the unique split-level Tower Room, with eagle-eye views over the waterfront. Private parking. €190

Tre Re Via Boldoni 20 ☎031 265 374, ⓦhoteltrere .com; map p.192. Decent three-star in the centre – modest in both size and ambition, but with spacious,

contemporary rooms, a touch of character, and good value for money. €125

Villa Flori Via Cernobbio 12 ☎031 33 820, ⓦhotelvillaflori.it; map p.190. Beautiful lakeside villa 2km north of the city centre on the western shore, a little beyond the Villa Olmo gallery. The house dates from the nineteenth century, and has many period fittings and decorations, although the rooms now have all mod cons, as well as balconies looking over the water. The gardens are lovely, shaded by fragrant citrus trees. Private parking. €240

HOSTEL
Ostello Villa Olmo (HI hostel) Via Bellinzona 2 ☎031 573 800, ⓦostellocomo.it; map p.190. Decent hostel located within the grounds of the Villa Olmo; to get there from the main train station, either take bus 1, 6 or 11, or turn left at the bottom of the long flight of steps in front of the station and walk for about 1.5km along Via Borgo Vico. The hostel serves evening meals, has laundry facilities, rents out bikes and provides a discount on the funicular. Closed Dec–Feb. Dorms €19

CAMPING
Camping Internazionale Via Cecilio ☎031 521 435, ⓦcamping-internazionale.it. Como's only campsite, a plain little site (with pool) in an unromantic location 4km south of the centre, near the Como Sud autostrada exit and Grandate-Breccia train station. Closed Nov–March. Pitch €12

EATING AND DRINKING

Como is not renowned for its **culinary** depth, but a little hunting through the old-town lanes will turn up somewhere both affordable and appealing to dine. **Bars** lie dotted through the lanes behind Piazza Duomo, as well as on and around Piazza Volta and along the waterfront Lungo Lario Trieste near the funicular station. All listings below are marked on the Central Como map.

CAFÉS
Da Pietro Piazza Duomo 16 ☎031 264 005. Decent café opposite the Duomo, with terrace tables on the square and a quiet *Sala da The* indoors. Simple menus are around €23, or plump for the daily special (*piatto del giorno*) at around €12. Closed Mon.

★**Dei Viaggiatori** Via Giovio 13 ☎031 271 415. Easy-going daytime café at the eastern end of the old town, with tables on Piazza Pinchetti and a range of mid-priced light bites. Closed Sun.

Mariett Via Vittorio Emanuele II 86 ☎031 267 106.

Old-fashioned locals' café and meeting-point in this jovial neighbourhood (once Como's Jewish quarter) behind the San Fedele church. Closed Wed.

Maya Via Luini 53. Cool, modern coffee bar, serving a great choice of coffees and delectable hot chocolate from 6.30am. Closed Sun.

RESTAURANTS AND BARS
Antica Trattoria da Angela Via Foscolo 16 ☎031 431 0534. Moderately priced local restaurant near the Piazza Matteotti bus station, serving inspired regional cuisine

---

DAY-TRIPPING IN SWITZERLAND

The **Swiss border** lies just 5km northwest of Como city centre; it's easy to day-trip into Switzerland by train or car – perhaps visiting Lugano (see p.166), stopping at Capolago for the rack-railway up Monte Generoso (see p.176) or exploring pretty Swiss lakeside villages such as Morcote (see p.177) or Gandria (see p.173). Everything, from an ice cream to a hotel room, can be paid for in euros (you'll get any change in Swiss francs).

5

using seasonal ingredients. Well worth a look. Closed in the evening on Sun, Mon & Wed.

Il Pomodorino Via Cinque Giornate 62b ☎031 240 384, ⓦristoranteilpomodorino.it. A decent, mid-range pizza and pasta restaurant, with pleasant ambience and overlooking an internal courtyard. The grilled meats are excellent, the desserts are home-made, and there are draught beers to accompany. Reckon on €25 or so per head. Closed Mon.

★**I Tigli in Theoria** Via Bianchi Giovini 41 ☎031 305 272, ⓦtheoriagallery.it. The *I Tigli* restaurant merged in 2014 with the Theoria art gallery. Amid leather sofas and stone-flagged floors in this fifteenth-century courtyard *palazzo*, sample upmarket modern Italian cuisine; green ravioli with ricotta (€20) followed by red snapper or loin of lamb (around €30) for instance. Upstairs is a super-cool lounge bar, serving light bites, and there's a rather lovely daytime tea-room on the top floor. Lovebirds should book ahead to secure Como's most romantic table, in a private dining space on a bridge spanning two wings of the building, high above the cobbles. Closed Sun eve & Mon.

★**La Colombetta** Via Diaz 40a ☎031 262 703, ⓦcolombetta.it. A classy, expensive little fish restaurant, with contemporary styling and a small but adventurous menu. The choice starter is the *crudo di pesce* (mixed raw fish) and you could move on to spaghetti *ai ricci di mare* (with sea urchin) or *rombo al forno* (baked turbot). As well as *orata* (gilthead bream) and *branzino* (sea bass), you may

see *pescatrice* (monkfish). Mains are around €25; the *menù degustazione* around €50. Daily until 1am.

★**Le Colonne** Piazza Mazzini 12 ☎031 266 166, ⓦalbergodelduca.it. A really nice, modestly priced little family-run restaurant attached to *Albergo Del Duca* on this quiet old-town square, away from the hubbub of Piazza Cavour and the Duomo. Pizzas are especially good, with an extra-long list to choose from, but the quality of all the familiar pasta, salads and meat staples is excellent. Service is warm, courteous and efficient. Open daily.

Osteria del Gallo Via Vitani 16 ☎031 272 591, ⓦosteriadelgallo-como.it. Atmospheric wine bar great for an aperitif, or evening drink, one of several nearby offering a choice of tasty nibbles with a fine selection of wines. Closed Sun & Mon eve.

Riva Via Cairoli 10 ☎031 264 325. Slick little restaurant just back from the waterfront, with a good selection of pizzas for around €8, lots of grilled meat options (€18 or so), and a range of novelty main-course salads, including American (with rocket and bacon), Norwegian (with cream cheese and smoked fish), Ligurian (with octopus) and Jamaican (with prawns), for about €13. Closed Mon.

Sociale Via Rodari 6 ☎031 264 042, ⓦristorantesociale .it. Classy, informal restaurant in a pleasant, historic building just north of the Duomo, complete with stone vaulting and a frescoed upper hall. The menu of classic Milanese cooking is around €16, or you can choose from a broad range of à la carte dishes for around €25 per head. Closed Tues.

The lake near Como

Spreading north from the city waterfront, Como's branch of the lake is the stuff of tourist brochures. Wooded mountain slopes protect the villages that are crammed onto the narrow shoreline from extremes of temperature, creating perfect conditions for an abundance of subtropical flora. These little communities are almost all pretty, characterful places (or, at least, have pretty, characterful parts to them), and the views of the mountains hemming in the lake are spectacular.

On the western side, **Cernobbio** makes for an alluring distraction before you reach the lake's only island, **Isola Comacina**. On the eastern side, a succession of old villages – **Blevio**, **Torno**, **Nesso** – cling to the cliffs on the shore towards Bellagio. Many of the opulent villas that line this stretch of the lake are still privately owned by industrialists and celebrities (George Clooney is a much-celebrated resident of **Laglio**).

GETTING AROUND

By bus Buses C10 (Como–Menaggio) and C30 (Como–Bellagio) run about hourly (ⓦasfautolinee.it). There's also the Trombetta Express, a motorized tourist train which trundles between Ossuccio and Menaggio (see p.202).

By car Choose either the western shore from Como to Menaggio or the eastern shore from Como to Bellagio; both

offer narrow, frequently busy roads coiling along the rocky shoreline. Neither is an easy drive. There's nowhere to cross the lake with a vehicle until you reach the Cadenabbia–Bellagio car ferry.

By boat Boats cruising this way – a far more pleasant way to travel than by road – follow a zigzag route from shore to shore, stopping at each village.

Cernobbio

5

Served by frequent boats and buses from Como, **CERNOBBIO** centres on a compact quarter of old houses that is fortunately bypassed by both the SS340 (which plunges into a tunnel) and the Via Regina shoreline road. The old quarter – huddled behind a rather beautiful, broad lakeside piazza – takes in a handful of rather upmarket hotels and fashion boutiques, while above, the modern village spreads out on the slopes of Monte Bisbino, whose summit (1325m) marks the Swiss border; a tortuous road reaches almost to the top.

Villa Erba

🕿 031 3491, Ⓦ villaerba.it

Signposted on the southern approaches, Cernobbio's opulent **Villa Erba**, dating from 1901, is now a giant conference centre set in its own lakeside park. It is closed to the public – though you can book for a private tour of some of the grandest rooms; the film director Luchino Visconti grew up here, and returned in later life.

Villa d'Este

🕿 031 3481, Ⓦ villadeste.com

On the northern side of Cernobbio, tucked into an elbow of shoreline hills, stands the palatial **Villa d'Este**, commissioned in 1568 by Tolomeo Gallio, one of the chief cardinals under Pope Gregory XIII, owned by royals and aristocrats, and converted in 1873 into what is now the grandest of Lake Como's grand hotels. With its sumptuous gardens and interiors adorned with stucco, frescoes, marble, mirrors and gilding, the hotel effortlessly draws in the global super-rich. Accommodation and dining are priced accordingly – but, then again, a mere €25 buys you a champagne cocktail to enjoy in the chestnut-shaded gardens in front of the hotel's swimming pool, which floats just offshore.

ARRIVAL AND INFORMATION CERNOBBIO

By bus From Como bus C10 (towards Menaggio) and bus C20 (towards Lanzo) – both approximately hourly – serve Cernobbio (15min; Ⓦ asfautolinee.it).

By boat Boats stop in frequently on routes up and down the lake (see p.189). Timetables are at Ⓦ navigazionelaghi.it.

Cernobbio tourist office Villa Bernasconi, Via Regina 7 (April–Sept daily 10am–6pm; 🕿 031 334 7209, Ⓦ comune .cernobbio.co.it).

ACCOMMODATION AND EATING

Gatto Nero Via Monte Santo 69 🕿 031 512 042, Ⓦ ristorantegattonero.com. Charming hillside trattoria serving hearty, well-presented modern Italian cooking that doubles as an enticing A-list haunt. The terrace views are stunning, but with footballers, fashionistas and film stars as fellow diners, it's just as much about who's at the next table as what's on the plate. Closed Mon & lunch on Tues.

Miralago Piazza Risorgimento 🕿 031 510 125, Ⓦ hotelmiralagocernobbio.com. Four-star hotel in an

---

LA VIA DEI MONTI LARIANI

Following mule-tracks and footpaths that wind across the mountains on the western side of Lake Como, the walking itinerary **La Via dei Monti Lariani** covers 125km of epic scenery, mostly from an eagle-eye altitude of around 1000m. The signed and waymarked route begins in Cernobbio, rapidly climbing the slopes of Monte Bisbino (1325m) and into the Val d'Intelvi. Stage two extends to the Val Menaggio at Grandola ed Uniti, with stage three skirting some beautiful scenery towards the San Bernardo pass and down to Garzeno. The final stage mostly contours along the hills above Gravedona to end at Sorico, at the far north end of the lake. Despite the stage divisions, though, even fit walkers would be hard pushed to complete the route in four days; you should reckon on six or seven at least. The free tourist office brochure *Lake Como Trekking* (widely available locally, and downloadable at Ⓦ menaggio.com) describes the route in detail, with variations and shorter loops, and also pinpoints mountain huts and B&Bs along the way.

5

unbeatable location overlooking the lakefront piazza, a stroll from the landing-stage. The interiors are charmingly old-fashioned – rooms are small and modest but some on upper floors have balconies – though it scores with friendly service and a lovely terrace to sit out and watch the world go by. **€160**

Carate Urio, Laglio and Brienno

After pleasant, slow driving on the lakeside road past Cernobbio, through tiny **Carate Urio** and **Laglio**, squeezed between cliffs and water, one of the most atmospheric places to stop on this stretch is **Brienno**, a medieval hamlet bypassed by the main road; the lake washes up against the old houses, with narrow cobbled walkways winding around and between balconied buildings. Lake Como is at its narrowest and deepest near here, at **Torriggia** – just 650m wide, but 410m deep. Caves in the mountainsides on both shores were once home to prehistoric bears.

ARRIVAL AND DEPARTURE

CARATE URIO, LAGLIO AND BRIENNO

By bus From Como bus C10 (towards Menaggio) and bus C20 (towards Lanzo) – both approximately hourly – serve Laglio (25min) and Brienno (35min; ⓦ asfautolinee.it).

By boat Urio is served by around six boats daily; Brienno has two on Sundays only.

ACCOMMODATION AND EATING

CARATE URIO

★**Orso Bruno** Via Regina Vecchia 45 ☎031 400 136, ⓦ hotelorsobruno.com. Pleasant little hotel wedged onto the old lakefront road directly opposite Urio's titchy *imbarcadero*. Ten compact but bright and cosy rooms offer peace, quiet and – in some – balconies over the water. **€110**

Ristorante Acqua Dolce Via Regina Vecchia 26 ☎031 400 260, ⓦ ristoranteacquadolce.it. Opposite the *Orso Bruno*, this is a lovely, refined little hideaway set on its own terrace, with picture windows gazing directly out across the water. Opt for a lunch of salads and light bites, or a

dinner of well presented, perfectly prepared trout or salt cod, duck breast or shrimp ravioli. Unusually keen prices (mains €14–24) and excellent service from the husband-and-wife team. Closed Wed (Sept–June only).

LAGLIO

Antico Forno San Giorgio Via San Giorgio 4 ☎031 400 534, ⓦ bbafsangiorgio.it. Tiny, traditional old B&B occupying an eighteenth-century former bakery in the blink-and-you-miss-it village of Laglio. There are only two rooms, modest but cosy, sharing a bathroom, but the welcome is warm – and George Clooney lives 100m down the road. **€80**

Argegno and around

From **ARGEGNO**, just north of Brienno, a road branches west into the **Val d'Intelvi**, a high valley system of small, country churches and quiet walks. Roughly 8km of hairpin turns brings you up to the main town, **SAN FEDELE INTELVI**. A turn-off above San Fedele coils down to Osteno on Lake Lugano (see p.174), while the valley road climbs for another 12km through Lanzo to end at **Monte Sighignola** (1320m), dubbed the "Balcony of Italy" for its spectacular views of Lake Lugano and the Swiss Alps (see p.175). It's a great drive.

A relatively straightforward three-hour **walk** from Argegno begins with the little cable car (*funivia*) from Argegno up to panoramic **PIGRA** on the slopes above (daily every 30min 8.30am–noon & 2.30–6.30pm; slightly shorter hours in winter; €2.90; ⓦ aapigra.it). The route dips down into the Val Camogge, climbs to the village of Corniga, then continues past Cambrianico down to Colonno on the lake, from where a Roman path leads to Sala Comacina and Ossuccio.

Isola Comacina

Island: Mid-March to Oct daily 10am–5pm (July & Aug until 6pm) • **Antiquarium Museum**: Mid-March to Oct Tues–Wed & Fri–Sun 10am–3pm • Ticket for both: €6 (€4.50 with a lake ferry ticket) • ⓦ isola-comacina.it

A little north of Argegno rests **Isola Comacina**, Lake Como's only island. It lies

5

opposite the attractive old villages of **SALA COMACINA** and **OSSUCCIO**, across a mirror-calm stretch of water known as the *Conca dell'Olio* (in dialect, Zoca de l'Oli), or Basin of Oil. The island – only 600m long by 200m wide – is wild and unkempt, dotted with the ruins of nine abandoned churches. Occupied by the Romans, it later attracted an eclectic mix of dethroned monarchs, future saints and the pirate Federico Barbarossa. Eventually it allied with Milan against Como – which prompted Como to sack the island. Abandoned for centuries, it was bought by a local, Auguste Caprini, who outraged Italy by selling it to the King of Belgium after World War I. The island is now administered by a joint Belgian/Italian commission.

Drop in first at the **Antiquarium** on Via Somalvico in Ossuccio, a former hospital founded in 1169 which now houses a small museum of finds and a visitor centre. On the island itself, the modest Baroque church of **San Giovanni** displays some Roman remains, but otherwise the reason to come is to ramble between the ruins and explore the two-kilometre perimeter trail – or to dine at the island's famous (and famously overpriced) **restaurant**.

ARRIVAL AND DEPARTURE ISOLA COMACINA

By boat Taxi-boats to the island (€6 return) leave frequently from Sala Comacina and the Antiquarium in Ossuccio – and normal lake ferries also stop in on their zigzag route between Como and Menaggio. You can also arrange crossings with local motorboat operators, including ⓦ boatservices.it (Sala Comacina) and ⓦ taxiboatcernobbio .it (Cernobbio) as well as others in Como, Lenno, Bellagio and elsewhere. Alternatively, rent your own transport on the Ossuccio waterfront (motorboat €45/hr; canoe or kayak €10/hr; ☏ 329 214 2280, ⓦ hiringaboat.com).

EATING AND DRINKING

Locanda dell'Isola Comacina ☏ 0344 55 083, ⓦ comacina.it. An exclusive restaurant which has been drawing patrons to the island since 1947. The owner has made a selling-point of an elaborate "exorcism by fire" at the end of every meal, stemming from a curse supposedly laid on the island in 1169 by the Bishop of Como. It involves – essentially – flambéed liqueur coffee. To eat here at lunch or dinner you pay an all-in price (€68; no credit cards), which covers a set menu with wine – heavily overpriced for relatively ordinary food, but you're paying for the spectacle. Booking essential. Boat transport (which is guaranteed back to Sala Comacina until midnight) costs extra. June–Aug daily noon–2pm & 7–9.30pm. Closed Tues in March–May & Sept–Oct. Closed Nov–Feb.

The eastern shore: Como to Bellagio

The **eastern shore**, north of Como, is a wilder affair, with rugged cliffs and a narrow road winding between village communities. The boats that zigzag their way up the lake are as good a way as any of sampling the landscapes.

TORNO, a medieval rival of Como's, 7km north, retains some fine old buildings, including the Romanesque church of **San Giovanni** and the celebrated sixteenth-century **Villa Pliniana**, viewable only from the water. The villa has hosted a parade of romantic souls, including Byron and Shelley, Ugo Foscolo, Stendhal, Rossini and Bellini, but was named after Pliny's description of the curious intermittent waterfall in its grounds, a natural phenomenon that was studied by Leonardo da Vinci.

Some 10km north, past the cave systems at **Pognana**, is **NESSO**, where gorges cut into the mountains; the **Orrido di Nesso**, an especially high, gloomy example, marks the mouth of the Tuf and Nosè torrents. From Nesso, a narrow branch road twists up into the mountains past **Piano** (or **Pian**) **del Tivano**, eventually joining the Valassina at Asso.

The final 10km stretch into Bellagio is taken up with a series of hamlets wedged into the cliffs; one, **LEZZENO**, 7km before Bellagio, stands directly opposite the Isola Comacina and is a relatively frequent stop for boats. Our coverage of Bellagio falls later in this chapter (see p.211).

By bus From Como bus C30 (towards Bellagio; approx hourly) serves Torno (20min), Nesso (40min), Lezzeno (55min) and points in between (🌐 asfautolinee.it).

By boat Torno, Nesso, Lezzeno and other points are served by boats zigzagging up and down the lake (🌐 navigazionelaghi.it).

Tremezzina

Lake Como's most scenically attractive zone lies halfway up the lake. Sheltered by a headland, the stretch of shore between Lenno and Menaggio – known as the **Tremezzina** (see map opposite) after the main town hereabouts, **Tremezzo** – is where Como's climate is at its gentlest, the lake at its most tranquil and the vegetation most lush. Lined with cypresses and palms, it's lovely at any time of year, but unbeatable in spring, awash with colour and heady with the scent of flowering bushes.

Villa del Balbianello

Mid-March to mid-Nov Tues & Thurs–Sun 10am–6pm • House and gardens €13, or €3 to UK National Trust cardholders; gardens only €7, or free to UK National Trust cardholders • ☎ 0344 56 110, 🌐 fondoambiente.it

One of Lake Como's most seductive grand houses is the **Villa del Balbianello**, situated on the headland just outside **LENNO**, an old town with charm of its own.

The house is a classic eighteenth-century set piece, built over the remnants of a medieval convent and left to the nation by explorer Guido Monzino, who in 1973 became the first Italian to climb Everest. However, it's the romantic **gardens** that inspire, with their gravel paths between lush foliage (including magnolias, cypresses, plane trees and ilex), and stone urns and arches framing exquisite views across the water.

ARRIVAL AND DEPARTURE

VILLA DEL BALBIANELLO

By boat Access is chiefly by boat (small craft leave frequently from Lenno and Sala Comacina for about €7 return). Local motorboat operators include 🌐 taxiboat.net (based at Lenno).

By car On Tuesdays, Saturdays and Sundays you can park your car either in Lenno or at the gates at the end of the access road (signposted) and walk to the villa through the grounds – roughly 1km from Lenno, half that from the gates.

By tourist train A motorized mini tourist train called the Trombetta Express trundles to and fro along the lakeside road, from Lenno (Villa Balbianello) to Tremezzo, Villa Carlotta, Cadenabbia and Menaggio, making roughly hourly trips in each direction (May–Sept daily 9am–10pm; Fri & Sat until 11pm; €5 one-way, €8 return, €12 day pass). Ask at your hotel for exact timetable info.

ACCOMMODATION AND EATING

LENNO

Albergo Lenno Via Lomazzi 23 ☎ 0344 57 051, 🌐 albergolenno.com. Plum on the lakefront, this is a rather swanky four-star, recently updated inside. Everything is now bright, fresh, airy and clutter-free, with simple, modern rooms and smiling service. **€170**

LA FINE DELLA GUERRA – THE END OF THE WAR

As you move around the western shore of Lake Como – the area around Tremezzo and Menaggio, as far north as Domaso, and into the mountains around Lake Lugano and the Swiss border – you'll spot a series of roadside panels marked **La Fine della Guerra**, giving details of buildings or places that were the scene of notable events during the last years of World War II. This is a publicly funded project to highlight the civil and military resistance network that spread across northern Italy during the *Repubblica Sociale Italiana* (1943–45), a Nazi puppet state under the Fascist dictator Mussolini that was headquartered at Salò on Lake Garda (see p.292). For the full story, head to the excellent **Museo della Fine della Guerra** in Dongo (see p.218; 🌐 museofineguerradongo.it), whose website has more detail and maps, as does 🌐 www.lakecomo.com.

5

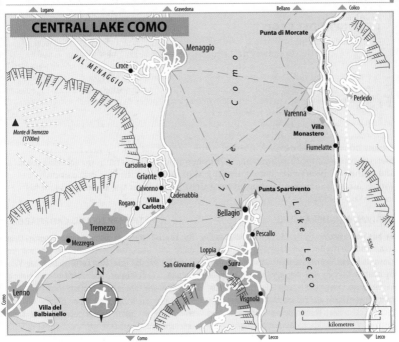

CENTRAL LAKE COMO

Lugano — Gravedona — Bellano — Colico

Menaggio
Punta di Morcate

VAL MENAGGIO

Croce

Lake Como

Perledo

Monte di Tremezzo
(1700m)

Varenna

Villa
Monastero

Fiumelatte

Carsolina
Griante
Calvonno
Rogaro   Cadenabbia
Villa
Carlotta

Punta Spartivento

Bellagio

Tremezzo

Pescallo

Mezzegra

Lake Lecco

Loppia

San Giovanni   Suira

N

Lenno

Visgnola

Villa del
Balbianello

Como

SS36

0   2

kilometres

Como — Lecco — Lecco

San Giorgio Via Regina 81 ☎0344 40 415, ⓦsangiorgiolenno.com. A lovely, quiet three-star hotel in a perfect location on the lake side of the main road – the tree-shaded gardens run down to a little lakefront beach, and balcony views across to Bellagio are gorgeous. Approaching its hundredth birthday, the hotel remains in the same family as from day one. Public areas have considerable character, with parquet floors and French windows, though the rooms are calmer and plainer. €150

Tremezzo and Cadenabbia

For more than 150 years, overseas visitors – particularly the British – have been holing up in **TREMEZZO** and neighbouring **CADENABBIA**. The latter's **Church of the Ascension** (communion Sun 10.30am, closed Nov–March; ☎0344 42 165, ⓦchurchonlakecomo .com), located directly opposite the car ferry dock, was the first Anglican church in Italy, completed in 1891, its interior sporting shimmering golden mosaics, marble columns and finely decorated barrel vaulting. The church hosts frequent concerts of classical music during the summer season.

The area remains popular, its hotels – enjoying splendid views of Bellagio's hills and the mountains behind, but regrettably cut off from the water by the busy lakefront road – hosting many repeat visitors. Wander through the shop-heavy lanes, or opt to climb the hills behind to discover a touch more character.

Rogaro, Griante and Mezzegra

Signposted above busy Tremezzo, the hamlet of **ROGARO** is another world – cool air, cows cropping Alpine pastures and steep walks offering epic views atop Monte Nava (850m). You could do worse than hole up here for a day or three.

Similarly, local tourist offices have details of walks that pass through quiet **GRIANTE**, on the hills above Cadenabbia. Many routes also link across to **MEZZEGRA**, renowned as the place where, on April 28, 1945, Italy's wartime partisan leader, Walter Audisio,

5

GREENWAY DEL LAGO

If some of the mountain trekking around Lake Como sounds a bit too much like hard work, indulge instead in the **Greenway del Lago** (ⓦgreenwaydellago.it), a path that stays mostly on the flat, with just a bit of gentle up and down over the 10.5km of beautifully scenic terrain between Colonno and Cadenabbia. The route is split into five short, easy strolls – described on the website, and on tourist-office handouts – but it doesn't take much to link them all together into a single walk, or to turn them around to follow in the opposite direction. The website also describes variations and other walks in the area.

caught up with – and shot – Mussolini at the gates of Villa Belmonte, before the dictator could escape into Switzerland. Euphemistic signposts from the lakeside road, and within the pretty village itself, direct you to the site of the "historical event", where, bizarrely, a memorial cross to the Fascist leader often still has flowers laid before it. The villa is closed to the public.

ARRIVAL AND DEPARTURE

By bus From Como hourly bus C10 (towards Menaggio) serves Tremezzo (1hr 5min) and Cadenabbia (1hr 10min; ⓦasfautolinee.it). From Menaggio, it's a 5–10min journey.
By boat Boats (see p.189) stop approximately hourly at Tremezzo, Villa Carlotta and – rarely – Cadenabbia on the route between Como and Bellagio/Menaggio/Varenna. In addition Cadenabbia is linked to Bellagio car ferries running about every 30min (which also take foot passengers).

TREMEZZO AND CADENABBIA

By tourist train A motorized mini tourist train called the Trombetta Express trundles to and fro along the lakeside road, from Lenno to Tremezzo, Villa Carlotta, Cadenabbia and Menaggio, making roughly hourly trips in each direction (May–Sept daily 9am–10pm; Fri & Sat until 11pm; €5 one-way, €8 return, €12 day pass). Ask at your hotel for exact timetable info.

INFORMATION

Cadenabbia tourist office Via Regina 1 (April–Oct Mon–Fri & Sun 9.30am–12.30pm; ☎0344 40 393, ⓦcadenabbiadigriante.com).
Tremezzo tourist office Via Regina 3 (April–Oct Mon &

Wed–Sun 9am–noon & 3.30–6.30pm; ☎0344 40 493, ⓦtremezzo.it).
Useful websites ⓦgriante.com & ⓦlakecomo.com.

ACCOMMODATION AND EATING

Tremezzo is a focus for package tourism, but not all of the hotels are quite up to snuff – and, in addition, the busy lakefront road runs between the village and the water; however good a restaurant may be, eating at terrace tables within metres of passing traffic won't be to everyone's taste.

TREMEZZO

Grand Hotel Tremezzo Palace Via Regina 8 ☎0344 42 491, ⓦgrandhoteltremezzo.com. One of the glitziest five-star hotels on the lake, a giant behemoth of a building with opulent though tastefully designed interiors – pastel colours, period furnishings – and tranquil grounds on the lakefront. Brace yourself for the prices. **€650**
La Darsena Via Regina 3 ☎0344 43 166, ⓦhotelladarsena.it. A stylish small hotel and restaurant on the lake side of the road near Tremezzo's landing-stage, with spacious, elegant rooms (many with balconies). Well worth a look – this is a breath of fresh air after the town's often uninspiring locales. **€160**
La Perla Via Romolo Quaglino 7 ☎0344 41 707, ⓦlaperlatremezzo.com. This modern hillside hotel, though undistinguished, has 17 rooms around a swimming

pool, tremendous views and helpful staff. The outlook – distinctly silver-haired – and decor – tiled floors, drapes, pelmets – won't appeal to all tastes, but it is nonetheless a bargain for the area. Shuttles head down to the lakefront every day. **€150**

CADENABBIA

★**La Marianna** Via Regina 57 ☎0344 43 111, ⓦla-marianna.com (hotel), ⓦlamarianna.com (restaurant). Wonderful old hotel-restaurant just north of Cadenabbia on the lakefront road. The restaurant, reminiscent of a nineteenth-century etching of a tavern, has an impeccable reputation for authentic, traditional lake cuisine, from stewed rabbit to fresh fish, accompanied by expert wine pairings. Two-course *menù* €35, or à la carte mains around €25. The atmospheric hotel has eight rustic

5

rooms. Big wardrobes, plants and knick-knacks lend a family feel throughout. Go for room 10, facing to the rear but – thanks to a long balcony around the building – also offering a lake view. Restaurant closed all day Mon, and Tues–Fri eves. **€95**

ROGARO

Al Veluu Via San Martino 11 ☎ 0344 40 510, ⓦ alveluu .com. Splendid fine-dining restaurant perched on a terrace viewpoint above Tremezzo, serving accomplished seasonal and organic dishes to a knowledgeable local clientele. Above the restaurant are two one-bedroom apartment suites – luxury boutique hideaways featuring wood beams, spacious terraces, fancy bathrooms and fully equipped kitchens. Normally let by the week (roughly €1300 in high season), they might be available by the day on request, for about €200. Restaurant closed Tues.

★ **La Fagurida** Via San Martino 15 ☎ 0344 40 676, ⓦ lafagurida.it. Charming, atmospheric family-run farmhouse restaurant specializing in home-produced *salumi*, polenta and roast rabbit. Well worth the journey up to Rogaro. Expect around €30–35 a head. Closed Mon.

Rusall Via San Martino 2 ☎ 0344 40 408, ⓦ rusallhotel .com. Perched high up on the hillside above Tremezzo, this family-run hotel draws in as many peace-seeking loafers as it does muddy-booted hikers; paths climb the hilly slopes behind the village – but what takes the breath away are the stupendous views from the hotel's pretty rear terrace, far out over the lake and the mountains beyond. The rooms are adequate three-star quality, the welcome is always cheery and the restaurant has a solid reputation for hearty local cooking. **€120**

GRIANTE

Casa Pini Via Brentano 12f ☎ 0344 37 302, ⓦ casapini .com. A pleasant little three-room family-run B&B in this quiet hillside village, with a lovely garden and home-cooked food. **€60**

Villa Carlotta

Via Regina 2, Tremezzo • April to mid-Oct daily 9am–6pm; March & mid-Oct to mid-Nov daily 10am–5pm • €9 • ⓦ villacarlotta.it

Located directly on the lakeside road between Tremezzo and Cadenabbia, **Villa Carlotta** is perhaps Lake Como's most famous attraction. It's best visited by **boat**; views of the house from the water are glorious.

Pink, white and exceptionally photogenic, this grand house was built in 1690 by Giorgio Clerici, a banker from Milan. In 1843, it passed to Princess Marianne of Nassau, wife of Albert of Prussia, who gave it to her daughter Carlotta as a wedding present – hence the name.

You approach through the formal terraced gardens in front, and up a distinctive triple-layered scissor staircase. The house displays a collection of eighteenth-century **painting and statuary** beloved of the Sommariva family, owners of the villa at the time of Napoleon. On the ground floor, the rear left-hand room is the one to aim for; here resides the meltingly romantic *Cupid and Psyche*, a copy in marble, done under Canova's direction, of his own original. Elsewhere, as you drift through the rooms, are paintings by Jean-Baptiste Wicar (*Virgil Reading Book VI of the "Aeneid" Before the Court of Augustus*) and Francesco Hayez (*Romeo and Juliet's Last Kiss*), as well as Canova's sculpture *Palamedes*, a fine figure of a man from every angle. Upstairs, rooms have been laid out with original furniture, mostly of the Empire period.

As much as the art or the building itself, though, Villa Carlotta is worth visiting for its expansive, fourteen-acre **gardens**, a beautifully ordered collection of camellias, rhododendrons and azaleas that stretches around and behind the house. You can use your ticket to come and go all day.

ARRIVAL AND DEPARTURE
VILLA CARLOTTA

By boat Boats (see p.189) stop at least hourly at Villa Carlotta on the route between Como and Bellagio/Menaggio/Varenna. Alternatively, you could stroll here from the landing-stages at Tremezzo (450m south) or Cadenabbia (900m north) – both are pleasant, attractive walks.

By tourist train A motorized mini tourist train called the Trombetta Express trundles to and fro along the lakeside road, from Lenno to Tremezzo, Villa Carlotta, Cadenabbia and Menaggio, making roughly hourly trips in each direction (May–Sept daily 9am–10pm; Fri & Sat until 11pm; €5 one-way, €8 return, €12 day pass). Ask at your hotel for exact timetable info.

Menaggio

MENAGGIO, 37km north of Como, is a bustling village resort with a good deal of character. Busy roads cut into a chunk of the upper town – the lakeshore routes and the road west to Porlezza and Lake Lugano – but below them, around the traffic-free **Piazza Garibaldi** and surrounding alleyways, Menaggio retains much of its poise; it is well kept, attractive and has a fine view east across the water to Bellagio and Varenna. It also sees more of a mix of tourists than many of its neighbours, with a reputation for sports and activities – hiking and cycling in the mountains, waterskiing and kayaking on the lake.

The old quarter

A tourist office booklet describes a self-guided **walk** of about an hour through Menaggio's hilly older streets. From Piazza Garibaldi, it passes the church of **Santa Marta** on Via Calvi – whose facade displays the gravestone of Roman noble Lucio Minicio Exorato – on a route up Via Castellino da Castello to the former site of Menaggio's castle, destroyed in 1523 (though the street still follows its perimeter walls). Passing a photogenic **bridge** on Via Strecioum, the route heads down to the public beach and pool at the **Lido** on Via Roma (late June to mid-Sept daily 9am–7pm) before returning to the Piazza.

ARRIVAL AND INFORMATION   MENAGGIO

By plane From Milan-Malpensa airport, reach Como Lago station by train (see p.195), then take bus C10 from Piazza   Matteotti outside the station direct to Menaggio (approx hourly; 1hr 10min). Alternatively, take the train from

MENAGGIO

Lake Como

ACCOMMODATION

Bellavista	4
Garni Corona	3
Grand Hotel Menaggio	5
Grand Hotel Victoria	2
Ostello Menaggio La Primula	6
Royal	1

RESTAURANTS & CAFÉS

Al Paladar de la Memoria	2
Crotto Da Gusto	1
Il Ristorante di Paolo	6
Il Vapore	4
Osteria Il Pozzo	3
Pizzeria Lugano	5

0	100
metres	

5

Milano Centrale to Como San Giovanni station and pick up bus C10 to Menaggio from there (approx hourly; 1hr 5min).

By bus Menaggio's bus station is on Via Lusardi, served by the C10 from Como (1hr 10min) and all points in between, and the C12 from Lugano (55min) via Porlezza (25min), both hourly (ⓦasfautolinee.it). Timetables are at ⓦwww .muoversi.regione.lombardia.it.

By boat Boats and hydrofoils shuttle frequently from Como, Tremezzo, Bellagio and Varenna. There are also regular car ferries from Bellagio and Varenna (which also carry foot passengers). Menaggio's two landing-stages are beside each other just south of the centre; from there, the unromantic five-minute walk into town involves negotiating narrow pavements alongside busy Via IV Novembre. Timetables are at ⓦnavigazionelaghi.it. Local motorboat operators include ⓦmenaggioboat.com.

By tourist train A motorized mini tourist train called the Trombetta Express trundles to and fro along the lakeside road, from Lenno, Tremezzo and Cadenabbia to Menaggio, making roughly hourly trips in each direction (May–Sept daily 9am–10pm; Fri & Sat until 11pm; €5 one-way, €8 return, €12 day pass). Ask at your hotel for exact timetable info.

Tourist office Piazza Garibaldi 3 (daily 9am–12.30pm & 2.30–6pm; April, May & Sept closed Sun; Nov–March closed Wed & Sun; ☎0344 32 924, ⓦmenaggio.com & ⓦlakecomo.com).

ACCOMMODATION

Bellavista Via IV Novembre 21 ☎0344 32 136, ⓦhotel-bellavista.org. Decent, three-star lakefront hotel. Rooms have a whiff of style, with drapes and good fabrics, and there's a terrace restaurant, pool and parking. Service is good, though you may have to overlook some shortcomings in amenities and cuisine to savour the spectacular views – especially from upper-floor rooms – over the lake. **€140**

Garni Corona Largo Cavour 3 ☎0344 32 006, ⓦhotelgarnicorona.com. Family-run two-star on the lakefront, with 22 plain but adequately fitted-out rooms, some with lake views and balcony. The location is very central, bang on the main square, but the welcome is what makes this place; you feel like you're one of the family. "Garni" means it only serves breakfast; the restaurant down below on the square is a separate concern. Closed Nov–March. **€110**

★**Grand Hotel Menaggio** Via IV Novembre 77 ☎0344 30 640, ⓦgrandhotelmenaggio.com. In a superb location overlooking the twin landing-stages, this is the larger of Menaggio's two historic four-star hotels. Service is remarkably good and, for such a big place, it has few airs and graces, retaining its old-fashioned gentility and elegance. Rooms are spacious and well appointed, many with balconies offering wonderful lake views, and there is a pool and private parking. Closed Nov–March. **€180**

★**Grand Hotel Victoria** Lungolago Castelli 9 ☎0344 32 003, ⓦgrandhotelvictoria.it. Five minutes' stroll east of Piazza Garibaldi, this splendid old property, built in 1885, stands sheltered behind five immense cedar trees.

The ambience here is as engaging as at the *Grand Hotel Menaggio*, though quieter; the hotel grounds (with parking) are private and hardly any traffic passes. Old-fashioned standards prevail – in decor, facilities and quality of service – and the genial staff all speak English. Closed Nov–March. **€180**

Royal Largo Vittorio Veneto 1, Loveno ☎0344 31 444, ⓦroyalcolombo.com. Fine, well-run three-star hotel located in tranquil residential surroundings way up on the slopes overlooking Menaggio. The public areas are pleasantly upmarket, the rooms spotless and comfortable, and the whole complex (only eighteen rooms altogether) stands amid expansive gardens with a swimming pool. You're a long way from the lakeside bustle – but that's the point. Closed Nov–March. **€140**

HOSTEL

★**Ostello Menaggio La Primula** Via IV Novembre 106 ☎0344 32 356, ⓦlakecomohostel.com. Excellent HI hostel on the edge of town, a short walk from the landing-stage, with small, clean dorms, doubles and family rooms, as well as a bar and restaurant. It has bikes, kayaks and canoes for rent, offers guided hikes and climbs, sailing trips, cooking classes, weekend barbecues, even informal Italian language lessons. This is a popular spot; reservations are essential. Closed Nov–March. Dorms **€22**; doubles **€75**

CAMPING

Camping Europa Via Cipressi 12 ☎0344 31 187. Basic local campsite just north of town. Closed Oct–March. Pitch **€17.50**

EATING AND DRINKING

Aside from restaurants within the better hotels, Menaggio's lakefront square – a lively, sociable spot after dark – has several places laying out terrace tables. Restaurants, both here and in the lanes further back, serve late. The *gelaterie* on the square and Via Calvi round the corner compete on quality and reputation; a taste test is a must. Menaggio is also handy if you're self-catering, with a couple of supermarkets, including a handy deli-cum-general store 20m from the landing-stage.

5

ALPINE ADVENTURE: THE ST MORITZ LOOP

Menaggio is well placed for sightseeing in the **Swiss Alps**, with two epic panoramic routes by train and bus combining to form a loop to and from St Moritz. You could follow the route as described, or turn it around to follow it in reverse – but you can't do it all in a day; reckon on an overnight stay in St Moritz.

FROM MENAGGIO: THE PALM EXPRESS

One of the celebrated mountain routes of the Swiss **postbus** network, the **Palm Express** between Lugano and St Moritz, passes through Menaggio once a day in high season (mid-June to mid-Oct daily; rest of year Fri–Sun only). The route follows an epic drive around the northern end of Lake Como to **Chiavenna**, an attractive, low-key Alpine town, crossing the Swiss border to climb the beautiful Val Bregaglia to the Maloja Pass at 1815m, ending at St Moritz (2hr 50min). The standard fare from Menaggio is about €50 one-way, though discounts are often available (advance reservation essential; ⓦ postbus.ch).

ST MORITZ

Set 1856m above sea level in Switzerland's glorious Upper Engadine valley, **St Moritz** revels in, on average, 322 sunny days a year; blue skies reign supreme. It's undeniably posh – the village, piled on slopes above the train station, hosts dozens of designer-label boutiques – but there's plenty more to do than shopping. Take a stroll around the pine-forested lake, stop in at one or two of the small art museums, ride the Corviglia funicular to the summit of Piz Nair (3057m), or relax at a terrace table on one of the village squares. The tourist information site, with full accommodation options, is ⓦ stmoritz.com.

BACK TO MENAGGIO: THE BERNINA EXPRESS

For the return journey, you could opt for the epic **Bernina Express** route of Switzerland's Rhaetian Railway (ⓦ rhb.ch). From St Moritz, this heads up on a wild crossing of the ice-bound Bernina Pass (2328m), before easing down into the bucolic Val Poschiavo to terminate at the little border town of **Tirano**, where passport control separates the station's Swiss platforms from its Italian ones. Ordinary trains do the run for Fr.30/about €25 one-way, but check online for when special panoramic carriages operate – these are well worth the surcharge (Fr.14/ about €10).

Tirano – located at the end of the craggy Valtellina valley, 69km east of Lake Como – is best known for the opulent pilgrimage church Madonna di Tirano, 1km northwest of the centre, its shrine focused around a statue of Mary dressed in a silk and gold robe donated by local people in 1746. More information at ⓦ valtellinaturismo.com.

From Tirano, a Swiss bus follows the scenic journey down the Valtellina and back around Lake Como to Lugano – but it doesn't stop at Menaggio on the way. An easier (and cheaper) option is to take an ordinary Italian stopping train from Tirano direct to **Varenna** (approx hourly; 1hr 30min; €7), and then return to Menaggio by boat.

Al Paladar de la Memoria Via Al Lago 23 ☎0344 30 102. Modern, lively café-bar in the narrow lanes behind Piazza Garibaldi, open from breakfast until 2am and also serving snacks and light meals for €9–13. Closed Mon.

Crotto Da Gusto Monti di Gottro, Carlazzo ☎0344 70 040. If you can find this place, hidden away in the hills high above Menaggio, you're in for a treat; honest-to-goodness, unreconstructed, mountain cooking without any nod to modernity or compromise. Polenta, sausage, *pizzoccheri*, stews of boar, rabbit or pheasant, cheese made on the premises, local grappa – it's all here, and rarely for more than €25 a head. To find it, drive towards Porlezza, turn right at Grandola ed Uniti, head towards Naggar and then follow the mountain roads towards Gottro. Closed Tues & Nov–March.

Il Ristorante di Paolo Largo Cavour 3 ☎0344 32 133,

ⓦ ilristorantedipaolo.it. A fairly fancy, white-tablecloth place, serving well-prepared local cuisine with a modern European twist – *missoltini* (dried lake fish), *casonsei* (meat-filled ravioli) and more – alongside excellent wines. Mains €11–19; expect around €35 a head. Closed Tues.

Il Vapore Piazza Grossi 3 ☎0344 32 229, ⓦ albergoilvapore.it.gg. Pleasant little hotel restaurant in a quiet, central location serving mid-priced local dishes in the modest dining room or on the flower-decked terrace. No credit cards. Closed Wed.

Osteria Il Pozzo Piazza Garibaldi ☎0344 32 33. An attractive small terrace restaurant squashed into an alley just off the main square, serving decent local cooking, from salamis and cheeses to home-made pasta (mains €10–17). Expect around €30 per head. Closed Wed.

5

WALKS AROUND MENAGGIO

There's a wide choice of **walking** routes in the countryside around Menaggio, and the tourist office is well equipped to help, with maps, route descriptions and local knowledge. Shorter walks include the easy paths to the ex-fishing hamlet of **Nobiallo** (40min), with its leaning Romanesque bell tower, or around the eighteenth- and nineteenth-century villas of hillside **Loveno** (45min).

Starting from **Grandola ed Uniti** at 385m, reached on bus C12 above Menaggio, a fairly testing two-hour chunk of the **Via dei Monti Lariani** long-distance route (see p.199) leads up through the pretty village of **Codogna** to a steep mule-track amid pastures, continuing past La Piazza to finish at **Breglia** (749m), from where bus C13 heads back down to Menaggio. If you're feeling spry, a different path from Breglia climbs even higher to the **Rifugio Menaggio** hut (1hr 40min; ⓦ rifugiomenaggio.eu), perched at 1383m, where the nearby viewpoint Pizza Coppa takes in stupendous views over Lake Como, Val Menaggio and Lake Lugano.

IL SENTIERO DELLE QUATTRO VALLI

Breglia is also the starting-point for **Il Sentiero delle Quattro Valli** ("Four Valleys Trail"), a classic three-day mountain walk of about 50km which links Lake Como to Lake Lugano. Stage 1 (13km; about 6hr) from Breglia shadows the Via dei Monti Lariani initially but then branches off to enter the wild Val Sanagra, following cart-tracks through Alpine pasture to end at tiny **Malè** (1144m), where there is simple accommodation. Stage 2 extends to **Cavargna**, while Stage 3 ends at **Dasio**, above San Mamete in the Valsolda (see p.174). The route is described in detail in the free booklet *Lake Como Trekking*, available at the tourist office or downloadable at ⓦ menaggio.com.

★**Pizzeria Lugano** Via Como 26 ☎ 0344 31 664. A wonderful little family-run pizzeria just above the town centre, utterly unreconstructed. Strip lights overhead, net curtains and a conscious lack of décor only reinforce just how good these pizzas are – wood-fired, crispy and delicious. The parade of local families and old-timers stopping in – not to mention busy dads zipping by to collect early-evening takeaways – speaks volumes. €10 will see you right. Don't miss it. Closed Mon.

Val Menaggio: west to Lake Lugano

The stretch of shoreline north of Menaggio forms part of what we've called Northern Lake Como (see p.217). However, Menaggio also stands at the mouth of a route linking **west** through the mountains to Lake Lugano. This is a scenic byway, through some splendid countryside, and offers the chance to compare the two lakes; only 11km separate busy Menaggio on Lake Como from **Porlezza**, which faces along the beautiful, little-visited eastern arm of Lake Lugano. More enticing reasons to head this way include having a meal at the first Swiss village over the border, **Gandria** (see p.173), or spending time exploring pacy **Lugano** (see p.166), 29km from Menaggio. Walks crisscross the mountains hereabouts (see above).

Lago di Piano

After climbing out of Menaggio on tight switchbacks up to Croce, high on the ridge, the road scoots along the floor of the **Val Menaggio**, passing **Bene Lario** and 3km later reaching the small, reedy **Lago di Piano**, protected as a nature reserve and breeding place for water birds. Drop into the little information office beside the lake, or ask the Menaggio tourist office for the route description of a pleasant, almost flat two-hour walk here that takes in woodlands and a fortified cluster of medieval houses on a peninsula in the lake, known as Castel San Pietro. Porlezza on Lake Lugano (see p.174) is 4km further west.

ARRIVAL AND INFORMATION · LAGO DI PIANO

By bus Roughly hourly bus C12 from Menaggio towards Lugano stops at Lago di Piano (20min; ⓦ asfautolinee.it).

Tourist office Via Statale 117 (Mon, Tues & Sat 9am–noon, Wed 2–4pm; ☎ 0344 74 961, ⓦ riserva lagodipiano.eu).

Bellagio

5

Cradled by cypress-spiked hills on the tip of the Triangolo Lariano – the triangle of mountainous land between the Como and Lecco branches of the lake – **BELLAGIO** has been called the most beautiful town in Italy. It's not hard to see why. With a promenade planted with oleanders and lime trees, *fin-de-siècle* hotels painted shades of butterscotch, peach and cream, a spectacular mid-lake location and a crumbling core of stepped, cobbled alleyways, Bellagio is the quintessential Italian Lakes town.

This little place has a long history. The Roman statesman **Pliny the Younger** may have had a villa on Bellagio's promontory in the first century AD. The village is first mentioned in 835 as Belasio, and also appears as Bellaxio, Belacius and Bislacus; despite inevitable associations with modern Italian *bella* ("beautiful"), its name derives more prosaically from *bi-lacus*, Latin for "between the lakes". Bellagio's strategic location ensured its success throughout the **medieval** period, and by the early

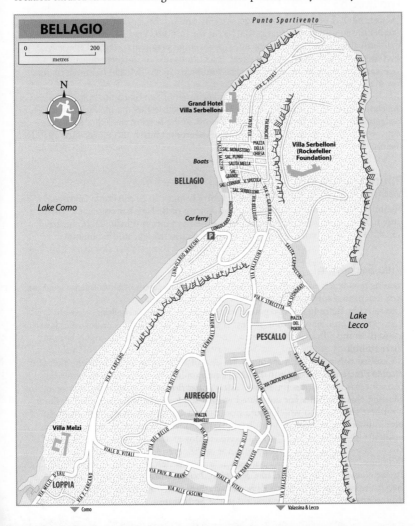

5

nineteenth century, the wealthy families of Lombardy – like their Roman forebears – were coming here simply to relax.

The waterfront

Bellagio's first hotel, the *Genazzini*, opened in 1825; its second, the *Florence*, opened in 1852. The two flank Bellagio's scenic **waterfront** to this day, and passenger boats dock midway between them (the *Genazzini* is now the *Metropole*, with a prominent sign commemorating its origins). Car ferries dock 100m to the south. The **views** from anywhere along the lakefront promenade westwards to the mountains above Cadenabbia are simply lovely; spending an afternoon watching the shadows lengthen, as the ferries parade to and fro, is pure Bellagio.

The Borgo

The central part of town – the **Borgo** – is tiny, laid out on a grid pattern; three streets parallel to the waterfront (Piazza Mazzini at the bottom, Via Centrale in the middle, Via Garibaldi at the top) are connected by seven perpendicular stepped alleyways. **Via Garibaldi**, the main shopping street, is a curious mix of touristy souvenirs, high-class silk outlets, and ordinary delis and pharmacies. Bellagio has more than its fair share of fey watercolourists.

At the top of the town is the Romanesque church of **San Giacomo**, built at the end of the eleventh century, alongside a tower (in Piazza della Chiesa) which is all that's left of Bellagio's medieval defences. Across the square, at the head of the Salita Monastero steps, was once a monastic institution attached to the church, occupied since 1919 by the *Bar Sport*.

Punta Spartivento

A short stroll 350m north of the village centre brings you to the **Punta Spartivento**, the "Point Which Divides the Winds", at the very tip of Bellagio's promontory. There's a little harbour here – nice for a cool dip – as well as a pleasant little restaurant from which to enjoy the unique panoramic vistas out over the lake and mountains.

Villa Serbelloni

Garden tours: April–Oct Tues–Sun 11am & 3.30pm • €9 • Minimum six people, maximum thirty people; cancelled in bad weather • Buy tickets 15min in advance from the Promo Bellagio office at the far end of Piazza della Chiesa

Confusingly, Bellagio has two grand houses known as **Villa Serbelloni** – one a luxury hotel on the waterfront, the other a privately owned mansion set amid lavish gardens on the hilltop above Bellagio. The two are entirely separate today, but once shared a link.

Shielded behind gates at the northern end of Piazza Mazzini stands the *Grand Hotel Villa Serbelloni*, built in 1852 as a private house and converted into a hotel twenty years later under the name *Grand Hotel Bellagio*. For the best part of a century, this palatial affair competed with Bellagio's equally grand *Hotel de la Grande-Bretagne* as to which could host the more sophisticated guests amid the more opulent surroundings, inspiring partisan loyalty among visitors and local residents alike (hundreds of whom were employed as hotel staff). In 1907, the *Grand Hotel Bellagio* acquired as an annexe the seventeenth-century mansion residence of the then-defunct Serbelloni family, which stood on top of the hill above Bellagio – and it changed its name to *Grand Hotel Villa Serbelloni* in celebration. Barely two decades on, the Wall Street Crash of 1929 forced the hotel to sell its hilltop annexe, although it clung on to the Serbelloni name. Today, with the

Grande-Bretagne long derelict (despite its beautiful location partway down the Salita Serbelloni steps in town), the *Grand Hotel* offers Bellagio's only five-star accommodation.

Meanwhile, in 1959 the real Villa Serbelloni on the hilltop above passed into the hands of the **Rockefeller Foundation**. Although the villa remains off-limits – it's an exclusive study centre for scholars and politicians – its gorgeous **gardens** can be visited on a guided tour. Formally designed in the nineteenth century on English and Italian lines, the gardens offer magnificent **views** over all three branches of the lake, and are liberally sprinkled with evocative grottoes and statuary. It is thought that Pliny's villa stood up here.

Villa Melzi

Lungolario Manzoni • Gardens: April–Oct daily 9.30am–6.30pm • €6.50 • ⓦ giardinidivillamelzi.it

Just beyond Bellagio's lido, the lake promenade continues south for about 500m to **Villa Melzi**, another of Lake Como's great houses, built in 1808 for Francesco Melzi D'Eril, vice president of the Italian Republic. The Neoclassical building is off-limits, but visitors can explore the extensive, luxuriant **gardens**, laid out in the English style and crammed with azaleas, rhododendrons, ornamental lemon trees, cypresses, palms, camellias and even a sequoia. Statuary dots the grounds, and you could hunt out the romantic little pond with Japanese water lilies, overlooked by cedar and maple.

ARRIVAL AND DEPARTURE   BELLAGIO

By plane From Milan-Malpensa airport, reach Como Lago station by train (see p.195), then take bus C30 from Piazza Matteotti outside the station direct to Bellagio (approx hourly; 1hr 5min). Alternatively, take the train from Milano Centrale to Como San Giovanni station and pick up bus C30 to Bellagio from there (approx hourly; 1hr 10min).

By bus Buses stop on Bellagio's waterfront, including the C30 from Como (approx hourly; 1hr 10min; ⓦ asfautolinee .it) and LB from Lecco (approx every 2hr; 50min; ⓦ lineelecco.it). Timetables are at ⓦ www.muoversi .regione.lombardia.it.

By car Bellagio is 30km from Como and 20km from Lecco, but both are treacherous, narrow roads that coil along the rocky cliffsides; reckon on a slow forty minutes to drive

either route, an hour or more if traffic is bad. An easier way to reach Bellagio is by car ferry – the most frequent service is from Cadenabbia, with slightly longer gaps in service from Varenna, plus a few departures each day from Menaggio. However, note that you are not permitted to drive through the centre of Bellagio unless you're unloading at a (pre-reserved) hotel. In town, a car is a liability.

By boat Boats (see p.189) shuttle frequently to Bellagio from Tremezzo/Villa Carlotta, Cadenabbia, Menaggio, Varenna and further afield. Passenger ships and hydrofoils dock at one of the landing-stages fronting Piazza Mazzini; car ferries (which also carry foot passengers) dock 100m south by the car park. Timetables are at ⓦ navigazionelaghi.it.

GETTING AROUND

On foot Bellagio's lanes are too narrow and steep for any vehicles to penetrate; walking is the only way.

By boat Local motorboat operators include ⓦ taxiboat .it, ⓦ bellagiowatertaxis.com and ⓦ barindellitaxi boats.it.

By tourist train For roaming slightly further afield, opt

for the motorized mini tourist train called the Trombetta Express, which goes on a circuit from Bellagio's waterfront to Pescallo, then Loppia (for Villa Melzi), San Giovanni (for the museum) and back to Bellagio (May–Sept daily 9.30am–5.30pm, about every 45min; €5). Ask at your hotel for exact timetable info.

INFORMATION

Tourist office At the landing-stage on Piazza Mazzini (April–Oct usually Mon–Sat 9am–12.30pm & 1–6pm, Sun 10am–2pm; rest of year usually Mon, Tues & Thurs 9am–12.30pm & 2.30–5pm, Wed 9am–1pm, Fri & Sat 9am–1pm & 3–6pm; ☏ 031 950 204, ⓦ bellagiolakecomo.com).

Promo Bellagio town information Piazza della Chiesa 14 (April–Oct Mon 9.30am–1pm, Tues–Fri 9.30–11am & 2–4pm (Wed closes 3.30pm), Sat & Sun 10–11am & 2–3.30pm; ☏ 031 951 555, ⓦ www.promobellagio.it).
Useful websites ⓦ bellagiopoint.com & ⓦ lakecomo .com.

5

ACCOMMODATION

Barchetta Salita Mella 13 ☎031 951 030, Ⓦristorantebarchetta.com. Four decent en-suite budget rooms attached to this famous old Bellagio restaurant – attractive, modern styling, good attention to detail and a great location in the cobbled lanes. **€95**

★**Bellagio** Salita Grandi 6 ☎031 950 424, Ⓦhotelbellagio.it. An appealing, modern boutique hotel, in one of Bellagio's tallest buildings. Contemporary rooms have huge picture windows, electric blackout shades, wood floors, flat-screen TVs, a/c and spotless en-suite bathrooms. Go for the rooftop vistas from the fourth floor; the corner rooms 401 or 404 are to die for. Cheaper rooms lower down have all the same fittings but less dreamy views. Managed by the family that also runs the *Hotel Du Lac*, with discounts offered at the *Du Lac* restaurant. **€120**

Belvedere Via Valassina 31 ☎031 950 410, Ⓦbelvederebellagio.com. A modern three-star hotel, in the same family since 1880 but now completely refurbished, set in its own parkland at the top of the village, with a swimming pool and wonderful views over the Lecco arm of the lake. Closed Dec–March. **€250**

★**Du Lac** Piazza Mazzini 32 ☎031 950 320, Ⓦbellagiohoteldulac.com. Directly opposite the landing-stage, this fine old hotel offers spacious three-star lake-view rooms in classic style. Service – rarely for Bellagio – is excellent, and the atmosphere is one of quiet, informal gentility, aided by the ministrations of the owner-manager Leoni family. Closed Nov–Feb. **€200**

Giardinetto Via Roncati 12 ☎031 950 168. Friendly but basic old one-star place at the top of Bellagio. Some of the recently renovated rooms have lake views and there's a garden where you can picnic, which lifts it above some of the other budget options. No a/c. Closed Nov–Feb. **€70**

Grand Hotel Villa Serbelloni Via Roma 1 ☎031 950 216, Ⓦvillaserbelloni.com. One of Italy's grandest and stuffiest luxury retreats (see p.212). Opulent nineteenth-century interiors with ornate ceilings and fittings, original artworks, chandeliers, frescoes and marble, all best appreciated to the nightly strains of the hotel orchestra. The visitors' book reads like an account of twentieth-century history, from Russian princes through Franklin D. Roosevelt to Churchill, King Farouk of Egypt on honeymoon, JFK and Prince Rainier of Monaco – via Mary Pickford, Clark Gable and Al Pacino. Amazingly, for such a huge property, there are only 73 rooms (and 22 suites); each is spacious, formal and unique. A swimming pool, luxury spa and fitness centre fill out the list of amenities. Closed Nov–March. **€500**

La Pergola Piazza del Porto 4, Pescallo ☎031 950 263, Ⓦlapergolabellagio.it. Stylish, modern en-suite rooms with balconies overlooking the lake and the vine-covered restaurant below, though you'll need your own transport to reach it, since it's just outside Bellagio in the neighbouring hamlet of Pescallo. Closed Dec–March. **€125**

★**Silvio** Via Carcano 12, Loppia ☎031 950 322, Ⓦbellagiosilvio.com. Outstanding little three-star hotel south of the centre near Villa Melzi, now in the fifth generation of the same family, completely refurbished with a fresh, modern style. Most rooms have views over the lake and villa gardens, the hotel restaurant is excellent and there are free shuttles to and from Bellagio. The owners take their fishing seriously, serving the daily catch in the hotel restaurant, and offering guests the chance to join them nightly as they set and collect their nets on the lake. Closed Nov–March. **€140**

CAMPING

Camping Clarke Via Valassina 170c ☎031 951 325, Ⓦbellagio-camping.com. A small, family-run campsite about 10min drive south of town into the hills. Closed Nov–April. Pitch **€15**

EATING AND DRINKING

Like everything in Bellagio, **restaurants** can be pricey. You'd do best to **book** a table – essential at weekends and in the summer peak period, when the lanes and promenades can be packed with visitors. As usual, hunting slightly further afield can pay dividends, with some lovely places to discover in Loppia and Pescallo, on either side of the peninsula. In winter (Nov–Feb) Bellagio's restaurants tend to either close or operate restricted hours.

★**Alle Darsene di Loppia** Via Melzi 1, Loppia ☎031 952 069, Ⓦristorantedarsenediloppia.com. A quiet, attractive fish restaurant on Loppia harbour, a little south of Bellagio, which blends classic lake cuisine with a Modern European approach. The *menù degustazione* is €45, with mains around €14–20. Closed Mon.

BELLAGIO FESTIVAL

From late June to early September, venues in and around Bellagio – as well as further afield, from Como and Menaggio to Varenna and even small villages in the hills – play host to classical music concerts and recitals as part of the *Festival di Bellagio e del Lago di Como*, or plain **Bellagio Festival** (Ⓦbellagiofestival.com), inaugurated in 2011. Almost all events are free; check online for listings.

GARDENS OF THE ITALIAN LAKES

5

With a climate that is more Mediterranean than Alpine, the Italian Lakes host some of the **finest gardens** in Europe, Bellagio's Villa Melzi and Villa Serbelloni among them.

GARDEN DESIGN

The design of Italian gardens had its roots in that of the gardens of ancient Rome – which, in turn, drew inspiration from older Hellenistic **paradeisoi**, or paradise gardens. The Greek word paradeisos comes from an ancient Persian term meaning "enclosed by a wall"; Alexander the Great saw walled gardens and royal hunting parks on campaign in Persia in the fourth century BC, and brought the idea back home. These developed into the Roman concept of countryside estates, landscaped with terraces, trees and abundant planting, and peristyle gardens, small, enclosed open spaces within a townhouse, often featuring statues and a central fountain.

The medieval period developed the **peristyle** garden tradition; gardens were inward-looking, focused around cloisters and private, walled retreats, often planted with kitchen herbs and other medicinal plants.

By the mid-fifteenth century, Renaissance ideas led to a revival among the wealthiest families of the Roman tradition of dividing life between a villa – that is, a grand country estate, suitable for otium (leisure) – and a *palazzo*, or noble townhouse, suitable for negotium (business). Design focused on the **taming of nature**, with elaborate geometric designs (imported from France), topiary (originally Dutch) and flat, grass lawns cut across by gravel paths (an English preoccupation). These principles held sway throughout Europe for three hundred years.

In the mid-eighteenth century, a new aesthetic emerged in England, based on appreciation of the irregularity of natural forms. Key characteristics were rolling lawns, irregularly shaped ponds, meandering streams and patches of woodland. This **English style** caught on around Europe – not least through the work of the famed landscape designer Capability Brown (1715–83) – and remained popular into the Victorian era.

From the mid-nineteenth century, the English style heavily influenced the design of many Italian Lakes gardens. At many sites (as with the Borromeo islands of Lake Maggiore, or the Palazzo Estense in Varese), a formal Italian garden is juxtaposed with a wilder English garden alongside.

PERFECT CONDITIONS

The **climate** and **topography** of the lakes lend themselves to gardens. These southern foothills of the Alps are slightly lifted above the foggy, marshy plain of the River Po – thickly humid in summer, bone-chillingly dank in winter – to catch plenty of clear, warm sunshine all year round. Water both heats up and cools down slower than land, moderating extremes of temperature. Maggiore and Garda (Italy's two largest lakes) are big enough to act as giant solar batteries, storing the sun's energy all summer long and then releasing it slowly during the winter to keep their shores balmy and frost-free.

Several places – such as Gardone on Lake Garda, Pallanza on Lake Maggiore and Lugano on Lake Lugano – feature a rocky wall of cliffs shielding a narrow strip of south-facing lakeside land from cold northerly winds, thereby creating a protected **microclimate** that lends itself particular well to subtropical exotics. All these locations harbour superb gardens open to the public: Giardino Hruska at Gardone, Villa Taranto at Pallanza and Parco degli Ulivi at Lugano. There are many similar spots (see p.17).

PLANTING

The extent and variety of plants on show in the gardens of the Italian lakes is simply dazzling. There are hundreds, probably thousands, of varieties; this little account omits far more than it could ever include.

You'll be unlikely to miss ubiquitous **bougainvillea**, window-boxes of **geraniums**, camellias, azaleas, laurel, holm oaks, cypress, horse-chestnut, figs and olives. Lake Garda is known for its **lemon trees**, but you'll find citrus trees on lakes Maggiore, Lugano and Como, too.

Many gardens feature mixtures of evergreen and deciduous trees: Villa del Balbianello has oaks as well as firs, while **Villa Melzi** – the first garden on the lakes to be designed in the English style, in 1808 – boasts a promenade of plane trees in addition to exotic pines, Japanese maples and palms. Lilacs, jasmine and magnolia have been imported to Italy since the sixteenth century.

5

Barchetta Salita Mella 13 ☎031 951 389, ⓦristorantebarchetta.com. A fixture since 1887 in the heart of the old lanes, serving excellent local cuisine; opt for the *pesce del giorno* in the Terrazza restaurant (mains €12–25), or go for perfectly authentic, wood-fired Neapolitan pizza (€7–12) in the more informal *Forma e Gusto* pizzeria section downstairs. Open daily.

★**Bellagio Point** Salita Plinio 8 ☎031 950 437. Genial little spot which offers the intriguing combination of internet access and wine tasting, along with snacks and light bites (under €10). Open daily.

Bilacus Salita Serbelloni 9 ☎031 950 480, ⓦbilacusbellagio.it. Opposite the *San Giacomo* (see below), but more formal and slightly more expensive, with an attractive pergola for alfresco dining on fresh pasta, fillet of lake perch, steaks and the like. Mains around €9–21. Open daily.

Cava Turacciolo Salita Genazzini 3 ☎031 950 975, ⓦcavaturacciolo.it. Pleasant wine bar just off the waterfront near the car ferry, which knows its vintages and how to present them with knowledge, warmth – and top-quality nibbles. Open nightly until 1am. Closed Wed.

★**Du Lac** Piazza Mazzini 32 ☎031 950 320, ⓦbellagiohoteldulac.com. The restaurant of this fine hotel spreads beneath the arcades opposite the landing-stage – surprisingly good for such an obvious location, with carefully prepared daily specials, fair prices (about €18–21), and a touch of chic atmosphere after dark. Open daily.

La Grotta Salita Cernaia 14 ☎031 951 152, ⓦlagrottabellagio.com. Decent, budget-priced wood-fired pizza (€7–12) and lake fish dishes (mains €11–18) at this cosy place which serves late until 1am. Credit cards accepted over €25. Closed Mon.

Mella Via Rezia 1, San Giovanni ☎031 950 205, ⓦristorantemella.it. A family-run trattoria in San Giovanni, near Bellagio – good local cooking, in a genial atmosphere, concentrating on fresh-caught lake fish done a hundred different ways, prepared with skill and presented with charm. *Menù* around €26. Closed Tues.

Mistral At Grand Hotel Villa Serbelloni ☎031 956 435, ⓦristorante-mistral.com. Bellagio's top spot for fine dining, spreading over a beautiful lakeside veranda. It has a Michelin star for its light, creative Italian and Mediterranean food, and they are very proud of their "molecular cuisine" – a Heston Blumenthal-style approach bringing science into the kitchen; prawns with guacamole, turbot fried in sugar, ice cream frozen using liquid nitrogen… The full *menù degustazione* is €140. Or you could just have a normal meal of soup, pasta, fish and/or steak (mains €24–50). Dress code smart-casual. Closed Wed.

La Punta Punta Spartivento ☎031 951 888, ⓦristorantelapunta.it. Five minutes' walk north of town, and serving excellent food – especially lake fish – at mid-range prices. Lovely views over the Punta Spartivento. Closed Wed.

San Giacomo Salita Serbelloni 45 ☎031 950 329, ⓦtrattoriabellagio.it. A romantic trattoria at the top of the Salita Serbelloni, with tables on the steps outside, serving good local dishes such as ravioli with sage butter and fresh lake fish off a small menu with decent wines. A meal is about €30 a head. Closed Tues.

★**Silvio** Via Carcano 12, Loppia ☎031 950 322, ⓦbellagiosilvio.com. One of Bellagio's most pleasant, attractive dining spots, located just above nearby Loppia. This is an excellent, modern restaurant attached to a fine old hotel; the views are beautiful, and the fish – freshly caught by Silvio himself – is superbly prepared (mains around €18). Also gluten-free options. Open daily.

Around Bellagio

It's worth venturing out of central Bellagio; the villages flanking the peninsula – Loppia and San Giovanni on the west, Pescallo on the east – offer a rustic tranquillity that's hard to find in town. South of Bellagio, the hilly triangle of land between the two branches of the lake – known as the Triangolo Lariano (ⓦtriangololariano.it) – is lushly forested and often sunny, sometimes busy in a few places on the shore but with plenty of quiet villages speckling the highland interior.

Museo degli Strumenti per la Navigazione

Piazza Don Miotti, San Giovanni • May–Oct daily 10am–1pm • €5.50 • ⓦbellagiomuseo.com

On the west side of Bellagio's peninsula, the Villa Melzi gardens extend south to the characterful harbourside hamlet of **Loppia**, a relatively quiet retreat after Bellagio, from where you can continue for a further ten minutes' stroll to neighbouring **SAN GIOVANNI**, another attractive little village that hosts the **Museo degli Strumenti per la Navigazione** (Navigational Devices), a diverting collection of compasses, telescopes and marine chronometers. San Giovanni has its own landing-stage, where boats stop in on the scheduled route between Bellagio and Villa Carlotta/Tremezzo.

Pescallo

On the eastern side of Bellagio's peninsula, a fifteen-minute walk from the centre on an attractive footpath through vineyards leads to the charming little harbour of **PESCALLO**, a fishing port since Roman times. It can also be reached by car, on a turn-off from the Via Valassina heading south out of Bellagio. As well as a couple of little restaurants, Pescallo offers a tremendous view of the Grigne mountains looming over the Lecco branch of the lake.

Madonna di Ghisallo

Magreglio • June–Aug Mon–Fri 9.30am–5.30pm, Sat & Sun 9am–6pm; April–May & Sept–Oct same hours, closed Mon; March & Nov Sat & Sun 9.30am–5.30pm; closed Dec–Feb • €6 • ⓦ museodelghisallo.it • Bus C36 (3–4 daily; 30min)

South of Bellagio, after the point at which the SS583 branches off to hug the shoreline towards Lecco, the SP41 Via Valassina begins an epic climb on a twisting course up into the mountains, bound eventually for Erba, on the Como–Lecco road 28km south of Bellagio. This is a lovely drive, chiefly through cool, damp forest, green and quiet. The views over the lake from the peak of **Monte San Primo** (1686m), a steep walk of a couple of hours from the end of its signposted branch road, are much photographed – a breathtaking panorama, with Bellagio on the tip of its triangle down in front.

On the SP41 at the top of the ridge behind Bellagio, near **Magreglio**, is the church of **Madonna di Ghisallo**, patron saint of **cyclists** – a diminutive building but a hugely popular draw for weekend day-trippers; the **museum** alongside is packed with trophies, jerseys and cycling memorabilia of all kinds. If you fancy the time-honoured approach (on a bicycle), be prepared for an exceptionally tough climb on slopes of fourteen percent – reckon on two hours or more to cover the 12km from Bellagio. Up here, too, is a café and a monument to cyclists marked "Then God created the bicycle".

Asso

Beyond Madonna di Ghisallo, the road heads down the gently sloping **Valassina** (or **Vallassina**) – not to be confused with the Valsassina near Lecco – for the final 16km to Erba, passing through the quiet little town of **ASSO**, after which the valley was named. Asso is the terminus for stopping trains on a slow line into Milan's Cadorna station.

Northern Lake Como

The northern reach of Lake Como – dubbed **Alto Lario** – can be something of a letdown. Whereas lakes Maggiore and Garda become increasingly attractive the further north you go, the opposite is true on Lake Como. Here, the jagged cliffs and sheer slopes that characterize the lower two-thirds of the lake retreat from the water's edge; instead, the shores comprise marshy plains and reedy inlets, backed by a horizon of peaks. But the main difference is in the towns; there is nowhere here to compare with the charm of a Bellagio or a Varenna. Campsites and caravan parks abound, catering chiefly to holidaying families from northern Europe; venture this way to seek out some quiet corners, and for the excellent museum at **Dongo**.

Rezzonico and Pianello

On the drive north of Menaggio, fast tunnels tempt you inland. Instead, follow *lungolago* signs onto the slow, narrow lakeside road. That way, you'll stumble across **REZZONICO**, a

5

sleepy hamlet of cobbled lanes woven around a thirteenth-century castle, with a steep path leading down past a trickling stream and grazing sheep to the stony beach – one of the quietest bays on the lake (swimming is banned). Adjacent **PIANELLO** is about as tourist-free as Lake Como gets; there's a small campsite here, but otherwise the pedestrianized waterfront features local families strolling, kids playing and old-timers soaking up the rays. Occasional ferries stop by the picturesque fifteenth-century campanile of San Martino. Grab lunch at the village pizzeria, or picnic on the shore.

ARRIVAL AND DEPARTURE	REZZONICO AND PIANELLO
By bus Roughly hourly bus C10 from Menaggio stops at Rezzonico (15min) and Pianello (20min; ⓦ asfautolinee.it). **By boat** Ferries stop at Pianello on the route between	Menaggio/Varenna and Colico (see p.189). Local motorboat operators include ⓦ blueeasyrent.it, who also rent small craft from €30–60/hr.

ACCOMMODATION AND EATING	
Lauro Rezzonico ☏ 0344 50 029, ⓦ hotellauro.com. Tasteful little eco-friendly hotel in a sixteenth-century house just down from Rezzonico's castle, also serving up	decent country cooking in a friendly, welcoming environment. Restaurant closed Mon. €55

Dongo

Past shoreside cliffs roughly 12km north of Menaggio, **DONGO** is another peaceful, fairly downmarket little community at the mouth of the River Albano. A working town for most of its history – iron ore has long been extracted from these hills, exploited by a foundry and steelworks – but Dongo is best known as the place where, on April 27, 1945, the Fascist dictator Mussolini was captured by resistance partisans as he fled towards neutral Switzerland. Mussolini was taken away and shot the next day in Mezzegra, above Tremezzo (see p.203), while fifteen of his loyalists met their end in Dongo's main square. Palazzo Manzi, the former town hall on the square, now hosts one of the area's best museums.

Museo della Fine della Guerra (End of the War Museum)

Piazza Paracchini 6 • Tues–Sun 10am–1pm & 3–6pm • €5 • ⓦ museofineguerradongo.it

Once called Museo della Resistenza (Museum of the Resistance) – but renamed, reportedly by a mayor sensitive to accusations of left-wing sympathies – this splendid little museum was revamped and reopened in 2014 as the **Museo della Fine della Guerra**. It stands as the focus of a region-wide project (see p.202) designed to give greater prominence to the Italian anti-fascist partisans of World War II, who were active in the hills around Lake Como. The museum could fill an absorbing couple of hours, its information boards enlivened with displays of memorabilia and lots of visual interest. Outstanding multimedia exhibits include music, archive recordings and – best of all – video interviews with local figures who were involved in the resistance, giving eyewitness accounts (subtitled in English) of Alpine smuggling escapades and the moment Mussolini was identified and arrested.

ARRIVAL AND INFORMATION	DONGO
By bus Roughly hourly bus C10 from Menaggio stops at Dongo (25min; ⓦ asfautolinee.it). **By boat** Ferries (see p.189) stop at Dongo on the route between Menaggio/Varenna and Colico. Local motorboat operators include ⓦ rentland.it and ⓦ comolakeboats.it,	who both also rent small craft from €50–80/hr. **Dongo tourist office** In the museum (Mon–Sat 9.30am–12.30pm; ☏ 0344 82 572, ⓦ www.comune .dongo.co.it & ⓦ imagolario.com).

ACCOMMODATION AND EATING	
Antica Trattoria Vecchia Pira Via Cassia 5, Stazzona ☏ 0344 88 277. A tumbledown cottage restaurant in the	hills above Dongo that is simply picture-perfect, set above a rushing river, with geraniums in the window box and a

5

scenic terrace. It also delivers on culinary quality; the menu, around €25, features smoked trout, quiche and artichoke risotto alongside local specialities including polenta and *pizzocheri*. Open evenings only & Sun lunch; closed Wed.

Camping Le Vele Via Case Sparse 244, Domaso ☎0344 965 049, ⓦlevele.domaso.it. There's not much to choose between the thirty-odd campsites strung along the northern shores between Pianello and Colico – but this one

stands out for its slightly higher quality, lakefront location and decent sports amenities. Closed Nov–March. Pitch €18

La Trave Via Selva, Stazzona ☎0344 88 688. A friendly little local restaurant in this hillside village reached on twisting roads above Dongo, with its own *salumi* featuring on a €25 house *menù*. Sit out on the shaded terrace to take in the spectacular views. Closed Tues.

Gravedona

ⓦ gravedona.it

GRAVEDONA, 17km north of Menaggio, is one of the few towns on the lake as old as Como, with a lazy waterfront set around a curving bay. Wordsworth set off on a moonlight hike from here, got lost and was unable to sleep, "tormented," he wrote, "by the stings of insects". Nowadays, it's a pleasant enough town for a stroll, though the main reason to stop is to admire the fine twelfth-century carving of a centaur pursuing a deer – an early Christian symbol for the persecution of the Church – which adorns **Santa Maria del Tiglio**, a handsome, striped church on the lake originally built as a baptistry for the adjacent parish church of San Vincenzo. If it's closed, get the key from the green house on the road nearby.

Colico and around

At the northeastern tip of Lake Como, where the lake gives way to the high Alps, stands **COLICO**, the final stop for most ferries and hydrofoils. Just to the north, roads and rail tracks cross the River Adda to skirt the **Pian di Spagna**, a marshy plain named after the fortress built in 1603 by the Spanish ruler of Milan as a defence against the Austrians, whose main route into Italy was down the massive **Valtellina**, east of Colico pointing to the Dolomites. His **Forte di Fuentes** (Aug daily 10am–6pm; April–July & Sept–Oct Sat & Sun 10am–6pm; €5; ⓦfortedifuentes.it) survives in ruins, signposted down a country road off the SP72 behind Colico. Until Roman times, Lake Como extended across this plain; it withdrew to leave the **Lago di Mezzola** – a pleasant distraction if you're continuing north into the **Valchiavenna** and the high Alps. Signposted close to the fort is **Forte Montecchio Nord** (same hours; guided tours hourly; €7, joint ticket with Forte di Fuentes €9; ⓦfortemontecchionord.it), one of Europe's best preserved World War I fortifications, complete with four 149mm guns and a defensive tunnel network hacked out of craggy granite.

Piona

Contiguous with Colico to the south, the lakeside village of **PIONA** gathers around a west-facing suntrap cove. In front of the water there is a modest grass-and-gravel

---

WALKING ABOVE GRAVEDONA

Bus C18 from Dongo and Gravedona heads up to **Peglio** (Mon–Sat every 2hrs; 15–20min; first bus 6.30am), starting-point for the final stage of the **Via dei Monti Lariani** long-distance trail (see p.199) – be prepared for some difficult terrain on this testing walk to Sorico (22km; 8hrs). After a couple of hours meandering through the farming villages of Livo and Barro, the up-and-down begins, crossing streams and tracking through steep-sided valleys past Puii and Trobbio to an Alpine hut on Montalto and onwards, taking in panoramic views from Sass Olt before the final descent through chestnut forests to Sorico, a stopping-point on the C10 bus to Menaggio (approximately hourly; 45min; last bus from Sorico 8pm).

5

beach, a café, a couple of campsites and the Kite Zoo **kiteboarding** school (ⓦkitezoo.it), perfect for kiteboarding fanatics. Boats stop in a few times a day, or it's a walk of barely three minutes from Piona's **train station** – on the Lecco-Varenna-Colico line – down to the beach.

Abbazia di Piona

Abbey: daily 9am–noon & 2–6pm; **Shop**: daily 9.30–11.55am & 2.15–5pm • Free • ⓦ abbaziadipiona.it

Perched on the Olgiasca headland that almost encloses Piona's little lagoon, directly opposite Piona beach, is the Cistercian **Abbazia di Piona**. Reach it via a minor road off the SP72 lakefront road, which leads you 2.6km down a rough cobbled track. The abbey, centred on a Romanesque church dating from the mid-twelfth century, is perfectly tranquil, remote and little visited. A shop at the gates sells bottles of the monks' fiery herb liqueur.

ARRIVAL AND DEPARTURE   **COLICO AND AROUND**

By train There are trains approximately hourly to Colico from Milano Centrale (1hr 25min), Lecco (45min) and Varenna (25min).

By bus Colico is the terminus for the approximately hourly

bus C10 from Como (2hr 15min) and Menaggio (1hr; ⓦasfautolinee.it).

By boat Boats and hydrofoils (see p.189) stop at Colico from points all round the lake.

ACCOMMODATION AND EATING

Agriturismo Forte di Fuentes Via Forte di Fuentes ☎0341 930 128, ⓦcompendiodifuentes.com. A lovely little place to hide away, set in 34 acres deep in the Pian di Spagna countryside beside Colico. This cooperative-run farm – within a stone's throw of the Ranch El Picadero equestrian centre – keeps goats, sheep, chickens, bees, Shetland ponies and other animals, and maintains the surrounding forest. It offers four simple, rustic rooms above the farm shop (Wed–Sun 10am–6pm), which sells honey,

cheese and other local products, and the little on-site restaurant (Wed–Sun by appointment only). Watch trains scoot along below the towering bulk of Monte Legnone (2609m) – snowcapped into June – gaze out across the meadows, catch the odd neigh and let time drift. €35

Camping Logasc Via Laghetto, Piona ☎0341 933 139, ⓦlogasc.com. Easy-going campsite plumb on Piona's beautiful little bay, with a little café/kiosk/bar attached. Pitch €10

Orrido di Bellano

Bellano • July & Aug daily 10am–7pm; April–June & Sept daily 10am–1pm & 2.30–7pm; March, Oct & Nov Sat & Sun 10am–12.30pm & 2.30–5pm; Dec–Feb Sat & Sun 2–5pm • €3 • ⓦ comune.bellano.lc.it

Roughly 13th south of Colico, and 4km north of Varenna, **BELLANO** is an easy-going old town of silk and cotton mills, served both by trains and boats. From the landing-stage, follow signs for the three-minute walk up behind Piazza San Giorgio to the **Orrido di Bellano**, a steep gorge threaded with a series of walkways suspended above a roaring river.

Varenna

Halfway up Lake Como's eastern shore, gazing back at Bellagio and Menaggio, **VARENNA** is perhaps the loveliest spot on the whole lake. Free of through traffic – which is diverted around the village – shaded by pines and planes, and almost completely devoid of souvenir shops, this little cluster of attractive old houses and waterfront cafés is set around steep, narrow alleyways stepping back from the old harbour. It's an unassuming little place which repays however much time you're prepared to devote to it – not least at sunset, illuminated by golden rays while its neighbours across the lake lie in shadow.

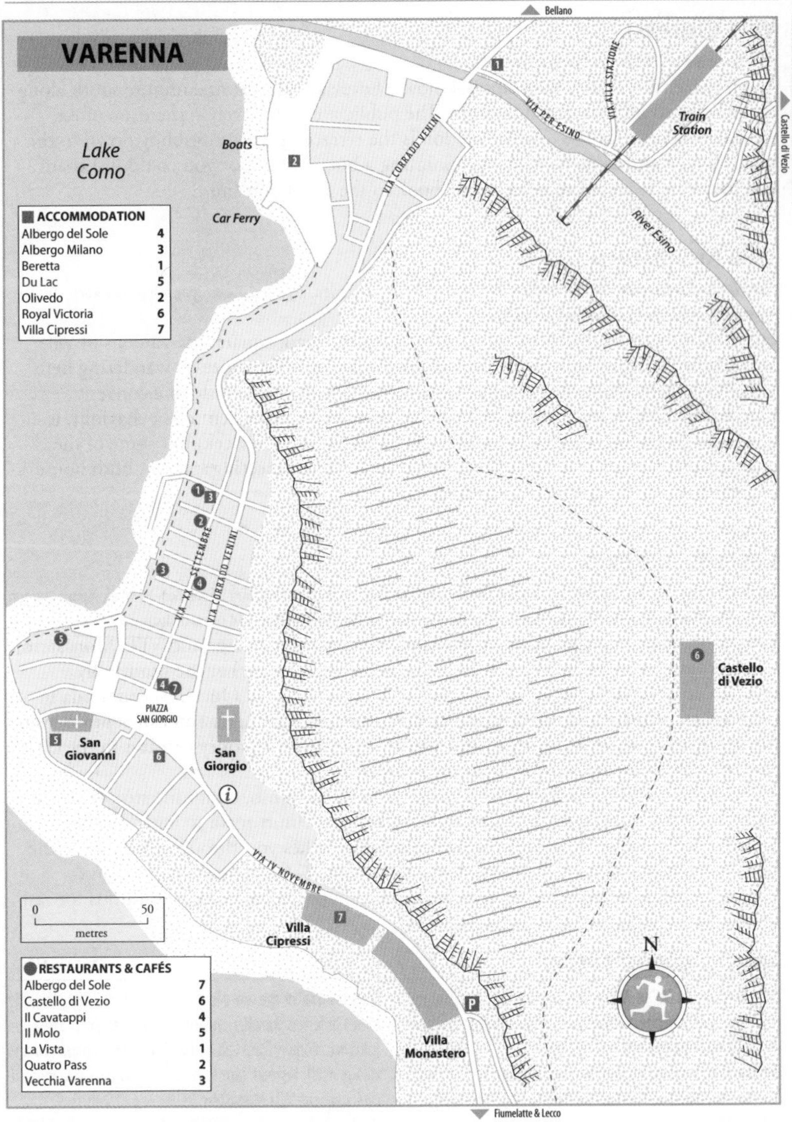

VARENNA

*Lake
Como*

Bellano

Boats

Car Ferry

Train
Station

VIA PER ESINO

VIA ALLA STAZIONE

Castello di Vezio

River Esino

ACCOMMODATION	
Albergo del Sole	4
Albergo Milano	3
Beretta	1
Du Lac	5
Olivedo	2
Royal Victoria	6
Villa Cipressi	7

VIA 20 SETTEMBRE

VIA CORRADO VENINI

PIAZZA
SAN GIORGIO

San
Giovanni

San
Giorgio

Castello
di Vezio

VIA IV NOVEMBRE

0	50
metres	

RESTAURANTS & CAFÉS	
Albergo del Sole	7
Castello di Vezio	6
Il Cavatappi	4
Il Molo	5
La Vista	1
Quatro Pass	2
Vecchia Varenna	3

Villa
Cipressi

Villa
Monastero

N

Fiumelatte & Lecco

Piazza San Giorgio

Thanks to Varenna's rocky shoreline, the village is split into two fragments. From Olivedo, a northern outpost where trains and boats arrive, follow the *passarella*, a scenic walkway which clings to the rocks down at lake level for some 300m, to reach the main part of the village; lanes from the old harbour climb to the main square, **Piazza San Giorgio**, ringed by hotels and cafés and overlooked by the thirteenth-century church of **San Giorgio**. Almost forgotten on a lower corner of the same square stands one of the oldest churches on the lake, the tenth-century **San Giovanni Battista**. Barriers at the south door stop you exploring inside, but you can lean over to see well-preserved, if fragmentary, frescoes inside.

5

Villa Cipressi

Via IV Novembre 18 • March–Oct daily 9am–7pm • €4

The nineteenth-century **Villa Cipressi**, now a hotel, stands just one minute south along the main road off Piazza San Giorgio. The public areas are lovely – there are often weddings here – but the main attraction is the terraced garden tumbling down to the lake. Hotel staff have a brochure pinpointing a botanic trail, or you could just roam and find a perfect spot to relax with a book in the afternoon sun.

Villa Monastero

Via Polvani 4 • **Garden only** March–Oct daily 9.30am–7pm • €5 **House & garden** Aug daily 9.30am–7pm; March–July & Sept–Oct Fri–Sun 9.30am–7pm • €8 • ⓦ villamonastero.eu

On the southern edge of Varenna, a stroll from the main square, the gardens of **Villa Monastero** are even more lavish than at neighbouring Villa Cipressi; wandering here feels like a secret discovery. The splendid house, occupying the site of a convent founded in 1200 but dissolved in 1569 because of its nuns' licentious behaviour, is now used as a conference centre and is off-limits during the week, but some of the most beautiful rooms are accessible at weekends. When meetings are on, both house and gardens can be closed at short notice.

Castello di Vezio

Vezio • July & Aug Mon–Fri 10am–7pm, Sat & Sun 10am–8pm; June daily 10am–7pm; April, May & Sept Mon–Fri 10am–6pm, Sat & Sun 10am–7pm; March & Oct Mon–Fri 10am–5pm, Sat & Sun 10am–6pm; closed in bad weather • €4 • ⓦ castellodivezio.it

Steep paths creep up the hillside from opposite the landing-stage and Villa Monastero, meeting (after a stiff climb of 30–40 minutes, perhaps longer) at the beautifully restored **Castello di Vezio**, allegedly founded by the Lombard Queen Theodolinda in the seventh century and offering spectacular views over the lake. You can venture inside to explore the towers and turrets, and also take in regular falconry displays in the castle gardens; schedules are published on the website.

The castle is also accessible by car; at the seventh hairpin bend up the steep hill past Varenna's train station, turn off at a sign for Vezio to climb again to a parking area outside Vezio village. A signposted stroll from here takes you through the lanes to the late-Romanesque church of **Sant'Antonio Abate** (Sat 2–6pm, Sun 10am–noon & 2–5pm), with fifteenth-century frescoes inside, above which a footpath climbs the last few puff-inducing metres to the castle itself.

ARRIVAL AND DEPARTURE

VARENNA

By plane From Milan-Malpensa airport, take the train or bus to Milano Centrale station, then catch a train from there direct to Varenna (approx hourly; 1hr).

By train Regular trains (approx hourly) serve Varenna from Milano Centrale (1hr) and Lecco (20min), on the line towards Colico. From Bergamo, take a local train to Lecco and change there. The station (titled "Varenna-Esino") is located on the hillside above Olivedo, a short walk on steep streets above the landing-stage. It is unstaffed; buy tickets on the train. Timetables are at ⓦ www.muoversi.regione.lombardia.it.

By car Varenna is 22km north of Lecco on the SS36

"superstrada" or the more leisurely (and scenic) SP72 lakeside road. Car ferries shuttle regularly from Menaggio and Bellagio (plus occasionally from Cadenabbia). There is no parking in the village itself; instead, aim for the large car park dug into the cliffs opposite Villa Monastero (€2/hr or €20/24hrs).

By boat Boats (see p.189) shuttle frequently to Varenna from Menaggio, Bellagio and other points. Passenger ships, hydrofoils and car ferries dock beside each other in Olivedo, a short walk from Varenna village itself. Timetables are at ⓦ navigazionelaghi.it. Local motorboat operators include ⓦ taxiboatvarenna.com and ⓦ boats2rent-varenna.net.

INFORMATION

Tourist office Piazza San Giorgio (May–Sept Tues–Sat 10am–1pm & 2–7pm, Sun 10am–1pm; restricted hours in winter; ☎0341 830 367, ⓦ varennaturismo.com &

ⓦ comune.varenna.lc.it).
Useful website ⓦ lakecomo.com.

5

ACCOMMODATION

Several of Varenna's **hotels** – tucked away in the web of narrow, stepped lanes running down from the main road to the rocky shore – are difficult or impossible to reach in a vehicle. If you are arriving by car, check arrangements in advance with reception staff.

Albergo del Sole Piazza San Giorgio 17 ☎0341 815 218, ⓦsolevarenna.altervista.org. Excellent three-star hotel in the village centre. Rooms are light, airy and modern – some with lake views, others overlooking the piazza – and service is warm and courteous. **€140**

★**Albergo Milano** Via XX Settembre 35 ☎0341 830 298, ⓦvarenna.net. One of Lake Como's friendliest, best-looking small hotels lies tucked away in the narrow lanes between the square and the waterfront. It's justifiably popular, not least for its modern design – a breath of fresh air amid fusty old lake hotels. Well run by a charming couple, it has great views from the rooms and terrace, and an effortless air of cool romance. Evening meals, out on that terrace, are memorable. The eight rooms in the main building are supplemented by the *Casa Rossa* (Red House) annexe nearby and two self-contained apartments. Closed Nov–Feb. **€150**

Beretta Via per Esino 1 ☎0341 830 132. Welcoming place above a locals' bar near the train station that is the best of the cheaper options in town. It's also the hotel most likely to have room if you haven't booked ahead. **€70**

Du Lac Via del Prestino 11 ☎0341 830 238, ⓦalbergodulac.com. Varenna's top hotel – a romantic 1823 villa hidden away in a corner of the village right on the waterfront. The renovations have retained much of the old charm; public areas are elegant but not stuffy, rooms are spacious and airy. Solid four-star quality. **€165**

Olivedo Piazza Martiri 14 ☎0341 830 115, ⓦolivedo .it. Cheery, atmospheric little family-run hotel opposite the landing-stage, stuffed with old prints and knick-knacks, with a busy terrace bar out front. The location is a plus if you love watching lots of comings-and-goings on the car ferries – or a minus if you're seeking romantic tranquillity. **€140**

Royal Victoria Piazza San Giorgio 2 ☎0341 815 111, ⓦroyalvictoria.com. Landmark hotel on the main square with spacious rooms, stunning lake views and amiable service. Recently renovated, it now sports interiors revamped in what is claimed to be original nineteenth-century colours and decor (that's debatable; the work is unmistakeably contemporary, and the bathrooms, thankfully, are resolutely up-to-date). **€220**

Villa Cipressi Via IV Novembre 18 ☎0341 830 113, ⓦhotelvillacipressi.it. Curiously characterless rooms for such a wonderful old house. There's absolutely nothing wrong with them – they're rather good three-star quality, modern and well maintained – but you can't help feeling such a gorgeous setting deserves more. That said, the villa is often booked out for events; reserve well ahead. **€170**

EATING AND DRINKING

Albergo del Sole Piazza San Giorgio 17 ☎0341 815 218, ⓦsolevarenna.altervista.org. Great little pizzeria attached to this small hotel on the main square, with a meal coming to €25 or less a head. Closed Wed.

Castello di Vezio ☎333 448 5975, ⓦcastellodivezio .it. In front of the castle, on the mountainside high above Varenna, there's a little terrace café-restaurant. You wouldn't go out of your way to eat here, but if you're visiting the castle, you could pause for lunch; the menu is decidedly rustic and simple, but it's tasty stuff and most of the ingredients come from nearby organic farms. Eat for around €12. Open during castle hours only (see p.222).

★**Il Cavatappi** Via XX Settembre ☎0341 815 349, ⓦilcavatappivarenna.it. Hidden away in the narrow lanes off the main piazza, Varenna's best place to eat is also its smallest – it has just five tables. Booking is essential for this delightful little restaurant, where the owner/manager/chef takes the time to discuss the menu with you before turning out simple, beautifully cooked dishes with first-

---

FIUMELATTE

A short walk south of Varenna, the hamlet of **FIUMELATTE** ("River of Milk") is named after the seasonal torrent which tumbles frothily through it for half the year – starting abruptly in March and running dry just as suddenly in October. Leonardo da Vinci was fascinated by the phenomenon, and tried to find out why it occurred; he drew a blank – as, indeed, have modern scientists. This is also the shortest river in Italy (and perhaps Europe), just 250m from source to outflow, though it's not easy to find, flowing in a narrow, steep channel between cottages. From Varenna's main square, head south for 200m, then take a path up the hillside to a cemetery, from where steps climb steeply to a higher path which contours south for 1km to the river's source.

5

class ingredients. A meal is around €30 a head. Closed Wed.

Il Molo Via Riva Garibaldi14 ☎ 0341 830 070, ⓦ barilmolo.it. Very pleasant little café-bar down on the old fishing harbour, with a broad selection of snacks, drinks, light meals, salads and desserts, served until 1am. Credit cards accepted over €25. Open daily.

La Vista At Albergo Milano, Via XX Settembre 35 ☎ 0341 830 298, ⓦ varenna.net. A spectacular terrace perched high above the lake is the perfect setting for a romantic dinner of light, tasty Mediterranean cuisine. Expect a bill around €35–40. Evenings only. Closed Tues & Sun.

Quatro Pass Via XX Settembre 20 ☎ 0341 815 091, ⓦ quattropass.com. Cosy little *osteria* occupying a vaulted cellar in the heart of the old lanes, serving authentic, well-presented local and seasonal cuisine. Prices are modest and the service is genuinely warm and outgoing; this place is not a secret, but it takes care to deliver a culinary experience to remember. Closed Mon–Wed in winter.

Vecchia Varenna Contrada Scoscesa 10 ☎ 0341 830 793, ⓦ vecchiavarenna.it. In an unbeatable location, tucked beneath the arcades on the lakeside promenade by the fishing harbour. Book ahead in summer for a table on the terrace – but the location beats the food, which is acceptable but not remarkable (mains €12–20). Closed Mon.

Lake Lecco

Flanked by mountains of scored granite, Lake Como's eastern fork is austere and fjord-like, at its most atmospheric in the morning mists. This the branch of the lake that terminates at Lecco; it's often dubbed "Lago di Lecco" (**Lake Lecco**), even though it is an integral part of the whole. It is quieter than elsewhere and much less visited – the villages wedged along the shoreline are generally fairly ordinary. Overshadowing it all are the craggy peaks of the **Grigne** range, which rise above the eastern shoreline to 2400m and culminate in the saw-like ridge of Monte Resegone (1875m) above the town of Lecco itself. Tourist offices can supply details of hikes in the **Valsassina**, an isolated rural valley that follows a curving course behind the Grigne peaks.

The road along Lake Lecco's **western shore** for the 20km between Bellagio and Lecco is slow and tortuous. Some 8km south of Pescallo, on Bellagio's outskirts, stands **OLIVETO**, with a sprinkling of small restaurants and views of the brooding peaks across the water.

Mandello del Lario

The main highway along Lake Como's **eastern shore** spends most of the 23km between Varenna and Lecco dipping in and out of tunnels, although a quiet minor road dawdles along the waterfront. **Lierna**, 6km south of Varenna, is a pretty little place, with its medieval adjunct of Castello occupying a picturesque, beach-girt peninsula, but the main settlement here is **MANDELLO DEL LARIO**, an industrial town that has been the production centre of Italy's famous **Moto Guzzi** motorbikes since 1921; there's a **museum** of vintage specimens at Via Parodi 57 (guided tours Mon–Fri 3pm; closed Aug; free; ⓦ motoguzzi.it). Just south is the old silk-town of **Abbadia Lariana**, much modernized.

Lecco

Located 30km east of Como at the foot of this branch of the lake, **LECCO** is a commercial town, though prettily spread around its little stretch of waterfront beneath towering mountains. The principal draw for Italians is that Lecco was the childhood home of the novelist **Alessandro Manzoni** (1785–1873), and was the setting for his classic work *I Promessi Sposi* (*The Betrothed*), published in 1827 – the first novel to be written in a pan-national Italian, and the first to paint Italian history in terms of its effect on ordinary individuals. It is required reading in Italian schools to this day. The tourist office and the town oblige with a torrent of Manzoniana; a brochure pinpoints the locations around Lecco of various scenes in the novel, while Piazza Manzoni in the

5

GIROLARIO: FROM LECCO TO BELLAGIO

The **GiroLario** day pass (June–Sept only; €15) covers a discounted boat journey from Lecco to Bellagio, another boat from Bellagio to Como, and a less romantic hour's bus ride from Como back to Lecco. It is outlined in detail at ⓦnavigazionelaghi.it. Because the buses run fairly late (last bus Como–Lecco 9pm in Aug, or 8.30pm in June, July & Sept), you can dawdle – or, alternatively, not start out from Lecco until mid-afternoon and still be back for dinner. However, you're not allowed to break the journey (other than at Bellagio and Como) and you can't backtrack. The route is also possible from and to Como.

centre holds a grand statue of the author. The **Villa Manzoni**, Via Guanella 1 – where the writer grew up – is open as a museum (Tues–Sun 9.30am–5.30pm; €5; ⓦmuseilecco.org).

All this leaves most non-Italian visitors cold, and Lecco has little else to offer other than natural beauty (though there's plenty of that). As you stroll the lakefront, past the **Torre Viscontea** – remnant of a medieval castle – at one end of the main Piazza XX Settembre, you could pop into the **Basilica**, which boasts a set of fourteenth-century Giotto-esque frescoes. The most attractive part of town is **Pescarenico**, an old fishermen's quarter located on the north bank of the River Adda as it flows out of Lake Como on its way into Lake Garlate. It's an atmospheric spot, with narrow alleys and a picturesque, sixteenth-century riverfront piazza.

ARRIVAL AND INFORMATION   LECCO

By train Lecco is served by trains from Varenna (approx hourly; 20min), Milano Centrale (approx hourly; 45min) and Bergamo (approx hourly; 45min). Two or three trains a day arrive from Como (1hr 5min). Timetables are at ⓦwww.muoversi.regione.lombardia.it.

By bus Lecco's main link with Como is the C40/D41 bus (approx every 30min; 1hr 10min; ⓦasfautolinee.it). Bus LB

serves Bellagio (approx every 2hrs; 50min; ⓦlineelecco.it).

By boat Boats run between Bellagio and Lecco every day in summer, and on Sundays only in spring and autumn. There's no service in winter. Timetables at ⓦnavigazionelaghi.it.

Tourist office Piazza XX Settembre (Mon–Sat 9am–1pm & 2–5pm; ☏0341 295 720, ⓦlakecomo.com).

ACCOMMODATION AND EATING

Don Abbondio Piazza Era 10 ☏0341 366 315, ⓦdonabbondio.com. With Como, Bellagio, Varenna and Bergamo close, there's not much need to stay in Lecco – but

this three-star option in Pescarenico, is a decent option, with a scenic riverside location, pleasant balconied rooms and a moderately priced restaurant. **€100**

Bergamo

Bergamo

Just 50km northeast of Milan, yet much closer to the mountains in look and feel, Bergamo is the second most important city on the Lombard plain. Having spent several centuries under Venetian rule, its art and architecture are noticeably different from much of Lombardy. Today, Bergamo is an appealing city that takes food and fashion seriously and the handsome medieval quarter, high on a hill overlooking the modern city, has a beguiling charm that makes it an essential stop on any visit to the region. In touch with the mountains too, Bergamo is surrounded by wooded slopes that hint at the great Alpine peaks just a few kilometres to the north, where the high valleys draw weekend skiers all winter long.

The city comprises two distinct parts – **Bergamo Bassa**, the modern city centre on the plain, and medieval **Bergamo Alta**, clinging to the rocky slopes 100m higher (the city's name derives from the Celtic *berg-heim*, or "home on the hill").

The Città Bassa is a harmonious mixture of medieval cobbled quarters blending into late nineteenth- and early twentieth-century town planning – but the historic Città Alta is one of northern Italy's loveliest urban centres, a favourite retreat for the work-weary Milanese, who flock here at weekends seeking solace in its fresh mountain air, picturesque lanes and the lively but easy-going pace of its life.

Bergamo owes much of its magic to the **Venetians**, who ruled here for over 350 years, building houses and palaces with fancy Gothic windows and adorning facades and open spaces with the Venetian lion, symbol of the republic. (The *bergamasche* like to say they still look east for their inspiration, conveniently showing their backsides to Milan in the process.) The Venetians' most striking legacy is the ring of gated **walls** that encircles the Città Alta. Now worn, mellow and overgrown with creepers, they kept armies out until the French invaded in 1796 and today enclose a dense network of cobbled alleyways weaving around the set-piece **Piazza Vecchia** and adjacent church of **Santa Maria Maggiore**. Just outside the walls in the Città Bassa, the **Accademia Carrara,** under renovation at the time of research, holds one of Italy's leading provincial art collections.

The upper town: Bergamo Alta

Bergamo's upper town, the **Città Alta** is a remarkably rich urban environment, still enclosed by its sixteenth-century Venetian walls. The appearance of the narrow, steep streets, flanked by high facades, remains largely as it was in the Middle Ages, but the main public spaces – **Piazza Vecchia** and adjacent **Piazza del Duomo** – combine medieval austerity with the grace of Renaissance design. The main street, beginning as **Via Gombito** and continuing as **Via Colleoni**, follows the line of the Roman *decumanus maximus*, topped and tailed by evidence of Bergamo's military past – the **Rocca** to the east, the **Cittadella** to the west.

The best place to start exploring is Piazza Mercato delle Scarpe, at the top station of the nineteenth-century **funicular** that rises from Viale Vittorio Emanuele II

| Treno Blu p.239 | Bergamo's B&Bs p.240 |

Highlights

❶ Bergamo Alta Bergamo's historic upper town makes for endlessly fascinating roaming and wonderful views. **See p.228**

❷ Funicular railway Trundle up past ornate villas and landscaped gardens for a bird's-eye view of the city and surrounding countryside. **See p.228**

❸ Piazza Vecchia The focal point of Bergamo Alta and one of Italy's great Renaissance squares. **See p.231**

❹ San Vigilio A world away from the lower town bustle, admire the glorious views from the very top of town. **See p.234**

❺ Accademia Carrara Bergamo's wonderful gallery that is among Italy's best, with works by Botticelli, Titian, Raphael and others. **See p.238**

❻ Polenta On a foggy winter evening there's nothing more comforting than a plate of steaming polenta with stew, salami or melted cheeses. Try some at *Lalimentari*. **See p.241**

❼ La Marianna An ice cream from Bergamo's famous *gelateria* is unbeatable. They claim to have invented *stracciatella*. **See p.241**

❽ Clusone This medieval mountain village with its Liberty houses and Danse Macabre frescoes gives a taste of the Bergamasco valleys rarely visited by foreigners. **See p.242**

HIGHLIGHTS ARE MARKED ON THE MAPS ON P.230, P.232 & P.235

(bus 1 serves its lower station). From here, the old town spreads up the hill in front of you. Alternatively, stay on bus 1 to **Colle Aperto**, at the top (western) end of the Città Alta, and then walk back down through the old streets. The bus and funicular both run frequently throughout the day and evening (see p.239).

The thirty-minute uphill **walk** from the Città Bassa is well worth doing; take bus 2 from the station (or any bus east from Porta Nuova along Via Camozzi), get off at

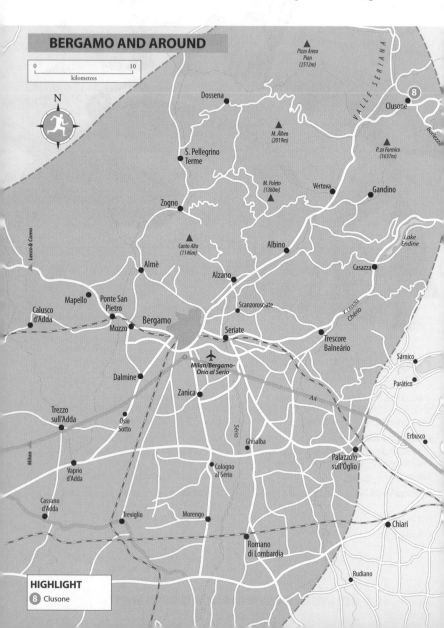

BERGAMO AND AROUND

HIGHLIGHT

8 Clusone

Via Pignolo and head left up this attractive street, lined with sixteenth- and seventeeth-century *palazzi*, to Porta Sant'Agostino (see p.236), from where Via Porta Dipinta climbs to Piazza Mercato delle Scarpe.

Piazza Mercato delle Scarpe

Piazza Mercato delle Scarpe – literally, Shoe Market Square – is an atmospheric introduction to Bergamo's medieval upper town, utterly removed from the bustle of the modern streets below. The funicular station is housed in the fourteenth-century Palazzo Suardi, subsequently the cobblers' guildhall (hence the square's title), faced by a now-disused fountain installed in 1486. Opposite, café tables spread out beneath an attractive medieval portico.

As in antiquity, this square marks a meeting of roads. With the funicular at your back, **Via Porta Dipinta** heads down to the right towards Sant'Agostino, while **Via San Giacomo** descends to the left to another gate in the walls; both of these are broad streets lined with *palazzi*. On the left, the attractive **Via Donizetti** climbs past the former mint (at no. 18) on its way towards Piazza Giuliani behind the Duomo. On the right, **Via Rocca** and, through a passage beside it, **Via Solata** both climb towards the Rocca (see p.236).

Via Gombito

The main street of the upper town, **Via Gombito**, is a narrow lane squeezed between five-storey buildings that leads off the top of Piazza Mercato delle Scarpe. Shops jostle for attention at street level, an intriguing mixture of delis and butchers, fashion boutiques, bars and places to eat. Look up to the higher floors to catch some beautiful examples of Venetian-influenced architecture – ornate balconies, arched windows and some faded frescoes. On the right, to one side of the fifteenth-century church of **San Pancrazio**, three fine medieval tower-houses survive in **Piazza Mercato del Fieno** (Hay Market), near the San Francesco museum (see p.234).

Torre del Gombito

Via Gombito 13 • Daily 9am–5.30pm • €7 • ☎ 035 242 226

The twelfth-century **Torre del Gombito** looms 52m above the main street and today the ground floor houses the tourist office. It's worth climbing up to the top of the tower for incredible views over the old town and the valley below – you'll have to book a time slot at the tourist office before heading up.

Piazza Vecchia

Bergamo's *coup de théâtre* is the magnificent Renaissance **Piazza Vecchia**, a broad, open square enclosed by a harmonious miscellany of buildings, ranging from wrought-iron-balconied houses containing cafés and restaurants to the opulent Palladian-style **Palazzo Nuovo**, now housing the civic library (on the right as you enter from Via Gombito). Stendhal rather enthusiastically dubbed this "the most beautiful square on earth", and certainly it's a striking open space. The piazza was the scene of joyous celebrations in 1797, when the French formed the Republic of Bergamo; the square, carpeted with tapestries, was transformed into an open-air ballroom in which – as a symbol of the new democracy – dances were led by an aristocrat partnered by a butcher.

Palazzo della Ragione

The medieval **Palazzo della Ragione**, a Venetian-Gothic building that stretches across the piazza directly opposite the Palazzo Nuovo, dates from the mid-twelfth century, though its splendid arched windows over the square were added in 1453. Court cases used to be heard under the open arcades that form the ground floor. A grand covered stairway – the piazza's most eye-catching feature, also dating from 1453 – rises from alongside to the palazzo's upper floor.

Torre Civica

Piazza Vecchia 8 • April–Oct Tues–Fri 9.30am–6pm, Sat & Sun 9.30am–8pm; Nov–March Tues–Fri 9.30am–1pm & 2.30–6pm, Sat & Sun 9.30am–6pm • €3; combined ticket with Museo Donizettiano, Museo Storico (Rocca) and Museo Storico (Convento di San Francesco) €7

It's worth heading up the massive **Torre Civica**, or **Campanone**, which you can ascend by lift or lots of stairs, for the wonderful views over the old city. Its seventeenth-century bell, which narrowly escaped being melted down by the Germans during World War II, still tolls every half-hour. At 10pm the bells ring out one hundred times as they have done since they pealed to warn everyone that the city gates were closing for the night.

Piazza del Duomo

The small **Piazza del Duomo** was almost certainly the site of the Roman forum. On the left is the incongruous 1886 facade of the **Duomo**, formerly the church of San

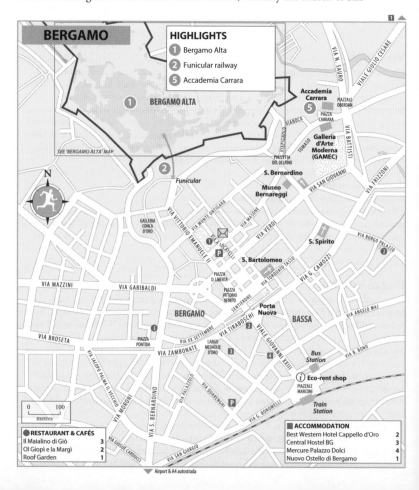

BERGAMO

HIGHLIGHTS
1. Bergamo Alta
2. Funicular railway
5. Accademia Carrara

RESTAURANT & CAFÉS
Il Maialino di Giò	3
Ol Giopì e la Margì	2
Roof Garden	1

ACCOMMODATION
Best Western Hotel Cappello d'Oro	2
Central Hostel BG	3
Mercure Palazzo Dolci	4
Nuovo Ostello di Bergamo	1

Vincenzo, dating from well before 1100. It's worth a brief look, though the interior was extensively mucked about with through the seventeenth and eighteenth centuries, from when much of the art dates.

Museo e Tesoro della Cattedrale

Piazza Duomo • Tues–Sun 9.30am–1pm & 2–6.30pm • €5 • ☎ 035 248 772, ⓦ fondazionebernareggi.it

A series of complex excavations between 2004 and 2012 revealed the presence of a Roman settlement, an early Christian cathedral and a subsequent Roman cathedral in the subsoil of the Duomo. The site had already been inhabited in the tenth century BC, and, between the first century BC and the fourth century BC, was occupied by a Roman quarter with commercial streets lined with stores, workshops and domus with beautiful decorations. In the fifth century BC, the largest sacred building of the city was built here – a sizeable cathedral dedicated to Saint Vincent, which corresponds to the perimeter of the present-day church. The ruins of the Roman citadel and the church's beautiful frescoes can be seen at this wonderful museum, along with findings and other precious objects from that time.

Santa Maria Maggiore

Piazza Duomo 3 • Mon–Sat 9am–12.30pm & 2.30–6pm, Sun 9am–1pm & 3–6pm; Nov–March closes 5pm • Free

The splendid twelfth-century Basilica of **Santa Maria Maggiore**, built over an eighth-century predecessor, has a Gothic north portal on the square, decorated with Romanesque lions and, above, an equestrian statue of Alexander, Bergamo's patron saint. It's worth walking round the exterior; this is one of Lombardy's best **Romanesque** churches, and the apse and minor portals are all beautiful examples of the style. The rather stubby interior – with a floor plan that is almost a Greek cross – is a different kettle of fish, dating from a late-sixteenth century makeover. It is extraordinarily elaborate, its ceiling marzipanned with ornament in the finest tradition of **Baroque excess**, encrusted with gilded stucco, painted vignettes and languishing statues. The confessional (1704), by Andrea Fantoni, displays stunning artistry, festooned with cherubs, saints and prophets and topped by a flaming orb. There's a piece of nineteenth-century kitsch, too – a monument to Bergamo's most famous son, **Donizetti** (see p.234), composer of comic opera, who died from syphilis here in 1848; bas-relief putti stamp their feet and smash their lyres in misery. More subtly, the intarsia biblical scenes on the choir stalls – designed by **Lorenzo Lotto**, and executed by a local craftsman – are remarkable not only for their intricacy but also for the incredible colour range of the natural wood.

Cappella Colleoni

Piazza Duomo • Daily 9am–12.30pm & 2–6pm; Nov–Feb closes 4.30pm & Mon • Free

Built onto Santa Maria in the 1470s, the Renaissance **Cappella Colleoni** chapel is an extravagant confection of pastel-coloured marble carved into an abundance of miniature arcades, balustrades and twisted columns, and capped with a mosque-like dome. Commissioned by Bartolomeo Colleoni, a Bergamo mercenary in the pay of Venice, it was designed by the Pavian sculptor Giovanni Amadeo (who was also responsible for the equally excessive Certosa di Pavia). The opulent interior, with a ceiling frescoed in the eighteenth century by Tiepolo, holds Colleoni's sarcophagus, encrusted with reliefs and statuettes and topped with a gleaming, gilded equestrian statue. There's also the more modest tomb of his daughter, Medea, who died aged 15. Note Colleoni's coat-of-arms on the gate as you enter; the smoothness of the third "testicle" (supposedly biologically true) bears witness to the local tradition that rubbing it will bring you luck.

Outside on the square is the free standing **Baptistry** (kept locked), which was removed from the interior of Santa Maria Maggiore in the seventeenth century when christenings were transferred to the Duomo. Behind, at the back of Santa Maria Maggiore, is the bulbous **Tempietto di Santa Croce**, dating from the tenth century.

Museo Donizettiano

Via Arena 9 · June–Sept Tues–Sun 9.30am–1pm & 2.30–6pm; Oct–May Tues–Fri 9.30am–1pm, Sat & Sun 9.30am–1pm & 2.30–6pm
· €5; combined ticket with Campanone, Museo Storico (Rocca) and Museo Storico (Convento di San Francesco) €7 · ☎ 035 247 116,
Ⓦ bergamoestoria.it

The Palazzo della Misericordia, tucked away off a series of picturesque narrow streets on the western end of town, is the home of the **Museo Donizettiano**, dedicated to the opera composer Gaetano Donizetti (1797–1848). Donizetti, who was born and died in Bergamo, was, along with Bellini and Rossini, one of the masters of the "bel canto" style, celebrated for his melodramatic lyricism, which reached a peak in *Lucia di Lammermoor*. The museum holds display cases of original letters and scores, as well as portraits of the maestro. Other rooms hold his imperial-style bed and a collection of musical instruments, including a harmonium and a rectangular-cased fortepiano belonging to Donizetti's patron and mentor, Simon Mayr.

Via Colleoni

Leading away from Piazza Vecchia, the narrow main street continues as **Via Colleoni**, lined with pastry shops selling chocolate and sweet polenta cakes topped with sugar-icing birds. Among the boutiques and shops, **Sant'Agata del Carmine** is an attractive single-naved church of the fifteenth century.

Via Colleoni leads into the rectangular, tree-shaded **Piazza Mascheroni**; to the right, views open out over the city and mountains. Passing beneath the **Torre della Campanella** (1355), you enter the **Piazza della Cittadella**, a military stronghold built by Barnabo Visconti that originally occupied the entire western chunk of the upper town. The remaining buildings now house a small theatre and two didactic museums, one of archaeology, the other of natural history.

Colle Aperto and San Vigilio

The **Colle Aperto**, with views out beyond the city wall across Bergamo Bassa, is accessed through the outer gateway of the Cittadella. Just through the **Porta Sant'Alessandro** to one side, a **funicular** rises on a short, steep course to **San Vigilio** – the walk alongside the track is also pleasant, up a steep, narrow road overlooking the gardens and villas. The view from the summit, topped by the **Castello** and a sprinkling of bars and restaurants, is wonderful. Wander left out of the funicular station round on Via San Vigilio to the panoramic viewpoint with lovely vistas across the ornate gardens of Bergamo's most prestigious summer retreats.

Returning to the Colle Aperto, you can either walk back through the Città Alta or follow the old **walls** around its circumference – the whole circuit takes a couple of hours. The most picturesque stretch is from the Colle Aperto to Porta San Giacomo, from where a long flight of steps leads back down into the lower city through the vegetable patches and orchards growing in the shade of the walls.

Ex Convento di San Francesco

Piazza Mercato del Fieno 6/a · June–Sept Tues–Fri 9.30am–1pm & 2.30–6pm, Sat & Sun 9.30am–7pm; Oct–May Tues–Sun 9.30am–1pm & 2.30–6pm · Free; prices vary for the temporary exhibitions · Ⓦ bergamoestoria.org

It's worth taking a quick look at the ex-convent of **San Francesco**, with its beautiful thirteenth-century cloister. In the nineteenth century the convent served as a barracks and prison, which sadly caused irreparable damage to the building. The adjacent building houses temporary exhibitions spanning the history of the city from the eighteenth century to 1945.

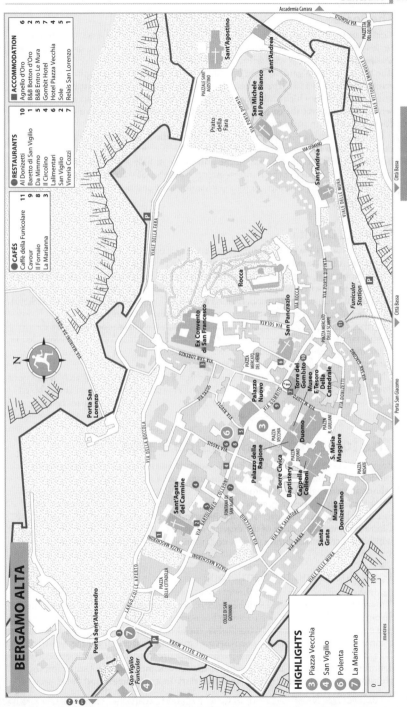

BERGAMO ALTA

Accademia Carrara

● CAFÉS
Caffè della Funicolare | 11
Cavour | 9
Il Fornaio | 8
La Marianna | 3

● RESTAURANTS
Al Donizetti | 10
Baretto di San Vigilio | 1
Da Mimmo | 5
Il Circolino | 4
L'alimentari | 6
San Vigilio | 2
Vineria Cozzi | 7

■ ACCOMMODATION
Agnello d'Oro | 6
B&B Botton d'Oro | 2
B&B Entro Le Mura | 3
Gombit Hotel | 7
Hotel Piazza Vecchia | 4
Sole | 5
Relais San Lorenzo | 1

HIGHLIGHTS

3 Piazza Vecchia
4 San Vigilio
6 Polenta
7 La Marianna

The Rocca

Piazzalle Brigata Legnano • **Grounds** April–Sept 9am–8pm; Oct & March 10am–6pm; Nov–Feb 10am–5.30pm • Free • **Museum** June–Sept Tues–Fri 9.30am–1pm & 2.30–6pm, Sat & Sun 9.30am–7pm; Oct–May Tues–Sun 9.30am–1pm & 2.30–6pm • €5; combined ticket with Campanone, Museo Storico (Convento di San Francesco) and Museo Donizettiano €7 • ⓦ bergamoestoria.it

The beautiful **Rocca** gardens were probably the site of the Roman Capitol, rebuilt and reinforced in the 1330s. The gardens make a great spot for a picnic with cannons and armoured vehicles which children can clamber over. The views from its grounds are sensational, out over the eastern parts of the Città Alta; the Gothic frontage of Sant'Agostino is in plain view far below.

Within the castle or Rocca itself is an outpost of the Museo Storico – the nineteenth-century section focusing on the Italian Wars of Unification, the Risorgimento. Bergamo is very proud of its role in the unification of Italy and is known as the "Città dei Mille" – "City of the thousand" – after the number of volunteers from the city who donned the famous red shirts to join Garibaldi's army and fight in Sicily and the south of the country.

Via Porta Dipinta

The elegant street **Via Porta Dipinta** is lined with seventeenth- and eighteenth-century *palazzi*. Past the church of **Sant'Andrea**, mentioned as early as 785 but rebuilt in 1840 – with a fine altarpiece of the *Madonna and Saints* by Moretto – stands the quiet little church of **San Michele al Pozzo Bianco** (daily 9am–noon & 2–5pm), overlooking a junction of streets. The atmospheric interior – with a supporting structure of medieval arches – holds an array of frescoes, including works by Lorenzo Lotto.

Further down, Via Porta Dipinta skirts the open, grassy **Fara**, dominated by the Gothic facade of the deconsecrated **Sant'Agostino**, a beautiful, lofty church founded in 1290 and now used for temporary art exhibitions. The adjacent ex-convent houses the Faculty of Letters and Philosophy of Bergamo University.

Just below, cars and buses line up at traffic lights to shoot the central arch of the stout **Porta Sant'Agostino**. From outside the gate, **Via Pignolo** and the stepped and cobbled **Via della Noca** head down into the twisting streets of the medieval quarter below.

The lower town: Bergamo Bassa

Bergamo's lower town – the **Città Bassa** – spreads north from the train station in a comfortable blend of Neoclassical ostentation, Fascist severity and leafy elegance. Wandering through the **Sentierone**, an open, tree-lined piazza alongside the central **Porta Nuova**, is the best way to get a feel for the area. From here, it's a pleasant walk east into the medieval quarter of **Borgo Pignolo**, with an atmosphere that presages the Città Alta lanes. At the top of the district, a short walk from the upper town walls, stands the **Accademia Carrara** gallery, under renovation at the time of writing.

Porta Nuova and the Sentierone

At the heart of the busy, trafficy lower town, midway along the main Viale Papa Giovanni XXIII, the mock-Doric temples of the **Porta Nuova** mark the **Sentierone**, a favourite spot for Bergamo's citizens to meet and stroll beneath the trees. The area was laid out by Roman architect Marcello Piacentini in the 1920s with a plan focused on traditional elements – loggias, porticoes and piazzas – that preserved the Sentierone, a Bergamasque rendezvous since the 1620s, and maintained a visual and aesthetic connection between the upper and lower towns. Piacentini's arcades still flank this pleasant spot, along with the eighteenth-century **Teatro Donizetti** and the church of

San Bartolomeo, which holds a *Madonna with Child* by Lorenzo Lotto (1516). Frowning down on the square is the **Palazzo di Giustizia**, built in the bombastic rectangular style of the Mussolini era, while the rather more elegant **Torre dei Caduti** (1924) rises ahead, above Piazza Veneto. Off to the west is pedestrianized Via XX Settembre, the city's main shopping street, leading to the medieval porticoes of Piazza Pontida at its western end.

6 Via Pignolo

From the Sentierone, **Via Torquato Tasso** leads east into the oldest part of the Città Bassa. Marking the junction with the old medieval thoroughfare of **Via Pignolo** is the Renaissance church of **Santo Spirito**, originally fourteenth-century, with Lorenzo Lotto's altarpiece of the *Blessed Virgin Enthroned* (1521) and an eight-section polyptych by Ambrogio Bergognone (1507). The Borgo Pignolo formed in the Middle Ages as overspill from the upper town, and its main artery, Via Pignolo, has a largely unchanged appearance and ambience; narrow, broody and atmospheric, with many surviving architectural features such as balconies and mullioned windows.

Museo Diocesano Bernareggi and San Bernadino

Via Pignolo 76 • Tues–Sun 3–6.30pm • €5 • ⓦ fondazionebernareggi.it

In among the rooms of ecclesiastical treasures and liturgical vestments of the **Museo Diocesano Bernareggi** nestles the odd gem – a ninth-century Longobard silver crucifix here, a Trinity by Lotto there. Diagonally across the street, at the junction of Via Pignolo with Via Verdi is the small, unremarkable church of **San Bernardino**, with Lotto's altarpiece of the *Blessed Virgin.*

Piazzetta del Delfino

Via Pignolo continues past the marble facade of **Sant'Alessandro della Croce** to the attractive **Piazzetta del Delfino**, occupied by a dolphin fountain built in 1526. Ahead, Via Pignolo leads to the Porta Sant'Agostino, while **Via San Tomaso**, packed with galleries, antiques shops and cafés, heads right towards the Accademia Carrara.

Accademia Carrara

Piazza Carrara 82 • ⓦ accademiacarrara.bergamo.it

Just below the upper town, close to the city walls, stands the **Accademia Carrara** – Bergamo's best art gallery and one of Lombardy's leading collections. At the time of writing, the gallery was closed for a top-to-toe refit, and was due to reopen in spring 2015. Among the collection are **Titian**'s remarkable *Virgin and Child*, painted at the age of 27, a touchingly effeminate *St Sebastian* by the young **Raphael**, and **Botticelli**'s startlingly modern *Portrait of Giuliano de' Medici*, painted in the 1470s – several hundred years ahead of its time. Other noteworthy pieces include **Mantegna**'s wistful *Virgin and Child*, **Bellini**'s wrenching *Dead Christ Between Mary and St John* and a portrait of a cadaverous *Doge Leonardo Loredan* by **Vittore Carpaccio.**

Galleria d'Arte Moderna e Contemporanea (GAMeC)

Via San Tomaso 82 • Tues–Sun 10am–1pm & 3–7pm • Temporary exhibitions €5 • ☎ 035 270 272, ⓦ gamec.it

The **Galleria d'Arte Moderna e Contemporanea (GAMeC)** offers temporary exhibitions, often of world-class stature, plus a small **permanent collection**. Among paintings by Kandinsky and Graham Sutherland are bronzes by the twentieth-century Bergamo-born sculptor Giacomo Manzù and a collection of abstract works by Atanasio Soldati, Luigi Veronesi and Alberto Magnelli.

ARRIVAL AND DEPARTURE

BERGAMO

By plane Bergamo's Orio al Serio airport (airport code BGY; ☎035 326 323, ⓦorioaeroporto.it) – also called "Milan-Bergamo" – is 4km southeast of Bergamo city centre. To reach Bergamo centre, take city bus 1 (daily every 20min 6am–midnight; 15min; one way €2.10, day pass €5, three-day pass €7; ⓦatb.bergamo.it). All stop at the bus station, with most continuing to the funicular base station and into the Città Alta. A taxi (☎035 451 9090) is around €30 into Bergamo, over €100 to Milan. The following companies connect the airport to Milano Centrale station (1hr): Orioshuttle (☎035 330 706, ⓦorioshuttle.com; every 30min 4.25am–12.10am; €5), Autostradale (☎035 339 10794, ⓦautostradale.it; every 30min 7.45am–12.15am; €5) and Terravison (☎331 299 9450, ⓦterravision.eu; every 30min 4am–1am; €5). The website ⓦsacbo.it lists bus times to all destinations from the airport. Journey times to major points from this and other airports are covered in Basics (see p.20).

By train Bergamo's train station is at the southernmost end of the Città Bassa's central avenue, Viale Papa Giovanni XXIII, a long walk from the Città Alta but well linked by bus (1) with the airport, the upper town and the funicular station. Left-luggage facilities are a two-minute walk away just outside the bus station (see below). There are trains from Milan (Centrale and Lambrate) and Brescia, and slower ones from Como, Cremona and Lecco.

Destinations Brescia (hourly with no services 9am–noon; 50min); Como San Giovanni (with a change in Monza; hourly; 1hr 25min); Cremona (via Treviglio or Milan; every 30min; 2hr) Lecco (hourly; 40min); Milano Centrale or Porta Garibaldi (every 40min; 50min).

By bus The bus station is behind the lower town tourist office, opposite the train station. There is a secure, automatic luggage deposit facility just outside the bus station (€4/24hr).

Destinations Clusone (11 daily; 1hr); Lovere (hourly; 1hr 10min); Sarnico (hourly; 55min).

By car The A4 autostrada runs from Milan to Bergamo and on to Brescia, while the SS342 is a useful but heavy-traffic link with Lecco and Lake Como.

GETTING AROUND

Public transport is well organized with simple bus and funicular links between the upper and lower towns. Consult the machines to buy an ordinary ticket (valid 75min; €1.25) or a *biglietto turistico giornaliero* (24hr; €3.50) – both usable on buses and funiculars within the city centre (€5 including the airport). You can get a *biglietto turistico 3 giorni* (valid for three days; €7) from outlets listed at every stop (as well as the bus stop, the tourist office at the airport, and from the machines at the train and funicular stations).

By bus City bus 1 runs frequently (every 20mins) between the airport and the train station continuing on to the funicular stations and Colle Aperto in the Città Alta (every 5–10 mins between the train station and Colle Aperto) – though some services stop short or follow route variations; check timetables carefully.

By car Città Alta is closed to cars and motorbikes April–Nov Sun 10am–noon & 2–7pm; Fri & Sat 9pm–1am. Parking is pricey in the lower town and difficult to find (and expensive) in the upper town, it's easier to use public transport – or your legs.

By funicular A funicular (daily 7am–12.30am) runs every few minutes on the steep route between Viale Vittorio

Emanuele II in the Città Bassa (the extension of Viale Papa Giovanni) and Piazza Mercato delle Scarpe in the Città Alta. A separate funicular also runs from just behind Colle Aperto in the upper town up to San Vigilio.

By tourist train The tourist train Gulliberg links the Upper Funicular Station (Città Alta) to the Colle Aperto (every 30min 2–7pm; €2 one way).

By bike, scooter and micro-car Electric bikes, scooters and micro-cars take the puff out of the city's hills. Available for good-value rates from Eco-rent (Viale Papa Giovanni XXIII 57, c/o Urban Center; ☎035 529 3888, ⓦeco-rent.it) by the bus station in the lower town.

INFORMATION AND TOURS

Tourist information Offices can be found in the Orio al Serio airport arrivals hall (daily 8am–9pm ☎035 320 402, ⓦturismo.bergamo.it), in the Urban Center, Piazzale Marconi, opposite the train station in Città Bassa (daily 9am–12.30pm

TRENO BLU

On Sundays in April, May & Sept only, the vintage **Treno Blu** (ⓦferrovieturistiche.it) chugs along through the Lombard countryside to the rail junction at Palazzolo and then on the short but scenic stretch along the Oglio river to Parático on **Lake Iseo** (see p.246). Boats connect from Sarnico (by Paratico) to Iseo, Monte Isola and around the lake. Return fares including lunch cost €50.

& 2–5.30pm; ☎035 210 204, ⓦprovincia.bergamo.it /turismo) and at Via Gombito 13 at the base of the Torre Gombito in Città Alta (daily 9am–5.30pm; ☎035 242 226).

Tours The Gruppo Guide Turistiche Città di Bergamo on

Piazza Mercato delle Scarpe can arrange guided walking tours of the old town (Wed, Sat & Sun 3pm; 2hr; €10; ☎035 344 205, ⓦbergamoguide.it). Tours leave from just outside the tourist office at Via Gombito 13.

ACCOMMODATION

Bergamo is not somewhere to arrive without a reservation, even out of season; **accommodation** is pricey and, in the centre, fairly limited. There are a handful of atmospheric hotels in the Città Alta with mostly business hotels in the Città Bassa.

HOTELS

CITTÀ ALTA

Agnello d'Oro Via Gombito 22 ☎035 249 883, ⓦagnellodoro.it. This warm and cosy two-star hotel jam-packed with trinkets and curios offers simple, excellent value rooms, some with balconies, in the heart of Bergamo's Città Alta. **€111**

★**Gombit Hotel** Via Mario Lupo 6 ☎035 247 009, ⓦgombithotel.it. A fashionable design hotel housed in a thirteenth-century building with a stone tower and stylish interiors featuring exposed walls and pastel coloured furnishings. **€210**

Hotel Piazza Vecchia Via Colleoni 3 ☎035 253 179, ⓦhotelpiazzavecchia.it. Right in the heart of town, this peaceful hotel in a fourteenth-century building offers comfortable rooms featuring fresh, contemporary decor brightened up by the owner's colourful paintings. Private parking. **€190**

Relais San Lorenzo Piazza Mascheroni 9A ☎035 237 383, ⓦrelaisanlorenzo.com. This luxury hotel features sleek, stylish rooms in shades of brown and cream looking onto a peaceful cloister. Its atmospheric restaurant is a must visit for non-guests too, carved into the basement with seating amid ancient Roman and medieval walls. Facilities include a spa and a lovely terrace overlooking the lower city. **€265**

Sole Via Colleoni 1 ☎035 218 238, ⓦilsolebergamo .com. In a great location steps from the main square, this family-run hotel offers bright en-suite two-star rooms with little balconies looking over a back courtyard or the private garden. The bustling restaurant with a pleasant garden patio serves good local dishes. **€100**

CITTÀ BASSA

Best Western Hotel Cappello d'Oro Viale Papa Giovanni XXIII 12 ☎035 422 2711, ⓦhotelcappellodoro .it. Just a few hundred metres from the train station, this pet friendly four-star hotel offers welcoming rooms with tasteful decor. Facilities include a sauna and gym, and discounts at selected local shops. At breakfast there's a choice of organic and gluten free cereal and croissants. **€140**

Mercure Palazzo Dolci Viale Papa Giovanni XXIII 100 ☎035 227 411, ⓦmercure.com. This four-star chain hotel just a short walk from the train station offers comfortable, stylish rooms with modern amenities. Excellent value. **€160**

HOSTELS

Central Hostel BG Via Ghislanzoni 30 ☎035 211 359, ⓦcentralhostelbg.com. Right in the centre of the lower town and handy for the train station, this hostel offers simple dorms as well as privates. There's an in-house pub that's open until 1am, a TV room with projector, free international calls, parking and free bike rental. Dorms **€25**, doubles **€56**

Nuovo Ostello di Bergamo Via Ferraris 1 ☎035 361 724, ⓦostellodibergamo.it. A large concrete building outside of town offering simple spacious rooms, all with private bath, a pleasant roof terrace and laundry facilities. There is no kitchen, but ready-made meals are available for purchase. Take bus 6 from Porta Nuova (direction Monterosso/San Colombano; every 20min; 15min), and get off at the 'Leonardo da Vinci' stop. From here, the hostel is at the top of the steps. Alternatively, reach it on the direct bus 3 from Piazza Mercato delle Scarpe in the Città Alta to the Ostello stop (every 40min; 20min). Dorms **€19**, doubles **€50**

EATING AND DRINKING

One of the pleasures of Bergamo is its food and drink, easily enjoyed whether you assemble **picnics** from the many *salumerie* and bakeries in the old town, or opt to graze around the city's terrific **osterie**. The town's signature dish is

---

BERGAMO'S B&BS

Bergamo's hotels are popular but can be bland, pricey or poorly located, so it's worth looking at the growing band of **B&B** rooms and apartments available. The website ⓦbedandbergamo .it is useful, while *Entro le Mura* (Via San Lorenzo 26; ☎035 2331 89, ⓦbedandbreakfast-elm.it; **€80**) and *Botton d'Oro* (Via Colleoni 30; ☎349 7806 584, ⓦbottondoro.com; **€74**) are attractive, well-priced B&Bs in the heart of the upper town.

polenta often served with veal or local game although polenta *taragna* is a creamy cheese and butter combination. *Casoncelli* – ravioli stuffed with sausage meat and served with sage and melted butter – are another justified favourite. With Bergamo's popularity it's always worth **booking ahead** – it's essential at weekends.

CAFÉS AND SNACKS

CITTÀ ALTA

Caffè della Funicolare Piazza Mercato delle Scarpe ☎ 035 210 091. In the funicular station, this is a lovely spot to enjoy a morning coffee or an afternoon snack; the terrace has spectacular views over the Città Bassa. Lunch is served here, too. Mains €11. Wed–Mon 8am–2am, Tues 6pm–2am July & Aug only.

Cavour Via Gombito 7 ☎ 035 243 418. This elegant old-fashioned *pasticceria* has been going strong since 1880 and is one of the most attractive cafés in town – don't miss their thick hot chocolate on a cold winter's day (€4). Mon, Tues & Thurs–Sat 7.30am–9pm, Sun 8am–8pm.

Il Fornaio Via Colleoni 3 ☎ 035 249 376. In the heart of the Città Alta, this bakery's large window displays all manner of delectable pizzas – there are thirty different options. A great spot for a quick lunch or a snack as you explore town. Daily 8am–8pm.

La Marianna Largo Colle Aperto 4 ☎ 035 237 027, ⊛ lamarianna.it. Bergamo's historic ice-cream parlour is allegedly where the flavour stracciatella was invented. In summer there are about twenty-five different ice creams to choose from and enjoy on the outdoor patio. Tues–Sat 7.30am–midnight, Sun 8am–midnight.

CITTÀ BASSA

Il Maialino di Giò Piazza Pontida 37 ☎ 035 215 840, ⊛ ilmaialinodigio.it. A lively little deli and bar with hams hanging from the ceiling that is particularly popular at *aperitivo* time for its tasty cold cut platters (€8). It's a great spot to grab a sandwich (€4), too. Mon–Sat 10am–10pm, Sun 10am–2.30pm.

RESTAURANTS

CITTÀ ALTA

Al Donizetti Via Gombito 17a ☎ 035 242 661, ⊛ donizetti.it. Located in what was formally a cheese market, this pleasant bar with seating on a breezy shaded portico offers tasty cheese and cold cut platters (€11.50) that go down a treat with a glass of one of the many wines on offer. Choose from goat's cheeses, *prosciutti crudi*, Bresaola, *salumi d'oca* (goose) and more. Daily 11am–midnight, Sat until 12.30am.

Baretto di San Vigilio Via al Castello 1 ☎ 035 253 191, ⊛ baretto.it. A stylish, classic restaurant opposite the top station of the San Vigilio funicular with tables lining the pavement and overlooking the valley below. The *menù degustazione* will set you back €45 per head. Primi €14, secondi €20. Mon–Fri 11am–2.30pm, Sat 10am–1am, Sun 9am–1am.

★ **Da Mimmo** Via Bartolomeo Colleoni 17 ☎ 035 21 85 35, ⊛ ristorantemimmo.com. Located in a former post office building, this excellent family-run restaurant –where recipes have been passed down for generations – serves hearty dishes and exquisite pizzas on a large shaded terrace in the summer months, or in the welcoming interior on cold winter days. Try the excellent Regina Margherita pizza with buffalo mozzarella (€9). Daily noon–2.30pm & 7–11pm; closed Tues lunch.

Il Circolino Vicolo Sant'Agata 19 ☎ 035 218 568, ⊛ ilcircolinocittaalta.it. This laidback informal place has a huge leafy garden with a bowling green where the elder generation often enjoy a game or two. The restaurant serves up large portions of excellent low-priced local dishes. Daily noon–2.45pm & 6.30pm–1am.

Lalimentari Via Tassis 3a ☎ 035 233 043, ⊛ lalimentari.it. A friendly little restaurant and wine bar serving traditional regional cuisine with high quality seasonal ingredients – including a number of polenta-based dishes (€12) and hearty rabbit mains (€14). Cheeses and cold cuts are all from the area, as are the majority of wines they stock (the extensive wine list features over 900 labels). Tues–Sun 11am–3pm & 6–11pm.

San Vigilio Via San Vigilio 34 ☎ 035 253 188, ⊛ ristorantepizzeriasanvigilio.it. This friendly restaurant and pizzeria offers a range of local dishes, including hand-made *casoncelli* (€11), wood-fired pizzas (€5.50) and home-made desserts, on a lovely terrace and garden dotted with apple trees that overlooks the valley. Daily noon–3pm & 7–11.30pm; Jan, Feb & Nov closed Wed.

Vineria Cozzi Via Colleoni 22 ☎ 035 238 836, ⊛ vineriacozzi.it. The interior of this lovely wine bar has largely remained unchanged since 1848. The food is all home-made, and there's a network of pretty dining rooms where traditional dishes are served, such as risotto with foie gras (€19). Customers can order a lovely two-course picnic meal (€30), served in a pretty picnic basket with tablecloths and cutlery. Daily 10.30am–3pm & 6.30pm–midnight.

CITTÀ BASSA

Ol Giopì e la Margì Via Borgo Palazzo 27 ☎ 035 242 366, ⊛ giopimargi.eu. A warm and welcoming place with a cavernous interior in what was once a stable, this delightful family-run restaurant serves authentic regional cuisine using local products – try the delicious risotto with taleggio cheese (€15). There's a good value set lunch menu for €19; set dinner menu €48. Tues–Sat 12.30–2.30pm & 7.30–10.30pm, Sun 12.30–2.30pm.

Roof Garden Hotel Excelsior San Marco, Piazza Repubblica 6 ☎ 035 366 159, ⓦ roofgardenrestaurant .it. The top (eighth) floor of this four-star hotel hosts an expensive haute cuisine restaurant. Expect international fine dining, nouvelle-style (tiny portions, creatively presented) in contemporary surroundings with spectacular views of the floodlit walls of the old town. Taster menus start at €75 per person; vegan menu €60 per person. An open-air terrace runs around the exterior. Mon–Fri 12.30–2pm & 7.40–10pm, Sat 7.40–10pm.

Bergamo's valleys

Northwest of Bergamo the **VAL BREMBANA** follows a mountain-fringed route that was well trodden in the Middle Ages by caravans of mules transporting minerals from the Valtellina down to the cities of the plain. The road is now frequented mostly by weekend skiers heading up to Foppolo (1508m) at the head of the valley, and by less energetic Italians en route to **San Pellegrino Terme** to take the waters. San Pellegrino (source of the famous bottled water) has been Lombardy's most fashionable spa since the early 1900s; it's from this period that its extravagant main buildings – the grand hotels and casino – date. Redevelopment is under way; a local entrepreneur is planning to relaunch the town as a getaway for Milan's super-rich with a seven-star hotel and luxury spas.

The valley just outside Bergamo houses factories and rather unattractive apartment blocks, although travelling northeast are the verdant rolling hills of the **VALLE SERIANA**, home to lovely walks through forests and mountains that are sprinkled with towns from a bygone era.

Clusone

CLUSONE, a picturesque hilltop town 35km northeast of Bergamo, is worth visiting for a stroll along its winding cobbled streets. With its medieval core and attractive Liberty mansions, the town centre is worth a wander, especially on Mondays when the steep curving streets are taken over by a market selling local sausage and cheeses. The central **Piazza dall'Orologio** is named after the sixteenth-century clock on the Palazzo Comunale, which shows the time (backwards), the date, sign of the zodiac, duration of the night and phase of the moon.

From Clusone it's a scenic 17km downhill to Lovere on Lake Iseo (see p.248).

Basilica di Santa Maria Assunta
Via Brasi 11 • Daily 8.30am–noon & 2.30–6.30pm

Consecrated in 1711, the imposing **Basilica di Santa Maria Assunta** is not to be missed. The basilica's porch, connected to the street below by three staircases, is surrounded by a balustrade decorated with tall marble statues; from here, there are wonderful views of the valley. The opulent interior consists of eight side chapels separated by arches that rest on Corinthian columns. Sculptor and woodcarver Andrea Fantoni created the beautiful high altar, while the altarpiece depicting the Assumption of Mary is a masterpiece by Venetian painter Sebastiano Ricci.

Oratorio dei Disciplini
Via dell'Arena 24 • Daily 8.30am–noon & 2.30–6.30pm

Right by the Basilica is the **Oratorio dei Disciplini** with its fifteenth-century exterior frescoes. The upper fresco, *The Triumph of Death*, portrays three noblemen discovering an open tomb containing the worm-infested corpses of the pope and emperor, overlooked by a huge laughing skeleton, representing Death and symbolising our inability to buy eternal life and death's inevitability for all. *The Dance of Death*, below, contrasts the corrupt nobility with a procession of contented, God-fearing commoners dancing their way happily towards death.

Museo Arte Tempo

Via Clara Maffei 3 • Fri 3.30–6.30pm, Sat & Sun 10am–noon & 3.30–6.30pm • Free • ☎ 03 462 2440, ⊛ museoartetempo.it

The lovely **Museo Arte Tempo** houses a collection of over eighty works of art, including paintings, sculptures and drawings, although the real draw here are the ancient tower clocks. The twenty specimens on display, among the sixty two that form part of the collection, take visitors on a journey from the fifteenth- to the twentieth-century, and include a late Gothic wrought iron device as well as more sophisticated clocks from the belle époque period.

6

ARRIVAL AND DEPARTURE

CLUSONE

By bus From Clusone, buses connect to Lovere on Lake Iseo (9 daily; 40min) and Bergamo (11 daily; 1hr).

INFORMATION AND ACTIVITIES

Bike rental You can rent a mountain bike from Cicli Pelligrini (€4/hr; half day €10; full day €14) in Piazza Santa Anna 8 (Mon–Sat 9am–noon & 3–7pm; in winter closed Wed too; ☎0346 21 017).

Horseriding Azienda Agricola Gaeni Monica (Via Valeda 15; ☎340 5233 469 or ☎333 215 9008) arranges treks into the countryside (€25/hr).

Tourist information Piazza Orologio 21 (Mon–Sat 9.30am–noon & 3.30–6.30pm, Sun 10am–noon & 4–6.30pm; ☎0346 21 113, ⊛www.turismoproclusone .it). If you fancy exploring the surrounding countryside the tourist office can help with walking or trekking paths.

ACCOMMODATION AND EATING

B&B Del Centro Piazza Martiri della Libertà 3A ☎348 413 7640, ⊛bedincentro.it. This B&B offers four individually furnished rooms and one apartment in the heart of the historical centre. Staff are friendly and happy to help. €80

Della Torre Via Lattanzio Querena 37 ☎034 624 208. The creatively presented dishes at this restaurant and wine bar change on a monthly basis, and there's a good-value weekly set lunch (€8). On Sundays the brunch menu (€11) includes scrambled eggs, club sandwiches, Caesar salads and burgers. Thurs–Tues noon–3pm & 6pm–midnight.

Mas-ci Piazza Paradiso 1 ☎0346 21267, ⊛mas-ci.it. This cosy restaurant with a cavernous wooden interior serves local specialities including home-made pasta and polenta with wild mushrooms. In the summer you can eat on a pleasant vine-shaded terrace. There are also a few comfortable hotel rooms for rent (doubles €80). Fri–Wed 12.30–2pm & 7.40–10pm; open Thurs July & Aug only.

Lake Iseo

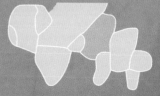

BELLAVISTA WINERY, FRANCIACORTA

Lake Iseo

Lake Iseo is the least known of the major lakes outside Italy and considerably smaller than its neighbours. This S-shaped chip of blue shaded by wooded mountains is popular with local tourists, bustling with day-trippers and second-homers on summer weekends and low-key out of season. It lacks the romance of Como and the grandeur of Garda but has a certain unreconstructed charm and far fewer visitors than its neighbours. Complete with its own inhabited island in Monte Isola, the lake also offers some great cycling and lovely hiking routes with fabulous views. Nearby, fascinating prehistoric rock carvings pepper the Val Camonica, and Lombardia's best-known secret, the bucolic wine-growing region, Franciacorta, lies just to the south.

7

Rising from the water mid-lake is **Monte Isola** (or Montisola), a giant wedge of an island offering a fine day-trip – or more – using one of the lake's many ferries. The lake's two other tiny islands are closed to the public and privately owned – one by the Beretta family, founders of the arms firm renowned for making James Bond's favourite gun.

Along much of the Bergamo or western shore, the mountains drop right down to the water's edge, while the eastern Brescian shore is more inviting with its rolling slopes and relaxed tourist villages. Stretching northwards, the broad **Val Camonica**, famous for its prehistoric rock carvings, reaches into the high Alps. Just south of the lake, **Franciacorta** is a beautiful area of rolling hills carpeted by award-winning vineyards and dotted with ancient castles and manor houses.

The western shore

The rugged western shore has just a handful of villages, the largest being **Sarnico** to the south and **Lovere** to the north both of which attract Sunday visitors with their lakeside promenades and ice cream parlours. Famed locally for its hair-raising coastal road, the western shore also offers the best watersports on the lake.

Sarnico and around

At the southernmost point of the western shore, **SARNICO** is an attractive old town, linked to its neighbour **Paratico** by a bridge over the River Oglio. The broad, waterfront piazzas of the contrada (the old quarter) give way to narrow, cobbled lanes climbing the hill behind.

In the hills around Sarnico are a number of Art Nouveau villas designed by the architect Giuseppe Sommaruga.

ARRIVAL AND INFORMATION   SARNICO

By train From April–Sept, a Sunday service runs from Bergamo to Paratico (a walk over the bridge from Sarnico). Steam trains sometimes cover the route (see p.239) – check ⓦ ferrovieturistiche.it for the latest timetables.

By bus Buses stop outside the town hall in the centre of town, just up from the lakefront.
Destinations Bergamo (hourly; 50min; limited service on Sun); Iseo (6 daily Mon–Sat; 15min).

Boats on Lake Iseo p.249
Festivals and events p.251

Hiking and biking p.253
Franciacorta wines and wineries p.255

MONTE ISOLA

Highlights

❶ Lake cruise Chug around the islands taking in the lakeside villages and enjoying the mountain panoramas. **See p.249**

❷ Monte Isola Follow the lakeside promenade on Europe's largest lake island for a couple of hours of peaceful retreat with glorious views. See p.250

❸ Settimana della Tinca Sample oven-baked tench, an Iseo speciality, during the lively, week-long Settimana della Tinca festival, celebrated with music and events around the lake. **See p.251**

❹ Via Valeriana Wander along slopes with splendid lake views retracing this ancient trade route among olive groves and chestnut trees. See p.253

❺ Cycling Whether you prefer lakeside cycle paths, challenging mountain-bike routes or freewheeling through vineyards, this region is best explored on two wheels. **See p.253**

❻ Prehistoric rock carvings Hundreds of fascinating rock carvings cover the wooded slopes of the Val Camonica. **See p.253**

❼ Wine tasting Visit the cellars of the famous Franciacorta region to sample and learn more about the quality sparkling wines made here. See p.254

HIGHLIGHTS ARE MARKED ON THE MAP ON P.248

By boat In summer, ferry and cruise services connect Sarnico to most villages on the lake but there are no services at all in winter (see box, p.249).

Tourist office Via Tresanda 1 (Tues–Sat 9am–12.30pm & 3–6.30pm; April–Sept also Sun mornings; July & Aug also Mon afternoons; ☎ 035 910 900, ⓦ prolocosarnico.it).

Lovere

The scenic route from Sarnico up the western shore (25km) – more scenic still when viewed from the water – passes below towering cliffs that often force the road into tunnels. Beyond **Tavernola Bergamasca** and **Riva di Solto**, both limestone quarrying towns, is the

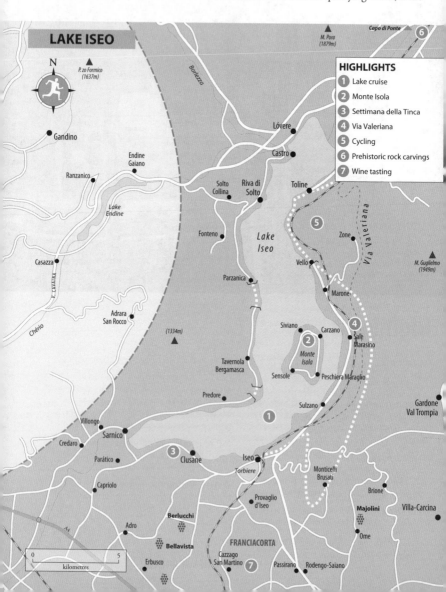

LAKE ISEO

HIGHLIGHTS
1. Lake cruise
2. Monte Isola
3. Settimana della Tinca
4. Via Valeriana
5. Cycling
6. Prehistoric rock carvings
7. Wine tasting

pretty town of **LOVERE** at the lake's northern tip, once a Venetian textile centre. It's worth climbing the 92 steps to the top of the Civic Tower on Piazza Emanuele II (June–Sept daily 10am–noon & 4–6pm; free) for wonderful views of the town and the lake.

Accademia Tadini

Via Taldini 40 • May–Sept Tues–Sat 3–7pm, Sun 10am–noon & 3–7pm; April & Oct Sat 3–7pm & Sun 10am–noon • €7 • ☎ 035 962 780,
Ⓦ accademiatadini.it

Located in a lakefront Neoclassical building, the **Accademia Tadini** gallery was commissioned by Count Luigi Tadini to display nineteenth-century works of art that he acquired during his travels in Italy and France. The gallery's masterpieces are works by his friend the sculptor Antonio Canova, whose early nineteenth-century marble *Stele Tadini* is located in the chapel within the grounds. The second floor, which opened in 2004, houses works of modern art. The gallery hosts concerts on Monday evenings from mid-April until the end of May.

Basilica di Santa Maria in Valvendra

Via Fratelli Pellegrini 7 • Mon–Fri 4–6pm, Sat & Sun 3–6pm; reduced hours in winter • Free

The interior of Lovere's imposing basilica reflects the town's prosperity during the fifteenth century, with invaluable works of art including two wonderful organ panels that depict the Annunciation. The portraits on the panels' interior were painted by Renaissance artist Alessandro Bonvicino.

ARRIVAL AND DEPARTURE   **LOVERE**

By bus Buses stop on the main road on Piazza XIII Martiri. Destinations Bergamo (every 30min; 1hr 10min; reduced services on Sun); Capo di Ponte (3 daily except Fri with only one journey; 1hr); Pisogne (3 daily excluding Sun; 15min).

By boat In summer, ferry services connect Lovere to most villages on the lake including Monte Isola. In winter, there are only regular ferries to Pisogne (see box below).

INFORMATION AND ACTIVITIES

Tourist office Piazza XIII Martiri 37 (July & Aug Mon–Wed 10am–12.30pm & 3.30–6pm, Thurs–Sun 9.30am–1pm & 2–7pm; reduced opening hours outside summer; ☎ 035 962 178, Ⓦ iataltosebino.it).

BOATS ON LAKE ISEO

Boats run by Navigazione Lago d'Iseo (☎ 035 971 483, Ⓦ navigazionelagoiseo.it) crisscross the lake from late March to late September. In winter there are connections to Monte Isola.

ROUTES

Service at **Iseo** is roughly every thirty minutes in each direction – south to **Sarnico**, north to **Monte Isola**, **Lovere** and **Pisogne** on weekends and daily from mid-June to the end of Aug. *Traghetti* (ferries) also shuttle continuously, 24 hours a day, to and from Monte Isola – from **Sulzano** to **Peschiera**, and from **Sale Marasino** to **Carzano**. **Various regular cruises** include the **Tour delle Tre Isole** (€7.50), which runs three times on summer Sundays (daily in mid-Aug) from Iseo around Monte Isola and its two minuscule offshoots, Isola di San Paolo and Isola di Loreto. The romantic **Crociera Notturna** is a serene four-hour glide after dark (June–Aug Sat 8.30pm from Iseo; Aug also Fri; €37, including dinner and drinks on board). Barcaioli Monteisola also runs its own cruises and **water-taxi** service (Ⓦ barcaiolimonteisola.it).

FARES

Tickets are charged on a complicated sliding scale. Each route is assigned a number, according to the distance involved; you then cross-check on the published list for how much that route-number (or tratta) costs. As an example, Iseo to Peschiera (or anywhere on Monte Isola) is given as tratta 2, which costs €3.10. Sarnico to Monte Isola is tratta 3, equal to €4.90. The most expensive ticket, tratta 4 (Iseo to Lovere), is €6.70. A return costs slightly less than two one-way tickets. There's a **supplement** of €1.25 for a suitcase, €2.50 for a bulky bag or **bicycle**. A **day pass** is €13.30.

Sports Sportaction (Solto Collina, Grè; ☎ 340 9843 097, ⓦ sportaction.it) offers sailing (€70) and windsurf (€95)

lessons (2–3hr), canoe (€8/hr) and stand-up paddle (€15/hr) rental.

ACCOMMODATION AND EATING

Hotel Lovere Via Marconi 97 ☎ 035 960 396, ⓦ hotel lovere.it. Located along the waterfront, this moderate four-star hotel offers spacious rooms, some with lake views (rooms in the new block are in substantially better shape than the old rooms). There's a pleasant rooftop terrace, as well as a gym and an attached spa with steam room and sauna. **€89**

Le Terrazze Piazzale Marconi 4 ☎ 035 983 533. The menu at this friendly restaurant includes handmade *casoncelli* (ravioli; €10), pizzas (€5) and meat and fish

dishes (€15); the real draw, however, is the pretty lakeside setting. Daily 9am–1am.

Zù Via XXV Aprile 53, Riva di Solto ☎ 035 986 004, ⓦ ristorantezu.it. In an unlikely location hugging the impossible western shore road just south of Lovere, this family-run restaurant with superlative lake and mountain views attracts those in the know from far and wide. Mains €16. Daily noon–2pm & 7.30pm–1am. Closed Tues lunch; Sept–June closed all day Tues.

7

Monte Isola (Mont'Isola or Montisola)

Amid Lake Iseo looms **MONTE ISOLA**, a huge chunk of mountain that is Italy's – and Europe's – largest lake island, over 3km long and 600m high. It's a peaceful spot and local day-trippers and summer tourists provide much of the island's income.

Ferries pull in to the little villages of **Peschiera Maraglio**, on the southeastern tip, and **Carzano** to the northeast as well as **Siviano** and **Sensole** on the western shore of the island, where it's worth visiting the **Museo della Rete** (Mon–Fri 9am–noon & 3–5.30pm; weekends advance bookings only ☎ 030 988 6336 or ☎ 345 91 43 707, ⓦ laretesrl.it; free), which provides an insight into lives past when the island produced hundreds of fishing nets (today it's mainly sporting nets and hammocks). The best way to explore Monte Isola is by bike (available for rent at Peschiera Maraglio; €3.50 per hour) or on foot. Cafés and restaurants dot the perimeter promenade around the island (9km by road, or about 15km following paths above the shore) and there are great views to be had from cycle-rides or the walking routes that crisscross the interior where stone hamlets cling to the slopes among vineyards, chestnut woods and olive groves. From the mountain-top village of **Cure**, at the end of the island's only bus route, stone steps lead through the woods to the fifteenth-century **Santuario della Madonna della Ceriola** poking out of the top of the island. The views from here are, naturally, breathtaking.

ARRIVAL AND INFORMATION
MONTE ISOLA

By boat There are four landing-stages around the island: Peschiera (nearest to Sulzano on the mainland) and Sensole on the south side, Carzano (opposite Sale Marasino) and Siviano on the north. Ferries shuttle over from Iseo and other points frequently (see box, p.249).

Tourist office Località Peschiera Maraglio 150 (July Fri & Sat 10am–4pm, Sun 10am–6pm; Aug Mon–Fri 10am–5pm, Sat & Sun 10am–6pm; mid-Sept–June Sat 10am–4pm, Sun 10am–5pm; ☎ 030 982 5088, ⓦ comune .monteisola.bs.it).

ACCOMMODATION AND EATING

Castello Oldofredi Via Peschiera Maraglio 58 ☎ 030 982 5294, ⓦ oldofrediresidence.it. Located on a hill in the picturesque village of Peschiera Maraglio, this four-star hotel in a restored medieval mansion offers welcoming doubles as well as apartments with modern amenities. Facilities include a swimming pool and a lovely restaurant with a welcoming terrace. Doubles **€115**, apartments **€150**

La Spiaggetta Via Sensole 26 ☎ 030 988 6141, ⓦ trattorialaspiaggetta.it. This laidback restaurant serves simple, traditional cuisine in a pretty lakeside setting on the southern end of Monte Isola. Meals are

enjoyed on a breezy veranda with uninterrupted views of the privately owned island of San Paolo. Primi €8, secondi €11. Wed–Mon noon–2pm.

La Torre Loc. Siviano 82, Sensole ☎ 030 982 5196. This welcoming restaurant with an airy terrace shaded by olive trees offers a selection of tasty local dishes. Tues–Sun 9.30am–3pm & 5–11pm.

★ **Villarzilla** Via Olzano 17, Olzano ☎ 329 117 8552, ⓔ villarzilla17@libero.it. Run by a warm and welcoming family, this lovely B&B with books scattered everywhere features natural materials such as wood and stone. The three warm rooms are filled with objects from the family's time living in India, and are decorated with mismatched rustic furniture (all made by the friendly owner). Book ahead. €70

Iseo town

At the southern curve of the eastern shore is **ISEO** town, an ancient trading post that was sacked by Federico I Barabarossa in the twelfth century. It's an attractive place for a stroll, along the narrow Via Campo, lined with flower-filled balconies, or into the web of lanes behind Piazza Garibaldi. On the northernmost side of the old town is Piazza del Sagrato, home to three pretty churches, including the Parish Church of **St Andrew's** with its Neoclassical interior and paintings by Francesco Hayez.

ARRIVAL AND DEPARTURE ISEO TOWN

The town is served by slow trains on the Brescia–Edolo line and buses from Brescia as well as local buses from along the lake. It is a ferry hub for the lake with regular services all year round. Iseo is off the main A4 Turin to Venice motorway and linked on a fast road to the Val Camonica by a series of tunnels.

7

By train The train station lies at the far eastern end of Via XX Settembre, 350m inland from the *imbarcadero*, which is at the western end.
Destinations Borgonato–Adro (4 daily; 6min); Bornato Calino (4 daily; 10min); Brescia (approx hourly; 30min); Edolo (8 daily; 1hr 30min); Pisogne (hourly; 30min); Rovato Città (4 daily; 20min).

By bus From Bergamo, head to Sarnico, or take a train to Rovato or Brescia, then switch to an Iseo-bound bus or train.

Destinations Lovere (2 daily; 45min); Pisogne (2 daily; 30min).

By boat Boats leave regularly from Iseo town for all points around the lake (March–Sept) including Monte Isola (see box, p.249). The village is also a departure point for the different cruise services. The *imbarcadero* is located just off the main square at the southern end of the village centre. Details of ferry services are listed earlier in the chapter (see p.249).

INFORMATION AND ACTIVITIES

Tourist office Lungolago Marconi 2 (Mon–Sat 10am–12.30pm & 3–5.30pm, Sun 9am–12.30pm; in winter closed Sat afternoon & Sun; ☎030 374 8733, ⓦ iseolake.info).
Bike hire Via per Rovato ☎340 396 2095,

ⓦ iseobike.com. One kilometre outside Iseo town at *Camping del Sole*, Iseobike offers mountain and electric bikes of various sizes for rental including helmets and children's seats for an extra fee (€4.50/hr; €17/day). April–Sept 9.30am–12.15pm & 2.30–7pm.

ACCOMMODATION AND EATING

BorgoLago Suites Via Sambuco 23 ☎030 982 2497, ⓦ borgolago.com. Located in a former textile storehouse, this building in the heart of the historical centre has been beautifully restored to house five welcoming suites with marble bathrooms and crisp linen. Each has a kitchenette and there's wi-fi throughout. €120
Del Muliner Via San Rocco 16, Clusane ☎030 982 9206, ⓦ trattoriadelmuliner.it. Located in Clusane, Iseo's

gastronomical hamlet is home to over twenty restaurants. This stylish trattoria offers creative takes on traditional staples including the lake's famous *tinca al forno* (oven roast tench). Wed–Mon noon–2.30pm & 7–10.30pm.
Hotel Rivalago Via Cadorna 7 ☎030 985 011, ⓦ rivalago.it. Five kilometres north of Iseo in the village of Sulzano, this four-star hotel with friendly staff offers warm and welcoming rooms right on the lakeshore. There are

---

FESTIVALS AND EVENTS

Festival dei Laghi Italiani (ⓦ festivaldeilaghi.it). Italy's largest event dedicated to Italian and European lakes takes place along the shores of Lake Iseo every year in May. The lively three-day festival includes art exhibitions, food markets, concerts, sporting, social and cultural events.
Franciacortando (ⓦ franciacortando.it). A two-day event in June celebrating street food in seven different locations of Franciacorta and designed by renowned multi-starred Italian chefs.
Settimana della Tinca A week-long festival in July with music and events on the lakeside and restaurants serving tinca al forno (oven-baked tench), a traditional Iseo speciality.

lovely views of Monte Isola and beyond from the lakeside garden, as well as a pleasant pool area. €142

Il Castello Via Mirolte 53 ☎030 981 285, ⓦtrattoriaalcastello.it. This welcoming restaurant offers alfresco dining in a pretty garden tucked away off Iseo's main artery. Meats are grilled in front of you (try the grilled duck breast with plum sauce; €14), and there are plenty of fish dishes to choose from too, including the lake's famed oven-baked tench (€9.50). Mon, Tues, Thurs & Fri 6.30–11pm, Sat & Sun noon–2.30pm & 6.30–11pm.

Le Palafitte & Co. Via Cesare Battisti 7, Sulzano ☎030 985 466, ⓦlepalafitte.net. With an enviable location right on the lake, this restaurant on stilts specialising in saltwater fish dishes (€18) has a breezy rooftop lounge and restaurant that is the perfect spot for a sundowner (on Wed & Sun the rooftop morphs into a nightclub). Tues–Sun 12.30–2.30pm & 8–11pm. Sun aperitivo from 7.30pm; Wed & Sun club open until 2am.

The eastern shore

On the **eastern shore**, the rugged mountains soften as they fall down to the lake and the wooded slopes give way to small-scale olive and grape cultivation that hasn't changed for centuries. The shore is sprinkled with pretty little villages including **Sulzano**, **Sale Marasino** and **Marone**, all with good ferry links to Monte Isola and ideal places for a refreshing dip in the lake. Up above the lake, the peaceful **Via Valeriana** (see box, p.253) winds through hamlets on an ancient commerce route, and just outside the hillside village of **Zone**, the landscape has been eroded into strange rock pyramids. On the northeastern tip is the larger **Pisogne**, where it's worth stopping off to explore the town's picturesque little streets and its wonderful **Church of Santa Maria delle Neve**.

Pyramids at Zone

Heading out of the village of **Marone**, midway up the eastern shore, a tortuous road climbs through chestnut woods to the village of **Zone**, in an area of rocky pyramids topped by granite boulders, a result of the rain erosion of glacial moraine deposits. Alongside the entrance, the twelfth-century church of San Giorgio (Easter–Sept daily 9am–5pm; limited hours out of season) is decorated with frescoes of Saint George.

Santa Maria delle Neve

Via Antica Valeriana • Daily 10am–6pm; reduced hours in winter • ☎036 488 0856

The little fifteenth-century church of **Santa Maria delle Neve**, in the village of Pisogne, where the artist **Romanino** painted a fresco cycle in 1534, is beautiful enough to have since been dubbed La Cappella Sistina dei Poveri ("the Poor Man's Sistine Chapel"). The basilica's interior walls are covered with Romanino's graceful art, the Passion to the west and south, and a trompe l'oeil design in the vaults of a sky crowded with prophets.

ARRIVAL AND DEPARTURE
THE EASTERN SHORE

By train A slow local train line linking Brescia and the Franciacorta to Edolo in the Val Camonica hugs the coast stopping at all the villages along the way. The best way to reach Pisogne is by train.

Destinations Brescia from Marone (hourly; 50min); Pisogne from Iseo (hourly; 30min).

By bus To reach the pyramids of Zone, catch a train to Marone and then a bus from the station up to Zone.

Destinations Zone from Marone (hourly; 15min).

By boat Sale Maresino and Sulzano are the two main ports for ferries to Carzano and Peschiera Maraglio on Monte Isola with services continuing through the winter. There are car parks by the ferry jetties.

Destinations Carzano from Sale Maresino (every 20min; 5min); Iseo from Sulzano (10 daily; 15min); Peschiera Maraglio from Sulzano (every 20min; 5min).

ACCOMMODATION AND EATING

El Giardí Via Monte Marone 9, Zone ☎030 982 7400, ⓦelgiardi.it. This warm and welcoming agriturismo with five rooms nestled under the pyramids of Zone offers delicious home cooking on a pleasant terrace. The menu includes a number of hearty wild boar dishes (the property houses a wild boar farm). Jams and olive oil are available for purchase, too.

HIKING AND BIKING

HIKING THE VIA VALERIANA

The ancient trading route between the plains of Lombardy and the Val Camonica and the Alps, the **Via Valeriana** is a 24km hike from Pilzone d'Iseo to Pisogne. It is divided into six stretches or the whole route could be spread comfortably over two days. Traversing the hillside on the eastern shore of the lake, it's a comfortable trek of never more than medium difficulty passing through vineyards, hamlets, olive groves and chestnut woods, alongside streams and ancient churches with glorious views of the lake beyond.

Starting and finishing points are linked by train and road connections. A couple of short 1km stretches are suitable for wheelchair users at Pilzone d'Iseo and Vesto Di Marone, paved with stone slabs and boulders, with a picnic area and disabled parking facilities. Every year on the third weekend in May, the **Sale Marasino** stretch sees re-enactments of the route's historical past.

A good bilingual map and route description is provided by the Comunità Montana del Sebino Bresciano (Ⓦcmsebino.brescia.it); available in Iseo from La Libreria bookshop in Via Duomo and the newsstand in Piazza Garibaldi.

BIKING

One of the best ways to enjoy this part of the world is on two wheels. There are details of **cycle routes** and paths online at Ⓦagenzialagoiseofranciacorta.it/percorsi_ciclabili.pdf as well as on various maps from the tourist offices (see p.251). Bicycles are available for rent from Iseobike (see p.251) and are also supplied by many hotels and B&Bs in the area. Most train and ferry services in the area allow bikes on-board.

7

Set meals from €23. Thurs, Fri & Sat 7.30pm–9.30pm & Sun noon–2pm; Oct–Easter Fri–Sun only. **€90**
Hotel Capovilla Via Papa Paolo VI 7, Pisogne ☎036 486 729, Ⓦhotelcapovilla.it. Each floor of this friendly

four-star hotel is decked out in a different theme and colour. The attached *Le Tentazioni* restaurant serves inviting dishes (mains €14) including excellent desserts (try the tiramisu; €6). **€85**

Val Camonica

The **VAL CAMONICA**, which stretches north of Lake Iseo for 50km up to Sonico just short of the border with Switzerland, is not only home to numerous parks and nature reserves harbouring rich alpine flora and fauna, but also to a large number of **prehistoric rock carvings** all the way up the valley. To date, over 180 rock art sites have been found, home to about 2400 decorated rocks. The engravings cover a period of 13,000 years, from the late Upper Paleolithic (13,000–10,000 years ago) to the Iron Age (1000 BC). The figures depict spiritual aspects, cult scenes and dances, as well as hunting and agricultural scenes. There are eight parks where engravings may be seen, although the **Parco Nazionale delle Incisioni Rupestri** is the best place to admire these incredible works of art. The little town of Capo di Ponte makes an ideal base.

Parco Nazionale delle Incisioni Rupestri

Naquane, Capo di Ponte • Tues–Sun 8.30am–1.30pm • €6 ticket grants free entry to MUPRE (valid for 30 days) • ☎036 442 140, Ⓦparcoincisioni.capodiponte.beniculturali.it

The **Parco Nazionale delle Incisioni Rupestri**, covering an area of over 140,000 square metres in the **Naquane** district near Capo di Ponte, is a lovely spot to spend a few hours strolling the park's wooden walkways shaded by chestnut, fir and beech trees. The park is home to 104 engraved rocks, mostly dating back from the Neolithic (5000 BC) to the Iron Age (1000 BC). Rock 50, with panoramic views of the valley, depicts praying figures, warriors, footprints and buildings, while rock 99 also features a Latin inscription, indicating that rock art continued after the Roman occupation of the valley.

Museo Nazionale della Preistoria (MUPRE)

Capo di Ponte · Mon–Sat 2–7pm · €6 tickets grants free entry to the Parco Nazionale delle Incisioni Rupestri (valid for 30 days) · ☎ 036 442 403, ⓦ mupre.capodiponte.beniculturali.it

The **Museo Nazional della Preistoria (MUPRE)** displays archaeological finds and rock engraved figures that provide an insight into the life of the valley's ancient inhabitants. The ground floor contains fifty engraved stelae and menhirs dating back to the Copper Age (4000–3000 BC), while the first floor houses archaeological finds.

ARRIVAL AND INFORMATION

CAPO DI PONTE

By train The local train from Brescia traces the eastern shore of Lake Iseo and then heads into Val Camonica stopping off at Capo di Ponte (every 2hr; 1hr 30min).
By bus Local and long-distance buses pull into the centre of the village.

Destinations Milan (2 daily; 2hr 30min).
Tourist office There is an Infopoint at Via Nazionale 1, Capo di Ponte (March–Oct Mon–Sat 9.30am–5.30pm, Sun 9.30am–12.30pm; Nov–Feb Mon–Sat 9.30am–4.30pm, Sun 9.30am–12.30pm; ☎ 036 442 104, ⓦ capodiponte.eu).

ACCOMMODATION

★ **Casa Visnenza** Via San Faustino 7, Cemmo di Capo di Monte ☎ 320 906 4557, ⓦ casavisnenza.it. This attractive B&B in an old silk mill has welcoming rooms with parquet floors, wooden beams and period furniture.

Books and curios are dotted about, and there's a lovely tranquil garden with deck chairs. The owners couldn't be friendlier and are full of suggestions for walks and sights in the area. **€76**

Franciacorta

Between Iseo and Brescia is **FRANCIACORTA**, a hilly wine-producing district rising from the built-up plain. It got its name from the religious communities that lived here from the eleventh century onwards; they were exempt from tax and known as the Corti Franche, or "free courts". Wine producers soon moved in, attracted by the possibility of owning vineyards in a duty-free haven. These days the area is no longer tax free, but the wine continues to flow, invigorated by the success of the award-winning sparkling wines produced here since the 1960s.

Erbusco is the de facto capital of the area and where many of the better known cantinas are located, although there are dozens throughout the area. One of the best ways to explore is by following sections of the well-signposted **Strada del Vino Franciacorta** (see box, p.255) which takes you along the most attractive routes through vineyards and tiny villages, past ancient farmhouses and international wineries.

This being a strategic area, there are castles and fortified manor houses as well as monasteries at every turn but most are closed to the public. On summer Sundays, however, the Medieval **Castello di Bornato** with a Renaissance interior (Via Castello 24, Bornato; mid-March to mid-Nov Sun 10am–noon & 2.30–6pm; ☎ 030 725 006, ⓦ castellodibornato.it) and the seventeenth-century **Palazzo Torri** (Via Sant'Eufemia 5, Nigoline di Franciacorta; April–Oct Sun 3–6pm; booking necessary; €6; ☎ 030 982 6200, ⓦ palazzotorri.it), where it's also possible to stay overnight, open their doors. To the north of the region is an ancient peat bog known as **Torbiere**, protected as a nature reserve and bird sanctuary and carpeted with water lilies in spring. It is watched over by the Romanesque monastery of **San Pietro in Lamosa** (church; Mon–Fri 2.30–5pm, Sat & Sun 9am–noon & 2–6pm; free; ⓦ sanpietroinlamosa.org), which has wonderful sixteenth-century frescoes in the Disciplina behind the church (April–Oct Sat & Sun 10am–noon & 3–6pm; Nov–March Sat & Sun 10am–noon & 2–5pm). Attractions of **Rodengo-Saiano**, on the Iseo–Brescia road, include not only the wonderful **Abbazia Olivetana**, a restored tenth-century abbey, but also the **Franciacorta Outlet Village** (ⓦ franciacortaoutlet.it), where brand-name stores sell discounted designer-label fashion.

FRANCIACORTA WINES AND WINERIES

This small area of Lombardy is best known for the **Franciacorta DOCG** (Denominazione di Origine Controllata e Garantita), Italy's most refined **sparkling wine**, produced according to Champagne methods. It was first produced in the 1960s and the secret lies in the second fermentation in the bottle which can last from 18 to 60 months. Usually a blend of Chardonnay and Pinot Noir or Blanc grapes, the sparkling wine comes in various types: Not Dosed/Pas Dosé (extremely dry), Extra Brut, Brut Satèn (a light silky-smooth mixture), Sec, Demisec and Rosé.

There are non-sparkling **Terre di Franciacorta DOC** – both bianco and rosso – and a host of lesser **IGT** (Indicazioni Geografiche Tipiche) wines available too. Some of the best known **Franciacorta sparkling wine producers** are Bellavista (ⓦterramoretti.it), Berlucchi (ⓦberlucchi.it), Ca' del Bosco (ⓦcadelbosco.com) and Monte Rossa (ⓦmonterossa.com), but all of the vineyards – and there are over one hundred of them – have their own story and often lovely headquarters in ancient farmhouses or villas. It's worth visiting the smaller, lesser-known wineries too, where you'll get a real taster for life in Franciacorta, such as Cortefusia (ⓦcortefusia.com) and Il Pendio (ⓦilpendio.com), which also produces exceptional olive oil. Most guided tours end with a tasting and very competitive prices are offered in the cantina shops, where they can usually arrange shipping back home for you too.

In mid-September on even years, the **Festival Franciacorta** sees wineries open for special tasting sessions and local restaurants offering themed seasonal menus.

THE STRADA DEL VINO FRANCIACORTA

Tourist offices and hotels stock a map of the **Strada del Vino Franciacorta** (ⓦstradadelfranciacorta.it), a route which winds for 80km through the area, passing visitable vineyards, hotels and restaurants along the way. There are well-thought out routes for cars, cyclists or walkers lasting for a couple of hours to a day or two. Contact details are given for wineries along the route, most of which offer tours and tastings; advance booking is preferred.

7

ARRIVAL AND DEPARTURE

FRANCIACORTA

By train Trains on the Brescia-Edolo line link Iseo with several small stations in the Franciacorta region. Bikes are permitted on board.

Destinations Borgonato–Adro (hourly; 5min); Bornato Calino (hourly; 10min); Cazzago San Martino (4 daily; 15–30min); Rovato (5 daily; 15–30min).

ACCOMMODATION

There are numerous B&Bs and agriturismi throughout Franciacorta, often in historic buildings or attached to vineyards. This area has only recently opened to tourism so most places are newly renovated with owners proud to showcase the best of the region. There are few hotels and private rooms or self-catering apartments are much more common.

Ca'minore & BB Camignone Via Diaz 7 ☎030 654 356 & ☎030 634 5496, ⓦcaminore.it & ⓦcamignone.it. Formally one large B&B, this building has now been converted into two separate establishments. Both offer comfortable rooms with modern furniture and pleasant gardens. *Ca'minore* has a swimming pool, too. **€90–110**

Villa Gradoni Via Villa 12, Monticelli Brusati ☎030 652 329, ⓦvillafranciacorta.it. A medium-sized winery and agriturismo offering good value apartments that line the hamlet of Borgo Villa. Facilities include a children's play area, bicycles and complimentary cellar tours for guests. One-bed apartment **€120**

EATING AND DRINKING

Proudly boasting a clutch of Michelin-starred restaurants, Franciacorta is somewhere to eat and drink well. Many of the wineries have good informal restaurants where you can try the house vintages with local dishes.

★**Al Rocol** Via Provinciale 79 ☎030 685 2542, ⓦalrocol.com. This family-run agriturismo offers outstanding home cooking in a welcoming trattoria. The seasonal menu includes traditional Italian staples. Fri & Sat 7–9pm, Sun noon–2pm & 7–9pm.

★**Due Colombe** Borgo Antica San Vitale, Via Foresti 13, Borgonato di Cortefranca ☎030 982 8227, ⓦduecolombe.com. Located in an ancient farmhouse now housing a grappa distillery, this Michelin-starred restaurant offers exceptional gourmet cuisine with its roots in Franciacorta traditions. Tasting menu €70–85 per head, mains €25. Tues–Sat 12.15–2pm & 7.45–10pm, Sun 12.15–2pm; July & Aug closed Sun lunch.

Brescia and Cremona

SANTA GIULIA, BRESCIA

Brescia and Cremona

The roads to Brescia and Cremona are the roads less travelled. To most Italians, Lombardy's second largest city, Brescia (pronounced *bresha*) means heavy industry or business meetings; Cremona is known for violins and its sticky pickle *mostarda*. To most outsiders, they're somewhere to be bypassed while plotting a route to or from the lakes. But for a contrast with picturesque waterside villages, or if the commerce of the lakes is starting to irritate, a dip into these attractive provincial towns on the Lombard plain could be just the ticket.

Brescia has the richer pickings with a surprising wealth of Roman ruins as well as an attractive jumble of medieval, Renaissance and Fascist architecture, although it is the outstanding museum complex of **Santa Giulia** that really makes the town stand out. Just down the road, low-key **Cremona** is for violin enthusiasts; it has an attractive Renaissance centre with a splendid main piazza and a fascinating heritage as the place where the modern violin was created. There are priceless instruments to be heard as well as a thriving industry of violin-makers crafting contemporary masterpieces.

8

Brescia

Lombardy's second city, hard-working Brescia is frequently cold shouldered by Italians and visitors alike, though its architecture is attractive, its food unique and its museum outstanding. What the city lacks in classic good looks it makes up for in history. Brixia – as it then was – was a major **Roman** city, designated *Colonia Civica Augusta* in 27 BC. Evidence is widespread, from the **Capitoline Temple** overlooking the forum to well-preserved mosaic floors of Roman villas in the **Santa Giulia** museum. Its rich medieval and Renaissance history under the Venetians left a Brescian school of painting and fine architecture in the main **Piazza della Loggia**, while neighbouring **Piazza Vittoria** holds as striking an ensemble of Fascist architecture as anywhere in the region.

Brescia has remained a success into the modern era, moving from silk production through railways to an iron and steel industry and the production of trucks and weapons. Yet it merits barely a footnote in most lakes itineraries; tourism is well down the city's list of priorities. This gives the handsome historic centre a uniquely unpretentious charm; in a region of spectacular natural scenery and legendary urban beauty, Brescia refuses to be pigeon-holed. It's just a serious, working city, almost completely free of tourists and with plenty to fill an absorbing couple of days.

Brescia's city centre comprises a network of shopping streets enclosing a compact cluster of piazzas. The ancient **Piazza della Loggia** is the heart of the city, though the adjacent Fascist-era **Piazza della Vittoria** is larger. Nearby **Piazza Paolo VI** holds the remarkable **Duomo Vecchio**. Just to the east rise a huge **Roman temple** and **theatre**. An outstanding museum adds to Brescia's allure; the ex-monastery complex of **Santa Giulia** houses excellent displays on the history of Brescia and a fine Renaissance art collection.

Mille Miglia p.261
Art in Brescia p.264

Violin concerts and festivals p.269
Luthiers in action p.270

Highlights

❶ Roman Brescia All over town, fragments of the wealthy Roman settlement are visible in mosaics, reconstructed walls and recycled building materials. **See p.258**

❷ Duomo Vecchio Wander this atmospheric sunken circular cathedral with its vivid Roman mosaics. **See p.261**

❸ Santa Giulia city museum With its fascinating strata of history, the Santa Giulia museum is a wonderful place to lose yourself in the history of Brescia, indeed Italy. **See p.262**

❹ Angel by Raphael This ethereally beautiful fragment of an altarpiece was painted when the artist was only seventeen. **See p.264**

❺ *Casoncei* Brescia's speciality pasta is stuffed with salami and served oozing with sage butter. **See p.266**

❻ Climb the Torrazzo Up the 502 steps to the top of the tower, there are expansive views over Cremona's rooftops. **See p.267**

❼ Luthier workshops Cremona is a magnet for the best violin-makers in the world. Many are happy to give you an insight into their art. **See p.270**

❽ *Mostarda di Cremona* A multi-hued spicy syrup with preserved fruit, delicious with cheese or boiled meats. **See p.270**

HIGHLIGHTS ARE MARKED ON THE MAPS ON P.260 & P.268

Piazza della Loggia

Brescia's main square is also its prettiest – **Piazza della Loggia**, which dates back to 1433, when the city invited Venice in to rule and protect it from Milan's power-hungry Visconti family. The Venetian influence is clearest in the fancy **Palazzo della Loggia** which dominates the west side of the square – and in which both Palladio and Titian had a hand – and in the ornate **Torre dell'Orologio** opposite, modelled on the campanile in Venice's Piazza San Marco. Around 1480, in a gesture of self-aggrandizement, the city authorities set bits of inscribed Roman

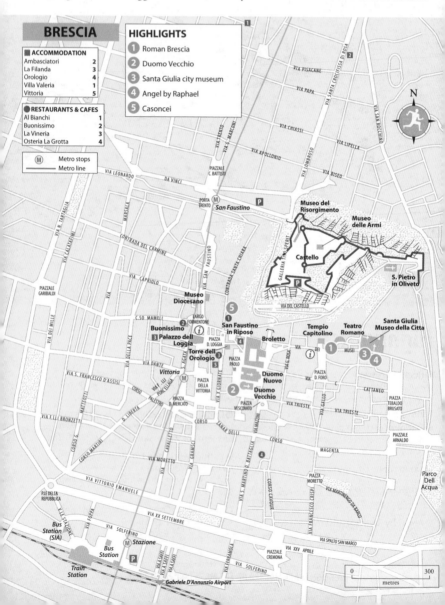

BRESCIA

HIGHLIGHTS

1 Roman Brescia
2 Duomo Vecchio
3 Santa Giulia city museum
4 Angel by Raphael
5 Casoncei

ACCOMMODATION

Ambasciatori	2
La Filanda	3
Orologio	4
Villa Valeria	1
Vittoria	5

RESTAURANTS & CAFES

Al Bianchi	1
Buonissimo	2
La Vineria	3
Osteria La Grotta	4

Ⓜ Metro stops
— Metro line

MILLE MIGLIA

According to Enzo Ferrari, the **Mille Miglia** is the "most beautiful" car race in the world. Every May this vintage contest sees hundreds of classic cars set off from central Brescia to Rome and back along the same route the race has been tracing since 1927.

An entertaining museum (Tues–Sun 10am–6pm; €7; ☎030 336 5631, ⊛museomillemiglia.it) showcases dozens of shiny classic vehicles and past winners in an atmospheric display with photos, posters and music of the era in a refurbished eleventh-century monastery, **Sant'Eufemia della Fonte**, on the eastern outskirts of town. There's also a stylish vaulted taverna (Tues–Sat 11am–3pm & 6–10pm, Sun noon–3pm).

stonework into the unified frontage of the shops lining the square's south side, later taken over by the **Monte di Pietà**, a kind of municipal pawnbrokers. The Roman chunks survive in the same facade today. Just nearby, below the Torre dell'Orologio, a **monument** commemorates the Fascist bombing, in 1974, of a trade-union rally here, in which eight people were killed and over a hundred injured. The terrorists left the bomb in a rubbish bin; you can still see the blast damage on the pillar. To the north is the **Porta Bruciata**, a defensive medieval tower-gate giving onto Via dei Musei (see p.262); insinuated into the gate itself is the tiny, conical church of **San Faustino in Riposo**.

Piazza della Vittoria

Long, Fascist-built **Piazza della Vittoria** sits under the stern gaze of the monumental post office building, its facade – like much of the square – done in contrasting shades of highly polished marble. The architect Piacentini's clinical arcades march off down the square in rigid formation, and grandiose corner steps struggle to mask the uneven topography.

Piazza Paolo VI

Once called the Piazza del Duomo, **Piazza Paolo VI** was renamed after the Brescian-born Pope Paul VI (1897–1978). It's one of the few squares in Italy to boast two cathedrals; alongside the Duomo Nuovo, to the north, stands the **Broletto**, the twelfth-century town hall that was the municipal seat of power before the construction of the Palazzo della Loggia.

Duomo Nuovo

Piazza Paolo VI • Mon–Sat 7.30am–noon & 4–7pm, Sun 8am–1pm & 4–7pm • Free

Frankly, Piazza Paolo VI would have been better off without this chilly, heavy Mannerist monument that took over two hundred years to complete, its grim Neoclassical facade concealing a tall cupola. An original design was by Palladio but the budget couldn't stretch so the building was completed by local architects. Inside among the cathedral's treasure, look out for the Renaissance sculpture *Arca di S.Apollino*.

Duomo Vecchio

Piazza Paolo VI • April–Oct Tues–Sun 9am–noon & 3–7pm; Nov–March Tues–Sun 10am–noon & 3–6pm • Free

The twelfth-century **Duomo Vecchio**, or **Rotonda**, a unique circular church of local stone, is by far the most appealing building on the square. Its fine proportions aren't easily appreciated from outside, as the building is sunk below the current level of the piazza.

You enter at the matroneum, the upper gallery previously reserved for women to pray, looking down over the interior. Here stands the tomb of Berardo Maggi, a thirteenth-century Bishop of Brescia, in red Verona marble. The transept and presbytery were added to the church in 1450, in a very late style of Gothic. As you look down, the chapel to the right holds two paintings by Romanino and four by Moretto, who also has a striking *Assumption* as the main altarpiece. Glass set into the transept pavement reveals the remains of Roman baths (a wall and geometrical and animal mosaics) and the apse of an eighth-century basilica, which burned down in 1097. The crypt is supported on a random array of reused Roman columns.

The Roman temple

Adjoining the Broletto to the north, **Via dei Musei** marks the line of the Roman *decumanus maximus*, the main east–west street. It's a narrow, undramatic thoroughfare today, although lined with some historic *palazzi*. A short walk east brings you to what was the centre of Roman Brixia, **Piazza del Foro**, built over the ancient forum (which was substantially larger than the current square). Dominating the area are the tall columns of the **Tempio Capitolino**, a Roman temple built in 73 AD, now partly reconstructed with red brick. Behind are three reconstructed *celle*, probably temples to the Capitoline trinity of Jupiter, Juno and Minerva. Adjacent to the east, reached by dodging around a side street, is a part-excavated Roman **theatre**; ongoing archeological work has revealed frescoes and remnants of an older temple beneath the current one. The complexes are currently closed to visitors while work continues but they are still visible to some extent from the road.

8

Santa Giulia: Museo della Città

Via dei Musei 81 • Tues–Sun: June–Sept 10am–7pm; Oct–May 9.30am–5.30pm • €10 • ⓦ bresciamusei.com

The fabulous civic museum of **Santa Giulia**, recognized by UNESCO World Heritage, is housed in the sprawling ex-Benedictine convent of San Salvatore and Santa Giulia. The convent was founded in 753 AD by Desiderius, king of the Lombards, for his daughter over what was, during the Roman period, a residential quarter of frescoed villas. The layers of history on show make this a fascinating place to spend a couple of hours; there is a vast amount to get through, so we've focused on specific **highlights**. These now include artworks from the **Pinacoteca Tosio Martinengo** (see box, p.264), which is closed indefinitely, ostensibly for restoration.

Roman galleries: Winged Victory and the Domusae

From the ticket desk, head right and down to the basement for the first **Roman** gallery; beyond a series of inscribed mileposts, a remnant of Brixia's *cardo maximus* is visible both inside and outside the monastery walls. Head up a short flight of stairs to galleries set out around the ground floor of the monastery's northern cloister. Room 3 holds a model of Brescia's Tempio Capitolino, while a museum highlight is in room 6 – a bronze, life-sized **Winged Victory** discovered in the temple. This was adapted in the second century AD from a pre-existing fourth-century BC statue of Aphrodite admiring herself in a mirror; the artist added a military tunic and wings and changed the goddess's mirror into a shield, on which Victory is inscribing her champion's name. The mirror and shield have long been lost, as has the helmet of Mars beneath the figure's left foot.

Signs lead round to a catwalk that passes through the (covered) excavation area of two **Roman houses** discovered beneath the monastery gardens. The colourful mosaic floors of each villa (known as a *domus*), and the remnants of frescoed walls, are amazingly well preserved; walking this close to them, tracing a path through the rooms they adorned, is a real treat.

There are more galleries with capitals and Roman glassware – and an exit to the cloister, which is lined with Roman funerary inscriptions.

Medieval galleries

A doorway leads to the **early medieval** galleries, displaying exquisitely embossed Lombard and Carolingian grave goods such as swords, pottery and gold crosses. Further on, the rooms devoted to the **city-states** (*comune* and *signorie*) begin, on the right, with two fine bronze wolves' heads, of about the twelfth century, taken from the Broletto – a rare example of secular Romanesque work.

San Salvatore

An exit here leads into the first of the museum's three churches, **San Salvatore**. Follow signs straight through on the right to climb to the upper-level **Coro delle Monache**, or **Nuns' Choir**. This soaring, barrel-vaulted space above the main floor of the San Salvatore church is covered in colourful frescoes, most of them executed in the 1420s by Floriano Ferramola. Overhead is *God the Father*, while the most striking image is a *Crucifixion* against an open landscape on the east wall (which has windows down into the church). Scenes from Christ's childhood adorn the upper panels all round the room. On the west side, moved here in the 1880s, is the dour marble mausoleum of the Martinengo family, excessively encrusted with ornament, beyond which is the church of **Santa Giulia**, now off-limits.

Returning down the stairs delivers you into San Salvatore itself, most of which is early medieval (parts date from the eighth century, visible through grilles in the floor) but there are more remnants of the Roman dwellings underneath visible through floor grilles. A circular route leads down to the ancient crypt and up again, to exit the church in the southeast corner.

From here, the itinerary continues to the **Venetian** galleries – with elegant reliefs and statues, as well as re-creations of aristocratic Brescian family homes of the period – and the **Applied Arts** galleries, with majolica and beautiful sixteenth-century Murano glassware.

Santa Maria in Solario

Signs deliver you back to the ticket desk, from where you can head left on the itinerary devoted to the history of the Santa Giulia monastery, and a gallery dominated by a seventeenth-century statue in Carrara marble of St Julia herself. Head outside into the southern cloister and left, to enter **Santa Maria in Solario**, a square twelfth-century church with an octagonal lantern. You arrive in a lower room housing the **Lipsanoteca**, a small, fragile, ivory reliquary casket from the fourth century, covered in superbly detailed carving in three bands: the top and bottom are devoted to stories from the Old Testament, while the central band details scenes from Christ's life.

Stone stairs lead up into the main chamber of the church, frescoed by Ferramola (1513–24). In the three apses of the east wall, Mary is flanked by St Catherine and St Benedict, while the north wall shows scenes from the life of St Julia. Overhead is a spectacular, midnight-blue **frescoed dome**, speckled with gilded brass stars.

Dominating the centre of the room is a glass case holding the **Croce di Desiderio**, an eighth-century wooden cross, covered in sheet metal and studded with more than two hundred gemstones, mostly Roman in origin. Desiderius was king of the Lombards, and this eye-popping item would have represented a significant part of his treasure – spiritual and material.

The exit, in the west wall, leads downstairs into the cloister of San Salvatore, facing the bell tower. Follow signs to the right back to the ticket desk.

The Castello

Castello Daily 8am–8pm • Free • **Museums** Tues–Sun: June–Sept 10.30am–6pm; Oct–May 9.30am–5pm • €5 • ⓦ bresciamusei.com /castello.asp

Behind Santa Giulia, Via Piamarta climbs the **Cydnean Hill**, the core of early Roman Brixia, mentioned by the poet Catullus. Fragments of a Roman gate survive just before

ART IN BRESCIA

Brescia's main art gallery, the **Pinacoteca Tosio Martinengo** at Via Martinengo da Barco 1, has been closed for restoration for several years. The collection – built up separately by two nineteenth-century Brescian noblemen, Paolo Tosio and Leopardo Martinengo (hence the name) – is now partially housed in **Santa Giulia**, with some works in the **Museo Diocesano** at Via Gasparo da Salò, 13. Below are some highlights; if you want to see particular works, enquire at the tourist office about their whereabouts – and check whether the pinacoteca has finally reopened.

RAPHAEL AND LORENZO LOTTO

Two of the star paintings in the collection are by Renaissance master **Raphael**. One is an ethereally beautiful *Angel* (1501), painted as part of a retable for the Umbrian abbey of San Nicolà da Tolentino; after an earthquake destroyed the church, the damaged retable was cut up. Three fragments survived: one is in the Louvre, another is in Naples, and the third – this angel – was discovered for sale in a Florentine market by Paolo Tosio and brought to Brescia. The virtuosity of this small portrait is dazzling – more so when you realize that Raphael was just 17 when he painted it. Another small work by Raphael, a *Risen Christ*, shows – in the accurate rendering of the body's musculature, the movement in the slightly turned stance and details such as a whisper of five o'clock shadow – the debt the young artist owed to Leonardo.

Alessandro Bonvicino was one of a trio of artists at the head of the Brescian Renaissance (the others were Moretto and Romanino), who brought techniques of colour and humanistic portraiture learned from Titian and other Venetian masters back to Brescia, blending them with local, Lombard styles. Bonvicino's *Salome* (c.1537) is an insightful portrait of Renaissance courtesan Tullia d'Aragona, whose mother was known for sexual impropriety. In an attempt to recover her own and her family's reputations, Tullia took to writing poetry, and the artist portrays her as a melancholy victim – as Salome was – of her mother's manipulations.

The collection also features a fine *Adoration of the Shepherds* (1530) by **Lorenzo Lotto**, a Venetian who lived in Bergamo and had great influence on the Brescian school. The tenderness of the Christ-child reaching out to a sheep, the bold colouring and the blue sky are all signs of a Venetian style, and here, unusually, the Virgin is shown kneeling in the manger. The artist has shown his two patrons, members of the wealthy Bagnoni family, as shepherds, incongruously dressed in the elegant clothes of noblemen.

PAINTINGS OF THE CINQUECENTO

An inscrutable, introspective portrait of a man by one of the leading figures of the Brescian school, **Romanino**, is *Boy with a Flute* by **Giovanni Gerolamo Savoldo** (c.1525). This

you reach the sixteenth-century church of **San Pietro in Oliveto**, named after the olive grove that surrounds it. The hill is crowned by the **Castello**, begun in the fifteenth century by Lucchino Visconti and added to by the Venetians, French and Austrians. The resulting confusion of towers, ramparts, halls and courtyards is difficult to interpret, though it makes a good place for an atmospheric picnic. There are two museums here – the **Museo delle Armi** with a large collection of weaponry from through the ages and the **Museo del Risorgimento**, which is dedicated to Italian Unification.

ARRIVAL AND DEPARTURE

BRESCIA

By plane The tiny Verona/Brescia-Montichiari (Gabriele D'Annunzio) airport (airport code VBS; ☎030 965 6599, ⓦ aeroportobrescia.it) is 23km southeast of Brescia near the town of Montichiari (and about 35km south of Lake Garda). It is named after the poet Gabriele D'Annunzio, and has also been dubbed "Verona-Brescia airport", even though Verona lies 50km east. Confusingly, the airport is referred to on signs and timetables by any of its four names, or a combination thereof. Buses run by CGA (☎030 965 6502, ⓦcgabrescia.it) to Brescia bus station and to Verona Porta Nuova train station. A taxi (☎030 996 0504) into Brescia costs €40 or more. There is a table in the guide with journey times to major points from this and other airports (see p.20).

By train The town is served by mainline trains from Milano Centrale, Verona and Desenzano/Sirmione, as well

arresting work shows a proud young musician, complete with a feather in his cap, stopping midway in a tricky passage to glance at the painter, his long fingers still in position on his recorder. Savoldo shows off his skill in handling light by pinning a half-folded sheet of music to the wall behind the flautist, and then expertly depicting the play of shadows.

You'll also see a double-sided work by Vincenzo Foppa, who painted under the patronage of the Visconti in Milan, Pavia and elsewhere. Foppa met Bramante and Leonardo in Milan, and is credited with introducing Renaissance ideas to Brescia after arriving here as an old man. His *Madonna with Saints* (1514) is backed by *St George, St Sebastian & St Rocco*. Rocco is a popular fixture in country churches around Lombardy; he was the patron saint of plague victims, and is always shown lifting his tunic to show the pustules on his thigh.

Romanino's raw *San Gerolamo Penitente* (c.1536) depicts the hermit-saint mortifying his flesh and his soul, and is juxtaposed with a more classical representation of Renaissance ideas – Moretto's *Exaltation of the Holy Cross* (c.1520), where the separation of the sacred from the profane is shown very literally as a horizontal layer of cloud.

In Savoldo's night-time *Adoration of the Shepherds* (c.1540), one shepherd gives his pal a leg-up to a high window so that he can lay eyes on the newborn Jesus, while in Moretto's chilling *Passion* (c.1550), a pale Christ is slouched on a flight of steps – perhaps before the crucifixion, perhaps already after death – with a terrible, reproachful look in his eyes, a frozen expression that is nonetheless tempered by knowledge of the victory over death that will come. Behind, an angel, his red garment the only splash of colour amongst shades of grey, holds up Christ's robe, his face twisted by angry tears. For all its age, this disturbing work comes across as shockingly modern.

GIACOMO CERUTI AND OTHER MASTERS

Giacomo Ceruti was known as "Il Pitocchetto" after the first work here, *Due Pitocchi*, or Two Paupers (c.1730–34), epitomizing the eighteenth-century shift into an awareness and depiction of the reality of daily life for ordinary folk. Ceruti's two characters – a bright-eyed chap with a withered arm, seated across from his chum in a ragged old army greatcoat, with a jug of wine and pouch of tobacco on the table between them – are matched by a snapshot of a washerwoman (c.1720) and other paintings of spinsters, cobblers and more. Ceruti's formal portrait of an old man (c.1724) demonstrates his maturity; even here, a noble visage unmistakeably shows the vagabond beneath.

A sequence of the *Four Seasons* by Rasio is executed in Arcimboldo style, with fruit and flowers used to compose the figures, while a collection of **drawings** includes a characteristic *Portrait of Lieven van Coppenol* by **Rembrandt** (c.1658), a marvellous *Adam and Eve* by **Dürer** (c.1504) and Venetian scenes by **Canaletto**.

as slower trains from Lecco, Bergamo and Cremona.

Destinations Bergamo (hourly; 50min); Capo di Ponte (8 daily; 1hr 55min); Cremona (hourly; 55min); Desenzano/Sirmione (hourly; 20min); Iseo (approx hourly; 40min); Lecco (hourly; 1hr 55min); Milano Centrale (every 30min; 1hr); Peschiera (hourly; 20min); Verona (every 30min; 35min).

By bus Flanking the train station are two bus stations – the main Stazione Autolinee, with buses from Verona, Mantua, Iseo, Bergamo-Orio al Serio airport and

Brescia-Montichiari airport, and the SIA bus station, with buses from Desenzano, Salo, Riva, Idro and Val Trompia.

Destinations Cremona (hourly; 1hr 15min); Desenzano (at least hourly; 1hr); Gargnano (every 30min; 1hr 25min); Iseo (8 daily; 40min–1hr); Mantua (hourly; 1hr 25min); Riva del Garda (3 daily; 2hrs 5min); Salo (at least every 30min; 55min); Verona (hourly; 2hr 20min).

By car Brescia has three exits off the main A4 autostrada which links Milan, Bergamo, Brescia, Verona and lakes Iseo and Garda.

GETTING AROUND

By bus To skip the dull fifteen-minute walk to the centre from the train station, hop on one of the buses from the stop opposite the train station (bus 1 direction Mompiano or bus 10 direction Marconi; tickets from the driver or from the shop by the bus stop are €1.40). Full details at ⓦ bresciamobilita.it.

By metro Brescia's new metro (ⓦ bresciamobilita.it) opened in 2013, with one line cutting through the city centre and serving outlying districts.

By car Having negotiated the ring roads and followed signs to the city centre, Brescia is straightforward to drive around, although the historical centre is closed to traffic so you'll need to park in the pricey but abundant on-road parking or in an underground car park like the one at Piazza della Vittoria.

By bike The city's bike-sharing initiative, bicimia, that you'll see around town is aimed at residents and takes over a month to register but bike rental from the station makes a good alternative to walking (Mon–Sat 7.30am–7.30pm; €1 for up to 5hrs; ☎030 306 1224, ⓦservice.bicimia.it).

On foot Central Brescia is compact and mainly pedestrianized making it safe and pleasant to wander on foot.

Trenino storico At weekends and during the summer, a naff-looking miniature train (€5, tickets and hours available on board or from the tourist office) leaves from outside the tourist office scuttling along the main thoroughfares of the old town.

INFORMATION

Tourist office Piazza della Loggia 13/b (Mon–Sat 9.30am–6.30pm, Sun 10am–6pm; ☎030 240 0357). Very well organized office with helpful staff, buckets of information and leaflets.

Provincial tourist office Via dei Musei 32

(Mon–Thurs 9am–noon & 2.30–4.30pm, Fri 9am–noon; ☎030 374 9916, ⓦbresciatourism.it). Collect info on Brescia Province which stretches from Val Camonica, Lake Iseo and Franciacorta over to the western shore of Lake Garda.

ACCOMMODATION

Brescia's **hotels** are a fairly undistinguished bunch, almost universally aimed at business travellers. At the lower end of the market, there's a cluster of rather nasty cheap hotels around the station and adjacent main roads that are best avoided. Book ahead if you're planning to be here in May, when the Mille Miglia vintage car rally attracts thousands to the city (see p.261).

Ambasciatori Via Crocefissa di Rosa 90 ☎030 399 114, ⓦambasciatori.net. A fine, family-run four-star in an unappealing modern building 1km north of the centre. The inside is attractive with spacious, air-conditioned rooms, an excellent restaurant and top-quality service. Children under 10 stay for free in their parents' room, there's free parking, and bus 1 from the station stops outside. **€100**

La Filanda Vicolo delle Cossere 6 ☎030 503 6006, ⓦlafilandadibrescia.it. An elegant but well priced B&B in the centre of the city, with three smart rooms and a breakfast buffet. It features timber ceilings and terracotta tiled floors, tea and coffee in the rooms and free wi-fi. **€70**

★Orologio Via Beccaria 17 ☎030 375 5411, ⓦalbergoorologio.it. Attractive boutique three-star in an old building beside the Broletto. Rooms have been carefully renovated with a good deal of taste, matching the warm welcome and genial service. **€125**

Villa Valeria Via Massimo D'Azeglio 16, ☎030 396 052, ⓦvillav.it. Three spacious, handsomely furnished B&B rooms in a grand family home with a lovely garden only ten minutes' walk from the centre. **€80**

Vittoria Via X (Dieci) Giornate 20 ☎030 280 061, ⓦhotelvittoria.com. Brescia's central five-star option, built in 1933 in Fascist style, has had a makeover and is a good-value, luxurious, contemporary hotel in an excellent location. **€160**

EATING AND DRINKING

Brescia has plenty of reasonably priced **places to eat** in the centre, specializing in local dishes such as *casoncei* (large meat-filled ravioli) or *brasato d'asino* (donkey stew). Many menus feature pasta stuffed with (or polenta smothered in) *bagòss*, a locally produced cheese – rich, spicy and flavourful. For *aperitivo*, head for lively Piazzale Arnaldo to the east of the centre, where a clutch of atmospheric **café-bars** fill up quickly after work and stay buzzing into the small hours.

RESTAURANTS AND CAFÉS

Al Bianchi Via Gasparo da Salò 30 ☎030 292 328, ⓦosteriaalbianchi.it. Historic restaurant dating from 1880 in a quiet location just off Piazza Loggia. A popular evening spot, serving a variety of tasty, local dishes at good prices, specializing in Brescian meaty mains (around €12), presented with home-made flair. Mon–Fri & Sun 11am–3pm & 6pm–1am, Sat 11am–1am.

Buonissimo Corso Mameli 23 ☎030 280 8245, ⓦbuonissimo-store.it. If you're feeling indecisive,

head to this four-storey foodhall including an informal, well-priced restaurant, wine bar and bookshop café where you can eat, relax and shop for goodies from across Italy all under one roof. Ideal if you're self-catering. Daily 9am–8pm.

La Vineria Via X Giornate 4 ☎030 280 543. Acclaimed little trattoria tucked beneath the arcades off Piazza Loggia. Emphasis is squarely on wines, but this is an *osteria con cucina*, also serving decent meals in its pleasant, contemporary interior. Around €40 per head. Mon, Thurs &

Sun 11.30am–3.30pm; Tues, Wed, Fri & Sat 11.30am–3.30pm & 6pm–midnight.

Osteria La Grotta Vicolo del Prezzemolo 10 ☎ 030 44 068, ⓦ osterialagrotta.it. Charming little place, dating from the 1920s, with an atmospheric interior and a menu centred on its own, high-quality *salumi* and other local specialities. Around €35 per head. Mon, Tues & Thurs–Sun 10am–3pm & 7pm–midnight.

Cremona

An attractive provincial town 55km south of Brescia, on the plain of the River Po, **Cremona** has some fine Renaissance and medieval buildings, and its cobbled streets make for some pleasant wandering, but it is best known for its violins. Ever since Andrea Amati established the first violin workshop here in 1566, followed by his son and grandson Nicolò and pupils Guarneri and – most famously – Antonio Stradivari (1644–1737), Cremona has been a focus for the instrument. Today, the city hosts an internationally famous school of violin-making, as well as frequent concerts – not least those dedicated to the city's other famous son, composer Claudio Monteverdi. It's a modest sort of place; a target for violin buffs or as a half-day trip from Brescia or Milan, on a looping route towards the richer pickings of Mantua.

Piazza del Comune

The centre of Cremona is the splendid **Piazza del Comune**, a narrow space dominated by monumental architecture. The west side is least dramatic, though its thirteenth-century buildings – the red-brick **Loggia dei Militia** (formerly headquarters of the soldiery) and the arched **Palazzo del Comune** – are lavish.

8

Torrazzo
Piazza del Comune • Tues–Sun 10am–1pm & 2.30–6pm • €5

In the northeast corner of the Piazza del Comune, visible from far and wide, looms the gawky Romanesque **Torrazzo**, at 112m one of Italy's tallest medieval towers. Built in the mid-thirteenth century and bearing a fine Renaissance clock dating from 1583, its 502 steps can be climbed for excellent views.

Duomo
Piazza del Comune • Mon–Sat 7.30am–noon & 3.30–7pm, Sun 10.30–11am & 3.30–5.30pm • Free

Adjacent to the Torrazzo stands the **Duomo**, connected by way of a Renaissance loggia. The huge facade, made up of classical, Romanesque and fancy Gothic elements, focuses on a rose window from 1274. Originally conceived as a basilica, transepts were added when the Gothic style became more fashionable, and the interior is rather oppressive – lofty and dim, marked by the dark stone of its piers, and covered by naïve sixteenth century frescoes including a trompe l'oeil by Pordenone on the west wall showing the *Crucifixion* and *Deposition*. Also of note are the fifteenth-century pulpits, decorated with fine reliefs.

Baptistry
Piazza del Comune • Tues–Sun 10am–1pm & 2.30–6pm • €3

The south side of Piazza del Comune features the octagonal **Baptistry**, dating from the late twelfth century. Its vast bare-brick interior is rather severe, though lightened by the twin columns in each bay and a series of upper balconies.

Collezione di Violini
Piazza del Comune • Tues–Sat 9am–6pm, Sun 10am–6pm • €6

The Palazzo del Comune – which also houses the tourist office – stands opposite the Torrazzo. There is a small museum of historic violins on the upper floor variously dubbed the **Collezione di Violini**, **Sala dei Violini** or **Gli Archi di Palazzo Comunale**. It is only visitable on guided tours (available in English), which run continuously; buy tickets from the bookshop in the courtyard.

After climbing the stairs, you are ushered past a stone-faced security guard – these violins are worth millions – into a room holding nine violins in glass cases. These include a very early example made by Andrea Amati in 1566 for Charles IX of France, and later instruments by Amati's pupils, Guarneri – plus, of course, Stradivari. The guide gives a spoken history and plays recordings of each violin. However, unless you're a violin nut, this is all rather over-reverent; instead, check with the tourist office to find out when one of the instruments is to be brought out

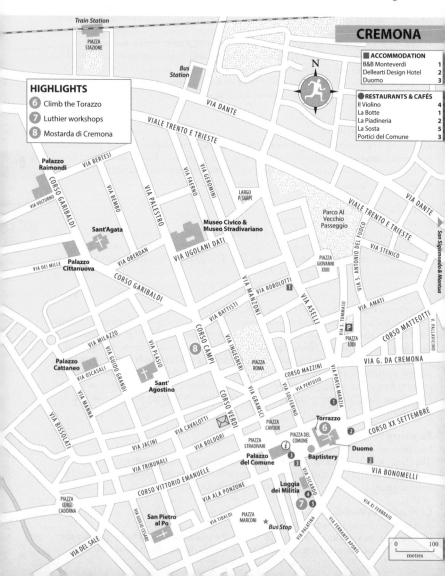

and **played**. This happens at least twice a day on weekdays, as long as at least fifteen people are in attendance.

Museo Civico, incorporating Museo Stradivariano
Via Ugolani Dati 4 • Tues–Sat 9am–6pm, Sun 10am–6pm • €7

The pilastered Palazzo Affaitati – a pleasant ten-minute stroll north of Piazza del Comune – holds the **Museo Civico "Ala Ponzone"**. The museum is strikingly designed, and forms an excellent setting; it's just a pity that much of the art is so uninspired. The star painting is *St Francis Meditating* by **Caravaggio**, showing the artist's typically deft handling of light. To find it, head into the *cinquecento* gallery; it's hanging in an alcove in the far left-hand corner. Beyond here, hunt out rooms 18 and 19, holding Chinese porcelain, Japanese ivories, Meissen ware and two little examples of eighteenth-century Wedgwood. From room 15, head upstairs for three rooms of nineteenth- and twentieth-century art, including *Le Nereidi*, a languid, mysterious work painted in 1906 by Cremona-born Emilio Rizzi (1869–1940).

From the ticket desk, separate stairs head up to the **Sezione Archeologica**, displaying Egyptian amulets, rather beautiful Greek vases and delicate Roman glassware.

Museo Stradivariano
Return to the stairs and head up again into a long hall, where, at the far end, a suite of eighteenth-century rooms – filled with the sound of recorded violin music – holds the **Museo Stradivariano**, displaying models, paper patterns, tools and acoustic diagrams from Stradivari's workshop, a letter to his patron dated August12, 1708, and more violins, violas, viols and cellos, hanging impotently in glass cases. An informative video helps to unravel the mysteries of the violin-maker's art.

8

San Pietro al Po
Piazza San Pietro • Daily 7.30–11.30am & 3.30–7pm • Free

The church of **San Pietro al Po**, southwest of Piazza del Comune, has better frescoes than the Duomo; its walls are coated with sixteenth-century art and stuccoes. Look for the trompe l'oeil work of Antonio Campi in the transept vaults, and Bernadino Gatti's hearty fresco of *The Feeding of the Five Thousand* in the refectory next door.

San Sigismondo
Via Giuseppina 3 • Daily 8am–noon & 3–6pm • Free • Bus 2 from Piazza Cavour

On the eastern edge of town is Cremona's most important religious complex after the cathedral. Built by Francesco and Bianca Sforza in 1441 to commemorate their

---

VIOLIN CONCERTS AND FESTIVALS
Besides the weekly opportunity to hear instruments being played in the Palazzo Comunale (see p.267), Cremona also hosts annual festivals with concerts by top international musicians.

Festival di Cremona Monteverdi May ⓦ teatroponchielli.it. Annual festival of concerts and operas taking place in churches and the Teatro Ponchielli.

Liuteria in Festival Mid-Sept to early Oct ⓦ fondazionestradivari.it. Annual programme of concerts, conferences and exhibitions organized by the Stradivari Foundation.

Mondomusica Early Oct ⓦ cremonamondomusica.it. An international festival of handcrafted instruments.

Triennale Internazionale degli Strumenti ad Arco ⓦ entetriennale.com. String instrument exhibition held every three years In October that also organizes occasional concerts throughout the year.

> ## LUTHIERS IN ACTION
>
> Cremona is a natural magnet for **violin-makers** of all nationalities. There are workshops across the city, many of which can be visited. The tourist office has details of open studios including Gaspar Borchardt at Piazza Zaccaria 11 (☎0372 319 69, ⓦborchardtviolins.com), just off the main square.

wedding – Cremona was Bianca's dowry – San Sigismondo's Mannerist decor is among Italy's best, ranging from Camillo Boccaccino's soaring apse fresco to Giulio Campi's *Pentecost* in the third bay of the nave, plagiarized from Mantegna's Camera degli Sposi ceiling at Mantua. Other highlights include Giulio's *Annunciation* on the entrance wall, in which Gabriel is seemingly suspended in mid-air, and the gory *John the Baptist* in the second left chapel, by Giulio's younger brother Antonio.

ARRIVAL AND DEPARTURE

CREMONA

By train The station is on Via Dante, ten minutes' walk north of Piazza del Comune; bus 1 runs regularly to Piazza Cavour.

Destinations Brescia (hourly; 55min); Mantua (hourly; 55min); Milano Centrale (6 daily; 1hr 10min).

By car Halfway between Milan and Mantua on the trafficy P415, Cremona makes a good place to stretch your legs. It is an easy half- or full-day from Brescia; a speedy drive on the A21 takes 40min. Piazza Lodi has the most central parking.

GETTING AROUND AND INFORMATION

On foot Cremona is a comfortable city to explore on foot, wandering the narrow lanes and pedestrianized areas. If you want to avoid the ten-minute walk from the station, bus 1 runs regularly to Piazza Cavour.

By bike To explore the narrow lanes of Cremona or perhaps head down to the river for a picnic, rent a bicycle

from Mata Store (Via Eridano 4; ☎0373 457 162; €20/day). **Tourist office** Piazza del Comune 5, opposite the Torrazzo (daily 9am–12.30pm & 3–6pm; June–Aug closed Sun pm; ☎0372 23 233, ⓦprovincia.cremona.it) has details of classical concerts around town as well as violin-makers' workshops that can be visited.

ACCOMMODATION

★**B&B Monteverdi** Via Robolotti 25 ☎0349 612 1624, ⓦmonteverdicremona.com. This is more of an apartment than a B&B, though breakfast is included and is served on a tray left outside your door. Located in a historic building near the old centre, the flat is spacious and elegant, furnished with handsome antiques and old paintings. **€90**

Dellearti Design Hotel Via Bonomelli 8 ☎0372 23 131, ⓦdellearti.com. Slightly incongruous in provincial Cremona, the contemporary styling of this self-fashioned art hotel offers comfortable, über-designed rooms, a small spa and courtyard café. Good discounts online. **€190**

Duomo Via Gonfalonieri 13 ☎0372 35 242, ⓦhotelduomocremona.com. A simple three-star hotel with air-conditioned en-suite rooms just off the main square. **€85**

EATING AND DRINKING

Numerous cosy *osterie* serve Cremona's excellent **local specialities**, especially *bollito misto* – a mixture of boiled meats, served with *mostarda di frutta* (also known as *mostarda di Cremona*), fruit suspended in a sweet mustard syrup. The excellent *gastronomie* that cluster around Corso Garibaldi and Corso Ca Api make good places to put together a picnic.

★**Il Violino** Via Sicardo 3 ☎0372 461 010, ⓦilviolino.it. Top choice for a gastronomic experience – a quality restaurant metres from the main piazza specializing in local dishes such as *tortelli* with sea bass or *risotto alla zucca*, followed by a variety of excellent fish dishes. Around €60 per head. Book in advance. Daily noon–2.30pm & 6–11pm.

La Botte Via Porta Marzia 5 ☎0372 29640, ⓦtavernalabotte.org. A young, local crowd come to this

taverna for plates of *affettati* (cold meats and cheeses) and other regional specialities. Tues–Sun noon–3pm & 8pm–1am.

La Piadineria Via Platina 20. Flatbread wraps at this central branch of a quality chain make a filling, fast snack. Tucked behind the cathedral on the square. Tues–Thurs 11.30am–3pm & 8–11pm, Fri 11.30am–3pm & 6pm–midnight, Sat 11.30am–3pm & 8pm–1am, Sun 5–10pm.

La Sosta Via Sicardo 9 ☎0372 456 656, ⓦosterialasosta.it. By the main piazza, this attractive *osteria* does a great line in Cremonese specialities at reasonable prices. Tues–Sun 12.15–2.15 pm & 7.30–10pm.

Portici del Comune Piazza del Comune 2 ☎0372 027 925. The nicest – and best-located – of the pleasant pavement cafés dotted around the main squares, in a plum position under the arches directly opposite the Duomo. Mon & Wed–Sun 9am–11pm.

8

Lake Garda

SIRMIONE

9

Lake Garda

Lake Garda (Lago di Garda, often called by its Latin name Benaco) is the largest and cleanest of the Italian lakes, the best-known abroad and also the most popular; roughly seven percent of all tourists to Italy head here. A body of water this big alters the local climate, which is milder and – thanks to a complex pattern of lake breezes – sunnier than might be expected, creating Mediterranean conditions well north of the Med itself.

Even more than its near-neighbours Como and Maggiore, Garda serves as a bridge between the Alps and the rest of Italy. The north of the lake, narrow and hard to reach, is tightly enclosed by mountains that drop sheer into the water; villages survive where they can, wedged into gaps in the cliffs. Further south, the lake spreads out comfortably, mountains replaced by gentle hills that precede the plain of the River Po. Whereas the north has dried ham and Alpine cheeses, the south has olive groves, vineyards and citrus orchards. The north is famous for windsurfing and sailing; the south boasts some of Italy's most luxurious spas.

It is this diversity which has fed a tourism industry that is very nearly succeeding in its efforts to devour every last usable bit of shoreline. Every summer, resorts in all corners of the lake are swamped by visitors; northern European holiday-makers tend to head for the northern and eastern resorts while Italian families tend to prefer the southern and western shores. Trying to move around on summer weekends is not easy, to say nothing of trying to enjoy the beauty and tranquillity of the lake itself. Making the best of the mild weather and visiting slightly out of season – in May to June, or September to October – allows you to appreciate the surroundings in relative peace and quiet.

In the south, the main draw is the spa village of **Sirmione**, though its neighbour **Desenzano** is a cheery spot and the old village of **Garda** retains much charm. On the western shore, **Salò** is lovely, a historic town on its own bay, while further north, **Gargnano** is one of the lake's best destinations, a small village that remains largely unspoilt.

In the northern section of the lake, **Limone** can be too busy for comfort, though nearby stands **Riva del Garda**, a charismatic small town with a long history and a centre on the lake for water and adventure sports. On the eastern shore, attractive **Malcesine** is another village that is too popular for its own good, though **Torri del Benaco**, further south, is another highlight – an attractive lakefront village that has avoided the worst of the crowds.

GETTING AROUND
LAKE GARDA

By train Timetables for all train routes in Italy are at ⓦ trenitalia.com.

By bus Full details of transport in Lombardy – including buses on the west shore of Lake Garda from Sirmione to

SAILING OFF RIVA DEL GARDA

Highlights

❶ Sirmione Medieval village squeezed onto a narrow peninsula; dodge the crowds and head out to the cliff-edge Roman ruins. **See p.282**

❷ Punta San Vigilio The quietest spot on Lake Garda, an isolated headland with an exclusive hotel at its tip. **See p.287**

❸ Salò Dignified old town, more worldly and interesting than its touristy neighbours. **See p.291**

❹ Lake Idro Isolated tarn in the mountains behind Gargnano, reached on the scenic "Four Lakes Drive". **See p.296**

❺ Gargnano Alluring lakefront village crowded in by mountains. **See p.298**

❻ Riva del Garda The lake's top destination, a holiday resort with a unique history and plenty of character. **See p.304**

❼ Lake Ledro Tiny dot of blue in a high valley above Riva; a perfect place to draw breath. **See p.308**

❽ Torri del Benaco Gracious old Veronese village on the lakefront with a beautiful crenellated castle and swims with a view. **See p.312**

HIGHLIGHTS ARE MARKED ON THE MAP ON PP.276–277

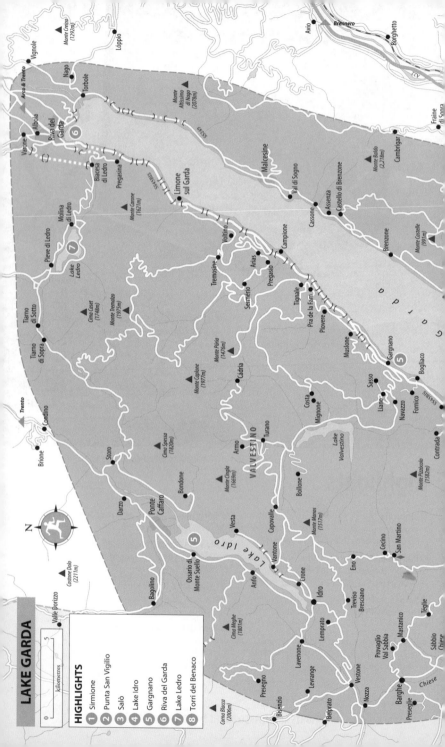

9

Limone, as well as Idro and Bagolino – are at ⓦwww .trasporti.regione.lombardia.it (click "*orari*"). Local buses for Riva del Garda and Lake Ledro are run by Trentino Trasporti (ⓦwww.ttspa.it). Buses from Riva down the eastern shore of Lake Garda are run by APTV (ⓦaptv.it);

those down the western shore are run by APTV and SIA (ⓦtrasportibrescia.it).

By boat The comprehensive boat and car ferries services are detailed on ⓦnavigazionelaghi.it (see below) and there is guidance on deciphering timetables in Basics (see p.27).

INFORMATION

Lake Garda is shared between three different provinces (in fact, three of Italy's twenty regions converge here). The northernmost tip of the lake, around Riva, is in the province of **Trento**, part of the region of Trentino. The western shore, from Limone to Sirmione, is in the province of **Brescia**, part of Lombardy. The eastern shore, from Malcesine to Peschiera, is in the province of **Verona**, part of Veneto. All three collaborate, along with a number of local hotel consortia, on the official tourism portal ⓦvisitgarda.com, which offers impartial information and hotel bookings for resorts all round the lake, along with useful extras like airport transfers. Other handy sites with English-language information include ⓦrivieradeilimoni.it and ⓦgardatrentino.it.

BOATS ON LAKE GARDA

Lake Garda's ferries are run by **Navigazione Lago di Garda** (☏800 551 801, ⓦnavigazionelaghi.it). There are almost thirty landing-stages and, since the shoreside roads are often busy with traffic, taking to the water is the easiest – and most scenic – way to get around. Boats run year-round, although outside the summer season (March–Oct), services are greatly reduced or, on some routes, halted.

Most boats are ordinary passenger vessels, marked on the timetable "**Batt**" for *battello*. Some are faster, marked "**Cat**" for *catamarano*. A few, marked with a red "**Sr**", for *servizio rapido*, are extra-quick hydrofoils; these command a small supplement. A blue "**T**" stands for *traghetto*, or car ferry. Services run daily, roughly 8am to 8pm.

ROUTES

Several routings make their way along the whole of Lake Garda, but the most frequent services link the lake's busiest resorts. In the north, boats shuttle at least hourly between **Riva**, **Limone** and **Malcesine**, while in the south, there is similar frequency on routes between **Desenzano**, **Sirmione** and **Garda**. Popular resorts in the centre of the lake, such as **Salò** and **Gardone**, are also well served, but quieter spots such as **Gargnano** have long gaps between boats.

The lake's two east–west **car-ferry** routes are timetabled separately as *traghetto autoveicoli*. These shuttle between **Maderno** and **Torri** (every 35min; 25min), and between **Limone** and **Malcesine** (hourly; 20min). Both accept foot passengers.

Services marked with a knife and fork generally (but not always) have a **restaurant** on board, serving a set meal (€25). There are no nonstop **cruises**, but timetables at each landing-stage publicize local routings as cruise excursions and it's easy to create an itinerary of your own. Check carefully the various symbols and colour-coded notes to identify each route's days of operation.

FARES AND PASSES

Fares are charged on a complicated sliding scale. Each route is assigned a number, according to the distance involved; you then cross-check on the published chart for how much that route-number (or *tratta*) costs. As an example, Torri to Salò is *tratta* 4, which costs €9.80 by boat or catamaran, or €13.80 on the *servizio rapido*. Desenzano to Sirmione is *tratta* 2 (€5/€7.60), while Garda to Malcesine is *tratta* 5 (€12/€16.60). The most expensive ticket, *tratta* 7 (Riva to Desenzano), is €15.10/€20.40. Taking a small/medium-sized **car** on either ferry costs €10.70 including the driver, plus €6.50 for each passenger.

For all these, a **return** costs twice the price of a one-way; the return half is valid on the day after purchase. EU citizens over 65 get a discount (Mon–Fri only), as do children aged 4–12.

A **biglietto di libera circolazione** gives unlimited journeys for one day; choose either the whole lake (*Intera Rete*; €34.40), or the lower lake between Desenzano and Gargnano (*Basso Lago*; €23.40), or the upper lake between Malcesine and Riva (*Alto Lago*; €20.50).

Basso Garda: the lower lake

9

BASSO GARDA – the southern third of the lake, before the mountains begin – comprises a big, apple-shaped bay, its shores curving to enclose a succession of holiday towns. The topography is gentle; this landscape of low, rolling hills and a lake-influenced Mediterranean climate are ideal for nurturing excellent wines and undemanding tourist resorts.

If you're approaching from Milan or Verona, the lower lake is likely to be your first encounter with Garda. In winter, and even at the top and tail of the season, this area can be bewitchingly beautiful, with snow on the peaks further north, a balmy climate, few hotels open and a lazy, introspective pace to life. But in midsummer, the lower reaches of Lake Garda can be as crowded as anywhere in northern Italy, with holiday-makers cramming the promenades and traffic clogging every road. The best advice, if you visit at this season, is to find yourself a bolthole-with-a-view and let the lake work its magic.

At the lake's southwestern corner stands **Desenzano**, a thoroughly likeable town with space to absorb the crowds. Nearby, little **Sirmione** occupies a peninsula projecting into the centre of the bay, its old streets heaving with sightseers. Further east, a succession of pretty and very busy lakefront villages line the shore around to the stylish little resort of **Garda**, beyond which rise the mountain slopes of Alto Garda (see p.290). A world away from the bustle of the lakeside roads, the rolling hills to the south of the lake are carpeted with vineyards and dotted with historical villages like **Solferino** and **Vallegio sul Mincio**.

Desenzano del Garda

Lake Garda's largest town, at its southwestern extremity, **DESENZANO DEL GARDA** is an engaging place that bustles with activity. If you're coming by public transport, it will probably be your first taste of the lake. The road north leads through some of the lesser visited parts of the lake (other – faster – roads zip straight to Salò and beyond) past vineyards and some good beaches up to the historical towns of the upper western shore.

Behind the attractive lakefront, lined with bars and restaurants, ordinary town life continues in the steep lanes leading up to the fourteenth-century **castle** (April to mid-June Tues–Sun 9.30am–noon & 3–6pm; mid-June to Sept Tues–Sun 9.30am–noon & 4.30–7.30pm; Oct–March Sat & Sun 10.30am–noon & 3–5.30pm; €3), from where there are spectacular views. The main square, **Piazza Malvezzi** – its terrace cafés watched over by a statue of St Angela Merici, founder of the Ursuline order – twists out to either side of the old harbour, which is fronted by some beautiful houses. Nearby, the seventeenth-century "**duomo**" (actually just the parish church; daily 8am–noon & 3.30–7pm) holds a crowded *Last Supper* by Giambattista Tiepolo (1743).

LAKE GARDA'S WINDS

Garda is swept by regular **winds** – so regular, you could virtually set your watch by them. The main wind is the **Pelèr** (also called **Suer** or **Vento**), which blows all year round from the north, starting in the small hours and lasting until midday. It begins gently, but by the time the sun is up, it can be felt across the whole surface, bringing fine weather along with a distinctive sequence of waves (small, large, then three wavelets).

The southerly **Ora** picks up after midday, lasting until dusk; it's felt mainly in the central and northern parts of the lake, often not blowing at all in the south in summer (though when it does, it can leave clouds on the mountain-tops).

Several lesser winds include the **Ponale**, which blows out of the Valle di Ledro, and the **Ander**, which blows from Desenzano towards Garda. If there is calm around Gargnano, a blustery **Vent da Mût** could be on the way. A southerly **Vinezza** sweeping from Peschiera towards Maderno in the afternoon signals bad weather to follow. The strongest is the **Balì**, a winter northerly gusting from the heights above Riva which causes a heavy chop but usually blows itself out after 24 hours.

DESENZANO DEL GARDA

ACCOMMODATION

Bonotto Hotel	1
Flowers Apartments	3
Park	2
Tripoli	4

RESTAURANTS

Bagatta alla Lepre	1
Cavallino	2
Pizzeria Vesuvio	3

Villa Romana

Via Crocefisso 22 • Tues–Sun 8.30am–7pm; Nov–Feb closes 4.30pm • €4

A short walk from the main square on Via Crocefisso is the entrance to the **Villa Romana**, one of Italy's most important late-Roman villas. As anarchy spread in Rome during the fourth century AD, those who could afford to retreated to grand country estates such as this one. Past the ticket desk and small museum, you come outside to the excavation area and, first, to Area A. An octagonal vestibule (room 1), with its mosaic floor largely intact, leads into what was a colonnaded porch (room 2), surrounded by mosaics of hunting scenes and chubby cupids and, under a modern brick shelter, through an atrium to the main dining area (room 4), with another decorative floor mosaic. A multitude of other rooms lie off to each side. A walkway leads over the mosaic pavement to Area B, with more elegant geometric mosaics (rooms 39–42). Areas C and D, in the far corner of the site, are still only partially excavated.

ARRIVAL AND DEPARTURE
DESENZANO DEL GARDA

By train The town has a good train service on the fast Milan–Brescia–Verona line.

Destinations Brescia (hourly; 20min); Milano Centrale (hourly; 1hr 10min); Venice (approx hourly; 1hr 40min);

Verona (every 30 min; 30min).

By bus Desenzano has its own exit on the nearby A4 autostrada, and buses arriving from Riva (5 daily; 1hr 50min), Salò (9 daily; 50min) and Sirmione (at least hourly; 20min).

By boat Regular ferries zip between Sirmione and the towns on the lower eastern shore while fast services leave several times a day for Riva at the top of the lake, pulling in at most larger villages on both shores along the way (see p.278).

GETTING AROUND AND INFORMATION

Bike rental Bikes can be rented at Piazza Einaudi 8, opposite the train station (☎030 914 2268), for around €15/day.
Tourist information Via Porto Vecchio 34, just off the main square on the old harbour (Mon–Fri 9am–12.30pm & 3–6pm, Sat 9am–12.30pm; ☎030 914 1510, ⓦvisitgarda.com).

ACCOMMODATION

Bonotto Hotel Via Gramsci 40 ☎030 912 1021, ⓦbonottohoteldesenzano.it. Well located just back from the waterfront, this friendly family-run hotel offers pleasant, good-value en-suite rooms with very comfy beds. Family rooms with extra bunks and free, covered parking make life easier. **€98**

★**Flowers Apartments** Piazza Malvezzi 20 ☎914 1840, ⓦbeautifulgarda.com. Well furnished, central and attractive, these apartments are perfect for families and groups of friends. The furniture is mostly modern, but terracotta floors and wooden ceilings add class. **€150**

Park Lungolago C. Battisti 19 ☎030 914 3351, ⓦparkhotelonline.it. This swish four-star with a range of sleek rooms is the smartest in the centre. There's an attractive pool with lovely lake views. **€180**

Tripoli Piazza Matteotti 18 ☎030 914 1305, ⓦhotel-tripoli.it. Surveying the bustling lakefront square, a decent three-star with small, comfortable rooms. **€135**

EATING AND DRINKING

★**Bagatta alla Lepre** Via Bagatta 33 ☎030 914 2313, ⓦristorantelalepre.com. This modern and elegant little back street restaurant is a highlight of the town, serving sophisticated dishes such as ravioli with duck and black truffles. Two-course set meal €30. Daily 12.10–2.30pm & 7.10–11pm.

Cavallino Via Murachette 29 ☎030 912 0217, ⓦristorantecavallino.it. An expensive temple to gourmet Gardesana cooking, positioned well back from the lakefront bustle. Innovative takes on lake fish dishes and Mediterranean seafood mark it out as worth a splash. Expect €60 or more per head. Tues–Sat 12.30–2.30pm & 7.30pm–midnight, Sun 12.30–2.30pm.

Pizzeria Vesuvio Via Mezzocolle 37 ☎030 914 0092. This is primarily a takeaway joint, but you can sit in and enjoy delicious pizza with a crispy crust, cooked – of course – in a wood-fired oven. Daily noon–2pm & 6–11pm.

North of Desenzano: the Valtenesi

A little north of Desenzano the lakefront road detours inland through the rolling hills of the **Valtenesi**, a bucolic region of vineyards and olive groves. The main settlement, **PADENGHE**, is a quiet, prosperous little town, very spick and span, though it's a different story up at the hilltop castle; venture through the gateway and you'll find the interior still crowded with ramshackle, claustrophobic houses. From Padenghe, a minor road detours inland for 6km to **PUEGNAGO**, where you can sample the chiaretto or rosé wines – Garda Classico DOC Groppello and Chiaretto – that the Comincioli vineyard has been producing since the sixteenth century.

The main road out of Padenghe makes a beeline north for Salò (see p.291), bypassing the photogenic harbour village of **Moniga** and the castle on the headland above the beaches around **Manerba**.

Isola del Garda

Guided tours only June–Sept daily Tues–Sun · €25–30 depending on where you start from · ⓦisoladelgarda.com · Boat departs from Salò (most frequently), Garda, Bardolino and Sirmione

Off the Valtenesi shore north of Manerba, the elongated **ISOLA DEL GARDA** is the lake's largest island, formerly the site of an ancient monastery once visited by St Francis. The old buildings were replaced around 1900 by a fanciful **villa** in Venetian neo-Gothic style. Italianate terraced **gardens** lead down to the lake, lush with lemon and pear trees, persimmons, jujube, pomegranates, bougainvillea and roses, while beyond, much of the island is covered by coniferous **woodland**, alongside Mediterranean shrubs, cypresses, cedars, bay trees and more.

9

The island remains privately owned – the Cavazza family live there all year round – and can only be visited on a **guided tour**. The fare covers return boat transport and a two-hour guided tour, including a tasting of local products.

Sirmione

Sirmio, gem of the peninsulas and islands
Which Neptune bears in liquid lakes or the vast sea –
How willingly and happily I visit you!

Catullus, 56 BC

Things have changed since the Roman poet Catullus scribbled a verse to celebrate coming home to his villa at **SIRMIONE**. This narrow promontory, extending 4km into the lake from the southern shore, is now occupied by an attenuated holiday resort, and the tranquillity which Catullus sought is consequently long gone. Little Sirmione – barely more than a village in size – creaks under the pressure of a million overnight stays every year, and is almost suffocated with hotels and touristy commerce. The town has Lake Garda's only mineral spring, rising 300m offshore on the lake bed, and several hotels and **thermal spas** take advantage, with many programmes of therapies for various ailments. Tens of thousands of people come for the traditional twelve-day cure.

Make no mistake: this is a beautiful, unusual spot, well worth a visit for the spectacular **castle** and equally spectacular ruined **Roman villa** on the steep-sided headland – but having to elbow a path through the crowded lanes of the old village to reach them may rapidly try your patience. If you can, pay the extra to enjoy the beauty of the setting while shielded behind the gates of a luxury hotel.

SIRMIONE

N

Grotte di Catullo

Lake Garda

Lido delle Bionde

San Pietro in Mavino

Punta Staffalo

Parco Maria Callas

Villa Cortine

Catullo Spa

PIAZZA D. A. PIATTI

PIAZZALE ORTI MANARA

PIAZZALE PORTO VALENTINO

PIAZZA FLAMINIA

Santa Maria Maggiore

Imbarcadero

PIAZZA CARDUCCI

PIAZZA CASTELLO

Rocca Scaligera

PIAZZALE PORTO

Lake Garda

Bus Station

Desenzano, Peschiera & **5**

0	200
metres	

■ ACCOMMODATION	
Eden	3
Grand Hotel Terme	4
Grifone	2
Ideal	1
La Casa di Marla	5

● RESTAURANTS & CAFÉS	
Al Torcol	1
Caffè Grande Italia	4
Grifone	3
La Rucola	2

Rocca Scaligera

Tues–Sat 8.30am–7pm, Sun 8.30am–1pm • €4

The only access into Sirmione is across a narrow, fortified bridge over an inlet. Looming beside are the battlemented walls of the **Rocca Scaligera**, a fairy-tale castle with boxy turreted towers almost entirely surrounded by water. It dates from the thirteenth century, when the Della Scala/Scaligeri family of Verona expanded and fortified their territory. You're free to roam around the walls – the enclosed harbour is especially photogenic – and climb the towers; 77 steps lead up to the keep, followed by another 92 to the top of the highest tower, from where views over the rooftops of Sirmione are lovely.

Via Vittorio Emanuele

Sirmione spreads out across a few piazzas either side of the narrow main street, **Via Vittorio Emanuele**, packed with cafés, *gelaterie*, postcard stands and a few fashion and jewellery shops. To one side is the fifteenth-century church of **Santa Maria Maggiore**, worth stopping at to admire the pretty seventeenth-century entrance arcade that reused ancient columns (including a fourth-century milepost), before pressing on to **Piazza Piatti** at the far end of the shopping area.

Via Catullo

From Piazza Piatti, the **trenino elettrico** (little electric train; €1.50) makes short work of the 750m or so along Via Catullo, past the cypresses and olive groves. If you walk, it's worth detouring up to the asymmetrical, hut-like church of **San Pietro**, which has thirteenth-century frescoes and an eleventh-century bell tower; its shady grounds make for a good picnic stop.

From partway along Via Catullo, a path heads down to water level and the pay beach **Lido delle Bionde** (May–Oct daily 8am–midnight; free, €8 for a sun lounger) where you can eat, drink, swim in the lake or sunbathe on the pontoon or nearby rocks.

Grotte di Catullo
Tues–Sat 8.30am–7pm, Sun until 5pm; Nov–Feb closes 4.30pm • €6

Occupying the tip of Sirmione's headland, perched on rocky slopes high above the lake, are the **Grotte di Catullo**, the remains of a large, first-century BC/AD Roman villa (167m by 105m). The connection to Catullus is unsubstantiated; he is known to have had a villa at Sirmione, and the ruins have been dated to the right era, but nothing links this particular house to the poet. Beside the ticket office stands a small museum displaying artefacts and mosaic fragments. From here, you can roam the open-air ruins freely; the setting, among olive trees, with birds singing and bees buzzing in the lavender, is lovely, with superb views across the lake towards the mountains, though – even with the help of maps and signboards – it's not always easy to tell which part of the villa is which.

ARRIVAL AND INFORMATION
SIRMIONE

By bus The bus station is at the end of Viale Marconi, by the tourist office and the entrance to the walled village.
Destinations Brescia (hourly; 1hr 20min); Desenzano (at least hourly; 20min); Verona (hourly; 1hr).
By car Sirmione has an exit on the Milan to Verona A4 autostrada. The old quarter of Sirmione stands at the far end of a slender peninsula, 4km north of the main Desenzano–Peschiera road. The village is closed to traffic and there is plenty of pay and display parking at the end of the approach road, Viale Marconi.

By boat The *imbarcadero* is on Piazza Carducci, a short stroll away from the tourist office. Regular boats link the resorts at the southern end of the lake, while a reduced number of boats also head to the towns to the north of the lake (see p.278).
Tourist office Viale Marconi 2 (Easter–Nov daily 9am–8pm; Dec–Easter Mon–Fri 9am–12.30pm & 3–6pm, Sat 9am–12.30pm; ☎ 030 916 114, ⓦ sirmionehotel.com).

ACCOMMODATION

Accommodation lines the approach roads to Sirmione and spreads all the way down the peninsula. The recommendations below concentrate on some of the more appealing choices that line the lanes of the old town. The *Borgo San Donino* agriturismo, 4km inland (p.288), makes a peaceful alternative to the hustle and bustle of Sirmione.

Eden Piazza Carducci ☎ 030 916 481, ⓦ cerinihotels.it. This was where Ezra Pound was staying when he met James Joyce in 1920. Now a fine four-star hotel, it's a modern, cool and comfortable retreat from the bustle of the village; opt for a lake-view room facing west, and muse on the glittering waters as the ferries come and go below you. Closed Nov–Feb. **€200**
Grand Hotel Terme Viale Marconi ☎ 030 916 261, ⓦ termedisirmione.com. Located just beside the castle, this is a palatial affair, with most rooms facing east away from the road, across the lake. It has a lovely pool and a private beach, as well as fitness facilities and its own thermal spa. Closed Feb. **€300**
Grifone Vicolo Bisse ☎ 030 916 014, ⓦ sirmionehotelgrifone.it. Probably the cheapest waterside rooms on the lake, this house-proud little

9

two-star is tucked down a quiet alley alongside the castle. Decor in the sixteen basic rooms is plain, but there's a warm welcome and this is a great spot away from the bustle to enjoy the lake. Ask for a room with a view of the castle; singles and triples are available. Closed Nov–Feb. €90

Ideal Via Catullo ☎030 990 4245, ⓦ hotelidealsirmione .it. A near-perfect location, on the top of the hill overlooking the very tip of the headland, with the lake and the Roman ruins just metres away. Rooms, however,

though decent, are uninspired; all the character comes from the vistas and the surroundings, viewable from the swimming pool. Closed Nov–March. €100

★**La Casa di Marla** Via Palazzo 3A ☎327 203 5258, ⓦ bblacasadimarla.wordpress.com. This old farmstead just south of Sirmione has a wonderfully homely feel, with bright walls, antiques, plants and Turkish carpets. It's run with warmth by Marzia and Laura who don't speak English; a rare chance to practice your Italian in this touristy region. Singles from €30. €60

EATING AND DRINKING

★**Al Torcol** Via San Salvatore 30 ☎030 990 4605. An elegant cut above its neighbours, this friendly place with a lovely vine-covered garden serves well-judged dishes to remember – the home-made pasta is to die for. Prices aren't bad for central Sirmione at around €40 per head. July & Aug Fri–Mon noon–2pm & 7pm–midnight, Tues–Thurs 7pm–midnight; Sept–June Tues–Sun noon–2pm & 7pm–midnight.

Caffè Grande Italia Piazza Carducci. Stands out for its history; it's been churning out ice-cream sundaes from a marble-topped bar since 1894, and continues to do so with a touch more panache than its neighbours. Tues–Sun

8.45am–midnight.

Grifone Vicolo Bisse 5 ☎030 916 097. Small, family-run restaurant with a romantic lakefront garden and simple, thoughtfully prepared food served with a smile. Fish dishes around €18. Mon & Tues–Sun noon–2.30pm & 7–10.30pm.

La Rucola Vicolo Strentelle 5 ☎030 916 326. A sophisticated little spot near the castle, this is the top restaurant in town with a refined menu of lake fish and meat specialities along with perfect pizzas from their wood oven. Prices are high; expect more than €80 per head. Daily 12.30–2pm & 7.30–10pm.

Peschiera del Garda

At the southeastern corner of Lake Garda, the old military town of **PESCHIERA DEL GARDA** guards the outflow of the lake into the River Mincio. Its impressive fortifications ("fair and strong", as Dante wrote in the *Inferno*) were revamped in the 1550s by the Venetians, and subsequently reinforced by the Austrians. The old town lies within them, on an island at the mouth of the river, with the modern town occupying the banks either side. Although it's an atmospheric place to wander, Peschiera can get extremely busy – not least with spillover from the nearby **theme parks** (see box opposite).

ARRIVAL AND INFORMATION
PESCHIERA DEL GARDA

By train Peschiera has a good train service on the Milan–Brescia–Verona line. The station is around a fifteen-minute walk to the east of the walled town.

Destinations Brescia (hourly; 30min); Milano Centrale (hourly; 1hr 40min); Venice (approx hourly; 1hr 30min); Verona (hourly; 20min).

By bus Buses head north from here through all the lakeside towns to Riva (see p.304) at the northwestern tip of the lake. Shuttle buses head to the theme parks just 2km north of town (see p.285).

Destinations Riva (hourly; 1hr 35min); Sirmione (at least

hourly; 20min); Malcesine (hourly; 1hr 10min); Torri del Benaco (hourly; 1hr).

By car Peschiera is an important access point to the lake with an exit on the A4 autostrada, so roads around the town get choked, especially in summer.

By boat The town is well linked by boats to the southern part of the lake, with some fast services to towns in the northern part of the lake too (see p.278).

Tourist information Piazza Betteloni (daily 9am–1pm & 3–6pm, July & Aug 4–7pm; ☎045 755 1673, ⓦ tourism .verona.it).

ACCOMMODATION AND EATING

Antica Locanda del Contrabbandiere Martelosio di Sopra, Pozzolengo ☎030 918151, ⓦ locandadel contrabbandiere.com. Family-run agriturismo with an excellent upmarket restaurant offering dishes such as

beef tenderloin with *stracchino* cheese and mustard fondue. The three comfortable rooms feature handsome wooden beds. €100

THEME PARKS: GARDALAND AND CANEVAWORLD

The **theme parks** just north of Peschiera are a good day out for all ages. The biggest is **GARDALAND** (daily: mid-March to late Sept 10am–6pm; mid-June to early Sept until 11pm; also weekends in Oct & Dec; €37.50, children under 10 €31, children less than 1m tall free; discounts for part-day and multi-day tickets; ☎045 644 9777, ⓦgardaland.it), which includes the nearby small but well-planned **SeaLife aquarium**. It's pricey but well thought out with lots of shade, water games and rides for all ages from around 3 upwards.

A little further north is **CANEVAWORLD** (☎045 696 9900, ⓦcanevaworld.it), comprising two adjacent parks: **Movieland** (mid-April to mid-Sept daily 10am–6pm, later opening at weekends and in July & Aug; also weekends in Oct), with fake movie-sets and shows revealing secrets of special effects; and **AquaParadise** (mid-May to mid-Sept daily 10am–6pm; July & Aug until 7pm), with slides, flumes, pools and a pirate island. One day's admission is €25 for one park (€19 for kids under 1.40m high), or €29/24 for both parks. Both parks in two days costs €33/27. Children under 1m go free.

ARRIVAL AND DEPARTURE

By bus Free buses shuttle every thirty minutes (mornings only) to Canevaworld from Peschiera station.
By car Parking at Gardaland costs an extra €5.

ACCOMMODATION

Gardaland Hotel Via Palù 11, Castelnuovo ☎045 640 4407, ⓦgardalandhotel.it. If you're in the market for giant friendly dragons and face painting, just down the road from the theme park, with free shuttle buses, the New England-style *Gardaland Hotel* offers very comfortable family-orientated accommodation. The gardens, pool area and entertainers will keep younger visitors entertained for hours. Online special offers available. Closed Nov–March. €150

Lazise

Nine kilometres north of Peschiera, the walled village of **LAZISE** was once a major port and retains a photogenic (but privately owned) **castle** and, on the harbour, an arcaded medieval **customs house**. Originally used for building and repairing boats for the Venetian fleet, it later served as a shelter for sheep, whose urine was a vital ingredient in gunpowder. Next door the small Romanesque church of San Nicolò holds thirteenth-century frescoes. Nowadays the village is lined with cafés, pizzerias and holiday-makers, but retains an appealing character, with some picturesque corners. Wednesday sees the main piazzas bustling with the weekly market. Out of season, when it reverts to being a sleepy lakeside village, the allure is stronger still.

ARRIVAL AND INFORMATION
LAZISE

By bus Lazise is on the main bus route from Verona to Riva del Garda, which runs throughout the year.
Destinations Malcesine (hourly; 1hr); Peschiera (hourly; 15min); Riva (6 daily; 1hr 25min); Torri del Benaco (hourly; 25min); Verona (6 daily; 55min).
By boat The *imbarcadero* is just by the little harbour at the pedestrianized centre of the walled village. Boats head for other resorts around the southern part of the lake; the service is greatly reduced in winter (see p.278).
Tourist information Via Francesco Fontana 14 (daily 9am–1pm & 3–6pm; ☎045 758 0114, ⓦtourism .verona.it).

Bardolino

About 5km north of Lazise is the spruce resort of **BARDOLINO**, home of light, red Bardolino wine. The town is at its most animated in mid-September during the bibulous **Festa dell'Uva**; otherwise, strolling the lush palm- and pine-shaded promenade is the main activity, especially on Thursdays, when it's taken over by the weekly market. The church of **San Zeno**, just above the main road, was built in the eighth century; its Latin-cross form and high domed ceiling became a prototype for later Romanesque churches.

9

If you have your own transport, grab a map from the tourist office and head off along the **Strada del Bardolino** (ⓦstradadelbardolino.com) to enjoy the inland countryside while taking in wineries and olive oil producers on the way.

Museo dell'Olio di Oliva and Museo del Vino

Celebrating the major industries of the region, a little south of town is the **Museo dell'Olio di Oliva** at Via Peschiera 54 (Mon–Sat 9am–12.30pm & 2.30–7pm, Sun 9am–12.30pm; free; ⓦmuseum.it), centred on a shop selling local oils, wines and vinegars but with an engaging display of old equipment. On the hillside above and well signposted from Bardolino, the **Museo del Vino** at Via Costabella 9 (March–Oct daily 9am–1pm & 2.30–7pm; free; ⓦzeni.it) is a similar concern, part of the Zeni winery and supplemented by ancient tools, free tastings and sales.

ARRIVAL AND DEPARTURE   BARDOLINO

By bus The bus 62/64 runs from Verona to Riva del Garda throughout the year, stopping at Bardolino en route. Other local bus routes add to the service.
Destinations Malcesine (hourly; 50min); Peschiera (hourly; 25min); Riva (6 daily; 1hr

15min); Torri del Benaco (hourly; 15min); Verona (6 daily; 1hr 5min).
By boat Bardolino is well linked with towns and villages up and down the lake with both regular and fast ferry services (see p.278).

INFORMATION AND ACTIVITIES

Horseriding On the eastern slopes of Monte Baldo near Porcino, *Ranch Barlot* (ⓣ348 723 4082, ⓦranchbarlot.com) offers guided horse-trekking through the hills. Book ahead.

Tourist information Piazzale Aldo Moro (daily 9am–1pm & 3–6pm; ⓣ045 721 0078, ⓦtourism.verona.it).

ACCOMMODATION AND EATING

Biri Via Solferino 13 ⓣ045 721 0873. Good-value local specialities served in this little back-street restaurant and washed down with quality local wines. Try the *tagliata di manzo al rosmarino* (roast fillet of beef in rosemary; mains €10–15) for a change from lake fish.

Cà Castellani Strada Galeazzo 1 ⓣ045 721 1698, ⓦagriturismocastellani.com. Among vineyards 2km from the lake, this attractive agriturismo has a handful of double rooms and bright modern apartments (sleeping from two to seven) with a large garden and pool. **€85**

Garda

The former fishing village of **GARDA**, 18km north of Peschiera, is an ancient settlement, recorded in the tenth century. It has a tight little historic quarter of narrow alleys squeezed between the main road and the lake, although – as in many of Garda's neighbours – the lanes are now characterized by snack bars and souvenir shops. Look for the **Palazzo Fregoso**, a charming sixteenth-century house on Via Spagna with its original external staircase and a double lancet window over an arched passageway. Across town, the Baroque church of **Santa Maria Assunta** is worth a peek.

Garda's chief pleasure, though, is strolling its long, curving lakefront promenade, which has plenty of benches from which to soak up the wonderful views southwest over the water. In summer, Garda is also a departure point for the pleasant excursion to the nearby **Isola del Garda** (see p.281). Barely half an hour's drive east of Garda, over the ridge beyond **Affi** (a junction on the A22 autostrada), the scenic **Valpolicella wine region** is perfect for vineyard walks and country restaurants (see box, p.335).

ARRIVAL AND INFORMATION   GARDA

By bus Garda is well connected by buses travelling north and south on the main lakeside road as well as those heading east into the Valpolicella region (see box, p.335).
Destinations Malcesine (hourly; 1hr); Peschiera (hourly;

30min); Riva (6 daily; 1hr 25min); Torri del Benaco (hourly; 15min); Verona (6 daily; 55min).
By boat Garda's position almost halfway up the lake means it is well positioned for boat services around the lake; services are at their most extensive in summer (see p.278).

Tourist information Piazza Donatori di Sangue 1, just above the main road (Mon–Sat 9am–7pm, Sun 10am–4pm, reduced hours in winter; ☎045 627 0384, ⓦ tourism.verona.it).

EATING AND DRINKING

Busy terrace cafés and restaurants abound on the lakefront promenade – even the fifteenth-century **Loggia della Losa**, originally a dock for the Palazzo Carlotti behind, is now a **gelateria** – but the quality of food in the town isn't great, with not much to choose between many places.

Caffe Amaro Piazzale Roma, 2 ☎346 633 2296, ⓦ osteriacaffeamaro.it. Rustic restaurant at the south end of town with mains such as braised beef in red wine with polenta for €14. You can eat outside on the tree-shaded terrace; book ahead in summer. Tues–Sun noon–11pm.

Taverna Fregoso Corso Vittorio Emanuele 37 ☎045 725 6622. A good-value little restaurant serving generous portions of decent pasta dishes, pizza and steaks (€10–15). Tues–Sun noon–11pm.

Punta San Vigilio

Marking the end of the southern part of the lake, **PUNTA SAN VIGILIO**, 3km west of Garda and 4km south of Torri del Benaco (see p.312), forms a prominent headland flanked by a lovely shingle pay beach. The main road passes well inland, behind a shelter of foliage, meaning that traffic noise down on the waterfront is minimal.

The promontory is private and consists of an attractive, well-equipped pay beach, the **Parco Baia delle Sirene** (April Sat & Sun 10am–7pm, €5; May to mid-June daily 10am–8pm, €9, or €6 after 3pm; mid-June to mid-Sept daily 9.30am–8pm, €12, or €9 after 2.30pm, or €5 after 4.30pm; ⓦ parcobaiadellesirene.it) plus a historic **hotel** and **taverna**. From the parking area, an avenue of cypresses leads to the entrance to the sunny beach where there are sun loungers and picnic tables scattered on grassy slopes planted with pines and planes, as well as table football, table tennis and a little bar. As an alternative, footpaths lead to smaller nearby (free) coves, one of which is unofficially nudist.

If you keep walking down the avenue of cypresses, you arrive at a beautiful sixteenth-century villa, surrounded by peaceful olive and citrus groves at the tip of the headland. This bewitching little corner of the lake is the location of one of Lake Garda's most exclusive **hotels** – *Locanda San Vigilio* – and, alongside at the tiny harbour, the sixteenth century *Taverna San Vigilio*.

ACCOMMODATION AND EATING   PUNTA SAN VIGILIO

★**Locanda San Vigilio** Punta San Vigilio ☎045 725 6688, ⓦ locanda-sanvigilio.it. An impossibly romantic hotel, a favourite with Churchill and various other heads of state, with just seven doubles and a handful of suites in a beautiful lakeside location amid olive groves and cypress trees. €550
Taverna San Vigilio Punta San Vigilio ☎045 725 6688, ⓦ locanda-sanvigilio.it. This tiny horseshoe harbour beside the sixteenth-century inn is the stuff holiday memories are made of. Prices are high for the day-long snacks but a sundowner prosecco or a morning coffee is worth every penny. On summer evenings there is a buffet laid out in the olive groves by the side. Closed Dec–Feb.

South of Lake Garda

The landscape of low hills south of Sirmione holds Lake Garda's finest **wine** country; the overlapping DOC areas of **Lugana**, **San Martino della Battaglia** and **Garda Classico** all produce excellent wines, sold widely in the region. The sleepy agricultural villages are full of history and the peaceful countryside makes a welcome contrast to the bustle of the lake in high season.

Torre di San Martino

Tower and museum March–Sept Mon–Sat 9am–12.30pm & 2.30–7pm, Sun 9am–7pm; Oct–Feb Tues–Sun 9am–12.30pm & 2–5.30pm • €5 • ⓦ solferinoesanmartino.it

The rolling hills and vineyards hereabouts experienced death on an appalling scale in

9

the wars surrounding the Risorgimento. On June 24, 1859, combined Italian and French forces under Napoleon III defeated the Austrian army under Emperor Franz Josef on two fronts. The first victory was won by the Italian King Vittorio Emanuele II near **SAN MARTINO** (subsequently suffixed "della Battaglia"), where a circular tower, built in 1893 to the memory of Vittorio Emanuele, now stands 70m high, dominating sightlines for miles around. There are wonderful views from the top of the tower accessed via a steep, winding ramp.

An ossuary chapel holds the bones of hundreds of the slain, and a small, touching **museum** displays bloodied uniforms, love letters, tattered flags and discarded weapons.

Solferino

Some of the bloodiest fighting on June 24, 1859, took place near **SOLFERINO**, 11km south of San Martino della Battaglia, where over 40,000 men were killed or wounded. A travelling businessman from Geneva, Henri Dunant, was shocked at the sight of injured soldiers left to fend for themselves, and subsequently called for the formation of a nursing corps to care for the victims of battle – an idea which evolved into the **Red Cross**.

Solferino today is a quiet town, its stout **Rocca** and nearby **museum** (March–Sept Tues–Sun 9am–12.30pm & 2.30–7pm; €2.50) displaying mementoes of the battle, its church ossuary filled with the bones of soldiers.

Valeggio sul Mincio

Once on the western border of the mighty Venetian Republic, **VALEGGIO SUL MINCIO** played a strategic role witnessed by the fourteenth-century Castello Scaligero that towers over the village. The Republic's enemy, the Duke of Milan's response was to build the fortified Ponte Visconteo, which presides over the pretty riverside neighbourhood of Borghetto.

Visitors come these days to enjoy Valeggio's culinary speciality – **tortellini** – small stuffed pasta served in over forty family-run restaurants (ⓦvaleggio.com) throughout the village. The third Tuesday in June sees the **Festa del Nodo d'Amore**, a huge open-air dinner seating four thousand at tables on the Ponte Visconteo.

Parco Giardino Sigurtà

Via Cavour 1 • March–Oct daily 9am–6pm • Park €12; bike rental €4/hr; golf cart rental €13–16/hr; tourist train €3/30min tour • ⓦ sigurta.it

The **Parco Giardino Sigurtà**, on the edge of Valeggio, is acclaimed as one of Italy's most beautiful gardens, spreading luxuriantly over 125 acres on the moraine hillsides above the river. Two footpaths (each 50min) wind through the park, or you can rent a bike or a four-person golf cart, or take the tourist train.

ARRIVAL AND DEPARTURE   SOUTH OF LAKE GARDA

By bus Services are slow and infrequent in this region; one of the most useful regular links is between Peschiera, Valeggio sul Mincio and Mantua.

Destinations Mantua (hourly; 45min); Peschiera (hourly; 20min).

ACCOMMODATION

SAN MARTINO

★**Borgo San Donino, Selva Capuzza** San Martino della Battaglia ⓣ030 991 0279, ⓦselvacapuzza.it. Eleven lovely self-catering apartments in stunning, peaceful surroundings. Part of the nearby winery and farmhouse restaurant (see p.290), there's plenty of open space, and a large pool. **€105**

VALEGGIO SUL MINCIO

La Finestra sul Fiume Corte Sega 2 ⓣ045 7950 556, ⓦlafinestrasulfiume.it. Three tasteful B&B rooms in converted mill buildings on the river's edge a ten-minute walk from Borghetto. Wonderfully peaceful surroundings, pretty garden and bicycles to rent. Five-night minimum stay in high season. **€120**

9

EATING AND DRINKING

SAN MARTINO

★**Cascina Capuzza, Selva Capuzza** San Martino della Battaglia ☏030 991 0279, ⓦselvacapuzza.it. This is a popular local secret, extended families crowding in to enjoy a slap-up meal in rustic converted farm buildings covered in ivy, all exposed brick and stone-tiled floors. There's no menu; choose based on your waiter's descriptions or go for the set four courses (around €35), washed down with award-wining local wine. Follow signs through country lanes from the roundabout by the A4 tollbooths, around 5km south of Sirmione. They also offer peaceful, attractive agriturismo apartments (see p.288). Closed Mon–Wed.

VALEGGIO SUL MINCIO

Antica Locanda Mincio Via Buonarroti 12, Borghetto ☏045 795 0059, ⓦanticalocandamincio.it. A stout waterside inn with a perfect location shaded by trees alongside an old footbridge over the weir. The grand interior features frescoes and decorated beams in the Sala del Camino, which is warmed by a roaring fire in winter. The cooking is Mantuan in spirit, with *agnolotti* (a local tortellini) in butter and porcini mushrooms featuring alongside lake fish and country cheeses. Closed Wed & Thurs.

Alto Garda: the upper lake

ALTO GARDA – the northern two-thirds of the lake – is a different kettle of fish from the south. Where the south has gentle shoreside hills, the north has mountain cliffs closing in, often dropping sheer to the water. Ease of access to the southern resorts such as Desenzano and Sirmione can make them almost suburban in ambience; by contrast, the best of the northern villages – **Gargnano** on the west shore, **Torri del Benaco** on the east – retain an elusive, romantic charm. Wherever you end up, the views are spectacular, with mountains rising on every side, cloud-capped or perhaps dusted with snow, and your eye able to pan effortlessly along miles of the long, straight shores, blue water below, blue sky above. **Salò**, on its own little bay, is the most dignified of lakeside towns, with Art Nouveau villas nestling discreetly above the shore towards and beyond its neighbour, **Gardone**.

A distinctive history, a spectacular cliff-girt location and a lived-in old quarter give **Riva del Garda** – the most popular holiday destination on the lake, at its northernmost tip – much to recommend it. Its neighbours, **Limone** and **Malcesine**, are two of the prettiest villages of all, but it can be hard to navigate a path through their crowds of holiday-makers, souvenir shops and mediocre restaurants. Behind Gargnano, roads climb precipitously to **Lake Idro**, a little smear of blue on the map which we've included in this chapter for its remote, mountain atmosphere.

The western shore: Salò to Limone

Do you know the land where the lemon trees grow?

Goethe, 1786

Garda's **western shore** holds some of the most dramatic scenery in the whole Lakes region. The entire area comprises the **Parco Alto Garda Bresciano** (ⓦparcoaltogarda.net), a diverse chunk of land that includes the lush beauty of the lakeshore road, lined with palms, bougainvillea and, further north, citrus trees, steep rock faces perched over the lake, hidden valleys and rugged mountains rising to 2000m. Monikered the "*Riviera dei Limoni*" by marketeers, this area is covered by the useful website ⓦrivieradeilimoni.it.

A little north of the old Venetian town of **Salò** – in the hills above the sedate resort of **Gardone Riviera** – stands Lake Garda's most idiosyncratic attraction, the eye-popping **Il Vittoriale** villa, former home of the poet Gabriele D'Annunzio. After **Gargnano** – the most attractive and unspoilt of the lake villages – the narrow road offers up tantalizing glimpses of the sparkling water from between the *gallerie* and the lemon trees on the beautiful approach to the nineteenth-century resort of Riva del Garda, north of **Limone** at the head of the lake. Engaging diversions head across the mountains to **Lake Idro**.

THE LAKESHORE ROAD

9

Garda's lakeshore road – dubbed **La Gardesana Occidentale** (SS45bis) on the west (Salò to Riva 45km), and **La Gardesana Orientale** (SS249) on the east (Torbole to Peschiera 61km) – is a narrow, ordinary route with one lane in each direction. It clings to the shoreline, often squeezed in a gap of a few metres between the cliffs and the water. On the southern part of the lake you can quite often detour onto a minor road or choose another way, but in the north there are no options; the topography dictates that there is only one road to follow. This can lead to unusually **heavy traffic**, with cars, lorries, buses, camper vans, motorbikes and – most dangerously – cyclists jockeying for position. On several stretches, the road passes through **tunnels**, all of them dimly lit, some totally unlit; if you're driving with sunglasses on, beware of being suddenly plunged into pitch blackness. The most demanding sections are between Gargnano and Limone, and between Torbole and Malcesine, where the tunnels are very narrow, sometimes lacking a white line dividing the lanes. This was where, in 2008, car-chase sequences in the James Bond movie *Quantum of Solace* were filmed, stunt drivers topping 200kmh in 007's custom-designed Aston Martin. Fantasy aside, those who lack the licence to kill are bound by a 50kmh speed limit.

Aside from the dangers of driving it, the lakeshore road also impacts on each of the communities it serves. Some, such as Torbole, suffer by having the road run directly through the centre, creating **noise** and **traffic** that cuts the village off from its shore. Others, such as Gargnano and Malcesine, benefit by having the road pass 100m or more inland, behind the village, thus leaving the shore traffic-free. This also impacts on visitors; a large proportion of **lake hotels**, up and down Garda, are built on the land side of the road, meaning that their views are tempered by the sight and sound of traffic passing just in front. Whenever possible, we've recommended hotels on the lake side of the road, where traffic doesn't impinge.

Salò

Tucked into the western shore, at the foot of Monte San Bartolomeo, **SALÒ** is splendidly sited on its own narrow bay. Capital of the Magnifica Patria – a grouping of lake communes – for more than four hundred years until the fall of the Venetian Republic in 1797, Salò today retains its old-fashioned hauteur. It's now something of a yachties' town, with a larger-than-usual marina of bobbing masts, but nonetheless has a less touristy profile than its neighbours, offering everything you'd want from a lakes town – a long, quiet waterfront promenade, great views, an alluring old quarter – but without the crowds and largely without the tat. Unlike Gardone or Desenzano, Salò is a small, elegant town, with ordinary shops and its own everyday concerns, transplanted to an extraordinary location on the lake. It is regularly at or near the top of the classification of Italian municipalities by income and quality of life.

The historic centre is bordered on the west by the sloping, tree-divided **Piazza Vittorio Emanuele II**, busy with traffic and known as the **Fossa** (ditch). At the top, the ancient city gate, dubbed the **Torre dell'Orologio** after renovation works added a clock in 1772, leads through to quiet **Piazza Zanelli**, overlooked by the mullioned windows of the sixteenth-century Casa Bersatti. Pedestrianized **Via San Carlo**, lined by dignified facades, leads down to the grand seventeenth-century town hall, directly on the lake. Alongside is the broad, pleasant **Piazza della Vittoria**, linked by narrow lanes to the unfinished Renaissance facade of the **Duomo** (daily 8.30am–noon & 3.30–7pm), which holds paintings by Romanino and Zenon Veronese, as well as an elaborate Gothic gilded altarpiece. More beautiful old *palazzi* crowd the nearby alleys, and the porticoed, sixteenth-century town hall **Palazzo della Magnifica Patria** fronts the broad lakeside promenade.

ARRIVAL AND INFORMATION

SALÒ

By bus Buses stop on Largo Dante Alighieri.
Destinations Brescia (every 30min; 1hr); Desenzano (7 daily; 50min); Gargnano (every 30min; 25min); Milan (3 daily; 2hr 40min); Riva (3 daily; 1hr 15min).

By car The SS45bis road links Salò directly to Brescia, but it has one lane in each direction and is plagued by summer traffic jams; you'd do well to avoid driving this route lake-bound on Fridays and city-bound on Sundays.

9

By boat The *imbarcadero* is at one end of Piazza della Vittoria. There are regular boats for destinations around the lake (see p.278).

Tourist information Behind the town hall on Piazza Sant'Antonio (Mon–Sat 10am–12.30pm & 3–6pm, Sun 10am–1pm & 3.30–6.30pm; ☎0365 21 423, ⓦ visitgarda.com).

ACCOMMODATION

Bellerive Via Pietro da Salò 11 ☎0365 520 410, ⓦ hotelbellerive.it. On the edge of the centre, this four-star offers pleasant, fresh rooms, many with lake views. Service is exceptional and *Ristorante 100km*, the restaurant, outstanding (see below). An annexe holds apartments for rent (minimum three-night stay). Closed Dec & Jan. €185

Benaco Lungolago Zanardelli 44 ☎0365 20 308, ⓦ benacohotel.com. A small family-run boutique hotel in the historic centre with a fine restaurant. €120

Laurin Viale Landi 9 ☎0365 22 022, ⓦ laurinSalò .com. A lovely, grand Art Nouveau villa boasting period features in the public areas – the beautiful restaurant has columns, frescoes and Liberty windows – though the guest rooms are lower key but comfortable. Pool and lovely lakeside location. Closed Dec–Feb. €200

EATING AND DRINKING

La Casa del Dolce Piazza Duomo 1. Salò's best ice cream, made using seasonal produce, is served at this little hole in the wall by the Duomo. Open 24hr.

Osteria di Mezzo Via di Mezzo 10 ☎0365 290 966, ⓦ osteriadimezzo.it. An atmospheric, old-fashioned tavern serving good home cooking with a slow-food ethos. Their six-course menu costs €40. Book ahead. Mon & Wed–Sun noon–3pm & 7–11.30pm.

Pizzeria Papillon Via Lungolago Zanardelli 69 ☎0365 41 429, ⓦ ristorantepapillon.it. Pizzas are served bubbling from the wood-fired oven but the pasta and fish options are good too (from €12). In summer reserve a table outside next to the lake. Tues–Sun noon–11pm.

Ristorante 100km In Hotel Bellerive, Via Pietro da Salò 11 ☎0365 520 410, ⓦ hotelbellerive.it. A classy,

THE REPUBBLICA DI SALÒ

Salò is resonant for Italians for its role in the short-lived Repubblica Sociale Italiana (RSI), commonly termed the **Repubblica di Salò**, the last-ditch attempt by Mussolini and Hitler to reorganize Italian Fascism. After the Allied invasion of southern Italy and Mussolini's escape northwards, the Nazis annexed the Trentino-Alto Adige region, bringing the Reich's borders down as far as Limone sul Garda. They installed Mussolini as head of a puppet regime in Salò, just 20km away; from September 1943 to April 1945, the town was the nominal capital of Italy. Mussolini established government ministries in several of the Liberty-style villas that dot this shore: Salò's Villa Simonini (now the *Hotel Laurin*) hosted the Foreign Ministry, while Villa Feltrinelli in Gargnano, also now a hotel (see p.299), became the residence of *Il Duce* himself. With the Allied liberation the republic collapsed. Mussolini fled, and was executed on April 28, 1945 on Lake Como (see p.203).

contemporary restaurant, where everything – ingredients, recipes, wines – is sourced from within a 100km radius of Salò. The menu focuses on classic

Brescian cuisine, including exquisite *coregone* (white lake fish), served with flair and innovation (*menù* around €50). Daily 11am–11pm.

Gardone Riviera

Just 2km east of Salò, **GARDONE RIVIERA** was once the most fashionable of Lake Garda's resorts and still retains its symbols of sophistication, though the elegant promenade, lush gardens, opulent villas and ritzy hotels (see box, p.294) now have to compete with more recent – less tasteful – tourist paraphernalia. Gardone Sotto, the old village on the lakeside, comprises a cobbled street and a couple of piazzas sandwiched between the busy Corso Zanardelli road and the lake. Gardone Sopra spreads across the hillside above, with a tiny centre at the chapel and piazza just by the entrance to Il Vittoriale.

Giardino Botanico André Heller

Via Roma 2, Gardone Sopra • March–Oct daily 9am–7pm • €10 • ⓦ hellergarden.com

Gardone's success as a health retreat and winter resort was in great part due to its famously consistent climate which has also encouraged the exotic **Giardino Botanico André Heller**, laid out just above Gardone Sotto in 1912 by Arturo Hruska, dentist to the Russian tsar, and now owned by Heller, an artist. This collection of flora from around the world includes bamboo, water lilies, orchids, tree ferns and banana plants, set amid artificial cliffs and streams. Sculptures from Morocco and India are displayed alongside installations by artists such as Roy Lichtenstein and Keith Haring.

San Michele

Three buses (Mon–Sat only) run from Salò and Gardone

In the mountains 500m above Gardone stands the pretty village of **SAN MICHELE**. The views along the road are splendid; the tourist office can advise on short cuts that divert onto hillside tracks if you choose to walk the hour or so uphill.

ARRIVAL AND INFORMATION
GARDONE RIVIERA

By bus Regular services connect Gardone with villages and towns along the western shore of the lake. Buses stop at several points along the main road; ask at the tourist office.
Destinations Brescia (every 30min; 1hr 5min); Limone (3 daily; 1hr); Riva del Garda (5 daily; 1hr 15min).
By boat The *imbarcadero* is just by Piazza Wimmer in

Gardone Sotto. Services leave for around the lake, with a reduced service in winter (see p.278).
Tourist office Corso Repubblica in Gardone Sotto (July & Aug Mon–Sat 9am–12.30pm & 3.30–6.30pm, Sun 9am–12.30pm; rest of year Mon–Sat 9am–12.30pm & 3–6pm; ⓣ 0365 20 347, ⓦ visitgarda.com).

ACCOMMODATION

Dimora Bolsona Via Panoramica 23 ⓣ 0365 21 022, ⓦ dimorabolsone.it. High above the lake this fifteenth-century manor house has been restored to provide a handful of rooms in a peaceful B&B amid a gorgeous garden. No children under 12. **€130**
Due di Moro Via Ceriolo 25 ⓣ 0365 20 101, ⓦ duedimoro.com. Exceptionally tasteful B&B above the town, featuring white linen bedspreads, terracotta tiled floors and chunky beamed ceilings. They have an organic restaurant, a pool with a lake view, bike rental – and they make their own olive oil. Unusually for Italy, vegans and vegetarians are well catered for. **€113**

★**Florida Residence** Corso Zanardelli 113 ⓣ 0365 21 836, ⓦ hotelvillaflorida.com. Thoughtfully run by a charming family, who are a wealth of information on the history of the area. The attractive rooms are good-sized suites with kitchen corners and balconies offering lovely lake views. Large pool and pretty grounds. **€175**
Locanda Agli Angeli Piazza Garibaldi 2 ⓣ 0365 20 832, ⓦ agliangeli.com. Small, family-run place with airy rooms with four poster beds, a veranda, and the peace and quiet of Gardone Sopra, just by Il Vittoriale. **€90**

9

GARDONE'S LUXURY HOTELS

Gardone Riviera – once Lake Garda's ritziest resort – specializes in opulent **luxury hotels**, many of which occupy grandiose Art Nouveau villas that were built, often in spacious park-like grounds, in the early years of the last century.

Grand Corso Zanardelli 84 ☎0365 20 261, ⊛www .grangardone.it. The largest of the hotels is the *Grand*, which takes up a huge stretch of the waterfront on the lake side of the main road. Its public areas remain as glitteringly opulent today as when the hotel opened in 1884 and the rooms – most of which have balconies over the lake – are pretty and pleasant. Churchill holidayed here in 1949. **€280**

Grand Hotel Fasano Corso Zanardelli 190 ☎0365 290 220, ⊛ghf.it. Perhaps the finest of the lot is the *Grand Hotel Fasano*, built in the nineteenth century as a hunting lodge for the Austrian imperial family and converted into a hotel around 1900. The interiors are spacious but not extravagant, characterized by a classic, traditionally styled comfort that – unusually for Lake Garda – avoids showiness. In the grounds, the waterfront *Villa Principe* is treated as a separate establishment with its own facilities, including a private beach. **€220**

Savoy Palace Corso Zanardelli 2 ☎0365 290 588, ⊛savoypalace.it. Churchill also stayed at the *Savoy Palace*, renovated from its 1920s heyday in a rather disappointingly modern style. The lakefront location remains dazzling. **€190**

Villa del Sogno Corso Zanardelli 107 ☎0365 290 181, ⊛villadelsogno.it. Occupying immaculate grounds just above the lakefront road is the *Villa del Sogno*, an Art Nouveau vision built by a Viennese silk tycoon in 1904 and now a favourite retreat for wealthy Germans and Americans on extended stays. Although everything is in place – interior grandeur, fragrant gardens, tennis courts – you can't shake the feeling that this is a luxury-hotel-by-numbers, with little warmth or character. **€370**

Villa Fiordaliso Corso Zanardelli 132 ☎0365 20 158, ⊛villafiordaliso.it. The most famous of the luxury hotels is *Villa Fiordaliso*, with just five suites. This is where Mussolini installed his mistress, Clara Petacci, during the Repubblica di Salò, and where they spent their last few weeks together in 1945; for around €700 a night you can sleep in their private suite. The villa and grounds are beautiful – and include the separate lakeside Torre San Marco, now a piano bar – but the road is just too close for comfort here, passing within metres of the rear of the building; traffic noise is an irritant. **€480**

EATING AND DRINKING

The lakeside **cafés** in Gardone Sotto are the perfect place to enjoy a coffee or an ice cream with dreamy views across the water. For a full **restaurant** meal, the quality is often better in the trattorias dotted around Gardone Sopra, although prices always reflect their popularity. It's best to book ahead in summer.

Agli Angeli Piazza Garibaldi 2 ☎0365 20 832, ⊛agliangeli.com. A good choice for top-quality lake fish and home-cured meats (from €15). Wed–Sun noon–2.30pm & 7–11pm.

La Taverna Corso Repubblica 34 ☎0365 20 412. A decent wine bar with inexpensive plates of typical local food from around €11. Mon & Wed–Sun noon–3pm & 7–11pm.

Trattoria Riolet Via Fasano Sopra 75, Gardone Riviera ☎0365 20 545. Hidden away at the top of a steep climb, this popular family-run trattoria offers pasta starters and grilled meats (from €12). The service can be brusque but the setting outside under the vines is very romantic. Mon, Tues & Thurs–Sun noon–2.30pm & 7–11.30pm.

Il Vittoriale

Just on the outskirts of Gardone, past the Neoclassical Villa Alba rising above the lakeside road, road signs point up the hillside towards one of Italy's most visited museums, **Il Vittoriale degli Italiani**. This is the former home of the poet and nationalist hero Gabriele D'Annunzio, preserved as it was when he died in 1938. It's an excessively grandiose spectacle – D'Annunzio was a shameless egotist and the house is a tribute to his desperate self-obsession – but has nonetheless been declared a national monument. Busloads of visitors (many Italian, and most of them school parties) turn up daily to crowd into the house and walk the garden footpaths.

Once D'Annunzio had had the house "de-Germanized", as he put it (the house had been confiscated from the German art critic Henry Thode), it didn't take him long to transform what was a gracious Art Nouveau villa into the showy spectacle it remains today.

VISITING IL VITTORIALE

Arrival and departure Within easy walking distance from the centre of Gardone, Il Vittoriale is equipped with various visitor car parks, although they do get full in summer.

Contact details ☎ 0365 296 511, ⓦ vittoriale.it.

Opening hours The Vittoriale comprises three elements, each with different opening hours: the gardens (daily: April–Sept 8.30am–8pm; Oct–March 9am–5pm); D'Annunzio's house, known as the Prioria (Tues–Sun 9.30am–7pm; Oct–March 9am–1pm & 2–5pm); and the Museo della Guerra, or War Museum (Tues & Thurs–Sun 9.30am–7pm; Oct–March 9am–1pm & 2–5pm). The scale

of visitors means that tickets can be restricted at peak times (Sun, national holidays, July & Aug), when you should arrive an hour or more before the opening time to be sure of entry. Even then, be prepared for a scrum.

Tickets and tours Entry to the gardens only is €8, or €13 including a tour of either the Prioria or the Museo della Guerra, or €16 including tours of both of them. Both the Prioria and the Museo della Guerra can be visited only with a guide; most speak Italian, but not English; ask first for an audioguide in English (free). Unless you're devoted to D'Annunzio, touring the house and having a quick wander round the gardens is enough.

The reception rooms

D'Annunzio's personality makes itself felt from the start in the two **reception rooms**, one a chilly and formal room for guests he didn't like, the other warm and inviting for those he did. When Mussolini visited in 1925, he was shown to the former (which is the first room on the tour; the latter is one of the last) – where the mirror has an inscription reputedly aimed at him: "Adjust your mask to your face, and remember you are merely glass against steel."

Nor was dining with D'Annunzio a reassuring experience; pride of place in the colourful Art Deco **dining room** was given, as a warning to greedy guests, to a gilded tortoise that had died of overeating. In fact D'Annunzio rarely ate with his guests, retreating instead to the **Sala di Lebbroso** (Lepers' Room), where he would lie on a bier surrounded by leopard skins and contemplate death.

The rest of the house

The rest of the house is no less bizarre, characterized by its extreme gloominess; D'Annunzio reportedly had an eye condition which meant daylight was painful to him. Every room has thick, opaque (often coloured) glass in the windows, and the combination of heavy drapes, thick rugs, dark woods and low, narrow passages – D'Annunzio stood just 5'4" tall (1.62m) – makes for a singularly claustrophobic experience. The **blue bathroom** has a tub hemmed in by over nine hundred objects,

---

GABRIELE D'ANNUNZIO

Born in 1863, Gaetano Rapagnetta – who took the name **Gabriele D'Annunzio** (Gabriel of the Annunciation) – was no ordinary writer, and is often acclaimed as one of Italy's greatest poets. He did pen some exquisite poetry and a number of novels, but he became better known as a soldier and socialite, leading his own private army and indulging in much-publicized affairs with numerous women, including the actress Eleonora Duse. When berated by his friends for treating her cruelly, he simply replied, "I gave her everything, even suffering." He was a fervent supporter of Mussolini, providing the Fascist Party with their (meaningless) war cry *ìeia! eia! alaláe* – though Mussolini eventually found his excessive exhibitionism an embarrassment. In 1921 he presented D'Annunzio with the Vittoriale villa – ostensibly as a reward for his patriotism, in reality to shut him up. D'Annunzio spent the next years expanding the villa and redesigning its interiors. He died in the house in 1938, of a brain haemorrhage while sitting at his desk in the Zambracca room, which remains untouched.

ABOVE GARGNANO: THE FOUR LAKES DRIVE

The only road through the lakeside mountains between Salò and Riva climbs from a turn-off at Gargnano. This is a spectacular drive through the hidden mountain scenery of the **Valvestino**, past a dammed lake and on, over a pass, to **Lake Idro**. Idro is utterly removed from the world of Lake Garda, a small, almost Alpine stretch of placid water squeezed between steep, rugged slopes; the dark, stone-built hamlet of **Bagolino**, above the lake, is a bewitching place to draw breath away from Garda's bustle.

This route can be done as the looping "**Four Lakes Drive**" – from Gargnano up past Lake Valvestino to Lake Idro, then down past Lake Ledro to Riva del Garda. It's 89km in total, easily doable as a leisurely day-trip, or split into two or more sections. Alternatively, from Gargnano to Idro then south down the Val Sabbia to Brescia is 84km. These are slow drives, on steep, switchbacking mountain roads, but the views and sense of escape are worth it.

THE VALVESTINO

Above Gargnano, the road concertinas its way up the mountainside in a series of hairpin turns on the way to **Navazzo** and on up to a small **dam** on the River Toscolano. This stretch takes twenty minutes to go 13.5km; you'll rarely be out of second gear. Behind the dam stretches **Lake Valvestino**, a narrow, forked tarn enclosed by the high valley walls. The road crosses the water twice before reaching the isolated inn *Al Mulì* at Molino di Bollone, a junction of roads 5.5km past the dam. Straight ahead lie the villages of the Valvestino – Gargnano tourist office holds maps of a lonesome circular walk (3hr 30min) through the meadows and hamlets above **Turano** – while at **Magasa** is the *Cima Rest*, a particularly attractive mountain restaurant – but the road continues on the second left (not Bollone) for 6km to **Capovalle**, the main settlement hereabouts, a modern town at 937m above sea level, surrounded by higher peaks. Beyond, over the pass, it's 11km down through the lush, wooded valley to Idro.

LAKE IDRO

Trapped in the higher reaches of the Val Sabbia above Brescia, the fjord-like **LAKE IDRO** (**Lago d'Idro**, also called by its Latin name **Eridio**) is both the highest of the major Italian lakes (368m above sea level) and the smallest, just 9.5km long by 2km wide. It's a pretty lake on a human scale, with wooded crags reaching down into cool, clear water, but its shores are occupied by rather too many bland little holiday suburbs and campsites to encourage much exploration.

The main town is **IDRO**, a collection of hamlets at the foot of the lake covering both shores. On the western side, amid shops and bars, is the **tourist office** and several **hotels**.

---

ranging from Persian ceramic tiles, through Buddhas, to toy animals; and the **Sala del Mappamondo** contains, as well as the huge globe after which it is named, an Austrian machine-gun and books, including an immense version of *The Divine Comedy*. Suspended from the ceiling of the **auditorium** adjoining the house is the biplane that D'Annunzio used in a daring flight over Vienna in World War I.

Museo della Guerra

The adjacent **Museo della Guerra**, reached up an external staircase from the courtyard, has displays on D'Annunzio's military adventures, including medals awarded to him, banners and photographs.

The battleship Puglia and the mausoleum

Rammed into the cypress-covered hillside above the house is the prow of the battleship **Puglia**, used in D'Annunzio's so-called "Fiume adventure". Fiume (now Rijeka), on the north Adriatic, had been promised to Italy before they entered World War I, but was eventually handed to Yugoslavia instead. Incensed, D'Annunzio gathered his blackshirted army, occupied Fiume, declared war, surrendered after a naval bombardment and returned home a national hero. Above, in the gardens at the top of the site, stands D'Annunzio's **mausoleum**, a Fascistic array of steps and angular travertine stonework installed in 1955.

For accommodation alternatives opt for one of the many rural B&Bs in the area. To the north, this road ends 5km on at **VESTA**'s gravel beach, where you can follow trails into the hills or walk the Sentiero dei Contrabbandieri (route 103) around the roadless headland. At the lake's northern end is **PONTE CAFFARO**, an unremarkable working town, though crossing its eponymous bridge still has a sense of occasion; until 1918, this marked the international border with Austria. Riva del Garda (see p.304) lies 39km ahead, beyond Lake Ledro.

BAGOLINO

On the western shore of Lake Idro, near **Anfo**, a turn-off (9km north of Idro, 3km south of Ponte Caffaro) heads steeply up, skirting Monte Breda (1503m) to climb into the Valle di Caffaro, with spectacular views back over the lake. Some 8km up this narrow road lies the captivating mountain village of **BAGOLINO** (bagolinoinfo.it). Many of its medieval houses are preserved, and 300m beyond the northern end of the village is the church of **San Rocco**, with a startlingly realistic cycle of fifteenth-century frescoes (the priest of San Giorgio in the village keeps the keys).

Winter sees Bagolino full of skiers, while the village is also famous for its Lenten **carnival**, originating in the sixteenth century and focused on costumed celebrations, music and dance.

INFORMATION AND ACTIVITIES

Activities Surfpoint in Vantone, near Vesta (June–Sept; 339 227 5994, surfpoint.it), rents canoes (€7/hr), windsurfing equipment, mountain bikes and motorboats.

Tourist office Via Trento 27, Idro (Mon–Wed, Fri & Sat 9am–12.30pm & 1.30–6pm; 0365 83 224, lagodidro.it).

ACCOMMODATION AND EATING

Al Poggio Verde Via Nazionale, Barghe 0365 824 591, alpoggioverde.it. The area's best restaurant, 12km west of Idro; follow the main Brescia road down the valley, then turn right at the big roundabout in Barghe (signposted Preseglie); the ranch-style property

is 500m up this road. _Menùs_ (€30–50) combine the local valley cuisine with influences from Lake Garda and further afield; fish arrives fresh daily. Tables on the veranda look out over the fields, and seven airy, pleasant hotel rooms (€72) add to the allure. Tues–Sun noon–3pm & 7–11pm.

Al Tempo Perduto Via San Rocco 46, Bagolino 0365 99 665, altempoperduto.it. A lovely hotel and restaurant, in a historic building on the main street, with attractive modern rooms and a warm welcome. **€80**

Hotel Milano Via Trento 17, Idro 0365 823 391, hotelmilano.bs.it. Decent rooms with a comfortable family feel. **€60**

Toscolano Maderno

Barely 3km east of Gardone, the road passes through the twin _comune_ of **TOSCOLANO MADERNO**, which straddles the delta of the Toscolano river. To the southwest, Maderno has the twelfth-century lakefront church of **Sant'Andrea**, while to the northeast, across the river, Toscolano – which, under the name Benacum, was the chief Roman settlement on the lake – has the ancient **Santuario della Madonna di Benaco**, with fifteenth-century frescoes. Between them is a good **beach**, while the valley behind has a tradition of paper-making going back to the fourth century; following the riverside road up into the beautiful, wooded valley brings you past many disused **paper mills** to the **Fondazione Valle delle Cartierie**, with a well-presented museum offering an insight into the processes and importance of the industry (mid-June to Sept daily 10.30am–6pm; April, May & Oct Sat & Sun only 10.30am–6pm; €5). This is also a lovely area for shady walks or picnics.

ARRIVAL AND DEPARTURE   TOSCOLANO MADERNO

By bus Local and longer-distance buses alike stop at various points along the main road.

Destinations Brescia (2 daily; 1hr 15min); Gargnano (3 daily; 10min); Riva del Garda (5 daily; 1hr).

By boat The _imbarcadero_ is just off the main road on Lungolago Zanardelli. Services run to villages round the lake (see p.278) and regular car ferries cross throughout the year to Torri del Benaco (see p.312).

9

●RESTAURANTS & BARS	
Bar Valentino	5
La Tortuga	2
Miralago	4
Osteria del Restauro	3
Villa Sostago	1

Gargnano

A little north of Toscolano, signs announce your arrival in the elongated *comune* of **GARGNANO**, though the road continues on through the outlying hamlets of **Bogliaco** and **Villa** before reaching Gargnano itself, 15km north of Salò.

This is a lovely spot, perhaps Lake Garda's most pleasant place to stay. Traffic runs a good way inland from the shore here, at a higher contour, leaving the old village itself noise-free. In addition, the narrow, difficult road northwards means tour buses heading south from Riva stop short at Limone and don't bother trying to reach Gargnano. Effectively sealed off by nature from the worse excesses of tourism, it feels like a haven. Gargnano is still more a working village than a resort, its empty lanes tumbling down the hillside from the main road to a little fishing port. Orange trees line the lakefront, greeting you off the boat. It's the perfect spot to unwind for a day or two and wander around the abandoned olive factory or the lakefront villas with their boathouses, or just to relax with an ice cream or a drink in one of the waterfront cafés. It was in Villa Igea, just south in the hamlet of Villa, that D.H. Lawrence stayed while writing *Twilight in Italy*, a work which is beautifully evocative of Lake Garda's attractions: "I sat and looked at the lake. It was beautiful as paradise, as the first creation."

San Francesco

Daily 8am–noon & 4–7pm; cloister closed to the public

Aside from the harbourside ex-**Palazzo Comunale**, which has two cannonballs wedged in the wall facing the lake – dating from the naval bombings suffered in 1866 during the war of independence from the Austrians – the main sight in Gargnano is the simple Romanesque church of **San Francesco**, built in 1289. The attached monastery became a citrus fruit warehouse at the end of the nineteenth century. Its cloister has columns carved with citrus fruits, a reference to the Franciscans' introduction of the crop to Europe, but it is currently a point of contention over developers' plans to turn the complex into luxury apartments.

San Giacomo di Calino

Via San Giacomo

A stroll along the road which leads north out of Gargnano from the harbour takes you for 3km past the beach and through olive and lemon groves, past the *Villa Feltrinelli* (see p.299), to the eleventh-century chapel of **San Giacomo di Calino**. On the side

---

CENTOMIGLIA

Every September hundreds of boats take to the waters off Gargnano for the round Garda yacht race, the **Centomiglia** (ⓦ centomiglia.it). It's been celebrated for over 60 years and attracts top international sailors and locals alike. The village celebrates with open-air concerts and markets.

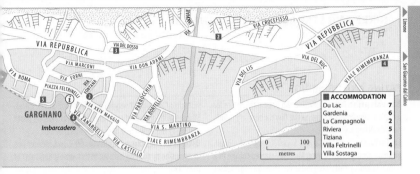

facing the lake, under the portico where the fishermen keep their equipment, is a thirteenth-century fresco of St Christopher, patron saint of travellers.

ARRIVAL AND DEPARTURE

GARGNANO

By bus Buses stop at Piazza Boldini on the main road, opposite the tourist office.

Destinations Brescia (3 daily; 1hr 10min); Desenzano (5 daily; 1hr); Riva (5 daily; 50 min);

Salò (5 daily; 30min).

By boat Ferries for regular services round the lake (see p.278) pull in to the *imbarcadero* by the little harbour on Piazza Feltrinelli.

INFORMATION AND ACTIVITIES

Activities OKSurf, Parco Fontanella (☎328 471 7777, ⓦoksurf.it), rents mountain and electric bikes (€21/day) and also runs windsurfing and kitesurfing courses for adults and children.

Tourist information Piazza Boldini (Mon–Sat 9.30am–12.30pm & 5–7pm, closed Wed pm; ☎0365 791 243, ⓦvisitgarda.com & ⓦgargnanosul garda.it).

ACCOMMODATION

Du Lac Via Colletta 21, Villa di Gargnano ☎0365 71 107, ⓦhotel-dulac.it. On the lakefront but 1km south of Gargnano, in the neighbouring community of Villa. A very pleasant, old-fashioned hotel, run by the same family as the *Gardenia* – standards are high, the welcome is warm and the rooms are comfortable and unfussy. Six of them look over the lake, with a balcony or terrace. Antique furniture, en-suite bathrooms and a/c come as standard. Closed Dec–Feb. **€160**

★**Gardenia** Via Colletta 53, Villa di Gargnano ☎0365 71 195, ⓦhotel-gardenia.it. A lovely family-run hotel in a nineteenth-century lakeside villa. The public areas feature beautifully maintained 1950s decor and fittings while the guest rooms have been completely renovated with big comfy beds, well-appointed bathrooms and airy lake views. Excellent garden restaurant too. Closed Nov–March. **€96**

La Campagnola Via Repubblica 38 ☎0365 71 191, ⓦfrassinehotels.it. Simple, attractively furnished apartments set in a lemon grove with lovely lake views, 300m from the village beach and two minutes' walk from the village centre. Apartment (four people for one week in high season) **€780**

Riviera Via Roma 1 ☎0365 72 292, ⓦgarniriviera.it.

Comfortable, good-value en-suite rooms in an enviable lakeside position in the village centre. Breakfast is served on the lovely waterside terrace. **€76**

Tiziana Via Dosso 51 ☎0365 71 342, ⓦalbergotiziana .com. Small, friendly, no-frills two-star, located slightly off the main road above the village. Rooms are comfortable, in modern style, most with lake views. Closed Nov–March. **€60**

Villa Feltrinelli Via Rimembranza 38 ☎0365 798 000, ⓦvillafeltrinelli.com. Built by local lumber magnates in 1892, this grand lakeside house is set in its own sizeable grounds – an elegant eleven-roomed villa with an enviable lakeside position just north of the village. Home to Mussolini and his family during the Republic of Salò (see p.292), this is now one of the world's top hotels where every detail has been stylishly considered. Minimum two-night stay. Closed Nov–March. **€900**

★**Villa Sostaga** Via Sostaga 19, Navazzo ☎0365 791 218, ⓦvillasostaga.com. On the hillside above Gargnano, this handsome villa is a wonderful bolthole with lovely rooms, spacious grounds and pool. The views are breathtaking, the welcome genuine and the seasonal cooking excellent (restaurant open to non-residents). **€250**

9

HIKES AND STROLLS FROM GARGNANO

The tourist office has details of various walks and hikes in the area, from following in the footsteps of D.H. Lawrence to striking out on old mule paths high into the mountains. The descriptions are also available online at ⓦgargnanosulgarda.com/Sport-Leisure/Walking-and-Hiking.html.

EATING AND DRINKING

Bar Valentino Piazza Villa 1/2. An unbeatable place for a drink or simple snack right on the tiny harbour in the Villa neighbourhood. Closed Tues.

La Tortuga Via XXIV Maggio 5 ☎0365 71 251. Small, intimate dining room serving Michelin-starred cuisine in a formal setting. Helpful staff guide you through gourmet set *menùs* showcasing local produce. Book well in advance. Closed lunchtime except Sun, also closed Tues & Mon in winter.

Miralago Via Zanardelli 5 ☎0365 71 209. A relaxed

waterfront restaurant serving excellent food at fair prices. Sit back with a glass of wine and a bowl of seafood pasta and enjoy the view – life doesn't get much better.

Osteria del Restauro Piazza Villa 19. Good, inexpensive local cuisine by the tiny harbour in this atmospheric part of the village. Closed Wed.

★**Villa Sostaga** Via Sostaga 19, Navazzo ☎0365 791 218, ⓦvillasostaga.com. The restaurant on this hillside hotel serves very well-judged local cuisine with flair. Reserve one of the tables by the window for stunning views.

Tignale, the Tremósine and around

About 4km north of Gargnano, a narrow road climbs away from the shore, coiling up the steep slopes. This forms a looping detour, roughly 30km of mountain driving through isolated hamlets and deep, wooded valleys before rejoining the main shoreside road at, or just before, Limone. You first reach the village of **TIGNALE**, occupying a plateau some 450m above the lake, with spectacular views – not least from the **Santuario di Montecastello**, accessed up a side road. The main route then descends into the deep Valle di San Michele before climbing out to cross the even higher plateau of the **TREMOSINE**; from the main village, **Vesio**, walking trails head out into the nature reserve of Bondo. The main route continues on a reasonable gradient down to Limone, or you can branch off to **Pieve**, perched on the edge of sheer cliffs above the lake, with yet more stunning views, from where the SP38, an exhilarating road – featured in countless car adverts, the 2008 James Bond film *Quantum of Solace* and once described by Churchill as the "eighth wonder of the world" – switchbacks sharply down through a dark ravine to rejoin the shore just north of tiny **Campione del Garda**, which is set in an amphitheatre of giant cliffs, has some excellent beaches and is one of the lake's main **surfing** and **windsurfing** centres.

Prà de la Fam

North of the turn-off to Tignale, where the lakeside road emerges from a tunnel, a headland marks the **Prà de la Fam**, or Field of Hunger, so named after medieval fishermen were stranded here for several days following a storm. It's a popular windsurfing area and boasts a fine old *limonaia* – a pretty little spot for relaxing and swimming alongside the beautiful B&B *Torre degli Ulivi*.

ARRIVAL

TIGNALE, THE TREMÓSINE AND AROUND

By bus A few local buses wind around among the hamlets of the Tremósine, with a slightly greater frequency in the summer months. Buses run from Vesio to Gargnano (2 daily; 1hr 10min) and Limone (2 daily; 35min), from Pieve to Gargnano (2 daily; 35min), Limone (2 daily; 55min) and Tignale (3 daily; 30min).

By car The Tremósine can only be reached by long, windy roads through Tignale or Bassanega or via the spectacular SP38 Porto to Pieve road, which is not for the faint-hearted driver. Once you've reached the plateau, driving is straightforward and attractive.

INFORMATION AND ACTIVITIES

Horseriding Individual or group lessons and treks in the Alpine landscape of the Tremósine can be arranged through Al Lambric (Via San Zenone 1, Prabione de Tignale ☎0365 73 402, ⓦwww.agrilambic.it).

Tourist information Piazza Marconi 1, Pieve (daily 9am–12.30pm & 3–6.30pm, afternoons only in winter; ☎0365 953 185).

ACCOMMODATION AND EATING

Al Lambic Via San Zenone 1, Prabione de Tignale ☎ 0365 73 402, ⓦ www.agrilambic.it. Deep in bucolic countryside, just 15min from the lake, this lovely agriturismo offers handsome B&B rooms or small apartments. There's a restaurant on summer evenings plus horseriding and a pool and playground just down the road. Closed Nov–Feb. €80

La Miniera Via Chiesa 9, Tignale ☎ 0365 760 225,

ⓦ gardaminiera.it. A traditional rustic trattoria serving meat or fish grilled over an open fire and home-made pasta. Tables outside in the garden in good weather. Mon & Wed–Sun 12.30–2pm & 6.30–10pm.

Torre degli Ulivi Via Gardesana Occidentale, Prà de la Fam ☎ 339 479 9834, ⓦ torredegliulivi.it. Set in its own gated grounds, this modern bungalow B&B has five modest, airy rooms. €180

Limone sul Garda

The last town in Lombardy, 20km from Gargnano and 9km from Riva, set among citrus groves on a tongue of land surrounded by rugged mountains, is **LIMONE SUL GARDA**. Although it is famous for its lemon cultivation – a commercial concern until the 1920s – its name derives not from the fruit, but from its location at what was the frontier (*limen* in Latin) of Roman control.

LAKE GARDA'S LEMONS

Lemons – and their rarer cousins, citrons – were introduced to Lake Garda from Genoa by Franciscan monks, resident at the monastery in Gargnano, in the thirteenth century. The industry flourished for hundreds of years, at its height exporting fruit as far afield as Poland and Russia. But disease in the 1850s, followed by the 1861 Unification of Italy, gave a lead to Sicily's lemon business, which soon cut into Garda's market. A combination of factors killed the industry off – the production of synthetic citric acid, the requisitioning of agricultural materials during the Great War, and finally a severe frost in the winter of 1928–29.

LEMON-HOUSES

Its remnants are still visible, embodied in the skeletal *limonaie* dotted all the way up this coast. These *limonaie* – or "lemon-houses" – were first built in the seventeenth century to protect the trees from the winter weather; Limone sul Garda was the most northerly point in the world producing lemons on a commercial scale. A **limonaia** comprises a grid of tall stone columns, set in between the trees on the sloping, terraced orchards. In winter, beams and roofs would be placed on the columns to cover the trees, with glass panes. This would moderate conditions; inside, during the day it could be cooler than outside, but at night it was always much warmer. Lighting fires within the *limonaie* to keep the trees warm was not unknown.

D.H. LAWRENCE

When the author **D.H. Lawrence** stayed at Gargnano in 1912–13, he recognized an industry on its last legs:

"I went into the lemon-house, where the poor trees seem to mope in the darkness. It is an immense, dark, cold place. Tall lemon trees, heavy with half-visible fruit, crowd together, and rise in the gloom. They look like ghosts in the darkness of the underworld, stately … There is a great host of lemons overhead, half-visible, a swarm of ruddy oranges by the paths, and here and there a fat citron. It is almost like being under the sea …

Looking at his lemons, the Signore sighed. I think he hates them. They are leaving him in the lurch. They are sold retail at a halfpenny each all the year round. 'But that is as dear, or dearer, than in England,' I say. 'Ah, but,' says the maestra, 'that is because your lemons are outdoor fruit from Sicily. One of our lemons is as good as two from elsewhere.'

It is true these lemons have an exquisite fragrance and perfume, but whether their force as lemons is double that of an ordinary fruit is a question. Oranges are sold at fourpence halfpenny the kilo – it comes to about five for twopence, small ones. The citrons are sold also by weight in Salò for the making of that liqueur known as Cedro. One citron fetches sometimes a shilling or more, but then the demand is necessarily small. So it is evident, from these figures, that the Lago di Garda cannot afford to grow its lemons much longer. The gardens are already many of them in ruins, and still more Da Vendere [For Sale]."

Limone is undeniably pretty, a stone-built village jammed onto a slender slope between the mountains and the lake. Steep, cobbled streets lead away from the wide lakeside promenade up into the shady lanes of the old village. Until the 1940s and the building of the road, the only way to get here was by boat, and this is still the best approach, with steep rock soaring above the town's waterfront terraces, and the striking sight of serried columns of ruined lemon houses (see box, p.301).

Now though, a million tourists a year stay here, not counting the vast numbers who visit for the day on the boats from Riva and Malcesine, and with a settled population of just one thousand, Limone can feel overrun

ARRIVAL AND INFORMATION

LIMONE

By bus Services link Limone with Riva to the north and Desenzano to the south of the lake throughout the year. Destinations Desenzano (6 daily; 1hr 30min); Gardone (7 daily; 1hr); Gargnano (hourly; 30min); Riva (hourly; 10min).

By boat Regular boat services call into Limone throughout

the year, including car ferries that cross the lake to Malcesine (see p.309).

Tourist information Via IV Novembre 29 (daily 8am–10pm; ☎0365 954 720, ⓦlimonehotels.com). The website ⓦvisitlimonesulgarda.com has information on the town.

ACCOMMODATION AND EATING

La Cantina del Baffo Via Caldogno 1 ☎0365 914 061, ⓦlacantinadelbaffo.it. A good time restaurant with a big personality and terrific food, including sturgeon from the lake cooked with foraged flowers and greens. Pasta dishes from €11, secondi from €17. Regular live music, including jazz nights. Tues–Sat 5pm–3am, Sun noon–2pm & 5pm–3am.
Monte Baldo Via Porto 29 ☎0365 954 021,

ⓦmontebaldolimone.it. Traditional family-run hotel with pleasant rooms in an atmospheric, tall, narrow building by the *imbarcadero*. Closed Nov–Feb. **€108**
Osteria Da Livio Via Tovo 4 ☎0365 954 203, ⓦosteriadalivio.it. Fine, mid-priced cooking in a friendly ambience among the olive trees in the hills high above town. Tues–Sun noon–3pm & 6pm–midnight.

APOLIPOPROTEIN A-1 MILANO

Little Limone, unlikely though it sounds, has made a uniquely valuable contribution to **medical science**, with far-reaching consequences.

The story began in 1979, when a railwayman, born in Limone but living in Milan for more than twenty years, was hospitalized for a check-up. Doctors discovered that his cholesterol levels were very high, yet he showed no sign of arterial damage or heart disease. They did a further investigation, whereupon Dr Cesare Sirtori discovered an anomalous protein in the patient's blood – dubbed **Apolipoprotein A-1 Milano**. This protein, it transpired, was continuously stripping fat from the patient's arteries, allowing it to be delivered to the liver to be broken down and eliminated; it was, in short, counteracting the effects of smoking and a high-fat diet.

Doctors tested the patient's close family, and discovered that his father and daughter carried the same protein. They then tested every inhabitant of Limone, and found it in dozens of local residents. Archivists set to work, and uncovered the fact that all present-day carriers of the gene are descended from a couple who married in 1644. For centuries many Limonesi – cut off from the outside world – had married close relatives; as is often the case in isolated communities, intermarriage had embedded a genetic anomaly in the local population. In Limone's case, though, the mutation was the beneficial "**wonder gene**" Apolipoprotein A-1 Milano.

Four major conferences at Limone followed, during the 1980s and 1990s, as scientists grappled with developing a treatment to eliminate heart disease using the protein. In 2000, teams in the US began **human trials**, and it rapidly became clear that the synthetic version of Limone's protein was highly effective, removing a significant percentage of fatty deposits in the arteries of high-risk coronary patients after just six weeks of treatment. Doctors returned to Limone in 2004 to retest the local population, and discovered that the number of carriers of Apolipoprotein A-1 Milano had grown to 36. Research and human trials are continuing.

CLOCKWISE FROM TOP MOUNTAIN BIKING AROUND LAKE GARDA; GARGNANO (P.298); LEMON GROVE, LIMONE SUL GARDA (P.301) >

9

Riva del Garda

At the northwest tip of the lake, 45km north of Salò, **RIVA DEL GARDA** is the best known of Lake Garda's resorts, and also one of the most rewarding. It is unmistakeably a holiday town – windsurfing (or watching others windsurf) is a major preoccupation – but the pedestrianized old quarter, within its ancient walls, is still full of character; its high, narrow lanes are flanked by medieval facades, with the main lakefront square, **Piazza III Novembre**, ringed by late fourteenth-century porticoes and loomed over by the massive cliffs of the Rocchetta.

Part of Austria until 1918, Riva is now Italian, yet it lies within an autonomous Alpine region (Trentino) which is left alone by Rome to set its own laws and conduct its own affairs. Amid these shifting political loyalties, the only constants are the ever-present lake and mountains.

This Teutonic influence in architecture and culture is what makes Riva different from anywhere else on the lake. The town is full of **tourists** and second-home-owners from across the Alps – turn on the radio and you'll catch news and local ads in German – but whereas some lake destinations can feel swamped, Riva has enough self-possession, and a large enough area, to emerge fairly unscathed.

Brief history

Little survives from Riva's days as a **Roman** settlement. It's the town's strategic importance in **medieval** times that is most evident today. After Riva gained autonomy in the twelfth century as a trading port, the Della Scala of Verona, Visconti of Milan and the republic of **Venice** battled for control, all losing out to the Prince-Bishops of

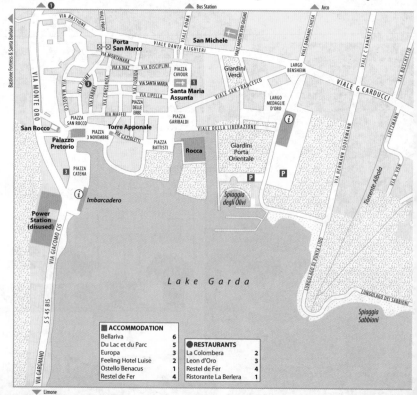

■ ACCOMMODATION	
Bellariva	6
Du Lac et du Parc	5
Europa	3
Feeling Hotel Luise	2
Ostello Benacus	1
Restel de Fer	4

● RESTAURANTS	
La Colombera	2
Leon d'Oro	3
Restel de Fer	4
Ristorante La Berlera	1

Trento, who took power in 1509 and kept it until the arrival of Napoleon.

From 1815 to 1918, Riva was part of the **Austro-Hungarian Empire**, serving as a fulcrum for trade between Germany and Italy and taking on a new role as a holiday playground. Archduke Albert, cousin of the emperor Franz Josef, built his winter residence at nearby **Arco** in the 1870s, and high society from all over German-speaking *Mitteleuropa* began flocking to the area, clutching their copies of *Die Italienische Reise* ("Italian Journey") – in which Goethe writes evocatively about his stay, in 1786, in Riva's neighbour, **Torbole**.

Piazza III Novembre

Riva's showpiece square, **Piazza III Novembre** (named to celebrate the arrival of Italian forces in 1918), is an attractive, cobbled space, its medieval, Lombard and Venetian facades lined up on three sides below the rugged face of Monte Rocchetta, the fourth side open to the lake. Its most striking feature is aural; the noise of footsteps, conversation and laughter bounces off the four-storey buildings and reverberates off the high Rocchetta cliffs to make an enclosed swirl of sound, graphically represented by *Percorsi*, a curious abstract spiral sculpture in bronze, by Osvaldo Bruschetti, on the waterfront.

Dominating Piazza III Novembre is the thirteenth-century **Torre Apponale**, 34m high and climbable for sensational lake views (March–Oct Tues–Sun 10am–6pm; June–Aug also Mon; €1). In the middle of the square are the Veronese **Palazzo Pretorio**, dating from 1375, and the Venetian **Casa del Comune**, completed in 1482, while to one side, behind the statue of San Giovanni Nepomuceno, co-patron of Riva, and the *imbarcadero*, looms a 1920s-era hydroelectric **power station**, complete with its network

RIVA DEL GARDA

9

of pipes that snake, Willy Wonka-like, over the hillside. This was designed to exploit the 500-metre drop in water level from Lake Ledro to this point; today, the generators are hidden within the mountain, and these buildings and pipes are only for show.

Marocco quarter

Behind Piazza III Novembre, and the adjacent Piazza San Rocco, stretches the **Marocco** quarter, Riva's oldest, named for the *marocche*, or debris, which used to tumble down off the mountain. Via Marocco itself is a long, curving alley of medieval houses, while alongside, **Via Fiume** – once Riva's Jewish quarter – remains a lively street, packed with shops and restaurants, leading to the massive **Porta San Marco** gate, beyond which cars and modern life take over. A trail from here climbs to the Bastione in about thirty minutes and Santa Barbara in a further hour.

The Rocca

Museo: March–Oct Tues–Sun 10am–12.30pm & 1.30–6pm; June–Aug also Mon • €2

The stout **Rocca**, originally built in 1124 but much altered since, not least by the Austrians, who lopped some height off the main tower in 1852 and turned the fortress into a barracks, is a short walk behind the Torre Apponale. It now houses the **Museo Civico**, with temporary exhibits on the ground floor, a modest *pinacoteca* upstairs and displays of archeology and local history upstairs again.

Monte Rochetta

Prominently towering over the western side of town is the **Bastione** fortress, erected in record time in 1508 – but not quickly enough to save the Venetians from losing Riva the year after. Even higher, nestled into the crags 585m up, is **Santa Barbara**, a small white church built in the 1920s that is visible from afar and eerily floodlit at night.

ARRIVAL AND INFORMATION

By bus Riva's bus station is about 1km north of the lakefront, on Viale Trento, but all intercity buses drop off at the *imbarcadero* (if approaching from Limone) or Viale Carducci (if approaching from Torbole).
Destinations Brescia (3 daily; 2hr 5min); Desenzano (3 daily; 1hr 50min); Malcesine (approx hourly; 25min); Salò (3 daily; 1hr 15min); Torbole (approx every 30min; 5min); Torri del Benaco (approx hourly; 1hr); Verona (approx hourly; 2hr 20min).
By car It's a slow drive to Riva along either shoreline, 45km from Salò or 65km from Peschiera. From the A22 autostrada, exit at Rovereto Sud and follow the SS240 west

for about 18km through the mountains down to Torbole. There's lots of parking but it gets very busy in season and there can be queues. Come by boat if you have the choice.
By boat The *imbarcadero* stands beside Piazza III Novembre. Riva is one of the hubs for lake ferries, with fast services heading for the larger villages and resorts around the lake. It is also served by numerous cruises in season (see p.278).
Tourist information The tourist office is at Largo Medaglie d'Oro (daily 9am–7pm; ☏ 0464 554 444, ⊛ gardatrentino.it) and there's an information kiosk at the *imbarcadero* (May–Sept daily 10am–1pm & 2–5.30pm; closed Wed; ☏ 0464 550 776).

ACCOMMODATION

Bellariva Via Franz Kafka 13 ☏ 0464 553 620, ⊛ www .hotelbellariva.com. Modest holiday hotel and apartments away from the centre but barely 100m from the lakeshore across a lawn; grab a room on the top floor for a bargain balcony with views. Closed Nov–Feb. **€150**
Du Lac et du Parc Viale Rovereto 44 ☏ 0464 566 600, ⊛ dulacetduparc.com. Riva's grandest hotel, a magnificent building set in its own lakefront park, was the destination of choice for German-speaking intellectuals around the turn of the last century, from Nietzsche and Freud to Kafka and Thomas Mann. It remains a high-class, traditionally styled establishment, modernized – and the

gardens are heavenly. Closed Nov–March. **€225**
Europa Piazza Catena 9 ☏ 0464 555 433, ⊛ hoteleuropariva.it. A good mid-range *Best Western*, occupying a tall, historic building on the main portside square by the *imbarcadero*, with a pleasant terrace café-restaurant. Rooms are modern and well furnished, with lake-view or town-view options. Closed Nov–March. **€160**
Feeling Hotel Luise Viale Rovereto 9 ☏ 0464 550 858, ⊛ hotelluise.com. A chic, modern boutique hotel just out of the centre with good service, children's activities and nice pool. Private parking. **€150**

Ostello Benacus (HI hostel) Piazza Cavour 10 ☎ 0464 554 911, ⓦ ostelloriva.com. Very central hostel, well run, with two-, four- and multi-bedded rooms. Parking €3/24hr. Closed Nov–Feb. Dorms €19, doubles €46

★ **Restel de Fer** Via Restel de Fer 10 ☎ 0464 553 481, ⓦ resteldefer.com. A real find, in the quiet back streets

out of the centre. This was once a farmhouse, isolated in the fields (named after the iron gate which still stands in front); Riva has grown up around it, but the Meneghelli family are still here, 600 years on. There are five simple rooms, comfortably furnished with individual touches and an excellent restaurant (see below). €100

EATING AND DRINKING

Riva's lakefront is lined with **places to eat**, from terrace cafés and *gelaterie* to smarter restaurants. As usual, though, for higher quality it pays to explore away from the waterfront. Although there is still plenty of lake fish on the *menùs*, the influence of the mountains and northern European traditions means you'll see game and filling winter dumplings too.

La Colombera Via Rovigo 30 ☎ 0464 556 033, ⓦ lacolombera.it. Among the vineyards on the edge of Riva this excellent, mid-priced country restaurant is crowded nightly with locals and others in the know. The *menù* comprises hearty, straightforward food served with gusto in a cheery, unpretentious setting. They also have pleasant, simply furnished rooms (€90). Closed Wed.

Leon d'Oro Via Fiume 28 ☎ 0464 552 341. Welcoming restaurant on a busy pedestrianized street, a handy place for good-quality, moderately priced pizza and fish dishes in the heart of the old quarter. Daily noon–2pm & 6–11pm.

★ **Restel de Fer** Via Restel de Fer 10 ☎ 0464 553 481,

ⓦ resteldefer.com. Local produce is used to create delicious takes on traditional recipes in this relaxed, family-run *locanda* (see above). Organic meat, game and fish are complemented by home-made bread and olive oil, plus well-chosen wines. Summer closed Wed; winter closed Mon–Thurs.

Ristorante La Berlera Localita Ceole, 8/B ☎ 0464 521149, ⓦ laberlera.it. At taxi ride north of the city centre, this restaurant has a wonderful location in a cave beneath a lofty medieval building. Good country cooking, including Trentino specialities (from €11). Mon, Tues & Thurs–Sun noon–midnight, Wed 9am–5pm.

Around Riva

There are several good options for exploring beyond Riva. Head up to the Alpine pastures of **Lake Ledro** for a break from the crowds or the attractive village of **Arco** with its hilltop castle. For thrills, make for the waterfall in **Varone** in spring or take to the waters in **Torbole**. Everywhere you go round here you will be spoilt for choice for **outdoor activities** – from rock climbing in Arco, canyoning or watersports around Torbole to cycling and hiking around Lake Ledro.

Parco Grotta Cascata Varone

May–Aug daily 9am–7pm; April & Sept daily 9am–6pm; March & Oct daily 9am–5pm; Nov–Feb Sun 10am–5pm • €5.50 • ⓦ cascata -varone.com • About 45min on foot from Riva waterfront, along Via Ardaro/Marone, or slow bus 862 from Riva bus station (40min)

Three kilometeres north of Riva, the **Parco Grotta Cascata Varone** is a gorge and waterfall system where you penetrate the canyon on a series of catwalks, as the waters of the River Magnone thunder down from almost 100m above. The most pleasant approach is on foot; it's reachable in under an hour from Riva's waterfront.

Arco

About 5km north of Riva is the old town of **ARCO**, a pleasing maze of cobbled streets and piazzas dominated by its twelfth-century **castle**, which teeters dramatically on top of a rocky outcrop, though there's not much to see inside today. Arco, once more favoured as a winter retreat for Central European nobility than Riva, has several lovely gardens, including a beautiful **public garden** opposite the Casino on Viale delle Palme, filled with hollyhocks, Chinese scented honeysuckle, other exotics and several varieties of palm, cypress and cedar. A short walk north is the **Parco Arciducale** (daily: April–Sept 8am–7pm; Oct–March 9am–4pm; free), the arboretum of the Habsburg Archduke Albert's winter palace, built in 1872 and filled with trees from six continents.

It is also a centre for **rock climbing**, hosting the World Championships in 2011, and for adventure sports in general (see p.308).

9

SPORTS AND ACTIVITIES

All around Lake Garda – as well as lakes Idro and Ledro – there are horseriding stables and you can rent out canoes, mountain bikes and often windsurfing equipment at reasonable prices. The northern shore around **Riva**, **Arco** and **Torbole**, however, is the real hub for sporting activity. All prices below are approximate; check directly or with local tourist offices.

WATERSPORTS

Top of the list is watersports, with a clutch of local outfits offering **windsurfing**; first-timers can get individual tuition (€45/1hr) or there are group lessons at various grades (€70/3hr). If you're already proficient, you can rent equipment for €60 a day. **Sailing** is also popular, with beginners' courses in a dinghy or catamaran (€70/2hr) and rental (€90/half day, depending on the size of boat). Shop around; local operators include ⓦ pierwindsurf.it, ⓦ vascorenna.com, ⓦ sailingdulac.com, ⓦ surfsegnana.it, ⓦ surflb.com and ⓦ gscharter.com. You can **rent canoes** (€35/day for two people) at the Sabbioni beach in Riva.

CLIMBING, TREKKING AND CANYONING

With over a dozen good locations within easy reach of the lake, **canyoning** is a good bet (April–Oct only; half-day €40–65, full-day €75–110; ⓦ canyonadv.com and ⓦ outdoorplanet .net). Several companies offer more traditional **Alpine activities** – free-climbing, ice-climbing, *via ferrata*, trekking and so on; check ⓦ friendsofarco.it, ⓦ alpinguide.com and ⓦ guidealpinearco.com for details.

PARAGLIDING

Paragliding – notably off Monte Baldo above Malcesine – is a spectacular way to get an eagle's-eye view of the lake (ⓦ paraglidingmalcesine.com; €130).

Torbole

TORBOLE, 4km east of Riva at the head of the lake, was thrust into the spotlight during the war between the Milanese Visconti and the Republic of Venice. In 1439, the Venetians organized an army and 240 oxen to drag a fleet of warships from the River Adige over the mountains to Torbole, launching them into the lake (and subsequently seizing Riva). These days, though, there's not much left of the town's historical character; the main diversions are **sailing** and **windsurfing** (see above). You'll find Torbole's many bars and restaurants packed with toned bodies and suntanned faces; enthusiasts come here from all over Europe, attracted by ideal wind conditions. In the mornings, when the wind is gentler, the water is full of wobbling novices attempting to circle their instructors. Although the town is busy with traffic, the view from the waterfront promenade is even better than from Riva, with a direct line of sight due south down the funnel of the lake and west to the formidable cliffs.

Lake Ledro

One of the most pleasant excursions from Riva is up to the little mountain-bound **LAKE LEDRO**, only 3km long – a good bolthole where you can escape the crowds on the Garda shore. It's a scenic, sunny spot, flanked by wooded slopes; traffic passes on the northern side, but the southern shore is quiet and there are some good hideaways to be discovered. Several streams fill the lake, but only the Ponale emerges for the short, steep tumble down into Lake Garda; its deep gorge, with a picturesque waterfall, is a spectacular sight from the deck of the boats into or out of Riva. Lake Ledro lies near the end of the long "**Four Lakes Drive**" from Gargnano (see p.296), which can, of course, also be done in reverse.

The old route into the Ponale valley branched off the shoreside road south of Riva. That is now a cycle route and footpath (the walk up from Riva takes about four hours); cars must head north out of Riva on Viale dei Tigli, to be directed into a **tunnel**, 4km long, beneath Monte Rocchetta.

Museo delle Palafitte
March–Nov Tues–Sun 9am–5pm; July & Aug daily 10am–6pm • €3.50 • ⓦ palafitteledro.it

UNESCO-recognized Bronze Age stilt or pile dwellings have been discovered in the lake at **Molina di Ledro**. The **Museo delle Palafitte** has interesting reconstructions of the houses and displays of the site's jewellery and artefacts.

ARRIVAL AND INFORMATION AROUND RIVA

By bus Local buses from Riva shuttle round this area throughout the year, running to Arco (every 30min; 30min), Ledro (2 daily; 35min) and Torbole (every 30min; 10min).

By car The "Four Lakes Drive" which begins in Gargnano arrives in Riva via Lake Ledro – or vice versa (see box, p.296).

Torbole tourist office On the lakefront between the town centre and the landing-stage (April Tues–Sun 9.30am–12.40pm & 2.30–6.30pm; May–Sept Mon–Sat

9am–1pm & 3–7pm; Oct–March Mon–Sat 9.30am–12.40pm & 2.30–6pm; ☎ 0464 505 177, ⓦ gardatrentino.it). The tourist office and their website have a good list of the many self-catering apartments and *residences* nearby.

Lake Ledro tourist office Via Nuova 7, Pieve di Ledro (Mon–Fri 8.30am–12.30pm & 2.30–6pm, Sat 9am–noon & 3–6pm, Sun 9am–noon; ☎ 0464 591 222, ⓦ valledileldro .com). Lots of information online and at the office on hikes in the area including tracing WWI trenches.

ACCOMMODATION

ARCO
Camping Zoo Via Legionari Cecoslovacchi 24 ☎ 0464 516232, ⓦ campingzoo.it. Well-located site in an olive grove along the river Sarca with a swimming pool and shady plots. As well as camping pitches, there are comfortable static caravans sleeping four. Camping €11, caravans €90

TORBOLE
Lido Blu Via Foci del Sarca 1 ☎ 0464 505 180, ⓦ lidoblu .com. On an elongated spit of land at the mouth of the River Sarca, away from the traffic, this four-star hotel has some great beaches and the bright, fresh rooms are popular with families on holiday. Has its own windsurf school. Cut-price deals in the low season (open year-round). €150

Villa Verde Via Sarca Vecchio 15 ☎ 0464 505 274, ⓦ hotel-villaverde.it. Decent modern three-star hotel in a peaceful setting also near the river, with its own pool and garden. €95

LAKE LEDRO
Al Sole Via Maffei 127, Ledro ☎ 0464 508 496, ⓦ campingalsole.it. Attractive campsite on the lakefront with camping pitches as well as wooden chalets sleeping four, plus a swimming pool, small spa and pizzeria. Camping €19, chalets €120

Mezzolago Lungolago 1, Mezzolago, halfway between Pieve and Molina ☎ 0464 508 181, ⓦ hotelmezzolago .it. House-proud, three-star hotel with standard rooms, all of which have balconies over the lake. €95

The eastern shore: Malcesine to Torri

A short way south of Torbole, the shoreside road leaves Trentino and enters Verona province, part of the Veneto region. The main resorts of Garda's **eastern shore** struggle to match the charm of the villages opposite. Holiday hotels and campsites line much of the lakeside road but they are overlooked by the ridges of Monte Baldo, topping 2100m – its treeless summit poking out of lushly wooded slopes – which offer myriad opportunities to hike, mountain bike and even paraglide while enjoying the glittering lake below.

The first settlement, **Malcesine**, has an attractive centre but is incredibly popular and swamped by holiday-makers in season; you'll need to work hard to carve out some individuality to a stay here. Heading south, **Brenzone** offers some quieter corners, while **Torri del Benaco** is one of the loveliest places on this shore, an old village with charm and character in spades.

Malcesine

Occupying a headland backed by the slopes of Monte Baldo, the small lakefront village of **MALCESINE**, 14km south of Torbole, boasts a pretty, historic core overlooked by the battlements of a medieval castle; it is a picture-perfect backdrop for an Italian Lakes

9

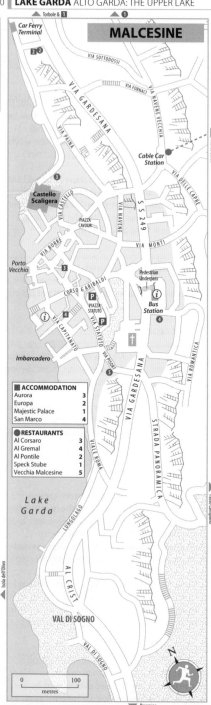

holiday – but that's the trouble. Malcesine is inundated with visitors (mostly British and German), including day-trippers from Riva and Limone, to such an extent that there is very little local life remaining in the village centre, which is filled with characterless shops and mediocre restaurants.

If you're booked to stay here – and there are some good deals to be had – but would prefer to sample somewhere a little more typically Italian, the best advice would be to make full use of boats and buses to explore up and down the shore; trips to Gargnano (see p.298) and Salò (see p.291) are easily done, and can show you a quite different Lake Garda. Verona (see p.316) is an hour and 45 minutes by bus. And, as always hereabouts, in hillside villages above the lake, such as Pai and Crero (see p.312), Gardesana life carries on regardless.

Castello Scaligera

Via Castello • Daily 9.30am–7pm; Nov–March Sat & Sun 11am–4pm • €6

Malcesine's main sight is the thirteenth-century **Castello Scaligera**, built, like Sirmione's (see p.282), by the Della Scala family of Verona. Goethe was imprisoned here briefly in 1786, having been arrested on suspicion of being a spy; he'd been caught making sketches of the castle's towers, which still loom over the old village.

Monte Baldo

Cable car: March–Oct daily every 30min 8am–7pm • €15 one way, €20 return • ⓦ funiviedelbaldo.it

For a change of perspective and a breath of mountain air, head up **Monte Baldo**. There are well-marked trails, or you can take the **cable car** (*funivia*), which rises more than 1600m in ten minutes. The trip alone is well worthwhile with slowly revolving cable cars giving splendid views. At the top, footpaths let you explore the summit ridge.

There are several special trips a day for cyclists to transport their bikes to the top; you can **rent a mountain bike** at G. Furioli in Piazza Matteotti

(☎045 740 045; €25 per day) and make a panoramic descent down easy trails to the shore. Be prepared for queues in summer for walkers, and in winter for skiers.

ARRIVAL AND INFORMATION   MALCESINE

By bus The bus station is on the main lakeside road; the old village spreads out below.
Destinations Riva (approx hourly; 30min); Torri del Benaco (approx hourly; 35min); Verona (approx hourly; 1hr 45min).
By boat From the central square, Piazza Statuto, stepped lanes head down to the old port and the *imbarcadero*. Car ferries cross to Limone (4 daily; 25min) and regular ferries

leave for destinations all around the lake (see p.278).
Tourist information The main tourist office is beside the bus station (Mon–Sat 9am–7pm, Sun 10am–4pm; ☎045 740 0044, ⬤visitgarda.com & ⬤tourism.verona.it), with a branch near the *imbarcadero* at Via Capitanato 8 (Mon–Sat 9am–1pm & 3–7pm; May–Oct also Sun 9am–1pm; ☎045 740 0837, ⬤malcesinepiu.it).

ACCOMMODATION

Many hotels in Malcesine are block-booked by tour operators; many others insist on half board and a three-night minimum stay in peak season around Easter and in summer. Although most hotels close down in winter, Malcesine always has a handful that remain open for those who want to enjoy the lake in cooler temperatures and without the crowds.

Aurora Piazza Matteotti 10 ☎045 740 0114, ⬤aurora -malcesine.com. Good, flexible budget option in the heart of the old lanes, with refurbished rooms and air conditioning. **€55**
Europa Via Gardesana 173 ☎045 740 0022, ⬤europa -hotel.net. Sleek, contemporary interiors herald this chic four-star hotel just north of town on the lake side of the main road. It has its own gravel beach, pool, parking, sauna and an excellent restaurant, *Al Pontile* (see below). Closed Nov–Feb. **€116**

Majestic Palace Via Navene Vecchia 96 ☎045 740 0383. Popular four-star holiday hotel in the hills just north of the centre, set among olive groves with a large pool. Room decor is a little standard but facilities are good and service welcoming. Used by many British tour operators. **€120**
San Marco Via Capitanato 9 ☎045 740 0115, ⬤sanmarcomalcesine.it. Pleasant three-star hotel overlooking the old harbour. The location is a little noisy and hectic in peak season but a prime spot otherwise for a simple, attractive room in the heart of the village. **€90**

EATING AND DRINKING

Most of central Malcesine's restaurants are pretty poor with slapdash service and spag bol the norm, although locations are often lovely. But choose carefully, or head out of the village centre, and you'll find some great cooking, service and atmosphere.

★**Al Corsaro** Via Paina 17 ☎045 658 4064, ⬤alcorsaro.it. Contemporary restaurant concealed at the base of the castle walls, on its own patch of beach and out of sight from anywhere but the water. The cooking is based on freshly caught lake fish, done a thousand different ways; a charming, relaxed, modern setting in which to enjoy a refined meal to remember. Expect to pay around €40 per head. Mon–Fri 7–10.30pm, Sat & Sun noon–2pm & 7–10.30pm.
Al Gremal Via Scoisse ☎045 657 0993. For a break from the old town, this attractive, contemporary-styled *enoteca*, perched on a terrace just above the main road, offers wines by the glass and light meals, along with tastings and sales of wines, grappas and oils. Daily 11am–11pm.
Al Pontile At Hotel Europa, Via Gardesana 173 ☎045 740 0022, ⬤europa-hotel.net. Stylish, beachfront

restaurant attached to this chic, modern hotel, serving innovative modern Italian cooking at moderate prices. Daily noon–11pm.
Speck Stube Via Navene Vecchia 139 ☎045 740 1177, ⬤speckstube.com. In a lovely rustic setting among olive groves, hearty portions of spit roast meat are served at wooden trestle tables and washed down by beer. Unusually the kitchen is open daily from noon to midnight. Daily 11.30am–11.45pm; Closed Nov–Feb.
★**Vecchia Malcesine** Via Pisort 6 ☎045 740 0469, ⬤vecchiamalcesine.com. The best food in town is served in a smart restaurant hidden away in its own grounds above Piazza Statuto. Views over the castle and the lake are sensational – as is the cooking – expect sophisticated flavours and creative presentation. Around €75 for a set menu. Closed Wed.

Brenzone and around

South of Malcesine, the elongated community of **BRENZONE** encompasses several lakeside villages dotted along 5km or more of shoreline, as well as a clutch of hamlets clinging to the mountainsides above – high and rugged enough to host decent **skiing** in winter. The tourist office in the waterfront hamlet of Porto has

9

maps and information about **walking** in the hills – including Path 33, which climbs (in about 2hr 15min) from just above Porto on a steep, scenic forest trail to **Prada Alta**, a village at 1000m.

A short way south of Porto lies the centre of Brenzone, sometimes called by its old village name, **Magugnano**. The main road diverts inland, leaving a little cluster of alleyways by the water free from traffic. It's a perfect spot for a quiet meal (see below); watch as ferries glide into the lake barely ten metres away. A kilometre or more south and – still within Brenzone – you come to **Castelletto** with a couple more recommended restaurants.

Pai and Crero

Castelletto's patch of shoreline is not Garda's most distinguished, the busy road flanked by holiday hotels and scrappy gravel beaches. As always on the lakes, venturing up into the hills pays dividends. From **PAI**, just south of Castelletto, a road squiggles up to **Pai di Sopra** – a beautiful, quiet hamlet with great views, and a bar, café and little hotel-restaurant ranged around a square.

Similarly alluring is tiny **CRERO**, accessed up an even skinnier turn-off from the lakeshore road a bit further south; signposted from the village square down a scenic footpath stands the the graceful, half-forgotten chapel of **San Siro**, built on these clifftops in the eighteenth century.

ARRIVAL AND INFORMATION

By bus Buses stop on the main lakeside road. Destinations Malcesine (hourly; 15min); Riva (hourly; 40min); Verona (hourly; 1hr 40min).

Tourist office On the main road as it runs through Porto (Mon–Fri & Sun 8.30am–12.30pm & 3–7pm, Sat 8.30am–7pm; ☎ 045 742 0076).

ACCOMMODATION AND EATING

Al Lago At the Hotel Brenzone, directly opposite the imbarcadero ☎ 045 742 0388, ⓦ hotelbrenzone.com. A perfect spot for a quiet meal gazing across the lake, watching the ferries glide into dock barely ten metres away. Specializes in freshly caught fish (from around €12), though with some more adventurous dishes including *fegato alla Veneziana* (Venetian-style liver and onions). Open mid-April to mid-Oct.

Alla Fassa Via B. G. Nascimbeni 13, Castelletto ☎ 045 743 3019, ⓦ ristoranteallafassa.com. Slightly formal, excellent fish restaurant with a delightful lakeside terrace. The highly regarded *menùs* offer creative Gardesana cuisine. €30–40 per person. Oct–June closed Tues.

★ **Al Pescatore** Via Imbarcadero 31, Castelletto ☎ 045 743 0702, ⓦ osteriaalpescatore.it. Overlooking the

picturesque little harbour bobbing with colourful boats, this small, family-run affair offers a handful of simple dishes using fresh lake fish in a cosy, authentic ambience.

Hotel Brenzone Directly opposite the imbarcadero ☎ 045 742 0388, ⓦ hotelbrenzone.com. Built in 1911 and still with an appealingly old-fashioned atmosphere to its public rooms; the bedrooms have been modernized and there's a genuine welcome from the Brighenti family who run it. Open mid-April to mid-October. **€120**

Locanda San Marco Piazza San Marco 22, Pai di Sopra ☎ 045 7260004, ⓦ locandasanmarco.it. In this little village above the lake, among hiking and cycling trails, this is a decent family-run inn with simple rooms. There's a small pool and restaurant serving local food too. **€90**

Torri del Benaco

TORRI DEL BENACO, 20km south of Malcesine, is one of the prettiest of the villages on this side of the lake. Part of its tenth-century walls still stand, notably the West Tower of the lakefront castle, which was overhauled in 1383 by the Della Scala of Verona. During the following centuries, Torri was a financial centre, controlling trade and imposing customs duties.

Although the main shoreside road passes within 100m of the shore here, Torri's old centre – which consists of one long cobbled street parallel to the lake, Corso D. Alighieri, crisscrossed with tunnelling alleyways and lined with mellow stone *palazzi* – is quiet and appealing. The swallowtail battlements of the **Castello Scaligero** stand guard over the quaint harbour at one end of the village, while there's a small sand beach with sun loungers and a bar in the centre, and a kids park and attractive shingle beach at the northern end.

Castello Scaligero

Daily: April, May & Oct 9.30am–12.30pm & 2.30–6pm; June–Sept 9.30am–1pm & 4.30–7.30pm • €5 • Ⓦ museodelcastelloditorridelbenaco.it

These days the castle buildings are home to an engaging display of local fishing and olive-oil making traditions as well as information on prehistoric rock carvings in the area (see box below). The castle also boasts one of the oldest working limonaie, or glasshouses on the lake, dating from 1760, built to protect the lemon trees inside during cold weather (see box, p.301).

ARRIVAL AND INFORMATION TORRI DEL BENACO

By bus Buses stop on the main road, by the post office; cross the street to Via Lavanda, which leads to the waterfront.
Destinations Malcesine (approx hourly; 35min); Riva (approx hourly; 1hr); Verona (approx hourly; 1hr 15min).
By car Park in the pay-and-display (free in winter) by the castle walls; the old centre is off-limits to cars.

By boat Regular services cover points across the lake and car ferries cross to Toscalano-Maderno throughout the year.
Tourist information Opposite the castle entrance (June–Aug daily 9am–1pm & 3–7pm; restricted hours at other times; ☎ 045 722 5120, Ⓦ visitgarda.com & Ⓦ tourism.verona.it).

ACCOMMODATION

Del Porto Lungolago Barbarani ☎ 045 722 5051, Ⓦ hoteldelportotorri.com. Stylish rooms with parquet flooring and swish bathrooms on the waterfront in the heart of the village. Also four attractive apartments in a villa with garden and pool away from the water. **€130**
Gardesana Piazza Calderini 20 ☎ 045 722 5411, Ⓦ hotel-gardesana.com. The harbourside classic *Gardesana* has hosted the likes of Churchill, Maria Callas, Laurence Olivier and Vivien Leigh. The three-star

rooms are comfortable and you can choose between a view of the harbour and castle or the lake (with or without a balcony). **€150**
★**Garni Onda** Via per Albisano 28 ☎ 045 722 5895, Ⓦ garnionda.com. Budget hotel 100m up from the centre. Each spotlessly clean room has its own balcony or terrace and the friendly owners provide a first-rate breakfast and lots of local knowledge on hikes, bike rides and local restaurants. Closed Nov–Feb. **€88**

EATING AND DRINKING

Many of the **restaurants** lining Torri's lakeside promenade have idyllic settings with lovely views across the water but the quality is generally poor. In the cobbled lanes just back from the water and in the olive groves on the hills above, there are a couple of relaxed gems that are worth seeking out for fresh, seasonal ingredients sourced locally.

Gardesana Piazza Calderini 20 ☎ 045 722 5411, Ⓦ gardesana.eu. You could hardly invent a more romantic setting for a meal (book for a table at the railing). Lake fish specials (from €15) are served in a refined but not stuffy ambience, with care taken over presentation and service. Daily 7–11pm.
Ristorante Le Gemme di Artesia Via Corrubio 18 ☎ 045 242 8622, Ⓦ legemmediartemisia.it. A real event restaurant in a private villa with intimate separate dining spaces and a stunning terrace with lake views. All

the food is seasonal and made in-house, and presentation is superb. All this doesn't come cheap, with set menus from €120 per person. Online bookings only. Open March–Nov.
★**Trattoria agli Olivi** Via Valmagra 7 ☎ 045 722 5483, Ⓦ agliolivi.com. Some of the tastiest food in the area is served at bargain prices (from €28 for three courses) in this lovely restaurant with a splendid lake-view terrace among the olive groves on the hillside above town. Daily noon–2.30pm & 7–11pm.

ANCIENT ROCK CARVINGS

In 1964, **rock carvings** dating back to the Bronze Age around 1500 BC were discovered in the hills between Torri and San Vigilio. Since then 250 rocks with over 3000 figures have been discovered in the area with more being unearthed all the time. The carvings often represent warriors, sometimes on horseback, as well as fishermen, boats and religious worship. There is more detail on the carvings in the castle museums at Torri (see above).

A 7km walk from Torri del Benaco (or slightly longer from Garda) takes you through oak woods on the slopes of hills behind the lake to see some of the carvings *in situ*. Ask at the tourist office for details.

Verona

PERFORMANCE AT VERONA'S ARENA

Verona

With its streets of pink-hued medieval *palazzi*, sublime Renaissance
art and architecture, and a long-standing tradition of excellence in food
and wine, Verona is a compelling destination. It's a vivacious place,
frenetic in parts but always amiable, and is not overwhelmed by the
tourist industry, crucial though that is to the local economy. Seduced
by Verona's role as the setting for Shakespeare's romantic tragedy
Romeo and Juliet, doe-eyed couples gather daily at the utterly fake
"Juliet's House" to gaze up at its balcony. More enticingly, every summer
the magnificent Roman Arena in the heart of the city is filled to capacity
for a prestigious open-air opera festival that has spread Verona's name
around the world.

The second-largest city in this book, Verona has a reputation within Italy for
being a rather hard-bitten working town, quite the opposite of its romantic
tourist persona. Its economic success – from Roman times onwards – was largely
due to its position on the River Adige, where trans-Alpine routes between Austria
and central Italy crossed over east–west roads between Milan and Venice. By the
twelfth century it had become a city-state, and in the following century approached
its zenith with the rise of the **Della Scala** (or **Scaligeri**) family, warlords and
cultivated patrons of the arts. Many of Verona's finest buildings date from their rule.
They were swept aside in 1405 by the Venetian Republic, which governed until the
arrival of Napoleon. A brief period of Austrian rule was ended by the Unification of
Italy in 1866.

The historic centre

There is no world without Verona walls
But purgatory, torture, hell itself.
Hence "banishèd" is banished from the world,
And world's exile is death.
Romeo

Today, Verona's sixteenth-century Venetian walls still enclose a sizeable chunk of the
city centre, whose southern limits are marked by a stretch of the earlier, fourteenth-
century Scaligeri-built walls near the central **Piazza Brà**, overshadowed by the huge
Roman **Arena**.
    North of Piazza Brà, the main shopping street, **Via Mazzini**, leads to elongated **Piazza
delle Erbe**, site of the Roman forum and now dominated by grand medieval
architecture. Further north still stand the churches of **Sant'Anastasia** and the **Duomo**,
though the main draw hereabouts is the bogus "**Juliet's House**". Make time for the
magnificent **Castelvecchio** fortress beside the River Adige, now housing Verona's main
art museum.

PONTE SCALIGERO, LEADING TO THE CASTELVECCHIO

Highlights

❶ Piazza Brà Verona's – and one of Italy's – largest city squares, always busy, always engaging; stroll around and soak up the atmosphere. **See p.318**

❷ The Liston An elegant curve of pavement cafés on the main square Piazza Brà – sit back and watch the city pass by. **See p.318**

❸ The Arena Giant Roman amphitheatre, plum in the heart of the city – monumental from the outside, epic within. **See p.319**

❹ Opera in Verona The historic Arena is a stirring backdrop to Verona's world-class opera

season, which consumes the city every summer. **See p.323**

❺ Castelvecchio Medieval riverside fortress that is now Verona's leading fine-art museum – devote at least a couple of hours to it. **See p.326**

❻ San Zeno Verona's most beautiful Romanesque church, in a western suburb of the city centre. **See p.330**

❼ Santa Maria in Organo Small, unsung church on the east bank of the River Adige which holds perhaps the most beautifully carved wooden choir-stalls in Italy. **See p.331**

HIGHLIGHTS ARE MARKED ON THE MAP ON PP.320–321

Porta Nuova

In plain view as you approach the city centre from the south (coming in from the Verona Sud autostrada exit, or the train station) stands Sanmicheli's impressive **Porta Nuova** gate in the Venetian walls, dating from the 1530s but rebuilt by the Austrians in 1854. It is now marooned in the centre of a huge roundabout, encircled by ceaseless flows of traffic. From here the kilometre-long Corso Porta Nuova boulevard charges northwards into the city towards Piazza Brà.

10

Piazza Brà

Beyond the crenellated double arches of the **Portoni della Brà**, which face along Corso Porta Nuova, promenading crowds fill **Piazza Brà**, one of Italy's largest squares, once an outlying meadow (*braida*). Immediately to the right is the **Palazzo Gran Guardia** (1610), a fearsomely blank-featured hulk paired with the equally bombastic Neoclassical **Palazzo Barbieri** (1838) across the way, the latter now housing the municipality. These two look out onto pretty tree-shaded gardens in the centre of the square, which is lightened by the long, gently curving, extra-wide pavement – in red Valpolicella marble – of the **Liston**. This is the focus of the Veronese *passeggiata*, a line of cheek-by-jowl cafés, *gelaterie* and restaurants, all with terrace tables beneath awnings, and all open late into the evening.

From Piazza Brà, it's a short walk west to the **Castelvecchio** museum (see p.326), where an impressive art collection is housed in a fourteenth-century fortress.

Museo Lapidario Maffeiano

Piazza Brà 28 • Tues–Sun 8.30am–2pm • €4.50; joint ticket with Arena €7; free with VC

At the Via Roma corner of Piazza Brà, reached through a passage beneath the arcades, is the **Museo Lapidario Maffeiano**. Founded in 1714, this is Europe's oldest museum of stone inscriptions, with a varied collection of chiefly Etruscan, Greek and Roman work, including many funerary reliefs.

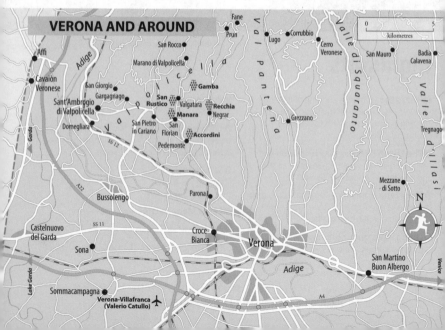

VERONA CARD (VC)

The great-value **Verona Card** (⊛veronacard.it) grants free admission to every church and museum in the city and free transport on all city buses. It comes in two versions – **two days** (€15) or **three days** (€20) – and is on sale at all the museums, monuments and churches and most hotels. Where it grants free admission, we've stated "**free with VC**".

VERONA'S HISTORIC CHURCHES

Separately, the **Associazione Chiese Vive** (⊛chieseverona.it) looks after four historic churches – San Zeno, Sant'Anastasia, San Fermo and the Duomo. Normal admission to each is €2.50 (though they're all part of the Verona Card scheme), but if you don't have a Verona Card you can buy a pass at any of them granting admission to all four for €6.

10

The Arena

Piazza Brà • Mon 1.30–7.30pm, Tues–Sun 8.30am–7.30pm; July & Aug until 5pm; last entry 1hr before closing • €6; joint ticket with Museo Lapidario €7; free with VC • ⊛arena.it

Dominating Piazza Brà is Verona's landmark monument, the superbly preserved **Arena**, the third-largest amphitheatre to have survived since antiquity (after the Colosseum in Rome and the theatre at Capua, near Naples). Its plan is elliptical, measuring 152m by 123m, and it was built in the first century AD just outside the walls of the Roman city. Earthquakes in 1117, 1118 and 1183 did little damage to the main structure, but effectively destroyed the entire outer encircling wall of the arena, all except for a three-storeyed section of four arches – now dubbed the "Ala", or wing, 31m high – which was left jutting up above the remaining walls at the northern side. With the original outer wall gone, what remains on view is a harmonious, two-storey line of arches, 72 in total, rising 20m above the square.

Inside the Arena

Inside – despite the three earthquakes, floods in 589 and 1239, and fire in 1172 – the Arena has survived more or less unscathed. As you walk out into the dusty pit, 73m long and 44m wide, the thought of what has gone on in this beautiful space, with its 44 tiers in white and pink marble, seating 30,000, is chilling. Aside from the Roman taste for gladiatorial combat, either man-to-man or against wild animals, the Arena has seen duels, public executions, bear-baiting and – an eighteenth-century attraction – bulls fighting men and dogs. Indeed, the word "arena" derives from the Latin for sand or dust, which was sprinkled liberally after shows to soak up the blood.

By 1890, the taste for public slaughter had eased; the Veronesi packed in, instead, to enjoy the spectacle of Buffalo Bill's touring Wild West Show. Today, rock concerts aside, the Arena is best known for hosting Verona's grand summer **opera** season, the *Stagione Lirica* (see box, p.323). It's worth clambering to the topmost tier for the panoramic views over Verona's rooftops.

Via Mazzini

The curving Liston plunges into narrow, traffic-free **Via Mazzini**, past window-displays of Gucci, Versace, Vuitton and Cartier into the heart of Verona's shopping quarter. Several hundred metres of bookshops and wine bars, lingerie shops and pharmacies lead into Verona's equally fascinating second square, Piazza delle Erbe.

Piazza delle Erbe

Site of the Roman forum, the long, narrow **Piazza delle Erbe** is still the heart of the city today. As the name suggests, the market here formerly sold vegetables, but it has

10

nowadays been largely taken over by souvenirs, knick-knacks and food stalls, the best offerings being the luxuriant takeaway *macedonie* (fruit salads).

The buildings framing the square are magnificent. As you emerge from Via Mazzini and look left into Piazza delle Erbe, at the far end rises the Baroque **Palazzo Maffei**, topped by six statues of Roman gods and goddesses and overlooked on the left by the **Torre del Gardello**, built in 1370. Lining the square's northeast side, to the right of the

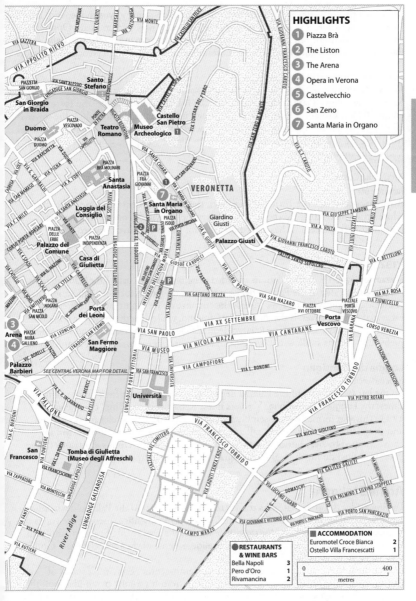

SEE CENTRAL VERONA MAP FOR DETAIL

Palazzo Maffei, is long **Casa Mazzanti**, its extensive sixteenth-century frescoes seen to best effect floodlit after dark. In front of it stands the **Fontana di Madonna Verona**, of the fourteenth century but incorporating an original Roman statue.

On the square's southwest side, at the corner with Via Mazzini, the **Domus Mercatorum** was founded in 1301 as a merchants' warehouse and exchange but ruined in an 1878 restoration. The very tall houses – six or seven storeys – at this end of the square formerly comprised part of Verona's **Jewish ghetto** (the nineteenth-century **synagogue**, with its monumental facade, is steps away on Via Portici, though now seldom used). Opposite the Domus Mercatorum, the twelfth-century **Palazzo del Comune** (or **Palazzo della Ragione**) is another unfortunate victim of restoration, now sporting a Neoclassical facade.

Torre dei Lamberti

Piazza delle Erbe • Daily 8.30am–7.30pm (June–Sept Sat–Thurs until 8.30pm, Fri until 11pm) • €8; free with VC

Soaring high above Piazza delle Erbe beside the Palazzo della Ragione, the **Torre dei Lamberti** looms to 84m. Begun in 1172 though not completed until 1463, the tower is climbable – there are five steps up to the lift, which then bypasses 238 steps. The views from here are splendid, but you can carry on to higher viewpoints; another 125 steps lead to the topmost level.

Arco della Costa

Piazza delle Erbe

An archway beneath the Torre dei Lamberti, the **Arco della Costa** is named after the whale's rib which hangs overhead. Legend says the rib will fall on the first honest person to walk beneath. It has stayed up there for more than five hundred years.

Piazza dei Signori

Piazza dei Signori is quieter than its crowded neighbour Piazza delle Erbe. On the right (southeast) is a side of the Palazzo del Comune that escaped Neoclassical alteration; its Romanesque courtyard survives. Across the entrance to Via Dante, with its stretch of excavated Roman street, is the **Palazzo del Capitano**, while directly ahead, closing the square on its northeast side, the **Palazzo degli Scaligeri** – much restored, and now the prefecture – sports swallow-tail battlements and an incongruous sixteenth-century portal.

Loggia del Consiglio

Piazza dei Signori

To the left (northwest) of the Palazzo degli Scaligeri is a monument to more democratic times: the **Loggia del Consiglio**, Verona's finest Renaissance building, completed in 1493. This was formerly the assembly hall of the city council; its elegant decoration and simplicity of design – eight tall arches at ground level, four mullioned windows above, topped by five statues of Roman notables (including Verona's illustrious native poet, Catullus) do much to give this square its sense of harmony.

Arche Scaligere

Passing under the arch that links the Palazzo degli Scaligeri to the Palazzo del Capitano, you come to the little Romanesque church of **Santa Maria Antica**, used by the rulers of Verona in the thirteenth and fourteenth centuries, the Della Scala/Scaligeri family. In front of the church are ranged the **Arche Scaligere**, some of the most elaborate Gothic funerary monuments in Italy.

Over the side entrance to the church, a fourteenth-century equestrian statue of **Cangrande I** ("Big Dog"; died 1329) gawps down from his tomb's pyramidal roof; this is a copy, the original being displayed in the Castelvecchio. The canopied tombs of the rest of the clan are enclosed within a wrought-iron palisade decorated with ladder motifs, the emblem of the family (*scala* means ladder). **Mastino I** ("Mastiff"; died 1277), founder of the dynasty, is buried in the simple tomb against the wall of the church. **Mastino II** (died 1351) is to the left of the entrance, opposite the most florid of the tombs, that of **Cansignorio** ("Top Dog"; died 1375).

A stroll 200m north of the Arche Scaligere brings you to the Gothic church of Sant'Anastasia.

OPERA IN VERONA

From late June to early September, Verona is consumed by its world-famous **opera festival** (the *Stagione Lirica*, or Lyric Season). Over half a million people attend the performances which take place almost nightly in the grand open-air setting of the 15,000-seat Roman **Arena**, in the heart of the city. The festival dates back to 1913, when *Aïda* was staged to celebrate the centenary of Verdi's birth. Since then, the season has always included *Aïda*, along with three or four other, no-expense-spared extravaganzas, invariably chosen from a roster of crowd-pleasers such as *Carmen*, *Tosca*, *La Traviata*, *Nabucco*, *Turandot*, *La Bohème* and *Madame Butterfly*. The stage is vast, stretching across the whole width of the Arena at one end, dominated by colourful scenery; the centrepiece of Franco Zeffirelli's 2002 *Aïda* was a golden pyramid 34m high. The acoustics are good (no microphones are used), and choruses hundreds-strong, as well as teams of horses, camels and even elephants on stage, make for quite a spectacle.

SEATS AND PRICES

Seating is divided into six areas. The best seats (**poltronissime gold**) are the first thirty rows in the front centre of the stalls. One block back and to the sides counts as **poltronissime**, with the furthest blocks to rear and side classed **poltrone**. Numbered places on the first fifteen rows of the Arena's stone steps are **poltroncina centrale di gradinata**; the two blocks flanking the stage are priced lower (**poltroncina di gradinata**). The cheapest seats are unreserved on the higher rows of stone steps (**gradinata**): blocks D and E are central, blocks C and F are lateral.

Expect to pay around €150 for a *poltronissima gold* seat. Each category costs roughly €20–30 less, down to around €20 for the cheapest seats. Weekend performances (Fri & Sat) cost more. People under 26 or over 60 and those in a wheelchair (plus a companion) are eligible for **discounts**.

BOOKING TICKETS

You can book online or by phone (☎045 800 5151, ⊕arena.it), or in person any time up to the start of the performance at the **Arena Ticket Office**, Via Dietro Anfiteatro 6b (on performance days 10am–9pm, on non-performance days 10am–5.45pm; Sept–June Mon–Fri 9am–noon & 3.15–5.45pm, Sat 9am–noon). In addition, agents around Italy can issue tickets to personal callers – a few agents in the lakes region include: **Brescia**: Tickets Point, Corso Zanardelli 52; **Desenzano**: Easy Lake, Via Mazzini 39; **Garda**: Lagotourist, Piazza Chiesa 20; **Lecco**: Saltours, Via Volta 10; **Limone**: Limtours, Via Comboni 42; **Malcesine**: Lagotourist, Via Capitanato 2; **Mantua**: Box Office, Via M. Giola 3; **Milan**: Teatro e Viaggi, Corso Porta Romana 65; **Riva del Garda**: ILG, Viale Rovereto 47.

ON THE NIGHT

Performances begin at 9pm (in Aug & Sept) or 9.15pm (in June & July), and – with long intervals – don't finish until well **after midnight**. Nights can get chilly; you should bring a coat or a shawl. It's a tradition for promenading crowds to fill the streets after the show, and many restaurants stay open until the small hours.

In the stalls seats, **black tie** is not out of place, with jackets and evening dress. Elsewhere, aim for relaxed **smart casual** – apart from in the cheapest seats, where nobody cares.

If you're in any seat other than *poltronissime*, bring a **cushion** (or rent one inside the Arena; about €5) – four hours on Roman stonework is unforgiving on the *gluteus maximus*. On the higher stone steps, where seating is unreserved, it is fine to come early and bring a **picnic dinner**, but beware that glass bottles, knives and other potential weapons will be confiscated; decant your wine into plastic first. Vendors up here sell ice cream, sandwiches, beer, wine and fizzy drinks. Binoculars to see detail on the stage are handy.

Even if it's raining, the performance is never **cancelled** before the scheduled start time. If, after a delay of up to two and a half hours, the show is called off before it's begun, you can get a refund by handing your ticket in to the Arena Ticket Office (see above for location) that evening or the following day – or by posting it within ten days (address on website). If the performance is abandoned after it has begun, no refunds will be given.

The Arena has **no cloakrooms** or left-luggage facilities. The **lost property** office is at Gate 5.

10

Casa di Giulietta (Juliet's House)

Heaven is here, where Juliet lives …   Shakespeare, Romeo and Juliet (III.3)

Via Cappello 23 • Mon 1.30–7.30pm, Tues–Sun 8.30am–7.30pm • €6; joint ticket with Juliet's Tomb €7; free with VC

The Immortal Bard is doubtless clutching his ribs in mirth at the nonsense his poetry has inspired. Leading south from Piazza delle Erbe is Via Cappello, a busy shopping street named after the family that Shakespeare turned into the Capulets. On the left you won't be able to miss the **Casa di Giulietta** – or, rather, an old, brick house that the municipality pressed into service in the 1930s to satisfy the demand for some visitable locations connected with *Romeo and Juliet*. There is not a shred of evidence to connect Juliet (a fictional creation), nor her family, the Cappelletti (real enough), with this or any other house.

You enter, first, a **courtyard** off the street, dominated by a much-photographed **balcony** that was freshly done up in Gothic style in 1935, to capitalize on the popularity of the "Romeo, Romeo, wherefore art thou, Romeo?" scene in a Hollywood movie of the day. It is, in short, fake – and unreachable from the ground, even for the most passionate Romeo.

Beneath the balcony stands a modern bronze **statue of Juliet**. Legend has it that if you rub Juliet's right breast you'll have a new lover within the year. Her gleaming bosom, the countless scrawls of love-graffiti, umpteen blobs of chewing gum, testify to the popularity of this slightly tawdry pilgrimage.

The **house** itself is a plain, much-restored fourteenth-century residence – also, once, an inn – filled out with a jumble of Shakespeariana and a Renaissance-style bed made in 1968. The only historic items are on the top floor – a few bowls and jugs. Unless you're dedicated to standing on that balcony, save your money.

San Fermo Maggiore

Stradone San Fermo • March–Oct Mon–Sat 10am–6pm, Sun 1–6pm; rest of year Tues–Sat 10am–5pm, Sun 1–5pm • €2.50; joint ticket with San Zeno, Sant'Anastasia and the Duomo €6; free with VC

Via Cappello leads south into Via Leoni with its Roman gate, the **Porta dei Leoni**, and a segment of excavated Roman street, exposed 3m below today's street level. At the end of Via Leoni rises the red-brick **San Fermo Maggiore**, whose inconsistent exterior betrays the fact that it comprises two churches built on top of each other. A church had existed here – where, in 304, saints Fermo and Rustico were martyred – for centuries before the Benedictines built, from 1065 to 1143, a grand upper church for religious ceremonies and a modest lower church to house the saints' remains (which were later transferred upstairs to avoid damage from flooding). Remodelled by the Franciscans in the fourteenth century, the vast Gothic upper church, with its splendid wooden ship's-keel ceiling of 1314, has a fine fresco of the *Annunciation* by Pisanello, while the dampish Romanesque lower church features impressive vaulting and some fragmentary thirteenth-century frescoes.

Sant'Anastasia

Piazza Sant'Anastasia • March–Oct Mon–Sat 9am–6pm, Sun 1–6pm; rest of year Tues–Sat 10am–5pm, Sun 1–5pm • €2.50; joint ticket with San Zeno, San Fermo and the Duomo €6; free with VC

Exiting Piazza delle Erbe at the northern end and turning right takes you onto Via Sant'Anastasia, which leads, in 300m, to Verona's largest church, **Sant'Anastasia**. Started in 1290 and completed in 1481, it's mainly Gothic in style, with undertones of the Romanesque in its proportions and design. The fourteenth-century carvings of New Testament scenes around the main doors are the most arresting feature of its bare, unfinished exterior; the soaring interior, with its fifteenth-century marble floor, is spare but elegant, with most of the interior vaulting frescoed. Just inside the main doors are two holy-water stoups, known as

ROMEO AND JULIET IN VERONA

To the continuing joy of Veronese tourism officials, their city is the setting for the world's greatest love story. Despite the lack of a factual basis to the tale, Verona plays on the association endlessly.

Shakespeare's version wasn't the first. That honour goes to the Vicenza author **Luigi da Porto** (1485–1529). His *La Giulietta*, written a few years before he died, was published in Venice in 1531, to great acclaim. Da Porto claimed he got the story while serving in the Venetian army, when he overheard a Veronese archer telling a tale of two doomed lovers, **Giulietta** (of the **Cappelletti** family) and **Romeo** (of the rival **Montecchi** family), who lived in Verona during the reign of Bartolomeo della Scala (1301–04). Da Porto may have been telling the truth, but the archer probably wasn't; no evidence has been found to authenticate the tale. Although it is known that both families were prominent in Verona at that time, much suggests that they were, in fact, allies rather than enemies.

Several versions appeared in the years following: it was a 1562 English translation of **Matteo Bandello**'s retelling which **William Shakespeare** adapted in 1596, retaining the setting in "fair Verona" but anglicizing the family names to **Capulet** and **Montague**. But the version which ultimately brought the legend to a worldwide audience was **George Cukor**'s Oscar-winning Hollywood production of 1936, starring Leslie Howard and Norma Shearer alongside stars such as John Barrymore and Basil Rathbone.

During pre-production, with MGM designers scouting the city for locations (they found none suitable), the Veronese authorities suddenly realized they were sitting on a golden egg. In 1935 the city's museum director, Antonio Avena, oversaw the purchase of the old house at Via Cappello 23. It was rapidly given a Gothic makeover – which included attaching a sawn-off Roman sarcophagus to the front as a balcony – and was officially renamed the **Casa di Giulietta**. Avena then lit upon a medieval-Gothic house of doubtful ownership at Via delle Arche Scaligere 2, which became the **Casa di Romeo** (now viewable only from the street). Then, at the convent of San Francesco al Corso, he polished up an old sarcophagus in red marble – which had, for some time past, been co-opted as Juliet's – installed it in a specially adapted subterranean room complete with Gothic accoutrements, and named the site **Tomba di Giulietta** (Juliet's Tomb).

Thus – hey presto! – Verona created for itself a bogus Romeo and Juliet pilgrimage trail in time for the movie première, initiating a wave of tourism which shows no sign of abating. Millions now visit, most completely unaware of how loose the links are, either to historical fact or even to Shakespeare's story (which, most people conveniently forget, ends with murder, suicide and a pile of corpses). As the 2010 Hollywood rom-com *Letters to Juliet* attests, lovelorn thousands even write to Juliet, the most plangent missives going forward for the "Dear Juliet" prize, awarded annually on St Valentine's Day (Ⓦ julietclub.com). It's hard to say where fiction ends and myth begins.

the *gobbi*, or hunchbacks; each features a crouched figure supporting the basin on his shoulders. Among the fourteenth- and fifteenth-century artworks around the church, the main highlight is Pisanello's delicately coloured fresco of *St George and the Princess*, high above the chapel arch to the right of the altar. It is damaged on the left side and placed so far up it's difficult to make out – the normally martial saint appears as something of a dandy.

Piazza Sant'Anastasia

Out on the little Piazza Sant'Anastasia, to the left of Sant'Anastasia's facade rises the eye-catching Gothic **tomb of Guglielmo di Castelbarco**, a *podesta* (high official) of Verona, built in 1320 in a style similar to that of the Arche Scaligere. To its left stands the church of **San Pietro Martire** (rarely open), deconsecrated since its ransacking by Napoleon. Numerous patches of fresco dot the walls, making for an atmospheric interior, though the highlight is the vast lunette fresco on the east wall, an allegorical account of the Assumption, featuring a bemused Madonna amid a bizarre collection of animals.

The Duomo

Piazza Duomo • March–Oct Mon–Sat 10am–5.30pm, Sun 1.30–5.30pm; rest of year Tues–Sat 10am–5pm, Sun 1.30–5pm • €2.50; joint ticket with San Zeno, San Fermo and Sant'Anastasia €6; free with VC

Modest Piazza Duomo is overlooked by the red-and-white-striped **Duomo**, almost at the tip of Verona's river-girt peninsula. Consecrated in 1187, the Duomo – dedicated to Santa Maria Matricolare – has a facade that is Romanesque in its lower parts, developing into Gothic as it goes up. The two doorways (under restoration at the time of writing) are twelfth-century; look for the story of Jonah and the whale on the south porch. The broad, well-lit interior, with its compound piers, has fascinating architectural details around each chapel and on the columns – particularly fine is the **Cappella Mazzanti** (last on the right). In the first chapel on the left, an *Assumption* by Titian occupies an architectural frame by Sansovino, who also designed the choir. Piazza Brà is a good twenty-minute walk (1.5km) south of the Duomo, while the Ponte Pietra (see p.330) is just a step away.

Porta dei Bórsari and around

Corso Porta Bórsari

From the northern side of Piazza delle Erbe, instead of turning right to Sant'Anastasia, if you turn left you enter **Corso Porta Bórsari**, a long, straight, pedestrianized street of fine *palazzi*, built over the Roman *decumanus maximus*. At its southern end stands another of Verona's impressive Roman remnants, the **Porta dei Bórsari**, a gateway that was as great an influence on the city's Renaissance architects as the Arena. Now reduced to a monumental screen straddling the road, it used to be Verona's largest Roman gate; the inscription dates it at 265 AD, but it's almost certainly older than that.

Corso Cavour – a busy traffic street – continues southwest beyond the gateway towards the Castelvecchio, while Via Oberdan cuts southwards into Piazza Brà.

San Lorenzo

Corso Cavour 30 • March–Oct Mon–Sat 10am–6pm, Sun 1–6pm; rest of year Tues–Sat 10am–1pm & 2–4pm, Sun 1–5pm • €2.50

Reached beneath an archway, the beautiful twelfth-century church of **San Lorenzo** is some 200m past the Porta dei Bórsari along Via Cavour. The lofty interior, in stripes of brick and tufa, is striking, and the church has two towers flanking the facade which hold spiral staircases up to the women's galleries.

Arco dei Gavi and Ponte Scaligero

The **Arco dei Gavi**, a first-century Roman triumphal arch that was rebuilt in 1930 after Napoleon's troops tore down the original is some 250m past the church of San Lorenzo, at the southern end of Corso Cavour. This is the best vantage point from which to admire the **Ponte Scaligero**, a fortified bridge over the Adige with distinctive swallow-tail battlements built by Cangrande II between 1355 and 1375 as a rat-run from the Castelvecchio, at a time when the Della Scala were losing the loyalty of the Veronesi. Like the Ponte Pietra, it survived until 1945, when the retreating Nazis blew it up – but, again, the stones were recovered from the riverbed and the bridge rebuilt. The stretch of shingle on the opposite bank is a popular spot for picnicking and sunbathing.

Castelvecchio

Corso Castelvecchio 2 • Mon 1.30–7.30pm, Tues–Sun 8.30am–7.30pm • €6; free with VC; audioguide €4 • Ⓦ comune.verona.it /castelvecchio/cvsito

The fortress from which the Ponte Scaligero springs – also easily reached on a short walk from Piazza Brà along Via Roma – is the **Castelvecchio**. The castle was commissioned by Cangrande II in 1354 and became the stronghold for Verona's

10

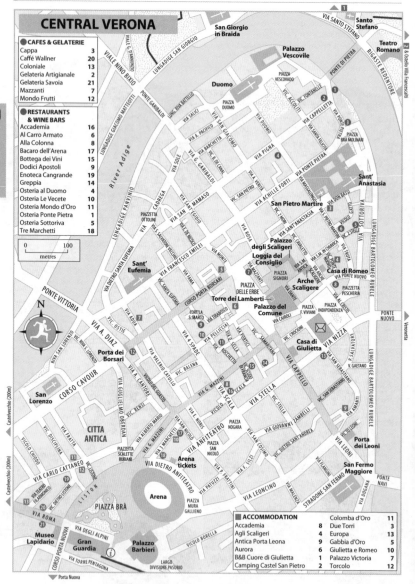

CENTRAL VERONA

CAFES & GELATERIE
Cappa	3
Caffé Wallner	20
Coloniale	13
Gelateria Artigianale	2
Gelateria Savoia	21
Mazzanti	7
Mondo Frutti	12

RESTAURANTS & WINE BARS
Accademia	16
Al Carro Armato	6
Alla Colonna	8
Bacaro dell'Arena	17
Bottega dei Vini	15
Dodici Apostoli	9
Enoteca Cangrande	19
Greppia	14
Osteria al Duomo	4
Osteria Le Vecete	10
Osteria Mondo d'Oro	11
Osteria Ponte Pietra	1
Osteria Sottoriva	5
Tre Marchetti	18

ACCOMMODATION
Accademia	8	Colomba d'Oro	11
Agli Scaligeri	4	Due Torri	3
Antica Porta Leona	9	Europa	13
Aurora	6	Gabbia d'Oro	5
B&B Cuore di Giulietta	1	Giulietta e Romeo	10
Camping Castel San Pietro	2	Palazzo Victoria	7
		Torcolo	12

subsequent rulers, incorporating part of the city walls along with substantial towers and fortifications.

The Castelvecchio now holds Verona's art museum, whose collection fills a labyrinth of chambers, courtyards and passages that is fascinating to explore in itself.

Ground floor: rooms 1 to 5

The first set of rooms is devoted to **sculpture**, mostly by unknown artists of the Middle Ages. Room 1 has a twelfth-century sarcophagus showing the graphic martyrdom of saints Sergius (decapitated) and Bacchus (clubbed to death), juxtaposed with a display case holding six pretty medieval spoons. A fine fourteenth-century St Catherine (room 2) and doleful St Libera (room 3) lead on to two violent, shocking pieces facing each other in **room 4**: a swooning Virgin, full of misery, and a screaming Christ opposite, eyes rolling in agony. The Renaissance panels in room 5 are limp by comparison.

First floor: rooms 6 to 12

The tour continues across the courtyard. Room 6 is the **dungeon** of the Torre del Mastio, now housing ancient bells. Climb the 33 steps here to enter the residential west wing, known as the Reggia, then turn left for **room 7**, where the frescoes include a flat, Gothic *Nursing Madonna* beside a perspectival, Giotto-esque *Madonna Enthroned*. Giotto himself is reported to have visited Verona in the 1310s.

10

Room 10 is full of Gothic art, including a beautiful, mystical *Madonna of the Rose Garden* attributed to Stefano da Verona and the ethereal *Madonna of the Quail* by Pisanello. **Jacopo Bellini**'s naturalistic *St Jerome* shows the saint praying in the desert amidst sharp-edged rocks, in Gothic-cum-Cubist style; room 11 – the elongated **Hall of the Reggia** – is dominated by his austere, starkly introspective *Crucifixion*.

Room 12, at the back of the hall, holds several Flemish works, including a *Portrait of a Woman* – thought to be the daughter of Philip II of Spain – painted by **Rubens** in Mantua in 1602.

Second floor: rooms 13 to 19

From the hall, climb the 31 steps then double-back and go through the doorway on the right for the Venetian paintings of **room 13**. Here, **Giovanni Bellini**'s *Madonna and Child* (1470) is displayed alongside a similar work by his studio assistant; one is wooden and predictable, the other is complex and alive, most notably in the central composition of Mary's crossed hands overlaid by the child's. **Room 14** holds Francesco Morone's *St Bartholomew* in, unusually, bright yellow against a black background.

Head now for small **room 18** at the rear, where hangs **Mantegna**'s superb *Holy Family* (1459), a tight cluster of four classical faces, Jesus as Dionysius, Joseph as an Old Testament prophet. Opposite is Jacopo da Valenza's Piero della Francesca-like *Risen Christ* – Jesus holds a flag of St George, while beneath lurk a sinister cross-eyed Roman soldier and his goitrous pal.

Room 19 holds a collection of **armour and weaponry**; from here, you can walk along the castle walls above the river and the Ponte Scaligero. Below, down some steps, strikingly displayed on a raised plinth is the equestrian figure of **Cangrande I**, removed from his tomb; his expression is disconcerting at close range, a simpleton's grin being difficult to reconcile with the image of the ruthless warlord.

First floor: rooms 20 to 25

Continue ahead to **room 20** and a *Passion* by Paolo Morando (known as *Il Cavazzola*), showing Verona in the background, alongside two portraits by Giovanni Francesco Caroto – a beaming boy holding up a drawing of a stick man (one of the few depictions in medieval painting of a child's work) and, in a rather more sombre vein, a Benedictine novice. Among the showy altarpieces in **room 21**, Caroto's simple, emotional *Pietà* stands out; opposite is an unflattering portrait of Savonarola by the Brescian artist Moretto, showing him as a shifty old sourpuss.

Rooms 22 and 23, with works by **Tintoretto** and a notable *Deposition* by **Veronese**, lead on to a *Portrait of a Man* in **room 24** by the local artist Marcantonio Bassetti (1626), full of insight for the subject's mortality. Room 25 has more seventeenth-century works, including a dark, tumultuous *Expulsion from Eden* by **Bernardo Strozzi**, full of vigorous movement on a sharp diagonal composition.

Beyond the city centre

Outside the central core of the city, attractions include the fine Romanesque church of San Zeno Maggiore to the west and the popular – if bogus – "Juliet's Tomb" to the south, though most interest lies over the River Adige to the north and east, in the unpretentious, largely residential neighbourhood of Veronetta – chiefly the splendid churches of San Giorgio in Braida and Santa Maria in Organo.

10

San Zeno Maggiore

Piazza San Zeno • Mon–Sat 8.30am–6pm, Sun 12.30–6pm; rest of year Tues–Sat 10am–5pm, Sun 12.30–5pm • €2.50; joint ticket with Sant'Anastasia, San Fermo and the Duomo €6; free with VC

Around 1km northwest of the Castelvecchio – best approached by a pleasant riverside walk of about fifteen minutes – is the church of **San Zeno Maggiore**, one of the most significant Romanesque churches in northern Italy and well worth the extra effort to reach.

A church was founded here, above the tomb of Verona's patron saint, as early as the fifth century, but the present building and its campanile were put up in the twelfth century, with additions continuing up to the late fourteenth century. Its large **rose window**, depicting the Wheel of Fortune, dates from the early twelfth century, as does the **portal**, whose lintels bear relief sculptures representing the months – look also for St Zeno trampling the devil. The reliefs to the side of the portal (from the same period) show scenes from the Old Testament on the right and New Testament on the left – except for the bottom two on both sides, devoted to the life of Theodoric. Bronze panels on the doors depict scenes from the Bible and the *Miracles of San Zeno*, their style influenced by Byzantine art; most on the left are from around 1100, most on the right from around 1200.

Areas of the lofty and simple **interior** are covered with beautiful frescoes, some superimposed on earlier works, others defaced by ancient graffiti. Diverting though these are, the most compelling image in the church is the high altar's luminous *Madonna and Saints* by Mantegna.

Juliet's Tomb and Fresco Museum

Via Pontiere 35 • Mon 1.30–7.30pm, Tues–Sun 8.30am–7.30pm • €6; joint ticket with Juliet's House €7; free with VC • Bus 71 from the centre

Roughly 700m southeast of Piazza Brà stands the picturesque ex-Capuchin monastery of San Francesco al Corso, a station on Verona's contrived Juliet pilgrimage trail (see p.325) for its **Tomba di Giulietta** (Juliet's Tomb). There is also a worthwhile museum of frescoes (**Museo degli Affreschi**) attached.

From the busy Via Pontiere, duck into a quiet, shaded garden – adorned with a bust of Shakespeare – to approach the old convent. At the top of the stairs, the **museum**'s outstanding works, frescoes notwithstanding, are two sculptures in marble by the nineteenth-century artist Torquato della Torre. *L'Orgia* is a reclining nude, radiating post-coital bliss, while *Gaddo* is so lifelike that critics accused della Torre of not sculpting the work but casting it from a living model. Downstairs, the church is now a gallery for large Renaissance and Baroque altarpieces, including a beautiful Mannerist *Archangels* by Francesco Caroto and four lusciously coloured semicircular panels by Louis Dorigny. You emerge into the cloister, and follow directions down to the **Tomba di Giulietta**, nothing more than an old sarcophagus, long touted as Juliet's (despite the fact she was a fictional creation), which was installed in this Gothified cellar in 1937.

Ponte Pietra

At the northernmost tip of Verona's peninsula sits **Ponte Pietra**, a fixture here since Roman times. The retreating Nazis blew the bridge up on April 24, 1945, but the Veronesi retrieved every stone from the riverbed after the war and faithfully rebuilt it.

SHAKESPEARE IN ITALIAN

The **Estate Teatrale Veronese** (W estateteatraleveronese.it) is a season of ballet, jazz and drama (including Shakespeare in Italian) staged chiefly at Verona's atmospheric open-air **Teatro Romano** (not the Arena) in July and August. Buy tickets at the box office in Palazzo Barbieri on Piazza Brà (entrance at Via Leoncino 61; Mon–Sat 10.30am–1pm & 4–7pm; ☎045 806 6485). Seats cost €25–30 in the stalls, €13–18 on the stone steps.

San Giorgio in Braida

10

Piazzetta San Giorgio • Daily 8–11am & 5–7pm • Free

On the north side of the Ponte Pietra, it's a short walk left past the twelfth-century church of Santo Stefano and along the embankments to **San Giorgio in Braida**, consecrated in 1447 and, in terms of its works of art, the richest of Verona's churches. The cupola was added in the sixteenth century by Sanmicheli, who also designed the unfinished bell tower. The house beside the church still sports bullet marks from fighting in 1805. Inside, a *Baptism* by Tintoretto hangs over the door, while the main altar, designed by Sanmicheli, incorporates a marvellous *Martyrdom of St George* by Veronese.

Teatro Romano and Museo Archeologico

Regaste Redentore 2 • Mon 1.30–7.30pm, Tues–Sun 8.30am–7.30pm • €4.50; free with VC

Overlooking the Ponte Pietra stands the first-century-BC **Teatro Romano**, much restored and now used for concerts and plays (see box above). High above it, reached by lift, the **Museo Archeologico** occupies the buildings of an old convent. Its well-arranged collection features a number of Greek, Roman and Etruscan finds, including a Roman bronze head. From the frescoed chapel at the top, the views across Verona are magnificent.

Santa Maria in Organo

Piazzetta Santa Maria in Organo • Daily 8am–noon & 2.30–6pm • Free

The church of **Santa Maria in Organo**, down at river level a short way southeast of the Teatro Romano, is one of Verona's treats. It possesses what Vasari praised as the finest choir stall in Italy. Dating from the 1490s, this marquetry was the work of a Benedictine monk, one Fra Giovanni, and is astonishing in its precision in depicting animals and use of perspective. There's more of his work in the sacristy, while in the crypt you can see reused upside-down Roman columns.

Giardino Giusti

Via Giardino Giusti 2 • Daily: April–Sept 9am–8pm; Oct–March 9am–5pm • €5 • Bus 72 from the centre

The Renaissance **Giardino Giusti** are the finest formal gardens in Verona. South of Santa Maria in Organo, they are full of fountains and shady corners, as well as a famous maze of box hedges designed in 1786. From here it's a short walk on Via Carducci down to cross the Ponte Nuovo back into the city centre.

ARRIVAL AND DEPARTURE

VERONA

BY PLANE

Verona/Valerio Catullo Verona's main airport (code VRN; ☎045 809 5666, W aeroportoverona.it) lies 13km southwest of the city and about 20km southeast of Lake Garda – it doubles as an international gateway for the lakes region. It is named Valerio Catullo (or just "Catullo") after the Roman poet Catullus, and is also sometimes suffixed Villafranca and/or Sommacampagna after two towns nearby – road signs and timetables might use any one of the subsidiary names without specifying Verona (the ATV bus company, for instance, calls it "Aeroporto Catullo di Villafranca"). Be sure not to confuse it with "Verona-Brescia" airport, 52km west at Montichiari (see p.264). Arrivals and departures share one terminal building. The Aerobus shuttles to/from Verona's Porta Nuova station (daily every 20min 6.30am–11.30pm; 15min; €6). A taxi (☎ 045 532 666) into town costs around €35. Journey times to major points from this and other airports are covered elsewhere in this guide (see p.20).

10

BY TRAIN

Verona Porta Nuova Verona's main train station is about 1km south of Piazza Brà. It is served approximately hourly by fast trains from Milano Centrale (1hr 30min), Brescia (45min) and Desenzano/Sirmione (30min), and slower ones from Mantua (45min). To walk into the centre (15min), turn right outside and cross the main roads to a busy roundabout where you'll see the triple-arched Porta Nuova gate; this faces along Corso Porta Nuova, which leads directly to Piazza Brà. Timetables for all train routes in Italy are at ⓦ trenitalia.com.

BY BUS

The bus station is at Porta Nuova train station, served by routes from nearby towns and villages, as well as bus 62/64 running roughly hourly from Riva del Garda (2hr 15min) and Malcésine (1hr 45min), and hourly bus LN026 from Brescia (2hr 20min), Desenzano (1hr 25min) and Sirmione (1hr). Verona's inter-urban buses are run by ATV (ⓦ www.atv.verona.it). Check timetables carefully for notes and arcane symbols (see p.27).

BY CAR

Two autostradas intersect just west of Verona. The north–south A22 (Modena–Brennero) has an exit marked "Verona Nord", 3km north of the intersection. The east–west A4 (Milano–Venezia) has the "Verona Sud" exit, 4km east of the intersection. You're allowed to drive into the historic centre (which is monitored by cameras) only if you have a booking at a hotel; otherwise, there are several paid car parks near the Arena (Cittadella is closest), while parking alongside the old city walls is free.

GETTING AROUND

Verona's historic centre is larger than you might think; the **walk** from Piazza Brà to the Duomo, for instance, is a solid twenty minutes. The **city buses** (ⓦ www.atv.verona.it), though, aren't much help. During the day (*feriali diurni*), one timetable operates. From 8pm to midnight (*serali*), and all day on Sundays (*festivi*), a completely different timetable operates, with different route numbers to boot. Maddeningly, they rarely connect places where visitors might want to go, and there's also a confusing one-way system, which means you often have to hunt for the right stop. Here's a summary.

Porta Nuova station to Piazza Brà Take bus 11, 12, 13, 51 or 73 during the day Mon–Sat (51 & 73 extend to San Fermo), or bus 90, 92, 93, 96, 97 or 98 at night or on Sun (96 & 97 extend to Piazza delle Erbe & Piazza Duomo).

Porta Nuova station to Castelvecchio & Porta Borsari Take bus 21, 22, 23, 24, 41, 42 or 61 during the day Mon–Sat, or bus 91, 94 or 95 at night or on Sun.

Other useful routes Otherwise, the most useful routes (which run every 30–40min on Mon–Sat daytimes) are

buses 70 and 71, which both link Piazza Brà (stop on Via Alpini) with Piazza delle Erbe & Piazza Duomo. Bus 71 extends south to Juliet's Tomb. Separately, bus 72 links Piazza Brà with Giardino Giusti.

Tickets All city buses are free with a Verona Card (see box, p.319). Otherwise buy a ticket (€1.30; valid 1hr) before boarding from the machines at Porta Nuova bus station or any local *tabacchi* (including those inside Porta Nuova station), and validate it in the machine on board the bus. A one-day pass is €4.

INFORMATION AND TOURS

TOURIST INFORMATION

Piazza Brà, Via degli Alpini 9 (Mon–Sat 9am–7pm, Sun 10am–4pm; ☎ 045 806 8680, ⓦ tourism.verona.it). As you enter Piazza Brà from Corso Porta Nuova, the office is on your right, easily missed against the old city walls.

There are further branches in the Arrivals hall of the airport (Mon–Sat 9am–6pm; ☎ 045 861 9163) and inside Porta Nuova train station. Note that on the first Sunday of the month in winter (Oct–May), admission to several major sights, including the Arena and Castelvecchio, is reduced to

---

CARNEVALE IN VERONA

One of the most enjoyable dates in the city's calendar is **Carnevale** (ⓦ carnevalediverona.it) on the Friday before Ash Wednesday; totally unlike its Venetian counterpart, this is a local event, without masks or posing – just lots of people dressing up, amid loud music and confetti. The festival dates back to 1531, and celebrates a local nobleman's donation of flour to make gnocchi during a time of food scarcity. Gnocchi in tomato sauce is handed out San Zeno's square, and the closing parade of the festival is led by the *Papa' de' gnocco*, who carries a staff topped with – you guessed it – a *gnocco*.

€1. The websites ⓦ veronatuttintorno.it and ⓦ verona.net are useful. For information on most of the city's sights, go to ⓦ comune.verona.it.

TOURS

Bus tours City Sightseeing has open-top buses following two different hop-on-hop-off circuits starting and ending at Piazza Brà (daily every 30min: May–Sept 9am–7.30pm; March, April & Oct 10am–6.30pm; 1hr; €19 for both; ⓦ www.verona.city-sightseeing.it.). Buy tickets on the bus or reserve through your hotel.

Horse-and-trap tours A more evocative way to get around is by horse-and-trap; Alberto Cipriani (☎ 338 621 9531) offers various circuits around the historic centre, from a short jaunt (20min; €25) to a Romeo & Juliet tour (1hr 20min; €90).

Walking tours A guided walk departs daily from the tourist office (Mon–Fri 2pm, Sat & Sun 11.30am; 1hr 15min; €10). Several guide companies run private tours on demand (roughly €100 for 2hr), including Assoguide Verona (☎ 045 810 1322, ⓦ veronacityguide.it) and Juliet & Co (☎ 045 810 3173, ⓦ julietandco.com).

10

ACCOMMODATION

Verona's **hotels** are pretty good, though options within the historic centre – which is where you'll spend all your time – are limited. Always book ahead, especially during the opera season (late June to early Sept) and the huge Vinitaly wine fair (late March/early April; ⓦ vinitaly.com/EN), when pressure on rooms is extremely tight. Verona Booking runs a free **booking service** for its partner hotels (☎ 045 800 9844, ⓦ veronabooking.com) and also has a desk inside the tourist office on Piazza Brà. There are dozens of **B&Bs**, or you could check with the tourist office for details of **self-catering apartments**. If you have your own transport, an alternative is to stay outside the city in the Valpolicella wine region; hotels such as *Villa del Quar* and *Byblos Art Hotel* (see p.335) lie less than 10km from central Verona.

Accademia Via Scala 12 ☎ 045 596 222, ⓦ accademiavr .it; map p.328. Elegant, 95-room, four-star hotel housed in a *palazzo* just off the main Via Mazzini, formerly an equestrian academy dating from 1565. The atmosphere is warm, service is smooth and efficient and it is often used as a venue for business meetings. The modernized interiors are lacking in old-world character, but an excellent location and comfortable facilities more than make up. **€180**

Agli Scaligeri Vicolo Ponte Nuovo 2 ☎ 0347 4765089, ⓦ agliscaligeri.it; map p.328. Beautiful B&B in a fabulous location, on a quiet side street steps away from Piazza dei Signori. The two rooms feature white linen, gleaming parquet floors and antique prints, and there's also a quirky apartment. Their excellent breakfast includes home-made cake, and the welcome is warm and genuine. **€115**

Antica Porta Leona Corticella Leoni 3 ☎ 045 595 499, ⓦ anticaportaleona.com; map p.328. Large four-star hotel close to Juliet's House, newly renovated with spacious interiors offering an enticing mix of sleek contemporary styling and traditional design touches – calligraphic poetry on the walls set off by club armchairs around the fireplace, matching cream and chocolate fabrics beneath ornate glittering chandeliers. A wide range of rooms means some unusual bargains can be had. **€280**

Aurora Piazza delle Erbe 2 ☎ 045 594 717, ⓦ hotelaurora.biz; map p.328. Upmarket, central two-star hotel with a warm atmosphere; the staff are friendly and knowledgeable and speak good English, and many of the simple rooms (some en suite) overlook the piazza. An excellent buffet breakfast and a lovely terrace above the square add to the attraction. **€180**

B&B Cuore di Giulietta Ippolito Nievo 15 ☎ 0327 475

5452, ⓦ cuoredigiulietta.it; map p.328. Warm-hearted B&B located just north of the Ponte Pietra. The three rooms are decorated in a plain but attractive modern style with splashes of colour, and the breakfast terrace looks over to Torricelle, the hill that overlooks the city. **€60**

Camping Castel San Pietro Via Castel San Pietro 2 ☎ 045 592 037, ⓦ campingcastelsanpietro.com; map p.328. This gorgeous hilltop site features city views through the foliage. There's a kitchen with a garden where you can pick your own herbs, a bar and mini-market, as well as three verdant terraces. Pitch **€20**

Colomba d'Oro Via Cattaneo 10 ☎ 045 595 300, ⓦ colombahotel.com; map p.328. Formerly a medieval monastery, set on a quiet back street behind Piazza Brà, this is an elegant four-star option, with a variety of rooms displaying tasteful decor and good attention to detail. There is a small bar but no restaurant – though with the Liston just a few steps away, that's no hardship. Prices drop substantially either side of the summer peak. **€190**

Due Torri Piazza Sant'Anastasia 4 ☎ 045 595 044, ⓦ duetorrihotels.com; map p.328. Opulent grandeur in a restored thirteenth-century building alongside the church of Sant'Anastasia in the heart of the old town. All ninety rooms (of which eight are suites) are soundproofed with a/c, many featuring eighteenth-century antique furniture. Public areas are charming, adorned with frescoes and vaulted ceilings, and an effortless air of wealth and privilege pervades the place. **€380**

Euromotel Croce Bianca Via Bresciana 2 ☎ 045 890 3890, ⓦ euromotel.net; map pp.320–321. A great option if you're driving but don't want to worry about (or pay for) parking in the centre. Located in a residential suburb 3km west of Porta San Zeno – easily reached from the A22 autostrada, with bus links into the city – this is a cheery, family-run hotel with 67 simple rooms, all en suite with a/c. Service is outstanding; the multilingual staff fall over themselves to be helpful, suggesting excursions, providing maps, bus timetables and more. Free parking. **€80**

Europa Via Roma 8 ☎ 045 594 744, ⓦ veronahoteleuropa.com; map p.328. Decent three-star hotel round the corner from Piazza Brà. Interiors are a bit tired and some rooms are cramped, but everything is quite serviceable and the convenience of the location makes up for minor deficiencies. Private parking. Often surprising discounts. **€120**

Gabbia d'Oro Corso Porta Borsari 4a ☎ 045 800 3060, ⓦ hotelgabbiadoro.it; map p.328. An admirably expensive, exclusive small hotel, occupying an eighteenth-century *palazzo* just off Piazza delle Erbe. Public areas retain many original features, from exposed brick walls to wood-beamed ceilings and stone-tiled floors. The modernized guest rooms comprise nineteen suites and eight doubles, done up in rich reds and golds, with Turkish carpets and marble bathrooms. **€360**

★**Giulietta e Romeo** Vicolo Tre Marchetti 3 ☎ 045 800 3554, ⓦ giuliettaeromeo.it; map p.328. A well-run, very popular three-star hotel in a perfect central location just a few steps from the Arena. It's not big – only thirty rooms – but the ambience is of a much larger, more prestigious hotel, not least because of warmly attentive staff, stylish interiors and large modern bathrooms. **€110**

Ostello Villa Francescatti (HI hostel) Salita Fontana del Ferro 15 ☎ 045 590 360, ⓦ ostelloverona.it; map pp.320–321. Reasonable hostel 3km outside the centre, in a beautiful sixteenth-century villa behind the Teatro Romano (not the Arena!); take bus 73 (or bus 91 after 8pm and on Sun) to Piazza Isolo, then walk up the hill. No reservations possible, but with 242 beds (including some family rooms), there should be space. There's a midnight curfew, but you can arrange later admission if you've got tickets for the opera. Also does reasonably priced evening meals. The sister hostel *Santa Chiara*, at the bottom of the hill, is used as an overflow. Dorms **€18**

Palazzo Victoria Via Adua 8 ☎ 045 590 566, ⓦ hotel victoria.it; map p.328. One of Verona's nicer four-star hotels, housed in a complex of older buildings with a snazzy foyer. Well-equipped rooms are furnished in romantic style, with especially swanky superior doubles and suites. **€280**

★**Torcolo** Vicolo Listone 3 ☎ 045 800 7512, ⓦ hotel torcolo.it; map p.328. Nicely decorated, house-proud little two-star hotel, with comfy rooms (all en suite) and welcoming owners. With a handy location just behind Piazza Brà it's a favourite with the opera crowd, so book well ahead. **€150**

EATING AND DRINKING

One of Verona's great joys is **eating**; the city takes food and wine seriously, and there are dozens of excellent **osterie** – small, local tavern-like restaurants – as well as plenty of more aristocratic places to eat. On nights when there is opera at the Arena (late June to early Sept), many restaurants go into overdrive from midnight until 2 or 3am, servicing the promenading post-opera crowds. Conversely, in the week before and after the opera season, some close early or shut completely as the city takes a rest. Watch out, too, for the huge Vinitaly wine fair, held in late March or early April, when restaurants and wine bars are packed. With the renowned **wine** regions of Valpolicella (see box, p.335) and Soave on the city's doorstep, not to mention nearby Bardolino and Lugana, almost everywhere serves fine wines – often small amounts in large glasses to release the bouquet. Wine lists can be bafflingly long; if you're in any doubt order the house wine, frequently a Valpolicella (red) or Soave (white) of some character. All the main squares have terrace **cafés** and *gelaterie*, though those on Piazza Brà can be overpriced and bland. After dark, Piazza San Zeno, out to the west, comes alive with people crowding the nearby cafés and **bars**.

CAFÉS

Caffé Wallner Via Dietro Liston 1 ☎ 045 800 0673; map p.328. Tucked away to the left as you enter Piazza Brà, this stylish café essentially a *pasticceria*, with sublime cakes as well as fresh juices, a variety of coffees, ice cream, salads and snacks (around €4). It's a great spot to start the day with coffee and a brioche, either in the bright café itself or at the foliage screened outdoor seating. Mon–Sat 7.30–11pm, Sun 8–11pm.

Cappa Piazza Brà Molinari 1a ☎ 045 800 4549, ⓦ cappacafe.it; map p.328. Amiable riverside café in business for forty years, with vaguely Eastern trappings, sofas and floor cushions, a pleasant waterfront terrace and live jazz on Sun. Also decent, affordable food on a daily-changing *menù*. Daily 9am–2am.

Coloniale Piazza Viviani 14c ☎ 045 801 2647, ⓦ casa -coloniale.com; map p.328. Some of the best coffee and hot chocolate in the city, and good snacks too (under €10), in a mock-colonial café setting. Daily 9am–midnight; Sept–June closed Mon.

Gelateria Artigianale Ponte Pietra Via Ponte Pietra 23 ☎ 340 471 7294, ⓦ gelateriapontepietra.it; map p.328. Wonderful little family-run enterprise – the ice cream is made fresh every day. A real local favourite. Mon 2.30–7.30pm, Tues–Sun 2.30–10pm.

THE VALPOLICELLA WINE REGION

On the northwestern outskirts of Verona rise the fertile hills of the **Valpolicella** region. The red wines produced here – including Valpolicella itself, Recioto and Amarone – are some of Italy's most famous vintages, exported worldwide. These are not classic landscapes – Valpolicella is a hard-working region of large vineyards and neat, wealthy villages, hemmed in by high valleys – but taking a day or so to draw breath among the vines, cherry trees and olive groves can make for a memorable diversion.

Around half an hour by car or bus covers 15km from Verona to the modest town of **San Pietro in Cariano**, where you'll find a tourist office (see below). The **Pieve di San Floriano**, just to the east, is one of the region's most significant Romanesque churches, or you could head west to the town of **Sant'Ambrogio di Valpolicella**, above which – reached by a series of hairpin climbs – stands the beautiful Romanesque **Pieve di San Giorgio**, part of which has been dated to 712 AD. Several **walks** in the area follow old tracks, including a 3km circular route from **Gargagnago** village dubbed "Percorso delle Quattro Fontane" that passes four restored medieval fountains. From Sant'Ambrogio, it's only a half-hour's drive west through the hills – past **Affi**, a junction on the A22 autostrada – to reach Garda (see p.286) on the shores of Lake Garda.

Many **wine estates** welcome individuals for **tastings and purchases**. Tourist offices have complete lists; always phone ahead to check opening times. Here's a handful of traditional producers: **Accordini** (☎045 770 1985, ⓦaccordini.it); **Gamba** (☎045 680 1714, ⓦvinigamba .it); **Manara** (☎045 770 1086, ⓦmanaravini.it); **Recchia** (☎045 750 0584, ⓦrecchiavini.it); **San Rustico** (☎045 770 3348, ⓦsanrustico.it). Otherwise, you can buy a huge 1.5l bottle of supermarket Valpolicella for as little as €4.

ARRIVAL AND INFORMATION

By bus Bus 3 (ⓦwww.atv.verona.it) runs every 30min or so along the SP4 between Verona (Porta Nuova station) and Domegliara, stopping at every village mentioned above.

By car Driving from Verona, follow the SS12 northwest to Parona, from where the minor SP4 road meanders into the heart of the Valpolicella.

Tourist information There's a tourist office on the main road through San Pietro in Cariano, Via Ingelheim 7 (Mon–Fri 9.30am–1pm & 1.30–5.30pm, Sat 9am–1pm; ☎045 770 1920, ⓦvalpolicellaweb.it).

ACCOMMODATION AND EATING

There are fine country restaurants and charming little family-run trattorias throughout the Valpolicella – wherever you go you're likely to find a decent place to eat and, of course, drink. We've picked out a few below, and we've also included a couple of luxurious villa hotels, in case you fancy pushing the boat out.

Antica Osteria della Valpolicella Via Monti Lessini 35, San Rocco ☎045 775 5010, ⓦanticaosteriavalpolicella.com. Rather posh little country restaurant above San Floriano serving innovative, mid-priced woodland cuisine flavoured with local truffles, nuts and pickles (tasting *menù* around €35). Tues–Sun noon–3pm & 7–11pm.

Byblos Art Hotel Villa Amistà Via Cedrare 78, Corrubbio ☎045 685 5555, ⓦbyblosarthotel .com. Behind a grand, fifteenth-century facade, this five-star hotel's beautifully restored interiors host outlandish contemporary artworks by the likes of Sol LeWitt, Anish Kapoor and Cindy Sherman. Stroll the grounds with a glass of wine or sample expensive contemporary Italian cuisine at the hotel's chic *Atelier* restaurant. **€300**

Hotel Villa Del Quar Via Quar 12, Pedemonte ☎045 680 0681, ⓦhotelvilladelquar.it. Spectacular five-star luxury hotel occupying a sixteenth-century mansion on an estate producing its own wines. Stay in the opulent rooms or book ahead for a table at the two-Michelin-starred *Arquade* restaurant. **€390**

★ **Locanda '800** Via Moron 46, Negrar ☎045 600 0133, ⓦlocanda800.it. Lovely, family-run winery with a sleek, highly rated restaurant (around €20 per main) and four beautifully rustic rooms upstairs. **€130**

Trattoria Cadelapela 1 Cà De La Pela, Sant'Ambrogio ☎045 680 0245, ⓦtrattoriacadelapela.it. Charming old trattoria, highly regarded by local gastronomes – a great little spot for hearty local cuisine and good wine, also offering a wonderful terrace views over Lake Garda and the mountains. Signposted near San Giorgio. Mon & Wed–Sun noon–2.30pm & 7–11pm.

Gelateria Savoia Via Roma 1b ☎045 800 2211, ⓦgelateriasavoia.it; map p.328. Another favourite *gelateria*, a fixture since 1939 under the arcades just off

Piazza Brà – ice cream and whole *semifreddi* (€15) made fresh daily by hand. Daily 9.30am–9pm.

Mazzanti Piazza delle Erbe 32 ☎045 800 3217,

10

10

Ⓦcasamazzanticaffe.it; map p.328. The least touristy of the cafés on this square offering a broad *menù* of salads and light meals (with unusual offerings too – couscous, gazpacho, sushi). Stays open late as a lively bar. Tues–Sun 8am–2am.

Mondo Frutti Corso Porta Bórsari 57b Ⓣ045 803 6341; map p.328. Artisan Trentino concoctions served from a hole-in-the-wall just inside the Roman gate. Takeaway only. Mon–Tues 12.30–7pm, Wed–Sun 12.30–8.30pm.

RESTAURANTS AND WINE BARS

Accademia Via Scala 10 Ⓣ045 800 6072, Ⓦristoranteaccademia.com; map p.328. One of Verona's best addresses, a cool, top-class restaurant renowned especially for its fish and seafood; signature dishes include succulent turbot. Simple *menù* from €35, but most mains are €20–25. Mon–Fri 10am–1.30pm, 4–6pm & 8–10pm, Sat & Sun 10am–1.30pm.

★**Al Carro Armato** Vicolo Gatto 2a Ⓣ045 803 0175; map p.328. One of Verona's most atmospheric old *osterie*, on a narrow street behind Sant'Anastasia, with stone floors, barred windows, lanterns and wooden benches. The *menù* is small – local-style dishes, very affordable – washed down by excellent wines. Staff are friendly and there's occasional live music on Sun. Open as a bar until midnight or later. Tues–Sun noon–3pm & 7.30–11pm.

Alla Colonna Largo Pescheria Vecchia 4 Ⓣ045 596 718; map p.328. Simple but good food and a lively atmosphere in this packed trattoria behind Piazza delle Erbe – much favoured by extended Veronese families out for a slap-up meal. The prices are attractive too (*menù* €15). Mon–Sat noon–2pm & 6.30–11.30pm.

Bacaro dell'Arena (Pizzeria da Sergio) Vicolo Tre Marchetti 16 Ⓣ045 590 503, Ⓦbacarodellarena.it; map p.328. Large, popular canteen-like pizzeria, handily located on an atmospheric little street a short walk from Piazza Brà. Great for straightforward meals, pizzas (€9) and late-night bites (till 11pm). Tues–Sun noon–11pm.

★**Bella Napoli** Via Marconi 16 Ⓣ045 591 143, Ⓦbellanapoliverona.com; map pp.320–321. Great pizzas – the largest in Verona – served in a distinctly Neapolitan atmosphere in this cheery modern pizzeria outside the historic centre. Aim for the original shop at no. 16 – or head across the street to no. 11 for the newer, classier restaurant. Same quality pizzas at both, thankfully. Mon–Thurs & Sun noon–2.30pm & 6.30pm–1am, Fri & Sat noon–2.30pm & 6.30pm–2am.

★**Bottega dei Vini (aka Antica Bottega del Vino)** Vicolo Scudo di Francia 3a Ⓣ045 800 4535, Ⓦanticabottegadelvino.net; map p.328. Illustrious, much-loved wine bar and restaurant, just off Via Mazzini, with a long list of dishes, from fragrant *primi* such as *gnocchetti verdi al pecorino e timo* (spinach gnocchi with sheep's cheese and thyme) or *bigoli con anatra* (thick

spaghetti with roast duck) to succulent steaks – horse or Florentine beef. The interior is cosy and always busy with diners or chatty drinkers, and the wine list is one of the longest you'll find in Verona. Expect to pay around €35–40 per head. Mon & Wed–Sun noon–midnight (open until 3–4am during Vinitaly and the opera).

Dodici ('12') Apostoli Corticella San Marco 3 Ⓣ045 596 999, Ⓦ12apostoli.it; map p.328. Named after a group of twelve Piazza delle Erbe merchants who used to dine here in the 1750s, this is an atmospheric place to sample Roman- and Renaissance-style cuisine in an old-fashioned setting of tiled floors and frescoed walls. The visitors' book reads like a *glitterati* history: Bergman, Callas, Garbo, Olivier, Fellini, Mastroianni and others have eaten here; expect a bill to match – the set meal is €67. Closed Sun eve & Mon, plus two weeks in June/July.

★**Enoteca Cangrande** Via Dietro Listone 19d Ⓣ045 595 022, Ⓦenotecacangrande.it; map p.328. Attractive, candlelit wine bar behind Piazza Brà offering a selection of foodie delights – salamis, cheeses, caviar – to accompany its fine wines. Service (which is English-speaking) and quality are highly recommended. Worth booking for a post-opera nosh. Four-course set meal €39.50. Daily noon–3pm & 7–11pm.

Greppia Vicolo Samaritana 3 Ⓣ045 800 4577, Ⓦristorantegreppia.com; map p.328. Small family-run trattoria near the Piazza delle Erbe that has an excellent reputation and prices around €25–35 a head. Outside it's wreathed in vines, and inside are columns and vaulted ceilings. The food and service are excellent. Tues–Sun noon–2.30pm & 7–10.30pm.

Osteria al Duomo Via Duomo 7a Ⓣ045 800 4505; map p.328. Wonderful old-fashioned *osteria*-bar, impervious to changing fashion, and enlivened on summer Wednesdays (5–8pm) by live music. There's a small, inexpensive *menù* of decent local favourites, including traditional dishes like *bigoli con asino* (thick spaghetti in a bolognese-style sauce of chopped donkey-meat). Mon–Sat 11.30am–3pm & 7pm–midnight.

Osteria Le Vecete Via Pellicciai 32a Ⓣ045 594 748, Ⓦgrupporialto.it; map p.328. Atmospheric *osteria* a few steps off Piazza delle Erbe that does good food and excellent wines. Crowd in at its wooden tables or let the expert barman recommend some gems from the superb range of local wines. Don't be afraid to check the price on the blackboard behind him; the wines range from cheap to very expensive. The small list of gourmet dishes – including their trademark savoury tartlets – ranges either side of €12. Daily 7pm–1.30am.

Osteria Mondo d'Oro Via Mondo d'Oro 4 Ⓣ045 803 2679, Ⓦosteriamondodoro.it; map p.328. Pleasant, unassuming modern *osteria* just off Via Mazzini – a decent spot for a break and a light bite (pasta dishes €15) in the midst of sightseeing, with tables set out on the (pedestrianized) street in spring and summer. Tues–Sun 12.30–10.30pm.

★**Osteria Ponte Pietra** Via Ponte Pietra 26 ☎045 804 1929, ⓦristorantepontepietra.com; map p.328. Sip a glass of wine in the tiny terrace garden while enjoying a splendid view across the river. The interiors have an atmosphere of retro chic, while the kitchen turns out simple but elegantly prepared classics for around €22. Daily noon–3pm & 7.30pm–midnight.

Osteria Sottoriva Via Sottoriva 9 ☎045 801 4323; map p.328. Verona's traditional *osterie* don't come much more authentic than this place – rumbustious and full of locals, in a charming residential district near the river. Sit in the shade of ancient stone arcades and enjoy a delicious, affordable lunch or dinner amid the banter, though don't expect to hurry; service is unapologetically slow. Most dishes under €10. Mon, Tues & Thurs–Sun 11am–11pm.

Pero d'Oro Via Ponte Pignolo 25 ☎045 594 645, ⓦperodoro.it; map pp.320–321. Friendly, family-run trattoria across the river in Veronetta, serving well-priced,

authentic Veronese food – handmade pastas, home-cured meats, and so on. *Menù* €18. Closed Tues–Sun noon–11pm.

Rivamancina Vicolo Quadrelli 1 ☎045 594 976, ⓦrivamancina.com; map pp.320–321. Popular late-opening Veronetta cocktail bar across the Porta Nuovo bridge that does some light early-evening dishes too. Daily 6pm–2am.

Tre Marchetti ("Da Barca") Vicolo Tre Marchetti 19b ☎045 803 0463, ⓦtremarchetti.it; map p.328. Cosy little trattoria a couple of steps north of the Arena, with a classy ambience and a tasteful, old-fashioned interior featuring starched tablecloths and bow-tied waiters. The perfect spot for a pre- or post-opera dish of Veronese specialities, but be sure to book. Try the *baccalà alla Vicentina con polenta* (wind-dried cod) or the *fegato di vitello alla Veneziana* (calves' liver) – or classic local *primi* such as *fettuccine porcini e tartufo*, with truffles from nearby Lessinia. You might get away with €35, but a bill is more likely to be €60-plus per head. Mon–Sat noon–2.30pm & 7–11pm.

10

Mantua

MANTUA BY NIGHT

Mantua

Aldous Huxley called it the most romantic city in the world. With a skyline of domes and towers rising above three encircling lakes, Mantua (Mantova in Italian) is undeniably evocative. Birthplace of the Roman poet Virgil, this was where Romeo heard of Juliet's supposed death, and where Verdi set Rigoletto. Its history is one of equally operatic plots, most acted out by the Gonzaga, one of Renaissance Italy's richest and most powerful families. Its cobbled squares retain a medieval aspect, and there are two splendid palaces: the Palazzo Ducale, containing Mantegna's stunning frescoes, and Palazzo Te, whose frescoes by the flashy Mannerist Giulio Romano have entertained and outraged generations of visitors with their combination of steamy erotica and illusionistic fantasy.

For all its attractions, Mantua feels like a different world from the lakes. It's a sedate town, known, if at all, for its delectable local culinary speciality *tortelli di zucca* (pumpkin ravioli). We've included it in this book as a rewarding one- or two-day addition to an itinerary centred on Verona or Lake Garda; it is easily reached from both of them. Note that an earthquake in 2012 caused severe structural damage, with parts of the Palazzo Ducale remaining closed for two years and scaffolding shoring up the city's towers; if you see any remaining scaffolding this is probably the cause.

The centre

The centre of Mantua is made up of four attractive squares, each connected to the next. Lively **Piazza Mantegna** is overlooked by the massive **Sant'Andrea** church. Beside it is the lovely **Piazza Erbe**, with fine arcades facing the medieval **Rotonda** church. To the north, through medieval passageways and across **Piazza Broletto**, the long, cobbled slope of **Piazza Sordello** is dominated by the **Palazzo Ducale**, the fortress and residence of the Gonzaga, packed with Renaissance art – notably by Mantegna.

Sant'Andrea

Piazza Mantegna · Daily 8am–noon & 3–7pm · Free · ⓦ santandreainmantova.it

Dominating **Piazza Mantegna** – a wedge-shaped open space at the end of the arcaded shopping thoroughfares of Corso Umberto and Via Roma – is the facade of Leon Battista Alberti's church of **Sant'Andrea**, an unfinished basilica that says a lot about the ego of Lodovico II Gonzaga, who commissioned it in 1470. He felt that the existing medieval church was neither impressive enough to represent the splendour of his state nor large enough to hold the droves of people who packed in every Ascension Day to see the holy relic of Christ's blood which had been found on the site. Lodovico brought in the court architect, Luca Fancelli, to oversee Alberti's plans. There was a bitchy rivalry between the two, and when, on one of his many visits, Alberti fell and hurt a testicle, Fancelli gleefully told him: "God lets men

Highlights

❶ Piazza Erbe The centrepiece of Mantua's beautiful (and eminently strollable) medieval centre, a broad, good-looking square full of historic character. **See p.343**

❷ Palazzo Ducale This vast medieval palace of Mantua's Gonzaga dukes dominates the city visually, culturally and artistically. It is filled with superb Renaissance art – including stunning frescoes by Andrea Mantegna – and, by itself, makes the detour to Mantua worthwhile. See p.344

❸ Palazzo Te Gonzagan love-nest on the edge of Mantua, another rambling palace complex which, in any other city, would be the top-notch attraction for its vivid, bawdy Renaissance frescoes and the dramatic "Hall of the Giants". **See p.348**

❹ Tortelli di zucca Mantuan cuisine stands out – be sure you make time to dine on the famous local *tortelli di zucca* (ravioli stuffed with sweet pumpkin) at one of the city's restaurants. **See p.350**

HIGHLIGHTS ARE MARKED ON THE MAP ON P.342

11

punish themselves in the place where they sin." Work started in earnest after Alberti's death in 1472, and took more than two decades to complete.

The Classical facade is focused on an immense triumphal arch supported on giant pilasters. **Inside**, the vast, column-free space is roofed with one immense barrel vault, echoing the facade. The octagonal balustrade at the crossing stands above the crypt where the holy relic is kept in two vases, copies of originals designed by Cellini and stolen by the Austrians in 1846; to see them, ask the sacristan. The painter Mantegna is buried in the first chapel on the left, his tomb topped with a bust of the artist that is said to be a self-portrait. The wall-paintings in the chapel were designed by Mantegna and executed by students, one of whom was Correggio.

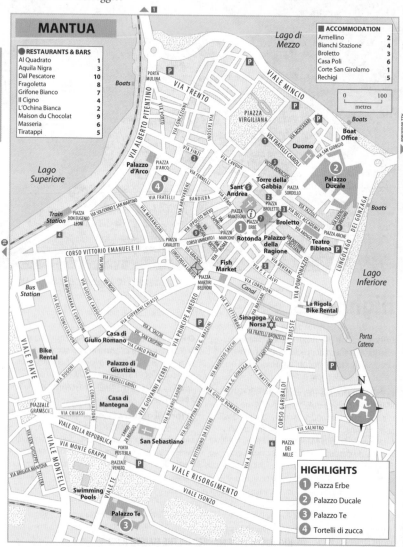

MANTUA

● RESTAURANTS & BARS
Al Quadrato	1
Aquila Nigra	3
Dal Pescatore	10
Fragoletta	8
Grifone Bianco	7
Il Cigno	4
L'Ochina Bianca	2
Maison du Chocolat	9
Masseria	6
Tiratappi	5

■ ACCOMMODATION
Armellino	2
Bianchi Stazione	4
Broletto	3
Casa Poli	6
Corte San Girolamo	1
Rechigi	5

HIGHLIGHTS
1 Piazza Erbe
2 Palazzo Ducale
3 Palazzo Te
4 Tortelli di zucca

THE GONZAGA

At the time of their coup of 1328, the **Gonzaga** family were wealthy local peasants, living outside Mantua on vast estates with an army of retainers. On seizing power in the city, **Luigi Gonzaga** nominated himself Captain of the People, a role which quickly became hereditary, eventually growing in grandeur to that of marquis.

Mantua's renaissance began in 1459, when a visiting pope complained that the city was muddy, marshy and riddled with fever. This spurred his host, **Lodovico II Gonzaga**, to give the city a facelift, ranging from paving the squares and repainting the shops to engaging **Andrea Mantegna** as court artist and calling in the prestigious architectural theorist **Leon Battista Alberti** to design the monumental church of Sant'Andrea, one of the most influential buildings of the early Renaissance. Later, Lodovico's grandson, **Francesco II** (1466–1519), swelled the family coffers by hiring himself out as a mercenary – money his wife, **Isabella d'Este**, spent amassing a prestigious collection of paintings, sculpture and objets d'art.

Under Isabella's son, **Federico II**, Gonzaga fortunes reached their height; his marriage in 1531 to the heiress of the duchy of Monferrato procured a ducal title for the family, while he continued the policy of self-glorification by commissioning an out-of-town villa – the **Palazzo Te** – for himself and his mistress. Federico's descendants were for the most part less colourful characters, one notable exception being **Vincenzo I**, whose debauchery and corruption provided the inspiration for Verdi's licentious duke in Rigoletto. After Vincenzo's death in 1612, the then-bankrupt court was forced to sell many of the family treasures to Charles I of England (many are still in London's V&A Museum), just three years before the arrival of the Habsburgs.

Piazza Erbe

Piazza Erbe is the town's most distinctive square, with a small daily market and cafés and restaurants sheltering in the arcades below the thirteenth-century **Palazzo della Ragione**, whose impressive wooden-vaulted main hall is viewable during occasional temporary exhibitions. Across from the tourist office is the **Casa del Bianco**, or Casa di Boniforte da Concorezzo, which still has its late-Gothic terracotta decoration and a beautiful portico supported on columns of Verona marble. It has long been occupied by a haberdashery run by the prominent Jewish Norsa family.

Rotonda di San Lorenzo

Piazza Erbe • Mon–Fri 10am–1pm & 2–6pm, Sat & Sun 10am–6pm • ⓦ casandreasi.it

Sunk below the present street level of Piazza Erbe, Mantua's oldest church, the eleventh-century **Rotonda di San Lorenzo**, narrowly escaped destruction under Lodovico's city-improvement plans. It lost its roof in the sixteenth century and was effectively turned inside out; houses were built surrounding it and their Jewish occupants (the church lay inside the ghetto boundary) used what is now the interior as an open courtyard. In 1908 the houses were demolished and the church rebuilt; it is now beautifully restored and still contains traces of twelfth- and thirteenth-century frescoes.

Piazza Broletto

At the north end of Piazza Erbe, a passage leads under the red-brick **Broletto**, or medieval town hall, into the smaller **Piazza Broletto**, where you can view two reminders of how "criminals" were treated under the Gonzagas. The archway to the right has metal rings embedded in its vault, to which victims were chained by the wrists, before being hauled up by a pulley and suspended in mid-air; while on your far left – actually on the corner of Piazza Sordello – the tall medieval **Torre della Gabbia** has a cage attached in which prisoners were displayed. A statue of Mantua's most famous son, the Roman poet Virgil, overlooks the square.

THE JEWS OF MANTUA

Jewish settlement in Mantua is recorded as early as 1145. Under the Gonzaga, Jews flocked to the city, chiefly from Rome and Germany; the Church had banned Christians from finance, so Jews (who were barred from politics) took on banking and money-lending to the Gonzaga court. By the mid-sixteenth century, two thousand – or over seven percent – of Mantua's population were Jewish. The community produced several notables in the fields of theatre, music, medicine and printing. As in Venice, where the first Jewish ghetto was created in 1516, in Mantua Jews were eventually enclosed within gates and forced to wear a yellow marker on their clothes. Even after emancipation in 1798, Jews remained in the area of the former ghetto, only being forced out around 1900 by the destruction of what was deemed unsanitary housing. Most moved to Milan, and many who remained were deported to death camps during World War II. The community today numbers about seventy.

It is possible to trace the remnants of a Jewish presence in Mantua. Behind the Rotonda, the corner of Piazza Concordia and Via Spagnoli – renamed from **Via degli Orefici Ebrei** (Street of the Jewish Goldsmiths) – marks the reused site of three adjacent synagogues. The huge **Banca d'Italia** on Via Castiglioni replaced what was the heart of the ghetto, while the **Hotel Rechigi** on Via Scuola Grande is built on the site of the Grand Synagogue, demolished in 1938. A stroll away, at Via Bertani 54, offices now occupy the tall, seventeenth-century **Casa del Rabbino** (House of the Rabbi), its facade decorated with stucco. Where Via Bertani meets Via Pomponazzo, you can see the hinges of the gates that were closed nightly, sealing off the ghetto. A short walk south, behind an anonymous facade at Via Govi 13, is the **Sinagoga Norsa**, the only one of Mantua's six synagogues to have survived; it was removed from its original location on Via Scuola Grande in 1904 and reassembled here. The interior, with its eighteenth-century fittings, is complete and is still used. It can be visited (Mon–Fri 9–11am; free) – but ask the tourist office (see p.350) to call ahead for you first.

Teatro Bibiena

Via Dell' Accademia 47 · Tues–Fri 10am–1pm & 3–6pm, Sat & Sun 10am–6pm · €2 · ⓦ societadellamusica.it

Teatro Bibiena is one of Mantua's final Baroque buildings – the work of Antonio Bibiena, whose brother designed the Bayreuth Opera House. This is a much smaller theatre, at once intimate and splendid, its curved walls lined with four tiers of boxes calculated to make their occupants more conspicuous than the performers. Mozart gave a concert here in 1770, a few days before his fourteenth birthday; his impression is unrecorded, but his father was fulsome in his praise for the building, calling it "the most beautiful thing, in its genre, that I have ever seen". Concerts are still staged here (the music conservatory is alongside).

The Duomo

Piazza Sordello · Daily 8am–noon & 3–7pm · Free

Cobbled **Piazza Sordello** is a large, sombre space, headed by the Baroque facade of the Duomo and flanked by touristy cafés and grim crenellated palaces built by the Bonacolsi (the Gonzagas' predecessors). The **Duomo**, or Cattedrale San Pietro, at the top of the square, boasts a rich, light interior, designed by Giulio Romano after a pre-existing church had been gutted by fire in 1545. Every year on the patron saint's day, March 18, the clothed, uncorrupted corpse of San Anselmo is wheeled out to worshippers.

Palazzo Ducale

Piazza Sordello · Tues–Sun 8.15am–7.15pm, last entry 6.20pm · €6.50 (audioguides €5) · ⓦ mantovaducale.beniculturali.it

Beside the Duomo on Piazza Sordello, the crenellated Palazzo del Capitano and Magna Domus were taken by Luigi Gonzaga when he seized Mantua from the Bonacolsi in 1328, beginning three hundred years of Gonzaga rule. They now form the core of the

Palazzo Ducale, an enormous complex that was once the largest palace in Europe. In its heyday it covered 34,000 square metres and had a population of over a thousand; when it was sacked by the Habsburgs in 1630, eighty carriages were needed to carry the two thousand works of art contained in its five hundred rooms.

The main highlight is the **Camera degli Sposi**, frescoed by Andrea Mantegna – a masterpiece. It lies in the farthest corner of the complex; reaching it and heading straight out again is the bare minimum for a visit, but that will take you the best part of a couple of hours, passing through most of the finest rooms on the way. Linger here and there, and you could easily spend a half-day in the palace.

VISITING THE PALAZZO DUCALE

Admission For conservation reasons, only 1500 people a day are allowed to visit the Camera degli Sposi (also called the Camera Picta). In the peak season for school trips (March 15–June 30 and Sept 1–Oct 15), individuals must book in advance for a timed slot for admission to this room, using the appointed ticket agents Teleart – either by phone (☏ 041 241 1897; Mon–Fri 9am–6pm, Sat 9am–2pm; €1 fee per person, payable on arrival) or online with a credit card (ⓦ ducalemantova.org).

Tours Our account follows the standard route through the palace complex. Other areas usually closed to the public – such as the frescoed bridal apartment of Isabella d'Este, the so-called "Summer Quarters", and Duke Guglielmo's apartments, which include a magnificent fretwork-vaulted Coffee House – can be visited on request (Sat & Sun only) as *Percorsi Aggiuntivi*, accompanied by a guide (free).

Rooms 1–14: the Corte Vecchia

You begin in the Corte Vecchia, the oldest wing of the palace. At the top of the Scalone delle Duchesse is the **Sala del Morone** (room 1), where you'll see a painting from 1494 by Domenico Morone showing the *Expulsion of the Bonacolsi* from Piazza Sordello, with the Duomo sporting its old, Gothic facade (replaced in the eighteenth century). In the **Sala del Pisanello** (room 3) are the fragments of a half-finished fresco by Pisanello, discovered in 1969 behind two layers of plaster and thought to depict either an episode from an Arthurian romance or the (idealized) military exploits of the first marquis, Gianfrancesco Gonzaga. It's a powerful piece of work, charged with energy.

The **Galleria Nuova** (room 5) is crammed with altarpieces from Mantuan churches suppressed by Napoleon, notably one of *St Francis* by Francesco Borgani with a view of Mantua behind. At the end, turn left for the splendid **Galleria degli Specchi** ("Hall of Mirrors"; room 6), which has a notice outside signed by Monteverdi, who worked as court musician to Vincenzo I; his *L'Orfeo*, the world's first modern opera, was premiered here on February 24, 1607. The room was originally an open loggia, bricked up in 1773; teams of horses are being driven across the barrel-vaulted ceiling from Night to Day.

Sala degli Arcieri and beyond

Vincenzo also employed Rubens, whose *Adoration of the Magi* in the **Sala degli Arcieri**, next door (room 7), shows the Gonzaga family of 1604, seated comfortably in the presence of God; notice Vincenzo with his handlebar moustache. The picture was originally part of a huge triptych, but Napoleonic troops carried off two-thirds of it in 1797 (one part is now in Antwerp, the other in Nancy) and chopped the remaining third into saleable chunks of portraiture; some gaps remain. Opposite is an even larger *Miracle of the Loaves and Fishes* by Domenico Fetti, while on the corbelling above squat nightmarish gargoyle figures. Around the room is a curious frieze of horses, glimpsed behind curtains.

Beyond the **Sala del Labirinto** (room 9), named after the maze on its painted and gilded wooden ceiling, adorned with *forse che sì, forse che no* ("maybe yes, maybe no"), the **Sala di Amore e Psiche** (room 11) is an intimate and characterful space, with a wooden floor and an eighteenth-century tondo of Cupid and Psyche in the ceiling.

From here, you enter the Corridoio dei Mori, but follow signs immediately left, down the stairs then right along the **Corridoio di Santa Barbara**. At the end, more signs point left, down the **Scalone di Enea** staircase (room 14), over a moat and into the fourteenth-century **Castello di San Giorgio** fortress.

Rooms 15–17: Camera degli Sposi

A spiral ramp (room 15) leads up to a holding chamber, where you may have to wait in order to view the adjacent **Camera degli Sposi** (room 17), which holds the palace's principal treasure: Mantegna's famous frescoes of the Gonzaga family, done in the period 1465–74. They depict the Marquis Lodovico and his wife Barbara with their family, and are naturalistic pieces of work, giving a vivid impression of real people, and of the relationships between them.

You enter from the south: facing the door, Lodovico discusses a letter with a courtier while his wife looks on; their youngest daughter leans on her mother's lap, about to bite into an apple, while an older son and daughter look towards the door, where an ambassador from another court is being welcomed.

The other fresco, on the west wall, depicts a landscape of weird rock formations and an imaginary city with the Gonzagan arms above the gate. Divided into three sections by fake pilasters, it shows Gonzagan retainers with dogs and a horse in attendance on Lodovico, who is welcoming his son Francesco back from Rome. In the background are the Holy Roman Emperor Frederick III and the King of Denmark.

The ceiling features a beautiful piece of trompe l'oeil, in which two women, peering down from a balustrade, have balanced a tub of plants on a pole and appear to be on the verge of letting it tumble into the room. Below them stand foreshortened chubby cherubs, comically clinging to the trompe l'oeil dome.

You exit to the adjacent **Stanza dei Soli** (room 16) and back down the spiral ramp to the Scalone di Enea.

Rooms 18–27: the Corte Nuova

Straight ahead from the top of the Scalone di Enea, you enter the sixteenth-century Corte Nuova wing, designed by Giulio Romano for Federico II Gonzaga. The first rooms are the huge, gloomy **Sala di Manto** (room 18), with a fine coffered ceiling, and the **Sala dei Cavalli** (room 19), whose irregular shape is disguised by a deftly designed ceiling. The **Sala delle Teste** (room 20) once featured eleven busts, all now gone, but its ceiling fresco remains, showing Jupiter in a thoughtful pose holding a thunderbolt. Through the **Sala di Troia** (room 21), with Romano's brilliantly colourful scenes from the *Iliad* and *Aeneid*, is the long **Galleria dei Marmi** (room 22), looking out over the Cortile della Cavallerizza (Courtyard of the Riding School), with its bizarre twisted columns.

Along the courtyard's long side runs the immense **Galleria della Mostra** (room 23), once hung with paintings by Titian, Caravaggio, Breughel and others, all now dispersed; in their place are 64 Roman marble busts of figures such as Virgil, Cicero, Nero and Marcus Aurelius.

Beyond are four small chambers, the **Camera del Fuoco**, **dell'Aria**, **dell'Acqua** and **della Terra** (Fire, Air, Water, Earth; rooms 24–27), collectively known as the **Galleria del Passerino**, painted with scenes from Ovid's *Metamorphoses* and formerly filled with displays of natural oddities: crystals, coral, resins, ostrich eggs and even the mummified corpse of Passerino Bonacolsi, pre-Gonzagan lord of Mantua.

Rooms 28–36: back through the Corte Vecchia

A sequence of corridors returns past a suite of miniature rooms long thought to have housed Isabella d'Este's celebrated troupe of dwarf jesters; in fact it is a scaled-down version of the St John Lateran basilica in Rome, built for Vincenzo. Stairs lead up to the **Corridoio dei Mori** (room 28), at the end of which is a sequence of rooms overlooking the unusual **Cortile delle Otto Facce** (Octagonal Courtyard).

Beyond, the stunning **Sala dello Zodiaco** (room 32), whose late sixteenth-century ceiling is spangled with stars and constellations, adjoins the Rococo **Sala dei Fiumi** (room 33), which features an elaborate painted allegory of Mantua's six rivers, flanked at either end by a mock garden complete with painted creepers and two ghastly stucco-and-mosaic fountains. The hanging gardens outside the window are considerably more attractive.

Save some wonder for rooms 34–36, beside the Sala dello Zodiaco. These comprise the **Stanze degli Arazzi**, three rooms (and a small chapel) altered in the eighteenth century to house a set of nine sixteenth-century Flemish tapestries, made from Raphael's cartoons (now in the V&A in London) for the Sistine Chapel depicting stories from the Acts of the Apostles. They are of exceptional virtuosity. At the end, the Scalone delle Duchesse returns you to the ticket desk.

Palazzo d'Arco

Piazza d'Arco • March–Oct Tues–Sun 10am–12.30pm & 2.30–6pm; Nov–Feb Sat & Sun 10am–12.30pm & 2–5pm • €5

On the western side of the town centre, dominating the compact Piazza d'Arco, the Neoclassical **Palazzo d'Arco** comprises the 1784 rebuilding of the residence of a noble family related to the rulers of Arco, a town near Riva del Garda. The main attraction is a wing of the fifteenth-century *palazzo* which survived in the gardens: its upper **Sala dello Zodiaco** (room 39) has frescoes dated 1520 by the Veronese artist Falconetto – twelve large panels depicting each sign (apart from Libra, which was destroyed when the fireplace was installed). Of the dozen or more rooms open in the main building, all with their original paintings and furniture, look out for room 15, the **Sala Andreas Hofer**, dedicated to a Tyrolean rebel executed in 1810; it features panels of wallpaper printed in 1823 with Italian landscapes, including a smoking Mount Etna.

South of the centre

A twenty-minute walk from the centre of Mantua, at the end of the long spine of Via Principe Amedeo and Via Acerbi, the **Palazzo Te** is the later of the city's two Gonzaga palaces. It's an easy walk, and you can take in a few of Mantua's minor attractions on the way.

First is Giulio Romano's **Fish Market**, to the left off Piazza Martiri Belfiori, a short covered bridge over the river which is still used as a market building. Located to the right off Via Principe Amedeo, at Via Poma 18, and overshadowed by the Palazzo di Giustizia, the **Casa di Giulio Romano** was also designed by Giulio; it was meant to impress the sophisticated, who would have found the licence taken with the Classical rules of architecture witty and amusing. A five-minute walk away on busy Via Giovanni Acerbi, the more austere brick is now used as a gallery for contemporary art (hours and admission vary; ⓦcasadelmantegna.it). **Casa del Mantegna** was designed by Mantegna both as a home and private museum; grand fireplaces and fresco friezes survive, and the circular courtyard, set within the rectangular building, is striking.

Tempio di San Sebastiano

Piazzale Vittorio Veneto • Mid-March to mid-Nov Tues–Sun 10.30am–12.30pm & 3–5pm • €1.50

Across the road from the Casa del Mantegna, the **Tempio di San Sebastiano** – the work of Alberti – is famous as the first Renaissance church to be built on a Greek-cross plan. Nikolaus Pevsner called it "curiously pagan". Lodovico II's son was less polite: "I could not understand whether it was meant to turn out as a church, a mosque or a synagogue." The bare interior – now deconsecrated – is dedicated to Mantua's war dead; the crypt, its forest of columns adorned with commemorative plaques, is especially atmospheric.

Palazzo Te

Viale Te • Mon 1–6pm, Tues–Sun 9am–6pm; last entry 5.30pm • €9 • ⓦ palazzote.it • Bus 1 from city centre to the stops "Risorgimento 3" or "Repubblica 1", either side of nearby Porta Pusterla

At the southern end of Via Acerbi, set in its own grounds, stands the **Palazzo Te**, a grand edifice designed in the 1520s for playboy **Federico Gonzaga** and his mistress, Isabella Boschetta. This is artist/architect **Giulio Romano**'s greatest work and a celebrated Renaissance pleasure-dome.

The palace originally formed an island, linked to the mainland only by bridge – an ideal location for an amorous retreat away from Federico's wife and the restrictions of life in the Palazzo Ducale. Although the upstairs rooms hold collections of Mesopotamian and Egyptian antiquities as well as a modest picture gallery, the main reason for visiting is to see Giulio's amazing decorative scheme in the ground-floor rooms – a voyage around Giulio's imagination, filling a sumptuous world where very little is what it seems.

11

Rooms 1–8

From the entrance hall, turn left beside the Cortile d'Onore to enter the north wing of the palace. The **Camera delle Imprese** (room 4) sets the tone; in the top right corner of the south wall is painted a salamander with the motto *Quod huic deest me torquet*. Salamanders were thought to be asexual, and Federico is saying here "What this lacks, torments me" – a nudge-nudge reference to his own legendary appetites. The salamander pops up with his catchphrase throughout the palace.

In the **Camera del Sole** (room 5), the sun and moon are represented by a pair of horse-drawn chariots viewed from below, giving a fine array of human and equine bottoms on the ceiling. In the **Sala dei Cavalli** (room 8), portraits of prime specimens from the Gonzaga stud-farm (which was also on the island) stand before an illusionistic background in which simulated marble, fake pilasters and mock reliefs surround views of painted landscapes through non-existent windows.

Room 9: Camera di Amore e Psiche

The function of the **Camera di Amore e Psiche** (room 9) is undocumented, but the graphically erotic frescoes, and the proximity to Federico's private apartments, are powerful clues. The ceiling paintings tell the story of Cupid and Psyche with more dizzying *sotto in su* ("from the bottom up") works by Giulio, among other examples clumsily executed by his pupils. The walls are more than a little racy, too, with orgiastic wedding-feast scenes, at which drunken gods in various states of undress are attended by a menagerie of real and mythical beasts. On the north wall, Mars and Venus are climbing out of the bath together, their cave watered by a river-god lounging above who is gushing with deliberately ambiguous liquid flowing from his beard, a vessel he's holding and his genitals. This is either what it seems – a glorying in bodily fluids – or is perhaps a punning reference to Giulio's second name, Pippi (The Pisser), along with encouragement to Federico who, according to his doctors, suffered from "the obstinate retention of urine". Other scenes show Olympia about to be raped by a priapic, half-serpentine Jupiter and Pasiphae disguising herself as a cow in order to seduce a bull – all watched over by the giant Polyphemus, perched above the fireplace, clutching the pan-pipes with which he sang of his love for Galatea before murdering her lover.

Rooms 10–22: Camera dei Giganti

Wander on through the couple of rooms either side of the beautiful **Loggia di Davide** (room 12), with views east across the gardens and west across the Cortile d'Onore, to the extraordinary **Camera dei Giganti** (room 15) at the southeast corner, where revenge is taken on Polyphemus. Its frescoes – "the most fantastic and frightening creation of the whole Renaissance", according to the critic Frederick Hartt – show the destruction of the giants by the gods, in a virtuoso display of artistic skill and imagination.

Unusually, there are almost no architectural interruptions to the frescoes; corners have been smoothed into curves, and the images come right down to the floor and go right up across the ceiling, in a sensational, IMAX-like effect. The destruction appears to be all around: cracking pillars, toppling brickwork and screaming giants, crushed by great chunks of masonry that appear to crash down into the room. The fireplace in the eastern wall was removed in the eighteenth century, but Vasari – who visited in 1541 – wrote that "when the fire is lit, the giants burn". That, and the sound of crackling, must have made this room the world's first multimedia fantasy experience, and the effect is little diminished today. Shout or stamp your feet and you'll discover the sound effects that Giulio created by turning the room into an echo chamber.

The remainder of the rooms in the south wing are pretty, but can barely match up.

ARRIVAL AND DEPARTURE
MANTUA

By train The train station – with roughly hourly services from Verona (45min), Milano Centrale (2hr 10min) and Cremona (55min) – is ten minutes' walk west of the centre. Timetables are at ⓦ trenitalia.com.

By bus The bus station is alongside the train station, with a roughly hourly service from Brescia (1hr 40min) and Peschiera via Valeggio (1hr 5min); note that buses from Verona (1hr 20min) drop off first at more convenient Piazza Sordello.

By car By car, the A22 autostrada zips south for 30km from Verona Sud to Mantova Nord. Mantua also lies on the SS249 36km south of Peschiera via Valeggio and on the SS236 47km southeast of Desenzano.

GETTING AROUND

By bus Bus 1 Circolare (ⓦ apam.it) runs frequently from the train and bus stations on a clockwise route east via Piazza d'Arco to the central squares, then south on Corso Garibaldi, west on Viale Risorgimento (stopping near Palazzo Te) and north on Viale Piave back to the train station. Tickets cost €1.40 (day-pass €3.50), buyable from *tabacchi*.

By bike Mantua has numerous signed cycle routes, from a gentle circuit of the lakes (14km) to a six-hour ride up the

---

TAKING TO THE WATER

Several companies offer **cruises** on Mantua's lakes – bulges in the course of the River Mincio – and on the river itself down to its confluence with the Po. All run daily but must be **booked in advance**; usually a day ahead, but sometimes an hour or so will do. Lago Inferiore, to the east of the city, and Lago di Mezzo to the north are linked, but Lago Superiore upstream to the west is 4m higher, behind a dam built in 1187. The scenery is flat, characterized by reeds and marshy inlets; lotus flowers abound, introduced in 1921, and you may see herons, egrets and storks. Many of the boats accept **bikes** so you can create a lazy day-trip – a morning on the boat, a picnic lunch at, say, Rivalta 10km upstream, then a gentle cycle-ride back in the afternoon.

TOUR OPERATORS

Motonavi Andes Negrini ☎0376 322 875, ⓦ www.motonaviandes.it. The leading company is Motonavi Andes Negrini, whose ticket office is at Via San Giorgio 2, three minutes' walk from its jetty on Lago Inferiore. Laghi di Mantova trips depart every couple of hours and meander around Lago di Mezzo, Lago Inferiore and a bit further south to the Vallazza lake (either 1hr, Mon–Sat €8, Sun €9; or 1hr 30min, Mon–Sat €9, Sun €10). An equally scenic cruise on Lago Superiore (1hr 30min; Mon–Sat €10, Sun €11) starts from the jetty by the Porta Mulina; the return journey, as Mantua's towers rise from the water, is a delight. Many other trips are offered, including a day cruise as far as Venice.

Navi Andes ☎0376 324 506, ⓦ naviandes.com.

A separate concern with ticket offices at Piazza Sordello 48 and by its jetty on Lago di Mezzo, runs similar trips for pretty much exactly the same prices. In effect, there's nothing to choose between them.

Barcaioli del Mincio ☎0376 349 292, ⓦ fiumemincio.it. Standard river trips can often be busy excursions, on large boats. The difference comes with the Barcaioli del Mincio, local boatmen operating small craft upstream from Mantua on Lago Superiore. Departures operate chiefly from Grazie, 8km upstream (1hr €8; 2hr €10), though they will pick up from Mantua on prior booking.

Olympusaquae ☎347 491 3437, ⓦ olympusaquae .it. The *Enigma* is a solar-powered boat that follows sightseeing itineraries starting from Rivalta, including full-moon and new-moon trips. Trips from €9.

11

wooded River Mincio to Peschiera del Garda (43km). You can rent bikes (around €10/day) from Mantua Bike, Viale Piave 22b (Mon–Sat 8am–12.30pm & 3–7.30pm; ☏ 0376 220 909, ⓦ mantuabike.it), and La Rigola on Via Trieste

(Mon–Sat 9.30am–12.30pm & 2.30–7.30pm; ☏ 0376 366 677).

On foot Mantua is compact enough to cover on foot; even the walk south to Palazzo Te is only twenty minutes.

INFORMATION

Tourist information This city-centre office at Piazza Mantegna 6 (daily 9am–6pm; Oct–March closes 5pm; ☏ 0376 432 432, ⓦ turismo.mantova.it) is large and well organized; there's also a small info-point at Piazza Sordello

23 (daily 9am–7pm) and a Mantua Tourism desk in the Arrivals hall of Verona-Villafranca (Valerio Catullo) airport (Mon–Sat 9am–6pm; ☏ 045 986 800). ⓦ cittadimantova .it and ⓦ mantova.com are useful tourist websites.

ACCOMMODATION

Armellino Via Cavour 67 ☏ 346 314 8060, ⓦ bebarmellino.it. Superior B&B with four attractively furnished double rooms (sharing two bathrooms) in an eighteenth-century palace right in the centre of town. There's a pretty garden for drinks, and breakfast is served in the period dining room. No credit cards. €85

Bianchi Stazione Piazza Don Leoni 24 ☏ 0376 326 465, ⓦ albergobianchi.com. A pleasant if unexciting family-run hotel by the train station with comfortable rooms and small suites – fifty altogether – arranged around an attractive garden. €80

Broletto Via Dell' Accademia 1 ☏ 0376 326 784, ⓦ hotelbroletto.com. Small three-star family-run hotel in the historic centre. Service is cheery and rooms are very pleasant, with a touch of contemporary style (all en suite, with a/c), even if some are a bit small. €89

★**Casa Poli** Corso Garibaldi 32 ☏ 0376 288 170,

ⓦ hotelcasapoli.it. Pristine four-star boutique hotel on a main road roughly 10min walk south of the centre. Rooms are done up in a chic, minimalist style, all wood floors and crisp cotton, with flat-screen TVs and hi-tech accoutrements. The location is not ideal but they offer good weekend discounts. €120

Corte San Girolamo Via San Girolamo 1, Gambarara ☏ 0376 391 018, ⓦ agriturismo-sangirolamo.it. Occupying a renovated watermill 3km north of town on the cycle route from Mantua to Lake Garda, this serene agriturismo has en-suite doubles plus a four-person apartment. Bicycles available. €90

Rechigi Via Calvi 30 ☏ 0376 320 781, ⓦ rechigi.com. Four-star hotel in the historic centre. The lobby is a little off-putting – all gleaming marble and sleek sofas, with contemporary art dotted about – but the rooms are calmer. Private parking. €180

EATING AND DRINKING

Mantua has plenty of excellent, reasonably priced restaurants dotted on and around the main central squares, many serving local specialities like *spezzatino di Mantova* (donkey stew), *agnoli in brodo* (pasta stuffed with cheese and sausage in broth) or the delicious *tortelli di zucca* (sweet pumpkin-filled pasta), the city's best-known trademark dish. The nicest spot for an alfresco drink and some people watching is one of the café-bars on Piazza Erbe.

Al Quadrato Piazza Virgiliana 49 ☏ 0376 368 896. A tranquil spot away from the fray, overlooking the Piazza Virgiliana park north of the centre. Serves good pizzas (around €8) and tasty fish dishes. Expect to pay around €25. Tues–Sun noon–3pm & 7–11pm.

Aquila Nigra Vicolo Bonacolsi 4 ☏ 0376 327 180, ⓦ www.aquilanigra.it. A formal restaurant housed in an elegant *palazzo* just off Piazza Sordello, serving delicious seasonal food complemented by an impressive wine list. The fish and, especially, seafood are highly regarded. *Menùs* are €70–80. Tues–Sat noon–3pm & 7.30–11pm.

★**Dal Pescatore** Località Runate, Canneto sull'Oglio ☏ 0376 723 001, ⓦ dalpescatore.com. Dedicated foodies should book weeks in advance for this award-winning country restaurant, located some forty minutes' drive west of Mantua (and currently boasting three Michelin stars). Local ingredients and methods rule, although the

husband-and-wife team are famed for their innovative take on classical Italian cuisine. Luxury and simplicity; it'll be a meal to remember, with a bill probably topping €200 a head. Wed 7–11pm, Thurs–Sun 12.30–3pm & 7–11pm. Closed Jan & Aug.

Fragoletta Piazza Arche 5a ☏ 0376 323 300, ⓦ fragoletta.it. Over towards the Lago Inferiore, this is a lively *osteria* shoehorned into a cramped little building. It's been around since 1748 and remains popular with locals for its well-priced regional cuisine. Expect to pay around €30. Tues–Sun noon–3pm & 8pm–midnight.

Grifone Bianco Piazza Erbe 6 ☏ 0376 365 423, ⓦ grifonebianco.com. The pick of the restaurants on this central square, a welcoming place serving excellent local specialities off a seasonal menu at moderate prices. Closed Tues, lunch on Wed & late June.

★**Il Cigno (Trattoria dei Martini)** Piazza d'Arco 1 ☏ 0376 327 101. Exceptional restaurant occupying a sixteenth-century mansion in a quiet corner away from the centre. The setting is refined; a tasteful old dining room, free from music, overlooks a beautiful private garden. And the cooking is out of this world – sweet, delectable *tortelli di zucca* with amaretti, delicately flavoured, melt-in-the-mouth *luccio con salsa* (dressed pike) and flavourful local meats (roast guinea-fowl is a signature dish). There are no prices on the menu; expect around €75 a head; set lunch €35. Wed–Sun noon–1.45pm & 7.30–9.45pm. Closed Aug.

L'Ochina Bianca Via Finzi 2 ☎0376 323 700, ⓦochinabianca.it. This cosy *osteria* where friendly staff serve tasty Mantuan dishes (€11–15) is a mainstay of the Italian "Slow Food" movement, dedicated to promoting quality and conviviality. Mon–Thurs 7.45–10pm, Fri & Sat 12.30–2.30pm & 7.45–10pm, Sun 12.30–2.30pm.

★**Maison du Chocolat** Via Oberdan 8 ☎0376 321 081, ⓦmaisonduchocolat.it. As well as the gourmet chocs and other sweet treats, this little shop tucked down a side street is probably Mantua's finest artisan *gelateria*, ladling out spectacular handmade ice cream. Tues–Sun 10.30am–12.30pm & 4–10.30pm.

Masseria Piazza Broletto 8 ☎0376 365 303, ⓦwww .istorantemasseria.it. A popular, lively place with good pizzas (around €7) as well as a wide selection of other moderately priced dishes served at outside tables. Daily noon–3pm & 7.30pm–midnight.

Tiratappi Piazza Alberti 30 ☎0376 322 366, ⓦristorantetiratappi.it. Atmospheric old wine bar on this little-visited square, down a concealed passageway beside the Sant'Andrea church. Its terrace tables are a sun trap – perfect for sampling Mantuan vintages on a slow afternoon. The cuisine is all local as well; mid-priced specialities (around €12) served with care. Daily noon–3.30pm & 7–11pm.

11

MONUMENT TO GARIBALDI, MILAN

Contexts

History

A specific Italian history is hard to identify – and a northern Italian history even more so. The country wasn't formally united until 1861, and the history of the peninsula after the Romans is one of warring city-states and annexation by foreign powers. Regional and local differences remain strong to this day. What follows is a brief description of key events.

From prehistory to the Romans

Some remains exist from the **Neanderthals** who occupied the Italian peninsula half a million years ago, but the main period of colonization began after the last Ice Age, with evidence of **Paleolithic** and **Neolithic** settlements dating from around 20,000 BC and 4000 BC respectively. There are remains of stilt dwellings on Lake Ledro dating from around 2000 BC. Successive inhabitants of the Val Camonica, north of Lake Iseo, left thousands of designs carved into the rocks, giving a unique picture of Neolithic – and, later, **Bronze** and **Iron Age** – life.

Other tribes brought Indo-European languages into Italy. The **Veneti**, in the northeast, and related **Liguri**, in the northwest, developed distinctive cultures and began moving down the peninsula from the north, but the rise of the **Etruscans** in central Italy, mirrored by the colonization of southern Italy by the **Greeks**, halted their progress. Some say the Etruscans arrived in Italy around the ninth century BC from western Anatolia, others that they came from the north, and a third hypothesis places their origins in Etruria. Whatever the case, by the sixth century BC, they were in control of central Italy, edging out the indigenous populations. **Mantua**, on the Po plain, was one of the northernmost Etruscan settlements.

Through the fifth and fourth centuries BC, Gaulish **Celtic** tribes migrated south across the Alps, frequently clashing with the Etruscans and, in 390 BC, almost taking **Rome**. This, though, proved a temporary reversal in the inexorable rise of the city; over the following century, virtually the whole peninsula came under Roman domination. The middle decades of the third century BC saw Rome taking Sicily, Sardinia and Corsica, as well as, in 222 BC, what they dubbed "**Cisalpine Gaul**" – that is, Gaul on this side of the Alps, referring chiefly to the area of the lakes and the Po valley.

The Gaulish Celts took a hand in the fightback against Rome, helping the Carthaginian general **Hannibal** cross the Alps in 218 BC (Hannibal continued south, gaining some victories but eventually being overcome by the legions). Their reward was complete subjugation by the Roman military machine, which moved into northern Italy in strength. New **coloniae** were founded, such as Brixia (Brescia) and Cremona, populated with army veterans. Meanwhile, existing Celtic settlements such as Mediolanum (Milan), Como and Verona were Romanized as **municipia**.

Peace and prosperity under **Augustus** and the subsequent first- and second-century AD emperors allowed the northern Italian communities to flourish; agriculture on the Po plain was strong, livestock grazed the hillsides and the cities grew in wealth and

8000–1000 BC	222 BC	100–200 AD	313 AD
Early civilizations in the Val Camonica leave their mark in rock paintings and stilt dwellings around Lake Ledro.	Rome conquers the Cisalpine Gaul area covering northern Italy.	Peace and prosperity under Roman rule sees agriculture and cities flourish and the wealthy build lakeside retreats.	Christianity is declared the state religion by Constantine in the Edict of Milan.

sophistication. Rome's moneyed elite established large estates on the lakes – most famously the elder and younger Plinys' villas on Lake Como.

Christianity and the collapse of Rome

In the middle of the third century AD, incursions by **Goths** in Greece and the Balkans, and **Franks** and **Alemanni** in Gaul foreshadowed the collapse of Rome. The persecution of Christians under Emperor **Diocletian** (284–305) produced many of the Church's present-day saints. Plagues had decimated the population, and problems of a huge but static imperial economy were compounded by the doubling in size of the army.

To ease administration, Diocletian **divided the empire** into two halves, east and west, basing himself as ruler of the western empire in Mediolanum (Milan). This measure brought about a relative recovery, coinciding with the rise of **Christianity**, which was declared the state religion by **Constantine** at the **Edict of Milan** in 313. Milan's bishop, Ambrose, became a key figure in the spread of the religion, building churches and establishing a theological orthodoxy. Constantinople (now Istanbul), capital of the eastern empire, became a thriving trading and manufacturing city, while Rome itself went into decline, as the enlargement of the senatorial estates and the impoverishment of the lower classes gave rise to something comparable to a primitive feudal system.

By the fifth century, many legions were made up of troops from conquered territories and several posts of high command were held by non-Romans. With little will or loyalty behind it, the empire floundered, and in late 406, **Vandals**, Alans and Sueves crossed the frozen Rhine into Gaul, chased by the Huns. By 408, the imperial government could no longer hold off **Alaric**, who went on to **sack Rome** in 410, causing a crisis of morale in the west. "The whole world perished in one city," wrote St Jerome.

The bitter end of the Roman Empire in the west came after **Valentinian III** was assassinated in 455. It limped on with his eight successors over the next twenty years until the Germanic invaders elected their general **Odoacer** as king in Pavia in 476.

During this time the **Christian Church** developed as a more or less independent authority. Continual invasions had led to an uncertain political scene in which the **bishops of Rome** emerged with the strongest voice – justification of their primacy having already been given by Pope Leo I (440–461), who spoke of his right to "rule all who are ruled in the first instance by Christ".

Lombards and Franks

During the chaotic sixth century, the **Lombards**, a Germanic tribe, were driven southwest into Italy, and by the eighth century, when the **Franks** arrived from Gaul, they were extending their power throughout the peninsula from their base at Pavia. The Franks integrated quickly and took over much of the provincial administration. Led by **Pepin the Short**, they saw an advantage in supporting the papacy, giving Rome large endowments and forcibly converting pagans in areas they conquered.

In 753 Pope Stephen II summoned the Frankish army. Pepin forced the Lombards to hand over treasure and 22 cities and castles, which then became the northern part of the **Papal States**. He died in 768, and divided the kingdom between his two sons. One died within three years; the other became known as Charles the Great, or **Charlemagne**.

410 AD	800 AD	1176	1200–1550
The decline of the Roman Empire leads to the Sack of Rome.	Charlemagne is crowned Holy Roman Emperor.	Battle of Legnano. An affiliation of northern cities defeats Barbarossa, making way for a string of independent city-states.	Powerful city-states like Milan, Mantua, Genoa, Venice and Florence keep relative peace, giving rise to the Renaissance.

An intelligent and innovative leader, Charlemagne was proclaimed King of the Franks and the Lombards, and patrician of the Romans, in 773. The treasure of the Lombard king he defeated, Desiderius, is on show in Brescia to this day. On Christmas Day 800, Pope Leo III expressed his gratitude for Charlemagne's political support by crowning him **Holy Roman Emperor**. By the time Charlemagne died, all of Italy from the northern lakes to beyond Rome was part of the huge **Carolingian Empire**.

The task of holding these gains was beyond Charlemagne's successors – who still ruled from Pavia. By the beginning of the tenth century the family was extinct and the rival Italian states had become prizes for which the western (French) and eastern (German) Frankish kingdoms competed. Power switched in 936 to **Otto**, king of the eastern Franks. In 962 he was crowned Emperor; his son and grandson (Otto II and III) set the seal on the renewal of the Holy Roman Empire.

Guelphs and Ghibellines

On the death of **Otto III** in 1002, Italy was again without a recognized ruler. In the north, noblemen jockeyed for power, while in Rome, a series of reforming popes began to strengthen the church. **Gregory VII**, elected in 1073, was the most radical, confronting the emperors and developing the papacy into the most advanced centralized government in Europe in the realms of law and finance. Holy Roman Emperor **Frederick I "Barbarossa"** besieged many northern Italian cities from his base in Germany from 1154; the issue of supremacy – papal or imperial – was to polarize the country for the next two hundred years, almost every part of Italy being torn by struggles between **Guelphs** (supporting the pope) and **Ghibellines** (supporting the emperor).

Meanwhile, trade was flourishing across northern Italy, not least in **Venice**, where a disparate band of refugees from the Lombard invasions had formed themselves into a powerful commercial bloc, trading as far afield as Syria and North Africa. In the eleventh century, revolts in many northern cities, including Pavia, Cremona and Milan, led to the establishment of **communal governments** across the region, many of which – in the face of Barbarossa's attacks – formed themselves into the united **Lombard League**. In 1176, the League defeated Barbarossa in a famous victory at Legnano, and by 1300, a broad belt of some three hundred virtually **independent city-states** stretched from central Italy to the northernmost edge of the peninsula.

In the middle of the century vast numbers died of the **Black Death** but the city-states survived, developing a participatory concept of citizenship quite different from the feudal lord-and-vassal relationship. By 1400 the richer and more influential states had swallowed up the smaller **comuni**, leaving four front-runners: Genoa, Florence, Venice and **Milan**, whose sphere of influence included Lombardy and much of central Italy. Smaller principalities, such as Mantua, supported armies of mercenaries, ensuring their security by building impregnable fortress-palaces.

Perpetual vendettas between the propertied classes often induced the citizens to prefer the overall rule of one **signore** to the bloodshed of warring clans. A despotic form of government evolved, sanctioned by official titles from the emperor or pope, and by the fifteenth century most city-states were under princely rather than republican rule; both

1498	1629–31	1796	May 23, 1805	1815
Leonardo da Vinci paints *The Last Supper* in Milan.	During the Great Plague of Milan, a bubonic plague epidemic decimates the towns of northern Italy.	Napoleon invades northern Italy.	Napoleon is crowned King of Italy in Milan's Duomo.	Settlement of Vienna. With Napoleon's decline the Austrians rule but unrest is rife.

Mantua and Milan became independent duchies, the former under the **Gonzaga**, the latter under the hugely powerful **Visconti**.

The commercial and secular city-states of late medieval times were the seed-bed for the **Renaissance**, when urban entrepreneurs and autocratic rulers enhanced their status through the financing of architectural projects, paintings and sculpture.

By the mid-fifteenth century the five most powerful states – Naples, the papacy, Milan, and the republics of Venice and Florence – reached a tacit agreement to maintain the new balance of power. Yet though there was equilibrium at home, the history of each of the independent Italian states became inextricably bound up with the power politics of other European countries.

French and Spanish intervention

In 1494, at the request of the Duke of Milan, **Charles VIII of France** marched south to renew the Angevin claim to the Kingdom of Naples. After his success, the kingdom was then acquired by Ferdinand II of Aragon, subsequently ruler of Spain.

Within three years of inheriting the Austrian and Spanish thrones, the Habsburg **Charles V** (1500–58) bribed his way to being elected Holy Roman Emperor. In 1527 his troops sacked Rome, a calamity widely interpreted at the time as God's punishment of the disorganized and dissolute Italians. The **French** remained troublesome opposition despite a defeat at Pavia in 1526, and the **Spanish** – granted the Duchy of Milan under the treaty of Château-Cambrésis in 1559 – were to exert a stranglehold on Italian political life for the next 150 years.

Social and economic troubles were as severe as the political upheavals. While the papacy combated the spread of the **Reformation** – aided, in Lombardy, by the archbishop **Carlo Borromeo** (1538–84), scion of the Borromeo family which remains pre-eminent in the lands around Lake Maggiore – the major manufacturing and trading centres were coming to terms with the opening up of the Atlantic and Indian Ocean trade routes, discoveries which meant that northern Italy would increasingly be bypassed. Mid-sixteenth-century **economic recession** prompted wealthy Venetian merchants to invest in land rather than business.

The seventeenth century was a low point in Italian political life, with little room for manoeuvre between the papacy and colonial powers. The Spanish lost control of their areas at the start of the eighteenth century when, as a result of the War of the Spanish Succession, Lombardy and Mantua came under Austrian control. The northern states advanced under the intelligent if autocratic rule of Austria's **Maria Theresa** (1740–80) and her son **Joseph II** (1780–92), who prepared the way for industrialization.

Lightning changes came in 1796, when the French armies of **Napoleon** invaded northern Italy. Within a few years the French had been driven out again, but by 1810 Napoleon was in command of the whole peninsula, crowning himself King of Italy in the Duomo at Milan; his puppet regimes – including a Cisalpine Republic in Lombardy – remained in charge until Waterloo. Napoleonic rule had profound effects, reducing the power of the papacy, reforming feudal land rights and introducing representative government to Italy. Elected assemblies were provided on the French model, giving the emerging middle class a chance for political discussion and action.

March 27, 1861	**1915**	**1918**	**1922**
Italy is declared a unified nation under King Vittorio Emanuele II.	Italy enters World War I on the side of Britain, France and Russia.	Ernest Hemingway stays on Lake Maggiore, an experience he will draw on when writing the novel *A Farewell to Arms*.	Mussolini becomes Prime Minister and within three years has declared himself *Il Duce*, dictator of Italy.

The Risorgimento: Italy's unification

The fall of Napoleon led to the Vienna Settlement of 1815, by which the Austrians effectively restored the old ruling class. **Metternich**, the Austrian Chancellor, did all he could to foster any local loyalties that might weaken the appeal of unity, yet 1820 to 1849 became years of revolution. In the north, the oppressive laws enacted by **Vittorio Emanuele I** in the Kingdom of Piemonte sparked off student protests and army mutinies in Turin. Vittorio Emanuele abdicated in favour of his brother, Carlo Felice, and his son, **Carlo Alberto**; the latter initially gave some support to the radicals, but Carlo Felice then called in the Austrians, and thousands of revolutionaries were forced into exile. Carlo Alberto became King of Piemonte in 1831. A secretive, excessively devout and devious character, he did a volte-face when he assumed the throne by forming an alliance with the Austrians.

One person profoundly influenced by the growing insurgencies was the radical **Giuseppe Mazzini**, founder in 1830 of the "**Young Italy**" movement, which also attracted **Giuseppe Garibaldi**, soon to play a central role in the **Risorgimento**, as the movement to reform and unite the country was known.

Crop failures in 1846 and 1847 produced widespread **famine** and **cholera outbreaks**, followed by rioting in Sicily, Piemonte and elsewhere. Rulers fled their duchies, and Carlo Alberto altered course again, prompted by Metternich's fall from power in Vienna; he granted his subjects a constitution and declared war on Austria. In Rome, the pope fled from rioting and Mazzini became a member of the city's republican triumvirate in 1849, with Garibaldi organizing the defences.

In Piemonte, Carlo Alberto abdicated in favour of his son **Vittorio Emanuele II**, but one thing that did survive was Piemonte's constitution, which throughout the 1850s attracted political refugees to this cosmopolitan state.

Nine years of radical change began when **Camillo Cavour** became prime minister of Piemonte in 1852. Napoleon III had decided to support Italy in its fight against the Austrians – the only realistic way of achieving unification – as long as resistance was non-revolutionary. The chance to provoke Austria into war came in 1859, when Cavour wrote an anti-Austrian speech for Vittorio Emanuele at the opening of parliament. His battle cry for an end to the **grido di dolore** ("cry of pain") was taken up over Italy. The Austrians ordered the Piemontese to demobilize; the Piemontese did the reverse.

The war was disastrous from the start, and thousands died in 1859 at Magenta and, most notably, **Solferino** near Lake Garda. A truce was quickly signed and, by 1860, following a series of plebiscites, Tuscany and the new state of Emilia (the duchies of Modena and Parma plus the Romagna) had voted for **union with Piemonte**. A secret treaty between Vittorio Emanuele and Napoleon III ceded Savoy and Nice to France, whereupon **Garibaldi** promptly set off for Nice with the aim of causing as much disruption as possible, only to be diverted when he reached Genoa, where he heard of an **uprising in Sicily**. Commandeering two old paddle-steamers and obtaining just enough rifles for his thousand-strong army, the Red Shirts – many of whom were from Lombardy – he headed south. Garibaldi's army outflanked the Neapolitan troops to take the island. After that, they easily occupied Naples, then struck out for Rome. Cavour, anxious that he might lose the initiative, hastily dispatched a Piemontese army to **annexe the Papal States**, except for the Patrimony around Rome. Cavour and Vittorio Emanuele then travelled south to Rome, thanked Garibaldi for his trouble and took command of all territories. In February 1861, the members of the new parliament formally announced the **Kingdom of Italy**.

1940	**September 8, 1943**	**September 23, 1943**
Italy declares war on France and Britain, announces a Tripartite Pact with Japan and Germany and invades France, Albania and Greece.	Italy declares an armistice with the Allied forces.	Mussolini is rescued from Italian captivity by German forces and established in a puppet government in Salò on Lake Garda.

Cavour died the same year, before the country was completely unified (Rome and Venice were still outside the kingdom). Garibaldi marched unsuccessfully on Rome in 1862, and again five years later, by which time Venice had been subsumed. It wasn't until Napoleon III was defeated by Prussia in 1870 that the French troops were ousted from Rome. Thus, by 1871 **Unification** was complete.

Into the twentieth century

After the Risorgimento, some things still hadn't changed. The ruling class were slow to move towards a broader-based political system, while living standards had worsened in some areas. When Sicilian peasant farmers organized themselves into **fasci** – forerunners of trade unions – the prime minister sent in 30,000 soldiers, closed down newspapers and interned suspected troublemakers without trial. In the 1890s capitalist methods and modern machinery in the Po valley created a new social structure, with rich **agrari** at the top of the pile, a mass of farm labourers at the bottom, and an intervening layer of estate managers.

In the 1880s Italy's **colonial expansion** began, initially concentrated in bloody – and ultimately disastrous – campaigns in Abyssinia and Eritrea in 1886. In 1912 Italy wrested the Dodecanese islands and Libya from Turkey, a development deplored by many, including the radical **Benito Mussolini**.

World War I and the rise of Mussolini

Italy entered **World War I** in 1915 with the chief aims of settling old scores with Austria and furthering its colonial ambitions through French and British support. A badly equipped, poorly commanded army took three years to force Austria into defeat. Some territory was gained – including the Alpine lands north of Lake Garda that became Trentino-Alto Adige – but at the cost of over half a million dead, many more wounded, and a mountainous war debt.

The middle classes, disillusioned with the war's outcome and alarmed by inflation and social unrest, turned to Mussolini, now a figurehead of the Right. In 1921, Mussolini – recently elected to parliament – formed the Partito Nazionale Fascista, whose **squadre** terrorized their opponents by direct personal attacks and the destruction of newspaper offices, printing shops, and socialist and trade union premises. By 1922 the party was in a position to carry out an insurrectionary **March on Rome**. Plans for the march were leaked to Prime Minister Facta, who needed the king's signature on a martial law decree if the army were to meet the march. The king feared civil war and refused. Facta resigned and shortly afterwards Mussolini was handed the prime ministership. Only then did the march take place.

Zealous **squadristi** now urged Mussolini towards **dictatorship**, which he announced early in 1925. Political opposition and trade unions were outlawed; the free press disintegrated under censorship and Fascist takeovers; elected local governments were replaced by appointed officials; powers of arrest and detention were increased; and special courts were established for political crimes. In 1929, Mussolini ended a sixty-year feud between Church and State by reorganizing the **Vatican** as an autonomous Church state within the Kingdom of Italy. By 1939, the motto

April 25, 1945	April 28, 1945	1946	1958
Milan is liberated although hand-to-hand fighting continues throughout northern Italy.	Mussolini is executed and strung up from a petrol station in Milan.	Italians vote for a republic and an end to the monarchy.	Italy is a founder member of the European Economic Community (EEC) which eventually becomes part of the European Union (EU) in 2009.

"Everything within the State; nothing outside the State; nothing against the State" had become fact, with the government controlling the larger part of Italy's steel, iron and ship-building industries, as well as every aspect of political life.

Even today many Italians hark back to Mussolini's dictatorship as an era during which "the trains ran on time". Supporters say he was a great modernizer, draining the malarial swamps in the south, establishing new towns both in Italy and abroad in a confident Neoclassical style, and gradually breaking the Mafia. His racism, social divisiveness, military incompetence and love of authoritarian red tape – legacies which hobble Italy to this day – are conveniently overlooked.

World War II

Mussolini's involvement in the **Spanish Civil War** in 1936 brought about the formation of the "**Axis**" with Nazi Germany. In terms of dress and ceremony Mussolini proved an inspiration to Hitler. **Racial laws** were passed in 1938 discriminating against the Jews, for example banning them from owning more than 100 hectares of land or companies with more than 100 employees. Italy entered **World War II** unprepared and with outdated equipment, but in 1941 invaded Yugoslavia to gain control of the Adriatic coast. As well as deporting Jews and other minorities to Nazi death camps in Eastern Europe, Mussolini set up his own **death camps**, including the notorious San Sabba in Trieste.

Before long, though, Mussolini was on the defensive. Tens of thousands of Italian troops were killed on the Russian front in the winter of 1942, and in 1943 the Allied forces gained a first foothold in Europe, when Patton's US Seventh Army and the British Eighth Army under Montgomery landed in Sicily.

In the face of these and other reversals Mussolini was overthrown by his own Grand Council, who bundled him away to the isolated mountain resort of Gran Sasso, and replaced him with the befuddled **Marshal Badoglio**. The Allies wanted Italy's surrender, for which they secretly offered amnesty to the king, Vittorio Emanuele III, who had coexisted with the Fascist regime for 21 years. On September 8, 1943 a radio broadcast announced that an **armistice** had been signed, and on the following day the Allies crossed to the mainland. As the Anglo-American army moved up through the peninsula, German divisions moved south to meet them, springing Mussolini from jail to set up the Fascist **Republic of Salò** on Lake Garda. It was a total failure, and increasing numbers from Communist, Socialist and Catholic parties swelled the opposing **partisan** forces to 450,000. In April 1945 Mussolini fled for his life, but was caught by partisans before reaching Switzerland. He was shot, as was his lover, Claretta Petacci, and both were strung up, feet first, in Milan's Piazzale Loreto.

The postwar years

A popular mandate in 1946 abolished the monarchy, declaring Italy a republic; Alcide de Gasperi's **Democrazia Cristiana** (DC) party formed a government. During the 1950s Italy became a front-rank industrial nation, massive firms such as Fiat and Olivetti helping to double the GDP and triple industrial production. US financial aid – the Marshall Plan – was an important factor in this expansion, as was the availability of a large and compliant workforce, much of which was from southern villages.

December 12, 1969	**May 28, 1974**	**March 16, 1978**
A bomb in Milan's Piazza Fontana kills 17 people and marks the beginning of a dark period of unrest lasting over ten years.	A bomb in Piazza della Loggia, Brescia, kills 8 people and injures over 90.	Aldo Moro, leader of the Christian Democrats and ex-prime minister, is kidnapped and murdered by Red Brigade terrorists.

The DC at first operated in alliance with other right-wing parties, but in 1963 they were obliged to share power for the first time with the **Partito Socialista Italiano** (PSI). The DC politician responsible for sounding out the socialists was **Aldo Moro**, the dominant figure of Italian politics in the 1960s, and prime minister from 1963 to 1968. The decade ended with the **autunno caldo** ("hot autumn") of 1969, when strikes, occupations and demonstrations paralysed the country. More extreme forms of unrest broke out, instigated in the first instance by the far right, who were almost certainly behind a bomb that killed sixteen people in **Piazza Fontana**, Milan, in 1969.

The situation continued to worsen through the 1970s. A plethora of left-wing terrorist groups sprang up, many of them led by disaffected intellectuals at the northern universities. The most active of these were the **Brigate Rosse** (Red Brigades), who reached their peak in 1978, when a group kidnapped and killed Aldo Moro. The bombings continued throughout the 1970s, including that of Piazza della Loggia, Brescia in 1974, reaching its hideous climax in 1980, when 85 people were killed and 200 wounded by a bomb planted at Bologna train station by a neo-Fascist group.

Inconsistencies and secrecy have beset those trying to clarify the terrorist activities of the 1970s. One Red Brigade member who served eighteen years in jail for his part in the assassination of Aldo Moro recently asserted that spies working for the **Italian secret services** masterminded the operation. A report prepared by the PDS (Italy's party of the democratic left) in 2000 reiterated the beliefs of many; it alleged that in the 1970s and 1980s the Establishment pursued a "**strategy of tension**" and that indiscriminate bombing of the public and the threat of a right-wing coup were devices to stabilize centre-right political control of the country. Italy was the only European country to consistently give the Communist party around a third of the vote, and there were Establishment fears that it may have become another pawn in the Cold War. The perpetrators of bombing campaigns were rarely caught, said the report, because "those military actions had been organized or promoted or supported by Italian state institutions and US intelligence". Valter Bielli, one of the report's authors, added: "Other bombing campaigns were attributed to the left to prevent the Communist Party from achieving power by democratic means." The report drew furious rebuttals from centre-right groups and the US Embassy.

Scandals and corruption

By whatever means, the DC government clung to power through the 1970s, but the early 1980s saw a series of **scandals** that severely damaged their reputation, notably when masonic links were discovered between corrupt bankers, senior DC members and fanatical right-wing groups. These events were to set the tone for the next twenty and more years of Italian public life with accusations, investigations and trials of public figures becoming the norm.

Italy's first-ever Socialist prime minister, **Bettino Craxi** – premier from 1983 to 1987 – was at the centre of the powerful Socialist establishment that ran Milan, when in 1992 a minor party official was arrested on corruption charges. This represented the tip of a long-established culture of kickbacks and bribes that went right to the top of the political establishment, not just in Milan – nicknamed **Tangentopoli** ("bribesville") – but across Italy. By the end of that year thousands were under arrest in what came to be known as the **Mani Pulite** (Clean Hands) investigation. In 1999, Craxi was

August 2, 1980	1994	2001–06	2002
A bomb in Bologna train station kills 85 people.	Silvio Berlusconi's Forza Italia party wins the general election with the National Alliance and the Lega Nord. It falls after eight months.	A second government headed by Silvio Berlusconi becomes the longest post-war government.	The Euro replaces the Lira as Italy's currency.

convicted, with twenty others, of **corruption**. He was sentenced to five years in prison, but died a year later in exile in Tunisia.

Giulio Andreotti, perhaps the most potent symbol of the sleazy postwar years, seven times prime minister and a senator for life, was also brought to the dock to answer charges of a long-term conspiracy with the Mafia. He denied any association, and was acquitted – partly on technicalities – in 1999 aged 80. In 2002, however, he was charged with complicity in the murder of a journalist suspected to have been blackmailing him, found guilty and sentenced to 24 years in prison – yet after a series of appeals the conviction was quashed.

A brave new world

The late 1980s and early 1990s saw the emergence of several new political parties, as many Italians became disillusioned with the old DC-led consensus. One was the right-wing **Lega Nord** (Northern League); its autocratic leader, **Umberto Bossi**, capitalized on a feeling held by many northerners that the state was supporting a corrupt south on the back of the hard-working, law-abiding north. The Fascist MSI, renamed the **Alleanza Nazionale** (AN), and a coalition of right-wingers, gained ground.

The after-effects of Tangentopoli affected all levels of politics and civil administration, almost entirely wiping out the established parties in the municipal elections of 1993. The 1994 national elections saw a new political force emerge: the centre-right **Forza Italia** ("Come On, Italy"), led by the Milan-based media magnate **Silvio Berlusconi**. Berlusconi used the power of his TV stations to build support, and swept to power as prime minister in a populist alliance with Bossi's Lega Nord and the post-Fascist Alleanza Nazionale. The fact that Berlusconi was not a politician was perhaps his greatest asset, and most Italians, albeit briefly, saw this as a new beginning – the end of the old, corrupt regime and the birth of a truly modern Italian state. However, as one of the country's top northern industrialists, and a pal of Craxi's, Berlusconi was as bound up with the old ways as anyone. Although he went on to win three elections in the following fourteen years and was head of Italy's **longest-lasting postwar government**, Berlusconi proved to be no more successful at ruling the country than any of his predecessors. Not only did he resist all attempts to reduce the scope of his media business and its conflict of interest with his premiership, but his time in the public eye has also been accompanied by a constantly evolving charge-sheet covering money-laundering, corruption, sex scandals, gerrymandering and forcing through backdated legislation to get himself out of sticky court cases. After numerous convictions and appeals, in 2013 Italy's highest court upheld Berlusconi's sentencing for tax fraud, prompting his expulsion from the Senate – though he remains unlikely to serve jail time because of his age.

Perhaps more worrying is the state of the nation; the media-mogul-turned-politician's promises of freedom and prosperity have been shown to be empty. Economic decline, social stagnation and stifling bureaucracy have modern-day Italy in a stranglehold. Both Berlusconi's governments and the various left-wing coalitions that have also been in power in the last decade have been too preoccupied by self-promotion, scandal and in-fighting to begin to resolve the malaise of the country. Italians, on the whole, have been left bruised, cynical and disillusioned by their leaders. Italy barely avoided bankruptcy during the economic collapse, and a new left-right coalition took power in 2014 under the youthful **Matteo Renzi** with a campaigning promise of reform.

2002	2006	2011	2013	2014
George Clooney buys Villa Oleandra on Lake Como for a cool $10 million.	Italy wins the football World Cup for the fourth time (previously in 1934, 1938 and 1982).	Berlusconi resigns as Italy teeters on the edge of bankruptcy.	Giorgio Napolitano is re-elected as president.	A left-right coalition government takes power under 39-year-old Matteo Renzi.

Books

Below is a selection of books that give a sense of the place, history and culture of northern Italy with particular relevance to the lakes region. Titles marked ★ are particularly recommended.

TRAVEL WRITING AND FICTION

Anne Calcagno (ed) *Travelers' Tales: Italy*. Crammed with evocative period detail as well as specifically commissioned contemporary writing by Tim Parks, Lisa St Aubin de Terán and others, this makes a perfect introduction to the richness and variety of Italy.

Ernest Hemingway *A Farewell to Arms*. Hemingway's first novel is partly based on his experiences as a teenage ambulance driver on Italy's northeast front during World War I. Some of the scenes are set in Milan and on the lakes.

Henry James *Italian Hours*. Urbane travel pieces from the young James with a couple of pages on Milan and Lake Como; perceptive about monuments and works of art, superb on the different atmospheres of Italy.

D.H. Lawrence *D.H. Lawrence and Italy*. Lawrence's three Italian travelogues collected into one volume. *Twilight in Italy* was written on Lake Garda and is infused with the atmosphere of the lake while combining the author's seemingly natural ill-temper when travelling with a genuine sense of regret for a way of life visibly passing.

★**Tim Parks** *Italian Ways, Italian Neighbours, An Italian Education* and *A Season with Verona*. Writer Tim Parks has lived in Italy since 1981. Through deftly told tales of family life, his books examine what it means to be Italian, and how national identity is absorbed. In *A Season with Verona*, Parks spends the 2000–01 football season seeing his beloved team play every game – home and away. The vivid characterizations, backed by highly attuned insight into Italian and Veronese society, make it an engaging page-turner.

★**Edith Wharton** *Italian Backgrounds*. Beautiful descriptions of the lakes and the other landscapes Wharton found in her travels. She is at once elegantly enthusiastic and highly informed about the country's art and architecture.

HISTORY, SOCIETY AND POLITICS

Baranski and West (ed) *Cambridge Companion to Modern Italian Culture*. Despite the textbook style, this compilation of essays is a useful way to get to grips with contemporary Italian society, from fashion and music to politics and identity.

R.J.B. Bosworth *Mussolini*. Bosworth paints a vivid picture of *Il Duce*, while also explaining the context of Fascism, and examines Mussolini's legacy, warning of the strong fascination for him that still exists in Italy today.

★**John Foot** *Milan since the Miracle: City, Culture and Identity*. Hugely enjoyable and rigorous work that sets out to explore the social questions and sense of identity in this beguilingly complex city.

David Gilmour *The Pursuit of Italy: A History of a Land, Its Regions and Their Peoples*. A highly readable analysis of whether Italy has or could ever really work as a unified country. Discussed by way of the cuisine, geography and culture of the country as well as historical facts.

Paul Ginsborg *A History of Contemporary Italy, Italy and Its Discontents* and *Silvio Berlusconi: Television, Power and Patrimony*. The first two are scholarly but very readable accounts of postwar Italian history, illustrating the complexity of contending economic, social and political currents. In the latter, Ginsborg again manages to make the intricacies and contradictions of Italian politics fathomable, this time while tracing the life and career of Berlusconi and his effect on the lives of Italy's citizens.

★**Tobias Jones** *The Dark Heart of Italy*. Written over three years in Parma, this interconnected sequence of essays deals with various aspects of modern Italian society, from the legal and political systems to the media and football.

The Longman History of Italy. This eight-volume series covers the history of Italy from the end of the Roman Empire to the present, each instalment comprising a range of essays on all aspects of political, social, economic and cultural history. Invaluable if you've developed a special interest in a particular period.

Denis Mack Smith *The Making of Italy 1796–1866* and *Italy and Its Monarchy*. The former is an admirably lucid explanation of the various forces at work in the Unification of Italy, while the latter deals with Italy's short-lived monarchy. The same author has also written a couple of excellent biographies, *Mazzini* and *Mussolini*.

ART AND ARCHITECTURE

Milano: Allemandi Architectural Guide. A handy volume giving detailed information on the architecture of Milan, with brief descriptions and simple, black-and-white snaps of all the buildings, plus short essays by specialists from the Polytechnic of Milan.

★**Frederick Hartt** *History of Italian Renaissance Art*. If one book on this vast subject can be said to be indispensable, this is it. A huge, wonderfully illustrated hardback that's something of a bargain in view of its comprehensiveness and acuity.

Elizabeth Helman Minchilli *Villas on the Italian Lakes*. Lavishly illustrated coffee-table book that takes a peek inside the grandest of the private villas on lakes Garda, Maggiore and Orta. Architecture and decor are examined in detail, and the photography is exquisite.

★**Peter Murray** *The Architecture of the Italian Renaissance*. Begins with Romanesque buildings and finishes with Palladio – valuable both as a synopsis of the underlying concepts and as a gazetteer of the main monuments in towns including Verona, Mantua and Milan.

Manfredo Tafuri *History of Italian Architecture 1944–1985*. The history, politics and movements that have shaped modern Italian architecture in this seminal work by one of today's leading critics and historians.

Manfredo Tafuri (ed) *Guilio Romano*. This attractive hardback balances beautiful reproductions with insightful essays by Gombrich, Tafuri and others to give a full account of the artist's life and work.

ITALIAN LITERATURE

Catullus *The Poems of Catullus*. Although his name is associated primarily with the tortured love poems addressed to Lesbia, Catullus also produced some acerbic satirical verse; this collection makes an entertaining companion to a trip to Sirmione, where he had a villa.

Gianni Celati *Voices from the Plains*. A beautifully crafted novel that uses the simple premise of chance encounters on a walk along the Po river to provide the focus for these touching, atmospheric tales.

Gabriele D'Annunzio *The Book of the Virgins*. Self-regarding dandy, war hero and worshipper of Mussolini, D'Annunzio – who lived in the extraordinary Il Vittoriale on the shore of Lake Garda – was perhaps the most complex figure of twentieth-century Italian literature.

Umberto Eco *Foucault's Pendulum*. Set in Milan to a backdrop of Masons, Templars and cultural mythology, this rather impenetrable thriller has been described as the forerunner to novels like Dan Brown's *The Da Vinci Code*. *The Name of the Rose* has some similar themes but is decidedly more readable.

Dario Fo *Plays I*. The Nobel Prize winner fabulously weaves together contemporary politics, surreal farce and the traditions of *commedia dell'arte*. This collection includes a trio of Fo's most famous plays – *Accidental Death of an Anarchist* (inspired by the Piazza Fontana cover-up in Milan), *Mistero Buffo*, and *Trumpets and Raspberries* – along with two previously unpublished short works.

Alessandro Manzoni *The Betrothed*. The first modern Italian novel is no pool-side thriller, but a skilful melding of the romance of two young lovers and a sweeping historical drama set in Milan and Lecco during the plague.

FOOD AND DRINK

Nicholas Belfrage *Barolo to Valpolicella: Wines of Northern Italy*. Not as user-friendly as it might be – there are no vintage charts and few maps – this guide nevertheless manages to pack in a wealth of information on the producers and diverse wines of the region.

Elizabeth David *Italian Food*. The writer who introduced Italian cuisine to Britain. Ahead of its time when it was published in the 1950s, and imbued with all the enthusiasm and diversity of Italian cookery. An inspirational book.

Marcella Hazan *The Classic Italian Cookbook*. The best Italian cookbook for the novice in the kitchen is a step-by-step guide that draws from all over the peninsula.

Fred Plotkin *Italy for the Gourmet Traveller*. Comprehensive, region-by-region guide to the best of Italian cuisine, with a foodie's guide to major towns and cities, a gazetteer of restaurants and specialist food and wine shops, plus descriptions of local dishes, with recipes.

Claudia Roden *The Food of Italy*. A culinary classic, this regional guide takes in easy-to-follow local recipes from the people for whom they are second nature. Recently reissued in a 25th anniversary edition, it's full of fascinating facts about Italian cuisine.

SPECIALIST GUIDES

★**Helena Attlee and Alex Ramsay** *Italian Gardens*. Evocatively photographed (by Alex Ramsay), this is a handy pocket-sized guide to more than sixty of the peninsula's most beautiful gardens. It provides histories and descriptions, as well as detailed information on locations, facilities, opening times and accessibility.

Penelope Hobhouse *The Garden Lover's Guide to Italy*. Large, beautifully illustrated guide taking the reader through the highlights of the best-known and some little-discovered Italian gardens. Well designed with lots of extra features and context on each garden.

Leonardo da Vinci *Notebooks*. Miscellany of speculation and observation from the universal genius of Renaissance Italy; essential to any understanding of the man.

Italian

Although you're likely to have few problems finding an English speaker when you need one in the area covered by this book, try a little Italian and your halting efforts will often be rewarded by smiles and appreciation. Regional dialects are still very much in use in Italy today, and as the nationalist Lega Nord party has taken hold in the north, so the pride in local dialects has increased. Brown-coloured signs bearing the dialect name mark the entrance to towns and villages across the region, especially around Brescia and Bergamo. In the Swiss canton (region) of Ticino, English is generally a third language, behind Italian and German.

As well as some useful **vocabulary** below, we've included a **menu reader** to help you negotiate your way round what's on offer at the table, and a **glossary** of common Italian words.

Pronunciation

Words are spoken as they are written in Italian, and usually enunciated with exaggerated, open-mouthed clarity. The only difficulties you're likely to encounter are the few **consonants** that are different from English:

c before e or i is pronounced as in church, while **ch** before the same vowels is hard, as in cat.

sci and **sce** are pronounced as in sheet and shelter respectively.

The same goes with **g** – soft before e or i, as in geranium; hard before h, as in garlic.

gn has the ni sound of onion.

gl in Italian is softened to something like li in English, as in stallion.

h is not aspirated, as in honour.

Most Italian words are **stressed** on the penultimate syllable. In written Italian, **accents** (either ` or ´) have traditionally been used to denote stress on other syllables, but the acute (´) accent is more rarely used these days. Note that the endings -**ia** or -**ie** count as two syllables, hence trattoria is stressed on the **i**.

Italian words and phrases

BASICS

Good morning	Buongiorno	I'm fine	Bene
Good afternoon/evening	Buona sera	Do you speak English?	Parla inglese?
Good night	Buona notte	I don't understand	Non ho capito
Hello	Salve	I don't know	Non lo so
Hello/goodbye (informal)	Ciao	Excuse me	Scusami
Goodbye	Arrivederci	Excuse me (in a crowd)	Permesso
Yes	Sì	I'm sorry	Mi dispiace
No	No	I'm here on holiday	Sono qui in vacanza
Please	Per favore	I'm British/Irish/	Sono inglese/
Thank you (very much)	Grazie (mille)	Scottish/Welsh	irlandese/
You're welcome	Prego		scozzese/gallese
All right/that's OK	Va bene	American	americano/a
How are you? (informal/formal)	Come stai/sta?	Australian	australiano/a

From New Zealand	neozelandese/a	Here/There	Quà/Là Fine
From South Africa	sudafricano/a	Good/Bad	Buono/Cattivo
I live in …	Abito a …	Big/Small	Grande/Piccolo
Today	Oggi	Cheap/Expensive	Economico/Caro
Tomorrow	Domani	Early/Late	Presto/Tardi
Day after tomorrow	Dopodomani	Hot/Cold	Caldo/Freddo
Yesterday	Ieri	Near/Far	Vicino/Lontano
Now	Adesso	Quickly/Slowly	Velocemente/ Lentamente
Later	Più tardi		
Wait a minute!	Aspetta!	Slowly/Quietly	Piano
Let's go!	Andiamo!	Mr …	Signor …
With/Without	Con/Senza	Mrs …	Signora …
More/Less	Più/Meno	Miss …	Signorina …
Enough, no more	Basta		(il Signor, la Signora,
In the morning	Di mattina		a Signorina when
In the afternoon	Nel pomeriggio		speaking about
In the evening	Di sera		someone else)

DRIVING

Left/right	Sinistra/destra	Slow down	Rallentare
Go straight ahead	Sempre diritto	Road closed/under repair	Strada chiusa/lavori in corso
Turn left/right	Gira a sinistra/destra		
Car park	Parcheggio	No through road	Vietato il transito
No parking	Divieto di sosta/Sosta vietata	No overtaking	Vietato il sorpasso
		Crossroads	Incrocio
One-way street	Senso unico	Speed limit	Limite di velocità
No entry	Senso vietato		

USEFUL SIGNS

Entrance/Exit	Entrata/Uscita	Drinking water	Acqua potabile
Free entrance	Ingresso libero	Platform	Binario
Gentlemen	Signori/Uomini	Cash desk	Cassa
Ladies	Signore/Donne	Go/walk	Avanti
WC/Bathroom	Gabinetto/Bagno	Stop/halt	Alt
Vacant/Engaged	Libero/Occupato	Customs	Dogana
Open/Closed	Aperto/Chiuso	Do not touch	Non toccare
Arrivals/Departures	Arrivi/Partenze	Danger	Pericolo
Closed for restoration	Chiuso per restauro	Beware	Attenzione
Closed for holidays	Chiuso per ferie	First aid	Pronto soccorso
Pull/Push	Tirare/Spingere	Ring the bell	Suonare il campanello
Out of order	Guasto	No smoking	Vietato fumare

ITALIAN NUMBERS

1	uno	12	dodici
2	due	13	tredici
3	tre	14	quattordici
4	quattro	15	quindici
5	cinque	16	sedici
6	sei	17	diciassette
7	sette	18	diciotto
8	otto	19	diciannove
9	nove	20	venti
10	dieci	21	ventuno
11	undici	22	ventidue

30	trenta	100	cento
40	quaranta	101	centouno
50	cinquanta	110	centodieci
60	sessanta	200	duecento
70	settanta	500	cinquecento
80	ottanta	1000	mille
90	novanta		

ACCOMMODATION

Hotel	Albergo/hotel	Is breakfast included?	È compresa la
Is there a hotel nearby?	C'è un albergo qui		colazione?
	vicino?	Do you have anything	Ha niente che costa
Do you have a room…	Ha una camera…	cheaper?	meno?
for one/two/three	per una/due/tre	Full/half board	Pensione completa/
person/people	persona/e		mezza pensione
for one/two	per una/due/ tre	Can I see the room?	Posso vedere la camera?
three night/s	notte/i	I'll take it	La prendo
for one/two week/s	per una/due	I'd like to book a room	Vorrei prenotare una
	settimana/e		camera
with a double bed	con un letto	I have a booking	Ho una prenotazione
	matrimoniale	Can we camp here?	Possiamo
with a shower/bath	con doccia/bagno		campeggiare qui?
with a balcony	con un balcone	Is there a campsite nearby?	C'è un campeggio
hot/cold water	acqua calda/		qui vicino?
	fredda	Tent	Tenda
How much is it?	Quanto costa?	Youth hostel	Ostello della gioventù

QUESTIONS AND DIRECTIONS

Where? (Where is/	Dove? (Dov'è/	How far is it to…?	Quant'è lontano…?
Where are…?)	Dove sono…?)	Can you give me	Mi può dare un
When?	Quando?	a lift to…?	passaggio a…?
What? (What is it?)	Cosa? (Cos'è?)	Can you tell me when to	Mi può dire quando
How much/many?	Quanto/Quanti?	get off?	devo scendere?
Why?	Perchè?	What time does it open?	A che ora apre?
Is it/is there …?	C'è…?	What time does it close?	A che ora chiude?
What time is it?	Che ora è/Che ore	How much does it cost?	Quanto costa?
	sono?	(… do they cost?)	(… Quanto costano?)
How do I get to…?	Come arrivo a…?	What's it called in Italian?	Come si dice in italiano?

TRAVELLING

Aeroplane	Aereo	Can I book a seat?	Posso prenotare un
Bus	Autobus/pullman		posto?
Train	Treno	What time does it leave?	A che ora parte?
Car	Macchina/automobile	When is the next bus/	Quando parte il
Taxi	Taxi	train/ferry to…?	prossimo pullman/
Bicycle	Bicicletta		treno/traghetto
Ferry	Traghetto		per…?
Hitch-hiking	Autostop	Do I have to change?	Devo cambiare?
On foot	A piedi	Where does it leave from?	Da dove parte?
Bus station	Autostazione	What platform does	Da quale binario
A ticket to…	Un biglietto per…	it leave from?	parte?
One-way/return	Solo andata/	How many kilometres	Quanti chilometri
	andata	is it?	sono?
	e ritorno	How long does it take?	Quanto ci vuole?

| What number bus is it to…? | Che numero di auto bus per…? | Next stop please | La prossima fermata, per favore |
| Where's the road to …? | Dov'è la strada per…? | | |

Menu reader

LOCAL SPECIALITIES

Bigoli	Local variety of thick spaghetti		bone and its marrow
		Pan d'oro	Verona's variation of panettone, often in a star shape
Bollito misto	Mixture of boiled meats usually served with *mostarda*		
		Panettone	Dome-shaped egg sponge filled with candied peel and sultanas. Originally from Milan, it is ubiquitous at Christmas time.
Burro fuso	Melted butter, usually with sage leaves		
Casoela	Pork chop, cabbage and sausage casserole, usually served with polenta		
		Persico fritto	Floured, fried perch
Casoncelli	Ravioli stuffed with sausage-meat	Pizzoccheri	Buckwheat pasta ribbons, usually served with cheese, spinach and potatoes
Coregone	White lake fish (lavaret)		
Costoletta/Cotoletta alla Milanese	Veal cutlet battered in breadcrumbs and fried in butter		
		Polenta	Cornmeal (or grits), served boiled, or boiled and then sliced and grilled
Mostarda	Marinated fruit and vegetables mustard, accompanying roasts and *bollito*		
		Rane in umido	Steamed frog-meat
		Risotto alla Milanese	Saffron risotto
Nervetti con cipolle	Cold starter of calf cartilage and onion dressed with oil and vinegar	Spiedo (spiedino)	Spit-roasted skewers, usually of meat
		Tortelli alla zucca	Ravioli stuffed with pumpkin
Osso buco alla Milanese	Braised veal including		

BASICS AND SNACKS

Aceto	Vinegar	Olive	Olives
Aglio	Garlic	Pane	Bread
Biscotti	Biscuits	Pane integrale	Wholemeal bread
Burro	Butter	Patate fritte	Chips (French fries)
Caramelle	Sweets	Patatine	Crisps (potato chips)
Cioccolato	Chocolate	Pepe	Pepper
Formaggio	Cheese	Riso	Rice
Frittata	Omelette	Sale	Salt
Grissini	Bread sticks	Uovo/Uova	Egg/eggs
Maionese	Mayonnaise	Zucchero	Sugar
Marmellata	Jam	Zuppa	Soup
Olio	Oil		

PIZZAS

Calzone	Folded pizza, often with cheese, ham and tomato	Frutti di mare	Seafood, usually mussels, prawns, squid and clams
Capricciosa	Literally "capricious"; usually including baby artichoke, mushrooms, ham and capers	Margherita	Cheese and tomato
		Marinara	Tomato and garlic; no cheese

Napoli/Napoletana	Tomato, cheese, anchovy, olive oil and oregano	Quattro Stagioni	"Four seasons", usually including ham, pepper, onion, mushrooms, artichokes and olives
Quattro Formaggi	"Four cheeses", usually including mozzarella, fontina, gruyère and gorgonzola		

ANTIPASTI AND STARTERS

Antipasto misto	Selection of starters, usually including cold meats, fish or vegetables	Lardo	Paper-thin slices of pork fat
Bresaola	Dried, salted beef, sliced thinly	Melanzane alla parmigiana	Baked aubergine with tomato and parmesan cheese
Caponata	Mixed aubergine, olives, tomatoes and anchovies	Peperonata	Green and red peppers stewed in olive oil
Caprese	Tomato and mozzarella salad with basil	Pomodori ripieni	Stuffed tomatoes
Insalata russa	Salad of diced vegetables in mayonnaise	Prosciutto cotto/crudo	Boiled ham/dried ham
		Salame	Salami
		Speck	Smoked ham

THE FIRST COURSE (IL PRIMO)

SOUP

Brodo	Clear broth	Pappardelle	Wide, flat pasta ribbons
Minestrina/minestra	Clear broth with small pasta shapes	Parmigiano	Parmesan cheese
Minestrone	Thick vegetable soup	Pasta al forno	Baked pasta with minced meat, eggs, tomato and cheese
Pasta e fagioli	Pasta and bean soup	Penne	Smaller version of *rigatoni*
Stracciatella	Broth with egg	Pesto	Sauce with ground basil, garlic and pine nuts

PASTA

Amatriciana	Cubed bacon and tomato sauce	Pomodoro	Tomato sauce
		Puttanesca	Spicy tomato, anchovy, olive oil and oregano sauce
Arrabbiata	Spicy tomato sauce, with chillies		
Cannelloni	Large tubes of pasta, stuffed	Ragù	Meat sauce, known in the UK as Bolognese
Carbonara	Sauce of pancetta, pecorino, pepper and beaten egg	Ravioli	Filled parcels of egg pasta
		Rigatoni	Large, grooved tubular pasta
Farfalle	Butterfly-shaped pasta	Salvia	Sage
Fettuccine	Narrow pasta ribbons	Tagliatelle	Pasta ribbons
Funghi	Mushrooms	Tortellini	Small rings of pasta, stuffed with meat or cheese and pasta sauce
Gnocchi	Small potato dumplings		
Panna	Cream	Vongole	Clams

THE SECOND COURSE (IL SECONDO)

MEAT (CARNE)

Agnello	Lamb	Coniglio	Rabbit
Anatra	Duck	Cotechino	Pork sausage
Asino	Donkey	Costoletta or coteletta	Cutlet, chop
Bistecca	Steak	Fegatini	Chicken livers
Carpaccio	Thin slices of raw beef	Fegato	Liver
Cervella	Brain, usually calves'	Involtini	Stuffed rolls of meat
Cinghiale	Wild boar	Lepre	Hare
		Lingua	Tongue

Maiale	Pork	Calamari	Squid
Manzo	Beef	Cefalo	Grey mullet
Osso buco	Shin of veal	Coda di rospo	Monkfish
Pancetta	Bacon	Cozze	Mussels
Pollo	Chicken	Dentice	Sea bream
Polpette	Meatballs	Gamberetti	Shrimps
Rana	Frog	Gamberi	Prawns
Rognoni	Kidneys	Granchio	Crab
Salsiccia	Sausage	Laverello	White freshwater lake fish
Saltimbocca	Veal with prosciutto	Luccio	Pike
	and sage	Merluzzo	Cod
Spezzatino	Stew	Ostriche	Oysters
Stufato	Stewed meat	Pesce persico	Perch
Tacchino	Turkey	Pesce spada	Swordfish
Trippa	Tripe	Polpo	Octopus
Vitello	Veal	Sampiero	John Dory
		Sardine	Sardines

FISH (PESCE) AND SHELLFISH (CROSTACEI)

		Sgombro	Mackerel
		Sogliola	Sole
Acciughe	Anchovies	Tinca	Tench
Anguilla	Eel	Tonno	Tuna
Aragosta	Lobster	Triglia	Red mullet
Baccalà	Dried salted cod	Trota	Trout
Branzino	Sea bass	Vongole	Clams

VEGETABLES (CONTORNI), HERBS (ERBE) AND SALAD (INSALATA)

Asparagi	Asparagus	Melanzane	Aubergine (eggplant)
Basilico	Basil	Origano	Oregano
Capperi	Capers	Patate	Potatoes
Carciofini	Artichoke hearts	Peperoni	Peppers
Cavolfiore	Cauliflower	Piselli	Peas
Cavolo	Cabbage	Pomodori	Tomatoes
Ceci	Chickpeas	Prezzemolo	Parsley
Cetriolo	Cucumber	Radicchio	Red salad leaves
Cipolla	Onion	Rosmarino	Rosemary
Fagioli	Beans	Rucola	Rocket (arugula)
Fagiolini	String beans	Salvia	Sage
Finocchio	Fennel	Spinaci	Spinach
Funghi	Mushrooms	Zucca	Pumpkin
Insalata verde/mista	Green salad/mixed salad	Zucchine	Courgettes
Lenticchie	Lentils		

COOKING TERMS

Affumicato	Smoked	Ben cotto	Well done
Ai ferri	Grilled without oil	Bollito/lesso	Boiled
Al dente	Firm, not overcooked	Brasato	Cooked in wine
Al forno	Baked	Congelato	Frozen
Al sangue	Rare	Cotto	Cooked
Alla brace	Barbecued	Crudo	Raw
Alla griglia	Grilled	Fritto	Fried
Alla Milanese	Fried in egg and	Grattuggiato	Grated
	breadcrumbs	In umido	Stewed
Allo spiedo	On the spit	Pizzaiola	Cooked with
Arrosto	Roast		tomato sauce

Ripieno	Stuffed	**Stracotto**	Braised, stewed
Spiedino	Skewer or kebab	**Surgelato**	Frozen

SWEETS (DOLCI), FRUIT (FRUTTA), CHEESE (FORMAGGIO) AND NUTS (NOCI)

Amaretti	Macaroons	**Mascarpone**	Smooth, rich, soft cheese
Ananas	Pineapple	**Mela**	Apple
Anguria	Watermelon	**Parmigiano**	Parmesan
Arancia	Orange	**Pecorino**	Strong, hard sheep's cheese
Cachi	Persimmons		
Ciliege	Cherries	**Pescha**	Peach
Cocomero	Watermelon	**Pinoli**	Pine nuts
Crostata	Jam tart	**Provola/Provolone**	Mild cheese made from buffalo or sheep milk, sometimes smoked
Dolcelatte	Creamy blue cheese		
Fichi	Figs		
Fragole	Strawberries	**Ricotta**	Soft, white cheese
Gelato	Ice cream	**Taleggio**	Creamy, soft cheese
Grana Padano	Local version of Parmesan cheese	**Tiramisù**	Trifle-like dessert
		Torta	Cake, tart
Gorgonzola	Soft, strong, blue-veined cheese	**Uva**	Grapes
		Zabaglione	Dessert with eggs, sugar and marsala wine
Macedonia	Fruit salad		
Mandorle	Almonds	**Zuppa inglese**	Trifle

DRINKS

Acqua minerale	Mineral water	**Litro**	Litre
gassata	sparkling	**Mezzo**	Half
naturale	still	**Quarto**	Quarter
Acqua tonica	Tonic water	**Salute!**	Cheers!
Bicchiere	Glass	**Secco**	Dry
Birra	Beer	**Spremuta**	Fresh fruit juice
Bottiglia	Bottle	**Spumante**	Sparkling wine
Caffè	Coffee	**Succo**	Concentrated fruit juice with sugar
Caraffa	Carafe		
Cioccolata calda	Hot chocolate	**Tè**	Tea
Dolce	Sweet	**Vino**	Wine
Ghiaccio	Ice	**Bianco**	White
Granita	Iced drink, with coffee or fruit	**Rosato**	Rosé
		Rosso	Red
Latte	Milk		

Glossaries

USEFUL ITALIAN WORDS

alimentari grocery shop
anfiteatro amphitheatre
autostazione bus station
autostrada motorway
biblioteca library
cappella chapel
castello castle
centro centre
centro storico historic centre/old town
chiesa church

comune an administrative area; also the local council or town hall
corso avenue or boulevard
duomo/cattedrale cathedral
entrata entrance
festa festival, holiday
fiume river
lago lake
largo a kind of square
lungolago lakefront road or promenade

mercato market
municipio town hall
paese country, village
palazzo palace, mansion or block of flats
parco park
passeggiata the customary early-evening walk
piazza square
pinacoteca picture gallery
ponte bridge
santuario sanctuary

sottopassaggio subway
spiaggia beach
stazione station
strada road
teatro theatre
tempio temple
torre tower
traghetto ferry
uscita exit
via road

ARTISTIC AND ARCHITECTURAL TERMS

ambo A raised pulpit, popular in Italian medieval churches.

apse A vaulted semicircular or polygonal termination of a church, usually eastern.

architrave Lintel or the lowest part of the entablature.

atrium Inner courtyard.

Baroque Exuberant architectural style of the seventeenth century, characterized by ornate decoration, complex spatial arrangements and grand vistas. Also applies to the period's sumptuous style of painting and sculpture.

basilica Originally a Roman administrative building, adapted for early churches; distinguished by lack of transepts.

belvedere A terrace or lookout point.

campanile Bell tower, sometimes detached, usually of a church.

capital Top of a column.

cella Sanctuary of a temple.

chancel Part of a church containing the altar.

chiaroscuro The balance of light and shade in a painting, and the skill of the artist in depicting the contrast between the two.

cornice The top section of a Classical facade.

cortile Galleried courtyard or cloister.

crypt Burial place in a church, usually under the choir.

decumanus maximus The main street of a Roman town. The second cross-street was known as the *cardo maximus*.

entablature The section above the capital on a Classical building, below the cornice.

ex-voto Painting or object presented in thanksgiving to a saint.

fresco Wall-painting technique in which the artist applies paint to wet plaster for a more permanent finish.

Gothic Architectural style of the thirteenth and fourteenth centuries, with an emphasis on verticality, characterized by pointed arches, ribbed vaulting and flying buttresses.

Liberty Italian version of Art Nouveau.

loggia Roofed gallery or balcony.

Mannerism Sixteenth-century style characterized by stylization of Renaissance rules, theatrical motifs and technical skill.

nave Central space in a church, usually flanked by aisles.

Neoclassicism A rigorous architecture of pure geometrical forms based on Classical rules, prevalent in the late eighteenth century.

piano nobile Main floor of a palace, usually the first level above ground.

polyptych Painting on several joined wooden panels.

portico Covered entrance to a building, or porch.

presepio A Christmas crib.

putti Cherubs.

reliquary Receptacle for a saint's relics, usually bones. Often highly decorated.

Renaissance Fifteenth- and sixteenth-century Italian-originated movement in art and architecture, inspired by the rediscovery of Classical ideals.

Romanesque Solid architectural style of the late tenth to mid-thirteenth centuries, characterized by round-headed arches and a penchant for horizontality and geometric precision.

sgraffito Decorative technique whereby one layer of plaster is scratched to reveal a darker-coloured layer beneath.

stucco Plaster made from water, lime, sand and powdered marble, used for decorative work.

thermae Baths, usually elaborate buildings in Roman villas.

triptych Painting on three joined wooden panels.

trompe l'oeil Work of art that deceives the viewer by means of tricks with perspective.

Small print and index

A ROUGH GUIDE TO ROUGH GUIDES

Published in 1982, the first Rough Guide – to Greece – was a student scheme that became a publishing phenomenon. Mark Ellingham, a recent graduate in English from Bristol University, had been travelling in Greece the previous summer and couldn't find the right guidebook. With a small group of friends he wrote his own guide, combining a highly contemporary, journalistic style with a thoroughly practical approach to travellers' needs.

The immediate success of the book spawned a series that rapidly covered dozens of destinations. And, in addition to impecunious backpackers, Rough Guides soon acquired a much broader readership that relished the guides' wit and inquisitiveness as much as their enthusiastic, critical approach and value-for-money ethos.

These days, Rough Guides include recommendations from budget to luxury and cover more than 120 destinations around the globe, as well as producing an ever-growing range of ebooks.

Visit **roughguides.com** to find all our latest books, read articles, get inspired and share travel tips with the Rough Guides community.

Rough Guide credits

Editor: Lucy Cowie
Layout: Anita Singh
Cartography: Rajesh Chhibber
Picture editor: Roger Mapp
Proofreader: Norm Longley
Managing editors: Natasha Foges, Alice Park
Senior editor: Rachel Mills
Assistant editor: Payal Sharotri

Production: Janis Griffith
Cover design: Nicole Newman, Emily Taylor, Anita Singh
Photographer: Helena Smith
Editorial assistant: Rebecca Hallett
Senior pre-press designer: Dan May
Programme manager: Gareth Lowe
Publisher: Joanna Kirby
Publishing director: Georgina Dee

Publishing information

This fourth edition published May 2015 by
Rough Guides Ltd,
80 Strand, London WC2R 0RL
11, Community Centre, Panchsheel Park,
New Delhi 110017, India
Distributed by Penguin Random House
Penguin Books Ltd,
80 Strand, London WC2R 0RL
Penguin Group (USA)
345 Hudson Street, NY 10014, USA
Penguin Group (Australia)
250 Camberwell Road, Camberwell,
Victoria 3124, Australia
Penguin Group (NZ)
67 Apollo Drive, Mairangi Bay, Auckland 1310,
New Zealand
Penguin Group (South Africa)
Block D, Rosebank Office Park, 181 Jan Smuts Avenue,
Parktown North, Gauteng, South Africa 2193
Rough Guides is represented in Canada by Tourmaline
Editions Inc. 662 King Street West, Suite 304, Toronto,
Ontario M5V 1M7
Printed in Singapore

Help us update

We've gone to a lot of effort to ensure that the fourth
edition of **The Rough Guide to Italian Lakes** is accurate
and up-to-date. However, things change – places get
"discovered", opening hours are notoriously fickle,
restaurants and rooms raise prices or lower standards. If
you feel we've got it wrong or left something out, we'd like
to know, and if you can remember the address, the price,
the hours, the phone number, so much the better.

Please send your comments with the subject line
"Rough Guide Italian Lakes Update" to ✉ mail
@uk.roughguides.com. We'll credit all contributions and
send a copy of the next edition (or any other Rough Guide
if you prefer) for the very best emails.

Find more travel information, connect with fellow
travellers and plan your trip on ⓦ roughguides.com.

ABOUT THE AUTHORS

Lucy Ratcliffe is a freelance travel writer and editor. She has been visiting and writing about the Lakes region of Northern Italy for over fifteen years and is the author of several guides to the area. She now shares her time between Bergamo and Barcelona, where she lives with her family.

Matthew Teller (⊚ matthewteller.com) is a freelance journalist and travel writer based in the UK. He has written for Rough Guides for more than fifteen years, contributing to many titles as author, updater or editor. He blogs at ⊚ quitealone.com and tweets @matthewteller.

Acknowledgements

Matthew Teller would like to thank Alessandra Smith and Adriana Vacca at the Italian State Tourist Board in London; Monica Neroni at Provincia di Como; Silvia Lorenzini at Distretto dei Laghi in Verbania; Sara Roloff at Switzerland Tourism in London; Jasmin Haslimeier at Ticino Turismo in Bellinzona; and particularly Rosanna Melaragni, Rachel Roots and Stephanie Elkington at Sunvil. Special thanks to Sarah and Luca in Stresa; to my brilliant co-updaters this time, Helena and Kiki; to Lucy in Barcelona for all the fun times on past editions; and to our super-efficient, sharp-eyed editor Lucy Cowie, who leaves this book better than when she found it.

Kiki Deere would like to thank Anna for her wonderful company and help at Lake Iseo; Andrea for joining in the fun; Milena for helping out with transport details and other queries; Massimo for his warm hospitality at *Casa Visnenza* and plethora of tips on the area; Enrica Puppi and Alessandra Pitocchi from Turismo Bergamo for all their support and assistance; Francesco Tanasini for the fun and company and for tucking into feast after feast in the span of twelve hours; Laura Benzoni for her knowledge of the Basilica of Clusone; Alessandra from Promoserio for coordinating my schedule and for such a terrific lunch; Elena Marchese for all her top Milan suggestions without whose help the Milan chapter wouldn't be as it is; a huge thanks goes to Francesca Potente from Assolombarda for coordinating my stay in Milan; and last but not least Budgie for all his support over the years and for putting up with a partner who is never around.

Readers' updates

Thanks to all the readers who have taken the time to write in with comments and suggestions (and apologies if we've inadvertently omitted or misspelt anyone's name):

Catherine Fulvio, Camilla Haw, David and Rhian Liddell, Elena Ponzini, Lynn Priebe, Gianfranco Scanferato, Martin Sury, Ian Tipping, Steve Vickers.

Index

Maps are marked in **grey**

W

Z

Map symbols

The symbols below are used on maps throughout the book

▬▬ ▪	International boundary	⌣	Bridge	P	Parking	↑	One way
▬▬ ▪	Province boundary	⊠	Gate	∴	Ruins	⊞	Church
▬ ▬ ▬	Chapter division boundary	▲	Mountain peak	⚓	Swimming pool	▨	Building
	Major road	◆	Place of interest	⛰	Rocks	◯	Stadium
	Minor road	★	Bus stop	//\	Hill	⬚	Park
	Motorway road	☖	Viewpoint	✡	Synagogue	☐	Beach
	Pedestrian road	♟	Castle	●-●-●	Cable car	⊞	Cemetery
▬▬▬	Railway	♟	Monastery	⊪⊪⊪	Funicular		
▬ ▬	Ferry route	⚠	Campsite	⊠	Post office		
	River	✈	Airport	ⓘ	Tourist office		

Listings key

■ Accommodation

● Restaurants/cafés

■ Bars/clubs

● Shops